AF552548

HISTORY OF SANSKRIT POETICS

HISTORY OF
SANSKRIT POETICS

P.V. Kane

MOTILAL BANARSIDASS PUBLISHERS
PRIVATE LIMITED • DELHI

6th Reprint: Delhi, 2019
Fourth Edition: Delhi, 1971

ISBN: 978-81-208-0274-2

MOTILAL BANARSIDASS
41 U.A. Bungalow Road, Jawahar Nagar, Delhi 110 007
1 B, J S Compound, Kennedy Bridge, Nana Chowk, Mumbai 400 007
203 Royapettah High Road, Mylapore, Chennai 600 004
236, 9th Main III Block, Jayanagar, Bengaluru 560 011
9, Panchanan Ghosh Lane, 1st Floor, Kolkata 700 009
Ashok Rajpath, Patna 800 004
Chowk, Varanasi 221 001

Printed in India

by RP Jain at NAB Printing Unit,
A-44, Naraina Industrial Area, Phase I, New Delhi–110028
and published by JP Jain for Motilal Banarsidass Publishers (P) Ltd,
41 U.A. Bungalow Road, Jawahar Nagar, Delhi-110007

PREFACE

The last edition of this work was published in 1951. As all copies were sold out, there was a great demand for a new edition. As my hands were full owing to the writing and printing of the 5th (the last) volume of the 'History of Dharmaśāstra, I could not find time for several months to revise the book. During the last nine years a good deal has been written on the subject of this work. I tried to read as much as I could and have made substantial additions and changes in this edition. But I am unable to say that I read everything that has been written during the last nine years on Sanskrit Poetics. I hope, however, that I have not missed much of valuable matter. In the last edition I thanked all those who helped me in various ways. In preparing this edition Dr. V. Rāghavan made valuable suggestions, many of which I have accepted. As in the preface to the last edition I express my deep gratitude to him. It gives me great satisfaction that this history which I first wrote over fifty years ago still continues to be popular with students of Sanskrit Poetics.

P. V. Kane

ABBREVIATIONS

(ENGLISH)

A. B.=Abhinavabhāratī, com. on Nāṭyaśāstra.
Ānan. ed.=Ānadāśrama (Poona) edition.
Āp. Dh. S.=Āpastamba—dharmasūtra.
A. S. W. I.=Archaeological Survey of Western India.
B. I.=Bibliotheca Indica Series.
B. O. R. I.=Bhandarkar Oriental Research Institute.
B. S. S. or Bom. S. S.=Bombay Sanskrit Series.
C. C.=Catalogus Catalogorum.
Chan.=Prof. Chandorkar's edition of the Kāvyaprakāśa I, II.
Cal. O. J.=Calcutta Oriental Journal.
Ch. ed.=Chowkhamba Sanskrit series edition.
D. C.=Deccan College.
E. I.=Epigraphia Indica.
Gode=Studies in Indian Literary History, Volumes I-III.
G. O. S.=Gaikwad Oriental Series.
H. of Dh.=History of Dharamśāstra.
H. S. D.=Keith's Sanskrit Drama.
H. S. L.=History of Sanskrit Literature.
H. S. P.=History of Sanskrit Poetics by Dr. De.
I. A.=Indian Antiquary.
I. H. Q.=Indian Historical Quarterly.
I. O. Cat.=India Office Catalogue of S. mss. by Eggeling.
J. A. H. R. S. or J. Āndhra H. R. S.=Journal of Āndhra Historical Research Society.
J. A. S. B.=Journal, Asiatic Society of Bengal.
J. B. B. R. A. S.=Journal, Bombay Branch, Royal Asiatic Society.
J. O. R.=Journal of Oriental Research.
J. I. H.=Journal of Indian History.
J. R. A. S.=Journal of the Royal Asiatic Society, Great Britain.
K. D. or Kāvyād=Kāvyadarśa of Daṇḍin.
K. M.=Kāvyamālā series, Bombay.

K. P.=Kâvyaprakāśa.
K. P. Pr.=Kāvya-Pradīpa-Prabhā.
Kuval.=Kuvalayānanda of Appayya.
New I. A. or N. I. A.=New Indian Antiquary.
Nai=Naiṣadhīya-carita of Srīharṣa.
Nir. or Nirṇ.=Nirṇaya-sāgar Press edition.
N. S.=Nāṭyaśāstra of Bharata.
P. L. M.=Parama - laghu - mañjūṣā of Nāgeśabhaṭṭa.
P. O.=Poona Orientalist.
Ṛg.=Ṛgveda.
R. G.=Rasagaṅgādhara.
Raghu.=Raghuvaṁśā of Kālidāsa.
Ru.=Rudraṭa's Kāvyālaṅkāra.
S. B. E.=Sacred Books of the East (edited by Max Müller).
S. D.=The Sāhityadarpaṇa.
S. K. A.=Sarasvatīkaṇṭhābharaṇa of Bhoja.
Subhā.=Subhāṣitāvali (ed. by Peterson).
Tri. S.=Trivandrum Sanskrit (series).
Ul.=Ullāsa.
Vā.=Vāmanācārya's edition of the Kāvyaprakāśa.
V. O. J.=Vienna Oriental Journal.
Z. D. M. G.=Zeitschrift Deutschen Morgenlandischen Gesselschaft.

(SANSKRIT)

अग्नि or अग्निपु.=अग्निपुराण (Ānan. ed.).
अ. भा.=अभिनवभारती (G. O. S.).
अभिधा० or अ. भा. = अभिधावृत्तिमातृका (Nir.)
अलं. स. or अल. स.=अलङ्कारसर्वस्व (K. M. ed.)
आश्व. गृ.=आश्वलायनगृह्यसूत्र
का. प्र. or काव्यप्र.=काव्यप्रकाश (ed. by Vāmanāchārya)
काव्यमी.=काव्यमीमांसा of राजशेखर (G.O.S. ed.)
काव्या०=काव्यादर्श of दण्डिन्
काव्या. सू. = काव्यालंकारसूत्र of वामन
कुव०=कुवलयानन्द of अप्पय्यदीक्षित
गाथा०=गाथासप्तशती of हाल (Nir.)
चि. मी.=चित्रमीमांसा of अप्पय्यदीक्षित
छा. उ.=छान्दोग्योपनिषद्
ध्व. or ध्वन्या.=ध्वन्यालोक (Nir. ed. of 1935)
नवसा०=नवसाहसाङ्कचरित

नाट्य०=नाट्यशास्त्र of भरत (Ch. ed.)
ना. ल. र. को. = नाटकलक्षणरत्नकोष
पा.=पाणिनि's अष्टाध्यायी
बालरा.=बालरामायण of राजशेखर
बृह. उ. भा. वा.= बृहदारण्यकोपनिषद्-भाष्यवार्तिक of सुरेश्वर.
भा. प्र. or भावप्र.=भावप्रकाशन
या० or याज्ञ.=याज्ञवल्क्यस्मृति
रसग. or रसगं.=रसगङ्गाधर of जगन्नाथ (Nir. ed.)
राज० or राजत० or राजतर०=राजतरङ्गिणी
वक्रोक्ति०=वक्रोक्तिजीवित
वि०, विम०, or विमर्शिनी=अलङ्कारसर्वस्वविमर्शिनी of जयरथ (K. M. ed.)
विद्ध०=विद्धशालभञ्जिका of राजशेखर
विष्णुपु.=विष्णुपुराण
शार्ङ्ग०=शार्ङ्गधरपद्धति edited by Peterson
सं. र =सङ्गीतरत्नाकर
सर. क.=सरस्वतीकण्ठाभरण (Nir. ed.)
सा. द.=साहित्यदर्पण
सि. कौ.=सिद्धान्तकौमुदी of भट्टोजि
सुभा०=सुभाषितावलि of वल्लभदेव ed. by Peterson
सा. मी.=साहित्यमीमांसा (Tri. S. S.)
सूक्तिमु =सूक्तिमुक्तावलि of जल्हण (G. O. S.)
स्मृतिच.=स्मृतिचन्द्रिका of देवण्णभट्ट (ed. by Mr. Gharpure)
हर्ष०=हर्षचरित of बाण

CONTENTS

PART I

PART II

The History of Sanskrit Poetics

The History of Alaṅkāra Literature can naturally be divided into two parts. The first part would have to be devoted to an account of the important works on the Alaṅkāraśāstra, a brief analysis of the contents and the chronology of writers on the Alaṅkāraśāstra and other kindred matters. More space would have to be devoted to early writers. The second part would comprise a review of the subjects that fall to be treated under the Alaṅkāraśāstra, attempt to show how from very small beginnings various theories about Poetics and literary criticism were evolved, dilate upon the different aspects of an elaborate theory of Poetics and trace the historv of literary theories in India.

Part I

1. As in many other branches of Sanskrit Literature, so in the Alaṅkāraśāstra also, we come across many writers whose works have not come down to us and who are no more than mere names to us. राजशेखर, for example, in his काव्यमीमांसा (p.1), tells us how the science of Poetics could claim to have been proclaimed by Śiva to Brahmā, from whom it was handed down to others and how it came to be divided into eighteen sections (अधिकरणs), each of which taught in this world by a particular teacher : 'तत्र कविरहस्यं सहस्राक्षः समाम्नासीत्, औक्तिकमुक्तिगर्भः, रीतिनिर्णयं सुवर्णनाभः, आनुप्रासिकं प्रचेतायनः, यमकानि चित्रं चित्राङ्गदः, शब्दश्लेषं शेषः, वास्तवं पुलस्त्यः, औपम्यमौपकायनः, अतिशयं पाराशरः, अर्थश्लेषमुतथ्यः, उभयालङ्कारिकं कुबेरः, वैनोदिकं कामदेवः, रूपकनिरूपणीयं भरतः, रसाधिकारिकं नन्दिकेश्वरः, दोषाधिकारिकं धिषणः, गुणौपादानिकमुपमन्युः, औपनिषदिकं कुचुमारः, इति.' It is doubtful how far this list is authentic or whether most of the writers named are mythical. It is, however, to be noted that सुवर्णनाभ and कुचुमार appear as teachers of the सांप्रयोगिक and औपनिषदिक sections of Erotics in the कामसूत्र (I. 1. 13 and 17), while Bharata's work dealing with Rūpakas (plays) has come down to modern times. सुवर्णनाभ is frequently mentioned by the कामसूत्र (vide I. 5. 23; II. 2. 23; II. 5. 34; II. 8. 7 &c.). Nandikeśvara is said in the above passage to have written a treatise on Rasas. This is probable. The last chapter in the Kāvyamālā edition of the Nāṭyaśāstra ends with the words

नन्दिभरतसङ्गीतपुस्तकम्. On p. X of the Introduction to the second volume of the अभिनवभारती (GOS) the editor quotes the following from Abhinavagupta's comment on chapter 29 'यत्कीर्तिधरेण नन्दिकेश्वरमतमत्रागमित्वेन दर्शितं तदस्माभिः साक्षान्न दृष्टं तत्प्रत्ययात्तु लिख्यते संक्षेपतः...एवं नन्दिकेश्वरमतानुसारेणायं चित्रपूर्वरङ्गविधिरिति निबद्धः।.' Abhinava says that he has not himself seen Nandikeśvara's work, but relying on Kirtidhara he would briefly point out what Nandikeśvara means. Abhinava knows *Nandimata* from which he quotes a verse on the *aṅgahāra* called *recita* (vide GOS. vol. I. p. 171). The भावप्रकाशन of शारदातनय (chap. 3) says that Nandikeśvara taught nāṭya to Bharata and asked the latter to teach it to *bharatas* (actors). A work called अभिनयदर्पण in 324 verses attributed to नन्दिकेश्वर has been edited (with an English translation and a learned Introduction) by Prof. Manomohan Ghosh in the Calcutta S. Series (1934). The first verse is : आङ्गिकं भुवनं यस्य वाचिकं सर्ववाङ्मयम्। आहार्यं चन्द्रतारादि तं नुमः सात्त्विकं शिवम् ॥[1]. It refers to the legend of Brahmā delivering the नाट्यवेद to भरत and mentions भरतमुनि and his doctrines by name in numerous places (e. g. verses 12, 128, 149, 159, 162 &c.). This work differs from the Nāṭyaśāstra in certain particulars, but, as it mentions Bharata and his *āgama* frequently, it must be much later than the present Nāṭyaśāstra. A work called भरतार्णव is described in the Catalogue, vol. XII, of the Govt. mss. at the BORI at pp. 460-463. It deals with *abhinaya* and *tāla* and appears to be a compilation made from the work of Nandikeśvara by one Sumati. Kāśyapa is recognized as a *muni* that preceded Bharata and his opinion on *rāgas* is cited by Abhinava (Intro. p. X to 2nd Vol. of अभिनवभारती, G. O. S.). Three verses of Kāśyapa are quoted by कल्लिनाथ on सं. र. II. 2. 31. काश्यप is cited as an authority on metrics in Agnipurāna chap. 336. 22. Vide Dr. De in HSP vol. I. p. 2 note 2. In the ms. 41 of 1924-28 of the A. B. at the Bhandarkar O. Institute pp. 384-391 about 75 verses are quoted from Kaśyapamuni.[2] The भावप्रकाशन (I. p. 2) quotes a number of

---

1 This verse occurs in सं. र. VII. 1 also.

2 'अत्र टीकाकारः शङ्कते योऽयं जात्यंशकानां विनियोग उक्तः स कश्यपमुनिमतादिभिर्विरुध्यते। ...अत्राहुः। काश्यपाद्यैस्तावन्मालव-कैशिकानां तत्तच्चित्तवृत्त्या जीवनौचित्यं दृष्ट्वा विनियोग उक्तः।'; see अभिनवभारती on chap. 29 p. 384. Then about 75 verses follow, the last half of which is: इत्येष कश्यपाद्युक्तो विनियोगो निरूपितः।

expounders of नाट्य such as सदाशिव, गौरी, वासुकि, नारद, अगस्त्य, व्यास, आञ्जनेय and the pupils of भरत. The सङ्गीतरत्नाकर (I. 15-19) mentions a host of divine, semi-divine and human authors among whom we have सदाशिव, ब्रह्मा, भरत, कश्यप, मतङ्ग, कोहल, नारद, तुम्बर, आञ्जनेय, नन्दिकेश्वर. नान्यदेव wrote a work called भरतभाष्य or सरस्वतीहृदयालङ्कारहार which is a commentary in verse on chapters 28-33 of the भरतनाट्यशास्त्र (dealing with music) and mentions मतङ्ग, विशाखिल, काश्यप and वृद्धकाश्यप, नन्दिन्, दन्तिल as ancient authorities. नान्यदेव is identified with king नान्यदेव of मिथिला (1097-1133 A. D.). Vide description below of D. C. ms. No. 111 of 1869-70 described in Des. Cat. of Govt. mss. at B. O. R. I. Vol. XII pp. 377-383 and Mr. Ramkrishna Kavi's paper on the same in J. A. H. R. S. vol. I. pp. 56-63. It is possible that Parāśara in the above quoted passage of काव्यमी० means बादरायण, who is mentioned as a भरतपुत्र in the नाट्यशास्त्र I. 32 (बादरायणि in Ch. ed.) and whose views on नान्दी and तोटक are quoted by सागरनन्दिन (in ना. ल. र. को. ll. 1091, 2770, 3202-3). The हृदयङ्गमा, a commentary on the काव्यादर्श, informs us that काश्यप and वररुचि had composed works on Poetics before the काव्यादर्श – 'पूर्वेषां काश्यपवररुचिप्रभृतीनामाचार्याणां लक्षणशास्त्राणि संहृत्य पर्यालोच्य' (on I. 2) and 'पूर्वसूरिभिः काश्यपवररुचिप्रभृतिभिः' (on II. 7). The com. श्रुतानुपालिनी on the काव्या० mentions काश्यप, ब्रह्मदत्त and नन्दिस्वामी as the predecessors of Daṇḍin. The Simhalese *siya-bas-lakara*, a work on rhetoric, after paying homage to ब्रह्मा, शक्र and बृहस्पति, refers to a sage काश्यप (J. R. A. S. 1905 p. 841). All these works are no longer available. Vide मत्स्यपु. X. 25 for वररुचि as नाट्यवेदपारग.

The question naturally arises :—what is the most ancient extant work on the Alaṅkāraśāstra ? Some comparatively modern writers on Alaṅkāra have put forward the Agnipurāṇa as the original source of all later teachings on this *śāstra*. There fore, the claims of the अग्निपुराण must be carefully examined.[1]

2. **The Agnipurāṇa.** महेश्वर in his काव्यप्रकाशादर्श says 'सुकुमारान्राजकुमारान् स्वादुकाव्यप्रवृत्तिद्वारा गहने शास्त्रान्तरे प्रवर्तयितु**मग्निपुराणा**दुद्धृत्य काव्यरसास्वादकारणमलङ्कारशास्त्रं कारिकाभिः संक्षिप्य भरतमुनिः प्रणीतवान्.' Similarly, the कृष्णानन्दिनी, a commentary on the साहित्यकौमुदी of विद्याभूषण, says 'काव्यरसास्वादनाय **वह्निपुराणा**दिदृष्टां साहित्यप्रक्रियां भरतः संक्षिप्ताभिः कारिकाभिर्निबबन्ध.'

---

1 For detailed discussion of this question, *vide* my paper in I. A. vol. 46, 1917, pp. 173 ff.

The अग्निपुराण has been frequently printed in India (in the B. I. series, Ānandāśrama series and at the Veṅkaṭeśvara Press in Bombay). Chapters 336-346 of the B. I. edition deal with subjects falling within the province of Poetics. Chapters 336-346 of the B. I. edition correspond to chapters 337-347 of the Ānan. ed. of the Agnipurāṇa; unfortunately, the readings of the Agnipurāṇa presented in the Ānan. ed. are much worse than those in the B. I. ed. In this work the B. I. text has been followed. The edition brought out by the Veṅkaṭeśvara Press, Bombay, follows the Ānan. ed. of the Agnipurāṇa in the numbering of the chapters. It may be noted that, according to the Matsyapurāṇa 35. 28-30 and Skandapurāṇa VII (Prabhāsakhaṇḍa) 1. 2. 47-50 (यत्तदीशानकल्पस्य वृत्तान्तमधिकृत्य च। वसिष्ठायाग्निना प्रोक्तमाग्नेयं तत्प्रचक्षते ॥...तच्च षोडशसाहस्रं सर्वक्रतुफलप्रदम् ॥), the Agni is 16000 verses in extent, deals with the incidents of Īśānakalpa and is narrated to Vasiṣṭha by Agni. The extant Agni states (in chap. 271. 11) that its extent is 12000 ślokas and that it expounds all the *vidyās*. In the first chapter Vasiṣṭha requests Agni (verse 12) to instruct him in the essence of *vidyās*, by knowing which a man may become omniscient. The extant Agnipurāṇa has about 11500 verses (and not 16000). In the last chapter (382. 51-54) it states that all *vidyās* have been dealt with and it enumerates the several subjects treated of such as the *avatāras*, Gītā, Rāmāyaṇa, Bhārata, Harivaṁśa, the Āgamas, āśauca, prāyaścitta, rājadharma, vyavahāra, vratas &c. Chapters 122-148 contain a summary of युद्धजयार्णव. We have hardly any means for judging which parts were in the original Agnipurāṇa and which were interpolated later. The commentary of Maheśvara and that on Vidyābhūṣaṇa quoted above apparently make no distinction between Agnipurāṇa and Vahnipurāṇa. But there is a Vahnipurāṇa that is different from the extant Agnipurāṇa as Eggeling's Catalogue of India Office Sanskrit mss. part 6 pp. 1294 ff clearly shows. Vide Prof. Hazra's papers 'On present Agni' in I. H. Q. Vol. XII pp. 683-691, 'Studies in genuine Āgneya alias Vahnipurāṇa' in 'Our Heritage' vol. I part 2 pp. 209-245, and vol. II part 1 pp. 70-109 and 'Discovery of genuine Āgneyapurāṇa' in JOI (Baroda) vol. V (1956) pp. 411-416. Most of the passages quoted in the दानसागर and अद्भुतसागर of बल्लालसेन (3rd quarter of 12th century A. D.) from the Agnipurāṇa are not found in the present Agnipurāṇa, and in many extracts the interlocutors are Vasiṣṭha and king Ambarīṣa (and not Agni and Vasiṣṭha as in the current Agni). It appears that the old Agnipurāṇa was recast and then it assumed the present form. Vide J. O. R., Madras, Vol. XII p. 129 at pp. 134–135 (for the paper 'Purāṇas known to Ballālasena'). Chapter 336 (=337 of Ānan. ed) defines a *Kāvya*, classifies *Kāvyas* into संस्कृत and प्राकृत (of three sorts) into गद्य, पद्य and मिश्र; subdivides these and defines in particular कथा, आख्यायिका, महाकाव्य. Chapter 337 deals with topics of dramaturgy (such as twelve kinds of dramas, उपरूपकs, प्रस्तावना, the five अर्थप्रकृतिs, the five सन्धिs). Chapter 338 speaks of the *rasas* together with the स्थायिभावs, अनुभावs, व्यभिचारिभावs, the आलम्बनविभाव and उद्दीपनविभाव, the various kinds of heroes and their companions and the heroines (नायिका), the eight qualities of heroes and the twelve *vibhāvas* of heroines. Chapter 339 speaks of the four *rītis*, पाञ्चाली, गौडी, वैदर्भी and लाटी and the four वृत्तिs, भारती, सात्त्वती, कौशिकी (कैशिकी?) and आरभटी. Chapter 340 contains a description of the various natural movements of the principal limbs (head, hands, feet &c.) and other parts of the body (eyebrows &c.) in dancing. Chapter 341 dilates upon the four kinds of अभिनय (acting), सात्त्विक, वाचिक, आङ्गिक and आहार्य. Chapter 342 defines and divides शब्दालङ्कारs, viz. अनुप्रास, यमक (of ten kinds), चित्र (seven varieties), 16 kinds of प्रहेलिकाs, *bandhas* called गोमूत्रिका, सर्वतोभद्र &c. Chap. 343 deals with अर्थालङ्कारs (such as उपमा, रूपक सहोक्ति &c, their definitions and sub-divisions). Chap. 344 is spoken of as dealing with शब्दार्थालङ्कारs, but therein are included such figures as आक्षेप, समासोक्ति, पर्यायोक्त. Chapters 345 and 346 dwell respectively upon the गुणs and दोषs of काव्य. There are in all 362 verses in these chapters.

It is not possible to give here even a brief analysis of the contents of the 11500 verses of the Agnipurāṇa. It is an encyclopaedia dealing with all sorts of subjects in which mediaeval India was interested.

The evidence for determining the date of the Agnipurāṇa (and particularly of the *sāhitya* portion) and for examining whether it can be regarded as the oldest extant work on Poetics is as follows:—

(a) The अग्निपुराण refers to the seven kāṇḍas of the रामायण, to the हरिवंश, to पिङ्गल (327. 1, 336. 22), पालकाप्य, शालिहोत्र, धन्वन्तरि and सुश्रुत. It contains (chap. 380) a short summary in 58

श्लोक्s of the भगवद्गीता by combining half verses of the latter. Chapters 359–366 contain lexical matter almost the whole of which is identical with the verses and portions of verses of the अमरकोश. It cannot be supposed that all these works (the गीता, अमरकोश &c.) borrowed from the अग्निपुराण. It must be supposed that the अग्निपुराण in its desire to give summaries of every branch of literature drew upon the lexicon that was most popular when the *purāṇa* was compiled. Various dates have been assigned to अमरसिंह. Prof. Macdonell (H. S. L. p. 433) thinks it not improbable that he flourished about 500 A. D. Max Müller says that the अमरकोश was translated into Chinese in the 6th century (India; what can it teach us ? lst. ed. p. 232). Dr. Hoernle (JRAS 1906 p. 940) places the अमरकोश between 625 and 940 A. D. rather on shadowy grounds. Mr. Oak places it in the 4th century A. D. Taking even this early date, the अग्निपुराण, if it borrowed from the अमरकोश, cannot be earlier than the 6th or 7th century A. D., as a good deal of time must have elapsed before the अमरकोश could attain a pre-eminent position as a lexicon.

(b) The अग्निपुराण says that the *rīti* Bhāratī was so called because it was promulgated by भरत (भरतेन प्रणीतत्वाद्भारती रीतिरुच्यते। chap. 339. 6). भरत says that he promulgated the four *vṛttis* by order of Brahmā and that the भारतीवृत्ति was so called after the *Bharatas* (मया काव्यक्रियाहेतोः प्रक्षिप्ता द्रुहिणाज्ञया ॥ ...स्वनामधेयैः भरतैः प्रयुक्ता सा भारती नाम भवेत्तु वृत्तिः॥ नाट्य. 22. 23 and 25, K. M. ch. 22. 23 and 25=GOS ed. chap. 20. 24–26. This shows that the अग्निपुराणं had before it the नाट्यशास्त्र of भरत (or at least the portion dealing with वृत्तिs). Though the नाट्यशास्त्र knows works of the *purāṇa* class (अन्येऽपि देशाः प्राच्यां ये पुराणे संप्रकीर्तिताः। नाट्य. 14. 46, K. M. 13. 46), yet it nowhere alludes to the अग्निपुराण.

(c) There are numerous verses in the अग्निपुराण that are identical with verses of the नाट्यशास्त्र. Compare नाट्य. 6. 36 first half and अग्नि. 338. 12; नाट्य. 6. 39 and अग्नि. 348. 7–9; नाट्य. 22. 28–29 and अग्नि. 337. 11–12; नाट्य. 17. 63–65 and अग्नि. 342. 15–17. Taking the express statement of the Purāṇa that it was to be an encyclopaedia of all vidyās and the character of the two works into consideration it will have to be conceded that it is the अग्निपुराण that borrows.

(d) The definitions of रूपक, उत्प्रेक्षा, विशेषोक्ति, विभावना, अपह्नुति and समाधि given by the अग्निपुराण (343, 23, 24–25, 26–27, 27–28,

344. 18, 13 respectively) are almost the same as those of the काव्यादर्श (II. 66, 221, 323, 199, 304, I. 93 respectively). Besides these, there are many phrases and half verses that occur in both works, e. g.—पद्यं चतुष्पदी तच्च वृत्तं जातिरिति त्रिधा (अग्नि. 336. 21 and काव्या. I. 11); सा विद्या नौस्तितीर्षूणां गम्भीरं काव्यसागरम् (अग्नि. 336. 23 and काव्या. I. 12); अग्नि. 336. 29 and काव्या. I. 16; अग्नि. 336. 25 and काव्या. I. 15. It has not been possible to point out (except in two instances, viz. काव्या. II. 226, the well known verse लिम्पतीव &c. and 276 अद्य या मम &c.) that Daṇḍin borrows his definitions or even examples from others. Daṇḍin belongs, as will be shown later on, to the latter half of 7th century. So the अग्निपुराण, if it borrows from the काव्यादर्श, must be later than this date.

(e) The definitions of रूपक, आक्षेप, अप्रस्तुतप्रशंसा, समासोक्ति and पर्यायोक्त are almost identical in भामह (II. 21, 68, III. 29, 8, II. 79) and the अग्निपुराण (343. 22; 344. 15; 344. 16; 344. 18; 344. 17). भामह distinctly states that he composed his own examples and also himself settled the definitions of figures (स्वयंकृतैरेव निदर्शनैरियं मया प्रकॢप्ता खलु वागलंकृतिः। भामह II. 96; गिरामलङ्कारविधिः सविस्तरः स्वयं विनिश्चित्य धिया मयोदितः। III. 58). भामह, as shown below, is not earlier than 700 A. D.

(f) It appears that the अग्निपुराण was aware of the theory of *dhvani* promulgated in the Dhvanikārikās and elaborately set forth in the Dhvanyāloka. It says that ध्वनि will be included in some one out of पर्यायोक्त, अपह्नुति, समासोक्ति, अप्रस्तुतप्रशंसा, आक्षेप; स आक्षेपो ध्वनिः स्याच्च ध्वनिना व्यज्यते यतः and एषामेकतमस्येव (स्यैव ?) समाख्या ध्वनिरित्यतः। अग्नि. 344. 14 and 18. This shows that though the अग्निपुराण knew the theory of ध्वनि it was not willing to subscribe to it. This view of the अग्निपुराण is similar to the view of भामह and उद्भट as said by the अलङ्कारसर्वस्व—'इह हि तावद्भामहोद्भटप्रभृतयश्चिरन्तनालङ्कारकाराः प्रतीयमानमर्थं वाच्योपस्कारकतयालङ्कारपक्षनिक्षिप्तं मन्यन्ते। तथाहि—पर्यायोक्ताप्रस्तुतप्रशंसासमासोक्त्याक्षेपव्याजस्तुत्युपमेयोपमानन्वयादौ वस्तुमात्रं गम्यमानं वाच्योपस्कारकत्वेन स्वसिद्धये पराक्षेपः परार्थं स्वसमर्पणमिति यथायोगं द्विविधया भङ्ग्या प्रतिपादितं तैः' (p. 3). *Vide* also ध्व० 'पर्यायोक्तेऽपि यदि प्राधान्येन व्यंग्यत्वं तद्भवतु नाम तस्य ध्वनावन्तर्भावः। न तु ध्वनेस्तत्रान्तर्भावः।' (p. 45-46). Therefore, it can be argued that the portion on Poetics in the अग्निपुराण is not much later than the ध्वन्यालोक. The latter work, it will be seen, was composed in the latter half of the 9th century. It is further to be noted that two verses (अपारे काव्यसंसारे &c. and शृङ्गारी चेत्कविः &c.) occur in the अग्निपुराण (338. 10-11 = 339.

10–11 of Ānan. ed.) and in the ध्वन्यालोक (p. 278). In the latter these verses are introduced with the words तथा चेदमुच्यते and so it is argued that the ध्वन्यालोक is merely quoting from another work. But these verses are followed, by a brief dicussion which winds up with the words ध्वनिरेव प्राधान्येन काव्यमिति स्थितमेतत् (pp. 278-9). In this connection it has to be remembered that on the very preceding page (277) the ध्वन्यालोक introduces two verses with the words तदिदमुक्तं which are explained by अभिनवगुप्त as मयैवेत्यर्थः, thereby showing that those verses are of आनन्दवर्धन himself. One fails to see any difference between तदिदमुच्यते and तदिदमुक्तम्. So the two verses on p. 278 of the ध्वन्या. should be deemed to be आनन्दवर्धन's own and and it should be held that the लोचन did not add 'by me the author of ध्वन्या.', because it had explained two verses occurring in the same context as composed by आनन्दवर्धन and because the occurrence of च (in तथा चेदमुच्यते) at the time of quoting the two verses on p. 278 and its non-occurrence on p. 277 (तदिदमुक्तम्) indicate that the two verses on p. 278 are the author's own. Dr. De. (in H. S. P. vol. I. p. 103) holds, without assigning any substantial reason, that it is Ānandavardhana that borrows from the Agnipurāṇa. Dr. De (H. S. P. vol. II p. 255 n.) persisted in his view that Ānandavardhana borrows the two verses on p. 278 from the Āgnipurāṇa, though it was brought to his notice by the late Prof. Sovani that Abhinava expressly ascribes the authorship of one of the two verses to Ānandavardhana in his comment on the Nāṭyaśāstra VI. 36–37 (G. O. S. ed. vol. I p. 295) "कविर्हि सामाजिकतुल्य एव। तत एवोक्तं 'शृङ्गारी चेत्कविः' इत्याद्यानन्दवर्धनाचार्येण". Therefore, I am of opinion that the Agnipurāṇa not only knew the Dhvani theory but actually borrowed two verses from the Dhvanyāloka. Prof. Batuknath Bhattacharya (Department of Letters, Calcutta University, vol. IX p. 129) states that 'the Agnipurāṇa shows no trace of the Dhvani theory.' But in this he is quite wrong as the above discussion will show. In chap. 339 (Ānan ed) the अग्निपुराण names the Rasas, the sthāyi-bhāvas, sāttvika-bhāvas (i. e. the रस theory) and in chap. 345. 18 it includes ध्वनि under such alaṅkāras as समासोक्ति, अपह्नुति, पर्यायोक्त 'पर्यायोक्तं यदन्येन प्रकारेणाभिधीयते। एषामेकतमस्यैव समाख्या ध्वनिरित्यतः।'.

(g) In the 5th chap. of S. K. Ā. the first four verses present in a brief compass Bhoja's Rasa theory of one Rasa Śṛṅgāra as Ānanda-Ahaṅkāra-Abhimāna-Rasa. This is propounded at great length in the Śṛṅgāra-prakāśa in chap. XI. The Agnipurāṇa (in chap. 338. 1-4) briefly touches this doctrine: अक्षरं परमं ब्रह्म सनातनमजं विभुम्। वेदान्तेषु वदन्त्येकं चैतन्यं ज्योतिरीश्वरम् ॥ आनन्दः सहजस्तस्य व्यज्यते स कदाचन। व्यक्तिः सा तस्य चैतन्यचमत्काररसाह्वया ॥ आद्यस्तस्य विकारो यः सोऽहङ्कार इति स्मृतः। ततोऽभिमानस्तत्रेदं समाप्तं भुवनत्रयम् ॥ अभिमानाद्रतिः सा च परिपोषमुपेयुषी। व्यभिचार्यादिसामान्याच्छृङ्गार इति गीयते ॥ तद्भेदाः काममितरे हास्याद्या अप्यनेकशः (अग्नि॰ 338. 1-5); vide Agnipurāṇa, 341. 3 also. But the Agnipurāṇa, caring only for presenting the essence of several theories, tries to round off the theory of Ānanda-Ahaṅkāra-Abhimāna-Rati by introducing in verses 7-9 the usual theory of eight or nine rasas based on Bharata's Nāṭyaśāstra. It is not possible to believe as Dr. De does (in H. S. P vol. II p. 334) that Bhoja built his all-embracing and elaborately worked out theory on the confused verses of the Agni (chap. 338). In chap. 338. 54 and 339 (verses 1-4) the Agnipurāṇa deals with four kinds of रीतिs (styles), viz. पाञ्चाली, वैदर्भी, गौडी, and लाटी. The functions of these closely resemble what Bhoja says in the Śṛṅgāra-prakāśa (vide Dr. Raghavan in J. O. R, Madras vol. X p. 768-779 wherein he criticizes some of the statements of Prof. P. C. Lahiri in I. H. Q. vol. IX pp. 448 ff, and in his Śṛṅgāra-prakāśa vol. I part I pp. 196-201). It is therefore proper to hold that the Agnipurāṇa which is not an original work on any subject but a mere encyclopaedic compilation most probably derived its inspiration from Bhoja.

It has been shown by me in my H. of Dh. vol. I pp. 170-173 that the Vyavahāra chapters (252-257) of the Agni borrow about 30 verses from Nāradasmṛti in chap. 252 and about 280 verses from the Yājñavalkyasmṛti in the other chapters.

The foregoing discussion goes to establish that the अग्निपुराण is later than the 7th century at least and that the section on Poetics was certainly compiled about or a little after 900 A. D. and probably after 1050 A. D.

It is significant that no early writer on Poetics quotes from or refers to the Agnipurāṇa. मम्मट quotes from the विष्णुपुराण but nowhere refers to the अग्निपुराण. The first Alaṅkāra writer of note who distinctly mentions the अग्निपुराण as an authority on Poetics is विश्वनाथ (14th century), who quotes अग्नि 336. 3-4 (in साहित्यदर्पण under I. 2) and 337. 7 (त्रिवर्गसाधनंनाट्यं), although works on धर्मशास्त्र such as अपरार्कटीका and the अद्भुतसागर of बल्लालसेन (begun in 1168 A. D.) refer to the Agnipurāṇa as an authority. But भरत's नाट्यशास्त्र is quoted with reverence by the ध्वन्यालोक, the लोचन and other early writers. Even भामह and दण्डी appear to refer to him as an authority as will be shown later on. Therefore, the अग्निपुराण is later than भरत, भामह, दण्डी, the ध्वन्यालोक and probably भोज and has no claim to be regarded as an original work on the अलङ्कारशास्त्र. Moreover, mediaeval writers, guided by their reverence for Purāṇas in general, because they were ascribed to the mythical Vyāsa, naturally looked upon the अग्निपुराण as the most ancient work on the अलङ्कारशास्त्र.

3. The Nāṭyaśāstra of Bharata. For several reasons the Nāṭyaśāstra must be regarded as the oldest extant work on the theory of Sanskrit Poetics. The work contains the first exposition of the *rasa* theory (for which see part II) and also contains considerable information upon many topics pertaining to the Alaṅkāraśāstra.

When I wrote this history of Alaṅkāra Literature in 1923 for prefixing it as an Introduction to my edition of the Sāhityadarpaṇa the only complete edition of the Nāṭyaśāstra that was available was the one in the Kāvyamālā series. Later on in 1929 Pandit Batuknath Sharma and Pandit Baladeva Upādhyāya published in the Kashi Sanskrit Series (often cited as the Chowkhamba S. Series) a complete edition of the Nāṭyaśāstra based on two mss. that appear to have been different from those used for the original K. M. edition. In 1929 Mr. Ramkrishna Kavi brought out the first volume of the Nāṭyaśāstra containing chapters 1-7 together with the very important and learned commentary of Ācārya Abhinavagupta in the Gaekwad Oriental Series. The 2nd volume containing chapters 8-18 together with the commentary called Abhinavabhāratī in the colophons as well as by later writers such as Rāghavabhaṭṭa in his com. on the Śākuntala was published in 1934. The third volume containing chapters 19-27 with the Abhinavabhāratī, edited by Mr. Kavi, was published in the G. O. S. in 1954. Prof. Manmohan Ghosh has brought out a translation of chapters 1-27 of the Nāṭyaśāstra for the Asiatic Society of Bengal (1950) with a lengthy Introduction, pp. XXXV—L of which deal with the attempts of scholars to publish various chapters of the Nāṭyaśāstra and the remaining pages deal with many matters such as the meaning of nāṭya, vṛttis, literary structure, kinds of plays, plot and its development, play-house, costumes and make-up, early and later writers on Drama, the two recensions and commentators of the Nāṭyaśāstra.

In this brief Introduction it is impossible for want of space to go deeply into the question of the text of the Nāṭyaśāstra. Certain important points alone will be noted. The mss. and the editions do not agree as to the number of ślokas in each chapter, about the number of chapters and also about their places in the book. The recent K. M. edition contains 37 chapters, while the Ch. edition contains 36, the last chap. combining into one the two chapters of the K. M. edition viz. 36 and 37. Abhinava in his 2nd Introductory verse (षट्त्रिंशकं भरतसूत्रमिदं विवृण्वन) and on p. 8 of vol. I (मध्ये षटत्रिंशाध्याय्यां) says that there are 36 chapters. Abhinava further says that the extent of the Nāṭyaśāstra is 6000 ślokas (each śloka being taken as equal to 32 syllables); further, no two corresponding chapters of the two editions have the same number of verses (except chap. 6 and chap. 19 of K. M.=21 of Ch. on Sandhyaṅgas). Chapter IX of K. M. edition is split into two chapters IX and X in the Ch. ed. Therefore, the numbering of the chapters in the two editions differs from that stage onwards. Some of the verses of chapter 24, sāmānyābhinaya, of the K. M, edition, occur as chap. 34 in the Ch. ed. and the rest (verses 90–115) are placed in chap. 35 of the Ch. ed.

Some portions of the text of the Nāṭyaśāstra were published from time to time during the last 85 years. Hall in his edition of the Daśarūpa of Dhanañjaya (B. I. series, 1865) added at the end four chapters of the Nāṭyaśāstra viz. 18, 19, 20 (which correspond with chapters 18–20 of K. M. edition, the verses in Hall's edition being respectively 132, 133 and 63 as against 198, 133, 66 of the K. M. edition) and chap. 34 having 121 verses (which corresponds with chap. 24 of K. M. ed. that has only 116 verses and with chap. 34 and a portion of chap. 35 of the Ch. edition). In Annales du Musee Guimet, vol. II pp. 69 ff. P. Regnaud published two chapters of the Nāṭyaśāstra on Metrics, viz. 15th and 16th (with 68 and 160 verses), corresponding with chapters 14 and 15 of the K. M. ed. (with 120 and 172 verses) and chapters

15 and 16 of the Ch. ed. (with 119 and 169 verses respectively) and chap. 14 and 15 of the G. O. S. ed. (with 133 and 227 verses respectively). The same scholar published in his 'Rhetorique Sanskrite' (1884) the 6th and 7th chapters of the Nāṭyaśāstra in Roman characters and translation in French. The verses in these two chapters of Regnaud's edition are 84 and 123 (while K. M. has 84 and 130 and Ch. has 83 and 124 respectively).

The above statement is quite sufficient to show that the text of the Nāṭyaśāstra is unsatisfactory and has been tampered with in almost every chapter. Those who want to go into the question of the additions and alterations made in the text of the Nāṭyaśāstra may read Mr. Kavi's Intro. to vol. I and II of the Abhinavabhāratī. Here again striking variations alone can be noted.

I. From a verse in the Vikramorvaśīya of Kālidāsa (II.18) it follows that in his day Bharata-muni was credited with having declared that the *rasas* in Nāṭya were eight and that he represented a play before Indra with Apsarases as actresses (मुनिना भरतेन यः प्रयोगो भवतीष्वष्टरसाश्रयः प्रयुक्तः। ललिताभिनयं तमद्य भर्ता मरुतां द्रष्टुमनाः सलोकपालः ॥). The chief points of this verse are found in the extant Nāṭyaśāstra (vide Ch. ed. chap. I for the instruction of Bharata in the Nāṭyaveda, performance of a play with the help of Apsarases, verses 47–50, the presence of Śakra and Lokapālas verses 55 ff. and chap. 6. 15 for the eight rasas 'शृङ्गारहास्यकरुणरौद्रवीरभयानकाः। बीभत्साद्भुतसंज्ञौ चेत्यष्टौ नाट्ये रसाः स्मृताः ॥'). The Ch. edition closes the 6th chapter with the verse (एवमेते रसा ज्ञेयास्त्वष्टौ लक्षणलक्षिताः। 83). The काव्यादर्श (II. 292 इह त्वष्टरसायत्ता रसवत्ता स्मृता गिराम्) shows that even in the 7th century the recognized *rasas* were only eight. Abhinavagupta notes that some people did not recognize nine rasas but only eight and that in old mss. he found a disquisition on *śānta rasa* and its *sthāyibhāva śama*. 'ये पुनर्नव रसा इति पठन्ति तन्मते शान्तस्वरूपमभिधीयते। G. O. S. vol. I p. 333; and again "तस्मादस्ति शान्तो रसः। तथा च चिरन्तनपुस्तकेषु 'स्थायिभावान् रसत्वमुपनेष्यामः'—इत्यनन्तरं 'शान्तो नाम शमस्थायिभावात्मकः' इत्यादि शान्तलक्षणं पठ्यते।" G. O. S. vol. I p. 340. Regnaud's edition of chap 6. reads त्वष्टौ नाट्यरसाः स्मृताः. This establishes that Śānta had not been recognised as a *rasa* at the time of Kālidāsa (between 350–450 A. D. at the latest) but had been recognized long before Abhinavagupta (i. e. centuries before 1000 A. D.) and that Abhinava knew that there were two recensions of N. S. Udbhaṭa in his काव्यालङ्कारसारसंग्रह (IV. 5.) mentions nine rasas (शृङ्गारहास्य...नकाः । बीभत्साद्भुतशान्ताश्च नव नाट्ये रसाः स्मृताः ॥). The भावप्रकाशन (G. O. S. ed., pp. 46-48) appears to hold that Vāsuki added Śāntarasa. Apart from the question whether any reliance is to be placed on this piece of information, it would follow from the facts brought out above that Śāntarasa was recognized in the mss. of the Nāṭyaśāstra at some time after 400 A. D. and before 750 A. D.

II. At the end of chapter 5 about 40 verses (KM 181-220, Ch. 176-215) are omitted in several mss. and it is noteworthy that Abhinava does not comment on them. They were probably taken over from Nandikeśvara (vide Intro. to vol. I p. 10).

III. Chapters 9 (verses 207) and 10 (verses 55) of the Ch. ed. form one chapter 9 (verses 267) in K. M. edition. Abhinavagupta also puts the two as one.

IV. At the beginning of the 15th chap. on metres, Abhinava notes that there were two recensions: तत्रेहाध्याये भरतमुनिकृतमिति त्रिकैर्मकारादिभिः कैश्चित् किंचिल्लक्षणं स्वीकृतमिति द्विविधः पाठो दृश्यते । मध्ये च चिन्तनाय (? चिरन्तनेषु) पुस्तकेषूभयमपि पठ्यते इति । अ. भा. vol. II pp. 252-253. The original KM ed. agrees with the latter.

V. In chap. 16 of the K. M. ed., and chap. 17 of Ch. ed., the 36 *Lakṣaṇas* of Nāṭya are enumerated in five anuṣṭubh verses, but in chap. 16 of the G. O. S. edition the enumeration is made in four Upajāti verses. Further, the order of the 36 Lakṣaṇas is not the same in the two lists and only 17 names are common in both. A. B. remarks that Bharata himself employs other names for the Lakṣaṇas which are different from those enumerated by him, that it is due to this that in the mss. there is variation in the names and order of Lakṣaṇas and that it follows the tradition of the author's *guru* (Tota) as to the names and order (तथा च मतान्तरेण भरतमुनिरेवान्यथाप्युद्देशलक्षणेन नामान्तरैरपि च व्यवहारं करोति तत एव पुस्तकेषु भेदो दृश्यते तं च दर्शयिष्यामः । पठितोद्देशक्रमस्त्वस्मदुपाध्यायपरम्परागतः । on XVI. 4, vol. II p. 298). This shows that in अभिनव's day there were two recensions of the chapter on लक्षणs. Vide Dr. Raghavan's paper on Lakṣaṇas in J. O. R. Madras, vol. VI pp. 54-82. धनिक on दशरूप 4. 78 and राघवभट्ट in अर्थद्योतनिका set out the enumeration in Upajāti, while the Sāhitydarpaṇa and some others give the names as in the Anuṣṭubh verses.

VI. It has already been stated that chap. 24 of the K. M. ed. is distributed among two chapters 34 and 35 of the Ch. ed. and that chap. 36 and 37 of K. M ed. become one chapter (36) in Ch. ed. and in अभिनवभारती.

VII. In the K. M. edition there are 334 verses in chapter 31, while in the Ch. ed. there are 545 in the same chapter. The new K. M. edition notes (on p. 520). that a block of 92 verses is added in one ms. after the verse आकारवृत्तमन्यत्स्यात् चतुष्कं त्रिकमेव वा । (verse 293 in K. M. ed. and 397 in Ch. ed). Mr. Kavi notes (in Intro. to vol. II p. XIV) that Abhinava's text omits only about half of these verses. Mr. Kavi (Intro. to vol. I p. 7) states that he secured 40 mss. of the text of the Nāṭyaśāstra and admits that no two of them agree completely (*ibid.* p. 9). He also says that there are according to him two recensions of the text of the Nāṭyaśāstra, the northern one and the southern one. The latter is, according to him, the earlier one and the former later.

From the statements Mr. Kavi makes in his two Introductions to the two volumes already published and in the footnotes in the two volumes, it appears that the mss. material for the constitution of the text of the Abhinavabhāratī is quite unsatisfactory. There is no ms. which contains the full text of the Abhinavabhāratī on the 36 chapters. The commentary अभिनवभारती itself sometimes appears in two recensions and differs from भरत himself. Vide a paper by Prof. Manmohan Ghosh in I. H. Q. vol. X pp. 161-163 for some examples. Mr. Kavi was not able to secure Abhinavagupta's commentary on the 7th and 8th chapters of the Nāṭyaśāstra (except a few passages at the beginning of the 7th). As the text of the commentary has to be constituted from different incomplete mss. found at places far apart, the text of the commentary presented would be a patched-up and eclectic one and, therefore, unsatisfactory from a critical point of view. As a portion of Abhinava's commentary on the last verses of the 5th chapter of the Nāṭyaśāstra was not available, Mr. Kavi added his own comment thereon (vol. I pp. 253-264). This has misled some scholars into thinking that it was Abhinava's commentary, in spite of Mr. Kavi's note at the bottom of p. 253. He should have given, if at all, his commentary in an Appendix at the end. On p. 10 of the Intro. to vol. I Mr. Kavi admits that he gave his own commentary in three other cases in the 4th chapter. This is most unfair. An unwary reader, if he has not gone carefully over the Introduction, would easily be misled.

In the circumstances described above about the text of the Nāṭyaśāstra and of the Abhinavabhāratī thereon two questions, that are rather puzzling and difficult of solution, arise, viz. what is the original Nāṭyaśāstra and who is the author.

The striking features of the extant Nāṭyaśāstra[1] are:

(1) There are prose passages in chapter 6th, 7th (very long ones in both), 14th (about 9 lines on प्रवृत्ति, K. M. chap. 13, p. 216), 15th (four lines on p. 170 on स्वर and व्यञ्जन, K. M. chap. 14 pp. 221–22), 19th (pp. 221–222, 224–25), 28th (several long passages on pp. 318–322 and 326, K. M. chap. 28, pp. 432–439), 33rd (pp. 433–435, 436, 438–39 several passages of a few lines each, K. M. chap. 34, pp. 611 ff); 35th (p. 466 two lines on सूत्रधारगुण, K. M. chap. 24, p. 400).

(2) There are at least 15 ślokas and 16 āryās described as *ānuvaṁśya*.

(3) Several verses are introduced with the words सूत्रानुबद्धे आर्ये भवतः

(4) About 100 verses are cited with nothing more than the words भवन्ति चात्र श्लोकाः, or अत्रार्ये भवतः, or अत्र श्लोकाः.

(5) There are over 5000 verses, most of which are in the śloka metre, a few being in other metres such as āryā or upajāti.

Each of these features calls for some explanation.

(1) The prose passages resemble passages of the Nirukta and are in the sūtra and bhāṣya style. For example, the well-known Rasasūtra passage in chap. VI may be cited here : 'विभावानुभावव्यभिचारिसंयोगाद्रसनिष्पत्तिः। को वा दृष्टान्त इति चेत्, उच्यते। यथा नानाव्यञ्जनौषधि...रसत्वमाप्नुवन्ति। ऋषय ऊचुः। रस इति कः पदार्थः। अत्रोच्यते। आस्वाद्यत्वात्।'. Here the first sentence looks like a sūtra and what follows has the appearance of a bhāṣya. To take another example: 'व्यभिचारिण इदानीं वक्ष्यामः। अत्राह व्यभिचारिण इति कस्मादुच्यन्ते। वि अभि इत्येतावुपसर्गौ। चर गतौ धातुः।' &c., chap. VII p. 84. Such passages may be compared with the Nirukta (e. g. III. 1 अपत्यं कस्मात् अपततं भवति नानेन पततीति वा।) or with Śabara's bhāṣya on Jaimini's sūtras

1 The references are throughout made to the Ch. edition except where it is expressly stated to the contrary.

(e.g. को धर्मः कथंलक्षणः काऽन्यस्य साधनानि कानि साधनाभासानि किंपरश्चेति p. 9, Ānan. ed.). It may be noted that Abhinava-gupta calls the Nāṭya-śāstra 'Bharatasūtra'. The extant work itself suggests (in chap. VI. 9-13 and 31) that it contains sūtras, bhāṣya, saṅgraha, kārikās, nirukta (exposition)[1] &c. Abhinava explains that 'sūtra' means 'definition' and *bhāṣya* means 'investigation or examination that will make clear the sūtra' (सूत्रं लक्षणं भाष्यं तद्व्यक्तिकरणरूपा परीक्षा, vol. I p. 256). On the word *kārikā* Abhinava remarks that sūtra also may be called kārikā and the śloka, that is put down after the sūtra having relation to the latter and clarifying the meaning of the latter for easy comprehension, is also called kārikā: सूत्रतः सूत्रणेन तेन सूत्रमपि कारिका। तत्सूत्रमपेक्ष्य या अनु पश्चात्पठिता श्लोकरूपा सापि कारिका। vol. I p. 266. On सूत्रग्रन्थविकल्पनम् (VI. 31 of Ch. ed. and 34 of GOS. ed.) Abhinava says 'सूत्रं सूत्रकं लक्षणं वक्ष्यामि। तेनैव च कारिका संगृहीता। ग्रन्थो भाष्यं तत्कृतं च विकल्पनमाक्षेपप्रतिसमाधानात्मकमिति परीक्षा निरुक्तशब्दवाच्या प्रतिज्ञाता। सूत्रविवरणस्वभावा तु कारिका सूत्रमपि प्रकाशयन्ती बहुतराक्षेपसमाधानव्याकुलशिष्यजनस्थितिपक्षं निरूपणेनोपकरोतीति भाष्यस्य पश्चादस्याः पाठः।' vol. I. p. 273. On 'विभावानु...निष्पत्तिः' the A. B. remarks 'एवं क्रमहेतुमभिधाय लक्षणसूत्रमाह—विभा०'. On 'को दृष्टान्तः, अत्राह यथा हि०'... A. B. observes 'अत्र प्रश्ने भाष्येण प्रतिवचनमाह यथेत्यादिना आप्नुवन्तीत्यन्तेन' vol. I. p. 289. Another example of सूत्र and भाष्य may be given. On pp. 301-302 (vol. I chap. VI) we read : तत्र शृङ्गारो नाम रतिस्थायिभावप्रभव उज्ज्वलवेषात्मकः। &c. The अभिनवभारती notes (p. 303) 'अत्र रतिस्थायीति सूत्रभागं भाष्येण स्पष्टयति स चेत्यादिना।'.

Note has to be taken of the fact that Bhavabhūti in his Uttararāmacarita (IV) refers to Bharata as 'tauryatrikasūtra-kāra.' It should not be supposed that a sūtra work must be entirely in prose. Even such ancient works as the Aitareya and Śatapatha Brāhmaṇas contain verses and Gṛhyasūtras and Dharmasūtras[2] (of Āpastamba, Baudhāyana and Vasiṣṭha)

---

1. विस्तरेणोपदिष्टानामर्थानां सूत्रभाष्ययोः। निबन्धो यः समासेन संग्रहं तं विदुर्बुधाः ॥ रसा भावा ह्यभिनया धर्मीवृत्तिप्रवृत्तयः। सिद्धिः स्वरास्तथातोद्यं गानं रङ्गं च संग्रहः ॥ अल्पाभिधानेनार्थो यः समासेनोच्यते बुधैः। सूत्रतः सा तु विज्ञेया कारिकार्थ-प्रयोगिनी ॥ ... एवमेषोऽल्पसूत्रार्थो व्यादिष्टो नाट्यसंग्रहः। अतःपरं प्रवक्ष्यामि सूत्रग्रन्थ-विकल्पनम् ॥ नाट्य. on VI. 9-11 and 31.

2. Vide for verses in Ap. Dh. Sūtra I. 4. 14. 23, I. 6. 16. 13 (two verses), I. 6. 19. 14-15, I. 9. 25. 10-11, I. 9. 27. 17-11, II. 4. 9. 13. The आश्व. गृ. (I. 3. 10 and IV. 7. 14) has verses and so has the Kauśikagṛhyasūtra 6. 34 (अत्रापि श्लोकौ), 68. 37(तत्र श्लोकौ).

contain verses. In mediaeval times the kārikās in such works as the Kāvya-prakāśa were called sūtras. Therefore, it is quite possible that the original kernel of the Nāṭyaśāstra was in mixed prose and verse.

Next we have to consider the significance of the words 'ānuvaṁśya' in citing certain āryā and anuṣṭubh verses. In the first place it is important to note that verses headed by these words occur mostly in the 6th and 7th chapters and very rarely in others (such as in chap. 19 verses 46–58 of the Ch. ed. and chap. 17 verses 107–119 of the K. M. edition). The expression आनुवंश्यश्लोक occurs very frequently in the Mahābhārata, e. g. in Ādiparva 95.9, 27, 30–31, 46. In the M. B. simply the word आनुवंशं is also used, e. g., वनपर्व 87. 16 'यत्रानुवंशं भगवाञामदग्न्यस्तथा जगौ। विश्वामित्रस्य तां दृष्ट्वा विभूतिमतिमानुषीम् ॥'. In वनपर्व 88. 5 we have the word आनुवंश्या applied to गाथा. Vide also वनपर्व 114. 10, 192. 27–29, 193. 13–15. In वनपर्व 129. 8 we read 'अत्रानुवंशं पठतः शृणु मे कुरुनन्दन', which is explained by the commentator नीलकण्ठ as 'परम्परागतमाख्यानश्लोकम्'. The मत्स्यपुराण 271.15 also has an आनुवंश्यश्लोक. On अत्रानुवंश्यौ श्लोकौ भवतः occurring before VI. 35–36 A. B. remarks: अत्रेति भाष्ये। अनुवंशभवौ शिष्याचार्यपरम्परासु वर्तमानौ श्लोकाख्यौ वृत्तविशेषौ सूत्रार्थसंक्षेपप्रकटीकरणेन कारिकाशब्दवाच्यौ भवन्तौ पठति यथेत्यादि। vol. I. p. 290. It should be noted that अ. भा. (vol. I p. 290) on the prose words preceding verses 35–36 (called आनुवंश्यश्लोकs) explains अत्र as भाष्ये, i. e. it regards the prose passage as भाष्य on the सूत्र 'विभावा...निष्पत्तिः'.

From this it follows that the verses cited as 'ānuvaṁśya' had already been composed and had been traditionally handed down from father to son or from teacher to pupil in relation to dramaturgy and were included in the Nāṭyaśāstra, but that they were not the composition of him who composed the Nāṭyaśāstra.

As regards the words सूत्रानुविद्धे (v. l. सूत्रानुबद्धे) आर्ये भवतः, they mean that the verses are closely connected with the sūtra that precedes (अनुबद्ध) or that they contain in easy language the meaning of the sūtra (अनुविद्ध). It may be said that such verses are the composition of the author himself. A. B. remarks on 'अपि च सुख०' (vol. I. p. 311–12): एवं सूत्रार्थे परीक्ष्य स्थापिते तदर्थस्य सुखग्रहणार्थं सूत्रार्थविवरणरूपत्वात्सूत्रसमीपेष्वुपचितपाठात्कारिकामधुना पठति अपि चेति। न केवलं सूत्रं परीक्षापि यावदियं कारिकेति एवं सर्वत्र मन्तव्यम्। तामेव कारिकां पठति सुखेति।'. These remarks may be applied also to the āryās quoted as sūtrānubaddha.

On अत्रार्या: (vol. I. p. 327–28) अभिनवगुप्त says that former teachers had composed and collected together āryās relating to *rasas* and matters connected with them from which Bharata took verses and inserted them at the proper places under different *rasas* 'ता एता ह्यार्या एकप्रघट्टकतया पूर्वाचार्यैर्लक्षणत्वेन पठिताः। मुनिना तु सुखसंग्रहाय यथास्थानं निवेशिताः।' (vol. I. p. 328). Though the prevailing metre in the Nāṭyaśāstra is Anuṣṭubh it frequently uses other metres also, as e. g. उपजाति (in chap. 20. 26, 41, 53 defining वृत्तिs), आर्या in 20. 64, 22. 274–279, 23. 42–62, 25. 95-103. Here G. O. S. ed. is used. Pages slightly vary in ed. of 1956.

This shows that at least according to Abhinava the Nāṭyaśāstra contains Āryās not composed by Bharata. The भावप्रकाशन quotes a verse from Vāsuki, which is entered in the extant Nāṭyaśāstra among five verses introduced with the words 'भवन्ति चात्र श्लोकाः।' or अत्र श्लोकाः in the editions and in mss. (vide Ch. ed. chap. VI. 34–38, K. M. ed. chap. VI. 35–39, and G. O. S. ed. chap. VI. 38–42). नानाद्रव्यौषधैः पाकैर्व्यञ्जनं भाव्यते यथा। एवं भावा भावयन्ति रसानभिनयैः सह। इति वासुकिनाप्युक्तो भावेभ्यो रससम्भवः। (भा. प्र. pp. 36–37). In the Ch. ed. (6.35) it reads 'नानाद्रव्यैर्बहुविधैर्व्यञ्जनं... यथा। एवं...सह॥'; vide same verse in G. O. S. ed. vol. I. p. 294.

As regards the rest of the portion of the extant Nāṭyaśāstra it has been already shown that in some cases the number of verses varies by several hundreds in different mss. Therefore, it is very difficult to say what the original Nāṭyaśāstra contained. If a very tentative theory may be advanced I would state it as follows: The present 6th and 7th chapters, chapters 8–14 dealing with *abhinaya* of various kinds, movements and gaits, chap. 17 to 35 were put together at one time. The prose portions in the 6th and 7th chapters and the Āryā verses which Abhinava says were taken from older ācāryas were probably composed about 200 B. C. and were taken up into the work when the other chapters were composed. The reasons for this date are as follows: The Gautamadharmasūtra mentions (in XI. 19) Upavedas. Four Upavedas corresponding to the four Vedas are mentioned from very ancient times : viz. Āyurveda, Dhanurveda, Gāndharvaveda and Arthaśāstra (or Sthāpatya according to some).[1] In the Vanaparva (91. 14–15) it is said that

1 Vide विष्णुपुराण III. 6. 28 for the four उपवेदs including अर्थशास्त्र and भागवत III. 12. 38 for them, the 4th being अर्थशास्त्र in

Arjuna learnt from Chitrasena, son of Viśvāvasu, Gandharvaveda which consisted of *sāma* chants, singing, dancing and playing on musical instruments. The Śāntiparva 168. 58 says the same thing, while Śānti 210.21 states that Nārada first propounded Gāndharvaveda. There is a difference between Gāndharvaveda Nāṭyaveda. The first is an Upaveda of a restricted nature, while the latter as the fifth Veda meant for all varṇas (including śūdras) was far more comprehensive and, as song and dance were only a part of it, it took over the teachings of the Gāndharvaveda, as expressly stated by the Nāṭyaśāstra. The Nāṭyaśāstra states that Gāndharva which was first propounded by Nārada (as said by the Śāntiparva quoted above) has been declared by him (in chap. 32).[1] The Nāṭyaśāstra declares that Śṛṅgāra is excited by flowers, Gāndharva and the reading of kāvya &c.[2] Too much emphasis should not, therefore, be laid (as done in I. H. Q. vol. VI. pp. 72–80) upon the fact that Gāndharva and Nāṭya are separately mentioned in some places by the Nāṭyaśāstra as in chap. 36. 49, 78 (गान्धर्वं चैव नाट्यं च यः सम्यगनुपश्यति। verse 78). This separate mention is due to the सामान्यविशेषन्याय or ब्राह्मणपरिव्राजकन्याय. The Nāṭyaśāstra states in the very beginning that Brahmā created the Nāṭyaveda which was connected with tne Vedas and Upavedas and which had grace and tenderness as its essence (वेदोपवेदैः सम्बद्धो नाट्यवेदो महात्मना। एवं भगवता सृष्टो ब्रह्मणा ललितात्मकः॥ I. 18).

The Hathigumpha Inscription of Khāravela styles Khāravela (the king of Kaliṅga) as 'Gāndharvaveda-budhaḥ' (E.I.vol. XX p. 71 at p. 79). That inscription is generally assigned to the 2nd century B. C.[3] Therefore, the गान्धर्ववेद must have been recognized.

---

the latter. अनुशासनपर्व 104. 49 states: गान्धर्वशास्त्रं च कलाः परिज्ञेया नराधिप। पुराणमितिहासाश्च तथाख्यानानि यानि च॥.

1 गान्धर्वमेतत्कथितं मया हि पूर्वं यदुक्तं त्विह नारदेन। कुर्याच्च एवं मनुजः प्रयोगं संमानमग्र्यं कुशलेषु गच्छेत्॥ नाट्य० 32. 484.

2 ऋतुमाल्यालङ्कारैः प्रियजनगान्धर्वकाव्यसेवाभिः। उपवनगमनविहारैः शृङ्गाररसः समुद्भवति॥ नाट्य० 6. 47.

3 Dr. D. C. Sircar places the inscription at the beginning of the Ist century A. D., but his arguments are vague, unconvincing and rather subjective. Vide I. H. Q. vol. 15 at p. 41 for his views. The words of the inscription are: ततिये पुन वसे गंधर्ववेदबुधो दपनटगीतवादितसंदसनाहि उसवसमाजकारापनाहि कीडापयति नगरिं. Should we read रूपनट० for दपनट० ? रूप may mean 'a dumb show' as in शान्तिपर्व 295. 4 or रूप may mean a play represented on the stage.

some centuries before Christ and the नाट्यवेद which includes its principles and practices may very well be placed about 200 B.C.

It appears that the first chapter of the present Nāṭyaśāstra and probably the next four were added some centuries before the 5th A. D., as Kālidāsa, Bhavabhūti and Dāmodaragupta refer to the legend af Bharata being the promulgator of Nāṭyaśāstra. That most of the chapters now found were in existence from at least the 3rd or 4th century A. D. follows from several considerations.

Abhinavagupta who wrote his commentary on the Nāṭyaśāstra about 1000 to 1030 A. D. notes several interpreters of the N. S. He mentions that Udbhaṭa read one verse in the 9th chapter differently.[1] In the 18th chapter अभिनव reads 'वृत्तानि समवकारे कविभिस्तानि प्रयोज्यानि' (verse 76) and remarks that Udbhaṭa read 'वृत्तानि समवकारे कविभिर्नैव प्रयोज्यानि (vol. II. p. 441).[2] On chap. 19 v. 42 A. B. (vol. III. p. 28) notes that Udbhaṭa speaks of *vimarśa* as *avamarśa* and explains it. In the same chap. on v. 69 A. B. (III p. 36) criticises Udbhaṭa for the order of the aṅgas in the *sandhi*. Udbhaṭa flourished, as will be proved below, in the latter half of the 8th century. So the 9th and 18th chapters of the present text existed long before the 8th century. On VI. 10 A. B. (vol. I. p. 266) notes that Lollaṭa criticized the view of Udbhaṭa. A. B. quotes the readings adopted by Lollaṭa several times (vide vol. II. pp. 415, 423, 452). A. B. quotes the explanation of Śaṅkuka on N.S. 3. 21–22 (vol. I. p. 75), four verses from N. S., out of which two have different readings (which are, however, the same as those of Ch. ed. chap. 29 verses 123–124). A. B. quotes (vol. II. pp. 411, 414) the commentary of Śaṅkuka on 18. 10 and 12 (Ch. ed. 20. 10 and 12). Śaṅkuka is mentioned by A. B. on chap. 19–42 (vol. III p. 28). So at least in the 8th century A.D. the principal chapters of the N. S. were in existence. We can push back the existence of the principal chapters a century or two before Udbhaṭa if we consider what the Kāvyādarśa (II. 281, 283, 286) says, viz. that रति, क्रोध, उत्साह, are स्थायि-

1 The verse is उत्तानो वर्तुलस्त्र्यस्रः स्थितोऽधोमुख एव च । पञ्च प्रचारा हस्तस्य नाट्यनृत्तसमाश्रयाः ॥ नाट्य० 9. 182 (GOS. ed.). The अ. भा. says 'उत्तानोऽथस्तलस्त्र्यश्रोऽग्रगोधोमुख एव च । पञ्च प्रचारा हस्तस्येति भट्टोद्भटः पठति' vol. II. p. 70. Vide Ch. ed. 9. 171–172 for the same verse.

2 Vide Ch. ed. chap. 20. 80 which reads नैव प्रयोज्यानि.

भाव s of शृङ्गार, रौद्र and वीर and that what are called सन्ध्यङ्ग, वृत्त्यङ्ग and लक्षण in another tradition or authoritative work are regarded by it as alaṅkāras.[1]

We can carry the matter back still further if we consider the implications of two verses in the Kumārasambhava of Kālidāsa VII. 91 and 95.[2] These refer to certain verses of the 6th, 21st and 22nd chapters of the extant Nāṭyaśāstra. Accepting the first half of the 5th century as the date of Kālidāsa (on which most scholars are agreed), it follows that the present Nāṭyaśāstra existed at least a century or two earlier than 350-450 A. D., i. e. in the 3rd or 4th century, if not earlier.

It may further be noted that in the drama (*prakaraṇa*) called Śāriputraprakaraṇa, fragments ofwhich were recovered by Prof. Lüders, there is a remarkably close coincidence between its technique and that of the Nāṭyaśāstra. In the present state of our knowledge the only work which could have been drawn upon by Aśvaghoṣa (who flourished about 100 A. D.) must be deemed to be the Nāṭyaśāstra. Vide Keith's H. S. D. p. 82-85 for this play and two others and Dr. B. C. Law on 'Aśvaghoṣa' p. 33 ff.

Songs and instrumental music occupied a very high place in Vedic times as will be briefly pointed out in part II. Before Pāṇini Naṭasūtras had been composed by Śilālin and Kṛśāśva (IV. 3. 110, 111). But they appear to have been altogether forgotten and I have not been able to find their names mentioned in any work on dramaturgy. Their names survive only in Śailālin and Kṛśāśvin (and Bharata) as synonyms for naṭa (acc. to the Amarakośa). The अमरकोश vesrse is 'शैलालिनस्तु शैलूषा जायाजीवा कृशाश्विनः । भरता इत्यपि नटाश्चारणास्तु कुशीलवाः ॥'. The words

---

1 यच्च सन्ध्यङ्गवृत्त्यङ्गलक्षणाद्यागमान्तरे। व्यावर्णितमिदं चेष्टमलङ्कारतयैव नः ॥ काव्यादर्श II. 367. Vide नाट्यशास्त्र 21. 58-69 for 64 सन्ध्यङ्ग s, 22. 25-64 for वृत्ति s and their aṅgas, chap. 17. 1-42 for 36 लक्षण s. The commentators are agreed that आगमान्तरे means भरते.

2 तौ सन्धिषु व्यञ्जितवृत्तिभेदं रसान्तरेषु प्रतिबद्धरागम्। अपश्यतामप्सरसां मुहूर्तं प्रयोगमाद्यं ललिताङ्गहारम् ॥ कुमारसंभव VII. 91; 'प्रमथमुखविकारैर्हासयामास गूढम्' ॥ VII. 95. The five सन्धि s are named in नाट्यशास्त्र 21. 37, the वृत्ति s in 22. 24-57 and 65 (for कैशिकी in शृङ्गार). नाट्यशास्त्र 22. 17 has the words सुललितैरङ्गहारैः. नाट्यशास्त्र VI. 44 is शृङ्गारो विष्णुदैवत्यो हास्यः प्रमथदैवतः'. So हास्य comes naturally to प्रमथ s.

for नट, शैलालिन् and कृशाश्विन्, are provided for by Pāṇini himself. क्षीरस्वामिन् derives भरत meaning 'नट' as भरतस्यापत्यं बिदाद्यञि बहुत्वे लुक्'. Acc. to it भरत proclaimed a नाट्यशास्त्र; those who studied it (and so may be called his sons or अपत्यs) would be called भरताः. The two Pāṇini sūtras would be अनृष्यानन्तर्ये बिदादिभ्योऽञ् (IV. 1. 104) and यञञोश्च (II. 4. 64.) It is tempting to suggest that भरत originally meant नट, then भरत came to mean नटशास्त्र; and so when a नटशास्त्र was composed an author भरत was invented for it. But the present author cannot accept such a conjecture. भरत is a very ancient Vedic name. Vide ऋग्वेद III. 33. 11 and 12, III. 53. 12 and 24 (भरतस्य पुत्राः), VII. 33. 6 and भरत-दौष्पन्ति (दौष्यन्ति ?) is mentioned in शतपथ-ब्राह्मण XIII. 5. 4. 11 and 13 and also in ऐ. ब्रा. 39. 9; याज्ञ. स्मृति III. 162 uses भरत in the sense of नट. If a conjecture is to be hazarded it would be more plausible to say that after Pāṇini and some centuries before Kālidāsa a person called Bharata composed a work on the dramatic art (not necessarily the present नाट्यशास्त्र) which was improved into the present work. Gradually, orthodox opinion stiffened against actors, dancers and singers in the times of the Dharmasūtras and early Smṛtis. Āp. Dh. Ś. (I. 1. 3. 11–12) prescribes that a student was not to see dancing and not to frequent *sabhās* and *samājas*. Manu II. 178 provides that a student was to avoid dancing, singing and instrumental music. Gautama (15. 18) prescribes that those brāhmaṇas that practised dancing, singing, playing on musical instruments and beating time were not to be invited to a dinner in honour of gods or Manes. Manu VIII. 102 recommends that brāhmaṇas who are carpenters or actors should be treated as śūdras, holds (VIII. 65) that they were not fit to be witnesses and that an actor was unfit for being invited to a religious rite (III. 155). शान्तिपर्व (295. 4–5) allows a śūdra to resort to the stage and take the parts of women and to exhibit dumb shows (रङ्गावतरणं चैव तथा रूपोपजीवनम् ।). Naṭa was a low caste and was included among the seven *antyajas* (vide History of Dharmaśāstra vol. II. pp. 70, 84). The Nāṭyaśāstra makes a valiant attempt to raise the status of the dramatic art, places it on a very high pedestal and infuses a spiritual and religious element in it. t is with this view that probably the first five chapters were added. Abhinavagupta, a very erudite scholar and a great Śaiva philosopher, takes a very reasonable, highly practical and philosophic view of the noble art of the drama (vol. I pp. 3-4). For want of space only a small part is quoted here: "एतेन 'कामजो दशको गणः' इति वर्जनीयत्वेन नाट्यस्यानुपादेयतेति यत्केचिदाशशङ्किरे तदयुक्तीकृतम्। याज्ञवल्क्य-स्मृतिपुराणादौ चास्य प्रशंसाभूयस्त्वश्रवणात्। न चागमादृते धर्मोनुमानगम्य इति न्यायात्। एतत्तु वृथैवास्थानभीरून् प्रति शङ्काशमनार्थमभिधीयते नाम। तथाहि **नटानां तावदेतत्स्वधर्माम्नायरूपतयानुष्ठेयमेव। न चास्माकं तच्चेष्टितं विचार्यम्।** सोमक्रयोपदेशिनो हि वाक्यस्य न तद्विक्रयिब्राह्मणान्तरगततकृत्याकृत्यविचारणोद्योगो युक्तः। न चाप्यस्योपदिश्यते गायेन्नृत्येदिति।". एतेन refers to नाट्यशास्त्र 36. 74–75 which promise the same reward for those who listen to or study the Nāṭyaveda or who perform a drama according to its rules as for one who studies the Veda or performs sacrifices or makes gifts. मनु VII. 47 speaks of ten things which men do for pleasure and asks the king not to be addicted to them, viz. मृगयाक्षो दिवास्वप्नः परिवादः स्त्रियो मदः। **तौर्यत्रिकं** वृथाट्या च कामजो दशको गणः॥.

Taking into consideration all that has been stated above one may say that at least sometime before the 3rd or 4th century A. D. there was a recast[1] made by one man in which were included prose passages in sūtra-bhāṣya style, ancient āryā verses and ślokas together with kārikās composed by the recaster. Then in different places and at different times some verses came to be added here and there by people learned in the śāstra.

The problems of the text of the Nāṭyaśāstra, its authorship and its date will remain puzzles and matters of conjecture till the earlier dramatic works such as those of Kohala, Nandikeśvara and the commentaries of Udbhaṭa and others are discovered.

Turning to the question of the authorship of the Nāṭya-śāstra, many difficulties arise. Long before Abhinava's day there were people who held that the first six verses of chap. one[1] were composed by a pupil of Bharata and that the questions and answers in the body of the work also were composed by a pupil and the text by Bharata. Abhinavagupta emphatically discards this idea and holds that the whole work is Bharata's as there is no evidence for holding that it is the outcome of composite authorship and as authors very often employ the third person for themselves.[2] He further combats the view of some teachers that were foremost among *nāstikas* that the Nāṭyaśāstra was com-

---

1 Vide Dr. De's History of Sanskrit Poetics vol. I pp. 23–36 for views on the text of the Nāṭyaśāstra.

2 एकस्य ग्रन्थस्यानेकवक्तृवचनसन्दर्भमयत्वे प्रमाणाभावात् स्वपरव्यवहारेण पूर्व-पक्षोत्तरपक्षादीनां श्रुतिस्मृतिव्याकरणतर्कादिशास्त्रेष्वेकविरचितेष्वपि दर्शनात्। अभिनव-भारती vol. I. p. 9.

posed for establishing that out of three expounders, viz. Sadāśiva, Brahmā and Bharata, the views of Brahmā were the most substantial (एतेन सदाशिवब्रह्मभरतमतत्रयविवेचनेन ब्रह्ममतसारताप्रतिपादनाय मतत्रयीसारासारविवेचनं तद्ग्रन्थखण्डप्रक्षेपेण विहितमिदं शास्त्रं न तु मुनिविरचितमिति यदाहुर्नास्तिकधुर्योपाध्यायास्तत्प्रत्युक्तम्, सर्वानपह्नवनीयाबाधितशब्दलोकप्रसिद्धिविरोधाच्च। अभि. भा. I. p. 8).[1] As stated above, the K. M. edition has at the end the words that the work is that of Nandi and Bharata and is concerned with *saṅgīta*. It appears that Nandi (Nandikeśvara ?) had, according to some mss., something to do with the Nāṭyaśāstra. Then there is Kohala whose relation with the Nāṭyaśāstra is not quite clear. In chap. I. 26 among the hundred sons or pupils (at least 105 or 106 are actually enumerated in Ch. ed. I verses 26–39), whom Bharata is said to have instructed in Nāṭyaveda and its practice, 'Śāṇḍilya, Vātsya, Kohala and Dantila' are the first four. In the last chapter (36. 65) in a prophetic vein it is stated that Kohala will treat of all matters left out (in the Nāṭyaśāstra) in a later (or additional) treatise and again (in 36. 71) it is said that the Nāṭyaśāstra was practised by Kohala, Vātsya, Śāṇḍilya and Dhūrtila. It appears that Kohala's work influenced the redactors of the Nāṭyaśāstra. Vide Mr. Kavi's Intro. pp. VI–VIII to vol. II. and Dr. De (H. S. P. vol. I. p. 25) for some works ascribed to Kohala. The A. B. very frequently mentions Kohala and in some places regards him as coeval with Bharata.[2] Vide A. B. vol. I. pp. 25 (where both Bharata and Kohala are brought together in relation to the Nāndī in Ratnāvalī), 173 (where one pāda of Kohala's work appears to be quoted), 182 (two verses of Kohala quoted), 183 (one verse quoted), 266, vol. II. pp. 55, 130, 133, 142, 144, 146, 151, 155, 407, 410, 416–17, 421, 434, 452, 459. Considerations of space forbid me from going into any details about these passages. But I should like to clear up one passage of A. B. which has been misunderstood by Dr. Manomohan Ghosh

1 It is somewhat strange that Mr. Kavi writes (Intro. p. 6 to vol. I) : 'Abhinava...clearly says that it represents three different schools of opinion: viz. of Brahmā, Sadāśiva and, lastly, Bharata, i. e. the author's own views'. The above passage makes it clear that it is not Abhinava's view but of some नास्तिकधुर्योपाध्यायs.

2 E. g. Vol. I. P. 48 ब्रह्मेव कविः शक्र इव प्रयोजयिता भरत इव नाट्यानामाचार्यः कोहलादय इव नटाः... । on chāp. II. 1.

(I. H. Q. vol. X. pp. 161 ff). He thinks that there is a conflict between Bharata and Abhinava, since on VI. 10 the latter says नाट्य is पञ्चाङ्ग and अभिनयs are three.[1] When Dr. Manomohan Ghosh refers to N. S. VIII. 12 for नाट्य being षडङ्ग he is wrong. In VIII. 12 the reference is not to नाट्य in general but to आङ्गिकाभिनय which is spoken of in the preceding verse. Similarly, the view that नाट्य is पञ्चाङ्ग is not that of अभिनव but of the औद्भटs who hold that that was the view of Bharata and also hold that VI. 10 is not Bharata's view but Kohala's. That Abhinava does not subscribe to the views either of the Audbhaṭas or of Lollaṭa is clear from the last sentence of the passage quoted. Kohala is mentioned in the same breath with Bharata as an authority on dancing in Dāmodargupta's Kuṭṭanīmata (latter half of the 8th century A. D..).[2] In the बालरामायण of राजशेखर there is a नाट्याचार्य कोहल who addresses Rāvaṇa with the words 'परमेष्ठिनो मानसभुवः प्रथमपुत्रस्य नाट्ययोनेर्भरताचार्यस्य कृतिरभिनवं सीतास्वयंवर इति नाटकं प्रयोक्तव्यम्' (before Act III. 12)[3]. The रसार्णवसुधाकर of शिङ्गभूपाल mentions भरत, शाण्डिल्य, कोहल, दत्तिल and मतङ्ग as authors of works on नाट्य (I. 50–52). The कुट्टनीमत (in verses 122–123) mentions दत्तकाचार्य (v. l. दन्तिलाचार्य) along with कामशास्त्र writers like वात्स्यायन and दन्तिल along with भरत and विशाखिल. A Dattakasūtravṛtti is mentioned in Epigraphia Carnatica vol. IX. D. B. 68 of 517 A.D. as composed by Mādhava son of Koṅgaṇivarma from whom Avinīta was 4th in decent and whose son made the grant in Ep. Car. Whether the two are identical is doubtful. दन्तिल is one of the भरतपुत्रs (नाट्य. I. 26). Mr. Kavi (in J. A. H. R. S. vol. III. p. 24) says that Dattila is authoritative on ध्रुवाs and तालs and that his work is called गान्धर्ववेदसार and is available.[4]

Mr. Kavi (Intro. to vol. I. p. 6) quotes a passage from the

---

1 संग्रहं दर्शयति **रसा भावा** इत्यादिना । ...अभिनयत्रयं गीतातोद्ये चेति पञ्चाङ्गं नाट्यम् -.......अनेन तु श्लोकेन कोहलमते एकादशाङ्गत्वमुच्यते न तु भरते। तत्सङ्गृहीतस्यापि पुनरत्रोद्देशाद् निर्देशे चैतत्क्रमव्यत्यासनादित्यौद्भटाः । नैतदिति भट्टलोल्लटः । ...वयं त्वत्र तत्त्वमग्रे वितनिष्याम इत्यास्तां तावत् । vol. I. pp. 265–266.

2 विटखटके का नृत्यति कोहलभरतोदितक्रियया ॥ 81.

3 Vide my paper 'Fragments from Kohala' in Proccedings of All India O. Conference at Patna (1930) pp. 577–580.

4 अभिनवगुप्त (vol. I. p. 205) quotes an अनुष्टुभ् verse from दत्तिल on a ध्रुवा (G. O. S. ed. नाट्यशास्त्र IV. 326 p. 205=Ch. ed. IV. 316–317.

Yamalāṣṭakatantra in which it is said that the Upaveda Gāndharva comprises 30000 ślokas. The Bhāvaprakāśana (G. O. S. ed., X. 34–35) states that Bharatas made up two epitomes from the Nāṭyaveda, one containing 12000 ślokas and the other containing 6000 ślokas. Mr. Kavi asserts (in J. A. H. R. S. vol. III. at p. 23) that वृद्धभरत wrote a work in 12000 *granthas* a part of which is now available, while Bharata produced the Nāṭyaśāstra in 6000 ślokas. The भावप्रकाशन of शारदातनय (1175–1250 A. D.) says that Bharata dealt with rasas in Nāṭyaveda and that Bharatavṛddha with the prose portion, of which it gives a sample (एवं हि नाट्यवेदेऽस्मिन् भरतेनोच्यते रसः। तथा भरतवृद्धेन कथितं गद्यमीदृशम् ॥ यथा नानाप्रकारैर्व्यञ्जनौषधैः पाकविशेषैश्च &c.).[1] In the B. O. R. I. cat. of mss. (vol. XII. p. 453) there is a work called नाट्यसर्वस्वदीपिका, that professes to be a commentary on आदिभरत which comprised five *skandhas* (समवाय, शिक्षा, भाव, उल्लास, वैशेषिक) divided into 32 chapters, 221 prakaraṇas and which contained 6000 ślokas. Some commentators of Sanskrit dramas quote verses from both आदिभरत and भरत. For example, Rāghavabhaṭṭa in his commentary अर्थद्योतनिका on the शाकुन्तल quotes at least 17 times verses from आदिभरत (most of which are either found in the extant Nāṭyāśāstra or have their parallels in the present work) and at least eleven times from Bharata. It is to be noted that when quoting from Bharata he often makes a reference to the chapter and then quotes a verse or verses,[2] but in the case of Ādibharata he merely quotes a verse or verses and refers to no chapter. It is possible that Rāghavabhaṭṭa had before him two separate mss., of which one was called आदिभरत and the other भरत, though many passages were common to both. In one place he has the following interesting pássage 'सूत्र–मूलभरतटीकाकाराभिनवगुप्ताचार्यसंमता अवान्तररूपाष्टपदा मूलकारेण स्वयमेव द्वादशपदोदाहृता'. It appears that he makes a distinction between सूत्र and मूलभरत. It is generally comparatively later writers that make a distinction between आदिभरत and भरत. For example, बहुरूपमिश्र in his commentary on the दशरूपक

---

1 This गद्य is very like the passage 'यथा नानाव्यञ्जनौषधिद्रव्यसंयोगाद् &c. (in chap. VI. p. 71 after the रससूत्र in Ch. ed.).

2 भरतः प्रथमाध्याये 'पूर्वं कृता मया नान्दी°'. (I. 57); पञ्चमाध्याये च 'सूत्रधारः पठेन्नान्दीं°' (V. 106–107); पञ्चमाध्याये भरतः–नमोस्तु सर्वदेवेभ्यः° (V. 107–111); तथा च षोडशाध्याये भरतः–विभूषणं चाक्षरसंहतिश्च (K. M. 16. 1–4 footnote).

quotes a षट्सहस्रीकार (i. e. भरत's नाट्यशास्त्र) 'सूत्रणं सकलाङ्गानां श्रेयमङ्कसुखं बुधैः—इति षट्सहस्रीकारः' and another from द्वादशसहस्रीकार 'समाप्यमान एतस्मिन्नितराङ्कस्य सूचनम्। समासतो हि नाट्यज्ञैरङ्कावतर इष्यते॥ इति द्वादशसहस्रीकारः.' Vide J. O. R., Madras, vol. 8 pp. 321–334 (Dr. Raghavan on बहुरूपमिश्र) at pp. 329–30. Vide Dr. Raghavan on 'Later Saṅgīta Literature' in Journal of Music Academy of Madras p. 82 and Dr. S. K. De. in Our Heriltage, I, part 2. In other branches of literature also the same work is sometimes styled बृहद् or वृद्ध. For example, the विष्णुधर्मसूत्र (17. 4–16 अपुत्रधनं पत्न्यभि. &c.) is cited as वृद्धविष्णु by the मिताक्षरा on या. II. 135–136 and the व्यवहारसार (p.252) and as बृहद्विष्णु in the स्मृतिच. II. 298, व्यवहारप्रकाश, मदनरत्न. It is possible that two different mss. of भरत containing different numbers of verses were styled आदिभरत and भरत. On this question of आदिभरत and भरत vide Prof. D. R. Mankad on 'आदिभरत and नाट्यसर्वस्वदीपिका' in ABORI vol. XIII pp. 173, 179, Prof. P. K. Gode on the so-called MS. of आदिभरत in the Mysore Govt. Library in ABROI vol. XIII pp. 92–93 and Prof. Manomohan Ghosh on the quotations of आदिभरत and भरत from the commentary of राघवभट्ट in ABORI vol. XV pp. 89–96. The net result of these papers is that the view of the present author in the preceding sentence is greatly supported.

In the Nāṭyaśāstra itself the word भरत is used in the sense of actor: पृष्ठे कृत्वास्य कुतपं नाट्यं युञ्ज्के यतोमुखं भरतः। सा पूर्वा मन्तव्या प्रयोगकाले तु नाट्यज्ञैः॥ 14.65 (K. M. 13. 61, G. O. S. 13. 66). From the above discussion it would be clear that it is very difficult to say who the author of the original kernel of the Nāṭyaśāstra was. Holding as I do that the first five chapters were later additions, it is not possible for me to say who the author of the prose passages and the versified chapters about *abhinaya*, daśarūpaka, and other closely allied subjects was. When the first five chapters were added it was easy to say that Bharatamuni who had access to the heavenly world as well as to the mundane world was the author of the Nāṭyaśāstra. In this connection attention must be drawn to the fact that the word '*bharata*' means an actor in the comparatively old smṛti of Yājñavalkya (III. 162) 'यथा हि भरतो वर्णैर्वर्णयत्यात्मनस्तनुम्। नानारूपाणि कुर्वाणस्तथात्मा कर्मजास्तनूः॥'.[1] This verse is explained by all commentators including Viśvarupa.

---

1 This verse occurs almost in the same words in बृहत्पराशर p. 294 (Jiv.)

It is quite possible that some one who had mastered the traditional lore of the histrionic art and was well-disposed to *bharatas* (actors) put together most of the present Nāṭyaśāstra and in order to glorify the tribe of *bharatas* passed it on as the work of a mythical hero. Such things are common in Sanskrit Literature. The whole of the vast Purāṇa literature is foisted on Vyāsa, but hardly anyone can believe that the 18 Purāṇas and 18 Upapurāṇas are the work of one man called Vyāsa. The word आनुवंश्य used with regard to certain āryās and ślokas points in the direction of a mass of verses being already available for inclusion in a formal treatise on *nāṭya*. The extant Nāṭyaśāstra mentions that it summarizes the views of ancient ācāryas on शब्दलक्षण 'पूर्वाचार्यैरुक्तं शब्दानां लक्षणं तु विस्तरशः । पुनरेव संहृतार्थं लक्षणतः संप्रवक्ष्यामि ॥' (Ch. ed. 15. 22, K. M. 14. 22; but G. O. S. 14. 24 omits reference to पूर्वाचार्य). The भावप्रकाशन (10th अधिकार pp. 285-287) narrates a legend about the origin of the नाट्यवेद. It states that Śiva ordered नन्दिकेश्वर to teach नाट्यवेद to ब्रह्मा before whom appeared Bharata with five pupils, to whom Brahmā said 'bear this Nāṭyaveda' (तानब्रवीन्नाट्यवेदं भरतेति पितामहः). Therefore, the first actors were called Bharatas and they first staged a play before Manu who wanted some pastime to remove his weariness arising from governing the world. The Bharatas taking the elements from Nāṭyaveda made two epitomes, one in 12000 verses and the other in six thousand verses and so the latter came to be known after the Bharatas: 'नाट्यवेदाच्च भरतः सारमुद्धृत्य सर्वतः ।...एकं द्वादशसाहस्रैः श्लोकैरेकं तदर्धतः । षड्भिः श्लोकसहस्रैर्यो नाट्यवेदस्य संग्रहः । भरतैर्नामतस्तेषां प्रख्याता भरताह्वयाः ॥'. This legendary account probably shows that the author of भावप्रकाशन was not prepared to accept the extant Nāṭyaśāstra as the work of a mythical Bharata but that he ascribed its composition to *bharatas* who had studied Nāṭya. This gives support to my hypothesis stated above. स्वाति and नारद are mentioned as expounders of गान्धर्व and वाद्य (chap. 33. 3 and 32. 484). The extant N. S. mentions an author Guha on metrics (Ch. 16. 112, K. M. 15. 110; G. O. S. text adopts in vol. II. p. 281 a different reading for गुहादिना). Nārada is mentioned in connection with ध्रुवाs (Ch. 32. 1, K. M. 32. 1). In the extant work (Ch. ed. 4. 17–19) it is stated that Taṇḍu instructed Bharata in the representation of aṅgahāras together with various *karaṇas* (postures) and *recakas* (gestures). Abhinavagupta remarks that the words Taṇḍu and Muni employed in the N. S. stand for Nandin and Bharata (तण्डुमुनिशब्दौ नन्दिभरतयोरपरनामनी । श्र. भा. vol. I p. 90). The extant N. S. mentions Kāmatantra (a work on Erotics) in Ch. ed. 24. 182 and 25. 65 (=K. M. 22. 183 and 23. 52). कामसूत्र is mentioned in 24. 142 (but omitted in K. M.). The views of Bṛhaspati are relied on for reciting the qualifications of the king, the commander-in-chief, the ministers, the chief justice, &c. (बृहस्पतिमतादेतान् गुणांश्चाप्यभिलक्षयेत् । 34. 79 of Ch. ed., 24. 72 K. M.). In order to keep up the pretence or illusion of the revelation of the N. S. by Brahmā to Bharata, Kauṭilya, well-known as a human author, was probably ignored and Bṛhaspati (the *guru* of gods) was mentioned as a writer on Arthaśāstra.[1] A purāṇa is mentioned in connection with the names of countries 'अन्येपि देशाः प्राच्यां ये पुराणे संप्रकीर्तिताः । तेषु प्रयुज्यते त्वेषा प्रवृत्तिश्चौड्रमागधी ॥ (14. 46, K. M. 13. 42, G. O. S. 13. 48). There are in the N. S. references to others' views in the words अन्ये, अन्यैस्तु. While these pages were passing through the press a recent work by Shri K. M. Varma on 'seven words in Bharata : what do they signify' (Orient Longmans, 1958) came to the present author's hands. The writer takes up seven words viz. सूत्र, भाष्य, सङ्ग्रह, निरुक्त, कारिका, आनुवंश्य and निदर्शन (occurring in chap. 6 and 7 the नाट्यशास्त्र) and discusses their meanings and arrives at his own conclusions. They cannot be examined in detail here. His main conclusion (on p. 88) is that before Bharata there was already a sūtra work on nāṭya and a bhāṣya thereon and also a third work containing ānuvaṁśya verses based on that sūtra and its bhāṣya by authors now unknown and he gives at the end a long list of what portions were sūtras and bhāṣya. The most damaging argument against this is : when Bharata mentions Svāti, Nārada, Kohala, Vātsya, Dhūrtila and others why should not the names of the three or at least of one of them appear in नाट्यशास्त्र.

A brief outline of the contents of the Nāṭyaśāstra would not be out of place here. It is given here from the Ch. edition chapter by chapter. It is to be regretted that the numbering of the chapters and the total verses in the chapters differ very often in the Chaukhamba and the G. O. S. editions ; where no mention is made of any edition the reference is to the Ch.

---

1 Vide my History of Dharmaśāstra vol. I. pp. 123–125 for references to Bṛhaspati's work in Arthaśāstra.

edition, but it is possible that by oversight some mistakes occur for which indulgence is requested. The greatest divergence is in the vol. III. of G. O. S. ed.

1 Ātreya and other sages ask five questions of Bharata, viz. how the Nāṭyaveda came into existence, for whose sake, what its aṅgas (subsidiary matters) are, what are the means for arriving at sure conclusions, how it is to be represented on the stage (Abhinavagupta[1] says these questions are not dealt with *seriatim*, but the answers are scattered over the whole work). The Vedas cannot be studied by śūdras and so Brahmā ordered Bharata to produce a fifth Veda meant for all varṇas[2]; Bharata took the matter to be recited in dramas from the Ṛgveda, singing from the Sāmaveda, the *abhinayas* (acting) from the Yajurveda and the Rasas from the Atharvaveda. Bharata taught Nāṭyaveda to his 100 sons (pupils): 2 Details of the construction of a theatre (*nāṭya-maṇḍapa*, in verses 3 and 6, *prekṣāgṛha* in v. 7)[3]; columns (स्तम्भ) should be raised; the theatre should have two separate portions and should appear like a mountain cave; pictures should be drawn on the walls and seats for spectators should be made of bricks or wood; 3 worship of several deities such as महादेव, ब्रह्मा, विष्णु, बृहस्पति, गुह and seeking their blessings

---

1 'वयं तु ब्रूमः-नात्र क्रमः कश्चित्। अपि तु यथावसरं महावाक्यात्मना षट्सहस्री-रूपेण प्रधानतया प्रश्नपञ्चकनिरूपणपरेण शास्त्रेण तत्त्वं निर्णीयते न तु क्रमः कश्चित्। अभिनवभारती, I. p. 8.

2 न वेदव्यवहारोयं संश्राव्यः शूद्रजातिषु। तस्मात्सृजापरं वेदं पञ्चमं सार्ववर्णिकम्॥ नाट्य. I 12.

3 Vide Dr. Raghavan in 'Triveni' for 1931 on 'Theatre Architecture in Ancient India', last part, pp. 69-77 and vol. V. (for 1932-33) pp. 357-366 and Mr. D. R. Mankad in I. H. Q. vol. VIII. pp. 480-499 on 'The Hindu Theatre'. Acc. to नाट्य. 2. 8-11 theatres were of three kinds : विकृष्ट (elongated i. e. rectangular), चतुरस्र (square) and त्र्यस्र (triangular) and each of these was either ज्येष्ठ or मध्यम or अवर (of 108, 64 or 32 हस्तs or दण्डs) and each was measured in हस्तs or दण्डs (दण्ड=four हस्तs). मध्यम is the proper one for men and 64 हस्तs in length and 32 in breadth, as otherwise the speeches will be indistinctly heard. शारदातनय, author of भावप्रकाशन, states that he was taught नाट्यवेद by a brāhmaṇa दिवाकर who was नाट्यशालापति (भा. प्र. I. p. 2).

for the play; **4** performance of a play[1] called अमृतमन्थन before the gods and of त्रिपुरदाह before महादेव; तण्डु instructed Bharata as to the various अङ्गहारs (movements of the limbs), करणs (postures),[2] and रेचकs (gestures); origin and technique of the ताण्डव dance; dancing by itself serves no special purpose in dramatic representation, it lends charm to the songs sung;[3] **5** remarks on पूर्वरङ्ग, नान्दी,[4] ध्रुवा, प्रस्तावना; **6** five questions of sages, viz. why rasas are so called, what are भावs, संग्रहकारिका &c.; the eleven elements of the śāstra in a nutshell (saṅgraha) are Rasas, Bhāvas, Abhinayas, Dharmī, Vṛtti, Pravṛtti, Siddhi, Svaras, Ātodya, Gāna and Raṅga; meanings of kārika, nirukta; the eight (or nine) rasas,[5]

1 The Padmapurāṇa (V. 12. 81) states that Bharata staged a drama called Lakṣmīsvayaṁvara for the gods, in which Urvaśī acting the part of Lakṣmī forgot abhinaya, being engrossed in thoughts about Purūravas and was cursed by Bharata.

2 In the G. O. S. edition of the अभिनवभारती (vol. I. chap. 4) illustrations of the 108 karaṇas that are enumerated in verses 34–55 are given, being copied from figures cut into rocks in the east and west *gopuras* in the Naṭarāja temple at Chidambaram, where appropriate verses from the Nāṭyaśāstra are engraved under each posture. The figures were cut in the 13th century A. D. Vide the pictorial Journal 'Mārg', vol. V. No. 2 for 108 karaṇas drawn in line from the carved ones on a gopuram in the Chidambaram temple of Naṭarāja (pp. 52–71). The 108 dance (Karaṇas) poses in chap. 4 of Bharata's Nāṭyaśāstra are here carved systematically and each sculpture has an inscription (i.e. a verse from chap. 4) describing its structure. In G. O. S. ed. they are verses 61–169.

3 The नाट्यशास्त्र says: अत्रोच्यते न खल्वर्थं नृत्तं कंचिदपेक्षते । किं तु शोभां जनयतीत्यतो नृत्तमिदं स्मृतम ॥ प्रायेण सर्वलोकस्य नृत्तमिष्टं स्वभावत: । मङ्गल्यमिति कृत्वा च नृत्तमेतत्प्रकीर्तितम् ॥ विवाहप्रसवावाहप्रमोदाभ्युदयादिषु । विनोदकरणं चैव नृत्तमेतत् प्रकीर्तितम् ॥...गीतप्रयोगमाश्रित्य नृत्यमेतत् प्रनृत्यताम् । chap. 4. 260–263, 265.

4 Vide I. H. Q. vol. 17 (1941) pp. 359–369 for a historic treatment of Nāndī.

5 From the Abhinavabhāratī it appears that there were two recensions of the Nāṭyaśāstra, one dealing with nine rasas (including śānta), which is contained in the G. O. S. edition and the other speaking of only eight rasas by excluding *śānta* contained in the Chowkhamba edition. Vide a learned paper of

the eight sthāyibhāvas, the 33 vyabhicāribhāvas, eight sāttvika-bhāvas, four kinds of abhinaya(आङ्गिक, वाचिक, आहार्य, and सात्त्विक), two kinds of धर्मी (viz. लोकधर्मी and नाट्यधर्मी); four vṛttis (भारती, सात्वती, कैशिकी, आरभटी) ; the pravṛttis (आवन्ती, दाक्षिणात्या, ओड्रमागधी, पाञ्चाली); siddhi (of two kinds, दैवी and मानुषी), the seven svaras (ṣadja, ṛṣabha &c.), the four kinds of musical instruments (तत, अवनद्ध, घन, सुषिर), five kinds of gāna (singing), raṅga (maṇḍapa : square, elongated or triangular); how rasa is evolved by विभाव, अनुभाव and व्यभिचारिभाव; relation of rasas to each other and to bhāvas; colours and superintending deities (adhidaivata) of the rasas; detailed treatment of several rasas, their sthāyibhāvas; **7** detailed treatment of bhāvas, vibhāvas, sthāyibhāvas (viz. rati &c.) and vyabhicāribhāvas, viz. *nirveda*, *glāni* &c.(in all 33); the eight sāttvika bhāvas, viz. *stambha* &c.; **8** detailed description of the four kinds of acting, viz. *sāttvika* (already described as *stambha*, perspiration, tremor, horripilation &c.), *āngika*, *vācika* and *āhārya*; **9** the various movements and positions of the hands, the chest, the sides, the abdomen, the waist, legs and feet in nāṭya[1]; 24 postures of the hand such as *patāka*, *tripatāka* when not joined and 13 postures of the joined hands such as añjali, svastika; 27 *nṛttahastas;* definitions and employment of the above mentioned 64 movements and postures of the hands; other kinds of movements and hands may be employed in accordence with *rasa, bhāva, and actions*, the requirements of time and place; the postures of hands in dancing; **10** five kinds of the movements of the chest, the sides, the waist and other parts of the body, their definitions and employments on occasions; **11** definitions of Cārī (gait),[2] Khaṇḍa, Karaṇa, and Maṇḍala; definitions of 16 cārīs (called *bhaumyaḥ*, of *land*) and 16 of the sky and when they are to be employed; how archery is represented in a drama; who should not be made to undergo rapid movements and

Prof. K. C. Pandey on 'Dhanañjaya and Abhinavagupta' in N. I. A. vol. VI pp. 272-282 in which the arguments for and against śānta rasa are well marshalled.

1 On 9. 27 एवमेष प्रयोक्तव्यः स्त्रीपुंसाभिनये करः, the अ. भा. (vol. II. p. 31) remarks: स्त्रीपुंसयोरुभयोरपि अभिनेत्रोरभिनेययोर्वा. So, women also were engaged as actresses in Abhinava's day at all events. Vide also 9. 155.

2 एकपादप्रचारो यः सा चारीत्यभिसंज्ञिता । द्विपादक्रमणं यत्तु करणं नाम तद्भवेत् ॥ ...यदेतत्प्रस्तुतं नाट्यं तच्चारीष्वेव संज्ञितम् ॥ नाट्य. XI. 3 and 6.

great exertion in a dramatic part; **12** number of maṇḍalas and their definitions; **13** the proper gaits of characters according to the *rasa* and the place when they enter the stage to the accompaniment of the lute and other instruments and after the Dhruvāgāna has started; the time taken in traversing the stage in the case of characters supposed to be gods or kings, of men of middle rank and of women and men of lower rank; gaits in representing Raudra, Bībhatsa, Vīra and other rasas and movements of the body when representing wounds, cold or persons who are ascetics or are intoxicated or mad &c.; **14** the distribution of space in the *nāṭyamaṇḍapa* as regards musical instruments, as regards representation of houses, gardens, forests, land and water &c; each Act (aṅka) should depict action taking place in a moment or in a muhūrta, a watch, one day at the most; then, a new Act may be begun by skipping over eventss occurring in a month or a year; the four kinds of pravṛttis which depend upon the combinations of the country, the dress, the languages, the manners; the pravṛttis are Āvantī, Dākṣiṇātyā, Pāñcālī, Oḍra-māgadhī; the countries that are included under the four groups together with the vṛttis associated with each pravṛtti; two kinds of nāṭyaprayoga viz. sukumāra (graceful and delicate) and āviddha; the plays called, डिम, समवकार, व्यायोग and ईहामृग are known as आविद्ध and the rest of the ten rūpakas as सुकुमार; *lokadharmī* and *nāṭyadharmī* defined and[1] illustrated; **15** *Vācikābhinaya* based on *svaras* (vowels) and consonants; speech is the body of nāṭya and *āṅgika* acting, dresses and theatrical devices suggest the sense of what is being said; disquisition on svaras, consonants, nouns, verbs, *upasargas*, adverbs, compounds &c.; recitation (in a drama) is either in Sanskrit or in Prākṛt or both; metres (*chandas*) containing from one to 26 syllables; several varieties of each metre; their numbers are vast; the

---

1 Vide Dr. Raghavan's very lucid and detailed article on *Lokadharmī* and *Nāṭyadharmī* in Journal of Oriental Research, Madras, vol. VII. pp. 359-375 and vol. VIII. pp. 57-74. भरत defines: स्वभावभावोपगतं शुद्धं त्वविकृतं तथा। लोकवार्ताक्रियोपेतमङ्गलीलाविवर्जितम् ॥ स्वभावाभिनयोपेतं नानास्त्रीपुरुषाश्रयम्। यदीदृशं भवेन्नाट्यं लोकधर्मी तु सा स्मृता ॥...योयं स्वभावो लोकस्य सुखदुःखक्रियात्मकः। सोङ्गाभिनयसंयुक्तो नाट्यधर्मी तु सा स्मृता॥ नाट्य. 14. 70-71 and 78. कल्लिनाथ illustrates (सं. र. p. 629) 'वाक्याभिनये केवलवाक्योच्चारणं लोकधर्मी रागयुक्तवाक्योच्चारणं नाट्यधर्मी'.

scheme of eight gaṇas (such as bha, ma, ja); meaning of *guru*, *laghu*, *yati*; **16** the metres (*vṛtta*) to be employed in dramas, their definitions and examples; *sama* and *viṣama* metres, Āryās; **17** enumeration of 36 lakṣaṇas in *kāvya* that is to be represented on[1] the stage and their definitions; four alaṅkāras of Nāṭaka viz. Upamā, Rūpaka, Dīpaka and Yamaka and their sub-divisions and illustrations; the ten blemishes of kāvya (kāvyadoṣa); the ten guṇas of kāvya and their definitions; **18** Prākrit recitation in dramas is of three kinds, just like Sanskrit, vibhraṣṭa (in which vowels and consonants of Sanskrit are changed) and deśī; what characters are to speak Sanskrit, Prakrit or other dialects; Śauraseni to be the principal Prākṛt but there are six other (bhāṣās) prākṛts viz. मागधी, अवन्तिजा, प्राच्या, अर्धमागधी, बाह्लीका, दाक्षिणात्या that may be employed according to the desire of the actors; who are to use these; dialects of śabaras, ābhīras, cāṇḍālas, sacara (? śakāra), draviḍas, oḍras (Orissa people) and of forest tribes are called vibhāṣā; **19** the various modes of addressing high, middling or low characters, such as saying *ārya* to a brāhmaṇa and mahārāja to a king; names of persons of the three varṇas should respectively end in śarma, varma and datta; names of courtezans should end in dattā, mitrā and senā; the guṇas of pāṭhya; seven musical notes (*svaras* viz. ṣaḍja, ṛṣabha &c.), the three sthānas (chest, throat and head); four svaras viz. उदात्त, अनुदात्त, स्वरित, कम्पित; the two kinds of *kāku*; the alaṅkaras viz. उच्च, दीप्त, मन्द्र, नीच, द्रुत and विलम्बित); **20** disquisition on ten varieties of plays (noted below)[2]; description of contents and characte-

---

1 Vide Dr. Raghavan's paper on 'the concept of lakṣaṇas in Bharata' in J. O. R., Madras, vol. VI. pp. 54-82 and in 'Some concepts of the Alaṅkāra-śāstra' (1942) pp. 1-47; 'Doctrine of lakṣaṇas' in Poona Orientalist vol. XVI part 1, pp. 11-33 by Prof. S. P. Bhattācharya. भरत says in the last line of chap. 16 'काव्यबन्धास्तु कर्तव्याः षट्त्रिंशल्लक्षणान्विताः'. As observed by Abhinava himself these lakṣaṇas faded into the background and some of these like āśīḥ and dṛṣṭānta came to be names of अलंकारs: 'तत्र गुणालंकारादिरिति वृत्तयश्चेति काव्येषु प्रसिद्धो मार्गो लक्षणानि तु न प्रसिद्धानि' अ. भा. vol. II. p. 294. There were ten पक्षs about them: इदं तु दशपक्ष्यां वस्तु । vol. II. p. 297.

2 नाटकं सप्रकरणमङ्को व्यायोग एव च । भाणः समवकारश्च वीथी प्रहसनं डिमः ॥ ईहामृगं च विज्ञेयं दशमं नाट्यलक्षणम् । नाट्य. 20. 2-3.

ristics of the first variety (nāṭaka) out of the *daśarūpas*; what incidents may be represented or not represented on the stage[1]; the technique of *praveśaka* and *viṣkambhaka*; the characteristics of a prakaraṇa and the other kinds of dramatic representations and the definitions of their aṅgas; **21** the plot of the drama; it has a dominant part (ādhikārika) and a subsidiary one (prāsaṅgika); there are five *sandhis;* five *avasthās* (प्रारम्भ, प्रयत्न &c); five arthaprakṛtis viz. बीज, बिन्दु, पताका, प्रकरी, कार्य, and their definitions; sandhyantaras; the 64 aṅgas (constituents) of the five sandhis (viz. 12 each of *mukha* and *garbha*, 13 each of *pratimukha* and *vimarśa* and 14 of *nirvahaṇa*) and their definitions; five *arthopakṣepakas* (devices referring to incidents that have happened during the intervals of the Acts and that are not to be represented on the stage) viz. विष्कम्भक, चूलिका, प्रवेशक, अङ्कावतार and अङ्कमुख; there is no action, no knowledge, no lore, nor kalā and no craft that cannot be[2] represented or cannot be useful in a Nāṭaka; 22 (or chap. 20 of GOS ed.) the four vṛttis, called भारती, सात्वती कैशिकी, आरभटी, their mythical origin at the time of the fight of Viṣṇu with the *asuras* Madhu and Kaiṭabha; the origin of the four vṛttis[3] respectively from ऋग्वेद, यजुर्वेद, सामवेद and आथर्वणवेद; four sub-divisions (भेद) of each of the four vṛttis and their definitions; particular *rasas* for which each of the four vṛttis was to be employed[4]; 23 dramatic representation is centred in

1. क्रोधप्रसादशोकाः शापोत्सर्गोऽथ विद्रवोद्वाहौ । अद्भुतसंश्रयदर्शनमङ्कप्रत्यक्षजानि स्युः ॥ युद्धं राज्यभ्रंशो मरणं नगररोधनं चैव । अप्रत्यक्षकृतानि प्रवेशकैः संविधेयानि ॥ अङ्कप्रवेशके वा प्रकरणमाश्रित्य नाटकं वापि । न वधः कर्तव्यः स्याद्योऽभ्युदयी नायकः ख्यातः ॥ नाट्य. 20. 20-22. Vide अ.भा. vol.II. pp. 426-427 (chap.18) for several views on the question of representing death on the stage directly. अभिनव० (vol. II. p. 426) is against it (तस्माद्रङ्गे मरणमप्रयोज्यमेव).

2. न तज्ज्ञानं न तच्छिल्पं न सा विद्या न सा कला । न तत्कर्म न योगोऽसौ नाटके यन्न दृश्यते ॥ नाट्य. 21. 122. It is also नाट्य. I. 113-114. अ. भा. comments (vol. I. 42) 'ज्ञानमित्युपादेयमात्मज्ञानादि । ...विद्या दण्डनीत्यादि । ...योगो योजनं तेषामेव ज्ञानादीनां कलान्तानां स्वभेदैरन्योन्यस्वभेदैः । ...कर्मेति युद्धनियुद्धादिर्व्यापारः ।.'

3. या वाक्प्रधाना पुरुषप्रयोज्या स्त्रीवर्जिता संस्कृतवाक्ययुक्ता । स्वनामधेयैर्भरतैः प्रयुक्ता सा भारती नाम भवेत्तु वृत्तिः ॥ नाट्य० 22.25 (or 20.26 G. O. S. ed.) In अलङ्कार works वृत्ति has several meanings.

4. Vide Dr. Raghavan on vṛttis in J. O. R., Madras, vol. VI. pp. 346-370 and vol. VII. pp. 33-52 and 91-112 and in 'Some concepts of the Alaṅkāra-śāstra' pp. 182-193. The रसार्णव-

āhāryābhinaya which is based on *nepathya* (costumes, ornaments and devices of representing)[1]; *nepathya* is of four kinds, viz. पुस्त, अलङ्कार, अङ्गरचना सञ्जीव (G. O. S. ed. reads सज्जीव in 21. 5 and सजीव in 21.1 61); the definitions of these; *pusta* means figures made with cloth or hides for representing hills, carts, and the like; *alaṅkāra* includes garlands, ornaments (from head to foot) and clothes to be worn by male and female characters of various countries and cities, *tilaka*, collyrium in eyes, colouring the teeth and lip; aṅgaracanā includes painting the body in order to represent the complexions of kings, well-to-do people, of kirātas, āndhras, śakas, yavanas, śūdras &c.; training the moustache and beard; sañjīva means devices to represent four-footed animals, bipeds, birds, snakes; the upakaraṇas of *nāṭya* and artificial weapons; **24** (or 22 of G. O. S.) *Sāmānyābhinaya* (that acting that has not yet been described but must be described); outward manifestations of सत्त्व; alaṅkāras of young women which are *aṅgaja* are three viz. भाव, हाव, हेला; ten are स्वभावज, लीला, विलास &c. and 7 are अयत्नज viz. शोभा, कान्ति, दीप्ति, माधुर्य, धैर्य, प्रागल्भ्य and औदार्य; definitions of these; the manifestations of सत्त्व in males viz. शोभा &c.; *bodily abhinaya* in relation to rasa and bhāva; twelve kinds of abhinaya as to the recitation part of a drama, such as आलाप, प्रलाप, विलाप &c.; all these are वाक्याभिनय; representation of hearing, touch, seeing, tasting &c. and of desirable or undesirable matters how done; description of women of various types; ten कामावस्थाs viz. अभिलाष, चिन्तन, अनुस्मृति, गुणकीर्तन, उद्वेग, विलाप, उन्माद, व्याधि, जडता, मरण and the description of their representation; sending of दूती; eight kinds of नायिका viz, वासकसज्जा, स्वाधीनपतिका, अभिसारिका &c. how represented on the stage, since the spectators include fathers and sons, daughters-in-law and mothers-in-law[2];

सुधाकर (pp. 69-71) gives fanciful derivations of the names भारती &c.; from chap. 15 to 22 the नाट्यशास्त्र deals with वाचिकाभिनय.

1. आहार्याभिनयो नाम ज्ञेयो नेपथ्यजो विधिः। तत्र कार्यः प्रयत्नस्तु नाट्यस्य शुभमिच्छता ॥ नाट्य. 23. 2. or 21.3 in G.O.S. ed. and अ. भा. explains 'समस्ताभिनयप्रयोगचित्रस्य भित्तिस्थानीयमाहार्यम्. Vide Dr. G. S. Ghurye's brochure on 'Bhāratanāṭya and its costume' published by Popular Book Depot, Bombay 1958.

2 न कार्यं शयनं रङ्गे नाट्यधर्मं विजानता।...चुम्बनालिङ्गनं चैव तथा गुह्यं च यद्भवेत्। दन्तं नखक्षतं छेद्यं नीवीस्रंसनमेव च। स्तनाधरविमर्दं च रङ्गमध्ये न कारयेत्। भोजनं सलिलक्रीडां तथा लज्जाकरं तु यत् ।... पितृपुत्रस्नुषाश्वश्रूदृश्यं यस्मात्तु नाटकम्। तस्मादेतानि सर्वाणि वर्जनीयानि यत्नतः ॥ नाट्य. 24. 285-289 (22.296-298 G.O.S.).

how loving women are to address men in love or anger and jealousy; 25 (or 23 of G. O. S.) *Vaiśika* is one who excels in kalās and is clever in wooing women and *veśyās*; 33 natural and cultivated qualities of such a man; his friend and go-between (दूती); signs of women who are enamoured of a man or who hate him; four stages of the youth of women; five classes of men who love; five upāyas to win over women viz. साम, प्रदान, भेद, दण्ड, उपेक्षा; 26 (or 25 of G. O. S.) *Citrābhinaya* i. e. āṅgika abhinaya not described so far (and which is therefore a supplementary part of सामान्याभिनय); how to represent the sky, night, evening, darkness, heat &c.; how to represent joy, anger, pain and sorrow; meaning of आकाशवचन, आत्मगत, अपवारितक, जनान्तिक; how old men and children are to recite their speeches; how to represent that a man is dying; other gestures should be learnt from the people;[1] 27 *siddhi* (successfull dramatic performance); siddhi is मानुषी and दैवी; the audience should indicate that the performance is a success by gifts of clothes &c., by smiles, loud laughter (when the Vidūṣaka plays mischievous tricks), by saying 'sādhu' or 'aho' (in wonderful or love scenes), 'kaṣṭam' (in a pathetic scene); दैविकी सिद्धि consists in there being no noise nor disturbance, no ill omen and the audience hall being full; accidents and portents are such as fire, whirlwind, elephant, snake &c. or clapping of hands and throwing of cowdung or mud by persons who hate the actors, forgetting one's speech, the fall of a crown or of ornaments; qualifications of dramatic judges or critics; **28** musical instruments of four kinds, viz. तत (stringed like lutes), अवनद्ध (on which a hide is spread as in the case of a drum), घन (*tāla*), सुषिर (hollow like a flute); the seven स्वरs (षड्ज, ऋषभ &c.): four kinds of them viz वादी, संवादी, अनुवादी, and विवादी and their description, ग्रामs, मूर्छनाs, 22 श्रुतिs, जातिs; **29** What जातिs and स्वरs are to be employed in which *rasas*; four varṇas, आरोही, अवरोही, स्थायी and सञ्चारी and 33 alaṅkāras dependent on them and their definitions; gītis; **30** flutes; **31** ताल and लय; **32** discourse on ध्रुवाs (sung when a character enters the stage or leaves it, or sung at the end of an Act or sung in the course of the play or when a character falls

---

1 नोक्ता ये च मया तत्र लोकग्राह्यास्तु ते बुधैः॥ लोको वेदास्तथाध्यात्मं प्रमाणं त्रिविधं स्मृतम् ।...तस्मान्नाट्यप्रयोगे तु प्रमाणं लोक उच्यते।...कृतानुकरणं लोके नाट्यमित्यभिधीयते। लोकस्य चरितं यत्तु नानावस्थान्तरात्मकम्। तदङ्गाभिनयोपेतं नाट्यमित्यभिसंज्ञितम्॥ नाट्य. 26.111-115.

down, forgets his speech or faints &c.[1]; the language of the Dhruvās was to be Śaurasenī generally[2] (verses 408-410), though a few (chap. 32. 47-55 are) in Sanskrit; qualifications of the singer and of those who are to play on such musical instruments as वीणा, वंश (flute made from bamboo); singing comes naturally to women and playing on musical instruments to men[3]; six qualifications of the teacher of music and the pupil; **33** disquisition on the instruments called अवनद्ध such as मृदङ्ग, पणव दर्दुर; Svāti and Nārada promulgated *Gāndharva* and *Vādya*; occasions when all kinds of musical instruments are to be played; the superintending deities of musical instruments: **34** three kinds of prakṛtis among men and women,[4] viz. उत्तम, मध्यम and अधम and their characteristics; four kinds of heroes in plays viz धीरोद्धत, धीरललित, धीरोदात्त and धीरप्रशान्त and who are to be represented as falling in these classes; different kinds of women in plays such as महादेवी, देवी, नर्तिका, परिचारिका and the descriptions of these; attendants in the harem such as कञ्चुकीयs, वर्षवरs; characteristics of नृप, सेनापति, पुरोहित, मन्त्रिन्, सचिव, प्राड्विवाक, कुमार; **35** the assignment of various parts to the several members on the staff of a dramatic troupe and the characteristics required; artificial devices made with clay, wood and hides (नाट्यधर्मी) to represent a character with many hands and faces (like Rāvaṇa) or to represent animals (like lions and elephants &c.); about men taking the parts of women and *vice versa*; dramatic representation is of two kinds सुकुमार (in नाटक, प्रकरण, भाण, वीथी, अङ्क) and आविद्ध (in डिम and the rest); qualifications of सूत्रधार, पारिपार्श्विक, actors, विट, शकार,[5] विदूषक, चेट, नायिका, गणिका, नट and artisans and craftsmen (such as माल्यकृत्, वेषकर, रजक, कारुक); **36** The sages, Ātreya and others, ask Bharata

---

1. प्रावेशिकी तु प्रथमा द्वितीयाक्षेपिकी स्मृता । प्रासादिकी तृतीया च चतुर्थी चान्तरा ध्रुवा ॥ नैष्क्रामिकी च विज्ञेया पञ्चमी च ध्रुवा बुधैः ॥ नाट्य. 32. 23-24; vide also 32. 334, 340.

2. The Prākrit of the Dhruvā verses is rather corrupt. Dr. Manomohan Ghosh has edited all prākrit verses found in this chapter; vide I. H. Q. vol. VIII. at end pp. 1-52.

3. प्रायेण तु स्वभावात्स्त्रीणां गानं नृणां च वाद्यविधिः । स्त्रीणां स्वभावमधुरः कण्ठो नृणां बलत्वं च ॥ नाट्य. 32. 465.

4. एवं च शीलतो नृणां प्रकृतिस्त्रिविधा स्त्रियः ॥ नाट्य 34. 8.

5. उज्ज्वलवस्त्राभरणः क्रुध्यत्यनिमित्ततः प्रसीदति च । अधमो मागधभाषी भवति शकारो बहुविकारः ॥ नाट्य. 35. 56.

some questions, viz. what deity is worshipped in पूर्वरङ्ग, how nāṭya came down to the earth from heaven and how his descendants came to be called naṭas; Bharata's replies to these that his sons being intoxicated with their proficiency in nāṭyaveda engaged in mimicking the sages and composing dramatic pieces that were lewd and improper; sages were angered and cursed the *bharatas* that they and their descendants would be śūdras; Bharata said that they should transmit the Nāṭyaśāstra to other and better pupils and perform prāyaścitta; then Nahuṣa who had become Indra desired Bharata to promulgate Nāṭyaśāstra on the earth; Kohala will supplement the Nāṭyaveda; then the sons of Bharata taught to their own sons the śāstra and Kohala, Vātsya, Śāṇḍilya, Dhūrtila propagated it in the world; the nāṭyaśāstra is auspicious and holy and the gods are pleased more by a dramatic performance than by worship with flowers and sandalwood paste.

The above outline of the contents of the Nāṭyaśāstra, though meagre as compared with the large bulk of the work, is sufficient to show its encyclopaedic character. It contains an elaborate analysis of the sources of the aesthetic pleasure that one derives from seeing a performance; it treats of the architecture of the theatre, gives an exhaustive treatment of metres to be employed, the postures, movements and gestures of actors and of the mode in which they are to deliver their speeches, of the different kinds of dramas, the analysis of the structures of the dramas and their styles. It also furnishes directions about the songs to be sung and the musical instruments to be employed and treats in detail of the musical notes and their combinations. Above all, it insists on a high and noble purpose for the drama, forbids indecent behaviour, scenes or language and holds forth before the actors a high spiritual ideal by saying that if the actors dedicate themselves to their work in a spirit of devotion to their art and attain perfection therein, they will be doing a great service to society and will acquire merit for themselves. The Nāṭyaśāstra, as narrated in its last chapter, knew well that the drama and actors had come into great disrepute for their loose character and tries hard to raise the status of both. This work is probably unique in the world's literature on dramaturgy. Hardly any work on dramaturgy in any language has the comprehensiveness, the sweep and the literary and artistic flair of the Nāṭyasastra. It is sad to note that in spite of the noble words of the Nāṭyaśāstra, dramatic artists descended to very low depths in a few centuries after it as attested by Dāmodaragupta in his Kuṭṭanīmata (latter half of the 8th century A. D.). Verses 881-928 of the कुट्टनीमत (edited by Mr. Tanasukhram, Bombay) refer to a unique matter, viz. the actual representation of the first Act of the Ratnāvali of Śrīharṣa before a prince in a temple at Benares by accomplished veśyās led by a teacher of dancing. Both male and female parts were acted by the veśyās, one of whom named Mañjarī (verses 803-805) performed the part of Sāgarikā (or Ratnāvali) and another veśyā (not named) that of king Udayana. One verse, viz. Ratnāvali I. 24, is actually quoted by the Kuṭṭanīmata (v. 926). The veśyās are out for money and make no secret of their motives. The whole work, though written in mellifluous verse, depicts very graphically the laxity of morals prevalent among most people and particularly among the votaries of singing and dancing. It will be shown later on how the verses of the कुट्टनीमत shed abundant light on the text of the Nāṭyaśāstra as it stood in the last quarter of 8th century A. D. The राजतरङ्गिणी expressly mentions that king Jayāpīḍa of Kashmir made Dāmodaragupta, author of कुट्टनीमत, his chief councillor (स दामोदरगुप्ताख्यं कुट्टनीमतकारिणम्। कविं कविं बलिरिव धुर्यं धीसचिवं व्यधात्॥ राजतरङ्गिणी IV. 496). जयापीड ruled from about 779 to 813 A. D.

The date of the Nāṭyaśāstra

In the discussion about the original kernel of the Nāṭyaśāstra and its authorship some remarks have already been made which have a bearing on the date of the Nāṭyaśāstra. One matter must be made clear before starting further discussion of the date. Frequent additions have been made to the Nāṭyaśāstra and there are substantial discrepancies in the mss. of the work. Therefore, any discussion about the date of the work refers of necessity to a time when the principal structure and chapters of the work had been put up and takes no account of the insertion of some verse or verses here and there.

Various dates have been assigned to the Nāṭyśāstra. M. M. Haraprasad Shastri assigned it to the 2nd century before Christ (J. A. S. B. for 1913 p. 307). Prof. Levi, in a brilliant article translated in the Indian Antiquary vol. 33 p. 163 relying upon the use of such words as स्वामी, सुगृहीतनामन् and भद्रमुख in the works on Nāṭyaśāstra as terms of address, tried to establish that the नाट्यशास्त्र of Bharata was composed about the times of the Indo-Scythian Kṣatrapas some of whom like Nahapāna and Caṣṭana are styled *swāmin* and *bhadramukha* in their inscriptions (e. g. E. I. IX. p. 274 and E. I. XVI. at p. 238). In spite of the vigour and confidence with which the arguments are set forth the theory that the Sanskrit theatre came into existence at the court of the *Kṣatrapas* appears, to say the least, to be an imposing structure built on very slender foundations. In the first place, स्वामी is the term of address for a Yuvarāja in the Nāṭyaśāstra (19. 12) and not for a ruling king. In the the second place, an obvious reply is that the inscriptions might have been drafted by persons thoroughly imbued with the dramatic terminology of the नाट्यशास्त्र. भद्रमुख as a term of address does not occur in the नाट्यशास्त्र but in the साहित्यदर्पण. In the Indian Antiquary vol. 46 (1917) pp. 171—183 I discussed the question of the date and arrived at the conclusion that before 300 A. D. there existed a work on नाट्यशास्त्र ascribed to भरत and dealing with the *rasa* theory and dramaturgy in general. Prof. Keith (in HSD. p. 13) holds that 'we cannot with any assurance place it before the 3rd century A. D.' More recently Mr. Manomohan Ghosh (in Department of Letters, Calcutta University, vol. 25, Art. 4 pp. 1—54) dealt exhaustively with the question of the date from several points of view such as the linguistic data (Sanskrit, Prakrits in ch. 18 and the Dhruvās in chap. 32), the treatment of metres, the mention of only four figures of speech, the mythology, the geographical data, and came to the conclusion (p. 52) that the date of the Nāṭyaśāstra must be placed between 100 B. C. to 200 A. D. Although I do not agree with several things that he says,[1] the date he arrives at cannot, in my opinion, be far

1 For example, on p. 25 he says that दाक्षिणात्या, one of the seven भाषाs mentioned in chap. 18. 35-36 is not the महाराष्ट्री. भरत's words are : शौरसेनं समाश्रित्य भाषा कार्या तु नाटके ।... नानादेशसमुत्थं हि काव्यं भवति नाटके । मागध्यवन्तिजा प्राच्या शूरसेन्यर्धमागधी । बाह्लिका दाक्षिणात्या च सप्त भाषाः प्रकीर्तिताः ॥. What country, acc. to Mr. Ghosh, is meant by दाक्षिणात्या ? द्रविड and ओड्र are separately mentioned in v. 36. The काव्यादर्श (I. 34) mentions the भाषा of महाराष्ट्र as the best प्राकृत and states that सेतुबन्ध was composed in that language. The सेतुबन्ध

from the truth. Dr. D. C. Sircar (ournal of Andhra H. R. Society, vol. XII. p. 108 ff) opines that the fact that the present text mentions the countries of महाराष्ट्र (in 14. 38) and नेपाल (in 14. 43) definitely points to a date later than the 2nd century A. D., since नेपाल is first mentioned in Samudragupta-praśasti in the first half of the 4th century and महाराष्ट्र is mentioned first in the महावंश (5th century) and in the Aihole inscription (of 634 A. D.). This is a strange and unconvincing argument. Names of countries do not drop down all at once from heaven nor is there anything to show that the name was first coined by समुद्रगुप्त or his panegyrist or by some one else at a particular period. If नेपाल is mentioned about 325 A. D., no reason is given why it could not have existed as a name two hundred years earlier. The same reasoning applies to महाराष्ट्र. In 634 (Aihole inscription) महाराष्ट्र was a vast territory containing three provinces and 99000 villages).[1] In the Nāṇāghāt Inscription (A. S. W. I. vol. V. p. 60) the word Mahāraṭhi occurs (about 200 B. C.) which can very well be explained as meaning an inhabitant of Mahārāṣṭra, though it must be conceded that that word is differently interpreted by several scholars.

---

was composed at the latest in the 5th century A. D. in महाराष्ट्रीप्राकृत. Even if Bharata preferred Śaurasenī, which might have been due to his being a native of शूरसेन (the country round about मथुरा) or because the art of writing dramas was very much cultivated there before his time, no reasons are forthcoming to establish that महाराष्ट्री in which such an elegant poem as the Setubandha was composed in the 5th century at the latest could not have existed as a प्राकृतभाषा at all some centuries earlier. On p. 43 he says that the avatāras of Viṣṇu are not mentioned, but in chap. 13. 152 (Ch. ed.) we read या कृता नरसिंहेन विष्णुना प्रभविष्णुना and अभिनवगुप्त explains the verse (G. O. S. XII. 154, vol. II. p. 162). His views on महाराष्ट्री as a later phase of शौरसेनी (Department of Letters, Calcutta University, vol. 23) have been criticized by Dr. Ghatge in an informing paper 'on Mahārāṣṭrī Language and Literature' in Journal of the Bombay University (vol. II. part 6 pp. 19-70 at pp. 22-35). Vide also Dr. Ghatge on Śaurasenī in Journal, Bom. Un. vol. III. part. 6 pp. 44-62.

1 अगमदधिपतित्वं यो महाराष्ट्रकाणां नवनवतिसहस्रग्रामभाजां त्रयाणाम् ॥ E. I. vol. VI. p. 1 at p. 4.

The upper limit of the Nāṭyaśāstra cannot be fixed with any certainty. We can only try to fix some probable limit. The नाट्यशास्त्र mentions विश्वकर्मा on architecture and house—building (2. 7 and 12), Purāṇas (14. 46 and 27·59 in G. O. S.), Pūrvācāryas (15. 22 on शब्दलक्षण), कामतन्त्र (23·37 and 52 of G.O.S.), बृहस्पति (24.88 of GOS and 34.79 on अर्थशास्त्र), नारद (32. 1 on ध्रुवाs and 32. 484 on गान्धर्व), तण्डु (4. 17 on अङ्गहारs), पाशुपतs (in 13.85), शबर, आभीर and द्रविड (in 18. 36), शक (18. 40). But all these details cannot lead to any certain inference about the date of the नाट्यशास्त्र. They, however, make it probable that the present Nāṭyaśāstra is not much older than the beginning of the Christian era. The lower limit can be indicated with more assurance. The evidence for the lower limit may be briefly set out here :

(a) Kālidāsa's verse in the Vikramorvaśīya (II. 18) already noticed (p. 11) leads to the inference that before 450 A. D. at the latest Bharata had been regarded as founder of the नाट्यशास्त्र, had spoken of only eight *rasasa* and had performed a drama before the gods. So this vouches for the existence of the legend in the first chapter and the discussion about rasas in the 6th chap. In रघुवंश 19. 21 there is a reference to खण्डिता नायिका, which reminds us of the eight नायिकाs enumerated and defined in नाट्यशास्त्र 31. 109-110 and the following verses. Similarly, in रघुवंश 19. 36 (अङ्गसत्त्ववचनाश्रयं मिथः स्त्रीषु नृत्यमुपधाय दर्शनम्) there is a conscious following of नाट्यशास्त्र 24. 1 (सामान्याभिनयो नाम ज्ञेयो वागङ्गसत्त्वजः).

(b) The कुट्टनीमत speaks of the नाट्यशास्त्र as ब्रह्मोक्त (in v. 75), which is a reference to chapter one, and in verse 946 (भरतसुतैरुपदिष्टं क्षितिपतिनहुषावरोधनारीणाम् ।) there is a clear reference to the legend in the last chapter (36. 48-61) about नहुष and the sons of भरत. In numerous other places the कुट्टनीमत refers to subjects that are dealt with in different chapters of the present नाट्यशास्त्र, e. g. verses 791-92 refer to खण्डिता and कलहान्तरिता for which नाट्यशास्त्र 22. 216-217 (in vol. III of GOS.) and the following verses may be compared. Verses 881 and 928 refer to the singing of Dhruvā called Prāveśikī when the सूत्रधार is to enter the stage and the नैष्क्रामिकी ध्रुवा when all characters left the stage at the end of the 1st Act of the Ratanāvali. This is a pointed reference to chap. 32 verses 335 and 336 where both these occur and are described. Verse 805 of the कुट्टनीमत refers to सात्त्विकभावs (for which see नाट्यशास्त्र 7. 93) and verse 809 (सद्वरोप्यनुभावगणे करुणरसं विप्रलम्भतो भिन्नम्) refers to नाट्यशास्त्र VI. p. 73 where this matter is discussed. Therefore, it follows that the important chapters of the नाट्यशास्त्र from the first to the 36th existed before 800 A. D.

(c) आनन्दवर्धन in the ध्वन्यालोक says 'यदि वा वृत्तीनां भरतप्रसिद्धानां कैशिक्यादीनां' (p. 202) and 'यथा वेणीसंहारे विलासाख्यस्य प्रतिमुखसन्ध्यङ्गस्य प्रकृतरसनिबन्धनाननुगुणमपि भरतमतानुसरणमात्रेच्छया घटनं' (p. 185) ; so also 'अत एव च भरते प्रबन्धप्रख्यातवस्तुविषयत्वं प्रख्यातोदात्तनायकत्वं च नाटकस्यावश्यकर्तव्यतयोपन्यस्तम्' (p. 180) and 'एतच्च रसादितात्पर्येण काव्यनिबन्धनं भरतादावपि सुप्रसिद्धमेव' (p. 226). The vṛttis called Kaiśikī and others are described in the नाट्यशास्त्र (chap. 20 in G. O. S. vol. III and in chap.22 in other editions and mss.) and the *aṅga* named विलास is defined in chap.21.61 and 78-G.O.S. vol.III. 22.15. In defining नाटक (chap. 16. 16-12-G. O. S. ed. chap. 18·10–12) the very first half verse is 'प्रख्यातवस्तुविषयं प्रख्यातोदत्तनायकं चैव' (10). आनन्दवर्धन flourished in the latter half of the 9th century. The वेणीसंहार had been composed before him and the auther of that drama regarded Bharata as a paramount authority. Therefore, centuries before आनन्दवर्धन the नाट्यशास्त्र contained a treatment of *rasas*, heroes, वृत्तिs and such minute particulars as the *aṅga* of the प्रतिमुखसन्धि called विलास.

(d) The काव्यप्रकाश quotes from Bharata the sūtra 'विभावानुभावव्यभिचारिसंयोगाद्रसनिष्पत्तिः' (which occurs in the 6th chap. p. 71) and gives the interpretation of that sūtra by four scholars, भट्टलोल्लट, शङ्कुक, भट्टनायक and अभिनवगुप्त. Whether all these composed commentaries on the नाट्यशास्त्र will be discussed later. It will be seen later that अभिनवगुप्त's literary activity lay between 980–1030 A. D. and that भट्टनायक flourished between 900 and 925 A. D. शङ्कुक has probably to be identified with the poet शङ्कुक, author of भुवनाभ्युदय, mentioned in the राजतरङ्गिणी (IV.705) 'कविर्बुधमनःसिन्धुशशाङ्कः शङ्कुकाभिधः । यमुद्दिश्याकरोत्काव्यं भुवनाभ्युदयाभिधम् ॥'. This would assign him to about 840 A. D. सोमेश्वर in his commentary on the काव्यप्रकाश quotes a few verses of शङ्कुक on the above *sūtra* of Bharata and the criticism of Bhaṭṭa Tauta thereon. The exact date of Lollaṭa cannot be determined. But as शङ्कुक, नायक and अभिनवगुप्त are mentioned in chronological order, it is not unlikely that लोल्लट precedes all three. He wrote रसविवरण and सोमेश्वर quotes from लोल्लट (folio 155 b) 'यमकानुलोमतदितरच्चक्रादिभिदा हि रसविरोधिन्यः । अभिधानमात्रमेदगद(ड्ड?)रिकादिप्रवाहो वा ॥'. This verse is quoted by नमिसाधु also (on रुद्रट III. 59) without the author's name. Therefore, लोल्लट probably flourished before शङ्कुक i.e. between 750–800. The conclusion is that the 6th chapter of the नाट्यशास्त्र dealing with *rasas* had been the subject of several interpretations from the 8th century A. D.

(e) भवभूति (about 700–740 A. D.) looks upon Bharata as the author of तौर्यत्रिकसूत्र (i. e. नाट्यशास्त्र) and as a contemporary of Vālmiki, the author of the रामायण (*vide* उत्तररामचरित IV).

(f) Bāṇa in his कादम्बरी (para 71 of my edition) mentions the नृत्तशास्त्र composed by भरत as one of the branches of knowledge in which चन्द्रापीड became proficient. In the हर्षचरित also (III. para 5) he speaks of singing which followed the path laid down by Bharata.[1] In another place (हर्ष० II. 4) he speaks of actors in the आरभटीवृत्ति (रैणवावर्तमण्डलीरेचकरासरभसारब्धनर्तनारभटीनटाः). रेचक is defined in नाट्यशास्त्र (4. 240–246) and आरभटी (chap. 20. 65 of vol. III GOS).

(g) The याज्ञवल्क्यस्मृति, after stating that by reciting the Sāman songs according to rules and without mistakes the singer reaches Brahma (i.e. realises the Supreme Reality), extends the same reward to those who instead of the Vedic songs sing the seven kinds of non-Vedic songs called[2] अपरान्तक, उल्लोप्यक, मद्रक, प्रकरी, ओवेणक, सरोबिन्दु and उत्तर; further provides that the repeated singing of four kinds of other songs (mentioned below) also tend to *mokṣa* (enabling the mind to concentrate itself on the Supreme Soul) and those who know the essence of the playing on the

---

1 वंशानुगमविवादि स्फुटकरणं भरतमार्गभजनगुरु । श्रीकण्ठविनिर्यातं गीतमिदं हर्षराज्यमिव ॥ हर्षचरित III. verse 4; as to विवादी, vide नाट्यशास्त्र for the four kind of स्वरs, viz वादि, संवादि, अनुवादि and विवादि (28. 20) and 'विवादिनस्तु ते येषां विंशतिस्वरमन्तरम् । तद्यथा वृषभगान्धारौ धैवतनिषादौ' (नाट्य० chap. 28 after verse 21 p. 318). For करणs (of the hand) see नाट्य. 9. 198–207.

2 अपरान्तकमुल्लोप्यं मद्रकं प्रकरीं तथा । औवेणकं सरोबिन्दुमुत्तरं गीतकानि च । ऋग्गाथा पाणिका दक्षविहिता ब्रह्मगीतिका । गेयमेतत्तदभ्यासकरणान्मोक्षसंज्ञितम् ॥ वीणावादनतत्त्वज्ञः श्रुतिजातिविशारदः तालज्ञश्च प्रयासेन मोक्षमार्गं नियच्छति ॥; compare याज्ञ० III. 113-115. Compare ब्रह्मोक्तं सप्तरूपं हि समवेताद विनिःसृतम् । दैवताराधनं पुण्यमनन्तं गीतवादितम् ॥...ऋग्गाथापाणिकानां च प्रमाणानां तथैव च । अनेनैव विधानेन युग्मौजस्त्वं विभावयेत् ॥ नाट्यशास्त्र 31. 419, 421; K. M. 31. 324 is somewhat similar to the last verse. Again 31. 523 is ऋग्गाथा पाणिका चैव सप्तरूपं प्रकीर्णकम् । and 32. 2 is या ऋचः पाणिका गाथा सप्तरूपाङ्गमेव च ।.

lute, who are experts in the knowledge of the (22) *śrūtis* and (18) jātis and know tāla reach the road to *mokṣa*. It is interesting to note that the Mitākṣarā and Aparārka refer to Bharata in explaining these, while Viśvarūpa refers to Nārada and others and the Dīpakalikā to Viśākhila and others. The seven names occur in the Nāṭyaśātra 31. 287 (K. M. 31. 184) but with some variation. The Nāṭyaśāstra devotes over hundred and thirty verses to the treatment of these seven and winds up by saying that these seven promulgated by Brahmā are holy and propitiate the gods. The अभिनवभारती also (B. O. R. I ms.) devotes several pages (from p. 479 of the ms.) to the elucidation of the seven kinds of non-Vedic songs. The names of the seven acc. to the Nāṭyaśāstra are मन्द्रक, अपरान्तक, प्रकरी, रोविन्दक (for सरोबिन्दु of या.), ओवेणक, उल्लोप्यक, उत्तर. On several grounds it may be argued that the याज्ञवल्क्यस्मृति borrows from the नाट्यशास्त्र. The four early commentators are agreed that याज्ञवल्क्य has in view some work on गीतवाद्य, while the मिताक्षरा and अपरार्क refer to भरत alone. Besides, in याज्ञवल्क्य the verses are rather abruptly introduced, while their position in the नाट्यशास्त्र is natural. I am inclined to hold that the source of these verses in Yājñavalkya is the Nāṭyaśāstra. In that case the नाट्यशास्त्र will easily have to be placed not later than the first or 2nd century of the Christian era.

(h) The Sāptaśatī of Sātavāhana (or Hāla) says in a verse 344 (Weber's ed. 27) that embraces are the पूर्वरङ्ग of the drama of love.[1] This has in view the fifth chapter of the Nāṭyaśāstra which treats of पूर्वरङ्ग. It is generally held that the गाथासप्तशती was composed between 200 to 400 A. D. Vide Prof. Keith's H. S. L. p. 224.

(i) From Fleet's Sanskrit and Old Canarese inscriptions (I. A. vol. X. pp. 166–167) we find that two Sanskrit verses are incised on a pillar at Paṭṭadakal (the characters being of the 8th or 9th century A. D.) which were composed by one Achala (or Acalada), the second of which may be quoted here to indicate how even in Southern India dancers instructed in Bharata's doctrines were supposed to vanquish their competitors brought up in another or a rival school of dancing :

---

1 मानदुमपरुसपवणस्स मामि सव्वंगणिव्वुदिअरस्स । अवऊहणस्स भद्दं रइनाडअपुव्वरंगस्स ॥ सत्तसई (सप्तशती) 344 and IV. 44 (of Nirn. ed.).

'नटसेव्यभरतमतद्युतपद्धतरवचनाशनिप्रपातेन । कुटिलोन्नतनटशैलः स्फुटितानतमस्तकः पतति ॥'.

(j) All ancient writers on *alaṅkāra*, Bhaṭṭi (between 590-650 A. D.), दण्डी, Bhāmaha, उद्भट, define more than thirty figures of speech. भरत defines only four, which are the simplest viz. उपमा, दीपक, रूपक, and यमक. भरत has a long disquisition on metres and on the Prākṛts and would not have scrupled to define more figures of speech if they had been well-known then. Therefore, he preceded these writers by some centuries at least.

The foregoing discussion has made it clear that the नाट्यशास्त्र cannot be assigned to a later date than about 300 A. D. This does not mean that the extant नाट्यशास्त्र has come down to us intact from that date. But what is contended is that before 300 A. D. there existed a work going under the name of Bharata containing the *rasa* theory and dealing with dramaturgy; this cannot be disputed. As there is no other extant work on the theory of Poetics and allied topics as old as 300 A. D. the नाट्यशास्त्र must be regarded in the present state of our knowledge as the oldest work on the अलङ्कारशास्त्र.

धनिक in his commentary on the Daśarūpa (III. 56-60) quotess a verse from भरत "एतच्च 'इदं त्रिपुरदाहे तु लक्षणं ब्रह्मणोदितम् । ततस्त्रिपुरदाहश्च डिमसंज्ञः प्रयोजितः ॥' इति भरतमुनिना स्वयमेव त्रिपुरदाहेतिवृत्तस्य तुल्यत्वं दर्शितम् ". In the नाट्यशास्त्र only the latter half is found (IV. 10). The commentator on the सरस्वतीकण्ठाभरण (II. p. 254 Benares ed. =Nir. ed of 1934 p 268 on कारिका 109) says that, as regards मुरजबन्ध, भरत mentions the letters to be employed 'पाठाक्षराणि मुरजे लहकारौ तथदधाच्ङमौ रेफः। नणकखगत्रङाश्चेत्थं षोडश भरतादिकथितानि ॥'. There is nothing in the नाट्यशास्त्र on this point.

We must now turn to the commentaries on the Nāṭyaśāstra. The most famous and the most erudite is that of Abhinavagupta called नाट्यवेदविवृति and also अभिनवभारती in the colophons of its mss. and by commentators of Sanskrit dramas such as Rāghavabhaṭṭa[1] on the Śākuntala. A separate section will be devoted to Abhinavgupta later on. As noted above Mr. Kavi has brought out so far only three volums of the अभिनवभारती in the G. O. S. (up to chap. 27 on सिद्धिलक्षण-विधान). For the rest I

1 e. g. राघवभट्ट on शाकुन्तल (I) quotes नाट्यशास्त्र 5. 24-25 and 106-107 सूत्रधारः पठेन्नान्दीं...लङ्कृताम् ।) and remarks 'इदं पद्यमभिनवगुप्ताचार्यैर्भरतटीकायामभिनवभारत्यां व्याख्यातम्'.

have used a recent transcript which is ms. No. 41 of 1924–28 in the Bhandarkar Oriental Institute. It is rather corrupt and incomplete, as it extends only up to chap. 32, verse 376 (ध्रुवाध्याय of Ch. edition) and then breaks off. So far as I know no complete ms. of the अभिनवभारती on the whole of the नाट्यशास्त्र is available at present anywhere. But even this incomplete commentary of अभिनवगुप्त furnishes very valuable information about the commentators of Bharata and about writers on the histrionic art. In the following I propose to give a brief account of the commentators of the Nāṭyaśāstra.[1] According to the सङ्गीतरत्नाकर of शार्ङ्गदेव the expounders of Bharata were लोल्लट, उद्भट, शङ्कुक, कीर्तिधर and अभिनवगुप्त (व्याख्यातारो भारतीये लोल्लटोद्भटशङ्कुकाः। भट्टाभिनवगुप्तश्च श्रीमत्कीर्तिधरोऽपरः ॥ I. 19). A separate section will be devoted to Udbhaṭa, but here a few words may be said about his commentary on भरत. उद्भट is mentioned by अभिनव on the following points. (1) On नाट्यशास्त्र VI. 10 (quoted above) the views of औद्भटs are quoted and Abhinava says that लोल्लट did not accept them (vide अभिनवभारती G. O. S. vol. I. p. 266); (2) On नाट्य. IX. 182 अ. भा. (vol. II. p. 70) notes that उद्भट read the verse differently as 'उत्तानोधस्तलस्त्यश्रोग्रगोधोमुख एव च । पञ्च प्रचारा हस्तस्येति भट्टोद्भटः पठति'; (3) about समवकार (a kind of रूपक) the नाट्यशास्त्र (18. 76) reads 'उष्णिग्गायत्र्याद्यान्यन्यानि च यानि बन्धकुटिलानि । वृत्तानि समवकारे कविभिस्तानि प्रयोज्यानि ॥'. अ. भा. notes that उद्भट reads नैव प्रयोज्यानि for तानि प्रयोज्यानि;[2] (4) उद्भट appears to have criticized भरत himself as to the four वृत्तिs, भारती, सात्वती, कैशिकी and आरभटी. भरत (20. 99–100) defines the play called उत्सृष्टिकाङ्क as full of women's lamentations and as bereft of all वृत्तिs except भारती. But in करुण when there is a swoon or death there can be no speech and no भारतीवृत्ति (which acc. to नाट्य. 22. 25 is या वाक्प्रधाना &c. or 20. 26 in GOS ed.). For this and other reasons उद्भट gives up the four वृत्तिs and proposes only three वृत्तिs viz. न्यायचेष्टावृत्ति, अन्यायचेष्टावृत्ति and फलसंवित्तिवृत्ति (for मूर्छा and मरण) or

1 For some further information consult Dr. Raghavan's paper on 'Writers quoted in the Abhinavabhāratī' in J. O. R. Madras, vol. VI. pp. 149–170 and pp. 199–223.

2 नैव प्रयोज्यानीत्युद्भटः पठति स्रग्धरादीन्येव प्रयोज्यानि नाल्पाक्षराणीति स व्याचष्टे । अ. भा. vol. II. P. 441. The Ch. ed. (20. 80) reads as उद्भट does.

फलवृत्ति. अभिनव quotes a verse of उद्भट,[1] states that certain followers of a writer called शकलीगर्भ[2] held that there were five वृत्तिs, the four of भरत plus the वृत्ति called आत्मसंवित्ति (or फलवृत्ति of उद्भट) and that लोल्लट refuted those views of उद्भट and शकलीगर्भ. अभिनव does not agree with all the three and sticks to the four वृत्तिs of भरत; (5) In a corrupt passage (in GOS ed. अ. भा. reads यासावन्वेषण०) Abhinava refers to an exposition of Udbhaṭa about the 4th सन्धि called अवमर्श (नाट्य. 21. 42) and refutes it;[3] (6) उद्भट explained नाट्य. 21.17 as laying down that the several *sandhis* and their *aṅgas* must appear in a drama in the same order as is stated by भरत, but A. B. rejects this view as opposed to reasoning and also to the tradition of poets.[4] From the above it is clear that अभिनव mentions Udbhaṭa's comments on chapters so far apart as 6, 9, 19 of the नाट्यशास्त्र (G. O. S. ed) and so probably उद्भट commented on the whole of it. It will be shown that उद्भट flourished about 800 A. D. His views about the वृत्ति called आत्मसंवित्ति were accepted by शकलीगर्भ, who was criticized by लोल्लट. So the latter must have flourished between 800 to 840 A. D. It has already been shown that he criticised उद्भट in several places (e. g. on नाट्यशास्त्र 6. 10 and 18. 112). His views on the theory of

---

1 तस्मात्फलसंवित्त्याख्या वृत्तिः वाक्चेष्टयोः फलानुभव इति यस्या लक्षणं साभ्युपगन्तव्या । अवश्यं चैतत् अन्यथा मूर्छामरणादौ वाक्चेष्टयोरभावे निर्वृत्तिकतैव स्यात् ।...तस्माच्चेष्टात्मिका न्यायवृत्तिरन्यायवृत्तिर्वाग्रूपा तत्फलभूता फलसंवित्तिरिति त्रयमेव युक्तमिति भट्टोद्भटो मन्यते । यदाह । आद्ये वाक्चेष्टाभ्यां पुरुषार्थचतुष्टयेन चाष्टविधे । षोडशधा फलवृत्तिस्तद्द्वयतोऽनेकधा तु रसभेदात् । A.B. vol.II.p. 451.

2 यच्छकलीगर्भमतानुसारिणो मूर्छादावात्मसंवित्तिलक्षणां पञ्चमीं वृत्तिं सकलकार्यनिवृत्त्यनुमेयां......आत्मव्यापाररूपां मन्यन्ते...तन्मतं भावानां बाह्यग्रहणस्वभावत्वमुपपादयद्भिः भट्टलोल्लटप्रभृतिभिः पराकृतम् । अ. भा. (G. O. S. vol. II. p. 452). The editor regards शकलीगर्भ as a name of उद्भट, but this cannot be accepted, firstly, because अ. भा. mentions the name Udhaṭa half a dozen times and there is no reason given why a different name should be used and secondly, because the view attributed to शकलीगर्भ differs from उद्भट's view on वृत्तिs noted by. अ. भा.

3 यदाह भट्टोद्भटः । नासान्वेषणभूमिरवमृष्टिरवमर्श इति तच्चेदं व्याख्यानं लक्ष्यविरुद्धं युक्त्या च । p. 28 chap. 19 of G. O. S. ed. vol. III.

4 पुनरेषामिति पुनःशब्दो विशेषद्योतको लक्षण एवायं क्रमो न निबन्धने इति यावत् । तेन यदुद्भटप्रभृतयो अङ्गानां सन्धौ क्रमे च नियममाहुस्तद्युक्त्यागमविरुद्धमेव p. 36 of vol. III of GOS ed.

Rasa summarised on the Rasa sūtra ay अभिनव (G. O. S. vol. I. p. 274) will be dealt with in part II. Some of his other views are : (a) Acc. to लोल्लट *rasas* are numerous,[1] but only eight (or nine) are to be represented (on the stage) in accordance with the well-known theory of traditional works; (b) It appears that लोल्लट did not read the verse (यः कश्चित्कार्यवशाद्गच्छति पुरुषः प्रकृष्टमध्वानम् । तत्राप्यङ्कच्छेदः कर्तव्यः पूर्ववत्तज्ज्ञैः ॥ G. O. S. 18. 32, Ch. 20. 30, K. M. 18, 34);[2] (c) A. B. (vol. II. p. 134) mentions the view of लोल्लट and गोपाल on ध्रुवाताल; (d) on नाट्य० 13. 1 अभिनव refers to भट्टलोल्लट's view; (e) अभिनव states (18. 14) that लोल्लट read the verse as अङ्क इति गूढशब्दो भावैश्च रसैश्च रोहयत्यर्थान्,' while अभिनव reads रूढिशब्दो; (f) on नाट्य० (G. O. S. 18. 60, Ch. ed. 20. 63) A. B. mentions the view of लोल्लट that a नाटिका is षट्पदा, while शङ्कुक held that it was अष्टपदा;[3] (g) on 21. 29 (Ch. ed.) Lollaṭa's view is that portions of the life and doings of the hero of a patākā are called अनुसन्धि.[4] From the above it will be clear that Lollaṭa also must have composed a commentary on most of the chapters of the नाट्यशास्त्र such as 6, 13, 18, 21 (if not on all).

Two verses of Lollaṭa are quoted by हेमचन्द्र in his काव्यानुशासन (chap. V. p 215) 'यस्तु सरिदद्रिसागरनगतुरगपुरारिवर्णने यत्नः । कविशक्तिख्यातिफलो विततधियां नो मतः प्रबन्धेषु ॥ यमकानुलोमतदितरचक्रादिभिदा हि रसविरोधिन्यः । अभिमानमात्रमेतद्गड्डुरिकादिप्रवाहो वा ॥.' The first verse is ascribed to अपराजिति by the काव्यमीमांसा (p. 45) and the second is quoted by सोमेश्वर from लोल्लट in his commentary on the काव्यप्रकाश (folio 105b) and by नमिसाधु on रुद्रट (III. 59) without naming the author. The का. प्र. सङ्केत of माणिक्यचन्द्र (Mysore ed. p. 82) who wrote in 1159-60 A. D. says that the details of the theory of *rasa* should be learnt from the रसविवरण of लोल्लट and others and on p. 147 hits off all three (लोल्लट, शङ्कुक, and नायक) as follows : न वेत्ति यस्य गाम्भीर्यं गिरितुङ्गोपि लोल्लटः । तत्तस्य रसपाथोधेः कथं

---

1 तेनानन्त्येपि पार्षदप्रसिद्धयैतावतां प्रयोज्यत्वमिति यद्भट्टलोल्लटेन निरूपितं तदवलेपनापरामृश्येत्यलम् (?) । अ. भा. vol. I. p. 299; should we read अवलेपनापरामृष्टयेत्यलम् ? This last would mean 'because he (लोल्लट) was touched with vanity.'

2 अत एवैतद्भट्टलोल्लटाद्यैर्न पठितमेव । अ. भा. vol. II. p. 423.

3 षटपदेयं नाटिकेति संप्रहानुसारिणो भट्टलोल्लटाद्याः, श्रीशङ्कुकस्तु अयुक्तमेतदित्यभिधायाष्टधेति व्याचष्टे । अ. भा. vol. II. p. 436.

4 तथा लोल्लटाद्यास्तु मन्यन्ते परार्थे साधयितव्ये पताकानायकस्येतिवृत्तभागा अनुसन्धयः । p. 17 of अ. भा. vol. III (GOS).

जानातु शङ्कुकः ॥ भोगरत्यादिभावानां भोगं स्वस्योचितं ब्रुवन् । सर्वथा रससर्वस्वमर्मास्प्राक्षीन्न नायकः ॥

लोल्लट appears to have advanced his arguments on the basis of the पूर्वमीमांसा; vide e. g. अ. भा. vol. II. p. 196 'प्रत्येकप्रसक्तत्वलाभात् क्रमस्यापदार्थत्वान्नार्थप्रमाणकत्वान्मुख्यश्रौतपदार्थबाधकत्वमयुक्तं श्रुत्या वाक्यप्रमाणस्य बाधनादितितु भट्टलोल्लटोक्तं प्रकृते सिध्यति विरोधाभावाद् ।'. Compare the well-known sūtra of जैमिनि 'श्रुतिलिङ्गवाक्यप्रकरणस्थानसमाख्यानां समवाये पारदौर्बल्यं°' (III. 3. 14).

There is a श्राद्धप्रकरण of लोल्लटाचार्य in the Ānandāśrama collection of mss. at Poona (no. 3175), which frequently cites the views of मेधातिथि in verse. The reference is probably to the स्मृतिविवेक of मेधातिथि mentioned by the latter in his मनुभाष्य. It is doubtful whether the author of the श्राद्धप्रकरण is identical with the लोल्लट that wrote on रस, as the former must be held to have flourished after 900 A. D.

Sankuka's view on the theory of *Rasa* will be stated in part II. His date has already been given above (p. 43). He came after Lollaṭa and criticizes the latter's theory of *rasa* (vide A. B. vol. I. p. 274). He appears to have been a regular commentator of the नाट्यशास्त्र. (a) On chap. III. verses 21–22, A. B. vol. I p. 75 mentions Śankuka's views on रङ्गपीठ 'अतः चतुर्हस्तं रङ्गपीठपृष्ठे एव मण्डलमित्युक्तं भवति । शङ्कुकादिभिः षोडशहस्तावकाशाभावः आसनस्तम्भादिवशात्तस्मादकृत एव रङ्गपीठे इत्यादि वृथैव बहुतरमुपन्यस्तम् ।'; (b) On chap. 18. 10 (p. 411 of GOS ed.) (प्रख्यातवस्तुविषयं प्रख्यातोदात्तनायकम्) about नाटक, A. B. quotes शङ्कुक's explanation and rejects it; (c) On the verse नृपतीनां यच्चरितं नानारसभावचेष्टितं बहुधा । (18. 12 G. O. S.) Śankuka's explanation of what is intended by the word नृपतीनां is cited and rejected;[1] (d) Śankuka's view about नाटिका (18. 60, vol. II. p. 436) has been cited under लोल्लट; (d 1) On chap. 21. 40 (= K. M. 19. 40) अभिनव refers to the examples illustrating that verse about प्रतिमुखसन्धि given by शङ्कुक;[2] (e) On 21. 42 about विमर्शसन्धि (= K. M. 19. 42 the reading of which is followed by शङ्कुक)

1. श्रीशङ्कुकस्तु व्याचष्टे । विजिगीषुररिर्मध्यमोदासीनौ मित्रं मित्रमित्रमिति । एषां चरितमिति बहुवचनेन लभ्यते । Vide H. of Dh. vol. III. pp. 218-222 for विजिगीषु and the others; chap. 18.12 of अ. भा. (GOS. II) has नृपतीना यच्चरितं नानारसभावचेष्टितं बहुधा । सुखदुःखोत्पत्तिकृतं भवति हि तन्नाटकं नाम । This is the verse on which शङ्कुक commented.

2. उद्घाटितत्वाद् बीजस्य स्तोकमात्रं तु शङ्कुकादिभिरुदाहृतं यत्तदेकदेशलक्षणमिति द्रष्टव्यम् । p. 25 of अ. भा. vol. III GOS.

the A. B. mentions Śaṅkuka's view (p. 28 of अ. भा. vol. II GOS); (f) On 21. 91 (= K. M. 19. 87) about विद्रव, one of the aṅgas of गर्भसन्धि, the A. B. gives the reading adopted by Śaṅkuka and its explanation and the illustration given by him (अन्ये तु शङ्काभयत्रासैः कृतो यः स विद्रव इत्यादि तत्र च विशेष्यपदमन्वेष्यं, समुदाय एव विशेष्य इति श्रीशङ्कुकः, उदाहरति च कृत्यारावणे षष्ठेऽङ्के गर्भसन्धौ)' &c. (p. 52 of अ. भा. vol. III GOS.); (g) On chap. 24 (= K. M. 22 सामान्याभिनय) the views of शङ्कुक are quoted at some length (p. 147 of अ. भा. vol. III GOS.); (h) On chap. 24. 3 (= K. M. 22. 3) A. B. offers the explanation that Śaṅkuka gives (अव्यक्तरूपमित्यादिकं प्रबन्धं श्रीशङ्कुकादय इत्थं नयन्ति &c. p. 150 of अ. भा. vol. III GOS.); (i) On 24. 66-71 (=K. M. 22. 66-71) Abhinava shows how hundreds of अभिनयभेदs arise and then states that according to Śaṅkuka they come to forty thousand (ननु यथा श्रीशङ्कुकेनोक्तं चत्वारिंशत्सहस्राणीत्यादि, p. 180 of अ०भा० vol. III GOS); (j) On नाट्यशास्त्र 5. 20-21 the अभिनवभारती quotes several verses from chap. 29 (Ch. ed. and 28 of the text of अभिनव) and states that शङ्कुक had different readings in some of the verses (i. e. शङ्कुक read त्रिः शम्योपरिपाणौ तालोपि शेष निर्दिष्टः ।... भूयः शम्यातालानुगुणादुत्तरस्तथा द्विकलश्च ।, while अभिनव read तालावित्येवमेककलः and ब्वुत्तरस्तथा चैव). It may be noted that the readings in Ch. (29. 123-124) are those adopted by शङ्कुक. शङ्कुक is quoted in vol. I. pp. 293, 298, 318 on the रससूत्राध्याय. From the above it would be manifest that Śaṅkuka's comment on several chapters from 3 to 29 being quoted it should be presumed that he commented on the whole of the Nāṭyaśāstra.

Bhaṭṭa Nāyaka is very frequently quoted by अभिनव, but the question whether he wrote a commentary on the Nāṭyaśāstra or an independent work will be discussed below separately.

On the last verse (and on the word एवं therein) of chapter 4 of the नाट्यशास्त्र the view of कीर्तिधर is quoted, but it is doubtful whether the reference is to a commentary of his on the नाट्यशास्त्र. कीर्तिधर's mention of नन्दिकेश्वरमत has already been referred to above. There is not sufficient material to establish that कीर्तिधर wrote a regular commentary on the नाट्यशास्त्र.

There is an author frequently mentioned by अभिनव as टीकाकार or टीकाकृत्. He is twice quoted on the 6th chap. (vol. I. pp. 318, 328). His views are mentioned and generally rejected over a dozen times on pp. 286 (chap. 21. 3-5 = chap. 19 of अभिनव in GOS p. 3 as opposed to उपाध्याय's view), on

प्रासङ्गिक इतिवृत्त), 382 (on chap. 28 verses 8-10 on आतोद्य), 397 (on 29. 32), 399 (on 29. 76 where his guru is said to be श्रीपाद),[1] 420 (chap. 30 on सुषिरवाद्य), 423 (on 30. 4 one verse and a half are quoted from टीकाकार), 458 (on 31. 252). So he is mentioned on most of the chapters, if not on all. On the 12 kinds of interlocutions in the plot (22.51-53 GOS) such as आलाप, प्रलाप, उपदेश, अतिदेश, अ.भा. (p. 176) remarks that commentators have brought in tārkika and mīmāṁsaka technique in explaining upaveśa, atideśa and upamāna in the domain of *sāhitya* and have thereby deluded men of delicate intellect and led them astray: अत्रोपदेशातिदेशयोरुपमानस्य च साहित्यविषये तार्किकमीमांसकविषये विशेषप्रतिपादनं यत् टीकाकारैः कृतं तत्सुकुमारमनोमोहनं वृथाश्रमफलिकामात्रं प्रकृतानुपयोगादिहोपेक्ष्यमेव ।

Bhaṭṭayantra is menioned on p. 208 of vol. I of अ.भा. (on नाट्य and नृत्त), Priyātithi (on the लास्याङ्ग called सैन्धवक on p. 317 of the B. O. R. I. copy), Bhaṭṭavṛddhi (Ch. chap. 32. 45 on *tālas*, p. 514 of B. O. R. I. copy);[2] Bhaṭṭa Sumanas (as explaining at great length the three verses 46-48 of chap. 31, p. 434 of B. O. R. I. copy), Bhaṭṭa Gopāla (G. O. S. vol. II. p. 134 on ध्रुवाताल and on chap. 31 verse 510 of Ch. ed., on p. 502 of B. O. R. I. copy), Rudraka (Rudraṭa ?) on chap. 31 verse 357 (of Ch. ed. on *tāla*) at p. 488 of B. O. R. I. copy, Bhaṭṭa Śaṅkara, a devotee of God Śaṅkara, on वृत्तप्रकरण (chap. 32. 329 of Ch. ed., p. 524 of B. O. R. I. copy), Ghaṇṭaka on नायिकाभेद (G. O. S. vol. II. p. 436). On the materials available it is not possible to say whether these authors wrote commentaries on some part of the Nāṭyaśāstra or whether they wrote independent works in which Bharata's views were discussed.

Abhinava appeared to refer to Aṣṭāgama on chap. 32. 360 (of Ch. ed.) at p. 529 of B. O. R. I. copy.[3] The passage is cor-

---

1. टीकाकृद्भिस्तु सदाशिवमतादिग्रन्थान्तरालिखितं त्रयस्त्रिंशदिमे प्रोक्ता अलङ्कारा इत्यादि तनं (?) लिखितं ग्रन्थान्तरपरिवर्तने अनिष्टप्रसङ्गात् श्रीपादप्रोक्तादिति स्वगुरुमताद् &c.p. 399 of B. O. R. I. copy.

2. तथा च भट्टवृद्धितदत्तादिपाणितलयभङ्गलक्षणपुस्तकेषु सर्वत्र शता इति प्रस्तारो दृश्यते । p. 514. The passage is corrupt. Should we read भट्टवृद्धिदत्तिलादिप्रणीतलय० ?

3. प्रावेशिकोग्रहणमुपलक्षणार्थम् । नृणामिति चेष्टाबाहुल्यमम्भावनात् । अन्ये तु श्रियमपरत्वं व्याचक्षते तच्चाष्टागमपक्षविरुद्धमित्युपेक्ष्यमेव । p. 529. Dr. Raghavan kindly informs me that he holds that अष्टागम is a corruption by the copyist of अस्मदागम. I agree and I had already suggested it in the ed. of 1951.

rupt. Aṣṭāgama may mean 'eight authoritative or traditional works on Nāṭyaśāstra' or the word may be a copyist's error for अस्मदागम. An author called Rāhula is quoted several times in the अ. भा. e.g. a verse of his is quoted in which भरत is named. On नाट्य IV.267 (GOS vol I, 172) 37. अ.भा. says. यथाह राहुलः। परोक्षेपि हि वक्तव्यो नार्या प्रत्यक्षवत्प्रियः। सखी च नाट्यधर्मोऽयं भरतेनोदितं द्वयम् ॥. On p. 115 (G.O.S. vol. I) a verse of राहुलक on वैशाखरेचित is quoted. He is credited with having recognised मौग्ध्य, मद, भावविकृत, परितपन as अलङ्कारs of young ladies in chap. 24 in addition to भरत's[1] twenty (in 24. 5-30). Abhinava once quotes मातृगुप्त on पुष्प, a technical term for a particular way of the playing of the वीणा defined in नाट्यशास्त्र 29. 93 (Ch. ed.).[2] He appears to have been a poet and writer on Nāṭya and Saṅgīta. The भावप्रकाशन quotes his view that, though a Nāṭaka should have a plot based on past incidents, still it should have some incidents due to the poet's creative imagination.[3] Several verses of his are quoted in about 20 different places by राघवभट्ट in his अर्थद्योतनिका (commentary on शाकुन्तल) on सूत्रधारगुणs, on आर्यावर्त, on शौरसेनी being the dialect for women of all castes in dramas, on नाटकलक्षण (5½ verses), on बीज (3 verses), one verse on who were to speak Sanskrit in dramas, definition of भूषण (the first of 36 लक्षणs of नाट्य), on definition of यवनी attendants (1½ verses), definitions of सेनापति, of हसित, of स्मित, पताकास्थानक, कञ्चुकिन्, परिचारिका, कार्य, when संस्कृत may be spoken by those who are ordinarily to speak प्राकृत. The नाटकलक्षणरत्नकोष of सागरनन्दिन् quotes several verses of मातृगुप्त on pp. 5,14,20,21,23,50. In the वक्रोक्तिजीवित (p. 52) he is referred to as a great poet whose work is full of सौकुमार्य and the औचित्यविचारचर्चा quotes his verses (e.g. on p. 142). The राजतरङ्गिणी (III. 125-323) describes at great length how मातृगुप्त was the court poet of हर्षविक्रमादित्य, how he was a contemporary and patron of भर्तृमेण्ठ (राजतर. III. 260-262), how he became regent or king of Kashmir for about five years after हर्ष and how ultimately he became an ascetic (यति) at Benares (राजतर. III.

---

1. तेन मौग्ध्यमदभावविकृतपरितपनादीनामपि शाक्याचार्यराहुलादिभिरभिधानं विरुद्धमित्यलं बहुना। p. 164 of अ.भा. (vol. III GOS) on सामान्याभिनय ..

2. यथोक्तं भट्टमातृगुप्तेन। पुष्पं च जनयत्येको भूयोनुस्पर्शनान्वितः। इति। p. 402 of B. O. R. I. copy.

3. पूर्ववृत्ताश्रयमपि किंचिदुत्पाद्यवस्तु च। विधेयं नाटकमिति मातृगुप्तेन भाषितम् ॥ भा. प्र. p. 234.

320). It does not appear that he was a commentator of the Nāṭyaśāstra, though one may hold that the मातृगुप्त patronized by हर्ष may have written a work in verse dealing with the topics of dramaturgy. The राजतर० ascribes two verses to him (III. 181 and 252). The नाट्यप्रदीप of सुन्दरमिश्र composed in 1613 A.D. quotes the definition of नान्दी from भरत's नाट्यशास्त्र (5.25 and 106) and then remarks 'अस्य व्याख्याने मातृगुप्ताचार्यैः षोडशाङ्घ्रिपदापीयमुदाहृता' (vide I.O. Cat. of mss. part III. p. 348 No. 1199). But this remark by a late writer need not be taken too literally. All that it means may be that मातृगुप्त in his work on dramaturgy dealt with भरत's definition of नान्दी. Dr. De (H. of S.P. vol.I.p. 33) was inclined to hold that the poet मातृगुप्त of the राजतरङ्गिणी was different from the writer on dramaturgy, but he was not probably aware, when he wrote, that अभिनव quotes a half verse on पुष्प from मातृगुप्त who writes on dramaturgy. At one time it was thought by scholars such as Dr. Bhau Dāji (in J.B. B. R. A. S. for 1861 pp. 208 ff.) that मातृगुप्त was to be identified with कालिदास, but hardly anyone now holds that view. If we rely on the राजतर०, मातृगुप्त must have flourished in the first half of the 7th century. Prof. T. R. Chintamani collected 'the fragments of Mātṛgupta' in J. O. R. Madras vol. II pp. 118-128. Whether Bhaṭṭa Tauta, the teacher of Abhinava in the Nāṭyaśāstra, wrote a commentary on the Nāṭyaśāstra will be discussed later on. Utpaladeva, who was the teacher's teacher of Abhinava in the Pratyabhijñāśāstra, is frequently quoted by the A. B. on chapters 29. 31, 32 (on ध्रुवाs.). But it is difficult to say whether he wrote a commentary on these chapters or an independent work on music. On p. 436 (of the B. O. R. I. copy) Abhinava appears to differ from him (उत्पलदेवपादास्तु अस्मत्परमगुरवो व्याचक्षते... वयं तु मन्महे).

The लोचन on the ध्वन्यालोक (p. 217) quotes from भरत the verse बहूनां समवेतानां रूपं यस्य भवेद्बहु । स मन्तव्यो रसः स्थायी शेषाः सञ्चारिणो मताः ॥ (नाट्यशास्त्र GOS. ed. 20. 76 = Ch. 22. 68 which reads सर्वेषां for बहूनां), states that it was variously interpreted and sets out the view of भागुरि 'तथा च भागुरिरपि किं रसानामपि स्थायिसञ्चारितास्तीत्याक्षिप्याभ्युपगमेनैवोत्तरमवोचद्बाढमस्तीति' (लोचन p. 217). भागुरि as a commentator of भरत is not yet known from any other source.

A few words must be said about ancient writers on dramaturgy as their works have not yet been found. The सङ्गीतरत्नाकर (I.15-18) mentions many divine, semi-divine and human authors, such as सदाशिव, शिवा, ब्रह्मा, भरत, कश्यपमुनि, मतङ्ग, याष्टिक, कोहल, विशा-

खिल, दन्तिल, कम्बल, अश्वतर, नारद, तुम्बर, आञ्जनेय, मातृगुप्त, रावण, नन्दिकेश्वर, रुद्रट, नान्यभूपाल, भोज, सोमेश्वरपरमर्दी, जगदेकमहीपति. Kohala is one of them and a good deal has already been said about him above (pp. 24-25). He appears to have written on all topics of नाट्यशास्त्र especially on music, acting and dance. See my paper on 'the fragments of Kohala' in the proceedings of the 6th Session of the All India O. Conference at Patna pp. 577-580. Mr. Kavi (in J. Andhra H. R. S. vol. III. at p. 24) says that the सङ्गीतमेरु of कोहल is not now available except the chapter on ताल and अभिनय. It was Kohala who started the definitions of Uparūpakas like सट्टक (नाट्यदर्पण p. 25 and अभिनव vol. II.p. 407). That the Aubhatas thought that the verse रसा भावा (नाट्यशास्त्र 6.10) puts down the elements of the historionic art at eleven according to the view of कोहल has already veen stated (p. 24 n. 2). A. B. very frequently mentions the views of Kohala and quotes his verses also. On नाट्य 9. 4-6 (vol. II p. 26) Kohala is said to be नृत्ताचार्य (शुल्यभास्वरविद्युदाद्यभिनयविषये नृत्ताचार्यप्रवाहसिद्धः कोहललिखितोपि हस्तः सङ्गतो भवतीति). His views are mentioned on नाट्य॰ 9. 126 (vol II. p. 55), on 12. 2-3 (vol. II. p.130), vol. II. p. 142 (about a ध्रुवाताल being called सुभद्र), vol. II. p. 144 (modes of moving about called नर्तनक and उत्फुल्लक in रौद्ररस), vol. II. p. 146 (a लय called जम्भटिका), vol. II. p. 151, on नाट्य 12. 113 (vol. II p. 155 about gaits called खञ्जक, हेला, विलम्बित), on नाट्य 18. 1 (vol. II. p. 407, saying that if the word प्रयोगतः is properly interpreted, then तोटक, सट्टक, रासक and other उपरूपकs will be included), on 18. 7-8 (vol. II: p. 410) Kohala separately named several varieties of plays, but they are practically included in the definitions of the ten रूपकs); on 18. 14 (vol. II. pp. 416-17, the रूपक called अङ्क is of three kinds acc. to कोहल from whom $2\frac{1}{2}$ verses are quoted), on 18. 26 (vol. II. p. 421 कोहल spoke of five अर्थोपक्षेपकs), vol. II. p. 434 (quotes an आर्या from कोहल about विष्कम्भक), vol. II. p. 452 (कोहल's view 'शृङ्गारहास्यकरुणैरिह कैशिकी स्यात्' is opposed to भरत's), vol. II p. 459 (two आर्याs of कोहल quoted on वीथी), vol. II. p. 133 (an अनुष्टुभ् of कोहल on द्विपदी is quoted. On p. 72 of अ. भा. vol. III. G. O. S. it is said that rūpakas are of many varieties, acc. to Kohala on the basis of the languages employed and that Bharata must be regarded as holding the same view since he accepts a play called Saindhavaka composed in the Saindhava speech ((तेन दशरूपकस्य यद्भाषाकृतं वैचित्र्यं कोहलादिभिरुक्तं तददिह मुनिना सैन्धवा-

ङ्गनिरूपणे स्वीकृतमेव)[1] On p. 146. (chap. 22.) (and 24. 1 of Ch. ed.) of अ. भा. it is said that former writers who followed Kohala's doctrines regard that सामान्याभिनय is of six kinds and a verse of कोहल is quoted.[2] On chap. 25. 124. अ. भा. p. 289 says that one should study also the चित्राभिनयs well-known from Kohala's śāstra and cites over thirty explanatory verses.

The भावप्रकाशन frequently quotes Kohala's views (vide pp. 204, 210, 236, 245, 251). मार्कण्डेय, author of प्राकृतसर्वस्व, states in the third Intro. verse[3] that after studying the works of शाकल्य, भरत, कोहल, वररुचि, भामह, वसन्तराज and others he composed his work. This shows that कोहल wrote on Prakrits also, as did Bharata.

The रसार्णवसुधाकर of शिङ्गभूपाल (p. 8 verses 52-54) states that the sons of Bharata, viz. शाण्डिल्य, कोहल, दत्तिल and मतङ्ग wrote works on नाट्यशास्त्र.[4] In the कामसूत्र (I. 1. 11, VI. 2. 55, VI. 3. 44) mention is made of दत्तक who at the request of the *Gaṇikās* of Pāṭaliputra expounded the वैशिक section of कामशास्त्र. The कुट्टनीमत (verses 77, 122) mentions दत्तकाचार्य (v. 1. दन्तिलाचार्य). The अभिनवभारती (vol. I. p. 205, chap. 4. 326-327 on ध्रुवा) quotes a śloka from दत्तिलाचार्य. In the B. O. R. I. copy the verses of दत्तिलाचार्य are very frequently quoted on आतोद्य and ताल. Vide pp. 383 (on chap. 28. 10), 403 (chap. 29. 101 of Ch. ed.), 435, 439 (on chap. 31. 31), 442, 446, 447, 450, 478, 487, 489 (a verse on ओवेणक), 491. Mr. Kavi (in J. Andhra H. R. S. Vol. III. p. 24) stated that his work is called गान्धर्ववेदसार and is now available. दन्तिल and दत्तिल are clearly forms of the same name, but whether the दत्तक mentioned by the कामसूत्र is the same as दत्तिल of the नाट्यशास्त्र is doubtful. Matanga is mentioned as an expert in hollow musical instruments (such as a flute) by

---

1. Vide नाट्यशास्त्र 31. 513 (Ch. ed.) सैन्धवीमाश्रितं भाषां ज्ञेयं सैन्धवकं बुधैः । रूपकाद्यादिसंयुक्तं सैन्धवं स्यादथोद्धतम् ॥. The corresponding verse in K. M. 31. 315 presents a better reading in the second half as 'रूपवाद्यादिसंयुक्तं युग्मतालकृतं तथा'.

2. 'कोहलमतानुसारिभिर्वृद्धैः सामान्याभिनयस्तु षोढा भण्यते। तथाहि कोहलः। शिष्टं कामं मिश्रं वक्रं सम्भृतमेकयुक्तत्वम्। सामान्याभिनये यत् षोढा विदुरेतदेव बुधाः। इति।

3. The Vijagapatam ed. of प्राकृतसर्वस्व, 1927

4. Similarly, the रसरत्नप्रदीपिका (recently edited by Dr. R. N. Dandekar in the भारतीयविद्याभवन series) mentions numerous authors and works that the author of the work studied such as कश्यप, कोहल, मतङ्ग, दत्तिल, विशाखिल, नारद, तुम्बर, रावण.

दामोदरगुप्त.[1] So he is very much older than अभिनवगुप्त. The B. O. R. I. copy of A. B. p. 420 (on chap. 30, 1) states that formerly the sage मतङ्ग and others propitiated the great god Maheśvara (Śiva) by means of the flute made of a bamboo, that it became well-known as वंश, that any hollow tube made even of the Khadira tree can be called सुषिर आतोद्य[2] and then quotes a śloka to the same effect from मतङ्ग and says later on that मतङ्ग has made it clear that even hollow metallic flutes may be used "तथाहि मतङ्गमुनिना 'चत्वारो धातवो वंश इत्यादिना धातुविनियोगोपि प्रदर्शित एव.' On chap. 30 verse 11 the B.O.R.I. copy p. 426 quotes two verses (ślokas) of मतङ्ग. The सङ्गीतचूडामणि of जगदेकमल्ल (1138-1150 A.D.) refers to मतङ्ग and भोज as great writers before him (I. H. Q. vol. 20 p. 87). The सङ्गीतरत्नाकर (I. 15 ff) mentions many authors (p. 55). कल्लिनाथ on सं. र. I. 3.24 p. 38 states that मतङ्ग explained how the स्वरs called षड्ज and others are significant and on I. 3. 25 remarks 'सरिगादीनां मतङ्गाभिमत: उद्धारकक्रम: उच्यते.' On सं. र. I. 4. 9. कल्लिनाथ says that मतङ्ग and नन्दिकेश्वर speak of twelve मूर्छनाs. On सं. र. I. 8. 19 p.146 कल्लिनाथ states the view of मतङ्ग 'सामवेदे गीतप्रधाने आवृत्तिषु अर्था नाद्रियन्ते इति.' On सं. र. II. 1. 7 कल्लिनाथ remarks that मतङ्ग speaks of seven गीतिs taking into account भाषाs and dialects (विभाषा), while भरत speaks of only four viz. मागधी etc.[3] Mr. Kavi (J. Andhra H. R. S., vol. III. at p. 24) says that मतङ्ग is the author of बृहद्देशी about 2500 ślokas of which are now available. The बृहद्देशी has been referred to dozens of times in the भरतभाष्य of नान्यदेव (ms. 111. of 1869-70 at B.O.R.I. e. g. folios 86a, 86b, 107 &c.). Recently a work called भरतार्णव of नन्दिकेश्वर with translation in English and Tamil has been published in the Tanjore Sarasvati Mahal series No. 74 (1957). It deals with 'नर्तन' (Dance). The ms was incomplete and contains first fifteen chapter of over 800 verses out of 4000. विशाखिल

1. सुषिरस्वरप्रयोगे प्रतिपादनपण्डितो मतङ्गमुनिः । कुट्टनीमत verse 877.

2. पूर्वं भगवन्महेश्वराराधानं मतङ्गमुनिप्रभृतिभिर्वंशुमितं (वेणुना कृतं ?) ततो वंश इति प्रसिद्धः, वस्तुतस्तु छिद्रात्मकसुषिराभिव्यक्तस्वरविशेषरूपतयैवास्योपयोग इति खादिरादिनिर्मित व्यसनं (?) भवत्येव । तथा चोक्तम् । वंशे सृष्टं यदा पूर्वं वंशसक्ता तु वैणवी । वंशास्तु खादिरारोप्या: शंशावायत्क...इति ।

3. Vide नाट्यशास्त्र 29. 76–77 अत ऊर्ध्वं प्रवक्ष्यामि गीतीनामपि लक्षणम् ॥ प्रथमा मागधी ज्ञेया द्वितीया चार्धमागधी । सम्भाविता तृतीया च चतुर्थी पृथुला स्मृता ॥. These four are also mentioned in सं र. 1. 8. 14-16 and कल्लिनाथ says 'अस्या मगधदेशोद्भवत्वान्मागधीति निरुक्तिर्मतङ्गोक्ता.'

is cited as a writer on कलाs in वामन's काव्यालङ्कारसूत्रवृत्ति (I. 3. 7.). The कुट्टनीमत (v. 123) has भरतविशाखिलदन्तिलवृक्षायुर्वेदचित्रसूत्रेषु । पत्रच्छेदविधाने भ्रमकर्मणि पुस्तसूदशास्त्रेषु ॥. The A. B. (vol. I. p. 199 on chap. 4. 312) states that लास्यगान was expounded by विशाखिल. On नाट्यशास्त्र 28. 10 the A. B. (B. O. R. I. copy p. 383) states the view 'तथा च विशाखिलाचार्याः स्वरपदतालसमवाये गान्धर्वमिति.' On नाट्य 29. 81-83, B. O. R. I. copy p. 401 makes the following remarks and thereby suggests that अभिनव thought that भरत knew विशाखिल 'एककारेण चतुष्प्रहरणस्त्रिप्रहरणमङ्गुलीनां विभागो द्वे वृती समलेखा च त्रिलेखा इत्यादिकं विशाखिलाचार्यान्तरप्रोक्तं सर्वथैव ध्रुवागानज्ञानवैकल्प्योपयोगात् मया नोक्तमिति सूचयति ।.' विशाखिल is mentioned also on pp. 408, 422 (on 30. 3 अतएव शारीरवद्वंश्यानामारोहणमिवारोहणं वेति विशाखिलाचार्यः ।), 429, 431, 432, 497 (विशाखिलादिलक्षितं सर्वमेव लास्यगानं).

It appears that there was a work called Vārtika on the Nāṭyaśāstra. It was composed by one Śrīharṣa or Harṣa. He is frequently referred to sometimes as simply वार्तिककृत् and sometimes as श्रीहर्ष; (1) On नाट्य. II. 97-98 (A. B. vol. I. p. 67) the views of the वार्तिककृत् on the numbers of columns (स्तम्भ) to be erected in various parts of the नाट्यमण्डप are quoted in 1½ āryās that are rather mutilated. On p. 68 there are four more āryās with gaps that are also probably from the वार्तिक; (2) on नाट्य I. 84 नेपथ्यभूमौ मित्रस्तु, A. B. (vol. I. p. 31) mentions the view of वार्तिककार which cannot be made out clearly as the passage is corrupt; (3) on नाट्य 4. 267-268 (vol I. p. 172) the वार्तिककृत् asserts that in essence नाट्य and नृत्त are not different,[1] वाच्यानुगतेऽभिनये प्रतिपाद्येर्थे च गात्रविक्षेपैः । उभयोरपि हि समानः को भेदो नृत्तनाट्यगतः ॥; (4) The same view is enforced by another āryā from the वार्तिक (vol. I.

---

1. नाट्य means all dramatic performance. It comprehends drama, singing and dance. In several kinds of रूपकs drama predominates, in the other रूपकs and in उपरूपकs song and dance predominate. Sometimes a distinction is made between नाट्य, नृत्य and नृत्त. नाट्य is represented by several persons, नृत्य and नृत्त are the business of one (they are एकहार्य). नृत्य and नृत्त are also distinguished. Vide दशरूपक 1. 7-9 अवस्थानुकृतिर्नाट्यं ...दशधैव रसाश्रयम् । अन्यद् भावाश्रयं नृत्यं नृत्तं ताललयाश्रयम् ।'. The भावप्रकाशन p. 298 says: 'पदार्थाभिनयो नृत्यं डोम्बीश्रीगदितादिषु । अङ्गविक्षेपमात्रं यल्लयतालसमन्वितम् ॥ तन्नृत्तं &c.; also p. 45 नटकमैव नाट्यं स्यादिति नाट्यविदां मतम् । करणैरङ्गहारैश्च निर्वृत्तं नृत्तमुच्यते ॥. What is common to all three is अनुकृति or अनुकरण. The अमरकोश has तौर्यत्रिकं नृत्यगीतवाद्यं नाट्यमिदं त्रयम् ।'

p. 174 एवमवान्तरवाक्यैरुपदेशो रागदर्शनीयेषु। सिंहादिवर्णकैर्वा क्वचिदप्यर्थान्तरन्यासात्॥); (5) On IV. 331 (vol. I. p. 207) th same view is further asserted by a mutilated quotation from हर्षवार्तिक; (6) Śrīharṣa's view about the interpretation of the word पूर्वरङ्ग (नाट्य. 5. 7) and one ārya of his are quoted (vol. I. p. 211) श्रीहर्षस्तु रङ्गशब्देन तौर्यत्रिकं ब्रुवन् नाट्याङ्गप्रयोगस्य तस्यैव पूर्वरङ्गतां मन्यमानः पूर्वश्चासौ रङ्ग इति समासममंस्त। यदाह—दृष्टा येऽवस्थार्थे (वस्त्वर्थे ?) नाट्ये रङ्गाय पादभागाः स्युः। पूर्वं त एव यस्मिन् शुद्धाः स्युः पूर्वरङ्गोऽसौ॥; (7) On नाट्य. 5. 8-15 which mention th *aṅgās* of पूर्वरङ्ग, A.B. (vol.I p. 212) quotes a prose passage from the वार्तिक which is mutilated; (8) on नाट्य. 5. 180 श्रीहर्ष is quoted in connection with the प्रस्तावना in पूर्वरङ्ग (vol. I. p. 251, यदाह श्रीहर्षः—अत एव हासो नाम कविः कस्मिंश्चिन्नाटके 'दिवं यातश्चित्तज्वरेण कलिरित एवाभिवर्तते, अशक्यमस्य पुरतोऽवस्थातुम्' इत्यादि).[1]

From the above it follows that the हर्षवार्तिक probably dealt with all the chapters, that it was composed mostly in Āryā verses with prose passages and illustrations from dramatic Literature. Mr. Kavi (Intro. p. XXIII to vol. II.) says that a large fragment of वार्तिक on अङ्गहार has been recovered. Dr. Raghavan (in his paper on writers quoted in the Abhinivabhāratī in J. O. R. Madras vol. VI at p. 205) remarks 'Here also it is quoted only in the first six chapters. Not even a single reference to it is available in the remaining bulk of the Abhinavabhāratī.' This statement argues from silence and is therefore not to be taken as deciding for certain that there was no वार्तिक on any chapter after the book. We have no comment of Abhinava on the 7th (except on the first few verses) and 8th chapters and there are gaps in other chapters also and there is no commentry after chap. 32. The भावप्रकाशन quotes a view of Harṣa that तोटक differs from नाटक in this that in the former there is no विदूषक (p. 238). Dr. Śankaran in 'History of the theory of Rasa' p. 13 identified the great emperor हर्ष of Kanoj with this Śrī Harṣa. But this is mere conjecture.

The भावप्रकाशन (p. 238) speaks of सुबन्धु as a writer on dramaturgy who divided nāṭakas into five kinds viz. पूर्ण, प्रशान्त, भास्वर, ललित, and समग्र. The नाट्यशास्त्र (24. 41) divides शारीराभिनय into six varieties

---

1. The editor suggests that भास should be read for हास but there are no grounds to do so. हास may well have been the name of a dramatist, now unknown.

one of which is नाट्यायित (defined in verse 48). On this अ.भा. (vol. III. p. 172) refers to वासवदत्तानाट्यधार composed by the great poet Subandhu as an instance of नाट्यायित (तत्रास्य बहुतरव्यापिनो बहुगर्भस्वप्नायिततुल्यस्य नाट्यायितस्योदाहरणं महाकविसुबन्धुनिबद्धो वासदत्तानाट्यधाराख्यः समस्त एव प्रयोगः । तत्र हि बिन्दुसारः प्रयोज्यवस्तुके उदयनचरिते &c.) This drama of Subandhu appears to be referred to in A.B. (vol. II. 427) as वासवदत्तानृत्तधार. Whether the महाकविसुबन्धु and the writer सुबन्धु on dramaturgy (referred to by भावप्रकाशन) are identical is doubtful. Probably they are different.

In the Govt. collection of mss. (at B.O.R.I.) there is a ms. (No. 111 of 1869-70, described in Cat. vol. 12 pp.377-383) which is called भरतभाष्य or सरस्वतीहृदयालङ्कार (and also भरतवार्तिक in the colophon at the end) and which was composed by नान्यपति or नान्यदेव styled in the colophons महासामन्ताधिपति and धर्मावलोक, king of Mithilā. It was intended to be a huge work; the above deals only with one (viz. वाचिकांश) out of the four kinds of अभिनय. It is principally a com. on chapters 28 to 33 of the Nāṭyaśāstra, which deal with music. The author states that he was also called राजनारायण (folio 12a) and was a younger brother of कीर्तिराज (folio 199a). He mentions another work of his called ग्रन्थमहार्णव. The last verse on folio 221 ends 'तेनायं मिथिलेश्वरेण रचितोऽध्यायोवनद्धाभिधः'. He promises that in 17 chapters he will expound the वाचिकाभिनयs and gives a summary of the names and contents. The ms. (221 folios) is old and employs पृष्ठमात्राs and is written very closely but in a legible hand. There is some confusion in the ms. Chapters 5 (on अलङ्कार), 16 and 17 are wanting. The work is not a commentary on each verse of Bharata, bu the latter is profusely quoted hundreds of times. कश्यप, दत्तिल and नारद also are quoted hundreds of times. बृहत्कश्यप and वृद्धकश्यप are quoted on folios 111b and 114b respectively. बृहद्देशी, मतङ्ग, याष्टिक and विशाखिल are quoted dozens of times. Among the other authors and works quoted are नारदीयशिक्षाविवरणकृत् (folio 16b), देवराज (sometimes written as देदराज as on folios 69b, 70), मेर्वाचार्य (folio 70a), नन्दिमत (205a, 210b), स्वरसंहिताचार्य (197b), स्वाति (201 a, is called स्वरमुनिः), याज्ञवल्क्यस्मृति III. 112-116 (on folio 182a), तुम्बुरु (181b), कालिकापुराण (131a), भगवतपुराण or भागवतपुराण (138a, 138b). The author closely follows अभिनवगुप्त but rarely names him as on folios 10a, 184b. पाणिनि, नारद and अपिशालि (आपिशलि ?) are mentioned in one place (8b). He sometimes contrasts his own views with those of भरत, e.g. (13a) गान्धारग्रामश्च भरतेनालौकिकश्चात्रोपदर्शितः । अस्माभिश्चागमानुसारेण प्रदर्शितः ; 15a भरताचार्यस्यास्य शास्त्रे

...प्रयोगागता अस्माभिश्च कश्यपमतङ्गतुम्बरविशाखिलाद्याचार्यनिखिलमुनिवचनात् &c. In places the author quotes सूत्रs (e.g. on folios 21a, 39a, 43a on गान्धारपञ्चमीलक्षण, 43b on आन्ध्रीलक्षण). So also he quotes in classical Sanskrit *padas* and *catuṣpadīs* called ब्रह्मोक्त (folio 22b, 42a अस्यां ब्रह्मोक्तं चतुःपदी यथा—सोस्यां गौरीमुखाम्भोजरुहदिव्यतिलकपरिचुम्बिताचित &c.)

The date of the author of the भरतभाष्य, viz. of king Nānyadeva would not present any difficulty but for one circumstance. The 4th Introductory verse is 'लक्ष्यप्रधानं खलु शास्त्रमेतान्निःशङ्कदेवोपि तदेव वष्टि (वक्ति ?). Verse 23 of the first chapter (which is in उपजाति) also refers to निःशङ्क 'नोपाधि ददेश्यस्य (?) विकारभेदं निःशङ्कसूरिः खलु कूटताने। सर्वेषु तास्तेपि कृताश्च शुद्धाश्चतुर्दशैवेति मतं मदीयम् ॥.' निःशङ्क is a somewhat unusual name for an author. It was borne by the author of the सङ्गीतरत्नाकर who was called निशङ्कशार्ङ्गदेव and whose father सोढल was patronized by king Bhillama and also by Singhaṇa of the Yādavas of Devagiri. सिङ्घण ruled from about 1210 to 1247 A.D.So शार्ङ्गदेव would have to be placed about 1233 to 1270A.D. Then if नान्यदेव refers to निःशङ्कशार्ङ्गदेव, the former cannot be much than about 1280 to 1300 A. D. But there is no Nānyadeva, known at present, who ruled over Mithilā in the latter half of the 13th century. The king नान्यदेव of Mithilā was the founder of the Karṇāṭaka dynasty of Mithila and is said to have ruled from 1097 to 1147 A.D. Vide the Proceedings of the 14th session of the Indian History Congress 130-135 (by Mr. Radhakrishna Choudhury) on 'Nānyadeva and his contemporaries.' He was defeated by Vijayasena, king of Bengal, who ruled from 1095 A.D. to 1158 A.D. Vide the Deopara plate (E. I. vol. I. 305 at p. 314) and Dr. R. C. Majumdar in I.H.Q. vol. VII.pp. 679-687, where he says that विजयसेन came to the throne in 1095 A.D. This would indicate that this Nānyadeva flourished about 1100 A.D. Therefore, either the references to निःशङ्कदेव in the ms. of the भरतभाष्य are interpolations (which is quite possible, in view of the fact that the ms. is not complete and no other ms. is available at present for comparison) or the निःशङ्कदेव referred to in the भरतभाष्य is some one other than शार्ङ्गदेव or that there was some other नान्यदेव of Mithilā not yet discovered. The matter of the date of the भरतभाष्य will have to rest there for the present. At the end of the नाटकलक्षणरत्नकोश of सागरनन्दिन् occurs the verse श्रीहर्ष—विक्रमनराधिप—मातृगुप्त-गर्ग-अश्मकुट्ट-नखकुट्टकबादराणाम्। एषां मतेन भरतस्य मतं विगाह्य घुष्टंमया समनुगच्छत रत्नकोशम्॥ It appears that according to सागर नन्दिन् these seven authors had either written commentaries on Bharata's work or at least had treated of Nāṭyaśāstra topics in their works.

As the Nāṭyaśāstra of Bharata was spoken of as Bharata-sūtra by अभिनवगुप्त and others (vide above pp. 10-11, 26 &c.), it is natural that following the precedents of the śāstras of Grammar, Logic, Vedānta and the like certain works were composed on the Nāṭyaśāstra called Vārtika and Bhāṣya.

We had occasion above to say something about Mr. Kavi and his method (p. 14). In reply to criticisms, particularly of Dr. De, Mr. Kavi justifies his work at length in I. H. Q. vol. V. pp. 558-577. Dr. De's brief rejoinder may be read In I. H. Q. vol. V. pp. 786-789. Vide Dr. Raghavan's 'Number of Rasas', Adyar Library pp. 92-106 and 'Bhoja's Śṛṇgāraprakāśa' pp. 536-543 (Karnataka Publishing House) for a revised version of the अभिनवभारती and Adyar Library Bulletin, vol. XVIII. parts 3-4 pp. 196-209 for emendations in some passages from vol. I and II of the अभिनवभारती (G. O. S. edition)

4 **Medhāvin.** भामह twice mentions a writer on Alaṅkāra named Medhāvin who enumerated seven faults of Upamā (त एत उपमादोषाः सप्त मेधाविनोदिताः II. 40). In another place he says 'यथासंख्यमथोत्प्रेक्षामलङ्कारद्वयं विदुः । संख्यानमिति मेधाविनोत्प्रेक्षाभिहिता क्वचित्॥' (II.88). The latter half as printed means 'Utprekṣā has been in some places designated संख्यान by Medhāvin.' But this does not make good sense. संख्यान, we are told by Daṇḍin, is the name given to यथासंख्य by other writers ('यथासंख्यमिति प्रोक्तं संख्यानं क्रम इत्यपि' काव्यादर्श II.273). Therefore the passage in Bhāmaha's work seems to be corrupt. If we read मेधावी नोत्प्रेक्षा etc. then there is correspondence with Daṇḍin's words, the meaning being 'Medhāvin calls यथासंख्य by the name संख्यान and in some places (in some works on *alaṅkāra*) उत्प्रेक्षा has not been spoken of as an Alaṅkāra.' नमिसाधु in commenting upon Rudraṭa's काव्यालङ्कार (I. 2) says, ननु दण्डिमेधाविरुद्रभामहादिकृतानि सन्त्येवालङ्कारशास्त्राणि. The question is whether मेधाविरुद्र is one name or whether there were two writers on Alaṅkāraśāstra named Medhāvin and Rudra. No work on Alaṅkāra composed by Rudra has been referred to by another writer. The शृङ्गारतिलक of रुद्रभट्ट as its contents show cannot be called a work on the अलङ्कारशास्त्र. Therefore, it is probable that the full name is मेधाविरुद्र. धर्मकीर्ति and भर्तृहरि are often cited as कीर्ति and हरि; so there is no wonder if मेधाविरुद्र be cited as मेधाविन् (*vide* my article in J. R.A.S. 1908 at p. 545 on भामह and दण्डिन्). शार्ङ्ग॰ quotes a verse of मालवरुद्र (No. 1091) and of

कपिलरुद्र (No. 3787) and सुभा० of a कपिलरुद्र (1666). This shows that there were many Rudras. On रुद्रट (XI. 24) नमिसाधु again quotes मेधाविन् about the seven दोषs of simile and the manner in which he deals with this topic suggests that the examples he gives are taken from Medhāvin's work, 'अत्र च स्वरूपोपादाने सत्यपि चत्वार इति ग्रहणाद्यन्मेधाविप्रभृतिभिरुक्तं यथा लिङ्गवचनभेदौ हीनताधिक्यमसम्भवो विपर्ययोऽसादृश्यमिति सप्तोपमादोषाः...तदेतन्निरस्तम्.' नमिसाधु quotes seven verses illustrating the seven faults of Upamā mentioned by Medhāvin. Five of these seven occur in भामह's काव्यालङ्कार II.40, 47, 55, 58, 63. The two verses illustrating उपमानोपमेययोर्लिङ्गवचनभेद and हीनता that do not occur in भामह are, 'भक्षिताः सक्तवो राजञ्शुद्धाः कुलवधूरिव। परमातेव निःस्नेहा शीतलाः परकार्यवत् ॥' and स्फुरन्ति निखिला नीले तारका गगने निशि। भास्कराभीशुसंस्पृष्टा कृमयः कर्दमे यथा ॥.' नमिसाधु mentions the seven examples immediately after mentioning मेधाविन and does not name भामह with regard to them. नमिसाधु mentions भामह by name on रुद्रट 8.84. If the verses were भामह's he would have probably so stated. Therefore, भामह should be taken as quoting five verses from मेधाविन्. On p.9 (on रुद्रट II.2) नमिसाधु tells us that मेधाविरुद्र and others gave only four divisions of शब्द 'एत एव चत्वारः शब्दविधा इति येषां सम्यङ् मतं तत्र तेषु नामादिषु मध्ये मेधाविरुद्रप्रभृतिभिः कर्मप्रवचनीया नोक्ता भवेयुः'. The त्रिकाण्डशेष gives मेधाविरुद्र and कालिदास as synonyms. The काव्यमी० tells us that मेधाविरुद्र and कुमारदास were poets blind from birth (p. 12) and quotes कालिदास as a writer on Poetics (p. 14). The work of मेधाविन् has not come down to modern times.

5. A passage in the वासवदत्ता of Subandhu (Hall's ed.p. 235) 'बौद्धसङ्गतिमिवालङ्कारभूषिताम्' led many scholars like Aufrecht (Indische Studien, vol.16 pp. 205-207), Hall, Peterson (Preface to सुभा० p. 47 and J. B. B. R. A. S. vol. 16 p. 173) and Telang (in J. B. B. B. R. A.S. vol. 18 pp. 148, 150) to regard धर्मकीर्ति as one of the oldest writers on Alaṅkāra, following the explanation of शिवराम that अलङ्कार was a work of धर्मकीर्ति. But the Śrīrangam edition reads (p. 303), 'सत्कविकाव्यरचनामिवालङ्कारप्रसाधिताम्'. Moreover, there is nothing beside this passage to show that धर्मकीर्ति wrote a work on Poetics. Prof. Batukanath in 'Brief Survey of Sāhitya-śāstra' (J. of Dept. of Letters, Calcutta, vol. IX. p. 119) simply repeats what Aufrecht said. That the Buddhist Dharmakīrti was a poet appears to follow from quotations contained in the anthologies where he is often cited as भदन्तधर्मकीर्ति (शार्ङ्ग० No. 947, सुभा० 657; सुभा० 737, 1587, 1617, 2246, 3232). The ध्वन्यालोक (p. 270) quotes the

verse 'लावण्यद्रविणव्ययो न गणितः क्लेशो महानर्जितः स्वच्छन्दं चरतो जनस्य हृदये चिन्ताज्वरो निर्मितः। एषापि स्वयमेव तुल्यरमणाभावाद्वराकी हता कोऽर्थश्चेतसि वेधसा विनिहितस्तन्व्यास्तनुं तन्वता ॥' and says that some explained this verse as an example of व्याजस्तुति while it is really an example of अप्रस्तुतप्रशंसा. Then it remarks 'तथा चायं धर्मकीर्तेः श्लोक इति प्रसिद्धिः सम्भाव्यते च तस्यैव'. The reason assigned is that the verse quoted has underlying it a current of ideas similar to another verse which certainly was composed by धर्मकीर्ति. The verse is then quoted (ध्व.p.272). क्षेमेन्द्र (in औचित्यवि०), सुभाषितावलि and other anthologies follow the ध्वन्या० in ascribing the verse लावण्यद्रविण० to धर्मकीर्ति. So the Buddhist logician and philosopher धर्मकीर्ति may have been a poet, but there is nothing to substantiate the claim to regard him as a writer on Alaṅkāra.

It is quite possible that what सुबन्धु wrote was बौद्धसङ्गीतिमिवालङ्कारभूषिताम्. सङ्गीति means 'Council' (vide Introduction to धम्मपद S.B. E.vol. X. p. XXXI). It is also the name of that class of Buddhist Literature where in the very opening lines Buddha is introduced in an assembly of the faithful (vide Annals of B. O. R. I. vol. X. at p. 5n). Mrs. Rhys Davids explains 'saṅgīti' as 'standardized scriptural recital'. There are two works that have the title अलङ्कार, one is the सूत्रालङ्कार of अश्वघोष, which was translated into Chinese by कुमारजीव (405 A. D.) and is a compilation of stories that illustrate the retribution of *Karma* (vide Dr. B. C. Law on 'Aśvaghoṣa' p. 6, and Journal Asiatique for 1929 at pp. 270-280, and K. G. Saunders' 'Epochs in Buddhist History' p. 56, E. J. Thomas in 'Indian Culture' vol. XIII. pp. 143-146). The other is the महायानसूत्रालङ्कार attributed to असङ्ग and commented on by वसुबन्धु (in the 4th century A.D.). Prof. Ui tries to prove that the महायानसूत्रालङ्कार is a work of मैत्रेय (and not of असङ्ग) commented on by वसुबन्धु. Vide Zeitschrift für Indologie und Iranistik, vol.VI. for 1928 pp. 215-225 for Prof. Ui's article. M. Sylvain Levi edited the text of महायानसूत्रालङ्कार with French translation (1907 and 1911). In his Introduction (p. 16) Levi reads बौद्धसङ्गीतिमिवालङ्कारभूषिताम् and states that a commentator called नरसिंह explained अलङ्कार as 'śāstra bouddhique.' In spite of the fact there is no positive evidence so far for holding that धर्मकीर्ति wrote on Sanskrit Poetics, Prof. S. P. Bhattacharya in his paper called 'Neo-Buddhist nucleus in Alaṅkāraśāstra' J. A. S. B. vol. XXII, 1956, part I pp. 49-66 cannot help nourishing the hope that it might ultimately turn out that Dharmakīrti, did write on Poetics (p. 64).

Further, his reference to Śākyācārya Rāhula (m. by A.B.) on N. S. 22. 26-31, p. 164 of G.O.S. vol. III) and to Śauddhodani on whose Kārikās Keśavamiśra composed his Alaṅkāraśekhara (No. 37 below) are very slender reeds for building the theory of his paper. Rāhula is quoted in the three volumes of A. B. only 3 times and there is no reason to suppose that he is much earlier than the 10th century while Keśavamiśra is a late writer of 16th century and the Kārikās ascribed to Śauddhodani have been shown below to have been composed after 11th century. The science of Sanskrit Poetics had been solidly based without Buddhist help before these two writers flourished.

6. The **विष्णुधर्मोत्तरपुराण**. It is a matter for some surprise that, though the अग्निपुराण has come in for treatment at the hands of several scholars, this पुराण, which contains very valuable material on Dramaturgy and Poetics in its third section (*khaṇḍa*) has not been thoroughly studied by any scholar so far. Even Dr. Raghavan who has bestowed great labour and thought on the studies of numerous topics of नाट्यशास्त्र and काव्यालङ्कार refers to अलङ्कारs in this पुराण in one or two places (e.g. on p. 97 of his paper on 'the History of Svabhāvokti', and in 'Some concepts of Alaṅkāraśāstra, p. 97 he refers to वार्ता as mentioned in the विष्णुधर्मोत्तर)[1]. For reasons of space I cannot deal at great length with this work. The Purāṇa contains about 1000 verses on topics of नाट्यशास्त्र and काव्यालङ्कार, besides four chapters in prose, viz. 18, 19, 32, 36 on गीत, आतोद्य, मुद्राहस्तs, प्रत्यङ्गविभाग respectively. It may be noted that the knowledge imparted here on painting, image-making, dramaturgy and Poetics is called चित्रसूत्र[2]. The following account is based on a ms. of the पुराण in the Bhau Daji collection of the B.B.R.A.S. and the Veṅk.

1. Mr. Kavi on p. XX. of his Introduction to vol. II of the अभिनवभारती refers to विष्णुधर्मोत्तर on वृत्तिs (भारती &c.)

2. It is noteworthy that in the कुट्टनीमत, the technical चित्रसूत्र begins with III. 35 of विष्णुधर्मोत्तर and चित्रसूत्र is mentioned as one of the subjects studied along with भरत, विशाखिल and दन्तिल by the accomplished courtesan. दामोदरगुप्त probably refers to some ancient work on painting or he may have this पुराण in view. Verse 123 of कुट्टनीमत is : भरत-विशाखिल-दन्तिल-वृक्षायुर्वेद-चित्रसूत्रेषु । पत्रच्छेदविधाने भ्रमकर्मणि पुस्तसूदशास्त्रेषु ॥. From the nature of the विष्णुधर्मोत्तर, which is an encyclopaedia, it follows that it had some work on चित्रसूत्र before it.

Press edition of it (published in *śake* 1834). A brief account of some part of the 3rd section of the विष्णुधर्मोत्तर may be given here. The first chap. starts with a dialogue between वज्र and मार्कण्डेय in which the latter says that divinity dwells in the image of a *devatā*, which is manufactured according to the canons of चित्रसूत्र and which has a pleasing form and that a wise man should worship such an image : चित्रसूत्रविधानेन देवतार्चां विनिर्मिताम् । सुरूपां पूजयेद्विद्वान् तत्र संनिहिता भवेत् ॥ v. 7). It is stated in chapter 2 that प्रतिमालक्षण (the art of making images) cannot be understood except by one who has studied चित्रसूत्र, which) itself cannot be known without studying नृत्तशास्त्र; नृत्त does not exist without musical instruments and in these latter proficiency is unattainable without the study of singing (विना तु नृत्तशास्त्रेण चित्रसूत्रं सुदुर्विदम् ।...आतोद्येन विना नृत्तं विद्यते न कथंचन । न गीतेन विना शक्यं ज्ञातुमातोद्यमच्युत ॥). The सं. र. (I. 24) also says : नृत्यं वाद्यानुगं प्रोक्तं वाद्यं गीतानुवृत्ति च. Song is either in संस्कृत or प्राकृत or अपभ्रंश which last is endless, as the provincial dialects are numerous (अपभ्रष्टं तृतीयं च तदनन्तं नराधिप । देशभाषाविशेषेण तस्यान्तो नेह विद्यते ॥ अध्याय 2. 9-10). पाठ्य (recitation) is either in prose or in verse. Chap. 3 and 4 deal with metres and *vākya-parīkṣā* respectively. Chap. 5 defines सूत्र, the five अवयवs of a syllogism, the sixfold व्याख्या of a सूत्र, three प्रमाणs (प्रत्यक्षानुमानाप्तवाक्यानि) and their definitions, with what is authoritative, with स्मृति, उपमान, अर्थापत्ति. Chap. 6 is on तन्त्रयुक्ति[1] (the arrangement or plan of a treatise into topics or divisions). Chap. 7 deals with Prakrit (in 11 verses), chap. 8 with देवादिशब्दपर्यायवर्णन, chap. 9 and 10 deal with lexicography; chap. 11, 12, 13 (each in 15 verses) with nouns that are of feminine, masculine or neuter genders. Chap. 14 names and defines figures of speech (which are set out below on p. 71 and are only 17); chap. 15 speaks of kāvya, distinguishes it from शास्त्र and इतिहास (तदेव काव्यमित्युक्तमुपदे-

1. The 15th अधिकरण of the कौटिलीय is called तन्त्रयुक्ति and it is stated therein that there are 32 युक्तिs in the work such as अधिकरण, विधान, योग, पदार्थ, हेत्वर्थ, &c. Most of these words occur also in chap. 6 of the पुराण. Vide a paper on कौटिलीयतन्त्रयुक्तयः in J. O. R. Madras, vol. 4 for 1930 pp. 82 ff. The चरकसंहिता (Siddhisthāna, chap. 12 verses 40-45) speaks of 36 'tantrasya yuktayaḥ' and Suśruta (Uttara-tantra, chap. 65) names 32 tantrayuktis. The appellations of the yuktis in the two medical works substantially agree with those in Kauṭilya.

शैर्विना कृतम्) and it is stated that it should be endowed with nine rasas ((रसैः कार्यं समन्वितम् ॥ verse 14); chap. 16 names and defines 21 Prahelikās (15 verses); chap. 17 speaks of rūpakas which are of 12 varieties (नाटकादिषु रूपेषु कर्तव्यं द्वादशस्वपि, verse 60) and not ten as Bharata states (नाट्यशास्त्र 20. 1-3=G.O. S. vol. II chap. 18. 2-3). Verses 12-13 state that death (of the hero), loss of kingdom, the siege of a city, battles, should not be shown directly on the stage but should be narrated by means of Praveśakas.[1] Verses 56-59 of this chap. speak of the eight kinds of Nāyikās; chap. 18 (mostly in prose) treats of गीत, the स्वरs, ग्राम, मूर्छना; two verses of it (अपरान्तकमुल्लोप्यं मद्रकं प्रकरी तथा । उवेणकं सरोबिन्दुमुत्तमं गीतकानि तु ॥ ऋग्गाथा &c.) are the same as Yāj. III. 113-14 quoted above (p. 45, n. 2) and they read सरोबिन्दु (as विश्वरूप and मिताक्षरा do) for रोविन्दक of the नाट्यशास्त्र (31. 290); chap. 19 (in prose) deals with the four kinds of musical instruments and 20 with मण्डलs (two kinds of ten varieties each), अङ्गहारs (36 in verses 29-35, while the नाट्यशास्त्र speaks of 32 in chap. 4. 27), करणs (108 described in नाट्य० IV. 61-169), पिण्डीबन्धs, four वृत्तिs and four प्रवृत्तिs; the first verse of chap. 20 is that nāṭya is an imitation of another and nṛtta (dance) gives it polish and charm (परस्यानुकृतिर्नाट्यं नाट्यज्ञैः कथितं नृप । तस्य संस्कारकं नृत्तं भवेच्छोभाविवर्धनम् ॥1). It also speaks of लोकधर्मी and नाट्यधर्मी; the four kinds of अभिनय; chapters 21-23 deal with शय्या, आसन, स्थानक; chap. 24-25 deal with movements and postures of the hand and other limbs of the body; chap. 26 with 13 gestures of the joined hands (संयुतकर) and 22 of the unjoined hands (असंयुतकर); at the end it is stated 'सर्वं करायत्तमिदं हि नृत्तम्'; chap. 27 deals with आहार्याभिनय which is of four kinds प्रस्त (पुस्त ?) अलंकार, अङ्गरचना, सजीव (vide नाट्यशास्त्र[2] 23.5); chap. 28 on सामान्याभिनय (the last verse viz. 62 saying नाट्यं हि विश्वस्य यतोनुकारं कृत्स्नं ततो वक्तुमशक्यमीश ॥); chap. 29 on गतिप्रचार (gaits and manner of movement on the stage of several charaters); chap. 30 on रसवर्णन (in 28 verses, the first being हास्यशृङ्गार... नव नाट्ये रसाः स्मृताः); chap. 31 on 49 भावs in 58 verses (53 being

1. मरणं राज्यविभ्रंशो नगरस्योपरोधनम् । एतानि दर्शयेन्नाङ्के तथा युद्धं च पार्थिव ॥ प्रवेशकेन कर्तव्यं तेषामाख्यानकं बुधैः । विष्णुध० III. 17. 12-13; compare नाट्यशास्त्र 20. 21=GOS. vol. II. chap. 18. 38. and भावप्र० (VII.) p. 216 for a verse similar to the above.

2. Verses 21-25 of chap. 27 of विष्णुधर्मोत्तर are identical with नाट्यशास्त्र 23. 102-104 about the complexion of characters from various countries.

बहूनां समवेतानां रूपं यस्य भवेद्बहु । स मन्तव्यो रसः स्थायी शेषाः सञ्चारिणः स्मृताः ॥);[1] chap. 32 on मुद्राहस्तs (here even वेदाङ्गs like छन्दोविचिति are indicated by postures of hands); chap. 33 on नृत्तशास्त्रमुद्राs (in 124 verses); chap. 34 (in 32 verses) on how नृत्त arose when विष्णु killed the *asuras* मधु and कैटभ that had snatched away the Vedas;[2] verse 17 is नृत्तेनाराधयिष्यन्ति भक्तिमन्तस्तु मां शुभे । त्रैलोक्यस्यानुकरणं नृत्तं देवि प्रतिष्ठितम् ॥; verse 28 condemns him who makes dancing his livelihood or who sells dancing (i.e. makes a business of it) by employing actors; but other verses say that he who engages in dance for propitiating God secures all desired objects and finds the path to *mokṣa* and that such dancing is blessed, gives long life and heaven, it removes the sorrows of the distressed (देवताराधनं कुर्याद्यस्तु नृत्तेन धर्मवित् । स सर्वकामानाप्नोति मोक्षोपायं च विन्दति ॥ धन्यं यशस्यमायुष्यं स्वर्गलोकप्रदं तथा । ईश्वराणां विलासं तु चार्तानां दुःखनाशनम् । मूढानामुपदेशं तत् स्त्रीणां सौभाग्यवर्धनम्॥;[3] chap.35 winds up by saying that नारायण produced चित्रसूत्र and imparted it to विश्वकर्मन् and that there is imitation of the three worlds in painting as there is in nṛitta (यथा नृत्ते तथा चित्रे त्रैलोक्यानुकृतिः स्मृता । verse 5).It is not necessary to deal with the other chapters as they dilate upon painting (36-43), image-making (44-85), house-building (chap. 86 ff.).

The विष्णुधर्मोत्तर closely follows the नाट्यशास्त्र of भरत, though in certain matters such as the number of rūpakas and *rasas* it differs from it. So it is much later than the नाट्यशास्त्र. The other chapters of the विष्णुधर्मोत्तर such as those on dāna and śrāddha are quoted in works from the 12th century. For example, the हारलता of अनिरुद्ध quotes a verse from it which is found in the विष्णुधर्मोत्तर I. 142. 16-17.[4] The दानसागर of बल्लालसेन expressly states in the introductory verse 14 that it relies for its sources on the विष्णुधर्मोत्तर along with several other Purāṇas. In chap. 5 of the 3rd part there is

1. This verse is the same as नाट्यशास्त्र VII. 119 (GOS. ed. VII. 181) and XXII. 68 (GOS. ed. where नाट्य० has सर्वेषां for बहूनाम्.

2. Compare नाट्यशास्त्र chap. 22.1-23 (=GOS. ed. 20. 1-25) for a similar story.

3. Compare नाट्यशास्त्र 1. 110-13 for very similar verses on the benefits of नाट्य.

4. तथा च विष्णुधर्मोत्तरे मार्कण्डेयः । अच्छिन्ननाड्यां कर्तव्यं श्राद्धं वै पुत्रजन्मनि । अशौचोपरमे कार्यमथवापि नराधिप । हारलता p. 19 (B. I. ed.) For the dates of the हारलता and बल्लालसेन, vide H. of Dh. vol. I, pp. 337-341.

this half verse; सूत्रेष्वेव हि तत्सर्वं यद्वृत्तं (यद्वृत्तौ ?) समुदाहृतम्. This is almost the same as a verse quoted by Kumārila in the तन्त्रवार्तिक from a (predecessor सूत्रेष्वेव हि तत्सर्वं यद्वृत्तौ यच्च वार्तिके। सूत्रं योनिरिहार्थानां सर्वं सूत्रे प्रतिष्ठितम् ॥ इति ये वदन्ति तान्प्रत्युच्यते॥).[1] So this would indicate that the विष्णुधर्मोत्तर cannot be very much earlier than about 500 A. D. Besides, the युक्तिकल्पतरु of भोज (Calcutta p. 85) quotes six verses from the विष्णुधर्मोत्तर on precious stones. It is interesting to note that Alberuni who wrote his work on India about 1030 A. D. quotes about thirty passages from the विष्णुधर्मोत्तर of which 22 have been identified by Buhler in I. A. vol. 19 pp. 381-409. Buhler holds that the पुराण विष्णुधर्म (under which name Alberuni mentions the quotations) and विष्णुधर्मोत्तर were canonical works in Kashmir in Alberuni's time and that many of the passages quoted by Alberuni from Viṣṇudharma can be traced in the विष्णुधर्मोत्तर (but not all) . Vide I. A. vol. 19 pp. 402, 407. This indicates that the विष्णुधर्मोत्तर was regarded as a very authoritative work before 1000 A.D. In Hemādri's[2] व्रतखण्ड alone the विष्णुधर्मोत्तर is quoted about 150 times. The third काण्ड on image-making is often quoted. For reasons of space only two or three examples are set out. On व्रतखण्ड part I p. 123 seven verses about the image of महादेव are quoted from विष्णु; they occur in विष्णुध. III. chap. 44. 14-20. On p. 110 of व्रतखण्ड part I five verses are quoted about the image of विष्णु which occur in विष्णुध. III. 44. 9-13. On p. 108 of व्रतखण्ड eight verses are quoted from विष्णुध. on how the images of the four Vedas and of शास्त्रs like पाञ्चरात्र, पाशुपत, पातञ्जल, अर्थशास्त्र and कलाशास्त्र are to be made and all of them occur in chap. 73 of विष्णुध. (part III) at the end. So also seven verses about वरुण image quoted in व्रतखण्ड I pp. 145-146 occur in विष्णुध. III chap. 52. 1-7.

The दानसागर of बल्लालसेन quotes numerous verses of the विष्णुध० 3rd खण्ड. For example, verses 1-5 of chap.290 on ब्राह्मणप्रशंसा are quoted in it at the very beginning; similarly, 15 verses of chap. 307 on घृतधेनु are quoted in दानसागर and 15 verses from विष्णुधर्मोत्तर chap. 309 on जलधेनु; 15 verses of chap. 308 on तिलधेनु are also quoted therein. Mr. Bhabatosh Bhattacharya, who has now brought out the whole of the Dānasāgara (text in 3 parts and Introduction in 4th) for the B. I. series, originally conveyed to

---

1. Vide तन्त्रवार्तिक p. 602 (Anan. ed.) on जैमिनि II. 3. 16.
2. हेमाद्रि flourished about 1270 A. D.; vide H. of Dh. vol. I p. 357.

me this information. The दानसागर was composed in 1169 A. D. (vide H. of Dh. vol. 1, p. 341). Therefore, it follows that the third part of the विष्णुधर्मोत्तर was an integral part of it from early times.

There is another very important consideration which weighed with me in placing the विष्णुधर्मोत्तर even before Bhaṭṭi. According to the commentators Bhaṭṭi gives examples of about 38 figures of speech. Daṇḍin, Bhāmaha, Vāmana and Udbhaṭa all mention between 30 to 40 Alaṅkāras, while the विष्णुधर्मोत्तर enumerates and defines only 17 alaṅkāras in chap. 14, all the verses of which are set out here. The अलङ्कारs are :

एकैकस्य तु वर्णस्य विन्यासो यः पुनः पुनः। अर्थगत्या तु संख्यातमनुप्रासं पुरातनैः ॥१ अत्यर्थं तत्कृतं राजन् ग्राम्यतामुपगच्छति। शब्दाः समानानुपूर्व्या (ms. समाना भिन्नार्था) यमकं कीर्तितं पुनः ॥२ आदौ मध्ये तथैवान्ते पादस्य तु तदिष्यते। सन्दष्टकसमुद्गाख्यौ तथैव यमकौ मतौ ॥३ समस्तपादयमकं दुष्करं परिकीर्तितम्। उपमानेन तुल्यत्वमुपमेयस्य रूपकम् ॥४ रूपकाभ्यधिकं नाम तदैवैकगुणाधिकम्। गुणानां व्यतिरेकेण व्यतिरेकमुदाहृतम् ॥५ उपमानविरुद्धैश्च गुणैस्तदपरं मतम्। द्वित्र्यर्थवाचकैः शब्दैः श्लेष इत्यभिधीयते ॥६ अन्यरूपस्य चार्थस्य कल्पना यान्यथा भवेत्। उत्प्रेक्षाख्यो ह्यलङ्कारः कथितः स पुरातनैः ॥७ उपन्यासस्तथान्यः स्यात्प्रस्तुताद्यत् क्वचिद्भवेत्। ज्ञेयः सोर्थान्तरन्यासः पूर्वार्थानुगतो यदि ॥८ उपन्यासेन चान्यस्य यदन्यः परिकीर्त्यते। उपन्यासमलङ्कारं तन्नरेन्द्र प्रचक्षते ॥९ हेतुं विना विततां प्राप्ता सा तु विभावना। प्रोक्ता चातिशयोक्तिस्तु ह्यतुलैरुपमागुणैः ॥१० यथास्वरूपकथनं वार्तेति परिकीर्तितम् (ms.; स्वभावोक्तिः प्रकीर्तिता। Venk. ed.)। भूयसामुपदिष्टानां निर्देशः क्रमशस्तथा ॥११ यथासंख्यमिति प्रोक्तमलङ्कारं पुरातनैः। विशेषप्रथनादुक्ता (ed. has विशेषप्रापणा॰) विशेषोक्तिस्तथा नृप ॥ १२ या क्रिया चान्यफलदा विरोधस्तु स इष्यते। स्तुतिरूपेण या निन्दा निन्दास्तुतिरिहोच्यते ॥१३ निन्दास्तुतिस्तथैवोक्ता निन्दारूपेण या स्तुतिः। वस्तुनस्तूपमानेन (ed. has वस्तुना रूप्यमाणेन) दर्शनं तन्निदर्शनम् ॥१४ विना तया स्यादुपमा तु यत्र तेनैव तस्यैव भवेन्नृवीर। अनन्वयाख्यं कथितं पुराणैरेतावदुक्तं तव लेशमात्रम् ॥१५. The figures are : अनुप्रास, यमक, रूपक, व्यतिरेक, श्लेष, उत्प्रेक्षा, अर्थान्तरन्यास, उपन्यास,[1] विभावना, अतिशयोक्ति, वार्ता, यथासंख्य, विशेषोक्ति, विरोध, निन्दास्तुति, निदर्शन, अनन्वय. It must of course be said that it knew उपमा also. So at the most eighteen Alaṅkāras were thought worthy of being mentioned by the विष्णुधर्मोत्तर. We know from Bhāmaha II. 4 that certain predecessors of his named only five alaṅkāras viz. अनुप्रास, यमक, रूपक, दीपक and उपमा and that according to Udbhaṭa's काव्यालङ्कारसारसंग्रह

---

1. उपन्यास is probably the same as व्याजोक्ति of later writers or it may be the first अतिशयोक्ति of मम्मट ; वार्ता and स्वभावोक्ति may be taken to be the same.

some predecessors of his mentioned only eight[1] viz. पुनरुक्तवदाभास, छेकानुप्रास, अनुप्रास, लाटानुप्रास, रूपक, उपमा, दीपक, प्रतिवस्तूपमा. Therefore, the विष्णुधर्मोत्तर should be placed between भरत, (who spoke of only four figures of speech), the predecessors of भामह and उद्भट that enumerated only five and eight alaṅkāras on the one hand and भट्टि, दण्डिन्, भामह, उद्भट and वामन. (that enumerate between 30 to 40 अलङ्कारs) on the other. The विष्णुधर्मोत्तर not only quotes गीता, मनु, नाट्यशास्त्र, but also नारदस्मृति for several verses e.g. विष्णु० III. 333. 10 is नारद VII. 9, III. 336. 1. (पाषण्ड...जनपदेतथा) is नारद XIII. 2. If we hold that the 2nd section of विष्णुधर्मोत्तर is of the same date as the 3rd section, then it would follow that the पुराण is later than वराहमिहिर. विष्णुधर्मोत्तर II. 176. 9-11 are borrowed from the बृहद्योगयात्रा of वराहमिहिर, since the अद्भुतसागर pp. 494-5 quotes seven verses from the बृहद्योगयात्रा of which विष्णु० II. 176. 9-11 are three. Besides, विष्णु० II. 124. 15-26 are identical with बृहत्संहिता 45. 82-94 (Dwivedi's ed.) on उत्पातs. So the विष्णुधर्मोत्तर (3rd part) will have to be placed between 575 to 650 A.D., the period during which भट्टि most probably flourished or a little earlier. Dr. Miss Priyabala Shah recently edited (G. O. S. 1958) the 3rd khaṇḍa (118 chapters) of the विष्णुधर्मोत्तर based on four mss.'

I thank Mr. Bhabatosh Bhattacharya who drew my attention to the following verse from the कालिकापुराण chap. 92. 2 (Venkateshwar Press ed.) : 'विष्णुधर्मोत्तरे तन्त्रे बा ुल्यं सर्वतः पुनः । द्रष्टव्यस्तु सदाचारो द्रष्टव्यास्ते प्रसादतः ॥'.

7 **Bhaṭṭikāvya**. This poem in 22 cantos was composed mainly for illustrating the rules of Sanskrit grammar. It is divided into four sections, called प्रकीर्णकाण्ड (*sargas* I-V), अधिकारकाण्ड (VI-IX), प्रसन्नकाण्ड (X-XIII) and तिङन्तकाण्ड (XIV-XXII). In the प्रसन्नकाण्ड, Bhaṭṭi illustrates matters that fall to be treated in works on Poetics. In the tenth *sarga* (75 verses, 74 in मल्लिनाथ) he gives illustrations of 38 Alaṅkāras (including the two शब्दालङ्कारs of अनुप्रास and यमक). The 11th illustrates माधुर्यगुण (in 47 verses);

---

1. अनुप्रासः सयमको रूपकं दीपकोपमे। इति वाचामलङ्काराः पञ्चैवान्यैरुदाहृताः ॥ भामह II. 4; पुनरुक्तवदाभासं छेकानुप्रास एव च । अनुप्रासस्त्रिधा लाटानुप्रासो रूपकं चतुः ॥ उपमा दीपकं चैव प्रतिवस्तूपमा तथा । इत्यत एवालङ्कारा वाचां कैश्चिदुदाहृताः ॥ काव्यालङ्कारसारसंग्रह I. 1-2. The com. of तिलक on उद्भट says 'वर्गैर्वर्गैरलङ्कारोपादानं चिरन्तनालङ्कारकृतामल्पदर्शितां प्रकटयितुम् ।' (G.O.S. ed. p.1).

the 12th illustrates the figure भाविक (which is said to be प्रबन्धविषय by भामह III.53 and दण्डी II. 364) in 87 verses and the 13th elucidates भाषासम in 50 verses (where the same verse may be regarded as composed in Sanskrit as well as in Prakrit). On account of these four *sargas* Bhaṭṭi deserves at least a passing notice in the History of Alaṅkāra Literature. It will be seen from the comparative table in section 13 below that Bhaṭṭi illustrates almost the same figures as are defined by भामह and दण्डी. He treats the alaṅkāras generally in the order in which भामह defines the figures, though in a few cases he deviates from भामह. For example, भामह defines रूपक first (II. 21) and then दीपक (II. 25) and आक्षेप before अर्थान्तरन्यास; while भट्टि illustrates दीपक and अर्थान्तरन्यास before रूपक and आक्षेप respectively; भामह defines तुल्ययोगिता (III. 27) immediately after विरोध, (III.25) while भट्टि illustrates तुल्ययोगिता after उपमारूपक and before विरोध. भट्टि does not illustrate अप्रस्तुतप्रशंसा, which is defined by भामह; while भट्टि illustrates the figures हेतु and वार्ता to which भामह denies the status of *alaṅkāras*. The mss. of भट्टि mention X.74 as an example of the figure निपुण which is found in neither भामह nor Daṇḍin. भट्टि does not illustrate लेश and सूक्ष्म which are said to be excellent ornaments of speech by Daṇḍin (along with हेतु), while भामह denies to all three the position of alaṅkāras (II. 86). भट्टि devotes about 20 verses to the illustration of यमक and herein is similar to the treatment of यमक in the नाट्यशास्त्र and काव्यादर्श, while भामह is very brief on this point. From this it is clear that Bhaṭṭi does not follow either Bhāmaha or Daṇḍin, but bases his examples on some other work or works that were prior to both of them. It may be stated here that भट्टि (in 10th सर्ग) does not expressly name any figure of speech. It is the mss. that mention the several figures over the verses and the commentators differ among themselves as to the figures of speech in several verses. K. P. Trivedi in his Introduction to भट्टिकाव्य mentions thirteen commentaries on it. जयमङ्गला quotes the definitions of भामह (II and III) thirty-three times, quotes one verse of भामह (II. 27) on भट्टि (X. 23.), another verse of भामह (II. 87) on भट्टि (X. 46) and appears to refer to the काव्यादर्श II. 275 once about ऊर्जस्वि on X. 49 (the verse प्रचपलमगुरुं &c.). मल्लिनाथ who flourished in the 15th century and who often relies on such late works as the प्रतापरुद्रीय differs about 20 times at least from the जयमङ्गला and sometimes very harshly criticizes the latter. For example, on भट्टि X. 25 (गरुडानिलतिग्मरश्मय: पततां यद्यपि संमता जवे । अचिरेण कृतार्थमागतं

तममन्यन्त तथाप्यतीव ते ॥) which the जयमङ्गला regards as an example of दीपक (of the मध्य kind) मल्लिनाथ remarks (with biting sarcasm against the name जयमङ्गला) 'अत्र गच्छन्नित्यादिश्लोकत्रये क्रमादाद्यन्तमध्यावसानेषु क्रियापदप्रयोगादाद्यन्तमध्यदीपकानीत्युक्तं जयमङ्गलाकारेण तत्परममङ्गलं लक्षणापरिज्ञानात्'. Vide Dr. De's H. S. P. vol. I. pp. 50-57 and Prof. H. R. Divekar in J. R. A. S. for 1929 pp. 825-841 for comparison and contrast between भट्टि and भामह. Recently, Dr. C. Hooykaas contributed a learned and exhaustive paper on 'some arthālaṅkāras in the Bhaṭṭikāvya X' to the Sir Ralph Turner Presentation volume (1957) pp. 351-363. On p. 357 he sets out an exhaustive table of the arthālaṅkāras from Daṇḍin's Kāvyādarśa, from the Bhaṭṭikāvya and from Bhāmaha and adds valuable criticisms on individuals Alaṅkāras. For reasons of space it is not possible to enter upon a discussion of his translations and explanations. On p. 351 he points out that the Bhaṭṭikāvya was the prototype of the old Javanese Rāmāyaṇa.

The date of Bhaṭṭi can be settled within certain narrow limits. In the last verse he states that he composed the poem in Valabhi ruled by king Dharasena (काव्यमिदं विहितं मया वलभ्यां श्रीधरसेननरेन्द्रपालितायाम्). Bhaṭṭi gives no further information about himself. The commentary Jayamaṅgalā says that his father was श्रीस्वामिन्, while another commentator विद्याविनोद says that Bhaṭṭi's father was श्रीधरस्वामिन्. The name of the author himself is given in some mss. as भट्टस्वामिन् and as भर्तृ[1] in others. This has given rise to several speculations, which will be briefly indicated below. There are four kings of Valabhī (modern Valā in Kathiawad) that were named Dharasena. The जयमङ्गला reads 'श्रीधरसूनुनरेन्द्रपालितायां'. But this is not accepted by most mss. and commentators. There is no king called नरेन्द्र, son of श्रीधर, among the Valabhī rulers. At least one hundred copperplate grants of the Valabhī dynasty have been discovered. There are at least 13 plates of Dharasena II alone. The pedigree relevant for showing the relationship of the four Dharasenas is as follows :

---

1. In the Bulletin of the Ramavarma Research Intitute, vol. 13 for 1946 July pp. 23-24, Mr. Pattar states that in several mss. of the Bhaṭṭikāvya in Malayalam script at Trichur the poem is called भर्तृकाव्य and that at the end of each canto of the commentary the colophon is परमगुरुहरिविरचितकाव्यटीकायां and the commentator had three names जयेश्वर, जयदेव and जयमङ्गल.

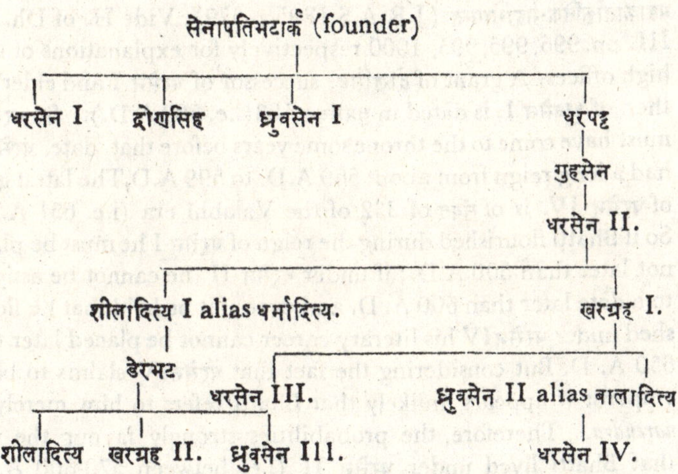

In the Palitana plates of Dharasena II dated Gupta-Valabhī-saṁvat 252 (i.e. 571 A.D.) both भटार्क and धरसेन I are styled सेनापति, while धरसेन II is styled महाराज. Vide I. A. vol. 15 pp. 335 ff. where a grant of धरसेन IV. dated in Valabhī saṁvat 330 (648 A.D.) is set out, in which धरसेन IV. is called चक्रवर्तिन्. A ms. of विशेषावश्यकभाष्य of जिनभद्र states that the work was finished at Valabhī in śaka 531 (608-9 A.D.) during शीलादित्य's reign. Vide P. O. vol. XI. parts 3-4 p. 29.

धरसेन II. styles himself महाधिराजाधिराज on his seal; vide Mr. A. S. Gadre's paper on five Valabhī grants in Journal of the Bom. University, vol. III. part. I. pp. 74 ff. The 5th plate was written by स्कन्धभट्ट son of दिविरपति (the Head of scribes) भट्टि. धरसेन IV describes himself as महाराजाधिराजपरमेश्वरचक्रवर्तिन् (vide I.A. vol. 15, p. 335 dated वलभीसंवत् 330 i.e. 649 A. D.). From the modest and colourless manner in which Bhaṭṭi speaks of his patron as *Narendra* (a king) it appears to me probable that Bhaṭṭi does not refer to धरसेन I, who is described in some of the Valabhī grants as सेनापति only (vide I.A. vol. VI. p. 9, a grant of धरसेन II dated वलभीसंवत् 269 i.e. 588A.D.) while his younger brothers द्रोणसिंह and धरपट्टare spoken of as महाराजand धरसेन II. is styled महासामन्तमहाराज. The Palitana plate of ध्रुवसेन, younger brother of धरसेन I (E.I.vol. XI. p. 109) and the Bhāvanagar plate of the same king (E. I. vol. XV. p. 255) describe him as महासामन्त-महाराज-ध्रुवसेन and both are issued in वलभीसंवत् 210 (i.e. 529A.D.); while another grant of his dated वलभीसंवत् 217 (536 A. D.) styles him महाप्रतीहारमहादण्डनायक

महाकार्तोकृतिक-महासामन्त (J.R.A.S.1895 p.379). Vide H. of Dh. vol. III. pp. 996, 995, 995, 1000 respectively for explanations of these high offices. A grant of द्रोणसिंह, successor of धरसेन I and elder brother of ध्रुवसेन I, is dated in गुप्तसंवत् 183 (i.e. 502 A.D.). So धरसेन I must have come to the throne some years before that date. धरसेन II had a long reign from about 569 A.D. to 599 A.D. The latest grant of धरसेन IV. is of संवत् of 332 of the Valabhī era (i.e. 651 A.D.). So if Bhaṭṭi flourished during the reign of धरसेन I he must be placed not later than 500 A.D.; if under धरसेन II he cannot be assigned to a date later than 600 A. D. and even if it be held that he flourished under धरसेन IV his literary career cannot be placed later than 650 A. D. But considering the fact that धरसेन IV claims to be an emperor it appears unlikely that Bhaṭṭi refers to him merely as *narendra*. Therefore, the probabilities strongly favour the idea that Bhaṭṭi lived under धरसेन II (i.e. between 570-600 A.D.) or under Dharasena III who succeeded Kharagraha I, who came after Dharasena II. Therefore it is very likely that Bhaṭṭi flourished between 590 and 650. Several persons named Bhaṭṭi appear in the Valabhī plates either as donees or as दिविरपति (chief of scribes) or राजस्थानीय. Vide I. A. vol. VI.p. 12 for grant of ध्रुवसेन alias बालादित्य for दिविरपतिवत्सभट्टि, J.R.A.S. for 1895 p. 379 (dated 217 वलभीसंवत् i.e. 536 A.D.) of ध्रुवसेन I for दूतक-राजस्थानीयभट्टि, I.A. 15 p. 335 (grant of धरसेन IV) for दिविरपति-वत्रभट्टिपुत्र-दिविरपति-स्कन्दभट्ट; E.I.vol.I.pp.89-92 for भट्टिभट (as donee). But there are no means beyond bare conjecture to identify any of these with the author of the भट्टिकाव्य. Prof. Keith favoured the view that Bhaṭṭi probably flourished under धरसेन I (vide J. R. A.S. 1909 p. 435 n.). The distance between the नाट्यशास्त्र which defines only four figures of speech and भट्टि who illustrates about 38 must be far greater than between Bhaṭṭi on the one hand and भामह and दण्डिन् on the other, who define a similar number of figures and are more systematic and scientific. It is not quite logical and appropriate to say that भट्टि might not have illustrated all figures that he knew just as he does not illustrate all the rules of Pāṇini but only a few. But the analogy is fallacious. There are thousands of Pāṇini's sūtras, while the well-recognized figures of speech up to the 8th century were not more than forty or so.

One circumstance not noticed so far by anyone of the scholars that have written about Bhaṭṭi may be mentioned here. One of the introductory verses of the काशिका commentary on Pāṇini's sūtras by Jayāditya and Vāmana is : वृत्तौ भाष्ये तथा धातुनामपारायणादिषु। विप्रकीर्णस्य तन्त्रस्य क्रियते सारसंग्रहः॥. The काशिकाविवरणपञ्जिका alias न्यास of जिनेन्द्रबुद्धि commenting on this verse says that चूल्लि, भट्टि and नल्लूर composed explanations of Pāṇini's sūtras before the काशिका. According to I-tsing who wrote his work in 691 A.D. Jayāditya died about 661 A.D. It is possible that Bhaṭṭi who wrote a mahākāvya for illustrating Pāṇini's aphorisms also composed a commentary thereon. If this turns out to be correct, then Bhaṭṭi must have flourished some years before the Kāśikā i.e. about 600 to 640 A. D. at the latest. This is a closer approximation about Bhaṭṭi's date than made a little above, but it depends upon the identity of Bhaṭṭi, mentioned in the Nyāsa, with the author of the Bhaṭṭikāvya.

The commentary जयमङ्गला is comparatively an old one. It quotes only such Alaṅkāra writers as भामह and दण्डिन्, but does not quote मम्मट. So the author who had three names (vide p. 74 note 1 above) flourished after 800 and before 1050 A.D. The author of the जयमङ्गला on भट्टिकाव्य appears to be different from the author of the commentary called जयमङ्गला on the कामसूत्र, as the latter is said to have been composed by यशोधर styled गुरुदत्तेन्द्रपाद. This latter also is an early work, as a ms. of it in the Bhau Daji collection in B. B. R. A. S. shows that it is a copy of a ms. in the भारतीभाण्डार (Library) of चालुक्य वीसलदेव (1243-1261 A. D.). Vide Mr. Trivedi's introduction to Bhaṭṭikāvya pp. XV-XVII for a discussion of the name of the author of the भट्टिकाव्य, wherein he comes to the conclusion that the author had three names, viz. भट्टि, भट्टस्वामिन् and भर्तृस्वामिन् and that most of the commentators speak of his father either as श्रीधरस्वामिन् or as श्रीस्वामिन्. In this connection it may be noted that the oldest of the mss. on which Mr. Trivedi's edition is based and which is dated *śake* 1326 (1404 A.D.) reads in the colophon 'श्रीधरस्वामिसूनोर्भट्टिब्राह्मणस्य कृतौ &c.

Some scholars identify the author of the भट्टिकाव्य with the donee भट्टिभट, son of बप्प, in a grant of ध्रुवसेन dated (वलभी) संवत् 344 (653 A.D.). Dr. Hultzsch objects to this identification (E. I. vol. I. p. 92). Mr. B. C. Mazumdar (J. R. A. S. 1904 pp. 395-397) identifies the author of the Bhaṭṭikāvya with the वत्सभट्टि of the Mandasor Sun temple Inscription (Fleet's Gupta Inscriptions No. 18) dated 473 A.D. on the ground of similarity between the verses of the inscription and the description of autumn (śarad) in the भट्टिकाव्य (*sarga* II). This would lead to the result that भट्टि flourished under धरसेन I or even earlier. Prof. A. B. Keith (J. R. A. S. 1909 p. 435) calls this identification a 'most unfortunate suggestion' and Mr. Majumdar (J. R. A. S. 1909 p. 759) replies that it is not so. Both Prof. Keith and Mr. Majumdar agree that Bhaṭṭi flourished before Bhāravi and Daṇḍin and that the Bhaṭṭikāvya is not the work of भर्तृहरि author of the वाक्यपदीय. I myself think that it is far-fetched to hold on the mere ground of similarity of verses that the वत्सभट्टि of the Mandasor inscription and the author of भट्टिकाव्य are identical.

There are numerous cammentaries on the भट्टिकाव्य out of which जयमङ्गला is published by the Nirn. Press and that of मल्लिनाथ was edited by Mr. K. P. Trivedi in the Bombay S. Series.

8. The काव्यालङ्कार of भामह. Out of deference to the opinions of a majority of scholars I dealt with Bhāmaha's work before that of Daṇḍin in the last edition. The same feature is preserved in this edition also. But it should by no means be supposed that I agree with the view of many scholars about the priority of Bhāmaha to Daṇḍin. I still hold that this view of the majority is wrong. The reasons will appear in the sequel.

Several scholars deal with the above question in a superficial manner and, I regret to say, are carried away by their enthusiasm and lack of balanced judgment. For example, Nobel in 'Foundations of Indian Poetry' (p. 16n.) had the hardihood to say that the theory of Daṇḍin's priority to Bhāmaha assumed by Prof. K. B. Pathak and others needs no further refutation and went so far as to say that Bhāmaha was prior even to कालिदास (pp. 14-15). Similar remarks would have to be made against certain conclusions in the introduction to the edition of भामह's काव्यालङ्कार written by Mr. Batuknath (in *saṁvat* 1985) and in his Sarasvati Bhavan studies, vol. VII. pp. 1-70 (1929). The last two works may be read with advantage for a historical *resume* of all the controversies that raged round Bhāmaha till 1920. Though Mr. Sarma in his Introduction (p. 37) pays me a handsome compliment by saying 'Mr. Kane, after stating and examining all such views with admirable impartiality, has come to the conclusion' etc. But, I regret to say that I cannot return the same compliment. I am sorry to find that he does not go deeply into the several questions raised, that he makes the uncritical and unhistorical statement (Intro. p. 39) that Prakrits had not 'perhaps' been so much in vogue in the time of भामह as they were in 'the time of दण्डी' and holds that भामह was separated from दण्डी not by decades but by centuries (Intro. p. 40). Mr. Sarma indulges in several conjectures and builds thereon his theory of Bhāmaha's being several centuries prior to Daṇḍin. They cannot be all dealt with here. As to Setubandha, he appears to have forgotten or ignored what the Harṣacarita says about it (Intro. verse. 14) कीर्त्तिः प्रवरसेनस्य प्रयाता कुमुदोज्ज्वला । सागरस्य परंपारं कपिसेनेव सेतुना ॥. Therfore, the सेतुबन्ध must have been composed at least a hundred years, if not more, before 600 A.D. Further, the same work in verse 13 praises the गाथासप्तशती of हाल containing 700 prakrit verses. That work is certainly earlier than the period (400-600 A. D.) assigned to Bhāmaha by Mr. Sarma. He is oblivious of the fact that, apart from Aśoka's inscriptions, most inscriptions in North and South India from 200 B.C. onwards for some centuries are in Prakrit. Bhāmaha himself divides Kāvya into three kinds (संस्कृत, प्राकृत, अपभ्रंश), the काव्यादर्श (I. 32) also divides वाङ्मय into संस्कृत, प्राकृत, अपभ्रंश and मिश्र and the नाट्यशास्त्र states that recitation in dramas is either संस्कृत, विभ्रष्ट or देशीगीत and also names शौरसेनी, मागधी, दाक्षिणात्या and other Prakrits. These grounds are enough to meet the conjectural speculations of Mr. Sarma. Further, the 3rd verse of the गाथासप्तशती says that Hāla compiled that work out of the crore of Prakrit verses that already existed. Allowing for exaggeration it is clear that in Hāla's time there existed a vast literature in Prakrit. Dr. A. Sankaran in 'Some aspects of literary criticism in Sanskrit' (1929) observes (on p. 25) 'His date (i. e. Daṇḍin's date) is one of the greatest puzzles in the History of Sanskrit Literature No definite data are yet forthcoming to solve the problem.' After making this candid statement Dr. Sankaran does not proceed to examine the several arguments advanced on the relative position of भामह and दण्डी for over a quarter of a century, but relies on a passage in a solitary ms. of the शृङ्गारप्रकाश of भोज at Madras, holds (p. 23 of his work) that passage is Daṇḍin's against the unanimous testimony of all editions of the काव्यादर्श based on numerous mss. and states that भामह is proved thereby to be prior to दण्डी. That passage is; 'तदुक्तम् । वक्रत्वमेव काव्यानां परा भूषेति भामहः । श्लेषः पुष्णाति सर्वासु प्रायो वक्रोक्तिषु श्रियम् ॥'. The latter half is काव्यादर्श II. 363. But the first half does not occur in any edition of the काव्यादर्श nor does Dr. Sankaran refer to any one of the numerous commentators. The first half is probably a quotation from some predecessor of भोज or it is a dictum of भोज himself and भोज supports it with a quotation from his favourite author दण्डी. With great respect to Dr. Sankaran I am constrained to say that this is a most perfunctory way of solving an admitted puzzle. Vide Dr. Raghavan on Śṛṅgāraprakāśa, vol. I part I p. 122 for further remarks on this passage. I am also surprised at the slipshod and somewhat dictatorial manner in which the acute and erudite scholar, Principal A. B. Dhruva, dismisses the question about the relative position of Daṇḍin and Bhāmaha in the Foreword to Mr. Batuknath's edition of भामह. He quotes भामह's verse (V. 3) 'स्वादुकाव्यरसोन्मिश्रं शास्त्रमप्युपयुञ्जते । प्रथमालीढमधवः पिबन्ति कटुभेषजम् ॥' and then quotes दण्डी (III. 127) 'प्रतिज्ञाहेतुदृष्टान्तहानिर्दोषो न वेत्यसौ । विचारः कर्कशः प्रायस्तेनालीढेन किं फलम् ॥'. Principal Dhruva thinks that this is a smashing reply of Daṇḍin who also uses the word आलीढ and asks the question 'is विचार ever said to be आलीढ ?' He thinks that the use of the word आलीढ with विचार is unusual. But Principal Dhruva seems to have forgotten that दण्डी had said in काव्या. I. 95 (निष्ठ्यूतोद्गीर्णवान्तादि गौणवृत्तिव्यपाश्रयम् । अतिसुन्दरमन्यत्र ग्राम्यकक्षां विगाहते ॥). The use of the word आलीढ with विचार in a metaphorical sense would be very charming and not unusual. The idea of conveying instruction in sweet poetic words is an old one; vide सौन्दरनन्द 18. 63 'यन्मोक्षात्कृतमन्यदत्र हि मया तत् काव्यधर्मात्कृतं पातुं तिक्तमिवौषधं मधुयुतं हृद्यं कथं स्यादिति ॥'. Principal Dhruva forgets that the root लिह् is given in the धातुपाठ (under अदादयः) as meaning आस्वादन and the root चर्व् is given as meaning अदन (in भ्वादिगण) and that nothing is more common in works on the रस theory than the words रसास्वाद and रसचर्वणा. Further, no less a writer than आनन्दवर्धन says: (ध्व० p. 237) "यथा वा वाणिश्रश्च हस्तिदन्ता' इत्यादि गाथार्थस्य 'करिणीवेहव्वकरो...वहइ' एवमादिष्वर्थेषु सत्स्वपि अनालीढतैव" and employs the word आलीढ with अर्थ. For these reasons also the use of the word आलीढ in relation to विचार would be very natural and charming.

The काव्यालङ्कार of भामह was for a long time known only from quotations (vide Col. Jacob in J. R. A. S. for 1897 p. 285). In 1906 Prof. Rangacharya kindly suplied to me a transcript of a ms. of भामह's work. Then in 1909 Mr. K. P. Trivedi published the work of Bhāmaha as an Appendix

(VIII) to his edition of the प्रतापरुद्रयशोभूषण in the B. S. S. In 1927 P. V. Nāganatha Sāstry of Tanjore published the text based on four mss. with an English translation, notes and an Introduction. In 1928 Messrs. Batuk Nath Sarma and Baladeva Upadhyaya published in the Kashi S. Series the text with a lengthy Introduction. Unfortunately all these printed editions (including the last) are unsatisfactory. The mss. material is meagre and the editors do not explain many knotty points, nor do they bring together all the various readings in Bhāmaha's text as quoted in many works and the explanations of his verses by numerous writers from the days of Udbhaṭa, the Dhvanyāloka and Locana onwards. Besides, the editors of the last edition have been severely criticized by Prof. Pathak for their peculiar methods in the Introduction and for their failure to see that the text printed by them is grammatically correct or to make suggestions for the correction of the text (vide Annals of the B. O. R. I. vol. XII. pp. 385-388, 392-395). A scholarly edition of Bhāmaha's work is a great *desideratum*. In the following I have used the edition of 1928. Prof. D. T. Tatacharya of Tiruvadi brought out an edition in 1934 with the textof Bhāmaha's work, a Sanskrit commentary called उद्यानवृत्ति composed by himself with an English and a Sanskrit Introduction and an English appendix on Ālaṅkārikas (pp. I-XXXIV) which is a brief rehash of what has been said by many scholars long before him. In the English Introduction he has introduced much matter quite irrelevant to the work criticizing Max Muller, Goldstuckor, Macdonell, Prof. Rajwade and M. M. Ananta Krishna Sastri. In the Sanskrit Intro. he attacks Prof. A. Sankaran, Prof. K. S. Ramaswami Sastri and the present author in footnotes. The most important point viz. the description of the mss. on which his edition is based is touched nowhere.

The काव्यालङ्कार of भामह is divided into six परिच्छेदs and contains about 400 verses (exactly 396, excluding the two verses at the end which roughly mention the number of verses on each of the five topics, viz. षष्ट्या शरीरं निर्णीतं शतषष्ट्या त्वलङ्कृतिः। पञ्चाशता दोषदृष्टिः सप्तत्या न्यायनिर्णयः॥ षष्ट्या शब्दस्य शुद्धिः स्यादित्येवं वस्तुपञ्चकम्। उक्तं षड्भिः परिच्छेदैर्भामहेन क्रमेण वः॥. In the Kashi edition the six परिच्छेदs have the following numbers of verses viz. 69, 96, 58, 50, 69, 66 (including the last two) i. e. in all 398. The verses are in the śloka metre except a few at the end of each परिच्छेद and a few in the body of the work. In the first परिच्छेद, after saluting Sārva, he states the purposes of poetry, the qualifications of a poet, the definition of काव्य and divisions of काव्य from different points of view into गद्य and पद्य, into संस्कृत, प्राकृत and अपभ्रंश; he divides काव्य into वृत्तदेवादिचरितशंसि, उत्पाद्यवस्तु, कलाश्रय and शास्त्राश्रय and again into five सर्गबन्ध, अभिनेयार्थ, आख्यायिका, कथा, अनिबद्ध. He then defines सर्गबन्ध, omits the treatment of अभिनेयार्थ (dramas, rāsakas &c.) because it has been dealt with by others, distinguishes between कथा and आख्यायिका, refers to the वैदर्भ and गौड styles and remarks that the distinctions drawn between the two styles by some are meaningless; and then speaks of some faults such as नेयार्थ, क्लिष्ट etc. In the 2nd परिच्छेद he speaks of three *guṇas*, माधुर्य, प्रसाद and ओजः and begins the treatment of Alaṅkāras which ends with the third परि०. The अलंकारs defined by him are (in order), अनुप्रास (refers to ग्राम्यानुप्रास and लाटीयानुप्रास of others), यमक (five varieties), रूपक (of two varieties), दीपक, उपमा (with its seven दोषs), प्रतिवस्तूपमा (as a variety of उपमा), आक्षेप (of two kinds), अर्थान्तरन्यास, व्यतिरेक, विभावना, समासोक्ति, अतिशयोक्ति, यथासंख्य, उत्प्रेक्षा, स्वभावोक्ति (according to some), प्रेयस्, रसवत्, ऊर्जस्वि, पर्यायोक्त, समाहित, उदात्त (of two sorts), श्लिष्ट, अपह्नुति, विशेषोक्ति, विरोध, तुल्ययोगिता, अप्रस्तुतप्रशंसा, व्याजस्तुति, निदर्शना, उपमारूपक, उपमेयोपमा, सहोक्ति, परिवृत्ति, ससन्देह, अनन्वय, उत्प्रेक्षावयव, संसृष्टि, भाविक, आशीः (according to some). He denies the status of अलंकारs to हेतु, सूक्ष्म and लेश (which must have been defined before him as figures by some writer on Poetics), as there is no वक्रोक्ति in them. After saying (in II. 83) that there can be no अलंकार without वक्रोक्ति he states that हेतु, सूक्ष्म and लेश are not accepted (by him) as अलंकारs because there is no वक्रोक्ति in them (II. 86). Then in II. 87 he refers to some people speaking of वार्ता as an alaṅkāra and giving as an instance of it the words गतोऽस्तमर्को भातीन्दुर्यान्ति वासाय पक्षिणः and asks 'do such words constitute Kāvya (his obvious meaning being that they do not). Then भामह says that some speak of स्वभावोक्ति as an alaṅkāra, defines it as अर्थस्य तदवस्थत्वं स्वभावोभिहितो यथा (II. 93) and gives an illustration (II. 94 आक्रोशन्नाह्वयन्नन्यानाधावन्मण्डलैर्नुदन् । गा वारयति दण्डेन डिम्भः शस्यावतारणीः) ॥. In order to make even a mere natural description as स्वभावोक्ति alaṅkāra, there must be some charm or strikingness as in the description of the boy preventing cows from entering into a field of growing crops, viz. he raised a hue and cry, called others to his help, ran about round and round and drove the cows and this does not exist in 'the sun has set, the moon rises and birds go to their nests'. भामह refuses to apply the name काव्य to such purely matter of fact statements. Such descriptions were called वार्ता by others (such as by विष्णुधर्मोत्तर p. 69). These words may mean 'these words are only news'. I prefer the first meaning, because भामह employs the word प्रचक्षते very frequently in enumerating or speaking of alaṅkāras or the opinions of other authors (II. 5, II. 93, III 54). In the 4th परिच्छेद he dilates upon eleven kinds of दोष (such as अपार्थ, व्यर्थ) in *kāvya*, defines and illustrates the first ten of them. In the fifth परि० he defines and illustrates the eleventh *doṣa* which arises from a faulty प्रतिज्ञा, हेतु or दृष्टान्त, the treatment being based upon a discussion of such Nyāya-Vaiśeṣika topics as the number and definitions of *pramāṇas*, definitions of प्रतिज्ञा and its varieties, of हेतु and its varieties, of दृष्टान्त etc. In the 6th परि० he gives some practical hints to poets for securing सौशब्द्य (grammatical purity) in poetry and in this respect resembles Vāmana who in the fifth अधिकरण of his काव्यालङ्कारसूत्र treats the same subject more elaborately.

Bhāmaha is deemed to be the oldest extant exponent of the Alaṅkāra school of *Poetics*. Of his personal history we know next to nothing. In the last verse he tells us that he was the son of Rakrilagomin 'अवलोक्य मतानि सत्कवीनामवगम्य स्वधिया च काव्यलक्ष्म । सुजनावगमाय भामहेन ग्रथितं रक्रिलगोमिसूनुनेदम् ॥'. This name रक्रिलगोमिन् has given rise to a heated discussion whether Bhāmaha was a Bauddha. Prof. M. T. Narasimhiengar (J. R. A. S. 1905 pp. 535-545) thinks that भामह was a Bauddha, as रक्रिल (his father's name) resembles some distinctly Buddhistic names such as Rāhula, Potala and that Gomin is a name of one of Buddha's disciples. Vide J. R. A. S. for 1908 p. 543 against this view. Prof. Pathak (I. A. 1912 p. 235) says that गोमिन् is not a contraction of गोस्वामिन्, but means 'venerable' (पूज्य) and that Rakrila was a Buddhist. He relies on a *sūtra* in the चान्द्रव्याकरण 'गोमिन् पूज्ये' (IV. 2. 144, गोमान् अन्यः ।). After all there is not much in a name. When Buddhists and followers of Brahmanism had lived together for a thousend years, there is no wonder even if distinctively Buddhist names were appropriated by Brahmanic people, since Buddha himself came to be recognised as an *avatāra* of Viṣṇu certainly before the

10th century. The same phenomenon is seen in modern India when Hindus adopt distinctively Mahomedan names and titles and *vice versa.* The Khoh copperplate ('Gupta Inscriptions' by Fleet No. 25 at p. 113) of 209 गुप्तसंवत् (528-529 A. D.) shows that a certain छोडुगोमिन् requested महाराज संक्षोभ to grant a village to a temple of goddess पिष्टपुरी. The Siroda plates of देवराज (in E. I. vol. 24 p. 143, about the 4th century A. D.) show that देवराज of the गोमिन् dynasty made a gift of tolls to two Brāhmaṇas. So here we have ancient evidence to show that गोमिन् was not a purely Buddistic appellation as early as the 4 or 5th century A. D. An author's religion must be judged from the contents of his books and not from his name. In the whole of the Kāvyālaṅkāra there is nothing that is peculiarly Buddhistic, nor is there any reference to the incidents of Buddha's noble life and to purely Buddhistic legends. The first verse salutes सार्व सर्वज्ञ. सर्वज्ञ is an appellation of शिव as well as of बुद्ध, while सार्व simply means 'सर्वस्मै हित' and is not given by अमर as an appellation of Buddha. भामह teaches the forms सार्व and सर्वीय in VI. 53 'हितप्रकरणे णं च सर्वशब्दात् प्रयुञ्जते । ततश्चमिष्टया च यथा सार्वः सर्वीय इत्यपि ॥' (compare 'सर्वपुरुषाभ्यां णढञौ' पाणिनि V. I. 10). भामह negative the अपोहवाद of the Bauddhas as regards the expressive power of words (VI. 16-17 'अन्यापोहेन शब्दोर्थमाहेत्यन्ये प्रचक्षते ।...यदि गौरित्ययं शब्दः कृतार्थोऽन्यनिराकृतौ । जनको गवि गोबुद्धेर्मृग्यतामपरो ध्वनिः ॥). Bhāmaha's three verses criticizing अपोहवाद (VI. 17-19) are cited in the तत्त्वसंग्रह of शान्तरक्षित (p. 291 verses 912-914), expressly attributed to भामह by the commentator कमलशील and severely criticized. शान्तरक्षित stigmatizes भामह, कुमारिल and others that denounce the theory of अपोह as कुदृष्टयः and दुरात्मानः (अन्यापोहापरिज्ञानादेवमेते कुदृष्टयः । स्वयं नष्टा दुरात्मानो नाशयन्ति परानपि ॥ verse 1003 of तत्त्वसंग्रह published in G.O.S.). So भामह was apparently beyond the pale of Buddhism according to the famous Buddhist writer शान्तरक्षित (deemed to have flourished about 705-762 A. D.; vide Intro. p. XXIII to the G. O. S. edition of the तत्त्वसंग्रह. This would establish that Bhāmaha cannot be placed later than about 750 A.D. The fact that भामह discarded the theory of अपोह and was branded as दुरात्मन् by a staunch Buddhist like शान्तरक्षित is one of the strongest arguments against holding that he was a Buddhist on the ground that he paid homage to सर्वज्ञ just as चन्द्रगोमिन् did in सिद्धं प्रणम्य सर्वज्ञं सर्वीयं जगतो गुरुम् ।. The late Principal A.

B. Dhruva thought that Bhāmaha was a Buddhist in spite of his diatribe against Apohavāda and in spite of the fact that nothing peculiarly Buddhistic is found in the body of his work. He relies upon the example of Hemacandra, who in his Kāvyānuśāsana makes use only of Brahmaṇic Literature. But the analogy does not go far enough. Hemacandra in his work leaves no doubt about his religion by putting in the forefront in the Maṅgalācaraṇa a reference to the founder of Jainism 'सर्वभाषापरिणतां जैनीं वाचमुपास्महे'. It is possible that Bhāmaha lived at a time when Gautama, the Buddha, had come to be regarded as an *avatāra* and wrote a मङ्गलाचरण verse which has two meanings, one applicable to शिव and the other to Buddha. He was probably a Hindu steeped in all the ancient Sanskrit culture but with an admiration for Buddha's noble life and therefore indulged in a double-meaning opening verse and also probably he had learnt Buddhist logic that was very much esteemed from the 5th to the 8th century. In IV. 49 (भूभृतां पीतसोमानां न्याय्ये वर्त्मनि तिष्ठताम्) he exemplifies what description given by a poet would be आगमबिरोधि. सोम was to be drunk by ब्राह्मणs alone but if a poet spoke of kings that always followed the right as drinkers of Soma that would be aganist what the Veda and Dharmaśāstras teach. This shows that भामह was steeped in the ancient Vedic traditions. Most of his examples refer to Brahmanical gods and heroes. He frequently alludes to the characters and incidents of the रामायण and महाभारत. For example, III.7 (कर्ण, पार्थ, शल्य), III. 11) उदात्तं शक्तिमान् रामो गुरुवाक्यानुरोधकः। विहायोपवनं राज्यं यथावनमुपागमत्' ॥), III. 5 (अद्य या मम गोविन्द' &c. to be quoted below), II. 41 (यदुप्रवीर and शार्ङ्ग), II. 55 (युगादौ भगवान् ब्रह्मा विनिर्मित्सुरिव प्रजाः), III, 24 (शम्भु and कुसुमायुध), III. 32 (रामः सप्ताभिनत् तालान् गिरिं क्रौञ्चं भृगूत्तमः), IV. 21 ,(रथाङ्गशूले बिभ्राणौ पातां वः शम्भुशार्ङ्गिणौ), V. 39 (भीम and रुधिरपान), V. 41-43 (प्रतिज्ञाs of दुर्योधन, युधिष्ठिर and भीष्म), V. 44. (meeting of परशुराम and राम), V. 37 (हनूमान् and सीता). Bhāmaha was in a way a modest man. At the end of the 4th परि० after pointing out the faults to be avoided in poetry he says 'न दूषणायायमुदाहृतो विधिर्न चाभिमानेन किमु प्रतीयते। कृतात्मनां तत्त्वदृशां च मादृशो जनोभिसन्धि क इवावभोत्स्यते ॥' (IV.50). But he was sometimes bitterly sarcastic; vide I. 31, IV. 45. He derived help from his predecessors, one of whom, Medhāvin, he names. He briefly summarises the sum of literary criticism that existed before him and says that in enumerating the figures of speech he saw various works of others (on Alaṅkāraśāstra) and thought over the matter himself. 'समासेनोदितमिदं धीखेदायैव विस्तरः । असङ्गृहीतमप्यन्यदभ्यूह्यमनया दिशा ॥' (II. 95) and 'इति निगदितास्तास्ता वाचामलङ्कृतयो मया बहुविधकृतीर्दृष्ट्वान्येषां स्वयं परितर्क्य च' । (V. 69). Vide I.13-15 'रूपकादिरलङ्कारस्तस्यान्यैर्बहुधोदितः । रूपकादिमलङ्कारं बाह्यमाचक्षते परे ।. The above references clearly show that before भामह flourished many writers on Alaṅkāra (including Medhāvin named by him) that had attained fame. It is probable as argued above that Bhāmaha quotes five verses of Medhāvin. At the end of the 2nd परि० occurs a verse which has been made much of by some scholars 'स्वयंकृतैरेव निदर्शनैरियं मया प्रक्लृप्ता खलु वागलङ्कृतिः ।' (96). What is the meaning of इयं वागलङ्कृतिः ? If these words refer to the whole of the work called काव्यालङ्कार, then the statement (said to be very emphatic on account of the occurrence of the word एव) must be qualified. There are several examples in the work that are obviously borrowed e. g. IV. 8 'दाडिमानि दशापूपाः षडित्यादि यथोदितम्' (for which see below); I. 41 हिमापहामित्रधरैर्व्याप्तं व्योमेत्यावाचकम्. Therefore, it cannot be asserted that every example in the book is Bhāmaha's own. If the words refer only to the examples of figures of speech, the verse should have occurred at the end of the third परिच्छेद. Besides, even in the second परिच्छेद he quotes many verses from other writers. It is true that he gives the sources from which those quotations are taken. But there is no qualifying clause in the verse (स्वयंकृतैरेव etc.) making an exception in favour of such borrowed verses. It is not unlikely that the names of some authors have been lost (if they occurred) in the lapse of centuries. The number of the mss. of Bhāmaha's work is not so large as to make one feel confident about the accuracy of the present text of Bhāmaha. For example, the लोचन (p. 87) says भामहेन हि गुरुदेवनृपतिपुत्रविषयप्रीतिवर्णनं प्रेयोलङ्कार इत्युक्तम्, but भामह nowhere defines प्रेयः and only cites an example which refers to देव (III. 5). राघवभट्ट in his अर्थद्योतनिका on शाकुन्तल I. 2 first quotes भामह's definition of पर्यायोक्त (III. 8) and cites यं प्रेक्ष्य as the illustration thereof given by भामह and states that it is taken from the work हयग्रीववध. This verse does not occur in the printed text. It is quoted by मम्मट under पर्यायोक्त. It is possible that राघवभट्ट is wrong in stating that the verse occurs in भामह. On शाकुन्तल I (कृष्णसारे), राघवभट्ट remarks 'नोपमानं तिङन्तेन' इति भामहोक्तेः. But these words occur in the काव्यादर्श II. 227 and *not* in भामह

and are taken from the महाभाष्य on पाणिनि III. 1. 7. The verse यं प्रेक्ष्य is quoted by उद्भटविवेक (p. 44) without name. No commentary on the work has been found. The only one that is known to have been composed, the भामहविवरण or भामहवृत्ति of उद्भट, has not been yet recovered. Therefore, too much emphasis cannot be laid on the words 'स्वयंकृतैरेव' etc. It is possible that most of the verses being his own compositions, he could say स्वयंकृतैरेव on the analogy of छत्रिन्याय.

भामह is expressly named twice by the ध्वन्यालोक p. 46 (about पर्यायोक्त) and p. 259 (about the verse सैषा II. 85). Vide under वामन.

Among the authors and works mentioned by name are the following :—अच्युतोत्तर of रामशर्मा (II. 19 and 58), अश्मकवंश (I. 33), कणभक्ष (V. 17), न्यास (VI. 36), पाणिनि (called also सालातुरीय, VI. 62-63), मेधाविन्, रत्नाहरण, (III. 8), राजमित्र (a work, II. 45, III. 10), शाखवर्धन (II. 47). Of these only five viz. अच्युतोत्तर, अश्मकवंश, रत्नाहरण, राजमित्र, and शाखवर्धन are names that are not known from other sources. From the अश्मकवंश no quotation is taken by भामह. It is doubtful whether रत्नाहरण is really the title of a work (उवाच रत्नाहरणे चैवं शार्ङ्गधनुर्यथा । गृहेष्वध्वसु वा नान्नं भुञ्ज्महे यदधीतिनः । न भुञ्जते द्विजास्तच्च रसदाननिवृत्तये ॥). The examples cited from शाखवर्धन and रामशर्मा are cited only for illustrating faults and they are quoted by नमिसाधु (on रुद्रट XI. 24) from मेधावी and in the काव्यप्रकाश (without name). Because these are deemed to be authors and works not referred to elsewhere, therefore it has been urged by some (e. g. Nobel in 'Foundations of Indian Poetics' p. 15) that भामह is very ancient. There is nothing of the sort. A few years ago even भामह's work was not found. We do not know what the future may discover to us and should be loth to dogmatise on the scanty data at present available. Besides, having decided to give illustrations composed by himself there was hardly any scope for quoting from ancient authors. Among the authors and works referred to but not named are भरत (I.24 'उक्तं तदभिनेयार्थमुक्तोऽन्यैस्तस्य विस्तरः), महाभाष्य of पतञ्जलि (VI. 31). Compar the very similar words of the काव्यादर्श I. 31 मिश्राणि नाटकादीनि तेषामन्यत्र विस्तरः. In IV. 22 he mentions सूत्रकृत् (पाणिनि), पदकार (कात्यायन) and इष्टप्रयोग (महाभाष्य). As regards other writers and works supposed to be quoted or referred to, vide below on the age of Bhāmaha. भामह refers to the story of वत्सेश (IV. 39) and of नरवाहनदत्त (IV. 49), both of whom are the principal characters in the बृहत्कथा. He very often cites the views of other rhetoricians under the words अपरे, अन्ये, केषांचित् (II. 6, 8, 87; III. 12, 54) and refers to other writers (on grammar and other śāstras) also (IV. 6; V. 6, 11, 60). He thought very highly of Pāṇini's system 'श्रद्धेयं जगति मतं हि पाणिनीयं' (VI. 63); at the beginning of the 6th परि० there is a fine रूपक on grammar 'सूत्राम्भसं पदावर्तपारायणरसातलम् । धातूणादिगणग्राहं ध्यानग्रहबृहत्प्लवम् ॥ नापारयित्वा दुर्गाधममुं व्याकरणार्णवम् । शब्दरत्नं स्वयंगममलङ्कर्तुमयं जनः ॥.. He refers to दण्डनीति (IV. 38) and to स्फोटवाद (VI. 12 'शपथैरपि चादेयं वचो न स्फोटवादिनाम् । नभःकुसुममस्तीति श्रद्दध्यात्कः सचेतनः:). In IV. 7 (गुरुभिः किं विवादेन) it is not clear to whom he refers as गुरुs. His verses are generally smooth and polished and about 100 of them have been quoted by the लोचन and other later writers.

The कामधेनु (वाणीविलास ed.) quotes many verses from भामह about definitions of सूत्र, वृत्ति and topics of Poetics which are not found in the काव्यालङ्कार. नारायण in his com. on the वृत्तरत्नाकर quotes long passages from भामह (pp. 5-6) which indicate that भामह wrote on metrics also. राघवभट्ट in अर्थद्योतनिका on शाकुन्तल I. 1 cites a half verse of भामह 'क्षेमं सर्वगुरुर्दत्ते मगणो भूमिदैवतः-इति भामहोक्तेः'. Whether the भामह who wrote the टीका on वररुचि's grammar is identical with our author is doubtful. Pischel in his Prakrit grammar (p. 35) holds that the two are identical and so does Prof. Pathak in his Intro. to कविराजमार्ग (p. 16). The देशीनाममाला of हेमचन्द्र (ed. by p. Rāmānujaswami, 1938) mentions on VIII. 39 भामह as follows 'अत्र सुगिम्हश्रो फाल्गुनोत्सव इति सुग्रीष्मकशब्दभवः । दृश्यते चायं संस्कृते । यद्भामहः । सुग्रीष्मकेन दृष्ट इति ।'. From what work of भामह this is taken cannot be stated. This is a पाद of an आर्या.

गोपाल in his commentary on काव्यप्रकाश called साहित्यचूडामणि (Tri. ed. p. 2) says 'उद्भटेनापि नम्रेण नायकेनोपलालितः । हृद्यो भाम इव क्षीणामल्पारम्भोपि भामहः ॥'. We know that उद्भट wrote भामहविवरण; but it is not possible to say what नायक had to do with भामह's work.

Before discussing the question of the age of Bhāmaha, it would be better, in order to clear the ground, to say a few words about the काव्यादर्श. Mr. Batuknath Śarma in the Intro. to his edition of Bhāmaha places Bhāmaha between 400 to 600 A.D. (p. 54). His main grounds will be discussed later on.

9 The **Kāvyādaśra** of **Daṇḍin**. The Kāvyādarśa has been often printed in India and Europe (at Calcutta in 1863 with

the com. of प्रेमचन्द्रतर्कवागीश, in 1890 by Bohtlingk with a German translation, in 1910 at Madras by Prof. Rangacharya with two commentaries, in Poona by Dr. Belvalkar and Shastri Rangacharya Raddi and by Pandit Rangacharya Raddi with his own commentary in 1938 (from B. O. R. I.). The work is divided into three परिच्छेदs; in Prof. Rangacharya's edition there are four परिच्छेदs, the third परि० of the other editions being split up into two. The fourth परिच्छेद in the Madras edition begins with the treatment of दोषs. There are in all 660 verses (in the Calcutta edition and in Pandit Raddi's ed.), while in the Madras edition there are 663 verses (the famous verse लिम्पतीव...गता being omitted in the 2nd परि०, 2 added at the end of its 3rd परि०, one added at the beginning of its 4th परि० and one more in the middle viz. the verse आधिव्याधिपरीताय अद्य श्वो वा विनाशिने । को हि नाम शरीराय धर्मापेतं समाचरेत् ॥' after III. 160 of the Calcutta edition). It is the edition of Pandit Rangacharya from which citations are made here.

The first परिच्छेद defines *kāvya*, divides the latter into गद्य, पद्य and मिश्र; defines सर्गबन्ध; refers to two varieties of गद्य viz. आख्यायिका and कथा and remarks that there is really no distinction between the two; divides literature into संस्कृत, प्राकृत, अपभ्रंश and मिश्र; speaks of the two styles वैदर्भ and गौड and of the ten *guṇas*; defines and illustrates अनुप्रास; mentions the three essentials that contribute to the making of a poet, viz. प्रतिभा (imagination), श्रुति (culture) and अभियोग (constant practice) The second परिच्छेद defines the word अलङ्कार, enumerates 35 *alaṅkāras* and illustrates them. The अलङ्कारs treated of are (in order) स्वभावोक्ति, उपमा, रूपक, दीपक, आवृत्ति, आक्षेप, अर्थान्तरन्यास, व्यतिरेक, विभावना, समासोक्ति, अतिशयोक्ति, उत्प्रेक्षा, हेतु, सूक्ष्म, लेश (or लव), यथासंख्य (or क्रम), प्रेयः, रसवत्, ऊर्जस्वि, पर्यायोक्त, समाहित, उदात्त, अपह्नुति, श्लेष, विशेषोक्ति, तुल्ययोगिता, विरोध, अप्रस्तुतप्रशंसा, व्याजोक्ति, निदर्शना, सहोक्ति, परिवृत्ति, आशीः, सङ्कीर्ण, and भाविक. The third परिच्छेद gives an elaborate treatment of यमक, defines and illustrates such चित्रबन्धs as गोमूत्रिका, अर्धभ्रम, सर्वतोभद्र, स्वरस्थाननवर्णनियम; gives 16 varieties of प्रहेलिकाs and illustrates ten kinds of दोषs.

Daṇḍin's Kāvyādarśa is to some extent an exponent of the Rīti school of Poetics and partly of the Alaṅkāra school. He gives, however, such an exhaustive treatment of

Guṇas and Alaṅkāras that it is not possible to identify him with any particular school. Of his personal history we know very little unless we are prepared to hold that the अवन्तिसुन्दरीकथा published by Mr. R. Kavi in 1924 in the Dakṣiṇabhāratī Series is a work of Daṇḍin. That work is full of gaps. It will be dealt with later on. Apart from the statements in the अवन्तिसुन्दरीकथा, he appears to have belonged to the Deccan or to some part south of the Narmadā. In the illustrations the following figure most prominently, मलयानिल (II 174; III. 165), कावेरी (III. 166), काञ्ची (III. 114 not actually named but suggested), चोल (III. 166), कलिङ्ग (III. 165), अवन्ती (II. 280, the name of वासवदत्ता). The occurrence of the word पश्य in I. 5. (आदिराजयशोबिम्बमादर्शं प्राप्य वाङ्मयम्। तेषामसन्निधानेऽपि न स्वयं पश्य नश्यति ॥) and in II. 172 (भगवन्तौ जगन्नेत्रे सूर्याचन्द्रमसावपि। पश्य गच्छत एवास्तं नियतिः केन लङ्घ्यते ॥') has led to the tradition that Daṇḍin wrote the work for some easy-going prince. But the word is probably a rhetorical device and used for the sake of the अनुप्रास (in पश्य नश्यति). The list of अलङ्कारs (II. 4-7) is suspected to be an interpolation by scholars like Dr. Belvalkar on the grounds of the use of the wrong from दीपकावृती (for ॰वृत्ती, which would mar the metre), the word लव for लेश and the somewhat strange अप्रस्तुतस्तोत्र and विशेष for अप्रस्तुतप्रशंसा and विशेषोक्ति. Though these blemishes are somewhat suspicious, still to regard the verses as interpolations on these grounds is going too far. Such lists of alaṅkāras always precede the treatment of them in ancient works. Bhāmaha, Udbhaṭa, and Rudraṭa have them (though not of all figurs in *one* place). To use syncnyms for the names of figures of speech is not an unknown proceeding. उद्भट (VI. 1) says 'काव्यदृष्टान्तहेतू चेत्यलङ्कारान्परे विदुः'. This shows that the figures are to be called काव्यहेतु and काव्यदृष्टान्त but when he comes to the definitions of these he uses the well-known terms काव्यलिङ्ग (and not काव्यहेतु) and दृष्टान्त (and not काव्यदृष्टान्त. This would explain the use of लव for लेश and ॰स्तोत्र for प्रशंसा and also of विशेष for विशेषोक्ति.

The Kāvyādarśa is throughout written in a flowing, mellifluous style. As compared with Bhāmaha, the palm of superiority in the sphere of poetic excellence must be given to Daṇḍin, though as regards precision and logical acumen Bhāmaha stands higher than Daṇḍin. Daṇḍin's examples bear the stamp of originality and, except in two or three cases, which will be discussed below, it has not been possible to point out that he borrows his examples from others.

The काव्यादर्श mentions the following works by name: छन्दोविचिति (I. 12), बृहत्कथा (I. 38 भूतभाषामयीं प्राहुरद्भुतार्थां बृहत्कथाम्), सेतुबन्ध (I. 34 'महाराष्ट्राश्रयां भाषां प्रकृष्टं प्राकृतं विदुः । सागरः सूक्तिरत्नानां सेतुबन्धादि यन्मयम् ॥).[1] The बृहत्कथा occurs in the verse 'कथा हि सर्वभाषाभिः संस्कृतेन च बध्यते । भूतभाषामयीं प्राहुरद्भुतार्थां बृहत्कथाम् ॥.' This means 'A kathā may be composed in all languages (Prakrits) and in Sanskrit, they say that the Bṛhatkathā which contains wonderful matter (stories) is composed in Bhūtabhāsā'

---

1 Dr. Manomohan Ghosh tries hard to establish that no Prakrit called Mahārāṣṭrī existed before 1000 A. D. and that 'Daṇḍin's praise of Mahārāṣṭrī was a patriotic exaggeration' (vide pp. 67, 75-76 of his Introduction to Karpūramañjarī, 1948). It would be irrelevant in this work to go into the question of the relation of Mahārāṣṭrī to Śaurasenī. But the 2nd remark about Daṇḍin's patriotic exaggeration must be dealt with here. No one would agree with Dr. Ghosh that Daṇḍin was an ignoramus in the matter of Prakrits. Daṇḍin definitely names (I. 34-35) महाराष्ट्री, शौरसेनी, गौडी and लाटी as different Prakrits and it is too much to say that a genius like Daṇḍin was not able to distinguish between शौरसेनी and महाराष्ट्री. Patriotism and false propaganda are a marked attitude of the last two hundred years or so. If the अवन्तिसुन्दरीकथा and its सार are to be believed, the family of दण्डी migrated from आनन्दपुर in the north-west of Āryadeśa (in modern north Gujarat) to अचलपुर in नासिक्यभूमि and दामोदर, great-grand-father of दण्डी, came to काञ्ची and acquired lands there. So four generations including दण्डी dwelt in काञ्ची. Which was the country about which दण्डी was to be patriotic, आनन्दपुर or अचलपुर or काञ्ची ? There is nothing to show that महाराष्ट्र ever extended up to आनन्दपुर or down to काञ्ची. He should ordinarily be supposed to love the country where four generations of his family lived i.e. काञ्ची. He could hardly feel warmth about नासिक्यभूमि which was only the stepping stone or second home of the family three generations before him. Therefore, the theory of patriotic exaggeration is absurd and if the facts do not fit in with one's theories or one's present knowledge, the theories must be given up and more knowledge awaited.

(Paiśācī). The 2nd half illustrates 'सर्वभाषाभिः'. Nobel in 'Fundations of Indian Poetry' p. 136 holds that this directly refers to भामह I. 28 (न वक्त्रापरवक्त्राभ्यां युक्ता नोच्छ्वासवत्यपि। संस्कृतं संस्कृता चेष्टा कथापभ्रंशभाक् तथा). Nobel begs the question. One may say on the contrary with equal reasons that भामह refers to the काव्यादर्श. Besides the verse of भामह is not clear. What does संस्कृतं refer to ? The latter half appears to mean Kathā is desired to be in Sanskrit and may be also in Apabhraṁśa. भामह himself says that काव्य may be पद्य or गद्य, again it may be in Sanskrit, Prākrit and Apabhraṁśa (I. 16). दण्डिन् refers to a कलापरिच्छेद, which he contemplated writing, probably as a part of his काव्यादर्श (इत्थं कलाचतुष्षष्टिविरोधः साधु नीयताम्। तस्याः कलापरिच्छेदे रूपमाविर्भविष्यति ॥' III. 171).[1] At one time eminent scholars thought that छन्दोविचिति was Daṇḍin's own work. छन्दोविचिति is, however, as shown by me in I. A. for 1911 p. 177, a name for the science of metrics and particularly for the Vedāṅga on metrics attributed to पिङ्गलनाग who is quoted even in the Śābarabhāṣya on जै. I. I. 5 (p. 54, Ānan.). The word छन्दोविचिति occurs even in कौटिल्य's अर्थशास्त्र (I. 3. 1) and in Āp. Dh. S. II. 4. 8. 11. The Bulletin of the London S. of Ori. and Afri. studies vol. XXII part I p. 192 reviews the publication of a work called 'Chandoviciti-Text

---

1 Vide Mr. S. L. Katre's paper in I. H. Q. vol. 24 pp. 118-122, where he brings together certain quotations from जगद्धर's commentary on मालतीमाधव, which are not found in the current काव्यादर्श. On कामसूत्र I. 3. 16 enumerating the 64 कलाs, the जयमङ्गला commentary in explaining दुर्वाचकयोगाः (30th कला in the list) quotes a verse from the काव्यादर्श viz. दंष्ट्राग्रद्धर्या प्राग्योद्राकल्पमामम्बन्तःस्थामुच्चिक्षेप। देवद्रुटूत्विद्ध्यत्विकस्तुत्यो युष्मान् सोऽव्यात्सर्पात्केतुः॥. Here सर्पात् means गरुड and सर्पात्केतुः is विष्णु; देवद्रुह् means असुर and देव... च्छित् means 'destroyer of Asuras'. While explaining काव्यसमस्यापूरण (which is कला No. 33 from the list of 64 kalās) जयमङ्गला quotes from the काव्यादर्श a quarter of a verse viz. आश्वासं जनयति राजमुख्यमध्ये which is given for समस्यापूरण and points out how the remaining *pādas* were composed. It appears from these examples that the जयमङ्गला knew of the काव्यादर्श as containing a treatment of kalās. This would be the कलापरिच्छेद and a part of the काव्यादर्श. Mr. Katre cites these passeges from Jaymaṅgalā on Kāmasūtra in a paper read at the 15th session of the All India Oriental conference.

zur Sanskrit Metrik, edited by Dr. Schlingloff from a single fragment found in central Asia (Turfan). I have not been able to secure a copy. It may further be noted that chapters 14–15 of the नाट्यशास्त्र (K. M edition=15-16 of Ch. ed.) deal with numerous metres and the colophon at the end of the 15th chap. (in G. O. S. ed.) is इति भारतीय-नाट्यशास्त्रे छन्दोविचितिर्नामाध्यायः पञ्चदशः. The following are among the authors and works not quoted by name: पतञ्जलि's महाभाष्य is quoted as आप्तभाषित 'नोपमानं तिङन्तेनेत्यतिक्रम्याप्तभाषितम्' (काव्या. II. 227); भरत's नाट्यशास्त्र seems to be referred to as another school (आगमान्तर) 'यच्च सन्ध्यङ्गवृत्त्यङ्गलक्षणाद्यागमान्तरे। व्यावर्णितमिदं चेष्टमलङ्कारतयैव नः॥' (II. 367). For सन्ध्यङ्ग, वृत्त्यङ्ग and लक्षण see chapters 21, 22, 17 of the नाट्यशास्त्र (Ch. ed.). In another place दण्डी says almost in the same way as भामह (I. 24 quoted above) 'मिश्राणि नाटकादीनि तेषामन्यत्र विस्तरः' (I. 31). He refers in general terms to former *Ācāryas* or learned men; 'पूर्वशास्त्राणि संहृत्य' (I. 2.; this is a common statement with writers; compare 'समाहृत्यान्यतन्त्राणि' अमर०); सूरयः occurs at I. 9 (former sages explained the body of poetry and its ornaments) and in II. 7 (इति वाचामलङ्कारा दर्शिताः पूर्वसूरिभिः); किं तु बीजं विकल्पानां पूर्वाचार्यैः प्रदर्शितम्' II. 2 and in 'एताः षोडश निर्दिष्टाः पूर्वाचार्यैः प्रहेलिकाः' III.106. He refers to the opinions of other writers on Poetics as केषांचित् or कैश्चित् (II. 227; I. 79) and एके (II. 268 about the definition of लेश). He quotes a half verse लिम्पतीव तमोऽङ्गानि वर्षतीवाञ्जनं नभः (II. 226) and holds an elaborate discussion on it, pointing out that some writers were misled into regarding that verse (well-known even in Daṇḍin's day) as an example of उपमा (as the word इव occurs in it thrice), but that the verse is an example of उत्प्रेक्षा (in the first half where two इवs occur). This discussion is pointedly referred to by प्रतीहारेन्दुराज on उद्भट (p. 26). The verse occurs in the मृच्छकटिक and also in two of the dramas discovered and ascribed to Bhāsa by M.M. Ganpatiśāstri, viz. चारुदत्त I. 19 and बालचरित I, 15. दण्डी refers to कापिल (III. 175), to सुगत (III. 174) and to न्याय which is called हेतुविद्या by him (III. 173).

In the शार्ङ्गधरपद्धति (No. 174) and in जह्लण's सूक्तिमुक्तावली p. 45 No. 74 a verse of राजशेखर is quoted which makes दण्डी the author of three works 'त्रयोऽग्नयस्त्रयो वेदास्त्रयो देवास्त्रयो गुणाः। त्रयो दण्डिप्रबन्धाश्च त्रिषु लोकेषु विश्रुताः॥'. Various scholars have taxed their ingenuity to find o ıt these three works. All that the verse means is that three compositions of Daṇḍin are well-known in all the worlds and not that Daṇḍin wrote only three works. Pischel made the desperate conjecture on account of not correctly understanding the discussion about the लिम्पतीव verse that the मृच्छकटिक was a work of दण्डी and along with the काव्यादर्श and the दशकुमारचरित made up the required number. But now we have two more works in which that verse occurs and they too will have Daṇḍin fathered on them if Pischel's reasoning is to be followed. Others like Peterson (Intro. दश० p. 5) and Dr. Jacobi (in Indische Studien, Vol. XVII) hit upon the छन्दोविचिति. as the third work. But this also has been shown to be wrong. Vide my article in I. A. vol. 40 (1911) pp. 177-78 on छन्दोविचिति. आप. ध. सू. II. 3. 7. 14-15 are षडङ्गो वेदः। छन्दःकल्पो व्याकरणं ज्योतिषं निरुक्तं शिक्षा छन्दोविचितिरिति; सुबन्धु in वासवदत्ता has 'छन्दोविचितिमिव भ्राजमानतनुमध्याम्' p. 235 (Hall's edition). छन्दःकल्प is one word and means कल्पसूत्रs. तनुमध्या is a metre. Some took the कलापरिच्छेद as the third work. It appears that दण्डी wrote a chapter on कलाs as a part of the काव्यादर्श and the कलापरिच्छेद is not his third work.

To add to the confusion there are scholars who seriously question the view that the दशकुमारचरित is a work by the same author that wrote the काव्यादर्श. Mr. Trivedi (Intro. to प्रतापरुद्र० XXXI), Mr. Agashe (in I. A. for 1915 p. 67 and more recently in his introduction to the दशकुमार० pp. XXV ff) argue that the author of the काव्यादर्श cannot be the author of the दशकुमार० also. This is not the place to examine their arguments in detail. But a brief reference must be made to some of them. Mr. Agashe's first argument is that the author of the काव्यादर्श was a fastidious critic, who warned all poets to eschew even the slightest blemishes (तदल्पमपि नोपेक्ष्यं काव्ये दुष्टं कथंचन। स्याद्वपुः सुन्दरमपि श्वित्रेणैकेन दुर्भगम्॥ I. 7) and condemned as ग्राम्य even such apparently harmless words as 'कन्ये कामयमानं मां न त्वं कामयसे कथम्। इति ग्राम्योयमर्थात्मा वैरस्याय प्रकल्पते॥' I. 63, while in the दश० there are numerous faults in the matter of good taste and grammar and direct references to sexual intercourse. Here two things have to be noted. There is always a great gulf between precept and practice, which has been admitted by all literary critics e. g. the व्यक्तिविवेक says about his method of finding fault with the greatest poets 'स्वकृतिष्वयन्त्रितः कथमनुशिष्यादन्यमयमिति न वाच्यम्। वारयति भिषगपथ्यादितरान् स्वयमाचरन्नपि तत्॥' (p. 37); similarly, क्षेमेन्द्र in his औचित्य० finds fault with his own compositions (under *kārikās* 20 and 21). Besides, the दश० may have been composed while दण्डी was comparatively young and inexperienced; while the काव्यादर्श is a product of mature years. Moreover, what दण्डी means when he styles the verse कन्ये &c. as ग्राम्य has not been clearly grasped. He condemns the downright, rough and outspoken mode of conveying one's meaning and prefers the suggestive method. This is illustrated by दण्डी himself in the next verse which conveys the same sense but in a different manner 'कामं कन्दर्पचाण्डालो मयि वामाक्षि निर्दयः। त्वयि निर्मत्सरो दिष्ट्येत्यग्राम्योर्थो रसावहः॥' (I. 64). The second point emphasized by Mr. Agashe is that there is great difference between the chaste and smooth diction of the काव्यादर्श and the somewhat slipshod style and the long-drawn compounds of the दश०. Here again there is a misapprehension. The काव्यादर्श being in verse did not allow much scope for long compounds; yet it approves of a compound extending over a half verse (I. 84 पयोधरतटोत्सङ्गलग्नसन्ध्यातपांशुका। कस्य कामातुरं चेतो वारुणी न करिष्यति॥), while the दश० being in prose exhibits long compounds and therein accords with the teaching of the काव्यादर्श which condemns long compouuds only in पद्य (ओजः समासभूयस्त्वमेतद्गद्यस्य जीवितम्। पद्येऽप्यदाक्षिणात्यानामिदमेकं परायणम्॥ I. 80). Subandhu's introductory verses to वासवदत्ता offer a great contrast to his prose. And so do the few verses in the दश०. Sufficient reasons have not been advanced for rejecting Daṇḍin's authorship of the दश०. The first verse of the दश० (ब्रह्माण्डच्छत्रदण्डः etc.) is quoted in जह्लण's सूक्तिमुक्तावलि p. 31 No. 86 and by the सरस्वतीकण्ठाभरण (परिच्छेद II under लाटानुप्रास p. 262) which profusely quotes from the काव्यादर्श also. The complexion of the whole problem is changed by the publication of the अवन्तिसुन्दरीकथा. The first verse contains obeisance to हिरण्यगर्भ (ब्रह्मा), ईशान (शिव) and हरि, who, though regarded as different (by many devotees), are really not so (हिरण्यगर्भमीशानमाद्यं च पुरुषं हरिम्। त्रीनप्यसत्यनानात्वान्वन्दे विश्वशरीरिणः॥). Then the author praises (in verses 2 to 21 that have many gaps) the following works and authors (as far as they can be made out): रामायण, महाभारत, सुबन्धु (who did not fall within the fetters of बिन्दुसार and whose heart was captivated by वत्सराज), बृहत्कथा, मूलदेव (?), शूद्रक, भास (and his dramas), सर्वसेन (and his हरिविजय), सेतु, कालिदास (who wrote in the वैदर्भमार्ग), नारायण (who wrote काव्यत्रय), then some blind poet (कुमारदास ?), बाण and मयूर, some poetess (probably विज्जका) who though dark was the abode of excellent svabhāvokti verses and guṇas (वर्णहीनापि या जाता जात्युत्कर्षगुणास्पदम् ॥), another poetess or work called मनोवती. Then verse 22 describes the author as a descendant of दामोदर, then four verses follow which are not clear; the last glorifies सरस्वती and the tribe of great poets. Then begins the story in prose. In the capital city named काञ्ची there was king सिंहविष्णु to whom an आर्या was recited by a गन्धर्व. The family of दण्डी migrated from आनन्दपुर to अचलपुर in नासिक्यभूमि (modern Ellichpur in Berar ?). The ancestor called दामोदरस्वामिन् (of the कौशिकगोत्र) following the advice of the great poet भारवि (who was a महाशैव) formed friendship with prince विष्णुवर्धन.[1] दामोदर met दुर्विनीत of the गाङ्गेय dynasty who was well-known for his wanderings. The आर्या that the गन्धर्व addressed to (पल्लव) सिंहविष्णु was दामोदर's.[2] सिंहविष्णु invited दामोदर to his court, got him

---

1 The passage as corrected by Dr. Raghavan from 'the Trivandrum mss.' and as communicated to me in a letter is 'महाशैवं महाप्रभावं गवां प्रभवं प्रदीप्तभासं भारविं रविमिवेन्दुः अनुरुध्य दर्श इव पुण्यकर्मणि विष्णुवर्धनाख्ये राजसूनौ प्रणयमन्वबध्नात् ।.' The printed text (of Mr. Kavi) is mutilated but the part पुण्य...बध्नात् (p. 6) is there. Vide I. H. Q. vol. III. pp. 169-171 for a similarly corrected passage by Mr. Harihar Sastri. The passage now appears on p. 10 of the T. S. S. ed.

2 The आर्या as given in the अवन्तिसुन्दरीकथासार (I. 16) is: दनुजपतिहृदय-भूधरविभेदविख्यातशक्तिनखकुलिशम् । जगदुदयहेतुविष्णोरवतु वपुर्नारसिंहं वः ॥. This applies both to नृसिंहावतार and to सिंहविष्णु, the Pallava king. This raises an important question, viz. whether this दामोदर, the ancestor of Daṇḍin, is the same as the poet दामोदर many of whose verses are quoted in the anthologies. Vide सुभाषितावलि of वल्लभदेव No. 2528 (ascribed to कपिलदामोदर) and कवीन्द्रवचनसमुच्चय pp. 43-46. It is not possible to give a definite answer to this question in the present state of our knowledge. It is suggested in a paper in the Bulletin of the D. C. Research Institute, Poona, (vol. I. pp. 421-424) that one of the Introductory verses of the Vāsavadattā contains a veiled allusion to Dāmodara as the *Guru* of Subandhu. The Introductory verse 6 of the अवन्तिसुन्दरीकथा mentions सुबन्धु but it is extremely doubtful whether he is the author of the extant prose romance called वासवदत्ता. He may be the महाकवि सुबन्धु, author of a play called वासवदत्तानृत्यधारा (धार) mentioned by अ. भा. Dr. A. N.

married and made to him a gift of lands. दामोदर had three sons of whom मनोरथ was the middle one, who had four sons, the youngest of whom was वीरदत्त. The latter married गौरी. Their only son was दण्डी whose mother died in his infancy and the father after upanayana. There was invasion, काञ्ची was devastated and दण्डी left काञ्ची. After some years दण्डी returned to the पल्लव court.[1] In a dream he had a vision of सरस्वती who blessed him and asked him to write the story of विद्याधर king राजवाहन. Next morning he narrated the story of अवन्तिसुन्दरी. The अवन्तिसुन्दरीकथा is the first portion of the whole story, the current दशकुमारचरित is the middle portion and there is one उच्छ्वास for the उत्तरपीठिका. अवन्तिसुन्दरीकथा was published in the Dakshinabhāratī Series (Madras) in 1924. For मातृदत्त as a friend of Daṇḍin as stated in अवन्तीसुन्दरीकथा, vide JOR (Madras) vol. 19 pp. 159-165. Vide JOR (Madras) vol. 17 (published in parts) and JOR (Madras) vol. XXV (supplement) for अवन्तिसुन्दरीकथासार edited by Mr. G. Nariharasastri with an Introduction and summary of contents. Vide Prof. V. V. Mirashi's paper on the 'Historical Data in the Daśakumāracarita' in ABORI. vol. 26 pp. 20-31, where he arrives at the conclusion that the political conditions described in the 8th Ucchvāsa of the Daśa-

---

Upadhye in the Poona Orientalist (vol. XI. parts 3 and 4 pp. 29-30) quotes a verse of जिनभद्र from his विशेषावश्यकभाष्य in which the two romances of वासवदत्ता and तरङ्गवती are mentioned and points out that a colophon of the ms. of that work shows that the latter was written in 531 śaka (i. e. 609 A. D.). This would mean that the author of the वासवदत्ता flourished sometime before 600 A. D. and would make it possible for us to hold that Dāmodara might have been Subandhu's guru.

1 Vide 'History of the Pallavas' by R. Gopalan (1928), where on p. 83 the pedigree is set out. I take only the relevant portion here. नन्दिवर्मन्—his sons सिंहविष्णु I and भीमवर्मन्—सिंहविष्णु's son महेन्द्रविक्रमवर्मन् I.—son नरसिंहवर्मन् I.—his sons महेन्द्रवर्मन् II. and परमेश्वरवर्मन् I. The मत्तविलासप्रहसन was written by पल्लव king महेन्द्रविक्रमवर्मन् I. son of सिंहविष्णु (vide p. 3 of the प्रहसन). Verse 22 of the प्रहसन is : 'विरोधः पूर्वसम्बद्धो युवयोरस्तु शाश्वतः। परस्परप्रीतिकरः किरातार्जुनयोरिव ॥'. In this there appears to be a pointed reference to the किरातार्जुनीय of भारवि, who was a contemporary of सिंहविष्णु acc. to the अवन्तिसुन्दरीकथा.

kumāracarita point to the inference that Daṇḍin must have flourished not long after 550 AD.

After the publication of the अवन्तिसुन्दरीकथा controversies arose about its being a work of Daṇḍin. Vide I. H. Q. vol. III pp. 169-171 (Harihar Shastri) and pp. 395-403 (Dr. De) and I. H. Q. vol. I. p. 31 ff. It was pointed out that, though भारवि is called a महाकवि in the work, there is no reference to the किरातार्जुनीय, which is somewhat surprising, since दण्डी is said to have been the great-grandson of दामोदर who was a friend of भारवि. In a paper on 'Problems of Identity' the great scholar, the late M. M. Prof. Kuppuswami, in J. O. R. Madras vol. I. pp. 191-201 appears to have entertained doubts about दण्डी being the author of the अवन्तिसुन्दरीकथा (pp. 200-201 and n 5). In J. O. R. Madras vol. V. part 2, p. 4. Dr. Raghavan points out that in a ms. of नामसंग्रहमाला of अप्पय्यदीक्षित (different from the famous Vedāntin) it is stated 'निरस्ता पल्लवेषु काञ्ची नाम नगरीत्यवन्तिसुन्दरीये दण्डिप्रयोगात्'. In J.O. R. Madras vol. XIII. part 4 at p. 294 Dr. Raghavan states that in some mss. of the सूक्तिरत्नहार of कालिङ्गराय (published in the Tri. S. Series) the verse मर्त्यंयन्त्रेषु (which is the 3rd Intro. verse of अवन्ति॰ praising the महाभारत) is ascribed to दण्डी. I find that the com. called श्रुतानुपालिनी on the काव्यादर्श (D. C. ms. No. 111 of 1919-24 entered in Des. Cat. vol. XII. No. 125 p. 137) while explaining काव्यादर्श I. 81 remarks (on folio 3) 'आख्यायिका शूद्रकचरितप्रभृतिः सा आदिः येषां (यासां?) अवन्तिसुन्दर्यादिकथानां तास्वित्यर्थः.' For the genealogy of Daṇḍin and further information about the Avantisundarī-kathā, vide vol. I. of the New Catalogus Catalogorum edited by Dr. Raghavan pp. 308-310 under Avantisundarī. Considering all that has been said by many scholars I am inclined to hold on the whole (though with some hesitation)[1] that the Avantisundarīkathā is a

---

1 The hestitation is mainly due to four circumstances viz. (1) non-mention of the किरातार्जुनीय or any other work as composed by भारवि; (2) the meagre extent of the printed अवन्तिसुन्दरीकथा as compared with the दशकुमारचरित; (3) the supernatural element about a गन्धर्व singing an आर्या verse of दामोदर; (4) difference between the style of अवन्तिसुन्दरीकथा and of दशकुमारचरित. The अवन्तिसुन्दरीकथासार must have been composed by some other person who based the story on the अवन्तिसुन्दरीकथा, as अभिनन्द wrote his कादम्बरीकथासार on बाण's कादम्बरी.

work of Daṇḍin (though not the सार)and constitutes the prelude to the current दशकुमारचरित. If this is accepted then the date of Daṇḍin can be settled within very narrow limits. Bhāravi had become as famous as Kālidāsa in 634 A. D. as the Aihole Inscription shows. He was a friend of the great-grandfather of दण्डी. As दामोदर the ancestor became a friend of चालुक्य विष्णुवर्धन, when the latter was only a *prince* (and not a crowned king) it must be held that the event cannot be placed later than about 590 A. D. and allowing 25 or 30 years for each generation, Daṇḍin, the great-grandson of Bhāravi's friend, should have his literary activity placed 75 to 90 years later (i. e. between 660 and 680 A. D.). Dr. S. K. Aiyangar's note on p. 229 of the History of Pallavas by Mr. Gopalan employs by inadvertence the word Gopāla for Dāmodara. विष्णुवर्धन was the younger brother of सत्याश्रय पुलिकेशिन् II. and founder of the Eastern चालुक्य dynasty of Āndhra and Kaliṅga and he reigned from 615 A. D. to 633 A. D. Vide 'Eastern Chalukyas' by Dr. D. C. Ganguly (Benares, 1937) p. 15 for authorities. The Gaṅga king दुर्विनीत had a long reign from 605 A. D. to 650 (Mysore Archaeological Reports for 1921 p. 28 and 'Eastern Chālukyas' p. 19). The कविराजमार्ग of नृपतुङ्ग (अमोघवर्ष) of the राष्ट्रकूट dynasty, which is the oldest extant work in the Canarese language (edited by Prof. K. B. Pathak in 1898) and which treats of Rhetoric (in three Paricchedas), takes, as Pathak points out, six verses on figures of speech in the काव्यादर्श and most of the verses in the 3rd परिच्छेद of the कविराजमार्ग are translations or adaptations of Daṇḍin. Prof. Pathak points out in I. A. vol. 41 p. 236 that the कविराजमार्ग copies in II. 59-85 most of the 33 varieties of उपमा in the काव्यादर्श. नृपतुङ्ग ascended the throne in śaka 737 (815 A. D.) and abdicated in śake 797 (875 A. D.). Therefore, it follows that the काव्यादर्श cannot be placed in any case later than 750 A. D., since considerable time must have elapsed before it became famous and could be translated into Canarese. Vide Prof. Pathak's Intro. to कविराजमार्ग p. 17 for Nṛpatuṅga's claim that he would follow ancient authorities on Alaṅkāra and pp. 18-19 for comparison between the two works and p. 13 for the express mention of हर्षचरित, कादम्बरी, नारायण, भारवि, कालिदास and माघ. On p. 16 of the Intro. Prof. Pathak asserted that Bhāmaha was frequently criticized by Daṇḍin, but changed that opinion later.

A Simhalese work called Siya-bas-lakara (स्वीयभाषालङ्कार) edited by Hendrick Jayatilak (Colombo 1892) possesses great importance on this question. Its first verse is the same as that of the काव्यादर्श. The 2nd verse is different and says 'Having bowed to Mahā-Brahmā, Indra, Bṛhaspati, the sage Kāśyapa, Vāmana and Daṇḍin and other eminent ācāryas who wrote on the science of poetics.' In the 3rd verse the author says that having condensed former books he composes his work in his own language. The 4th and 5th verses are the same as the 3rd and 4th verses of the काव्यादर्श I and almost all the verses of the two परिच्छेदs of काव्यादर्श are taken up in the Simhalese work, but the 3rd परिच्छेद of the काव्यादर्श is not translated. The last verse says 'this work was written by king Siri Silameghasena who comes of a royal race, who has a well-known following and who has lit with radiance from the rays of the jewels of the crown the inside of the white umbrella of sovereignty.' Dr. L. D. Barnett (in J. R. A. S. 1905 p. 841) refers to the Simhalese work, remarks that the author was king Sena I or Śilameghavarnasena. In the 'Early History of Ceylon' by Mr. G. C. Mendis and Prof. Geiger it is stated (on p. 50 of the 8th edition of 1947) that Sena I reigned from 831 to 851 A. D. Dr. Barnett refers to the opinion of Mr. Nevill who holds that the real author was probably Akbo (son of Kasup III) who ascended the throne in 741 A. D. Dr. Barnett further points out that two mss. of the Simhalese work in the British Museum read 'Bāmaha' for 'Vāmana' and holds that there were two traditions. In any case the Simhalese work is not later then 840 A. D. and so Daṇḍin cannot be placed later than about 750 A. D.

All these converging lines of historical data lead on to this that both Bhāmaha and Daṇḍin cannot be later than about 750 A. D. and that they are separated only by a few decades and not by centuries as Mr. Batuknath Śarma asserts (Intro. to काव्यालङ्कार on p. 40).

Therefore we must examine other evidence to settle their relative position.

The third work of Daṇḍin is the द्विसन्धानकाव्य ascribed to Daṇḍin by the Śṛṅgāraprakāśa. Dr. Raghavan kindly informs me that the Madras ms. of शृङ्गारप्रकाश vol. II. p. 444 mentions the द्विसन्धानमहाकाव्य of Daṇḍin as an illustration of प्रबन्धविषय

द्विसंधान (presenting in the same work the stories of both the epics viz. रामायण and the महाभारत). The द्विसंधान of दण्डी is mentioned also on pp. 168-69 of the same ms. and the same volume. Vide I. H. Q. vol. 24 at p. 117 for दण्डिद्विसंधान.

Seth Kanailal Poddar of Muttra wrote in Hindi an article 'संस्कृतसाहित्यमें अग्निपुराणका स्थान' in the Hindustani Academy's Quarterly for July 1931 (pp. 337-349), a copy of which he kindly sent to me in which he criticizes Dr. De and myself for holding that the Agnipurāṇa is a mere compilation and he tries to prove that Daṇḍin, Bhāmaha and the Dhvanyāloka all borrowed from the Agnipurāṇa. Answers to his arguments have been given in my remarks on the Agnipurāṇa and so I do not want to repeat them. But he appears to labour under two misapprehensions. The first is (at p. 347) that my History of Alaṅkara is largely based on Dr. De's work (एस्. के. देबाबू जिनके ग्रंथ पर श्री काणेका निबंध अधिकांशमें अवलम्बित है). For his information and for those who might not know, I desire to point out that my History of Alaṅkāra in two parts was published in 1923 June. Almost in the same month Dr. De's first volume of the H. S. P. appeared and the second volume appeared two years later. Further, in the I. A. for 1917 vol. 46 pp. 173 ff. I had discussed in detail the claims made for the अग्निपुराण at greater length than in my History of Alaṅkāra Literature and shown how the Agnipurāṇa borrows the very words of Daṇḍin in defining Alaṅkāras like Anuprāsa (Agni 343. 1 and Daṇḍin I. 55), Yamaka (Agni 343. 11-12 and Daṇḍin III. 1) and many arthālaṅkāras. So my views on the Agnipurāṇa were published six years before Dr. De's work (vol. I.) and Dr. De (in vol. I. p. 341, additions and corrections) refers to my paper in I. A. vol. 46 (for 1917). The 2nd misapprehension under which Mr. Poddar appears to labour is that I asserted that much of the Kāvyādarśa was included in the Agnipurāṇa (p. 337 ऐसी परिस्थिति में काव्यादर्श का अग्निपुराण में समावेश किया जाना किसी प्रकार भी सिद्ध नहीं हो सकता). What I said was that the Agnipurāṇa follows माधुकरी वृत्ति. It takes from several works what it chooses to take and that it is a mere compilation and not an original work. Simply because it differs in several cases from भामह or दण्डी, it does not follow that it did not borrow from them. Apart from the section on नाट्यशास्त्र and काव्यालङ्कार the अग्निपुराण borrows hundreds of verses from याज्ञवल्क्य and other works and borrows from

कुमारिल's तन्त्रवार्तिक p. 354 (Ānan. ed.) on जैमिनि I. 4. 20 the verse 'अभिधेयाविनाभूतप्रतीतिर्लक्षणोच्यते (अग्नि 344. 11). The learned writer has not adverted to all these points.

The following passages are common to both दण्डी and भामह word for word : (a) 'सर्गबन्धो महाकाव्यम्' काव्या. I. 14, भा. I. 19; (b) 'मन्त्रदूतप्रयाणाजिनायकाभ्युदयैरपि' काव्या. I. 17, भा. I. 20 (मन्त्रदूत... दयैश्च यत्); (c) 'कन्याहरणसंग्रामविप्रलम्भोदयादयः' काव्या. I. 29, भा. I. 27 (०दयान्विता); (d) 'अद्य या मम गोविन्द जाता त्वयि गृहागते। कालेनैषा भवेत्प्रीतिस्तवैवागमनात्पुनः॥' काव्या. II. 276, भा. III. 5 (both give it as an example of प्रेयः); (e) 'तद्भाविकमिति प्राहुः प्रबन्धविषयं गुणम्' काव्या. II. 364, भा. III. 53 (भाविकत्वमिति etc.); (f) 'अपार्थं व्यर्थमेकार्थं... विरोधि च।' काव्या. III. 125-126, भा. IV. 1-2; (g) 'समुदायार्थशून्यं यत्तदपार्थकमिष्यते' काव्या. III. 128 (v. l. र्थमितीष्यते), भा. IV. 8 ०र्थकमिष्यते; (h) 'गतोऽस्तमर्को भातीन्दुर्यान्ति वासाय पक्षिणः।' काव्या. II. 244, भा. II. 87; (i) 'आक्षेपोऽर्थान्तरन्यासो व्यतिरेको विभावना' काव्या. II. 4, भा. II. 66; (j) 'प्रेयो रसवदूर्जस्वि पर्यायोक्तं समाहितम्' काव्या. II. 5, भा. III. 1.

10 The relative position of Bhāmaha and Daṇḍin. There prevails a sharp conflict of views on this point and on the allied question of भामह and the न्यास and keen controversies have been going on for several years and it cannot be said that the question is definitely settled now one way or the other to the satisfaction of all scholars. Mr. Trivedi (Intro. to प्रतापरुद्र XXIII ff and I. A. vol. 42, 1913 pp. 258-274 and Bhandarkar Com. vol. p. 40), Dr. Jacobi (Z. D. M. G. 64 p. 134 and 139), Prof. Rangacharya (Intro. to edition of काव्यादर्श), Mr. Ganapati Śāstri (Intro. to स्वप्न० XXV), Prof. Pathak (Intro. to कविराजमार्ग p. 16) place भामह before दण्डी. Prof. M. T. Narasimhiengar (JRAS 1905 p. 535 ff) places दण्डी before भामह and Prof. Pathak also seems to have changed his earlier view (JBBRAS vol. 23 p. 19 and I. A. for 1912 p. 236 ff). Prof. Keith in H. S. L. pp. 375-376 and in 'Indian studies in honour of Lanman, pp. 167-185, where he criticizes Jacobi's views and also holds that Bhāmaha ridicules Bhaṭṭi (in the verse "Kāvyānyapi yadīmāni II 20") places Daṇḍin before Bhāmaha. I shall try to summarise the views of both sides and make remarks thereon as I proceed and make my own humble contribution to this subject.

Before proceeding further three points must be made clear and emphasized. One is that both भामह and दण्डी have several passages in common as specified above. The second point is that both expressly say that they had before them the works of older teachers on Poetics and भामह actually names one of them viz. मेधाविन्. This should warn us against jumping to the conclusion that one *necessarily* borrows from the other when they have identical verses or one appears to criticise the other when their views conflict. This fact and our ignorance of what went before भामह and दण्डी should make all of us reluctant to dogmatise and should dispose us to regard as probable the hypothesis that both are quoting from or criticizing older works now lost. The third point is that both are comparatively very early writers and vary near to each other in point of time. As उद्भट who flourished about 800 A. D. wrote a commentary on भामह's work, the latter cannot be placed later than about 750 A. D. The same lower limit is arrived at by the fact of the citation of three verses of भामह by शान्तरक्षित (vide above p. 84). दण्डी also cannot certainly be placed later than that date for the following reasons. The लोचन (composed about 1000 A. D.) names दण्डी and quotes his definition of चम्पू (p. 141) as it quotes भामह and उद्भट. So does प्रतीहारेन्दुराज (about 950 A.D.) quote (p. 26) the discussion of the verse लिम्पतीव in the काव्यादर्श II. 226-233. From the relation of the कविराजमार्ग and of the Simhalese work Siya-bas-lakara to the Kāvyādarśa it has been shown above (pp. 99-100) that Daṇḍin also cannot at all events be later than 750 A. D.

I shall now set out the grounds some or all of which are relied upon by those who place भामह prior to Daṇḍin.

(a) Mr. Trivedi and Prof. Rangacharya say that भामह is referred to as चिरन्तन by the अलङ्कारसर्वस्व (p. 3 quoted on p. 7 para f. above). His work is styled आकर by राघवभट्ट (शाकुन्तल p. 14) and he is styled 'ancient' in the प्रतापरुद्र० ('पूर्वेभ्यो भामहादिभ्यः', 'प्राचा भामहेन' pp. 4 and 11). The only place where according to Mr. Trivedi दण्डी is mentioned before भामह is by नमिसाधु on रुद्रट (I. 2) quoted above under मेधाविन् p. 63. I fail to see how this *proves* or even suggests the *priority* of भामह to दण्डी. भामह *is* an ancient writer and so there is nothing special in calling him पूर्व. Do these scholars mean that whenever reference is to be made to older writers all ancient names must be trotted forth ? Further, नमिसाधु is older than all the authors mentioned by Mr. Trivedi and therefore even a single positive reference where दण्डी is placed by a writer before मेधावी who preceded

भामह is sufficient to knock out all argument based upon mere silence. Besides, too much cannot be made of the views of authors belonging to the 12th or 14th century about the relative chronology of authors that flourished five or seven hundred years earlier. If we followed unquestioningly such later writers in chronological details, there would be a hopeless mess. The अलङ्कारसर्वस्व speaks of उद्भट also as चिरन्तन. Does Mr. Trivedi think that दण्डी is therefore later than उद्भट ? Mr. Trivedi forgets that जयरथ commenting upon the passage of the सर्वस्व specially includes दण्डी among the ancients. Such arguments must always be modestly and cautiously advanced. In the present case all the wind is taken away out of Mr. Trivedi's sails by a passage in अ. भा. On the *rasasūtra* in chap. VI (विभा... निष्पत्तिः) the अ. भा. first sets out the explanation of the sūtra by भट्टलोल्लट, then remarks that that very view is held by ancient writers and quotes as illustration two verses of Daṇḍin II. 281 and 283 (चिरन्तनानां चायमेव पक्षः। तथाहि दण्डिना स्वालङ्कारलक्षणेऽभ्यधायि रतिः शृङ्गारतां गता...इति, 'अधिरुह्य परां कोटिं कोपो रौद्रात्मतां गतः'।). Here a writer about 125 years older than the अलङ्कारसर्वस्व and belonging to the 1st quarter of the 11th century regards दण्डी as चिरन्तन. Further, प्रतीहारेन्दुराज in his commentary on Udbhaṭa's अलङ्कारसारसंग्रह (p. 26) names Daṇḍin and refers to his remarks on the verse लिम्पतीव (काव्यादर्श II. 226-233). प्रतिहारेन्दुराज says 'अत एव दण्डिना लिम्पतीव गतेत्यादेर्गर्भीकृतातिशयोत्प्रेक्षाभेदत्वमेव महता प्रबन्धेनाभ्यधायि'. It will be shown later on that प्रतिहारेन्दुराज flourished about 950 A. D.

(b) Daṇḍin's elaborate treatment of Yamaka and Śabdālaṅkāras in a separate chapter and his numerous sub-divisions of Upamā stamp him as a later writer; while भामह's divisions are not minute. I am of opinion that this puts the matter exactly the opposite way. भरत defines and illustrates ten varieties of यमक (17. 62-86), while भामह gives only five (II. 9). No one has made bold to place भामह before the नाट्यशास्त्र. The विष्णुधर्मोत्तर speaks of आदिमध्यान्तयमक, सन्दष्ट, समुद्ग, and समस्तपादयमक. यमक was highly thought of even by कालिदास (vide रघुवंश 9th *sarga*). It occurs even so early as in रुद्रदामन्'s Inscription of A. D. 150. It is precisely later writers that look down upon यमक. उद्भट ignores it altogether, though he defines अनुप्रास at some length, and मम्मट is very brief. The same remarks apply to शब्दालङ्कारs. Even Subandhu and Bāṇa knew शृङ्खलाबन्ध,

various puzzles like अक्षरच्युतक, प्रहेलिका etc. Daṇḍin's treatment of उपमा (of which he gives 32 varieties) is unscientific, but follows the lines of भरत (17. 44-55 GOS ed. 16. 46-59'), while भामह is the first of those who place the divisions of उपमा on a grammatical basis, as done later by उद्भट and मम्मट. From these very facts I would argue that Daṇḍin is earlier than भामह. It will be conceded by most scholars that both arguments are at least equally plausible. It is possible that दण्डी and भामह follow different traditions, the former having more affinity to भरत's school, while भामह follows a school that relies more upon mere *Arthālaṅkāras*. When there were differing views and works on a topic, later writers often pick and choose. For example, the कविराजमार्ग admits most of the varieties of उपमा (mentioned by दण्डी); vide II. 59-85 of कविराजमार्ग.

(c) The commentator तरुणवाचस्पति distinctly says that in some places Daṇḍin criticizes Bhāmaha (e. g. on दण्डी I. 23, 29; II. 235, 358 and III. 127). तरुणवाचस्पति is comparatively a late writer. He quotes from the दशरूपक (on दण्डी II. 281) and probably refers to the सरस्वती० in the sixfold division of *rītis*. The सूक्तिरत्नहार (Tri. S. series) of कालिङ्गरायसूर्य quotes two verses from तरुणवाचस्पति. In the Tri. Curator's Library there is a commentary called तात्पर्यनिरूपण by केशवभट्टारक, son of तरुणवाचस्पति (who was the *guru* of महाराजाधिराज रामनाथ, the same as Hoysala वीर रामनाथ that came to the throne in 1255). Vide Dr. Raghavan in J. O. R. Madras, vol. XIII pp. 293-306 (on the सूक्तिरत्नहार) at p. 305. So तरुणवाचस्पति flourished in the first half of the 13th century i. e. about 6 centuries after Daṇḍin. He found conflicting views and thinks that दण्डी criticizes भामह. A similar example will illustrate how unsafe it is to rely upon later commentators in the matter of chronology. चक्रवर्तिभट्टाचार्य in his commentary on the काव्यप्रकाश thinks that मम्मट criticizes the view of the अलङ्कारसर्वस्व on the verse राजति तटीयं० (10th उ.) and so says Nāgoji also; while जयरथ (who wrote about 1200 and was very near to both मम्मट and the सर्वस्व) thinks that the सर्वस्व criticizes the काव्यप्रकाश (p. 250 of सर्वस्व). Therefore तरुणवाचस्पति's remarks should carry hardly any weight with us in the absence of other very cogent evidence.

(d) भामह distinguishes between कथा and आख्यायिका, while

दण्डी says that the two are but different names for the same class of composition ('तत्कथाख्यायिकेत्येका जातिः संज्ञाद्वयाङ्किता' I. 28). It is supposed that दण्डी criticizes भामह. भामह makes the following points of distinction between the two (I. 25-27); (1) सोच्छ्वासाख्यायिका मता ॥; (2) वृत्तमाख्यायते तस्यां नायकेन स्वचेष्टितम् ।; (3) वक्त्रं चापरवक्त्रं च काले भाव्यर्थशंसि च ॥; (4) कवेरभिप्रायकृतैः कथा (थ?) नैः कैश्चिदङ्किता ।; (5) कन्याहरणसंग्रामविप्रलम्भोदयान्विता[1] (I take these two lines as part of the description of आख्यायिका). But a कथा is न वक्त्रापरवक्त्राभ्यां युक्ता (this is against No 3 above), नोच्छ्वासवत्यपि (against No I), अन्यैः स्वचरितं तस्यां नायकेन तु नोच्यते (against No 2 above). As भामह is silent about the points 4 and 5 in describing the characteristics of a कथा, it is not clear whether he means that they are to be absent in a कथा. दण्डी attacks all these points except one. According to दण्डी, some say that in an आख्यायिका the narrator is the hero himself while in a कथा the narrator may be the hero or someone else. This is not the distinction that भामह draws between कथा and आख्यायिका as shown above. 'तयोराख्यायिका किल ॥ नायकेनैव वाच्यान्या नायकेनेतरेण वा। अपि त्वनियमो दृष्टस्तत्राप्यन्यैरुदीरणात् । अन्यो वक्ता स्वयं वेति कीदृग्वा भेदकारणम् ॥' काव्या. I. 23-25. दण्डी remarks that even in आख्यायिकाs the narrators in some cases are others than the hero. On points 1 and 3 above he remarks "वक्त्रं चापरवक्त्रं च सोच्छ्वासत्वं च भेदकम् ॥ चिह्नमाख्यायिकायाश्चेत्प्रसङ्गेन कथास्वपि ॥ आर्यादिवत्प्रवेशः किं न वक्त्रापरवक्त्रयोः । भेदश्च दृष्टो लम्भादिरुच्छ्वासो वास्तु किं ततः ॥' I. 26-27. He says that as आर्याs are used in कथाs, so there is no reason why वक्त्र and अपरवक्त्र verses cannot be employed in them. Similarly, the sections of कथाs are called *lambhas* (lambakas in the बृहत्कथा): what difference does it make if they are called उच्छ्वास as in the case of आख्यायिका ? On points 4 and 5 दण्डी says that the topics कन्याहरण etc. occur in सर्गबन्ध (*i. e.* महाकाव्य) also and are not peculiar to आख्यायिकाs and that the use of some catchword (as the word श्री in the verses at the end of each *sarga* by माघ and अनुराग in the सेतुबन्ध) would not be a blemish in a कथा. 'कन्याहरणसंग्रामविप्रलम्भोदयादयः । सर्गबन्धसमा एव नैते वैशेषिका गुणाः ॥ कविभावकृतं चिह्नमन्यत्रापि न दुष्यति' काव्या. I. 29-30. It will be shown later on

1. The reading संस्कृतं संस्कृता चेष्टा कथापभ्रंशभाक् तथा (भामह I.28) is hard to construe. Probably it means that आख्यायिका must be in संस्कृत, while a कथा may be in संस्कृत or अपभ्रंश. Mr. Nāganath reads संस्कृते without mss. authority.

(Part II) that the two classes of works, कथा and आख्यायिका, were known to पतञ्जलि who named several of them, that long before the 6th century A. D. (as attested by सुबन्धु and बाण) आख्यायिकाs exhibited the special features on which भामह dwells. बाण designates his कादम्बरी as a कथा and states in the Introductory verses to the हर्षचरित that an आख्यायिका was divided into उच्छ्वासs and had some verses in the वक्त्र metre (उच्छ्वासान्तेऽप्यखिन्नास्ते वक्त्रे येषां सरस्वती। कथमाख्यायिकाकारा न ते वन्द्याः कवीश्वराः ॥ हर्षचरित Intro. verse 10). In verse 19 बाण expressly states that he is composing an आख्यायिका when he narrates हर्षचरित. Bāṇa's हर्षचरित remained unfinished. If one may conjecture, it was probably purposely left incomplete, because by the time Bāṇa came to write the 8th ucchvāsa, emperor Harṣa had been defeated by Pulikeśin as stated in the Aihole Inscription (I. A. vol. VIII. p. 237 at p. 242 भयविगलितहर्षो येन चाकारि हर्षः). Bāṇa did not like to hand down to posterity the defeat of his great patron. The defeat of Harṣa took place before 634 A.D. and so the हर्षचरित was composed about 630 A. D. long before both दण्डी and भामह flourished. Vide Bulletin of the London School of Oriental Studies, vol. III. pp. 507-517 for Dr. De's article on आख्यायिका and कथा. He agrees that the हर्षचरित does not conform to the pattern of an आख्यायिका defined by भामह (at p. 511). Dr. Nobel (p. 136 n 12 in his 'Foundations' &c.) gratuitouly surmises that बृहत्कथा was unknown to Daṇḍin. He has not properly understood काव्यादर्श I. 38 (भूतभाषामयीं प्राहुरद्भुतार्थां बृहत्कथाम्). What दण्डी meant is that the बृहत्कथा containing wonderful stories was not composed in संस्कृत (as he begins the verse as कथा हि सर्वभाषाभिः प्राकृतेन च बध्यते), but people said that the name of the Prākrit used in बृहत्कथा was भूतभाषा (पैशाची). In I. 34-35 the काव्यादर्श refers to महाराष्ट्री, शौरसेनी, गौडी, लाटी and other dialects, all of which, it says, are included under the word प्राकृत, महाराष्ट्री 'being the most eminent among Prakrits'. Bāṇa who preceded Daṇḍin knew the contents of the बृहत्कथा very well as the Introductory verse 17 and other references in the हर्षचरित and the कादम्बरी show. Nobel in his work (pp. 156-187) deals with कथा and आख्यायिका and indulges in many wrong translations and theories. Therefore, it is not necessary to suppose that दण्डी criticizes the dicta of भामह, particularly because one point of attack (about the narrator) in the काव्यादर्श is not exactly the opinion held by भामह.

(e) दण्डी (in II. 51 न लिङ्गवचने भिन्ने न हीनाधिकतापि वा। उपमादूषणायालं यत्रोद्वेगो न धीमताम्॥) refers to लिङ्गभेद, वचनभेद, हीनता and अधिकता between उपमान and उपमेय as blemishes in some cases, but not in all; while भामह (II. 39) speaks of seven blemishes in उपमा. But this cannot be made an argument for the priority of भामह. भामह himself says that मेधाविन् enumerated seven उपमादोषs (vide II. 40). So this was an ancient topic. One may rather use this as an argument for Daṇḍin's priority. Daṇḍin names only four[1] उपमादोषs (II. 51) while मेधावी knows seven and भामह follows the latter. So दण्डी was the pioneer. वामन speaks of six उपमादोषs (का. सूत्र IV. 2. 8). The अग्निपुराण (346.29) says 'विभक्तिसंज्ञालिङ्गानां यत्रोद्वेगो न धीमताम्। संख्यायास्तत्र भिन्नत्वमुपमानोपमेययोः'. It will be noticed that यत्रोद्वेगो न धीमताम् is common to both दण्डी and अग्नि०.

(f) दण्डी says that even the words 'गतोऽस्तमर्को भातीन्दुर्यान्ति वासाय पक्षिणः' are certainly good (poetry) in certain circumstances of time and situation (गतो...पक्षिणः। इतीदमपि साध्वेव कालावस्थानिवेदने' II. 244); while भामह says about those words 'are such words poetry ? (Some) designate them वार्ता.' His words may also mean 'such words are bad samples of poetry (गतो...पक्षिणः। इत्येवमादि किं काव्यं वार्तामेनां प्रचक्षते॥ II. 87). Prof. Rangacharya and Mr. Trivedi rely on this as proving Bhāmaha's priority. But the words इत्ये...चक्षते[2] show that भामह is quoting these words as an example of वार्ता given by others and these words are not his own composition (compare the use of the words इतीदमपि of दण्डी in connection with लिम्पतीव). Now वार्ता is a figure of speech illustrated by भट्टि (X. 45) according to जयमङ्गला. The विष्णुधर्मोत्तर 14. 11 defines वार्ता (in one ms.; vide above p. 71). Daṇḍin seems to

---

1. भामह(II. 38) finds fault with those who give several varieties of उपमा such as मालोपमा and states that such details are useless (मालोपमादि सर्वोपि न ज्यायान् विस्तरो मुधा). It is not in accordance with his own principles to have given instances of उपमादोषs and to have explained them in detail (as in II. 40-64) when मेधावी had already named the seven उपमादोषs and had exemplified them, as shown by नमिसाधु on रुद्रट XI. 24.

2. भामह frequently employs the verb प्रचक्षते for stating others' views. Vide II. 93 (about स्वभावोक्ति), IV. 12 (about एकार्थ), VI. 16 (about अपोह).

allude to it in the words 'तच्च वार्ताभिधानेषु वर्णनास्वपि दृश्यते' (I. 85). But Daṇḍin does not define the fignre वार्ता. He probably disapproved of it and included some examples of it under स्वभावोक्ति. He takes the example गतोऽस्तमर्कः cited by some old writer and says that even that example may be good poetry if the suggested sense be taken (but if the plain meaning is the only one intended it is not काव्य). Vide काव्यप्रकाश (5th उल्लास p. 240 of Vā.) for nine different meanings that these words may suggest[1] to different persons. These words गतोऽस्तमर्कः: are well-known examples (मूर्धाभिषिक्त) like the famous दशदाडिमादिवाक्य (which occurs in भामह at IV. 8) that is cited in the शाबरभाष्य (p. 47 and p. 1252 on जै. IV. 3. 10 Anan ed.) and महाभाष्य (vol. I. p. 38, ed. by Kielhorn) 'अनर्थकानि । दश दाडिमानि, षडपूपाः.'

(g) The verse अथ या मम गोविन्द is given by both as an example of प्रेयः. The argument of Mr. Trivedi is that Bhāmaha cites his authority if he is quoting from another, while दण्डी does not do so, as in the case of the verse लिम्पतीव. This argument does injustice to दण्डी. दण्डी *does* clearly indicate that he is citing another's verse 'viz लिम्पतीव' as a well-known example by using the words इतीदमपि in the latter half of काव्यादर्श II. 226. As remarked above (p. 86) भामह's text is not so immaculate as to inspire complete confidence. So the first part of the argument really begs the whole question. There are other considerations also. भामह does not even define प्रेयः and ऊर्जस्वि and cites one example (III. 5 and 7) of each; while दण्डी defines both and gives two examples of प्रेयः. The obvious conclusion is that भामह found both figures defined by some predecessor and was content simply to cite an example or probably he disapproved of these as figures of speech and following older authoritics simply cited examples. Therefore, it is going too far to say that दण्डी takes the example from भामह. One may perhaps more plausibly argue that भामह borrows from दण्डी one of the latter's two examples. The verse अथ या मम (काव्यादर्श II. 276) is similar in purport to the महाभारत 'या प्रीतिः पुण्डरीकाक्ष तवागमनकारणात्। सा किमाख्यायते तुभ्यमन्तरात्मासि देहिनाम् ॥' (उद्योग. 89. 24).

---

1 सोमेश्वर in his टीका on का. प्र. (folio 88b) says 'तथा गतो... पक्षिणः' इत्यादौ प्रसाद-श्लेष-समता-माधुर्य-सौकुमार्यार्थव्यक्तीनां गुणानां सद्भावेऽपि काव्यव्यवहाराप्रवृत्तेः ।'

(h) भामह defines उपमारूपक (III. 35), ससन्देह (III. 43), अनन्वय (III. 45) and उत्प्रेक्षावयव (III. 47) as separate figures of speech; while दण्डी does not regard them as separate figures, but includes उपमारूपक under रूपक, ससन्देह and अनन्वय under उपमा and उत्प्रेक्षावयव under उत्प्रेक्षा (अनन्वयससन्देहावुपमास्वेव दर्शितौ । उपमारूपकं चापि रूपकेष्वेव दर्शितम् ॥ उत्प्रेक्षाभेद एवासावुत्प्रेक्षावयवोपि च । II. 358-359). This has been used as an argument for भामह's priority. All these figures are separately illustrated by भट्टि; vide भट्टि X. 68-70 for ससन्देह, अनन्वय and उत्प्रेक्षावयव, X. 61 for उपमारूपक acc. to जयमङ्गला. There is no compelling reason why दण्डी must be regarded as referring to भामह and not to those Ālaṅkārikas who preceded भट्टि. There is one more reason which throws doubt on the theory advanced. उपमेयोपमा is separately defined by भामह (III. 37, while दण्डी does not define it but his अन्योन्योपमा (II. 18) is उपमेयोपमा. If दण्डी had the work of भामह before him, he would have said as he said in the other four cases that उपमेयोपमा was included under उपमा.

(i) Bhāmaha after enumerating ten *doṣas* (which are identical with Daṇḍin's) adds an eleventh *doṣa* in the words 'प्रतिज्ञाहेतुदृष्टान्तहीनं दुष्टं च नेष्यते' (IV. 2) and devotes one whole परि० (V) to the discussion of this *doṣa*. Daṇḍin says the discussion whether प्रतिज्ञाहेतुदृष्टान्तहानि is a *doṣa* or not is dry and abstruse and no purpose is served by entering upon it (प्रतिज्ञा......लीढेन किं फलम् ॥ III. 127 quoted above on p. 80). It is not to be supposed that discussions about logical matters in the province of Poetics were first started by भामह. Even the नाट्यशास्त्र enumerates ten *doṣas* of *kāvya* one of which is न्यायादपेत and defines as 'न्यायादपेतं विज्ञेयं प्रमाणपरिवर्जितम्' (नाट्य. 17. 93=GOS. ed. chap. 16. 93 p. 333). The प्रमाणs are the special province of logic. The काव्यादर्श, therefore, alludes if at all to the नाट्यशास्त्र or some *ālaṅkarika* who worked up the simple statement of the नाट्यशास्त्र into greater detail. It is more than doubtful whether, if दण्डी had the 5th परि० of भामह before him and was in a criticizing and fighting mood, he would have let off भामह with such a mild and suave remark 'तेनालीढेन किं फलम्'. The ten दोषs of the नाट्यशास्त्र (17. 88) are अर्थहीन, एकार्थ, गूढार्थ, अर्थान्तर, विसन्धि, शब्दच्युत (or शब्दहीन as in 17.94), विषम, भिन्नार्थ, अभिप्लुतार्थ and न्यायादपेत. The first seven correspond more or less with अपार्थ एकार्थ, ससंशय, अपक्रम, विसन्धि, शब्दहीन, भिन्नवृत्त (of भामह and दण्डी). The भिन्नार्थ of the नाट्य० is the same as असभ्य and ग्राम्य and अभिप्लुतार्थ is defined as

'यत्पादेन (यत्पादे न ?) समस्यते'. The यतिभ्रष्टदोष (of भामह) was probably included in the विषम (of the नाट्यशास्त्र) and व्यर्थ uuder the अर्थहीन (of भरत). The Alaṅkāra writers probably draw upon the न्यायसूत्र also for some of the names of the *doṣas*; compare न्यायसूत्र V. 2. 1 'प्रतिज्ञाहानिः प्रतिज्ञान्तरं प्रतिज्ञाविरोधः प्रतिज्ञासंन्यासः हेत्वन्तरमर्थान्तरं निरर्थकमविज्ञातार्थमपार्थकमप्राप्तकालं न्यूनमधिकं पुनरुक्तमननुभाषणमज्ञानमप्रतिभा... निग्रहस्थानानि.' The विष्णुधर्मोत्तर III. 15. 13 states ससंशय न वक्तव्यं प्रतिज्ञारहितं तथा । पूर्वापरविरुद्धं च यच्च लोकविगर्हितम् । and in III. 15. 11 mentions the cases in which पुनरुक्त is not a दोष.

I shall now mention the points relied upon for placing भामह after Daṇḍin.

(j) भामह says (I. 41) 'हिमापहामित्रधरैर्व्याप्तं व्योमेत्यवाचकम्,' while दण्डी gives the whole verse of which this is a part as an example of a kind of प्रहेलिका called परिहारिका 'विजितात्म(त्र. v. l.) भवद्वेषिगुरुपादहतो जनः। हिमापहामित्रधरैर्व्याप्तं व्योमाभिनन्दति ॥' (III. 120)). शार्ङ्ग० ascribes it to दण्डी and explains it.[1] This is a somewhat formidable argument in favour of the view that भामह borrows a verse of Daṇḍin and points out a *doṣa* in it and the only way of escaping from it is to assert that दण्डी is simply quoting from some older writer, whome भामह also quotes. But a few considerations even against this last reply may be urged. दण्डी has not been shown to quote any verse from another author except लिम्पतीव. The other verses suggested to be quotations are matters of controversy. It would be a gratuitous assumption to predicate of any verse in the काव्या० as another's simply because otherwise it leads to inconvenient results. The words 'दोषानपरिसंख्येयान्मन्यमाना वयं पुनः । साध्वीरेवाभिधास्यामस्ता दुष्टा यास्त्वलक्षणाः ॥' (काव्या० III. 107) appear to suggest that Daṇḍin gives his own examples of good प्रहेलिकाs and as the verse हिमापहा० is an example of a good प्रहेलिका and as भामह quotes only a part of it, it is a very weighty argument in favour of the view that he is later than दण्डी. Prahelikas were known long before the time of Bāṇa (first half of 7th century).

(k) Daṇḍin's treatment of Upamā is unscientific as compared with भामह's; so also दण्डी treats of अनुप्रास very concisely and dilates upon Yamaka at great length. But this is not such

---

1. शार्ङ्गधर explains 'विना गरुडेन जितः इन्द्रः तदात्मभवः अर्जुनः तद्द्वेषी कर्णः तद्गुरुः सूर्यः तत्पादहतः तत्किरणसन्तप्तः । हिमापहः अग्निः तदमित्रं पानीयं तद्धराः मेघाः' (तैर्व्याप्तं व्योम नभः).

a strong point after all. The Agnipurāṇa which borrows from भामह has a treatment of उपमा similar to Daṇḍin's and even comparatively early writers like Rudraṭa have treated of Yamaka at great length.

(l) There are many passages in Bhāmaha's work where he either refers to the views of other authors on Poetics or ridicules them. In most of these cases the views animadverted upon are found in Daṇḍin. भामह criticizes those who distinguish the two styles वैदर्भ and गौड and prefer the former to the latter and ironically calls them सुधियः. 'वैदर्भमन्यदस्तीति मन्यन्ते सुधियोऽपरे। तदेव च किल ज्यायः सदर्थमपि नापरम् ॥ गौडीयमिदमेतत्तु वैदर्भमिति किं पृथक्। गतानुगतिकन्यायान्नानाख्येयममेधसाम् ॥' (I. 31-32). The last half line is important. It means ignorant people should not be told (such a thing viz. that वैदर्भ and गौड are different मार्गs by blindly following what others have done). भामह means that in former times some Rhetoricians might have made a difference between styles as वैदर्भ and गौड, but it is not proper to persist and seriously teach such a difference to ignorant people. This shows that भामह knew that there were before him writers on Poetics, who thoughtlessly harped on the difference between वैदर्भ and गौड styles. Compare the well-known verse 'गतानुगतिको लोकः कुट्टनीमुपदेशिनीम्। प्रमाणयति नो धर्मे यथा गोघ्नमपि द्विजम् ॥.' The काव्यादर्श makes this distinction and shows its preference for वैदर्भमार्गः अस्त्यनेको गिरां मार्गः सूक्ष्मभेदः परस्परम्। तत्र वैदर्भगौडीयौ वर्ण्येते प्रस्फुटान्तरौ ॥...इति वैदर्भमार्गस्य प्राणा दश गुणाः स्मृताः। एषां विपर्ययः प्रायो दृश्यते गौडवर्त्मनि ॥ (I. 40 and 42). But these words (अनेको मार्गः) of Daṇḍin show that before him many styles had been recognised and as long as we do not possess all ancient works that preceded Daṇḍin we cannot assert with assurance that भामह criticizes Daṇḍin alone and no one else. It will be noticed that बाण also credits the Gauḍa style with pomposity 'गौडेष्वक्षरडम्बरः' (हर्षचरित, Intro. verse 7).

(m) Daṇḍin names ten *guṇas* (I.41-42) and the names are the same as those in the नाट्यशास्त्र (17-96). भामह has almost nothing to say on the *guṇas*. But he seems to be the first of those who like ध्वनिकारिका II. 8, 10, 11 and मम्मट reduced the *guṇas* to three and ridicules those who look upon ओजः as a profusion of compounds 'माधुर्यमभिवाञ्छन्तः प्रसादं च सुमेधसः। समासवन्ति भूयांसि न पदानि प्रयुञ्जते ॥ केचिदोजोभिधित्सन्तः समस्यन्ति बहून्यपि। श्रव्यं नातिसमस्तार्थं काव्यं मधुरमिष्यते ॥ आविद्वदङ्गनाबालप्रतीतार्थं प्रसादवत् ॥'

(II. 1-3). This shows, according to some, a distinctly later tendency, while Daṇḍin follows the ancient view of Bharata. The guṇa *ojas* is defined in नाट्यशास्त्र (GOS) 16. 105 as समासवद्भिर्बहुभिर्विचित्रैश्च पदैर्युतम् । सानुरागैरुदारैश्च तदोजः परिकीर्त्यते. अ. भा. comments on this verse, while in Kashi SS. edition the definition is different. But, when the tendency to reduce the *guṇas* began, no one knows. And the ten *guṇas* are enumerated by Vāmana who is certainly later than Bhāmaha. Besides, Daṇḍin does not distinctly say that माधुर्य and प्रसाद would not allow the use of long compounds, though he distinctly says 'ओजः समासभूयस्त्वं' (I. 89). It is possible to urge that very likely भामह is referring to a writer other than दण्डी. The present writer, however, feels that Bhāmaha is probably referring to Daṇḍin and that the treatment of guṇas in भामह savours of lateness in time.

(n) Bhāmaha says 'यदुक्तं त्रिप्रकारत्वं तस्याः कैश्चिन्महात्मभिः । निन्दाप्रशंसाचिख्यासाभेदादत्राभिधीयते ॥ सामान्यगुणनिर्देशात् त्रयमप्युदितं ननु । मालोपमादिः सर्वोपि न ज्यायान् विस्तरो मुधा ॥' II. 37-38. He refers to the threefold division of उपमा into निन्दोपमा, प्रशंसोपमा and आचिख्यासोपमा. These three varieties of उपमा occur in the same order in काव्या. (II. 30-32). The नाट्य० speaks of प्रशंसोपमा and निन्दोपमा (17. 51-52) but not of आचिख्यासोपमा. On the other hand it is urged that भामह's words, strictly interpreted, mean that उपमा was divided only into three varieties, while, दण्डी gives over 30 including these three. If he meant to refer to these three as a few out of many प्रकारs he would have said 'प्रकाराश्च एतेपि तस्या उक्ता etc.' There is some force in this latter argument. But it has to be noted that in the same breath (with these three) भामह speaks of मालोपमा and *other varieties* of Upamā as a mere superfluity. मालोपमा does accur in the काव्या. II. 42.

(o) The काव्यादर्श says 'हेतुश्च सूक्ष्मलेशौ च वाचामुत्तमभूषणम्' (II. 235), while भामह says 'हेतुश्च सूक्ष्मो लेशोथ नालङ्कारतया मत.' (II. 86). He puts his emphatic denial on the ground that they do not contain वक्रोक्ति. It may be argued that because भामह said that they were not even *alaṅkāras*, दण्डी equelly vehemently asserts that they are the best ornaments of speech.

(p) 'स्वभावोक्तिरलङ्कार इति केचित्प्रचक्षते । अर्थस्य तदवस्थत्वं स्वभावोभिहितो यथा ॥' भामह II. 98; दण्डी speaks of स्वभावोक्ति as the first of *alaṅkāras* and calls it जाति also 'नानावस्थं पदार्थानां रूपं साक्षाद्विवृण्वती । स्वभावोक्तिश्च जातिश्चेत्याद्या सालङ्कृतिर्यथा ॥ (II. 8.). It is true that भामह's definition has a very close verbal resemblance to Daṇḍin's; but स्वभावोक्ति is a very ancient अलङ्कार. बाण speaks of it as जाति. So this is not decisive.

(q) 'एतदेवापरेऽन्येन व्याख्यानेनान्यथा विदुः । नानारत्नादियुक्तं यत् तत् किलोदात्तमुच्यते ॥' भा. III. 12; दण्डी says 'आशयस्य विभूतेर्वा यन्महत्त्वमनुत्तमम् । उदात्तं... ॥ रत्नभित्तिषु संक्रान्तैः प्रतिबिम्बशतैर्वृतः । ज्ञातो लङ्केश्वरः कृच्छ्रादाञ्जनेयेन तत्त्वतः ॥ पूर्वत्राशयमाहात्म्यमत्राभ्युदयगौरवम् । सुव्यञ्जितमिति प्रोक्तमुदात्तद्वयमप्यदः ॥' काव्या. II. 300, 302-3. It will be noticed that Daṇḍin's example begins with the word रत्न, that भामह does not define the first variety of उदात्त and gives as an example Rāma's action of going into exile at his father's word (which also is Daṇḍin's example in spirit). But as against the theory that भामह refers to दण्डी it must be pointed out that उदात्त is an ancient figure. भट्टि gives two examples (X. 52-53) corresponding to the two varieties of the figure.

(r) भामह says 'आशीरपि च केषाञ्चिदलङ्कारतया मतः' (III. 55) and gives two examples. दण्डी says 'आशीर्नामाभिलषिते वस्तुन्याशंसनं यथा । पातु वः परमं ज्योतिरवाङ्मनसगोचरम् ॥' II. 337. भामह may or may not be referring to दण्डी. आशीः is a figure illustrated by भट्टि and आशीः is one of the 36 लक्षणs of नाट्य defined by भरत (16. 29 K. M. edition of 1894, GOS. ed. 16. 28, though not in Ch. ed.).

(s) 'पुनरुक्तमिदं प्राहुरन्ये शब्दार्थभेदतः ।...अत्रार्थपुनरुक्तं यत्तदेवैकार्थमिष्यते । ...तामुत्कमनसं नूनं करोति ध्वनिरम्भसाम् । सौधेषु घनमुक्तानां प्रणालीमुखपातिनाम् ॥ भा. IV. 12, 16. दण्डी says 'अविशेषेण पूर्वोक्तं यदि भूयोपि कीर्त्यते । अर्थतः शब्दतो वापि तदेकार्थं मतं यथा ॥ उत्कामुन्मनयन्त्येते बालां तदलकत्विषः । अम्भोधरास्तडित्वन्तो गम्भीराः स्तनयित्नवः ॥' III. 135-136. It will be noticed that the view ascribed to others in the word अन्ये is that of दण्डी and that भामह's example also is very similar to Daṇḍin's.

(t) As quoted above, नमिसाधु (रुद्रट 1. 2) refers to the अलङ्कारशास्त्रs composed by 'दण्डिमेधाविरुद्रभामहादिकृतानि'. It is argued that, as मेधाविन् certainly preceded भामह, नमिसाधु has purposely arranged the authors in chronological order and therefore दण्डी preceded even मेधावी. There is some force in the argument. But underlying it there is an assumption that नमिसाधु intends to arrange them chronologically. There is hardly any proof of such an intention. His only purpose is to assert that some authors wrote on अलङ्कार before रुद्रट. We shall have to attribute to him a double assertion (i. e. to use the language of the मीमांसकs there would be वाक्यभेद).

The upshot of the above discussion is that the reasons usually advanced by the partisans of Bhāmaha's priority fall very far short of what is required and are easily explicable without the hypothesis of Bhāmaha's priority and that the grounds so far urged for placing Daṇḍin before Bhāmaha, though of considerable force, are not so strong as to produce conviction in every unbiassed mind. It seems probable that भामह and दण्डी follow independent traditions, the former having more affinity with the अलङ्कार school and the latter with भरत's school. Whoever may be earlier, both are very near to each other and are to be placed between 650-750 A. D. If, however, it be said that from the materials collected above there is no option except to assert that one must be held to be borrowing from or criticizing the other and that the third alternative often suggested above about other ancient authors being referred to by both is not admissible, then I would declare myself in favour of Daṇḍin's priority over Bhāmaha. There is no use in repetition. I hold that the reasons so far assigned for Daṇḍin's priority are far more weighty (though not thoroughly decisive) than those assigned for Bhāmaha's priority.

(u) A few words must be said concerning the heated controversy about भामह and the न्यास. The two great protagonists here are Prof. Pathak and Mr. Trivedi. भामह says : शिष्टप्रयोगमात्रेण न्यासकारमतेन वा । तृचा समस्तषष्ठीकं न कथञ्चिदुदाहरेत् ॥ सूत्रज्ञापकमात्रेण वृत्रहन्ता यथोदितः । अकेन च न कुर्वीत वृत्तिं तद्गमको यथा ॥ (VI. 36-37). The straightforward meaning of the verses is : A poet should in no case employ (lit. utter) in his work a compound in which a word ending in the तृच affix (i.e. तृ) is compounded with another word that would be in the genitive (when the compound is dissolved), by merely relying on the usage of the śiṣṭas[1]

1. The word शिष्ट does not refer to Pāṇini at all. He is too great for that word. Prof. Pathak (I. A. vol. 41 at p. 235) is wrong in holding that शिष्ट means पाणिनि. The महाभाष्य (ed. Kielhorn, vol. III. p. 174) has a discussion on that word from which the following is taken:'के पुनः शिष्टाः ।...एवं तर्हि निवासत आचारतश्च । स चाचार आर्यावर्त एव । कः पुनरार्यावर्तः ।...एतस्मिन्नार्यनिवासे ये ब्राह्मणाः... किंचिदन्तरेण कस्याश्चिद् विद्यायाः पारगास्तत्रभवन्तः शिष्टाः । यदि तर्हि शिष्टाः शब्देषु प्रमाणं किमष्टाध्याय्या क्रियते । शिष्टज्ञानार्थाष्टाध्यायी ।' (on पा.VI. 3. 109, पृषोदरादीनि यथोपदिष्टम्). The Mahābhāṣya says that Pāṇini's work enables one to find out who are शिष्टs.

or on the opinion of the author of Nyāsa; as the word वृत्रहन्ता is employed by merely relying on the indication furnished by a sūtra of Pāṇini, one should not form a compound with a word, ending in अक as in the case of the word तद्गमक (तस्य गमक: तद्गमक:). It is not possible to go into all grammatical details here, but I shall say a few words which, I hope, will make the controversy clear to anyone having some knowledge of Sanskrit. पाणिनि says 'तृजकाभ्यां कर्तरि' II. 2. 15, which is an exception to his general rule 'षष्ठी' II. 2. 8 (a noun in the genitive may be compounded with another noun, as in राजपुरुष: which when dissolved becomes राज्ञ: पुरुष:). The exception means when affixes तृच् (तृ) and अक are added in the sense of the doer or agent, the words so formed cannot be compounded with another word in the genitive, e. g. we must say अपां स्रष्टा and ओदनस्य पाचक: (and not अप्स्रष्टा nor ओदनपाचक:). There are counter-exceptions such as those where words of the याजक group are concerned (याजकादिभिश्च-पा. II. 2. 9). One can say ब्राह्मणयाजक:, देवपूजक:. But poets often violate these rules as said in निरङ्कुशा: कवय: (by भट्टोजि on पा. III. 2. 138). For example, we have the well-known भोजप्रबन्ध verse 'घटानां निर्मातुस्त्रिभुवनविधातुश्च कलह:' (it should be त्रिभुवनस्य विधातु:). The commentators suggest several ways to get over this apparently ungrammatical use. One way to get over the difficulty is to hold that in विधातृ, the affix is not तृच्, but तृन् used in the sense of 'being in the habit of.' The sūtras are (आ क्वेस्तच्छीलतद्धर्मतत्साधुकारिषु । तृन् । पा. III. 2. 134-135; an example being कर्ता कटान्, one who habitually makes mats). But then another difficulty presents itself viz. पाणिनि forbids, among others, the employment of words formed by तृन् with a noun in the genitive (न लोकाव्ययनिष्ठाखलर्थतृनाम्) । पा. II. 3. 69).[1] To this a reply is given that Pāṇini's rules are not absolute, that there are indications (ज्ञापक) in his sūtras to that effect, since he gives such sūtras as जनिकर्तु: प्रकृति: (पा. I. 4. 30), 'तत्प्रयोजको हेतुश्च' (पा. I. 4. 55). Here कर्तृ (formed with affix तृ) is compounded with जनि which would be in the genitive case when the compound is dissolved; similarly प्रयोजक (formed with affix अक) is compounded with तत् which would be in the genitive when dissolved,

1. The word तृन् here is a प्रत्याहार and stands for all terminations beginning with तृ in शतृ in पा. III. 2. 124 and ending with तृन् (III.2.135).

तस्य प्रयोजकः तत्प्रयोजकः. Some writers hold that a compound of तृन् with षष्ठी does take place (vide Pathak in I. A. 41 pp. 234.)

Pāṇini's sūtras were commented upon by Jayāditya and Vāmana and the commentary is called काशिका, which in its turn was explained in a huge commentary (in 1149 printed pages) called काशिकाविवरणपञ्जिका or न्यास composed by जिनेन्द्रबुद्धि (published by the वारेन्द्र Research Society at Rajshahi, Bengal). If we can settle which work is the न्यास mentioned by भामह and when that work was composed भामह's date can be settled within narrow limits. Here comes the dispute among such scholars as the late Mr. Trivedi (in I. A. vol. 42 for 1913 p. 158 ff, my paper in J. B. B. R. A. S. for 1909 pp. 91-95, the late Prof. Pathak (in I. A. 1912 p. 232–237, and J. B. B. R. A. S. vol. 23 pp. 18-31, Annals of B. O. R. I. vol. XII. pp. 246 ff. and pp. 372-395) and Mr. R. Narsimhachar (in I. A. vol. 41 p. 91, who refers to a पूज्यपाद, author of a न्यास, that flourished about 500 A. D. according to Mr. Rice and in I. A. vol. 42 p. 204). The propositions clearly laid down by भामह are : (1) Śiṣṭas and न्यासकार allow the use of compounds in which the 2nd word is formed with तृच् or अक and the first is in the genitive; (2) that relying on सूत्रज्ञापक, a word like वृत्रहन्ता has been employed; (3) poets employ such compounds as तद्गमक, relying on पाणिनि's 'तत्प्रयोजको हेतुश्च'. Prof. Pathak takes the 2nd proposition as meaning that वृत्रहन्ता is employed among the people (लोके) and not in the न्यास of जिनेन्द्र० (which gives a different example viz. भीष्मः कुरूणां भयशोकहन्ता, v. l. हर्ता). Mr. Trivedi emphatically asserts that भामह ascribes propositions I and II to the न्यास, but the न्यास does not contain the example वृत्रहन्ता nor does the न्यास of जिनेन्द्रबुद्धि allow the compound of a word formed by तृच् with another noun in the genitive. Therefore, he argues that the न्यास mentioned by भामह is different from जिनेन्द्रबुद्धि's न्यास. From other evidence I have shown that भामह must have flourished before 750 A. D.; therefore the न्यास named by भामह must be one composed about or before 700 A. D. There is no other न्यास (though there are many grammatical works called न्यास) that can be assigned to this date except the न्यास of जिनेन्द्रबुद्धि. So I agree with Prof. Pathak so far. Prof. Pathak shows (I. A. 41 p. 235) that the work of पूज्यपाद to whom Mr. Narsimhachar referred (I. A. 41 p. 91) is not called न्यास by anyone. The passages of the न्यास on II. 2. 15-16 do show that the न्यास allowed a word in तृ to be compounded with a word that in dissolution would be in the genitive case. So भामह rightly says that न्यासकार allowed such compounds. I think that Mr. Trivedi is not right in insisting that वृत्रहन्ता must be found in the न्यास. भामह very often employs the word उदित for what is stated in a work or by an author.[1] So we should hold that वृत्रहन्ता was used in some work which भामह knew, but which we do not know. Prof. Pathak is not right in understanding लोके before उदित: (Annals B. O. R. I. vol. XII p. 390). Therefore we come to this conclusion that the न्यास of जिनेन्द्रबुद्धि was known to भामह.

We must now turn to the dates. I-tsing, in his 'Records of the Buddhist religion', describes the काशिका (at p. 175 of the translation by Dr. Takakusu, Oxford, 1896) and states that Jayāditya died nearly thirty years before. I-tsing wrote his work in 691 A. D. So Jayāditya died about 661-62. This date is corroborated by the fact that the काशिका on पा. I. 3. 23 quotes the किरातार्जुनीय of भारवि III. 14, viz. the पाद 'संशय्य कर्णादिषु तिष्ठते यः'. We find from the न्यास on the काशिका that numerous mss. were made of the Kāśikā and that the copyists of न्यासकार's days by mistake added a certain example to the original examples of the Kāśikā.[2] So that would require at least a generation or two. Hence the न्यास cannot be assigned to a date earlier than 700 A. D. The न्यासकार could not have been a contemporary of Jayāditya. As भामह expressly mentions न्यासकार, भामह must be placed after 700 and before 750 A. D. Prof. Pathak changed his original opinion of Bhāmaha's priority to Daṇḍin (expressed on p. 16 of Intro. to कविराजमार्ग) in ABORI vol. XII pp. 81-83. Prof. Pathak showed that Pātrakesari, Śāntarakṣita and Prabhācandra were more or

---

1. भामह II. 5 (यथोदितम् by himself), II. 19 (प्रहेलिका सा ह्युदिता रामशर्माच्युतोत्तरे), II. 45 (दृष्टं वा सर्वसारूप्यं राजमित्रे यथोदितम्), IV 8 (दाडिमानि दशापूपाः षडित्यादि यथोदितम्).

2. On पा. VI. 3. 79 the printed काशिका gives three examples, सकलं, समुहूर्तं, and ससंग्रहम्। On this the न्यास says: (p. 469) 'ससंग्रहमित्येतदुदाहरणं प्रमादादिदानींतनैः लेखकैर्लिखितम्'. The word इदानींतनैः is important. The editor (in Intro. to न्यास p. 21) furnishes other examples to show that काशिका and न्यास were separated by a good deal of time.

less contemporaries, that Prabhācandra was the latest of them and that they belonged to the 9th century and that Bhāmaha belonged to the middle of the 8th century. In his paper in the same vol. (pp. 372-395) he deals with the 5th chapter of Bhāmaha on logic, particularly verses 6-9 and shows that शान्तरक्षित quotes three verses of भामह (VI. 17-19) refuting the अपोहवाद and avers that शान्तरक्षित calls भामह 'दुरात्मा कुदृष्टिः' (p. 383). On pp. 389-390 he refers to हर्षचरित passage (कृतगुरुपदन्यासाः ff), states that Bāṇa was a contemporary of Jayāditya (author of Kāśikā) and his commentator Nyāsakāra (p. 390). But as to this (and particularly as to Nyāsakāra) the learned professor is wrong. The Harṣacarita breaks off in its treatment before Harṣa's defeat by Pulikeśin and Prof. Pāthak failed to notice that the Calcutta edition of Harṣacarita reads the passage quite differently (omitting all reference to वृत्ति). Vide Annals of B. O. R. I. vol. XII. where at p. 385 he says that जयादित्य died about 661 A. D. and न्यासकार flourished about 700 A. D. Vide also J. B. B. R. A. S. vol. 23 at pp. 248, 389 and I. A. vol. 41 pp. 19-31.

(v) I was the first to point out a passage from हर्षचरित of बाण 'प्रसन्नवृत्तयो गृहीतवाक्याः कृतगुरुपदन्यासाः न्यायवादिनः सुकृतसंग्रहाभ्यासगुरवो...लोक इव व्याकरणेपि' (III. para 5) and stated that Bāṇa knew both काशिकावृत्ति and न्यास. But I had not noticed that the हर्षचरित as printed in Calcutta in 1876 by Jivananda read the passage[1] as प्रसन्नप्रवृत्तयो गृहीतवाक्याः कृतगुरून्यासाः...सुकृतसंगृहीताभ्यासगुरवः. Therefore, the passage as printed in the Nirn. edition is of doubtful authenticity and must be left out of account in settling the date of the न्यास. It may have been an interpolation. It is rather strange that the editor of the न्यास understands (p. 25 Intro.) that what भामह meant was that the learned people and न्यासकार both condemned the use of the compound of a noun in तृच् with another and that a poet therefore should follow them. This interpretation is against the whole drift of Bhāmaha's words and particularly loses sight of the word 'मात्रेण'.

We may set out the chronology of some authors mentioned in the above discussion in a chain as follows: भारवि (about

1. The Intro. to काशिका-विवरणपञ्जिका (or न्यास) printed in 1913-16 at Rajshahi cites on p. 24 the हर्षचरित passage as noted above.

580-590)—भर्तृहरि[1] author of वाक्यपदीय (died about 650 A. D.)—जयादित्य author of काशिका (died 661 A. D.)—दण्डिन् (about 660-680)—न्यास of जिनेन्द्रबुद्धि (about 700)—भामह (about 725-750)—माघ (who in शिशुपालवध II. 112 mentions वृत्ति and न्यास) about 750 —नृपतुङ्ग, who names माघ in कविराजमार्ग I. 31, about 825-850.

(w) Attempts are made to fix the age of both भामह and दण्डी by reference to parallel passages from early writers and it is argued that they are later than those poets. Unless the very words are quoted I am not at all disposed to attach weight to parallelism of thought. There is no monopoly in the realm of thought as was observed by the ध्वनिकारिका (IV. 11. 'संवादास्तु भवन्त्येव बाहुल्येन सुमेधसाम्।') p. 306. It is said that दण्डी's (I. 45) 'इन्दोरिन्दीवरद्युति। लक्ष्म लक्ष्मीं तनोतीति प्रतीतिसुभगं वचः॥' is taken from the शाकुन्तल I. Similarly 'प्रभामात्रं हि तरलं दृश्यते न तदाश्रयः' (काव्या. II. 129) may be said to be a reminiscence of 'न प्रभातरलं ज्योतिरुदेति वसुधातलात्' (शाकुन्तल I). So also काव्या. II 286 is similar to verses in the कुमार॰ and रघु॰; and the words (अरत्नालोकसंहार्यमवार्यं सूर्यरश्मिभिः। दृष्टिरोधकरं यूनां यौवनप्रभवं तमः॥' (काव्या. II. 197) are supposed to have been suggested by बाण's words 'केवलं च निसर्गत एवाभानुभेद्यमरत्नालोकोच्छेद्यमप्रदीपप्रभापनेयमतिगहनं तमो यौवनप्रभवम्' (कादम्बरी, para 103 of my edition).

Prof. Pathak (I. A. vol. 41 for 1912 at p. 237) thinks that Daṇḍin's disquisition on the three kinds of कर्म (निर्वर्त्य, विकार्य and प्राप्य in काव्या. II. 240-241) is borrowed from the वाक्यपदीय. Supposing for argument that the वाक्यपदीय was the first to make this distinction, this argument is not worth anything. According to Itsing's rather confused statements (Dr. Takakusu p. 180) the author of the वाक्यपदीय died about 650 A.D. The काशिका on पा. IV. 3. 88 appears to refer to it as शब्दार्थसम्बन्धीयप्रकरणं वाक्यपदीयम्. So दण्डी, who, we have seen, flourished about 660-680 might have borrowed from the वाक्यपदीय.

In the words 'नासिक्यमध्या परितश्चतुर्वर्णविभूषिता। अस्ति काचित्पुरी यस्यामष्टवर्णाह्वया नृपाः॥' (काव्या. III. 112, an example of प्रहेलिका called संख्याता) the com. तरुणवाचस्पति sees a reference to काञ्ची and to the Pallavas. In another place Daṇḍin refers to a king

1. I-tsing (tr. by Takakusu p. 180) states that it was forty years since his death. The काशिका on पा. I. 3. 23 quotes from Bhāravi's किरातार्जुनीय the quarter संशय्य कर्णादिषु तिष्ठते यः (III. 14).

राजवर्म (रातवर्म according to some commentators), who had a vision of the Deity (II. 279). Prof. R. Narasimhachar (I. A. 1912 p. 90-92) and Prof. Belvalkar (notes pp. 175-178 on the काव्या० II. 279 and III. 112) regard राजवर्मा to be a पल्लव, putting the two verses together and identify him with नरसिंहवर्म II or राजसिंहवर्म (690-715 A.D.) and thus place दण्डी at the end of the 7th century. But this is a risky effort. Whether राजवर्मा or रातवर्मा (Dr. Belvalkar reads in काव्यादर्श II. 279 इति साक्षात्कृते देवे राज्ञो यद्रातवर्मणः) was a पल्लव we do not know. On the contrary the commentary श्रुतानुपालिनी says that he was a king of केरल.[1] राजवर्मा is a very general name. Bearing in mind that, if we rely on the अवन्तिसुन्दरीकथा, Daṇḍin was an inhabitant of काञ्ची and was at the पल्लव court, we may accept the view of the majority of commentators that the verse नासिक्यमध्या refers to काञ्ची and the पल्लवः. But we cannot accept as certain the identity of राजवर्म or रातवर्म with any पल्लव king who does not exactly bear that name.

Some think that the verses of भामह (I. 42-44 अयुक्तिमद्यथा दूता जलभृन्मारुतेन्दवः (?मारुतेन्दवः)। तथा भ्रमरहारीतचक्रवाकशुकादयः। अवाचो व्यक्तवाचश्च दूरदेशविचारिणः। कथं दूत्यं प्रपद्येरन्निति युक्त्या न युज्यते ॥) यदि चोत्कण्ठया यत्तदुन्मत्त इव भाषते। तथा भवतु भूम्नेदं सुमेधोभिः प्रयुज्यते ॥ contain a covert attack on or reference to the मेघदूत. Mr. T. Gaṇapati Śāstri, who has his own axe to grind as will be seen later on, vehemently protests against this theory (Intro. to स्वप्न० 1916 p. 7) and says that कालिदास in his fine verse (धूमज्योतिःसलिलमरुतां) condescends to administer a gentle rebuke to the extreme theorist भामह.

In another part of his work भामह refers to the story of वत्सेश (उदयन) and delivers a spirited attack against some poet or poets who so narrated Udayana's story as to run counter to the dictates of śāstra and worldly experience. 'अन्तर्योधशताकीर्णं सालङ्कायननेत्रकम्। तथाविधं गजच्छद्म नाज्ञासीत् स स्वभूगतम् ॥ यदि वोपेक्षितं तस्य सचिवैः स्वार्थसिद्धये। अहो नु मन्दिमा तेषां भक्तिर्वा नास्ति भर्तरि ॥ शरा दृढधनुर्मुक्ता मन्युमद्भिररातिभिः। मर्माणि परिहृत्यास्य पतिष्यन्तीति कानुमा ॥ हतोऽनेनमम

1. The words of the श्रुतानुपालिनी (Govt. collection of mss. at B. O. R. I. Cat vol. XII. No. 125 p. 137) are: केरलवंशाख्ये काव्ये रातवर्मणः इति रातवर्मा नाम केरलानामधिपतिरत्यन्तशिवभक्तः सोपि दिग्विजयवशेन कैलासं प्राप्तः पाशुपतमन्त्रेण पशुपतिं त्र्यम्बकमाराध्य दृष्टवान्, तदामुं श्लोकं प्रीतिप्रकाशनायोक्तवान्.

भ्राता मम पुत्रः पिता मम । मातुलो भागिनेयश्च रुषा संरब्धचेतसः ॥ अस्यन्तो विविधान्याजावायुधान्यपराधिनम् । एकाकिनमरण्यान्यां न हन्युर्बहवः कथम् ॥ नमोस्तु तेभ्यो विद्वद्भ्यो येऽभिप्रायं कवेरिमम् । शास्त्रलोकावपास्यैवं नयन्ति नयवेदिनः ॥ सचेतसो वनेभस्य चर्मणा निर्मितस्य च । अन्तरं वेद बालोपि कष्टं किं नु कथं नु तत् ॥' IV. 41-47). Mr. Gaṇapati Śāstri thinks that this is an attack against the प्रतिज्ञायौगन्धरायण of भास. His theory is that भामह preceded कालिदास and followed भास and he relies upon the fact that in the speech of हंसक (I Act p. 13) the words 'अय्येण मम भादा हदो अय्येण मम पिदा अय्येण मम सुदो मम वअस्सत्ति अण्णाहा भट्टिणो वअण्णअन्ता .etc.' are almost the same as the words 'हतोनेन मम भ्राता &c' (from भामह). This looks a plausible theory at first sight; but on closer examination it will be found that it is based on a very weak foundation. Several points in the passage from भामह have escaped the learned Śāstri's vigilance.

For want of space, all the points cannot be set out here. But the most important thing to note is that in the प्रतिज्ञा० उदयन is accompanied by *twenty* foot-soldiers who are all killed in the ambush except हंसक; while भामह uses the words एकाकिनं in IV. 44. Besides, the cries of the attacking party are not identical in both. In the प्रतिज्ञाo there is no reference to मातुल and भागिनेय which occur in भामह's work. It appears to me that the words of भामह 'नमोस्तु तेभ्यो &'c. amount to this that some poet first narrated the story of उदयन and then *others* (referred to as विद्वद्भ्यः) adapted (नयन्ति) the story for their own purposes (in a *mahākāvya* or drama), wherein they made the king unable to distinguish between a real elephant and a sham one and made him start on an adventure single-handed. Therefore, it seems that the original story is probably that of the बृहत्कथा (referred to as कवेः) and भामह is criticizing some drama or poem based thereon. In the बृहत्कथामञ्जरी (II. 2) where this adventure of उदयन is narrated, we are told that उदयन started alone with his वीणा (गजेन्द्रबन्धकुशलो विवेशैको महद्वनम् । verse 34) and the author क्षेमेन्द्र makes the sage reflection 'प्रायेण व्यसनासक्तिर्मोहाय महतामपि.' This is the real purport of the story to which probably भामह refers in the words (कवेरभिप्रायमिमम्). The कथासरित्सागर gives more details. But there also we have these statements that उदयन's detectives reported to him the discovery of a wonderful elephant (taking it to be real), that he entered the forest without his army (चारमात्रसहायस्तु... विवेश महाटवीम् II. 4. 15) and that he approached the elephant alone (एकाकी वादयन्वीणां, verse 17). Both the बृहत्कथामञ्जरी and the कथा० profess to be based upon the बृहत्कथा of गुणाढ्य. Therefore there is no force in saying that भामह refers to प्रतिज्ञा०, when besides the बृहत्कथा, there were about a dozen dramas and poems on the उदयन *saga* and when there are important discrepancies.

Mr. Trivedi relies upon the close resemblance between भट्टि 22. 34 (व्याख्यागम्यमिदं काव्यमुत्सवः सुधियामलम् । हता दुर्मेधसश्चास्मिन् विद्वत्प्रियतया मया ॥) and भामह II. 20 (काव्यान्यपि यदीमानि व्याख्यागम्यानि शास्त्रवत् । उत्सवः सुधियामेव हन्त दुर्मेधसो हताः ॥) for the latter's priority. Bhatti's verse has been misunderstood. This does not contain a boast. The Grammar of पाणिनि is difficult, भट्टि wrote the poem to illustrate it and thought that his work would be difficult and would require elucidation. To him learned men were dear. He would be satisfied if the learned appreciated, but he regrets that persons not clever enough to understand grammar would be disappointed. The words of भामह (in II. 20) refer to प्रहेलिकाs (mentioned in III. 19) and assert that they would not be real poetry ond would disappoint ignorant men, though they may give pleasure to the scholars. Though there is resemblance in the words, the purport is different. Further, भामह also says that a महाकाव्य should not be अतिव्याख्येय (I. 20). Besides, the two verses standing by themselves would rather suggest that भामह criticizes भट्टि. Moreover, we have already seen that Bhaṭṭi flourished between 590-650 A.D. and cannot be placed later than 650 A. D., while भामह's mention of the न्यास places him after 700. So it is भामह who attacks भट्टि. Dr. H. R. Divekar held, in J. R. A. S. 1929 pp. 825-842, that Bhāmaha preceded both Bhaṭṭi and धर्मकीर्ति. But the detailed discussion in the above pages will show that he is quite wrong.

(x) There were two points in connection with Bhāmaha's date which so far as I was aware had not been relied upon by any Indian scholar before I wrote thereon. The first is as follows : In the ध्वन्यालोक (4th उद्योत) it is expressly asserted that the same idea, though already expressed by one poet, appears new and charming when put in a suggestive garb by another poet and among several instances (pp. 296-7) occurs the following "तथा विवक्षितान्यपरवाच्यस्यैव शब्दशक्त्युद्भवानुरणनरूपव्यङ्ग्यप्रकारसमाश्रयेण नवत्वम् । यथा 'धरणीधारणायाधुना त्वं शेषः' (हर्षचरित IV. para 15 of my edition) इत्यादौ 'शेषो हिमगिरिस्त्वं च महान्तो गुरवः स्थिराः । यदलङ्घितमर्यादाश्चलन्तीं बिभ्रते क्षितिम् ॥' (भामह III. 28) इत्यादिषु सत्स्वपि तस्यैवार्थशक्त्युद्भवानुरणनरूपव्यङ्ग्यसमाश्रयेण नवत्वम्". In my desire to be fair to the opponents of the theory that Bhāmaha was posterior to Daṇḍin I put forward their possible defence on this question for the first time. But I had indicated my own view in such matters by scouting the idea that Daṇḍin's लक्ष्म लक्ष्मीं तनोतीति cited above under (w) is taken from the शाकुन्तल. I had not, however, stated my position as clearly and emphatically as I could and should have done. The purpose of several verses cited by the ध्वन्यालोक in IV. 2-7 is to show that the underlying idea may be one and the same in several verses; but if the poet has *pratibhā*, he can body forth the same idea in such a striking manner that the product of his imagination appears to be new and distinct from that of another. His object is not to declare that a certain poet is earlier or later than another. On IV. 4 the ध्वन्यालोक (p. 297) cites the verse एवंवादिनि from the कुमारसम्भव (IV. 84) and says that in spite of similar verses such as 'कृते वरकथालापे' the verse of Kālidāsa sheds new charm. No one has proved that the verse कृते वरकथालापे is earlier than कालिदास's. It should further be noticed that almost everywhere on pp. 294-298 the author of the ध्वन्यालोक uses the plural सत्स्वपि. For example, his words on the verse एवंवादिनि are : यथा एवंवादिनि देवर्षौ इत्यादि श्लोकस्य 'कृते वरकथालापे कुमार्यः पुलकोद्गमैः । सूचयन्ति स्पृहामन्तर्लज्जावनताननाः ॥' इत्यादिषु सत्स्वपि अर्थशक्त्युद्भवानुरणनरूपव्यङ्ग्यस्य कविप्रौढोक्तिनिर्मितशरीरत्वेन नवत्वम् (p. 297). These words show that he has several verses in mind that are as charming and striking as एवंवादिनि, but he does not mean that they were all composed prior to Kālidāsa's verse. Besides, there is another important consideration. The verse 'वाणिअअ हत्थिदन्ता occurs in हाल's गाथासप्तशती (Weber's ed. p. 500 verse 668) and is cited on p. 297 of ध्वन्या० and is said to have ideas similar to the verse करिणीवेहव्वकरो० (and others). But करिणीवेहव्वकरो itself occurs in गाथासप्तशती with the reading गअवहूवेहव्वकरो (गजवधूवैधव्यकरो) as No. 632 on p. 309 of Weber's ed. of 1881) No. question can arise in this case about priority of one verse to another. The same remark holds good in the case of the citations from बाण and भामह and we cannot presume that the

ध्वन्यालोक meant that भामह's verse and other verses (that the author had in mind) were composed before बाण. Supposing for the sake of argumentt hat the ध्वन्यालोक meant that भामह's verse is earlier than a passage from the हर्षचरित, there are obvious replies. बाण flourished about two hundred and fifty years before the ध्वन्यालोक and it is quite possible that the author of ध्वन्या० had no correct chronology about the two authors before him. He was more familiar with भामह who was his contryman and a rhetorician, while बाण hailed from distant Prītikūṭa on to be banks of the Śoṇa river and was only a poet. Besides, we should have to presume, if chronological conclusions were to be drawn, that the ध्वन्यालोक laid down two distinct propositions in the six cases where the words सत्स्वपि are used, viz. (1) that, though certain passages in the works of बाण, कालिदास and others are very similar in ideas to certain verses of भामह yet they possess charm and novelty that make them distinct (and not mere copies of each other) and (2) that one set of verses are later and others earlier. This in the languge of मीमांसा would be the fault of वाक्यभेद.

(y) In the the 5th परिच्छेद Bhāmaha devotes some verses to the elucidation of blemishes resting upon logic and philosophical doctrines. In the first two verses he promises that he would briefly describe such *doṣas* as प्रतिज्ञाहानि, दृष्टान्तहानि, that people of little learning are scared away by śāstra because of its being difficult and that in order to induce such people to look at śāstra he is going to say a little about logic. Then comes the verse स्वादुकाव्य० (quoted above on p. 80). Then he avers 'there is no word, nor sentence, nor logical reasoning nor kalā (art) that may not subserve the purpose of poetry and the poet carries a heavy burden' (न स शब्दो न तद्वाच्यं न स न्यायो न सा कला । जायते यन्न काव्याङ्गमहो भारो महान् कवेः ॥ V. 4).[1] Then he states that the pramāṇas are two, refers to the definitions of प्रत्यक्ष and अनुमान given by some, the meaning of प्रतिज्ञा and faults connected with it, then describes हेतु as त्रिलक्षण (v. 21), defines दृष्टान्त, speaks of जातिस (verse 29 जातयो दूषणाभासाः &c.), of प्रतिज्ञास based on धर्म, अर्थ, काम and क्रोध and of instances where they

1. Compare भरत's नाट्यशास्त्र 21. 122 quoted above on p. 35 n. 2 and रुद्रट's काव्यालङ्कार I. 19. नमिसाधु quotes 'न स शब्दो' (without name). With स्वादुकाव्य० (भामह V. 3) compare रुद्रट 12. 1.

were carried out and where they failed. It is not necessary to pursue this chapter further. I was probably the first Indian to point out that Bhāmaha quotes in this pariccheda the words of दिङ्नाग and probably of धर्मकीर्ति. Great controversies have raged round the question of the works of दिङ्नाग and धर्मकीर्ति and on the question of भामह's relation to them. I cannot here go into these. I shall only mention those works that are relevant for the date of भामह. Those who desire to make a detailed study of भामह 's brief dissertation on logic in relation to other works may read Prof. Pathak in B. O. R. I. vol. 12 pp. 372-387. भामह says 'प्रत्यक्षं कल्पनापोढं ततोऽर्थादिति केचन । कल्पनां नामजात्यादियोजनां प्रतिजानते' ॥' (V. 6). दिङ्नाग, the great Buddhist Logician, defines प्रत्यक्ष as प्रत्यक्षं कल्पनापोढं नामजात्याद्यसंयुतम् ।' (in प्रमाणसमुच्चय chap. I. quoted in Vidyābhuṣaṇa's 'History of the medieval School of Indian Logic', 1909 p. 85 and in History of Indian Logic, 1921 p. 277). अकलङ्कदेव quoted the latter half of the verse as 'असाधारणहेतुत्वादक्षैस्तद्व्यपदिश्यते[1] ।' (vide Prof. Pathak in annals of B. O. R. I. vol. XII. at p. 378). The प्रमाणसमुच्चय and its वृत्ति by दिङ्नाग in its original Sanskrit are lost, but early Tibetan translations are extant. The न्यायबिन्दु (ed. by Peterson in B. I. series, 1889 p. 103) of धर्मकीर्ति defines प्रत्यक्ष and explains it as follows : 'प्रत्यक्षं कल्पनापोढमभ्रान्तम् । अभिलापसंसर्गयोग्यप्रतिभासप्रतीतिः कल्पना तया रहितम् । तिमिराशुभ्रमणनौयानसंक्षोभाद्यनाहितविभ्रमं ज्ञानं प्रत्यक्षम्' ।[2] भामह quotes दिङ्नाग's definition and also explains what दिङ्नाग meant by कल्पना in the latter half viz. 'attributing to a thing a name, a genus and the like.' It appears that दिङ्नाग defined प्रत्यक्ष as कल्पनापोढ and धर्मकीर्ति added अभ्रान्तं to that definition. In the न्यायप्रवेश, which according to the Tibetan tradition is a work of दिङ्नाग and according to the Chinese tradition is a work of शङ्करस्वामिन् pupil of दिङ्नाग, the word अभ्रान्तं is absent. We may assume for this discussion that भामह is referring to the प्रमाणसमुच्चय of दिङ्नाग alone and not to

1. The न्यायप्रवेशवृत्ति (ed. by Prof. Dhruva in G. O. S. p. 35) also cites the latter half असाधारण...दिश्यते.

2. The न्यायबिन्दुटीका explains 'कल्पनाया अपोढमपेतं कल्पनापोढम् । कल्पनास्वभावरहितमित्यर्थः । अभ्रान्तमर्थक्रियाक्षमे वस्तुरूपेऽविपर्यस्तमुच्यते । p. 8 (B. I. series). The न्यायप्रवेश (p. 7 G. O. S. ed.) has तत्र प्रत्यक्षं कल्पनापोढं यज्ज्ञानमर्थे यथा रूपादौ नामजात्यादिकल्पनारहितम् on which हरिभद्र's वृत्ति (p. 35) is नामकल्पना यथा डित्थ इति जातिकल्पना यथा गौरिति'.

any other work. ततोर्थात् refers to another definition of प्रत्यक्ष given by वसुबन्धु. The न्यायवार्तिक of उद्द्योतकर (B. I. ed. 1887 p. 42) states 'अपरे पुनर्वर्णयन्ति ततोर्थाद्विज्ञानं प्रत्यक्षमिति'. On this the न्यायवार्तिकतात्पर्यटीका of वाचस्पति (who is deemed to have written his न्यायसूचिनिबन्ध in 841 A. D. and who composed authoritative works on many śāstras) says 'वासबन्धवं तावत्प्रत्यक्षलक्षणं विकल्पयितुमुपन्यस्यति अपरे पुनरिति ।' (p. 150). The न्यायवार्तिक of उद्योतकर again states (p. 44) 'अपरे तु मन्यन्ते प्रत्यक्षं कल्पनापोढमिति । अथ केयं कल्पना । नामजातियोजनेति । यत्किल न नाम्नाभिधीयते न जात्यादिभिर्व्यपदिश्यते ।'. On this the न्यायवार्तिकतात्पर्यटीका (p. 153 of the Kashi S. Series संवत् 1982) remarks संप्रति दिङ्नागस्य लक्षणमुपन्यस्यति अपरे इति । दूषयितुं कल्पनास्वरूपं पृच्छति अथ केयमिति । लक्षणवादिन उत्तरं नामेति ।'. लक्षणवादिन् is दिङ्नाग who defines प्रत्यक्ष as above. From these quotations it is clear that most eminent and early logicians like वाचस्पति ascribed the definitions of प्रत्यक्ष given by भामह to दिङ्नाग and वसुबन्धु (ततोर्थात्) respectively. For the present I shall leave धर्मकीर्ति aside. Two of दिङ्नाग's works were translated into Chinese between 557-569 A. D. Vide Dr. Vidyābhuṣan's 'Medieval School' &c. p. 80-81 and History of I. L. p. 272. So दिङ्नाग flourished before 550 and as he was a pupil of वसुबन्धु Dr. Vidyabhuṣan places दिङ्नाग's earlier limit at 480 (*ibid* pp. 81 and 273 respectively). Dr. Randle in 'Indian Logic in early school's (pp. 31-32) says that Vasubandhu's date is uncertain and that दिङ्नाग's date shares the uncertainty attaching to that of his master Vasubandhu and that Diṅgnāga may fall anywhere between 420 and 500 A. D. (ibid p. 27). Therefore भामह's reference to दिङ्नाग does not help any one much. There are certain other *indicia* which have been relied on for saying that भामह refers to धर्मकीर्ति. In V. 5 भामह says 'सत्वादय: प्रमाणाभ्यां प्रत्यक्षमनुमा च ते । असाधारणसामान्यविषयत्वं तयो: किल ॥'. This may be compared with न्यायबिन्दु 'द्विविधं सम्यग्ज्ञानं प्रत्यक्षमनुमानं च ।...तस्य (प्रत्यक्षस्य) विषय: स्वलक्षणम् ।...अन्यत्सामान्यलक्षणं सोनुमानस्य विषय:' (परिच्छेद I. p. 103 Peterson). Similarly, भामह V. 11 (त्रिरूपाल्लिङ्गतो ज्ञानमनुमानं च केचन ।) may be compared with न्यायबिन्दु 'अनुमानं द्विधा स्वार्थं परार्थं च । तत्र स्वार्थं त्रिरूपाल्लिङ्गाद्यदनुमेये ज्ञानं तदनुमानम्' (परिच्छेद II p. 104); so also the words 'दूषणं न्यूनतायुक्ति:' (भामह V. 28) are the same as न्यायबिन्दु (परि० III. p. 118) and 'जातयो दूषणाभासा:' (भामह V. 29) are the same as न्यायबिन्दु 'दूषणाभासास्तु जातय:' (III p. 118). It looks likely that भामह may be quoting from धर्मकीर्ति, though he may not agree with him in some details. No one has found out any work on logic by भामह nor has any quotation been taken by any one from भामह's work as a logician either in Sanskrit, Tibetan or Chinese; while धर्मकीर्ति is regarded as the most eminent among Buddhist logicians, probably equalled only by दिङ्नाग. One may argue that भामह is not necessarily referring to धर्मकीर्ति but to one of his predeoessors; to suggest however (as Mr. Batuknath does in his Intro. to भामह at p. 46) that it may be equally cogent to say that धर्मकीर्ति was indebted to भामह smacks too much of enthusiastic partisanship. Dharmakīrti flourished according to Dr. Vidyabhushan[1] about 635-650 (p. 103 of his History of Medieval Indian logic and of his History of Indian logic pp. 303-305). It may be noted that Yuan Chwan who was in India from 629 to 645 does not mention धर्मकीर्ति, while I-tsing who travelled in India during 671-695 A. D. and composed his work in 691 declares how धर्मकीर्ति made further improvements in Logic (Takakusu's translation p. 182). I-tsing gives three classes of Buddhist *savants* viz. नागार्जुन, देव, अश्वघोष, 'of an early age'; वसुबन्धु, असङ्ग,, संघभद्र, and भवविवेक 'in the middle ages' and जिन, धर्मपाल, धर्मकीर्ति शीलभद्र &c. 'of late years' (Takakusu's tr. p. 181). So धर्मकीर्ति (who was a pupil of धर्मपाल) as said above flourished about 650 or 660. It is not necessary for our purposes to establish positively that भामह refers to धर्मकीर्ति. It has already been shown from other evidence that भामह could not have flourished earlier than 700 A. D. Therefore it is quite possible that he borrows Dharmakīrti's words. The matter may be allowed to rest there.

(z) The date of Daṇḍin can also be arrived at in another manner. शार्ङ्ग० (No. 108), जह्लण (सूक्तिमुक्तावलि p. 47) and other anthologies quote a verse of a poetess विज्जका 'नीलोत्पलदलश्यामां विज्जकां मामजानता । वृथैव दण्डिना प्रोक्तं सर्वशुक्ला सरस्वती ॥'.[2] She quotes in this verse the last *pāda* of the first verse of the काव्यादर्श. धनददेव is quoted in the शार्ङ्ग० (No. 163) as enumerating विज्जा among poetesses. In the verse नीलोत्पल० cited above the word

1. vide Vidyabhushan in J. R. A. S. for 1914 pp. 601-606 and also I. H. Q. XI pp. 1-31 for the relation of उद्योतकर and धर्मकीर्ति.

2. Vide 'Sanskrit Poetesses Vijjā and Morikā' by Dr. J. B. Choudhuri in I. H. Q. vol. XVI pp. 543-560.

अजानता, it may be argued, conveys the idea that Daṇḍin did not know the poetess and that she was not a contemporary of Daṇḍin. But the word may also convey only the idea that Daṇḍin had not seen the complexion of that accomplished lady. If that idea be accepted, she may be deemed to be his contemporary (though probably a younger one). We have to find who this Vidyā or Vijjakā was. For that purpose the verse सरस्वतीव० is helpful. We have two names विज्जिका or विद्या[1] and विजया, both of which cannot be later that 900 A. D. No ancient or medieval author says that there were two different poetesses that flourished almost about the same period. It is possible that the poetess was known as विज्जा and राजशेखर sanskritized the name as विजया, while others sanskritized it as विद्या. Therefore, it is very likely that विज्जका and विजया are the same. If that be conceded, then the verse सरस्वतीव० indicates that विज्जिका was a कार्णाटी (a princess of Karṇāṭaka or a resident thereof) and that she wrote a work or works in the Vaidarbha-mārga rivalling Kālidāsa. No work expressly ascribed to her has yet been found. If the poetess विजया was a princess, then it is probable that she is the same as the famous queen विजय-महादेवी. The Nerur grant (I. A. VII p. 163 of विजयभट्टारिका, queen of महाराजचन्द्रादित्य, eldest son of सत्याश्रय पुलकेशिन् II. and brother of विक्रमादित्य) is referred to *śaka* 581 (659 A. D.). The Kochreṁ plate (I. A. VIII. p. 45) of same date speaks of her as विजयमहादेवी. Thus, if this identity be accepted (as I submit it should be), her grants being dated in 659 A. D., there is confirmation of the date of Daṇḍin as between 660-680 arrived at above (p. 120). Prof. K. C. Chattopadhyaya in I. H. Q. vol. 14 pp. 582-606 (on Kaumudīmahotsava) at p. 604 does not accept my identification of the poetess Vijjā or Vijjakā with the Queen Vijayā on the ground that a reigning queen could not have written the two verses भूपाला: शशिभास्करान्वयभुव: and यश:पुञ्जं देव ascribed to Vijjakā in some anthologies (e. g. in सदुक्तिकर्णामृत). They might be, from a modern scholar's point of view, indecent. But there are several answers. We

1. She is quoted under various names such as विज्जका, विज्जाका, विज्जिका, विज्जाका, विद्या. विद्या is a Sanskritized form of विज्जा or it may be also *vice versa* i. e. the name was विद्या, and विज्जाका, विज्जिका and विज्जका were popular or affectionate names.

should not foist our 20th century notions on a poetess of the 7th or 8th century. Besides, if one tolerates a verse like धन्यासि as Vijjākā's, there is no reason why the two verses mentioned above could not have been composed by the महादेवी. Moreover, the verse भूपाला:[1] is ascribed to मयूर in सुभाषितावलि (No. 2515); and further the plain sense is harmless enough, the sexual suggestion comes in only when we look into the puns on the words. The second verse यशःपुत्रं देव is decent enough from any point of view. On the subject of Vijjākā the following articles may be consulted viz, Dr. Raghavan in Quarterly J. of Mythic Society (Bangalore) vol. 25 at pp. 52-55, Quarterly Journal of Mythic Society vol. 24 pp. 156-159 (by Mr. V. K. Raghavacharyulu), Indian Culture, vol. XI. pp. 86-88. Vide also 'Sanskrit Poetesses' part A by Dr. J. B. Chaudhuri and English translation and Introduction by Dr. Roma Chaudhuri pp. XXXVIII-XLV, where it is pointed out that 29 verses are ascribed to विद्या or विज्जका in the anthologies and that they are composed in very fine language and deal with many topics such as love, seasons, damsels. Dr. Roma Chaudhuri in Intro. to 'Sanskrit Poetesses' part A p. LVIII states that the following verse is traditionally ascribed to विजयाङ्का[2] viz. 'एकोऽभूत्नलिनात्ततश्च पुलिनाद् वल्मीकतश्चापरस्ते सर्वे कवयो भवन्ति गुरवस्तेभ्यो नमस्कुर्महे। अर्वाञ्चो यदि गद्यपद्यरचनैश्चेतश्चमत्कुर्वते तेषां मूर्ध्नि ददामि वामचरणं कर्णाटराजप्रिया ॥.' This verse composed by a Karṇāṭa queen breathes great self-confidence and contempt for most writers other than ब्रह्मा, व्यास

1. The verse is : भूपालाः शशिभास्करान्वयभुवः के नाम नासादिता भर्तारं पुनरेकमेव हि भुवस्त्वामेव मन्यामहे। येनाङ्गं परिमृश्य कुन्तलमपाकृष्य व्युदस्यायतं चोलं प्राप्य च मध्यदेशमचिरात्काञ्च्यां करः पातितः ॥. The words अङ्ग, कुन्तल, चोल, मध्यदेश and काञ्ची primarily refer to countries, but by श्लेष sporting with a woman is suggested. It is ascribed to विद्या in सदुक्तिकर्णामृत III. 15. 1 p. 196 (Punjab Oriental Series, 1933). Compare for almost the same double-meaning words रुद्रटकाव्यालंकार X. 10.

2. Dr. Raghavan in Journal of Mythic Society, vol. 25 at p. 55 and Miss Sakuntala Rao in 'Indian Culture' vol. XI p. 86 also cite the verse एकोऽभूत्नलिनात् as विजयाङ्का's, but none of them points out the anthology or source in which it is so ascribed. Hardly any verse is found ascribed to विजया or विजयाङ्का in anthologies. This is a very significant circumstance.

and वाल्मीकि. So she must have been a great poet indeed. It is विज्जा alone that has many charming verses to her credit. Therefore, it may quite plausibly be argued that the कार्णाटीविजयाङ्का (or विजया) and विज्जा are identical, that she was a queen of कर्णाट and that she is to be identified with the विजयमहादेवी of the grants mentioned above p. (129). One very beautiful verse attributed to her in शार्ङ्ग० (No. 582) where the sound is an echo to the sense may be quoted here viz. the one that refers to corn-threshing by young women : 'विलासमसृणोल्लसन्मुसललोलदोःकन्दली-परस्परपरिस्खलद्वलयनिःस्वनोद्बन्धुराः । लसन्ति कलहुंकृतिप्रसभकम्पितोरः—स्थलत्रुटद्गमकसङ्कुलाः कलमकण्डनीगीतयः ॥'[1] (शार्ङ्ग०p. 94 and सरस्वतीकण्ठाभरण V. p. 602). She is the greatest of poetesses.

A further question about विज्जा or विज्जका arises whether she is the author of the drama कौमुदीमहोत्सव, which Mr. R. Kavi published some years ago. The name of the author is not fully preserved but in the single ms. on which Mr. Kavi bases his edition we have the following passage in the prologue 'यत्तदस्यैव राज्ञः समतीतचरितमधिकृत्य...कया निबद्धं नाटकम्'. This indicates that the name of the writer ended in का and that the writer was a lady. Mr. Kavi holds that the writer was विज्जिका. Until other mss. are found no final opinion can be given. But one verse in the drama (Act IV. 19) is rather striking viz. जयति प्रथमं विजया जयन्ति देवाः स्वयं महादेवः । श्रीमन्तौ भगवन्तावनन्तनारायणौ जयतः ॥'. The plain meaning here is that विजया, the goddess presiding over the Kaumudi festival in Śarad season, is glorious, but it is possible that there is a veiled reference to the author विजया (or विज्जिका). It is not necessary for our purposes to go into this question. For the controversies about the authenticity, the date and authorship of the कौमुदीमहोत्सव, vide Annals of B. O. R. I. vol. XII pp. 50-55, Festschrift Moriz Winternitz pp. 382-406 (Prof. K. C. Chattopadhyaya), J. Andhra H. R. S. vol. VI pp. 139-141 (by Mr. Raghavacharyulu) and vol. XI. pp. 63-67 (Dr. D. C. Sircar), Indian Culture, vol. XI. p. 87 ff., I. H. Q. 14 pp. 582-606, Journal of Bombay University vol. X. pp. 141-147 (Prof. Mankad on

1. In the सदुक्तिकर्णामृत II. 18. 3 p. 145, this verse is ascribed to योगेश्वर, while शार्ङ्गधर (No. 582) ascribes it to विज्जका and the सरस्वतीकण्ठाभरण does not mention the name of the author.

मुद्राराक्षस and कौमुदीमहोत्सव, who supports Jayaswal's views). Numerous verses are ascribed to this विज्जका in the anthologies, two of which दृष्टिं हे प्रतिवेशिनि (No. 500 कवीन्द्र०) and धन्यासि या कथयसि (298 कवीन्द्र०) ascribed to विद्या are very frequently quoted in *alaṅkāra* works. Vide Intro. to कवीन्द्रवचनसमुच्चय edited by Dr. Thomas (pp. 106-108) for all verses attributed to her. Both of them are quoted in मम्मट's शब्दव्यापारविचार and the second in the काव्यप्रकाश (IV). The verse दृष्टिं हे प्रतिवेशिनि occurs in the दशरूपावलोक (II. 21) and in मुकुलभट्ट's अभिधावृत्तिमातृका (p. 12). मुकुल as will be shown later on wrote about 900-925 A. D. So विज्जका could not have flourished later than 850 A. D. and Daṇḍin is earlier still. राजशेखर, as quoted in the सूक्तिमुक्तावलि of जह्लण, speaks of a Canarese poetess 'सरस्वतीव कार्णाटी विजयाङ्का जयत्यसौ । या विदर्भगिरां वासः कालिदासादनन्तरम् ॥' (*vide* शार्ङ्ग० 184, जह्लण's सुक्तिमुक्तावलि p. 47 verse 93, and in the शृङ्गारप्रकाश without name). The words विजयाङ्का सरस्वतीव means 'she was as if सरस्वती named विजया'. The words may also mean that in her compositions she used the word विजय as a catch-word. For the use of words like अङ्क or अङ्कित, vide verses like the following 'व्यासगिरां निर्यासं सारं विश्वस्य भारतं वन्दे । भूषणतयैव संज्ञां यदङ्कितां भारती वहति ॥'. Since Bhāmaha flourished (as shown above) after 700 A. D. and Daṇḍin about 660-680 A. D. it is not possible to hold that Daṇḍin criticizes भामह. It is possible that भामह may have been a much younger contemporary of Daṇḍin and the bitter sarcasms in which he reveals when criticizing views such as those held by Daṇḍin are explicable more easily on the hypothesis that he is criticizing a far-famed living author and probably was jealous.

Dr. Hooykaas in his paper on 'some arthālaṅkāras in the Bhaṭṭikāvya X' in Turner Presentation volume, at p. 358 n. 1 suggests an argument in favours of my view that Daṇḍin preceded Bhāmaha. Bhaṭṭi X. 63 cites as an example of निदर्शना the verse 'न भवति महिमा विना विपत्तेरवगमदन्निव पश्यतः पयोधिः । अविरतमभवत् क्षयेऽक्षयेऽसौ शिखरिपृथुप्रथितप्रशान्तवीचिः ॥. भामह on III. 33 defines निदर्शना as क्रिययैव विशिष्टस्य तदर्थस्यापि दर्शनात् । ज्ञेया निदर्शना नाम यथेववतिभिर्विना ॥. भामह requires that in निदर्शना the words यथा, इव, वत् must not occur, but इव occur is Bhaṭṭi's example. The काव्यादर्श II. 348 says nothing about यथा or इव. Dr. Hooykaas holds that the writer who vetos the use of certain characteristics must be later than him who says nothing. Some may argue that there is not much in this.

The 6th century had been accepted by many scholars as the date of Daṇḍin. Vide Max Müller (India; what can it teach us; 1st edition p. 332), Weber (H. S. L. p. 232 n), Prof. Macdonell (H. S. L. p. 434) and Col. Jacob (JRAS 1897 p. 284). That date must now be given up in favour of the view that Daṇḍin's literary activity lay between 660-680 A. D.

Among the commentaries on the काव्यादर्श are: (1) the व्याख्या of तरुणवाचस्पति (edited by Prof. Rangacharya), (2) the com. हृदयङ्गमा by an anonymous author (edited by Prof. Rangacharya) on the first two परिच्छेदs only; (3) a टीका called मार्जन by महामहोपाध्याय हरिनाथ, son of विश्वधर and younger brother of केशव (Govt. mss at B. O. R. I. Cat. vol. XII. No. 24, copied in संवत् 1746); (4) काव्यतत्त्वविवेचककौमुदी by कृष्णकिङ्कर तर्कवागीश of गोपालपुर in Bengal (I. O. cat. p. 221); (5) the श्रुतानुपालिनी of वादिघङ्गल (D. C. ms. No. 111 of 1919-24, cat. vol. XII No. 125); (6) वैमल्यविधायिनी by मल्लिनाथ, son of जगन्नाथ; and a few more mentioned by Aufrecht. For तरुणवाचस्पति's date vide above p. 105. हरिनाथ tells us that he wrote a com. on the सरस्वतीकण्ठाभरण called मार्जन (folio 5b in D. C. ms No. 373 of 1895-96). He quotes विश्वकोश, शाश्वतकोश, हारावली and विदग्धमुखमण्डन. There is a com. by विजयानन्द (vide Cat. of Govt. O. mss. at B. O. R. I. vol. XII. No. 123). There is another com. by यामुन (ibid. No. 126) who divides the काव्यादर्श into four परिच्छेदs, the 4th being formed of verses dealing with काव्यदोषs. Recently (in 1957) Prof. Anantlal Thakur of the Mithila Institute has published the काव्यलक्षण of Daṇḍin with a commentary called रत्नश्री by रत्नश्रीज्ञान from Ceylon.

11 The अलङ्कारसारसङ्ग्रह of उद्भट. This work was transliterated by Col. Jacob in JRAS 1897 pp. 829-847. It has been issued by the Nirṇayasāgara Press (1915) with the commentary (called लघुवृत्ति) of प्रतीहारेन्दुराज; and Mr. N. D. Banhatti has edited it for the Bombay Sanskrit Series (1925) with the commentary of प्रतीहारेन्दुराज, an Introduction and notes. Here the references are to the Nirn. Ed. The work of उद्भट is divided into six chapters (called *vargas*) and contains about 79 *kārikās* defining 41 *alaṅkāras* and over 90 illustrations. They are taken, as we are told by the commentor प्रतीहारेन्दुराज, from the author's own work styled कुमारसम्भव 'अनेन ग्रन्थकृता स्वोपरचितकुमारसम्भवैकदेशोऽत्रोदाहरणत्वेनोपन्यस्तः । तत्र पूर्वं दीपकस्योदाहरणानि । तदनु-

सन्धानाविच्छेदायात्र उद्देशकमः परित्यक्तः। उद्देशस्तु तथा न कृतो वृत्तभङ्गभयात्।' (p. 15—p. 16 of B. S. S. ed.). The *alaṅkāras* defined and illustrated are the following (in order); I (वर्ग), पुनरुक्तवदाभास, छेकानुप्रास, अनुप्रास (of 3 kinds, परुषा वृत्ति, उपनागरिका, ग्राम्या or कोमला), लाटानुप्रास, रूपक (four varieties), उपमा, दीपक (आदि, मध्य, अन्त), प्रतिवस्तूपमा; II. आक्षेप, अर्थान्तरन्यास, व्यतिरेक, विभावना, समासोक्ति, अतिशयोक्ति; III यथासंख्य, उत्प्रेक्षा, स्वभावोक्ति; IV प्रेय:, रसवत्, ऊर्जस्वि, पर्यायोक्त, समाहित, उदात्त (of two kinds), श्लिष्ट (of two kinds); V अपह्नुति, विशेषोक्ति, विरोध, तुल्ययोगिता, अप्रस्तुतप्रशंसा, व्याजस्तुति, विदर्शना, उपमेयोपमा, सहोक्ति, सङ्कर (of four kinds), परिवृत्ति; VI. अनन्वय, ससन्देह, संसृष्टि, भाविक, काव्यलिङ्ग, दृष्टान्त. It will be noted that the *alaṅkāras* are enumerated almost in the same order as that of भामह. उद्भट omits a few अलङ्कारs which भामह defined such as यमक, उपमारूपक, उत्प्रेक्षावयव; while he adds a few अलङ्कारs to those that were either defined or alluded to by भामह, viz. पुनरुक्तवदाभास, सङ्कर, काव्यलिङ्ग and दृष्टान्त. It is noteworthy that उद्भट employs the term विदर्शना for निदर्शना (unless it is due to copyist's mistake) and illustrates only one of the two varieties of that figure and his commentator had to cite an illustration of the second variety from भामह "यत्र तु पदार्थसमन्वयउपमानोपमेयभावकल्पनया स्वात्मानमुपपादयति तस्य विदर्शनाभेदस्योदाहरणमुद्भटपुस्तके न दृश्यते तस्य तु भामहोदितमिदमुदाहरणम् (भामह III. 34) 'अयं मन्दद्युतिर्भास्वानस्तं प्रति यियासति। उदयः पतनायेति श्रीमतो बोधयन्नरान्॥' इति" (p. 62 and p. 67 of B. S. S. ed.). The विवेक of तिलक on उद्भट's work also notices that उद्भट's work contains no example of the 2nd kind of विदर्शना (p. 45 G. O. S. ed.).

On comparing उद्भट's definitions with भामह's it will be seen that the definitions of आक्षेप, विभावना, अतिशयोक्ति, यथासंख्य, पर्यायोक्त, अपह्नुति, विरोध, अप्रस्तुतप्रशंसा, सहोक्ति, ससन्देह, अनन्वय are word for word the same in both and the definitions of several other figures such as अनुप्रास, उत्प्रेक्षा, रसवत्, भाविक contain closely similar phraseology. This is probably due to the fact that उद्भट wrote a commentary भामहविवरण or भामहवृत्ति on the काव्यालङ्कार of भामह. प्रतीहारेन्दुराज says (p. 13) "एकदेशवृत्तीत्यत्र हि एकदा अन्यदा ईशः प्रभविष्णुर्वो वाक्यार्थस्तद्वृत्तित्वं रूपकस्याभिमतम्। विशेषोक्तिलक्षणे च भामहविवरणे भट्टोद्भटेन एकदेशशब्द एवं व्याख्यातो यथेहास्माभिर्निरूपितः। तत्र विशेषोक्तिलक्षणं 'एकदेशस्य विगमे या गुणान्तरसंस्तुतिः। विशेषप्रथनायासौ विशेषोक्तिर्मता यथा॥ (भामह III. 23)." The work भामहविवरण seems to have been an elaborate one and it appears that the अलङ्कारसारसंग्रह was only a summary of that work, as its very name indicates. Later writers very frequently refer to the भामहविवरण of उद्भट; e. g. the

लोचन (ध्व. p. 12) says "भामहोक्तं 'शब्दश्छन्दोभिधानार्थं' (भामह I. 9.) इत्यभिधानस्य शब्दाद्भेदं व्याख्यातुं भट्टोद्भटो बभाषे शब्दानामभिधानमभिधाव्यापारो मुख्यो गुणवृत्तिश्च इति'; लोचन p. 47 'यत्तु विवरणकृद् दीपकस्य सर्वत्रोपमान्वयोस्तीति बहुनोदाहरणप्रपञ्चेन विचारितवांस्तदनुपयोगि नितरां सप्रतिक्षेपं च'; on the verse 'आहूतोपि सहायैरेमीत्युक्त्वा विमुक्तनिद्रोपि। गन्तुमना अपि पथिकः सङ्कोचं नैव शिथिलयति' (quoted in ध्व० p. 45 as an example of अनुक्तनिमित्ता विशेषोक्ति) the लोचन remarks 'शीतकृता खल्वार्तिरत्र निमित्तमिति भट्टोद्भटः'. प्रतीहारेन्दुराज (p. 49—p. 53 of B. S. S. ed.) seems to be quoting from the भामहविवरण when he says "एषां च शृङ्गारादीनां नवानां रसानां स्वशब्दादिभिः पञ्चभिरवगतिर्भवति। यदुक्तं भट्टोद्भटेन 'पञ्चरूपा रसाः' इति। तत्र स्वशब्दाः शृङ्गारादेर्वाचकाः शृङ्गारादयः शब्दाः।" (this last sentence is प्रतीहारेन्दुराज's comment on the words 'स्वशब्दस्थायिसञ्चारिविभावाभिनयास्पदम्' of the अलङ्कारसारसंग्रह 4th वर्ग); हेमचन्द्र (in विवेक p. 110) says "एतेन 'रसवद्दर्शितस्पष्टशृङ्गारादिरसोदयम्। स्वशब्द...स्पदम्॥' इत्येतद्व्याख्यानावसरे यद्भट्टोद्भटेन 'पञ्चरूपा रसाः' इत्युपक्रम्य 'स्वशब्दाः शृङ्गारादेर्वाचकाः शृङ्गारादयः शब्दाः' इत्युक्तं तत्प्रतिक्षिप्तम्"). It appears from this that हेमचन्द्र simply quotes the words of प्रतीहारेन्दुराज, had not the भामहविवरण before him and confounds the verse रसव...स्पदं, which is really उद्भट's own definition, with भामह's definition of रसवत्, which is simply 'रसवद्दर्शितस्पष्टशृङ्गारादिरसं यथा' III. 6). The काव्यप्रकाशसङ्केत of माणिक्यचन्द्र (p. 269 Mysore ed.) falls into the same confusion and savs 'एतेन शृङ्गाराद्याः शब्दाः शृङ्गारादेर्वाचका इत्युद्भटोक्तं निरस्तम्;' so also सोमेश्वर (folio 75 a) says एतेन रसवद्...स्पदमित्यस्य व्याख्यायां पञ्चरूपा रसा इत्युपक्रम्य तत्र स्वशब्दाः शृङ्गारादयः शृङ्गारादेर्वाचका इति भट्टोद्भटोक्तं निरस्तम्'; हेमचन्द्र (विवेक p. 17) "एतावता शौर्यादिसदृशा गुणाः केयूरादितुल्या अलङ्कारा इति विवेकमुक्त्वा संयोगसमवायाभ्यां शौर्यादीनामस्ति भेदः, इह तूभयेषां समवायेन स्थितिरित्यभिधाय 'तस्माद्गड्डरिकाप्रवाहेण गुणालङ्कारभेदः' इति भामहविवरणे यद्भटोद्भट्टोभ्यधात् तन्निरस्तम्;" माणिक्यचन्द्र (सङ्केत p. 289, Mysore ed.) says the same 'शब्दार्थालङ्काराणां गुणवत्समवायेन स्थितिरिति भामहवृत्तौ भट्टोद्भटेन भणनमसत्' and so does सोमेश्वर (folio 88 a); समुद्रबन्ध (on the सर्वस्व p. 89) says उद्भटेन च काव्यालङ्कारविवृतौ सत्कवित्वविरहिताया विदग्धताया अस्थैर्यस्याशोभनस्य च प्रतिपादनाय निदर्शनद्वयमिति वदता का श्रीरित्यस्य श्रीरस्थिरेत्यर्थोभिहितः'.

उद्भट exercised a profound influence over the Alankāra-śāstra. He eclipsed भामह and it is probably owing to his great fame that भामह's work remained in the background and was rarely to be had up till a few years ago. He is always quoted with respect by his successors, even when they differ from him. He is the foremost representative of the Alankāra school and his name is associated with several doctrines in the Alaṅkāraśāstra. In several important points he differs from भामह. For example, प्रतीहारेन्दुराज says: (p. 1) 'भामहो हि ग्राम्योपनागरिकावृत्तिभेदेन द्विप्रकारमेवानुप्रासं व्याख्यातवान् । तथा रूपकस्य ये चत्वारो भेदा वक्ष्यन्ते तन्मध्यादाद्यमेव भेदद्वितयं प्रादर्शयत् ।'; उद्भट speaks of three kinds of अनुप्रास and four varieties of रूपक; "भामहो हि तत्सहोक्त्युपमाहेतुनिर्देशात्त्रिविधं यथा' (भामह 3. 17) इति श्लिष्टस्य त्रैविध्यमाह" (प्रतीहारेन्दु. p. 47, while उद्भट divides श्लेष into two varieties); the लोचन says 'भामहेन हि गुरुदेवनृपतिपुत्रविषयप्रीतिवर्णनं प्रेयोलङ्कार इत्युक्तं... उद्भटमते हि भावालङ्कार एव प्रेय इत्युक्तः' (p. 87); भामह does not speak of three वृत्तिs viz परुषा, ग्राम्या and उपनागरिका, while उद्भट does (*vide* लोचन p. 6). For respect shown to उद्भट *vide* ध्व. p. 131 (तत्रभवद्भिरुद्भटादिभिः); अलङ्कारसर्वस्व) p. 3 (इह तावद्भामहोद्भटप्रभृतयश्चिरन्तनालङ्कारकाराः); व्यक्तिविवेकटीका (p. 3) 'इह हि चिरन्तनैरलङ्कारतन्त्रप्रजापतिभिर्भट्टोद्भटप्रभृतिभिः शब्दार्थधर्मा एवालङ्काराः प्रतिपादिता नाभिधाधर्माः'. It is not necessary to refer to the numerous passages where उद्भट is quoted or referred to by later writers.

Some of the doctrines that are peculiar to उद्भट are : (I) 'अर्थभेदेन तावच्छब्दा भिद्यन्ते इति भट्टोद्भटस्य सिद्धान्तः' प्रतीहारेन्दु० (p. 55.); (II) श्लेष is of two kinds, शब्दश्लेष and अर्थश्लेष and both are अर्थालङ्कारs. This view is severely criticized by मम्मट (9th उल्लास) 'शब्दश्लेष इति चोच्यते, अर्थालङ्कारमध्ये च लक्ष्यते इति कोयं नयः' (p. 527 Vā.). (III) श्लेष is stronger than other figures and that wherever other figures are combined with it, श्लेष is the principal figure and the apprehension of other figures is slight and dispelled by श्लेष, 'अलङ्कारान्तरगतां प्रतिभां जनयत्पदैः' as उद्भट says in (IV p. 54, p. 58 of B. S. S. ed.). The ध्व. (p. 116) refers to this view. मम्मट criticizes this view also. (IV) The काव्यमीमांसा (of राज०) says 'तस्य (वाक्यस्य) च त्रिधाभिधाव्यापार इति औद्भटाः.' (V) अर्थ is of two kinds 'किन्तु द्विरूप एवासौ विचारितसुस्थोऽविचारितरमणीयः । तयोः पूर्वमाश्रितानि शास्त्राणि तदुत्तरं काव्यानीत्यौद्भटाः' (काव्यमीमांसा p. 44); a somewhat similar view is attributed to उद्भट in the व्यक्तिविवेकटीका (p. 4) 'शास्त्रेतिहासवैलक्षण्यं तु काव्यस्य शब्दार्थवैशिष्ट्यादेव नाभिधावैशिष्ट्यादिति भट्टोद्भटादीनां सिद्धान्तः.' (VI) 'सङ्घटनाया धर्मो गुणा इति भट्टोद्भटादयः' लोचन p. 165. (VII) The later divisions of Upamā based upon grammatical considerations as in the काव्यप्रकाश seem to have been elaborated by उद्भट (वर्ग I q. in notes to साहित्यदर्पण p. 105). (VIII) उद्भट holds that रसs like शृङ्गार are manifested by their being expressly mentioned in so many words and in four other ways 'रसवत्...स्वशब्दस्थायिसञ्चारिविभावाभिनयास्पदम्', while, acc. to मम्मट, to mention a rasa like शृङ्गार by the use of the word शृङ्गार is a blemish (दोष).

Vide काव्यप्र. VII. 12 and 14 'व्यभिचारिरसस्थायिभावानां शब्दवाच्यता... रसे दोषाः स्युरीदृशाः' ॥.

Col. Jacob (JRAS. 1897 p. 847) thought that the verse रसाद्यधिष्ठितं काव्यं जीवद्रूपतया यतः । कथ्यते तद्रसादीनां काव्यात्मत्वं व्यवस्थितम् ॥' was Udbhaṭa's and that therefore Udbhaṭa subscribed to the view that *rasa* was the soul of poetry. But several circumstances militate against this view. The verse in question is introduced by प्रतीहारेन्दुराज with the words तदाहुः (p. 77, p. 83 of B. S. S. ed.) and therefore it is merely a quotation from some other writer that preceded प्रतीहारेन्दुराज. Besides, that verse would break the usual order followed by Udbhaṭa. That verse occurs in the comment on काव्यलिङ्ग. After defining काव्यलिङ्ग we naturally expect an illustration of it, which is the verse 'छायेयं तव शेषाङ्गकान्तेः किञ्चिदनुज्ज्वला । विभूषाघटनादेशान्दर्शयन्ती दुनोति माम् ॥', while, if Col. Jacob be followed, the verse रसाद्यधिष्ठितं काव्यं would be abruptly thrust between the definition of काव्यलिङ्ग and its example. Moreover, the view that उद्भट approved of *rasa* as the soul of poetry would be opposed to his own definition of रसवद् and the opinion of the अलङ्कारसर्वस्व (p. 9) 'उद्भटादिभिस्तु गुणालङ्काराणां प्रायशः साम्यमेव सूचितम् ।... तदेवमलङ्कारा एव काव्ये प्रधानमिति प्राच्यानां मतम्'. The printed edition (Nirn. ed. on p. 42) puts the verse तद्द्विगुणं त्रिगुणं वा in bold type, as if it were a कारिका of उद्भट; but it is really a verse of रुद्रट (VII. 35).

The कुमारसम्भव of उद्भट from which the example of Alaṅkāras are cited seems to have been a poem resembling the famous *mahākāvya* of कालिदास. There is a close correspondence between the two works not only in phrases and ideas, but even in incidents. For example, compare 'प्रच्छन्ना शस्यते वृत्तिः स्त्रीणां भावपरीक्षणे । प्रतस्थे धूर्जटिरतस्तनु स्वीकृत्य वाटवीम् ॥' उद्भट II. 10 with कुमार० V. 33 'विवेश कश्चिज्जटिलस्तपोवनं etc; 'अपश्यच्चातिकष्टानि तप्यमानां तपांस्युमाम् । असम्भाव्यपतीच्छानां कन्यानां का परा गतिः ॥' उद्भट II. 12 with कुमार० V. 2 'इयेष...पतिश्च तादृशः'; 'शीर्णपर्णाम्बुवाताशकष्टेपि तपसि स्थिताम्' उद्भट II. 17 with कुमार. V. 28 'स्वयं विशीर्णद्रुमपर्णवृत्तिता' etc.' It has already been stated above (pp. 48-49) that उद्भट wrote a commentary on the नाट्यशास्त्र of भरत.

The date of Udbhaṭa does not present much difficulty. He wrote a commentary on the work of Bhāmaha who, we have seen, flourished about or a little later than 700 A. D. Therefore he cannot be earlier than about 750 A. D. The author of the ध्वन्यालोक (latter half of 9th century) mentions him several times with respect (pp. 116, 131). Therefore, Udbhaṭa is earlier than 850 A. D. The Kashmirian tradition identifies him with a learned man called उद्भट who was the सभापति at the court of Jayāpīḍa, king of Kashmir (779-813 A. D.). The राजतरङ्गिणी says 'विद्वान्दीनारलक्षेण प्रत्यहं कृतवेतनः। भट्टोभूदुद्भटस्तस्य भूमिभर्तुः सभापतिः ॥ IV. 495'. If the tradition is accepted उद्भट must have flourished about 800 A. D. Even if the tradition be not accepted, no difference is made. In any case उद्भट flourished between 750 and 850 A. D.

The commentary of प्रतीहारेन्दुराज is among the oldest commentaries on Alaṅkāra works. He tells us that he was the pupil of Mukula (विद्वदग्र्यान्मुकुलकादधिगम्य विविच्यते । प्रतीहारेन्दुराजेन काव्यालङ्कारसंग्रहः ॥ Intro. 3rd verse). The last verse of the commentary bestows high praise upon मुकुल, who is said to have been deeply versed in मीमांसा, व्याकरण, तर्क and साहित्य. प्रतीहारेन्दुराज in that verse speaks of himself only as श्रीन्दुराज and as a कौङ्कण (an inhabitant of Koṅkan). The commentary of प्रतीहारेन्दुराज is concise, lucid and learned. He names अमरुक, उद्भट, कात्यायन, चूर्णिकार (पतञ्जलि), दण्डी, भामह, भामहविवरण of उद्भट, वामन and quotes frequently from the नाट्यशास्त्र, रुद्रट's काव्यालङ्कार and from the ध्वन्यालोक. As मुकुल flourished about 900-925 A. D. his pupil प्रतिहारेन्दुराज must have flourished about 950 A. D. That he is separated from उद्भट by a long period follows from the fact that he discusses various readings in उद्भट's examples e. g. on p. 4 he says (on स देवो दिवासान्निन्ये तस्मिन्शैलेन्द्रकन्दरे) 'निन्ये तस्मिन्' इत्यत्र 'निन्येन्यस्मिन्' इति पाठः. Whether he is identical with the इन्दुराज whose disciple was the great अभिनवगुप्त will be discussed later on.

The विमर्शिनी com. of जयरथ on the अलङ्कारसर्वस्व had been known to refer to राजानकतिलक as a commentator of Udbhaṭa's work and as further stating that the author of the अलङ्कारसर्वस्व generally followed the views of तिलक; एतच्चोद्भटविचारे राजानकतिलकेनैव सप्रपञ्चमुक्तमिति न तथास्माभिराविष्कृतम् । अलं. स. वि. p. 15; एतदेव राजानकतिलकेनाप्युक्तम् । कारणासामर्थ्यमिह बाधकत्वेनैव प्रतीयते कार्यानुत्पत्तिस्तु बाध्यत्वेनेति । ग्रन्थकृच्च प्रायस्तन्मतानुवर्त्येव । तदुक्तसमानन्यायोऽस्माभिः पाठो लक्षितः । अलं. स. वि. p. 158; उद्भट V. 4 is 'यत्सामर्थ्येऽपि शक्तीनां फलानुत्पत्तिनिबन्धनम् । विशेषस्याभिधित्सातस्तद्विशेषोक्तिरुच्यते ॥'; एतच्चोद्भटविवेके राजानकतिलकेन सप्रपञ्चमुक्तमिति... **चिरन्तनेति** (from अलं. स.)। अनेनास्माभिः सर्वत्रैव तन्मतानुसृतिरेव कृतेत्यात्मविषयमनौद्धत्यमपि ग्रन्थकृता प्रकाशितमिति। अलं. स. वि. p. 227. This commentary of राजानकतिलक on उद्भट's अलं. सा.

से. has been published in the G. O. series based on a single ms. (1931). From these quotations it follows that the commentary of Tilaka was called उद्भटविवेक or उद्भटविचार. The relevant reference in the com. of तिलक to the matter mentioned in the 1st quotation from the विमर्शिनी will be found at p. 22 of the com. of तिलक. I have not been able to find the second reference in the printed text of the उद्भटविवेक, unless the meagre explanation on p. 41 is treated as the one referred to. The word सामस्त्य appears in उद्भट's definition of विशेषोक्ति (V. 5) and not in तिलक's comment. The 3rd extract probably refers to p. 40 of the printed text (काव्ये दोषगुणालङ्काराणां च शब्दार्थगततयान्वयव्यतिरेकाभ्यां विभागः क्रियते । तिलक). In this case the अलं. स. (p. 257 तस्मादाश्रयाश्रयिभावेनैव चिरन्तनमतानुसृतिरिति) appears to differ from तिलक and follows older authors. The commentary of तिलक, though brief, is always to the point and acute. He criticizes प्रतीहारेन्दुराज several times and it appears that he had several commentaries on Udbhaṭa before him. रुचक who wrote the काव्यप्रकाशसङ्केत[1] learnt Poetics under तिलक and acc. to the colophon of the सहृदयलीला, the author रुचक whose another name was रुय्यक was the son of राजानकतिलक. As the अलं. स. was composed between 1135-1155, तिलक must have flourished about 1100-1125 A. D. He was probably a younger contemporary of मम्मट. I do not at all agree with the arguments, which look like special pleading, of the learned editor of the उद्भटविवेक (Intro. pp. 42-45) that मम्मट had read Tilaka's work and borrowed ideas from him. To me it appears that the truth is just the other way about. Similarly, the editor's attempt (Intro. pp. 38-39) to show that तिलक wrote some other work is based on nothing more solid than mere conjectures. The ms. of तिलक's commentary on उद्भट refered to by Dr. De in Bulletin of the London School of Oriental Studies, vol. 4 p. 279 is the same as the one on which the G. O. S. edition is based.

12. The काव्यालङ्कारसूत्र of वामन. This work has been edited several times, the best edition being that of the

---

1. The 2nd Introductory verse of the काव्यप्रकाशसङ्केत is : ज्ञात्वा श्रीतिलकात्सर्वालङ्कारोपनिषत्क्रमम् । काव्यप्रकाशसङ्केतो रुचकेनेह लिख्यते ॥. Vide Cat. of Govt. mss at B.O. R. I. vol. XII. No. 102 at pp. 108-109.

Vanivilas Press (1909). Dr. Cappeller brought out an edition at Jena in 1875 with a German Introduction. The work is divided into three parts, the *sūtras*, the author's own *vṛtti* thereon and examples. वामन himself says 'प्रणम्य परमं ज्योतिर्वामनेन कविप्रिया । काव्यालङ्कारसूत्राणां स्वेषां वृत्तिर्विधीयते ॥'. This is further corroborated by the fact that so early a writer as प्रतीहारेन्दुराज ascribes not only the sūtras (e. g. वामन III. I. 1·2 on p. 17 and IV. 3. 8 on p. 81) but also passages from the वृत्ति to वामन (e. g. the two verses युवतेरिव रूपमङ्ग काव्यं and यदि भवति which are cited by वामन under III. 1. 2 are ascribed to वामन on p. 76 and the words 'लक्षणायां हि झगित्यर्थप्रतिपत्तिक्षमत्वं रहस्यमाचक्षते' which occur in the वृत्ति on IV. 3. 8 are ascribed to वामन on p. 81 by प्रतीहारेन्दुराज. Similarly, the लोचन (p. 43) cites वामन's definition of आक्षेप and quotes the two instances given in the वृत्ति on IV. 3. 27. Most of the examples cited in the वृत्ति are taken from standard works as वामन himself says 'एभिर्निदर्शनैः स्वीयैः परकीयैश्च पुष्कलैः । शब्दवैचित्र्यगर्भेयमुपमैव प्रपञ्चिता ॥' (on IV. 3. 33). वामन's वृत्ति quotes about 250 verses or parts of verses. As वामन is comparatively a very early writer, his work, which is full of quotations, is of capital importance for settling the chronology of many Sanskrit writers. In this work I have given references to the Nirṇayasāgara edition of 1926.

Vāmana writes in the *sūtra* style and also borrows the terminology of *sūtra* writers in dividing his work into five अधिकरणs. Each अधिकरण is divided into two or three अध्यायs. There are in all 12 अध्यायs (the 1st and 4th अधिकरणs having three अ० and the rest two each) and 319 *sūtras*. It will be noticed that he reverses the relation of अध्यायs and अधिकरणs, but he appears to have followed कौटिल्य's अर्थशास्त्र and the कामसूत्र in this. Ancient सूत्रकारs divide their works into अध्यायs, each comprising several अधिकरणs. The first अधि० (called शारीर) of वामन speaks of the प्रयोजनs of काव्य, those who are properly qualified to receive instruction in Poetics, declares that *rīti* is the soul of poetry, speaks of three रीतिs, वैदर्भी, गौडी and पाञ्चाली, dilates upon the subsidiary aids to poetry and the divisions of poetry. The 2nd अधि० (called दोषदर्शन) speaks of the दोषs of पद, वाक्य and वाक्यार्थ; the third अधि० (called गुणविवेचन) distinguishes between गुण and अलङ्कार and defines and illustrates the ten *guṇas* (such as ओजस्) of words and of sense; the 4th अधि० (called आलङ्कारिक) treats of यमक and अनुप्रास, of उपमा and the six *doṣas* of उपमा, and treats of other अलङ्कारs based more or less upon उपमा; the fifth अधि० (called प्रायोगिक) speaks of certain conventions to be observed by poets, such as not employing the same word twice, observance of rules of सन्धि in the pādas of a verse except at the end of the first half, non-employment of words like खलु at the beginning of a पाद and points out how grammatical purity may be secured, examines and tries to explain away some apparent irregularities in the works of poets of old. The last अध्याय (on शब्दशुद्धि) resembles the 6th परिच्छेद of भामह's work. But there is a differencce between the two. भामह (in VI. 32-60) illustrates certain formations of words based on Pāṇini's sūtras that should be employed or not employed by poets and he generally follows the serial order of chapters and pādas of the Āṣṭādhyāyī; while Vāmana (in V. 2. 1-92) takes up words (but not in the order of the chapters of the Aṣṭādhyāyī) that have been used or are likely to be used and shows how the use is wrong or may in some cases be explained away. For example, (in V. 2. 1) he says that the use of the word रुद्रौ as an एकशेषद्वन्द्व (to represent रुद्रश्च रुद्राणी च) is not proper, if we read पा. I. 2. 67 with पा. IV. 1. 48. In the वृत्ति on V. 2. 1 he says the forms इन्द्रौ, भवौ, शर्वौ are not proper. This appears to be aimed at भामह VI. 32 (सरूपशेषं तु पुमान् स्त्रिया यत्र च शिष्यते। यथाह वरुणाविन्द्रौ भवौ शर्वौ मृडाविति॥). In V. 2. 15 वामन says that the word बिम्बाधर frequently used by poets should be अधरबिम्ब if we consider पा. II. 1. 56 (उपमितं व्याघ्रादिभिः सामान्याप्रयोगे), but that word can be justified if it is taken as a मध्यमपदलोपिसमास (बिम्बाकारोऽधरः बिम्बाधरः). The अलङ्कारs defined and illustrated (besides अनुप्रास, यमक and उपमा) are (in order): प्रतिवस्तूपमा, समासोक्ति, अप्रस्तुत०, अपह्नुति, रूपक, श्लेष, वक्रोक्ति, उत्प्रेक्षा, अतिशयोक्ति, सन्देह, विरोध, विभावना, अनन्वय, उपमेयोपमा, परिवृत्ति, क्रम, दीपक, निदर्शन, अर्थान्तर०, व्यतिरेक, विशेषोक्ति, व्याजस्तुति, व्याजोक्ति, तुल्ययोगिता, आक्षेप, सहोक्ति, समाहित, संसृष्टि, उपमारूपक, उत्प्रेक्षावयव (i.e. 33 in all). It will be noticed that वामन does not define such figures as पर्यायोक्त, प्रेयः, रसवत्, ऊर्जस्वि, उदात्त, भाविक, सूक्ष्म. Some of the definitions of वामन appear to be based on भामह e.g. उपमा (भामह II. 30, वामन IV. 2. 1), विभावना (भामह II. 77, वामन IV. 3. 13).

Among the authors and works that are expressly named are: कविराज (as a great poet, IV. 1. 10), कामन्दकीनीति (IV. 1.2.), कामशास्त्र, छन्दोविचिति, नाममाला (a lexicon. I. 3. 5), विशाखिल (a writer on कलाशास्त्र, I. 3. 7), शूद्रक (for works exhibiting श्लेषगुण, III. 2. 4), हरिप्रबोध for यमकs (IV. 1. 2). On III 2. 2 वामन says: 'साभिप्रायत्वं

यथा-सोयं संप्रति चन्द्रगुप्ततनयश्चन्द्रप्रकाशो युवा जातो भूपतिराश्रयः कृतधियां दिष्ट्या कृतार्थश्रमः ॥ आश्रयः कृतधियामित्यस्य (च सुबन्धु-v. l.) वसुबन्धुसाचिव्योपक्षेपपरत्वात् साभिप्रायत्वम्'. Round this a great controversy has raged as to what king is referred to as चन्द्रगुप्त and whether the proper reading is वसुबन्धुसाचिव्यो० or whether it is च सुबन्धुसाचिव्यो०. Vide I. A. vol. 40 (1911) p. 170 ff. (Prof. Pathak), p. 264 (Dr. Hoernle) and I. A. vol. 41 (1912) p. 1 (Prof. D. R. Bhandarkar) in favour of वसुबन्धु and I. A. 1911 p. 312 (Prof. Narasimhachar), I. H. Q. vol. I. p. 261, I. A. 1912 p. 15 (M. M. Haraprasāda Śāstrī) in favour of the reading च सुबन्धु.

It depends upon the reading one adopts what historical incident is referred to. If we read वसुबन्धुसाचिव्यो० then the reference would be to चन्द्रगुप्त, समुद्रगुप्त and वसुबन्धु and if we read it च सुबन्धुसाचिव्यो० then the reference is to चन्द्रगुप्तमौर्य, his son बिन्दुसार and his minister सुबन्धु. Vide Dr. Prof. Dasharatha Śarma in J.H.Q. vol. X. pp. 761 ff., who sees a close resemblance between this stanza quoted by वामन and the third stanza of the Mehrauli Pillar Inscription (Gupta Inscriptions p. 139, at p. 141). Now that the अभिनवभारती informs us of a play called वासवदत्तानाट्यधारा composed by महाकवि सुबन्धु, it is not necessary to hold that the reference to सुबन्धु in this verse quoted by Vāmana or the reference to वासवदत्ता by Bāṇa must necessarily be to the author of the prose romance called वासवदत्ता. On p. 172 of the G.O.S. edition vol. III. of the अभिनवभारती we find : तत्रास्य बहुतरव्यापिनो बहुगर्भस्वभावायिततुल्यस्य नाट्यायितस्योदाहरणं महाकविसुबन्धुनिबद्धो वासवदत्तानाट्यधाराख्यः समस्त एव प्रयोगः। तत्र हि बिन्दुसारः प्रयोज्यवस्तुत उदयनचरिते सामाजिकीकृतोपि &c. Vide Prof. Pathak in J. B. B. R. A. S. vol. 23 pp. 185-187 where he says that the verse quoted by वामन refers to कुमारगुप्त, son of चन्द्रगुप्त II (413-455 A. D.) परमार्थ (499-569 A. D.) says that वसुबन्धु died at the age of 80 during बालादित्य's reign. So वसुबन्धु flourished about 420-500 A.D. (J.R.A.S. for 1905 pp. 33-53). वसुबन्धु's अभिधर्मकोश is mentioned by बाण in हर्षचरित VIII. For more recent discussions, vide I. H. Q. vol. 18 pp. 373-375, vol. 19 pp. 69-72, vol. 20 pp. 85 and 366.

In the अवन्तिसुन्दरीकथा, सुबन्धु is mentioned immediately after वाल्मीकि, व्यास and one more (probably पाणिनि or पतञ्जलि) and before the बृहत्कथा, शूद्रक, भास, कालिदास, बाण. The poets are arranged more or less in a chronological order. Therefore, सुबन्धु in the अ. सु. कथा must be a very ancient author. The words (सुबन्धुः किल निष्क्रान्तो बिन्दुसारस्य बन्धनात् । तस्यैव हृदयं बद्ध्वा वत्सराजो...) in the intro.

verse of अ. सु. क. are not to be taken too literally. सुबन्धु did not literally escape from the prison of बिन्दुसार as some suppose; what is meant is that the story of वत्सराज captivated सुबन्धु's heart and that सुबन्धु did not become subservient to बिन्दुसार, but made the latter serve his own purpose and reduced बिन्दुसार to the position of a spectator. This, therefore, is probably a reference to वासवदत्तानाट्यधारा and the नाट्यायित therein mentioned by अभिनवगुप्त (p. 178 of G.O.S. ed. vol. III of अ. भा.). To me it appears that what Vāmana wrote was most likely वसुबन्धुसाचिव्यो०. The reading च सुबन्धु० does not convey the force of च. What does च connect? As time passed by, वसुबन्धु, a Buddhist writer, came to be forgotten and as सुबन्धु became more known the scribes either read वसुबन्धु as 'च सुबन्धु' or purposely read so in order to make the passage refer to a well-known author. The mere fact (on which M.M. Haraprasad Shastri relies) that many mss. read च सुबन्धु is not enough. Most of these mss. are later by several centuries than Vāmana. If there had been not a single ms. giving the reading वसुबन्धु, the matter would have been different. Among the works quoted from, though not actually named, are the अमरुशतक, उत्तररामo (इयं गेहे लक्ष्मीः on IV. 3. 6), [1]कादम्बरी, किरातार्जुनीय, कुमारसम्भव, मालतीमाधव, मृच्छकटिक (द्यूतं हि नाम पुरुषस्यासिंहासनं राज्यं on IV. 3. 23), मेघदूत, रघुवंश, विक्रमोर्वशीय, वेणीसंहार, शाकुन्तल, शिशुपालवध, हर्षचरित. The verse यासां बलिः (on V. 1. 3) occurs in the मृच्छकटिक (I. 9) as well as in the चारुदत्त (I. 2) ascribed to भास. The words 'यो भर्तृपिण्डस्य कृते न युध्येत्' (cited as an ungrammatical प्रयोग on V. 2. 13) occur in कौटिल्य's अर्थशास्त्र and in the प्रतिज्ञायौगन्धरायण (IV. 3). The verse 'शरच्छशाङ्कगौरेण वाताविद्धेन भामिनि। काशपुष्पलवेनेदं साश्रुपातं मुखं कृतम् ॥' cited as an example of व्याजोक्ति (IV. 3. 25) occurs with slight variations in the स्वप्नवासवदत्ता (IV. 8) ascribed to भास. The words मातङ्गं मानभङ्गुरं on वामन V. 2. 38 seem to be a misreading taken from भामह 'मदो जनयति प्रीतिं सानङ्गं मानभङ्गुरम्' II. 27. He refers to the view of other writers on अलङ्कार: उत्प्रेक्षैवातिशयोक्तिरिति केचित् (IV. 3. 10); अर्थान्तरन्यासस्य हेतुरूपत्वाद्धेतोश्चान्वयव्यतिरेकात्मकत्वान्न ततः पृथग् व्यतिरेक इति केचित् IV. 3. 21; उपमानाधिक्यात्तदपोह इत्येके—IV. 2. 18; 'अनयोर्दोषयोर्विपर्ययाख्यस्य दोषस्यान्तर्भावान्न पृथगुपादानम्। अत एवास्माकं मते षड् दोषा इति' on IV. 2. 11 (this seems to refer to मेधाविन् or to भामह II. 39). He often says श्लोकाश्चात्र भवन्ति (which are probably quota-

1 On सूत्र V. 2. 44 वामन' वृत्ति is 'अनुकरोति भगवतो नारायणस्य इत्यत्रापि मन्ये स्मशब्दः कविना प्रयुक्तो लेखकैस्तु प्रमादान्न लिखित इति'.

tions); *vide* III. 1. 25 'eleven verses' and III 2. 15 (three verses).

Vāmana is the protagonist of the *rīti* school. It was he who boldly asserted that *rīti* was the soul of poetry (रीतिरात्मा काव्यस्य । विशिष्टा पदरचना रीतिः । विशेषो गुणात्मा । I. 2. 6-8). Some of the other doctrines peculiarly associated with his name are ; I the distinction between गुणs and अलङ्कारs (काव्यशोभायाः कर्तारो धर्मा गुणाः । तदतिशयहेतवस्त्वलङ्काराः । III. 2. 1-2). This view is strongly criticized by the काव्यप्रकाश (VIII p. 471, Vā) ; II three styles वैदर्भी, गौडी and पाञ्चाली; III the inclusion of वक्रोक्ति as an अर्थालङ्कार and its definition as 'सादृश्याल्लक्षणा' (IV 3.8 उन्मिमील कमलं सरसीनां कैरवं च निमिमील मुहूर्तात् । अत्र नेत्रधर्मावुन्मीलननिमीलने सादृश्याद्विकाससङ्कोचौ लक्षयतः); IV the peculiar definition of विशेषोक्ति as एकगुणहानिकल्पनायां साम्यदार्ढ्यं विशेषोक्तिः' (IV. 3. 23), which according to जगन्नाथ and others is रूपक (दृढारोप) ; V the two meanings given to the figure आक्षेप (उपमानस्य आक्षेपः प्रतिषेधः तुल्यकार्यार्थस्य नैरर्थक्यविवक्षायामाक्षेपः, उपमानस्याक्षेपतः प्रतिपत्तिरित्यपि सूत्रार्थः), which respectively correspond to the प्रतीप and समासोक्ति of मम्मट and others.

The commentator सहदेव on the काव्यालङ्कारसूत्र tells us that वामन's work went out of vogue and भट्टमुकुल restored its tradition after obtaining a copy of it. 'वेदिता सर्वशास्त्राणां भट्टोभून्मुकुलाभिधः । लब्ध्वा कुतश्चिदादर्शं भ्रष्टाम्नायं समुद्धृतम् ॥ काव्यालङ्कारशास्त्रं यत्तेनैतद्वामनोदितम् । असूया तत्र कर्तव्या विशेषालोकिभिः क्वचित् ॥' (notes p. 117 to the काव्यमीमांसा of राजशेखर). राजशेखर in his काव्यमीमांसा speaks of an ālaṅkārika called Maṅgala and quotes a passage of his, viz. "ते च द्विधा अरोचकिनः सतृणाभ्यवहारिणश्च इति मङ्गलः । 'कवयोऽपि भवन्ति' इति वामनीयाः ॥" (p. 14). वामन says 'अरोचकिनः सतृणाभ्यवहारिणश्च कवयः' (I. 2. 1) which वामनs वृत्ति explains as 'अरोचकिसतृणाभ्यवहारिशब्दौ गौणार्थौ कोऽसावर्थः—विवेकित्वमविवेकित्वं चेति ।'. अरोचकिन: means persons who suffer from absence of appetite i. e. metaphorically 'persons who have a fastidious taste' and सतृणाभ्यवहारिणः means (literally) 'persons, that eat everything including grass' i. e. metaphorically 'persons who accept any kind of literature without discrimination'. राजशेखर quotes the views of मङ्गल on pp. 11, 16 and 20. The last is interesting. The question is about काव्यपाक. The view of मङ्गल is that *pāka* means परिणाम i. e. the grammatical purity of nouns and verbs. According to the followers of वामन, *pāka* means 'the difficulty or impossibility of putting other words in place of those that the poet has employed.' राजशेखर quotes two verses with the words तदाहुः, both of which are quoted in वामन's वृत्ति on

I. 3. 15 with the words अत्र श्लोकौ. The whole passage is quoted below from the काव्यमीमांसा.[1] हेमचन्द्र in his काव्यानुशासन quotes वामन many times and in one place states (p. 195) that वामन and मङ्गल held the same view. Daṇḍin defined the guṇa *ojas* as consisting in abundance of compound words[2] and further stated that *ojas* was the life of prose, while even in the poems of the Gauḍas compounds abounded. But Hemachandra says that Vāmana and Maṅgala hold the view that ojas being common to all three rītis viz. Vaidarbhī, Gaudīyā and Pāñcālī (Vāmana I. 2. 9 and 11), it is unreasonable to mention the Gauḍīyā alone in connection with *ojas* and therefore Vāmana defines '*ojas* as गाढबन्धत्वमोजः' (III. 1. 5.) and 'अर्थस्य प्रौढिरोजः' III. 2. 2. माणिक्यचन्द्र in his काव्यप्रकाशसङ्केत (Mysore ed. p. 292) refers to this difference of view between दण्डी on the one hand and वामन and मङ्गल on the other.[3] सोमेश्वर in his commentary on the काव्यप्रकाश also mentions the opposing views of भरत and मङ्गल on ओजस् (folio 89b).[4] It appears that दण्डी seized upon one part of

---

1. कः पुनरयं पाकः इत्याचार्याः । परिणामः—इति मङ्गलः । कः पुनरयं परिणामः—इत्याचार्याः । सुपां तिङां च श्रवः सैषा व्युत्पत्तिः—इति मङ्गलः । सौशब्द्यमेतत् । पदनिवेशनिष्कम्पता पाकः—इत्याचार्याः । तदाहुः । आवापोद्धरणे तावद्यावद्दोलायते मनः । पदानां स्थापिते स्थैर्ये हन्त सिद्धा सरस्वती ॥ आग्रहपरिग्रहादपि पदस्थैर्यपर्यवसायस्तस्मात्पदानां परिवृत्तिवैमुख्यं पाकः—इति वामनीया । तदाहुः । यत्पदानि त्यजन्त्येव परिवृत्तिसहिष्णुताम् । तं शब्दन्यायनिष्णाताः शब्दपाकं प्रचक्षते ॥ काव्यमी॰ p. 20. The printed वामन reads आधानोद्धरणे, पदस्य and शब्दन्यास॰ (in वृत्ति on I. 3. 15). For सौशब्द्य, compare भामह I. 14-15. Vide अग्निपुराण 346. 22-23 'उच्चैः परिणतिः कापि पाक इत्यभिधीयते । मृद्वीकानारिकेलाम्बुपाकभेदाच्चतुर्विधः । आदावन्ते च सौरस्यं मृद्वीकापाक एव सः ।.'

2. ओजः समासभूयस्त्वमेतद्गद्यस्य जीवितम् । पद्येप्यदाक्षिणात्यानामिदमेकं परायणम् ॥ काव्यादर्श I. 80.

3. दण्ड्युक्तं समासदैर्घ्यमोज इत्यपि न । रीतित्रयेप्योजसः साधारणत्वाद् गौडीयानिर्देशो न युक्तिमानिति वामनमङ्गलौ । काव्य. प्र. संकेत p. 292.

4. भरत defined ओजस् 'समासवद्भिर्बहुभिर्विचित्रैश्च पदैर्युतम् । सानुरागैरुदारैश्च तदोजः परिकीर्त्यते ॥' नाट्यशास्त्र 16. 105 (G. O. S. edition). अभिनवगुप्त explains this verse (अ. भा. vol. II. pp. 340-41), quotes the quarter विलुलितमकरन्दा मञ्जरीर्नर्तयन्ति cited by वामन under गाढबन्धत्वमोजः for illustrating the word सानुरागैः in भरत's definion and mentions the word गाढत्वं in connection with it. The definition of ओजस् in the Ch. ed. of the नाट्यशास्त्र (17. 103) is totally different from the one in the G.O.S. edition. It may further be noted that two

भरत's definition of ओजस् (viz. समासवद्भिर्बहुभिः) while वामन relied upon two others (viz. सानुरागैः and उदारैः) in defining ओजः as शब्दगुण and अर्थगुण respectively. Therefore, as Vāmana omits all reference to समासभूयस्त्व in defining ओजस् there is nothing 'irregular' (as Prof. Bhattacharya thinks in I. H. Q. vol. III p. 380 note 2) in Māṇikyacandra's putting Vāmana and Maṅgala together. What relation exists between वामन and मङ्गल it is difficult to say. राजशेखर speaks of वामनीयस (school of वामन) and माणिक्यचन्द्र says वामनमङ्गलौ and not मङ्गलवामनौ. From these two indications and from the fact that Maṅgala is very rarely mentioned while वामन is mentioned frequently by प्रतिहारेन्दुराज and अभिनवगुप्त, I infer that मङ्गल came after Vāmana and not before.

The date of Vāmana can be settled within very narrow limits. Vide my article in JBBRAS vol. 23 (1909 p. 91 ff.) राजशेखर in his काव्यमीमांसा quotes (pp. 14 and 20) the वामनीय school. राजशेखर flourished in the first quarter of the tenth century. प्रतीहारेन्दुराज, as shown above, quotes वामन frequently and so does the लोचन (pp. 9, 12, 224) and the अभिनवभारती vol. I p. 288 (where वामन I. 3. 30-31 are quoted). Therefore वामन flourished before 900 A. D. On the verse अनुरागवती सन्ध्या दिवसस्तत्पुरःसरः। अहो दैवगतिः कीदृक्तथापि न समागमः ॥ cited in the ध्वन्य० (p. 44) the लोचन remarks 'वामनाभिप्रायेणायमाक्षेपः, भामहाभिप्रायेण तु समासोक्तिरित्यमुमाशयं हृदये गृहीत्वा समासोक्त्याक्षेपयोरिदमेकमेवोदाहरणं व्यतरद् ग्रन्थकृत्.' So According to the लोचन, वामन preceded the ध्वन्य० (which was composed in the latter half of 9th century) and must have flourished before 850 A. D. The ध्वनिकारिका (III. 52 अस्फुटस्फुरितं काव्यतत्त्वमेतद्यथोदितम् । अशक्नुवद्भिर्व्याकर्तुं रीतयः संप्रवर्तिताः) probably refers to वामन. वामन quotes the verse इयं गेहे लक्ष्मीः (उत्तरराम० I) under रूपक (IV. 3. 6.) and the

---

out of the several examples of अर्थस्य प्रौढिरोजः in वामनसूत्रवृत्ति (viz अथ नयनसमुत्थं from रघुवंश II. 75 and ते हिमालयमामन्त्र्य from कुमारसम्भव IV 93) are mentioned by अभिनवगुप्त in explaining the word उदारैः in भरत's definition of ओजस्. सोमेश्वर says तत्रावगीतस्य हीनस्य वा वस्तुनः शब्दार्थसम्पादयदुदात्तत्वं निषिञ्चन्ति कवयस्तदोज इति भरतः। अनवगीतस्याहीनस्य वा वस्तुनः शब्दार्थयोरर्थसम्पदापदमुदात्तत्वं निषिञ्चति कवयस्तर्हि तदनोजः स्यादिति मङ्गलः। यथा ये सन्तोष०...मेरुर्न मे रोचते ॥ ...तस्मात्समासभूयस्त्वमोजस्तच्च गद्यविभूषणं प्रायेण वृत्तवर्त्मन्यपि गौडास्तदाद्रियन्ते । रीतित्रये...निर्देशो न युक्तस्तस्माद्गाढत्वमोज इति वामनः। (folio 89a and b). From this it appears that सोमेश्वर read the definition of ओजस् as in Ch. ed.

word 'पद्मालीपिङ्गलिम्नः' (on V. 2. 18) from the मालतीमाधव. भवभूति flourished at some time between 700 and 740 A.D. (*vide* Dr. Bhandarkar's preface to the मालतीमाधव pp. XIII-XVII ed. of 1905 and Smith in JRAS 1908 p. 793). Therefore, वामन is later than 750 A. D. The राजतरङ्गिणी says that a वामन was a minister of king जयापीड 'मनोरथः शङ्खदत्तश्चटकः सन्धिमांस्तथा । बभूवुः कवयस्तस्य वामनाद्याश्च मन्त्रिणः ॥' (IV. 497). Bühler (Kashmir report p. 65) is inclined to give credence to the tradition of the Kashmirian *pandits* that minister Vāmana whom जयापीड employed was the author of the काव्यालङ्कारसूत्र. If this were accepted it must lead to the result that Vāmana flourished about 800 A. D. and was a contemporary and probably a rival of उद्भट. It is remarkable that neither of them refers to the other. There is another way of arriving at the same date for वामन. He quotes some verses from माघ viz. उभौ यदि (शिशु III. 8 on IV 3. 10), सितं सितिम्ना (शिशु. I. 25 on V. 2. 9) and refers to खलूक्त्वा खलु वाचिकम् (शिशु. II. 70) in the *sūtra* 'न पादादौ खल्वादयः' (V. 1. 5). माघ refers to न्यास, वृत्ति and महाभाष्य in 'अनुत्सूत्रपदन्यासा सद्वृत्तिः सन्निबन्धना' (शिशु० II. 112). It has been shown above (p. 118) that the न्यास cannot be earlier than 700 A.D. and that माघ is praised by नृपतुङ्ग. So माघ flourished about 725-775. The author of काव्या० सूत्र cannot be identified with वामन, one of the authors of the काशिका, that was composed about 660 A.D. It is worthy of note that वामन holds the same views as the काशिका on certain grammatical points. For example, on the सूत्र 'ब्रह्मादिषु हन्तेर्नियमादरिहाद्यसिद्धिः' (काव्या० सूत्र V. 2. 35) वामन says ब्रह्मादिष्वेव, हन्तेरेव, क्विवेव, भूतकाल एवेति चतुर्विधश्चात्र नियमः'; the काशिका on ब्रह्मभ्रूणवृत्रेषु क्विप् (पा. III. 2. 27) says the same thing, while the महाभाष्य holds that there is a two-fold नियम only. On 'सुदत्यादयः प्रतिविधेयाः' काव्या० सू० (V. 2. 68) वामन mentions two ways of explaining away words like सुदती, the second of which seems to be the opinion of the काशिका (on 'स्त्रियां संज्ञायाम्' पा. V. 4. 143).

The commentary of गोपेन्द्रतिप्पभूपाल has been published several times. He belongs to the 15th century or is even a little later. He quotes the काव्यप्रकाश, विद्याधर, विद्यानाथ, विदग्धमुखमण्डन and other later writers. He quotes a verse in praise of तिप्पभूपाल (on V. 1. 3). The com. is called कामधेनु. He quotes a भट्टगोपाल who seems to have been a commentator on the काव्यालङ्कारसूत्र (on I. 3. 16). The other commentaries are those of महेश्वर (who wrote a commentary styled साहित्यसर्वस्व, I. O. cat. p. 321) and of सहदेव.

13 An Alphabetical list of ***alaṅkāras*** (omitting चित्रबन्धs) defiend or referred to by भट्टि, दण्डी, भामह, उद्भट and वामन.

अतिशयोक्ति found in all.

[1]अनन्वय defined by all except दण्डी who calls it असाधारणोपमा (II. 37).

अनुप्रास found in all.

अपह्नुति found in all.

अप्रस्तुतप्रशंसा found in all except भट्टि.

अर्थान्तरन्यास found in all.

आक्षेप found in all. But वामन's आक्षेप (IV. 3. 27) is either समासोक्ति or प्रतीप of later writers.

आवृत्ति treated by दण्डी alone (II. 116-119).

आशीः found in भट्टि, दण्डी II. 357 and भामह (केषाञ्चिदलङ्कारतया मतः in III. 55 and gives an illustration in III. 56).

उत्प्रेक्षा treated by all. वामन says (वृत्ति on IV. 3. 9.) that उत्प्रेक्षा is अतिशयोक्ति according to some.

उत्प्रेक्षावयव found in भट्टि, भामह (III. 47) and वामन (who treats) it as a variety of संसृष्टि IV. 3. 31-32). दण्डी includes it (II. 359) under उत्प्रेक्षा.

उदात्त found in all except वामन. (भट्टि called it उदार according to जयमङ्गला).

उपन्यास—m. by विष्णुधर्मोत्तरपुराण alone; vide p. 71 above.

उपमा found in all.

उपमारूपक found in भट्टि, भामह (III. 35), वामन (who treats it as a variety of संसृष्टि IV. 3. 31. दण्डी includes it under रूपक (II. 358).

उपमेयोपमा found in all except दण्डी (who calls it अन्योन्योपमा II. 18).

ऊर्जस्वि found in all except वामन.

काव्यलिङ्ग defined by उद्भट alone.

क्रम m. by वामन alone (IV. 3. 17); दण्डी says यथासंख्य was so called (II. 273).

छेकानुप्रास defined by उद्भट alone.

---

1. Even a great philosopher like सुरेश्वर makes use of the illustration of अनन्वय in his arguments. Vide बृह. उ. भा. वा p. 1149 verses 459-461 (on II. 4. 11 यत्र हि द्वैतमिव भवति) 'नैष दोषो यतो दृष्ट एकस्मिन्नपि वस्तुनि । उपमेयोपमाभावो दिग्धीरिव विहायसि ॥ रामरावणयोर्युद्धं रामरावणयोरिव । यथा प्रसिद्धो जगति तथैवेहापि गम्यताम् ॥. This example of अनन्वय is cited by वामन under अनन्वय (V. 3. 14).

जाति and स्वभावोक्ति are treated as synonyms by Daṇḍin (काव्यादर्श II. 8). बाण also appears to have known it (vide कादम्बरी Introductory verse हरन्ति कं...कथाः। निरन्तरश्लेषघनाः सुजातयो महास्रज &c).

तुल्ययोगिता found in all, but दण्डी adds that it must be स्तुतिनिन्दार्थं (II. 330).

दीपक defined by all.

दृष्टान्त defined by उद्भट alone.

निदर्शन or निदर्शना found in all, उद्भट calling it विदर्शना.

निपुण found in भट्टि X. 74 alone (may be included under उदात्त according to जय०, while the same verse is प्रेयः according to मल्लि०).

परिवृत्ति found in all, but भामह (III. 41) and भट्टि (acc. to जयमङ्गला) require it to be अर्थान्तरन्यासवती.

पर्यायोक्त found in all except वामन.

प्रतिवस्तूपमा found in all except भट्टि; भामह (II. 34) and दण्डी regard it as a variety of उपमा.

प्रेयः found in all except वामन.

भाविक ,, ,, ,, ,, ,, It is a प्रबन्धविषयगुण acc. to भामह (III. 53-54) and दण्डी (II. 364-366).[1]

यथासंख्य found in all, वामन calling it क्रम and दण्डी saying that it is styled संख्यान and क्रम also (II. 273).

यमक found in all except उद्भट.

रसवत् found in all except वामन.

रूपक found in all.

लव—same as लेश. Some commentators of काव्यादर्श read लव for लेश (यामुन and श्रुतानुपालिनी do so).

लाटानुप्रास defined by उद्भट alone and referred to by भामह (II. 8).

लेश defined by दण्डी alone (II. 265-267). It is the व्याजोक्ति of मम्मट. दण्डी also says that some defined it so as to make it the same as व्याजस्तुति. भामह (II. 86) denies that it is an अलं०. A later आलङ्कारिक रुद्रट defines and illustrates लेश (VII. 100-102).

वक्रोक्ति defined as a figure by वामन alone (IV. 3. 8); referred to by भामह (II. 85) and दण्डी (II. 220 and 363) as underlying all figures.

1. Vide Dr. Raghavan in 'Some concepts' &c on the history of भाविक pp. 117-130.

वार्ता found in भट्टि alone (acc. to जयमङ्गला on X. 46). भामह (II. 87) alludes to it and so does दण्डी (I. 85-86). विष्णुधर्मोत्तर III. 14. 11 has it, acc. to one ms; vide Dr. Raghavan in 'Some concepts' &c pp. 97-99 and सर. क. I. 142-143.

विभावना found in all.

विरोध found in all.

विशेषोक्ति found in all but वामन's वि० is defined differently (in IV. 3. 23) and is equal to रूपक.

व्यतिरेक found in all.

व्याजस्तुति found in all.

व्याजोक्ति defined by वामन alone, which was called मायोक्ति by others, as he says (IV. 3. 25).

श्लिष्ट found in all, वामन using the word श्लेष.

संसृष्टि found in all; दण्डी calls it सङ्कीर्ण and includes संसृष्टि and सङ्कर in it; वामन gives it a restricted scope recognising only two varieties उपमारूपक and उत्प्रेक्षावयव; उद्भट distinguishes it from सङ्कर.

सङ्कर defined by उद्भट alone (with four varieties).

संख्यान same as यथासंख्य acc. to दण्डी (II. 273), and भामह II. 80 says it was called संख्यान by मेधावी.

समासोक्ति found in all.

समाहित found in all, but the समाहित of दण्डी is different from उद्भट's and is the समाधि of later writers; वामन's समाहित is quite different from both. The verse in भट्टि that is समाहित according to जय० is स्वभावोक्ति according to मल्लि०.

ससन्देह found in all except दण्डी who includes is under उपमा calling it संशयोपमा; वामन uses the form सन्देह.

सहोक्ति found in all.

सूक्ष्म defined by दण्डी alone (II. 260); भामह denies that it is an अलं०.

[1]स्वभावोक्ति defined by दण्डी, उद्भट and भामह (II. 93) alone, the latter admitting it according to others and exemplifying it also (in II. 94) as आक्रोशन्नाह्वयन्नन्यानाधावन्मण्डलैर्नुदन्। गा वारयति दण्डेन गोपः सस्यावतारिणीः॥. It appears that भामह as a concession to his predecessors acceded to the view that

1. Vide Dr. Raghavan on 'the history of स्वभावोक्ति' in Indian Culture, vol. V. for 1938 pp.147-166 and in 'Some concepts &c.' pp. 92-116. (1942). In the latter he elaborates his former paper.

स्वभावोक्ति is an अलङ्कार and in II. 94 gave an appropriate example; दण्डी calls it जाति also. भट्टि's वार्ता included स्वभावोक्ति. अग्निपुराण 343. 3 calls it स्वरूप.

हेतु found in भट्टि and दण्डी (II. 235 ff); भामह denies (II. 86) it the position of अलं०. उद्भट would bring it under काव्यलिङ्ग.

14. The काव्यालङ्कार of रुद्रट. This work has been edited in the KM series with the commentary of नमिसाधु (the third edition of 1928 has been used here). The काव्यालङ्कार is an extensive work divided into 16 अध्यायs and reviews the whole field of Poetics. It is composed mostly in the *Āryā* [1]metre with a few exceptions here and there, particularly at the end of most chapters. All the examples are Rudraṭa's own. There are in all 734 verses, beside which 14 verses in the 12th अध्याय dealing with the eight kinds of नायिका and their sub-varieties are declared to be interpolations. The shortest chapter is the 13th containing only 17 verses and the longest are the 7th and 8th containing respectively 111 and 110 verses. The contents of the 16 chapters are;—1, obeisance to गणेश and गौरी, purposes and objects of काव्य, the essential requisites of a poet viz शक्ति, व्युत्पत्ति and अभ्यास, and definitions of these; 2, काव्यलक्षण, the five अलङ्कारs of शब्द viz. वक्रोक्ति, अनुप्रास, यमक, श्लेष and चित्र are enumerated, the four रीतिs वैदर्भी, [2]पाञ्चाली, लाटी and गौडी are briefly defined, six भाषाs (प्राकृत, संस्कृत, मागध, पैशाची, शूरसेनी and अपभ्रंश) in which काव्यs are composed are mentioned, then वक्रोक्ति and अनुप्रास are defined, divided and illustrated and five वृत्तिs (मधुरा, ललिता, प्रौढा, परुषा and भद्रा) of अनुप्रास are defined; 3, elaborate treatment of यमक in 58 verses; 4, श्लेष and its eight varieties (वर्ण, पद, लिङ्ग, भाषा, प्रकृति, प्रत्यय, विभक्ति and वचन and illustrations of भाषाश्लेष (same words in संस्कृत and प्राकृत, पैशाची, शौरसेनी etc); 5, treatment of चित्र, viz. such combinations and tricks of words as चक्रबन्ध, मुरजबन्ध, अर्धभ्रम, सर्वतोभद्र, मात्राच्युतक, प्रहेलिका etc.; 6, the *doṣas* of पद and वाक्य; 7, the four

1. गोपाल in his com. on the काव्यप्रकाश (Tri. ed. p. 2) has a paronomastic verse on रुद्रट referring to his partiality for the आर्या metre 'अतिलोकमलङ्कारमाविभ्रदमृतस्तुतम् (स्तुतम् ?) । आर्यानुरागी सर्वज्ञः सत्यं रुद्रः स रुद्रटः ॥'. सर्वज्ञ is an appellation of शिव also and आर्या means पार्वती and आर्या metre.

2. 'वृत्तेः समासवत्यास्तत्र स्यू रीतयस्तिस्रः ॥ पाञ्चाली लाटीया गौडीया चेति नामतोऽभिहिताः । लघुमध्यायतविरचनसमासभेदादिमास्तत्र ॥...वृत्तेरसमासाया वैदर्भी रीतिरेकैव ॥ काव्यालङ्कार II. 3, 4, 6.

bases of the figures of अर्थ viz. वास्तव, औपम्य, अतिशय and श्लेष and definitions of 23 figures based upon वास्तव; 8, 21 figures based on औपम्य; 9, 12 figures based upon अतिशय; 10, ten varieties of शुद्ध-श्लेष and two kinds of सङ्कर; 11, the nine *doṣas* of अर्थ and four *doṣas* of उपमा; 12, ten *rasas*, definition of शृङ्गार and its two varieties सम्भोग and विप्रलम्भ, qualities of नायक and his companions and varieties of नायक and नायिका; 13, सम्भोगशृङ्गार and characteristic actions of heroines at particular times and places; 14, characteristics of विप्रलम्भशृङ्गार, the ten दशाs of विप्रलम्भ, the six उपायs for winning over an offended lady, viz. साम, दान, भेद, प्रणति, उपेक्षा, प्रसङ्गभ्रंश; 15, characteristics of वीर and the other *rasas*; 16, various kinds of poetic compositions such as कथा, आख्यायिका and their plots and other characteristics.

रुद्रट was the first to attempt a scientific classification of figures as based upon certain definite principles, such as वास्तव, औपम्य, अतिशय and श्लेष. The result of rigorously following this classification has been this that the same figure occurs as an अलङ्कार based upon two or more from among the four bases of division. For example, the figures सहोक्ति and समुच्चय are spoken of as having two varieties based upon वास्तव and औपम्य (in VII. 11 and VIII. 3) and the figure उत्प्रेक्षा (VIII. 2 and IX 2) as having two varieties based upon औपम्य and अतिशय. Some of the figures separately defined by writers like भामह and उद्भट are not separately defined by रुद्रट, e.g. उपमेयोपमा and अनन्वय are regarded as mere varieties of उपमा (called उभयोपमा and अनन्वयोपमा, 7. 9 and 11). A few figures defined by both earlier and later writers appear in Rudraṭa under other names. For example, the figure called व्याजश्लेष (10. 11) is the same as the व्याजस्तुति of भामह and मम्मट, अवसर (7. 102) is the same as the 2nd kind of the उदात्त of उद्भट and मम्मट, the जाति of रुद्रट (7. 30) is the same as the स्वभावोक्ति of दण्डी and मम्मट, the पूर्व of रुद्रट (9. 3) is the same as the 4th variety of अतिशयोक्ति (कार्यकारणयोर्यश्च पौर्वापर्यविपर्ययः). Some of the figures defined by रुद्रट are not admitted as अलङ्कारs by other writers. हेतु (defined as 'हेतुमता सह हेतोरभिधानमभेदकृद्भवेयत्र' 7. 82) is said by मम्मट to be no अलङ्कार at all. रुद्रट defines an अलङ्कार called भाव (with two well-known varieties, 7. 38 and 40) and gives two instances : ग्रामतरुणं तरुण्या नववञ्जुलमञ्जरीसनाथकरम् । पश्यन्त्या भवति मुहुर्नितरां मलिना मुखच्छाया ॥; एकाकिनी यदबला तरुणी तथाहमस्मिन्गृहे गृहपतिश्च गतो विदेशम् । किं याचसे तदिह वासमियं वराकी श्वश्रूर्ममान्धबधिरा ननु मूढ पान्थ ॥'. The first is cited by मम्मट (I) and the second by the लोचन (p. 53).

In both there is व्यङ्ग्य sense which is subordinated to the वाच्य sense. Similarly, the figures मत (VIII. 69), साम्य (VIII. 105), पिहित (IX. 50) are not defined by other early writers.

About Rudraṭa we know very little. He seems to have been a Kashmirian as his name suggests[1]. At the beginning of his work he performs an obeisance to Ganeśa and Gaurī and at the end he praises भवानी, मुरारि and गजानन. While commenting upon V. 12-14 नमिसाधु says 'अत्र च चक्रे स्वनामाङ्कभूतोयं श्लोकः कविनान्तर्भावितो यथा-शतानन्दापराख्येन भट्टवामुकसूनुना । साधितं रुद्रटेनेदं सामाजा धीमता हितम् ॥'. This shows that रुद्रट was also called शतानन्द, that his father's name was वामुक and that he was a student of the सामवेद. रुद्रट does not mention any author by name. But he seems to refer to भरत's नाट्यशास्त्र by the word आचार्यैः (in 12. 4), to मयूर (I. 9 तुत्वा तथाहि दुर्गां केचित्तीर्णा दुरुत्तरां विपदम् । अपरे रोगविमुक्तिं वरमन्ये लेभिरेऽभिमतम् ॥). He refers to the opinions of others, as in II. 2 (and नमिसाधु says thereon that the reference is to मेधाविरुद्र and others who held that शब्द is of four kinds only and not five), VII. 17. One geographical reference (in VII. 105) to the river Śiprā and Mālava ladies is interesting.

रुद्रट must be regarded as a representative of the अलङ्कार school. Although he knows the *rasa* theory propounded by Bharata and although he says that *kāvya* must be endowed with रस (तस्मात्तत्कर्तव्यं यत्नेन महीयसा रसैर्युक्तम् । chap. 12. 2), still he looked upon *alankāras* as very important. It is a noticeable feature that he does not attach importance to the *rītis*, though he casually refers to them (II. 4-6, XIV. 37, XV. 20) and speaks of four *rītis*; and the *guṇas* are not defined and illustrated by him. The साहित्यदर्पण (IX. 2) quotes from रुद्रट an *Āryā* about वैदर्भी which is not found in the काव्यालङ्कार. Some of the special features of रुद्रट's काव्यालङ्कार are : (1) He was the first to propound some basis for the classification of Alankāras (viz. वास्तव, औपम्य, अतिशय, श्लेष) ; (2) to the nine well-known rasas he adds प्रेयस् (12. 3 and 15. 17) as the 10th रस, (3) he does not attach

1. There is no doubt that many Kashmirian names end in ट. But there is no monopoly in names. In a grant of the Gurjara Pratihāra king Bhojadeva of Kanoj dated in the Vikrama year 893 (i.e. 836-37 A.D.) an officer named रुद्रट is found; 'रुद्रटेन प्रयुक्तस्य शासनस्य स्थिरायतेः । दूतको बालादित्योत्र राज्यभट्टारिकासुतः ।.' Vide E. I. Vol. 19 p. 15 at p. 18.

much importance to रीतिs; (4) he omits the treatment of guṇas; (5) In his alaṅkāra called भाव he makes a very near approach to the theory of व्यङ्ग्य sense being the main point in a poem. The अलं. स. p. 6 refers to this special point about रुद्रट.

The सङ्गीतरत्नाकर (p. 82 of Ānan. ed.) mentions a रुद्रट as सङ्गीताचार्य. But there is nothing to show that he was the same as the author of the काव्यालङ्कार.

The date of Rudraṭa can be settled with a good deal of certainty. He defines more figures than भामह, दण्डी and उद्भट and his treatment is precise and scientific. He is, therefore, somewhat later than these writers. He is quoted by numerous writers from the tenth century downwards. राजशेखर in his काव्यमीमांसा (p. 31) mentions him by name 'काकुवक्रोक्तिर्नाम शब्दालङ्कारोयमिति रुद्रटः and quotes (on p. 57) the verse चक्रं दहतारं चक्रन्दहतारं (रुद्रट III. 4). प्रतीहारेन्दुराज frequently quotes the verses of रुद्रट without actually naming him (vide pp. 11, 31, 34, 42, 43, 49, where रुद्रट 8. 40, 8. 89, 8. 95, 7. 35, 7. 36 and 12. 4 are respectively quoted). In the दशरूपकटीका by धनिक (on IV. 35), रुद्रट (XII. 4) is quoted. The लोचन (p. 53) quotes रुद्रट's definition of भाव (VII. 38) and his example. मम्मट quotes him by name (IX p. 521 Vā.) and criticizes his views about हेतु, समुच्चय and व्यतिरेक (क्षीणः क्षीणोपि शशी etc.). Therefore रुद्रट is not later than about 900 A. D. उत्पल in his commentary on the first verse of the योगयात्रा of Varāhamihira (of which there is a ms. in the Bhau Daji collection in the B. B. R. A. S.) names रुद्रट and quotes his definition of अनन्वय and his example of it also (viz. काव्यालङ्कार 8. 11 and 12). At the end of his commentary on the बृहज्जातक published in the Harikrishna Nibandha series (Benares 1934) there are a few verses one of which says that the commentary was composed in śaka 888 (i.e. in 966 A.D.). But great doubt is cast on the genuineness of these verses by two matters, viz those verses are absent from Utpala's commentary in a ms. (D. C. No. 177 of A 1882-83) at the BORI, Poona. The 2nd matter is that in a paper by the great astronomer and expert in cuneiform texts in Babylon, Prof. Otto Neugebauer, published in the Bulletin of the Royal Academy of Belgium for 1957 (pp. 133-140) about the Greek translation of Abu Ma'shar's version on dreṣkāṇas where it is said on p. 134 n. 3 that Abu Ma'shar died in 886 A.D., that his translation contains a passage about the 3rd Dreṣkāṇa of Aries that belongs to Utpala's commentary. This would compel us to hold that Utpala must have flourished before 880 A.D. at the latest and that therefore Rudraṭa whom Utpala quotes must be placed before about 850 A.D.[1] The above conclusion is fortified by another consideration. It appears that Vallabhadeva who wrote a commentary on the Śiśupālavadha commented on रुद्रट. On Śiśu. II. 44 वल्लभदेव says 'नात्र भिन्नलिङ्गानामौपम्यं दोषायेति रुद्रटः'. On शिशु० IV. 11 वल्लभदेव says 'एतदस्माभी रुद्रजटालङ्कारे विवेचितम्'.[2] On शिशु II. 88 वल्लभदेव says 'उक्तं च शब्दार्थौ काव्यमिति'. This refers to रुद्रटकाव्यालङ्कार II.1 (ननु शब्दार्थौ काव्यं). वल्लभदेव's son's son कय्यट wrote a commentary on the Devīśataka of आनन्दवर्धन in गतकलि 4078 when भीमगुप्त was ruler of Kashmir (i. e. in 977 A. D.). Allowing 25 years for each generation वल्लभदेव must have been a grown-up man in 927 A. D. and was probably born about or before 900 A. D. Therefore, रुद्रट on whose work he commented must have flourished some time before 850 A.D. रुद्रट is quite unaware of the ध्वनि theory and has great affinity with भामह and उद्भट. He was probably a contemporary of or a little older than the author of the ध्वनिकारिका and flourished about 825-850 A. D.

The commentator नमिसाधु deserves more than a passing notice. He was a श्वेताम्बर जैन and pupil of शालिभद्र. He speaks of रुद्रट as सूत्रकार (8. 37, 6. 9). He composed his commentary in the year 1125 of the विक्रम era (i. e. 1068-69 A. D.). One old ms. gives the date as 1176 (i. e. 1119-20 A.D.). This latter date is wrong as नमिसाधु's com. called षडावश्यकटीका was composed in विक्रमसंवत् 1122 (1065-6 A.D.). Vide Peterson's Report III. p. 13. नमिसाधु is an early writer. He followed older commentators as he himself says 'पूर्वमहामतिविरचितवृत्त्यनुसारेण किमपि रचयामि' and refers to other explanations of रुद्रट's words (on II. 1, V. 23, VIII. 28 and 31). His commentary, though generally concise and to the point, contains many quotations. Among the authors and works either named or quoted from are the following :— अर्जुनचरित (16. 4), उद्भट (6. 33), कादम्बरी, किरातार्जुनीय, जयदेव (1. 18, as a writer on metrics), तिलकमञ्जरी (16. 3) दण्डी, नाममाला, पाताल-

1. Vide my paper on 'Varāhamihira and Utpala' in J. B. B. R. A. S., New Series, vol. 24-25 at pp. 22-23 and 26 for उत्पल and रुद्रट.

2. रुद्रजटालङ्कारे (in the Kashi S. Series which has been relied upon here) is obviously a wrong reading for रुद्रटालङ्कारे.

विजयमहाकाव्य of पाणिनि (2. 8.), पिङ्गल, बृहत्कथा (2. 12 peculiarities of पैशाची noted), भरत (12. 4 and 44), भर्तृहरि, भामह (8. 84, 10. 2), माघकाव्य (1. 20, VIII. 64), मालतीमाधव (7. 33), मृच्छकटिक (8. 1), मेधाविरुद्र (I. 2, II. 2), मेघदूत, रत्नावली (7. 33), वामन[1] (1. 20, 8. 10) विकटनितम्बा (6. 47), वेणीसंहार (7. 73), शिवभद्र (IV. 4), शिशुपालवध, हरि (on 2. 19, a writer in Prakrit on Poetics), हर्षचरित. There is a commentary on रुद्रट's work composed by आशाधर.[2] It has already been stated above that वल्लभदेव wrote a com. on रुद्रट; there is another commentary called रसतरङ्गिणी by गोपालभट्ट, son of हरिवंशभट्टद्राविड.

There is a work called शृङ्गारतिलक composed by रुद्रभट्ट. A keen controversy has raged for several years as to whether रुद्रभट्ट and रुद्रट are identical. Weber, Buhler (Kashmir Report p. 67), Aufrecht (Z. D. M. G. vol. 36 p. 376) and Pischel (in his Intro. to शृङ्गारतिलक p. 5 ff. and Z. D. M. G. 42, 1888, p. 296-304) held the view that they were identical, while Pandit Durgaprasad, Dr. Jacobi (VOJ 1888 vol. II. pp. 151-156 and Z. D. M. G. 42 pp. 425-435), Dr. Harichand in his work on Kālidāsa (pp. 91-95) think that they are distinct persons. This question must be briefly discussed here. The शृङ्गारतिलक has been published in the K. M. Series. It is divided into three परिच्छेदs. The first परि० deals with the nine *rasas*, the *bhāvas*, the various kinds of Nāyaka and Nāyikā. The second speaks of विप्रलम्भशृङ्गार, the ten stages of love in separation, the six *upāyas* for winning over one's offended beloved. The third treats of the other *rasas* and the four *vṛttis* कैशिकी, सात्वती,

1. On रुद्रट I. 20 नमिसाधु says 'तथा ह्यपिमिलि अर्थिवचिविलबप्रभृतयो धातवो धातुगणेषु पठिता अपि'. This I take is a reference to वामन's काव्यालङ्कारसूत्र V. 2. 2.

2. Dr. Bhandarkar's Report on the search for mss. for 1883-84 (pp. 391-93) contains an excerpt from a प्रशस्ति of आशाधर in धर्मामृतयतिधर्मटीका, where he describes himself as a Jain, as the son of सल्लक्षण and father of छाहड. Verse 15 mentions that he wrote a commentary on रुद्रट (रुद्रटस्य व्यधात् काव्यालङ्कारस्य निबन्धनम्). He was the author of several works such as a com. on. अमरकोश, on the अष्टाङ्गहृदय of वाग्भट, त्रिषष्टिस्मृतिशास्त्र, रत्नत्रयविधानशास्त्र and calls himself कलिकालिदास. He composed the प्रशस्ति in विक्रमसंवत् 1300 i. e. 1244 A. D. (verse 31). Vide E. I. vol. 9 at p. 107 for आशाधर.

आरभटी and भारती. रुद्रभट्ट says that he treats of *rasas* in their relation to *kāvya*, while Bharata spoke of them with reference to नाट्य; 'प्रायो नाट्यं प्रति प्रोक्ता भरताद्यै रसस्थितिः। यथामति मयाप्येषा काव्यं प्रति निगद्यते ॥' I. 5. The last verses are 'काव्या काव्यकथा कीदृग्वैदग्धी को रसागमः। किं गोष्ठीमण्डनं हन्त शृङ्गारतिलकं विना ॥ त्रिपुरवधादेव गतामुल्लासमुमां समस्तदेवनताम्। शृङ्गारतिलकविधिना पुनरपि रुद्रः प्रसादयति ॥'. The last verse is not found in some mss. That verse has been interpreted as meaning that रुद्रभट्ट composed another work called त्रिपुरवध. There is no doubt that there is a pun on the words त्रिपुरवध, शृङ्गारतिलक and रुद्र (god Śiva and the author रुद्र). It may be suggested as an alternative explanation that in त्रिपुरवध the author is not referring to his own work, but to a play (डिम) called त्रिपुरदाह said to have been performed by भरत before Śiva and his attendants (*vide* नाट्य० 4. 10) and धनिक's quotation on दशरूप IV. 57-60 'इदं त्रिपुरदाहे तु लक्षणं ब्रह्मणोदितम्। ततस्त्रिपुरदाहश्च डिमसंज्ञः प्रयोजितः ॥' इति भरतमुनिना स्वयमेव &c.

The mss. of the शृङ्गारतिलक sometimes give the name of the author as रुद्रट (*vide* I. O. cat. p. 321 No. 1131 and Madras Government mss. cat. 1918 p. 8697 No. 12955). The anthologies also make confusion and quote the verses of the काव्यालङ्कार as रुद्रट's and also as रुद्र's or रुद्रभट्ट's. For example, शार्ङ्ग० No. 3773 ('एकाकिनी यदबला' रुद्रट VII. 41) and No. 3778 ('मलयानिल०' रुद्रट II. 30) are ascribed respectively to रुद्र and भट्टरुद्र; Nos. 575 and 3473 correctly ascribe them to रुद्रट. शार्ङ्ग० Nos. 3567-68, 3579, 3670, 3675, 3754 are correctly ascribed to रुद्र (the author of शृङ्गारतिलक). The examples contained in the शृङ्गारतिलक appear to be the author's own and may be used for chronological purposes. The earliest authors who quote them are हेमचन्द्र (who quotes, for example, the verses यत्पार्श्विनं निवारितो० under शृ० I. 44 on p. 304 and गाढालिङ्गन० on p. 305 from the शृङ्गार० under I. 68) and विश्वनाथ. The very first verse (शृङ्गारी गिरिजानने ...इत्थं सर्वरसाश्रयः पशुपतिर्भूयात् सतां भूतये) of the शृ० is quoted and found fault with by हेमचन्द्र (p. 110). Therfore, the शृङ्गारतिलक must have been composed about or before 1100. A. D.

After the evidence I led in the History of Alaṅkāra Literature in 1923, it should not have been necessary to go into details to say that रुद्रट and रुद्र are not identical. But as even after that there are writers like the editor of the भावप्रकाशन (pp. 68-73 of Intro. GOS) who persist in treating the two as identical I have again to set out the whole evidence.

On an examination of all that may be urged for and against the identity of the two authors, it must be conceded that there are very weighty grounds for holding that the two are distinct authors. The reasons may be briefly stated. Chapters XII-XIV of रुद्रट cover almost the same ground as the शृङ्गारतिलक and very often in the same words. It does not seem very likely that the same author would write two works in this manner, the only important addition in the शृङ्गारतिलक being that of the illustrative verses. The शृङ्गारतिलक in a few cases gives more details, such as the treatment of the four *vṛttis*, the definition of the ten stages of love, the sub-divisions of Nāyikā and their definitions. But there are some points where रुद्रट gives more information e. g. रुद्रट 14. 22-24. There are some doctrines on which the views of the काव्यालङ्कार and of the शृङ्गारतिलक conflict. It is not likely that the same author will impart conflicting directions on vital points. The शृङ्गारतिलक (I. 10) says that there are nine *rasas* in काव्य; while रुद्रट says there are ten (12. 3). शृङ्गा° speaks of four वृत्तिs (कैशिकी etc. which are transferred from the realm of the drama to that of *kāvya* in general), while रुद्रट speaks of five वृत्तिs (called मधुरा, प्रौढा etc. II. 19) and is silent about the कैशिकी and other *vṛttis*. रुद्रट first classifies नायिका into स्वीया, परकीया and वेश्या and then says that all the three may be अभिसारिका or खण्डिता and sub-divides स्वीया into स्वाधीनपतिका and प्रोषितपतिका; while the शृङ्गार° speaks of eight kinds of नायिका in one place (I 72-73, KM ed.). रुद्रट (12. 39-40) has not one good word to say about courtesans, but the शृङ्गारतिलक, while admitting the justice of the strictures passed by some against them, puts in a defence on their behalf. Compare रुद्रट 12. 39 (सर्वाङ्गना तु वेश्या सम्यगसौ लिप्सते धनं कामात् । निर्गुणगुणिनोस्तस्या न द्वेष्यो न प्रियः कश्चित् ॥) with शृङ्गार° I. 62-63 (सामान्यवनिता वेश्या सा वित्तं परमिच्छति । निर्गुणेपि न विद्वेषो न रागोस्या गुणिन्यपि ॥ तत्स्वरूपमिदं प्रोक्तं कैश्चिद्वब्रूमो वयं पुनः ।' The शृङ्गार° winds up by saying about courtesans 'सर्वस्वमेतास्तदहो स्मरस्य (I. 69).' The words कैश्चित् in the शृङ्गार० is very suspicious. It seems almost certain that शृङ्गार° refers to रुद्रट's words. There is a slight difference between the words of रुद्रट 'साक्षाच्चित्रे स्वप्ने स्याद्दर्शनमेवमिन्द्रजाले वा । देशे काले भङ्ग्या साधु तदाकर्णनं च स्यात् ॥' (12. 31) and those of the शृङ्गार° 'साक्षाच्चित्रे तथा स्वप्ने तस्य स्याद्दर्शनं त्रिधा । देशे काले च भङ्ग्या च श्रवणं चास्य तद्यथा ॥' (I. 51). Barring such points of difference there is a remarkable coincidence of thought and phraseology between the two works, which cannot be explained away by the fact that the subject treated of is the same. There is also one very important point to be noted. रुद्रट is the name by which the author of the काव्यालङ्कार has been mentioned by writers from about 900 A.D. onwards and his काव्यालङ्कार quoted by राजशेखर, प्रतीहारेन्दुराज, वल्लभदेव, धनिक, लोचन, नमिसाधु (Intro. verse), मम्मट (on काव्यप्रकाश IX 'तथा चुक्तं रुद्रटेन 'स्फुटमर्थालङ्कारौ०' काव्यालङ्कार IV. 32), अलं. स. p. 6 (रुद्रटेन तु भावालङ्कारो द्विधैवोक्तः). It is very remarkable that none of these writers names रुद्रभट्ट or शृङ्गारतिलक. Even हेमचन्द्र who is the earliest writer on Poetics to quote from the शृङ्गारतिलक does not mention the name of the author. It is the anthologies that confuse the two names रुद्रट and रुद्र. The सूक्तिमुक्तावली of जल्हण (about 1258 A. D.) cites verses from the काव्यालङ्कार (such as किं गौरि० II. 15, एकाकिनी यदबला० VII. 41) and from the शृङ्गारतिलक only under रुद्र and does not even name रुद्रट or cite a single verse under his name. On the other hand the सदुक्तिकर्णामृत of श्रीधरदास (composed in 1205 A. D.) cites almost all verses even from the शृङ्गारतिलक under रुद्रट. As both these are among the earliest anthologies it follows that the confusion between the two names came to be made from about 1150 A.D. The editor of the भावप्रकाशन (Intro. p. 69) is wrong in thinking that the editor of the काव्यालङ्कार of रुद्रट arbitrarily omitted fourteen verses as spurious after काव्यालङ्कार XII. 40. They are not commented upon by नमिसाधु[1] as seen from the mss. in the B. O. R. I. The mere fact that the भावप्रकाशन (p. 95) states that रुद्रट speaks of 384 varieties of नायिका and that the verses called spurious do refer to 384 varieties does not prove anything. That is begging the question. To those who hold that the two writers came to be confounded by about 1150 A. D. the words of the भावप्रकाशन do not at all matter. This merely shows that the भावप्रकाशन which was composed between 1175-1250 A. D. even acc. to the editor (Intro. p. 76) himself confounds the two authors

1. Vide Cat. of Govt. Mss. at the BORI, Poona, vol. XII. No. 133-135 pp. 147-151. One of the mss. was copied in संवत् 1471 (1415 A. D.). The editor was perfectly justified in rejecting fourteen verses as spurious when such an old ms. contained no commentary on them.

just as the anthologies do. The number (384) is given in the शृङ्गारतिलक of रुद्र also (इत्थं शतत्रयं तासामशीतिश्चतुरुत्तरा । I. 88]. The भावप्रकाशन practically quotes the शृङ्गारतिलक I. 162, omits I. 63 and again quotes शृ. ति. I. 64 and ascribes them to रुद्रट (साधारणस्त्री गणिका सा वित्तं...गुणिन्यपि । शृङ्गाराभास एव स्यान्न शृङ्गारः कदाचन । इति द्विषन्तमुद्दिश्य प्राह श्रीरुद्रटः कविः । भावप्र० p. 95). The भावप्रकाशन (p. 96) quotes सर्वस्वमेतास्तदहो स्मरस्य from शृ. ति. I. 69. The रसार्णवसुधाकर (pp. 30, 87) falls into the same confusion and ascribes the verses ईर्ष्या कुलस्त्रीषु (शृ. ति. I. 69) and शृङ्गारहास्यकरुणरसातिशयसिद्धये (शृ: ति. III. 39) to रुद्रट.

The editor of the भावप्रकाशन (p. 70 Intro.) makes light of the difference in the number of *rasas* mentioned by रुद्रट and रुद्र; but that will not appeal to those who know the acute and long-standing controversies about the number of rasas.

To say that the वृत्तिs कैशिकी and others are अर्थवृत्तिs while the five वृत्तिs of रुद्रट are शब्दवृत्तिs does not deserve much weight on the question of identity. The शृङ्गारतिलक also (III. 38 and 40) in defining कैशिकी and आरभटी does emphasize the importance of proper letters, words and compounds : माधुर्ययुक्ताल्पसमासरम्या वाणी स्मृतासाविह कैशिकीति ॥. ओजस्विगुर्वक्षरबन्धगाढा ज्ञेया बुधैः सारभटीति वृत्तिः ॥. Besides, there is no apparent reason why when Rudraṭa spoke of ten *rasas*, referred to vyabhicāribhāvas like *nirveda*, set out Śṛṅgāra and heroes &c. (12-3-9 &c.) and prescribed (in 14. 37) the वृत्तिs मधुरा and ललिता and वैदर्भी and पाञ्चाली for शृङ्गार, he should not have spoken of कैशिकी and other वृत्तिs, which are described in the शृङ्गारतिलक immediately after the enumeration of व्यभिचारभावs in relation to each *rasa*. The only alternative is to suppose that one of the works is based on the other. Taking all the above circumstances together I think that रुद्र is later than रुद्रट, elaborates the dicta of रुद्रट with illustrations, bases his शृङ्गारतिलक on the काव्यालङ्कार and flourished between 950-1100 A. D.

धनिक in his comment on दशरूपक (IV. 60) says 'उत्स्वप्नायितो यथा रुद्रस्य-निर्मथने मयाम्भसि०'; this is found in neither of the two works. The प्रतापरुद्रयशोभूषण cites two quotations from रुद्रभट्ट (p. 11 and p. 335), which are found in neither of the two works. It cannot be ascertained whether the रुद्र who is mentioned as author of the त्रैलोक्यसुन्दरीकथा in the तिलकमञ्जरी of धनपाल (verse 35) is the same as the author of the शृङ्गार० (the verse is स मदान्धकविध्वंसी रुद्रः कैर्नाभिनन्द्यते । सुश्लिष्टललिता यस्य कथा त्रैलोक्यसुन्दरी ॥).

15 The ध्वन्यालोक. The work has been published in the KM series with the commentary, called लोचन, of अभिनवगुप्त, on the first three उद्द्योतs. Dr. S. K. De edited the commentary of अभिनवगुप्त on the 4th उद्योत from some mss, in the Journal of the Dept. of Letters, Calcutta University, vol. IX. pp. 15-42. Kashi S. S. [also called Haridas Sanskrit Granthamālā] published the whole of the Dhvanyāloka with Locana on all the four Uddyotas and a modern commentary called Bālapriyā. This was published in 1940. The ध्वन्यालोक is an epoch-making work in the history of Alaṅkāra Literature. It occupies the same position in the Alaṅkāraśāstra as Pāṇinī's sūtras in grammar and the Vedāntasūtras in Vedānta. The work shows great erudition and critical insight. It is written in a lucid and forcible style and bears the stamp of originality on every page. As the रसगङ्गाधर remarks (p. 425 ध्वनिकृतामालङ्कारिकसरणिव्यवस्थापकत्वात्), the ध्वन्यालोक settled the principles to be followed in Poetics.

The ध्वन्यालोक is divided into three parts: first come the कारिकाs, which are 129 in the K. M. (first) edition, then comes the वृत्ति in prose explaining (often at great length) the *kārikās*, and the examples, most of which are taken from previous poets. The work is divided into four उद्द्योतs. The first verse is a शार्दूलविक्रीडित, the 13th is an Āryā, the 4th and 6th Upajātis, and in the 3rd उद्द्योत there are four आर्याs, while all the other kārikās in the first three *uddyotas* are in the śloka metre; but in the 4th which contains only 17 कारिकाs, the last three verses are in the रसोद्धता, मालिनी and शिखरिणी metres.

All Sanskrit scholars owe a deep debt of gratitude to the Kāvyamālā series of the Nirṇaya-sāgar Press in Bombay for issuing hundreds of beautifully printed and cheap editions of Sanskrit works. The Dhvanyāloka with Locana was printed in that series for the first time over sixty years ago based on three mss. only. The text of the Dhvanyāloka and of the Locana as then printed was rather defective. And the same text has been reprinted by the Press in several editions [except omitting some verses as Kārikās]. Now many new mss. have become available. At the Bhandarkar Institute alone I found five mss. in Devanāgarī characters and two in Śāradā script. An edition based on these and other mss. available in the whole of India is a great *desideratum*. The

Calcutta Sanskrit Series brought out an edition of the ध्व॰ alone with a modern commentary called अवधान by Madhusudan Miśra. This edition does not specify the mss. on which they are based. Such editions are of little value and appear to be copies of the K. M. edition. The ध्व॰ was translated into German by Dr. Jacobi in Z. D. M. G. vol. 56 pp. 18-60, 311-343, 392-410, and vol. 57 pp. 586-615, 710-789. Dr. Jacobi made several suggestions about the correct readings and other matters, most of which have been accepted by later writers. One feels serious doubts about the genuineness of several verses printed as *kārikās* in the K. M. edition. Later on this will be discussed in connection with one or two kārikās. The kārikās in the 4th Uddyota appear to be later as pointed out by Prof. S. P. Bhattacharya in his paper (6th All India O. Conference pp. 613-622). There is apparently no reason why kārikās II. 18-20 should have been printed as kārikās, when they are introduced in the वृत्ति (p. 106) with the words 'अस्यैवार्थस्य संग्रहश्लोकाः' and they practically repeat the words and ideas of kārikās II. 15-17 and the वृत्ति thereon. This mistake has been acknowledged in the *corrigenda*. In the वृत्ति itself some portions arouse great suspicions. On p. 178 the वृत्ति as printed contains the आर्या 'इति काव्यार्थविवेको योयं चेतश्चमत्कृतिविधायी। सूरिभिरनुसृतसारैरस्मदुपज्ञो न विस्मार्यः ॥'. The K. M. editors note that out of their three mss. two do not contain this verse. They should have omitted it from the text and put it in a footnote. I find on consulting five Devanāgarī mss. and two Śāradā mss. (No. 256 and 257 of the collection of 1875-76 at B. O. R. I.) that none of them contains this verse. It is certainly spurious. Another noticeable feature is, that out of the 112 kārikās of the Nir. text in the first three Uddyotas only all—except eight as noted above—are in the śloka metre. But in the 4th Uddyota out of 17 kārikās the last three are in the रथोद्धता, मालिनी, and शिखरिणी metres. Besides, the Prakrit Gāthā (rather mutilated) which occurs on p. 297 (K. M. edition) is not commented upon by the लोचन as printed by Dr. De in Journal, Department of Letters, Calcutta, vol. IX. nor in the ध्वनिगाथापञ्जिका (ms. in the B. O. R. I.).

At the outset one is confronted by two questions viz. whether all the three parts of the work are by the same author and, if they are not, then who is the author of the कारिकाs and of the वृत्ति. That the वृत्ति and the citation of the examples proceed from the same author admits of no doubt. The real difficulty is about the authorship of the कारिकाs and the वृत्ति. The evidence on the subject of the identity of the कारिकाकार and the वृत्तिकार is both internal and external and further it is voluminous, I cannot go into all such evidence in detail for want of space. But the issue has been so much obscured by several half-digested, superficial and rather partisan writings, that I am reluctantly compelled to devote considerable space to this question. The learned reviewer of my 'History of Sanskrit Poetics' (1951) in JAOS vol. 72 (1952) pp. 129-130 finds fault with me for contentious repetitions about the kārikās and vṛtti (though he himself agrees that they are by different authors); but as even in the latest work of Dr. K. Krishnamoorthy (p. XVII of Introduction to the translation of the Dhvanyāloka, Poona, 1955) strong belief in the identity of the authors of the kārikā and vṛtti is affirmed, I have retained all the arguments advanced in the edition of 1951. The first Uddyota of the Dhvanyāloka with an English exposition by Prof. Bishnupada Bhattacharya has been published by the firma K. L. Mukhopādhyāya (Calcutta). It was I who first collected almost all important external evidence which was almost unanimous in holding the identity of the two. I should be glad if ultimately it be proved that the same person is the author of both कारिकाs and वृत्ति. I have pursued this subject in as detached a manner as I could. There are three stages in the case of a hypothesis, it is either proved, or not proved, or is disproved. I still hold that the hypothesis of non-identity cannot in the language of the law be said to be disproved. It is very near to being proved. It should not be supposed that the remarks of the लोचन are the mainstay of those who question the identity. All that they claim is that the लोचन is not helpful to the other side and rather goes against identity. The लोचन which was composed about 150 years after the ध्वन्यालोक is very frequently at great pains to distinguish between the author of the कारिकाs and the author of the वृत्ति. The following quotations will make this clear. From the days of Bühler (in Kashmir Report p. 65) about seventy-five years ago up to the present day the question whether the author of the kārikās and that of the vṛtti in the

ध्वन्यालोक is one and the same person has been discussed at great length and it cannot be said that it has been settled beyond cavil. In the limited space at my disposal I cannot deal with all the material that has gathered round this question. Those who feel deeply interested in this problem may read Dr. De in Bulletin of the School of O. Studies, vol. I part 4 pp. 1-9, and his H. S. P. 107-116, Prof. S. P. Bhattacharya in the proceedings of the 6th O. Conference pp. 613-622, Mr. K. Goda Varma in New I. A. vol. V. pp. 265-272 for the view that the author of the kārikās is different from that of the vṛtti, while M. M. Prof. Kuppuswami (in his उपलोचन p. 11), his pupil Dr. A. Sankaran in his 'The theories of Rasa and Dhvani' pp. 50-60, Dr. Satkari Mookerjee in B. C. Law vol. I. pp. 179-194, Dr. K. C. Pandey in his dissertation on 'Abhinavagupta' pp. 132-140, and Dr. K. Krishnamoorthy in I. H. Q. vol. 24. pp. 180-194 and pp. 300-311, Prof. Mankad in New Indian Antiquary vol.VI. p. 211 may be read for the theory of the identity of the two. I shall briefly reply to the important points raised by the latter group of scholars.

Before proceeding further I must make it clear that here and there some passages of the Locana and of the Abhinavabhāratī do imply that Ānandavardhana is the author of both the kārikās and the vṛtti. We know that eminent authors often follow the ancient or ordinarily accepted views. For example, compare the अलं. स. and साहित्यदर्पण on समासोक्ति. But this does not dispose of the matter finally. There are other passages which clearly lead to the inference that the लोचन felt that the authors were different. It would not do to gloss over such inconvenient passages not only in the लोचन, but in the वृत्ति, in the कारिकाs themselves and in writers like मुकुलभट्ट. So far as the Locana is concerned these passages that I quote below have not been satisfactorily explained by any of the scholars who are for the identity of the vṛttikāra and kārikākāra. All that Dr. Sankaran says after citing two passages from the अभिनवभारती and setting out a few passages which according to him indicate identity is as follows (in the 'Theories of Rasa and Dhvani' at p. 59): 'the only evidence which apparently favours the opposite view, viz. the distinction occasionally made by Abhinava between kārikākāra and vṛttikāra loses its force and it has to be explained differently. Probably Abhinava desired, in order to facilitate his comments, to keep the Kārikās distinct from the Vṛtti and he achieved it by referring to their author in two capacities as Kārikākāra and Vṛttikāra'. Dr. Sankaran has either failed to grasp the significance and force of the seven or eight passages quoted by me, particularly 2, 6 and 7 or he has shut his eyes to their implications. Morever, he does not consider many other matters which will be set out below. The references here are to the 4th edition of K. M. of 1935 A. D. With reference to passage 8 quoted from the लोचन, one wonders why the लोचन, if it firmly believed in identity, does not straightforwardly say 'यद्यप्यर्थानन्त्यमात्रे हेतुः कारिकायां नोक्तस्तथापि मया वृत्तौ उक्त एवेति भावः'. The important passages of the लोचन are : (i) 'अत एव **मूलकारिका** साक्षात्तन्निराकरणार्था न श्रूयते । **वृत्तिकृत्तु** निराकृतमपि प्रमेयसंख्यापूरणाय कण्ठेन तत्पक्षमनूद्य निराकरोति येपीत्यादिना ।......तेनात्र प्रथमोद्योते ध्वनेः सामान्यलक्षणमेव कारिकाकारेण कृतम् । द्वितीयोद्योते कारिकाकारोऽवान्तरविभागं विशेषलक्षणं च विदध-दनुवादमुखेन मूलविभागं द्विविधं सूचितवान् । **तदाशयानुसारेण वृत्तिकृ**दत्रैवोद्योते मूल-विभागमवोचत् etc. (लोचन. pp. 71-72.); (2) 'न चैत**न्मयोक्त**म्, अपि तु **कारिका-काराभिप्रायेणे**त्याह तत्रेति । भवति मूलतो द्विभेदत्वं **कारिकाकारस्यापि संमतमेवेति** भावः।' p. 73; (3) 'उक्तमेव ध्वनिस्वरूपं तदाभासविवेकहेतुतया **कारिका**कारो-ऽनुवदतीत्यभिप्रायेण **वृत्तिकृ**दुपस्कारं ददाति p. 149; (4) 'एतत्तावत्त्रिभेदत्वं न कारिकाकारेण कृतं वृत्तिकारेण तु दर्शितं न चेदानीं वृत्तिकारो भेदप्रकटनं करोति । ततश्चेदं कृतमिदं क्रियते इति **कर्तृभेदे** का सङ्गतिः । pp. 150-151; (5) कारिकाकारेण पूर्वं व्यतिरेक उक्तः । न च सर्वथा न कर्तव्योऽपि तु बीभत्सादौ कर्तव्य एवेति पश्चादन्वयः । वृत्तिकारेण तु अन्वयपूर्वको व्यतिरेक इति शैलीमनुसर्तुमन्वयः पूर्वमुपात्तः' (pp. 160); (6) on the words प्रतिपादितमेवैषामालम्बनम् in the ध्व. (p. 166) the लोचन says '**अस्मन्मूलग्रन्थकृतेत्यर्थः**'; (7) on the words in the ध्व. (pp. 169-170) 'एवमादौ च विषये यथौचित्यत्यागस्तथा **दर्शितमेवाग्रे**' लोचन remarks 'दर्शितमेवेति कारिकाकारेणेति भूतप्रत्ययः'. The last remark means this : if the कारिका and वृत्ति had been the work of the same author, he would have used the future tense in place of the past in the word दर्शितं, when referring to what was to be discussed later on; but as the कारिकाs were the work of a predecessor and were already before the वृत्तिकार when he wrote this passage, he employs the words दर्शितमेवाग्रे (कारिकाकारेण); (8) With reference to the वृत्ति on ध्व. IV. 3 लोचन says 'यद्यप्यर्थानन्त्यमात्रे हेतुर्वृत्तिकारेणोक्तस्तथापि कारिका-कारेण नोक्त इति ।' (Dr. De in Dept. of Letters, Calcutta Un. vol. IX at p. 29). For other places where the word वृत्तिकार occurs in the लोचन, thought not expressly in such opposition to the कारिका-

कार as in the above passages, *vide* लोचन pp. 57, 86, 103, 127, 132, 140. It has further to be noted that the लोचन generally applies the epithet ग्रन्थकृत् to the author of the वृत्ति and the examples and the word मूलग्रन्थकृत् or-कार to the author of the कारिकाs (as in the passage quoted above from p. 166). On the words 'तथा चान्येन कृत एवात्र श्लोकः' ध्व. (p. 10) the लोचन says 'ग्रन्थकृत्समानकालभाविना मनोरथनाम्ना'. If this मनोरथ be held to be identical with the मनोरथ mentioned above under Vāmana as having flourished in the reign of Jayāpīḍa (राजत० IV. 497) then it is impossible that he could have been a contemporary af आनन्दवर्धन. Dr. K. Krishnamoorthy supposes (I. H. Q. vol. 24 at p. 308) 'that the early age of आनन्द० and the old age of Manoratha synchronised'. Even this assumption has no foundation. Acc. to राजत० V. 34 the poet आनन्द० became famous as a poet in the reign of अवन्तिवर्म. The विषमबाणलीला, the अर्जुनचरित and the देवीशतक were, it appears, composed before the ध्वन्यालोक. That means that the ध्वन्यालोक was a work of a man of mature years and so आनन्दवर्धन as a critic (not as a poet) should be held to have become well-known probably about or after 875 A. D. If मनोरथ was to be a contemporary of आनन्द० and an adverse critic of आनन्दवर्धन's theory he must have lived right into the last quarter of the 9th century, while he began his life as a poet under जयापीड (779-813 A. D.) in the last quarter of the 8th century. So it would have to be supposed that he lived for more than 100 years and could at such an age ridicule आनन्दवर्धन. The ध्वन्यालोक names विषमबाणलीला and अर्जुनचरित; the देवीशतक also mentions these two, but it is itself not named or quoted in the ध्वन्यालोक. The देवीशतक is full of such tricks as यमकs, चित्रबन्धs. It was impossible for him to take pride in his देवीशतक when he delivered the following *dictum* in ध्व. pp. 277-278 'इदानीन्तनानां तु न्याय्ये काव्यनयव्यवस्थापने क्रियमाणे नास्त्येव ध्वनिव्यतिरिक्तः काव्यप्रकारः, यतः परिपाकवतां कवीनां रसादितात्पर्यविरहे व्यापार एव न शोभते'. So ध्व. must have been written many years after the देवीशतक, when आनन्दवर्धन had arrived at far-reaching conclusions about the purpose of poetry on the basis of the ध्वनिकारिकाs. On the words सहृदयानामानन्दः' (ध्व. p. 13) the लोचन says 'आनन्द इति च ग्रन्थकृतो नाम तेन स एवानन्दवर्धनाचार्य एतच्छास्त्रद्वारेण' etc.' p. 14; 'समासोक्त्याक्षेपयोरेकमेवोदाहरणं व्यतरद् ग्रन्थकृत्' (लोचन p. 44); 'एवमभिप्रायद्वयमपि साधारणोक्त्या ग्रन्थकृन्न्यरूपयत्' (p. 45); on the verse आहूतोपि सहायैः, 'अत एव ग्रन्थकारः सामान्येन' etc. (लोचन p. 70). The above quotations lead to the inference that the

लोचन really regarded आनन्दवर्धन as the author of the वृत्ति and that he was distinct from the author of the कारिकाs. We have to see how far this accords with the view of other early writers and what the name of the author of the कारिकाs was, supposing he was not identical with आनन्दवर्धन.

Of the above seven passages again 2, 6, 7 are most important. The passage 2 means (on the word प्रकाशितः in वृत्ति): this it not what I, the vṛttikāra, have stated out of my own head, but I have stated it in *accordance with the intention of the author of the kārikās* and so the word 'tatra' is used in the vṛtti ...(Dhvani) is first of two kinds (as stated in the first Uddyota) and this is also *approved of by the kārikākāra;* this is the meaning, (p. 73 of K. M. ed.). If the कारिका and वृत्ति had been the work of the same author, where was the necessity of the vṛttikāra saying that he follows the अभिप्राय of the कारिकाकार and that what he the वृत्तिकार did say is कारिकाकारसंमत ? He could have simply said 'what I meant by the कारिका is this'. In ordinary life if a man makes a statement in one place about a certain matter and makes a different statement about the same matter in another place, he does not speak of his own संमति to what he said before. He can simply say 'I am explaining what I said or what I meant to say or did not say'. No question of संमति arises when the same man makes two statements. Similarly, the passage on p. 166 of the Locana is utterly inexplicable on the theory of the identity of authorship. The passage relates to the relation between *guṇas* and *saṅghaṭanā*'. A question is asked by on objector in the vṛtti: What do you suppose is the substratum of *guṇas* ? If *saṅghaṭanā* is not the *āśraya* thereof, what is the āśraya ? The vṛtti gives the reply : 'the substratum of guṇas has already been propounded' and quotes kārikā II. 7. On this (i. e. on the word प्रतिपादितमेव) the Locana observes 'अस्मन्मूलग्रन्थकृता' (by the author of the original work on which my vṛtti is written). If the author of both कारिका and वृत्ति were the same person and लोचन firmly held that view, would not one expect अभिनवगुप्त to have explained प्रतिपादितं by the words मयैव द्वितीयोद्योते तमर्थं० इति कारिकायामित्यर्थः ? Why does the लोचन explain as अस्मन्मूलग्रन्थकृता (and not simply मत्कृतकारिकायाम् or मया कारिकायाम्) ? The लोचन does explain certain verses quoted in the vṛtti in this way. For example, on the two verses रसभावादिविषय० and रसादिषु विवक्षा तु० quoted on p. 277 with the words

तदिदमुक्तम्, the लोचन remarks मयैवेत्यर्थः i. e. states explicitly that those verses are the composition of the vṛttikāra himself. On p. 293 at the end of the 3rd Uddyota the K. M. edition read the words अनाख्येयांश॰ as a कारिका, but that was corrected in the ed. of 1935. The वृत्ति quotes that verse after तदिदमुक्तं (as on p. 277) and the लोचन explains उक्तमिति संग्रहार्थं मयैवेत्यर्थः. About the expression अस्मन्मूलग्रन्थकृता which is very inconvenient for the theory of identity, Dr. Mookerjee says (B. C. Law vol. I. 191) 'my thesis has been that the distinction is a matter of form, *lapse from which was very seriously regarded as an unpardonable offence*'. Where does the learned Doctor get this rule which he expresses in such strong language ? Dr. Krishnamoorthy who throughout take his cue from Dr. Mookerjee, remarks (on अस्मन्मूलग्रन्थकृता) that those words 'need not trouble us since the differentiation is but formal in accordance with the etiquette of exegesis'. I request the learned doctors to site at least one instance from their vast reading where the sūtras or kārikās and the vṛtti thereon being admittedly composed by one man, a commentator of the vṛtti explains some words of the वृत्ति resembling प्रतिपादितमेवैषामालम्बनम् with the words अस्मन्मूलग्रन्थकृता. Otherwise, all their remarks about the etiquette of exegesis and 'rules of the game' are entirely in the air and utterly baseless. Dr. Mookerjee complains (B. C. Law, vol. I, p. 190) that too much capital has been made of the words 'अस्मन्मूलग्रन्थकृता'. I do not understand why it should not be made. This sentence is one of the most critical passages that determine the real attitude of the लोचन on the identity or non-identity of authorship. In this connection we have to find out the exact meaning of the word ग्रन्थकृत् or ग्रन्थकार used by the Locana in numerous places. On p. 44 we have a decisive passage of the Locana on the verse अनुरागवती सन्ध्या cited in the vṛtti. The लोचन says 'वामनाभिप्रायेणायमाक्षेपः...एकमेवोदाहरणं व्यतरद्ग्रन्थकृत् । ......इत्यत्राशयोत्र ग्रन्थेऽस्मद्गुरुभिर्निरूपितः ।'. Here it is absolutely clear that the word ग्रन्थकृत् applies only to the वृत्तिकार, since the example occurs only in the वृत्ति. I hold that ग्रन्थकृत् is everywhere used by the लोचन for the वृत्तिकार. I request those who are for the theory of identity to point out some examples where the लोचन undoubtedly applies the word ग्रन्थकृत् to the कारिकाकार. Dr. Mookerjee protests (B. C. Law vol. I. p. 189) against equating वृत्तिकार with ग्रन्थकृत् and against holding that both have the same meaning or application in the लोचन. But that is a mere protest without warrant. He has not cited a single passage where the word ग्रन्थकृत् has been undoubtedly applied to the author of the कारिकाs by the लोचन. Why does the लोचन introduce the मङ्गल verse स्वेच्छाकेसरिणः with the word वृत्तिकारः? If both the कारिका and वृत्ति were the work of the same man in the opinion of the लोचन, why does it not introduce the मङ्गल verse with the word कारिकाकारः or even ग्रन्थकारः? It is noteworthy that the first कारिका is introduced on p. 3 as merely आदिवाक्य and nothing more. Similarly, on p. 45 (एवमभिप्रायद्वयमपि साधारणोक्त्या ग्रन्थकृन्न्यरूपयत्); p. 70 (अत एव ग्रन्थकार... ध्वनौ भक्तेरभावमभ्यधात्);[1] on p. 109 (ततश्च...अयं ग्रन्थकृत आशयः), on p. 289 (where the Prākrit verse अहिणअपओअरसिएसु is cited for illustrating ध्वनेः संसृष्टालङ्कारसंसृष्टत्व on which लोचन remarks ताभ्यां ध्वनेः सङ्कर इति ग्रन्थकारस्याशयः) the word ग्रन्थकृत् or ग्रन्थकार is applid to the वृत्तिकार alone. Therefore, in the two places on p. 14 of the लोचन where the word ग्रन्थकृत् occurs (आनन्द इति च ग्रन्थकृतो नाम and सहृदय...ग्रन्थकृदिति भावः) the same meaning must be taken. The 7th passage दर्शितमेवाग्रे is satisfactorily explicable only on the theory that the author of the kārikās is different from the vṛttikāra. Dr. Krishnamoorthy's reference to other places where the future is employed in the vṛtti will not explain away the use of the past tense in दर्शितमेवाग्रे. He merely echoes Dr. Mookerjee who refers to pp. 14, 23, 26, 34 of the old K. M. edition (pp. 18, 27, 31, 40 of ed. of 1935). These references are put forward merely because the वृत्ति contains a word in the future. But they are of no value. On p. 18 the वृत्ति says 'स त्वर्थो... वस्तुमात्रमलङ्कारा रसादयश्चेत्यनेकप्रभेदप्रभिन्नो दर्शयिष्यते.' This is not a reference to any कारिका but to the वृत्ति itself in the 2nd उद्योत. There is no single कारिका which expressly divides ध्वनि into वस्तु, अलङ्कार and रसादि. On p. 27 the वृत्ति says 'द्वितीयोपि प्रभेदो वाच्याद्विभिन्नः सप्रपञ्चमग्रे दर्शयिष्यते'. This again does not refer to a कारिका, but to his own वृत्ति as the word सप्रपञ्चं makes clear and लोचन understands it to be a reference to वृत्ति only (अग्रे इति द्वितीयोद्योते असंलक्ष्यक्रमव्यङ्ग्यः० इति विवक्षितान्यपरवाच्यस्य द्वितीयप्रभेदवर्णनावसरे). The same remarks apply to the passages on pp. 31, 40. They

1. तस्माद्भक्तिरलक्षणम्—these are the words in the वृत्ति (p. 67). कारिका I. 21 on which this वृत्ति० occurs does not employ the word भक्ति at all, but गुणवृत्ति. So लोचन must be held to refer to the वृत्ति.

contain only a reference to what would be discussed in the वृत्ति later on. As to दर्शयिष्यते on p. 26 of the वृत्ति the लोचन does not mention even a कारिका. Again on p. 40 (अग्रे दर्शयिष्यामः) the reference is to the elaborate treatment in four printed pages explaining III. 42-43 in which several verses of the वृत्तिकार himself are quoted. The two Doctors have not been able to shake the natural inference drawn from दर्शितमेवाग्रे in the वृत्ति and have merely deluded themselves into thinking that the वृत्ति refers to the कारिकाऽ by a verb in the future. Dr. Mookerjee (B. C. Law vol. I. pp. 187-188) in explaining these very inconvenient words 'दर्शितमेवाग्रे' makes this strange observation for which there is absolutely no authority beyond his own assertion 'the use of the future tense with the implication of personal identity as made out by M. M. Kane would be unjustifiable since the vṛttikāra is *required* to behave as a different person as a matter of form'. Where dose the learned Doctor get this ? A वृत्तिकार *may* speak of himself in the 3rd person but what law or rule lays down that he *must* do so. The only explanation that Dr. Satkari Mookerjee (in Dr. B.C. Law presentation vol. I. at pp. (180-182) puts forward is the plea that distinction between the author of sūtras or kārikārs and a vṛtti thereon by himself is 'a formal one' (p. 180) even when the same person is known to have composed both. Then he puts forward another proposition 'the role of the commentary is to explain what is implicitly contained in the original and it is an *offence* against the rules of exegesis to introduce matters foreign to the original. The offence is technically called 'utsūtravyākhyāna.' On p. 181 he concedes that 'authors of sūtras and kārikās when they happen to be the same person have not been sufficiently on their guard in their observance of this rule'. Admitting for the present the rule stated above, I fail to see from where Dr. Mukerjee got the proposition stated by him on p. 182 (in B. C. Law vol. I.) 'All internal evidence embodied either in the original text or in the gloss purporting or alluding to personal identity will be regarded as an offence against the rules of the game.' I totally deny that there is any such ancient rule of exegesis anywhere prohibiting a *commentator* from showing that the author of the sūtras or kārikās and of the vṛtti thereon are identical or different or any rule laying down that the violation of this supposed rule is condemned anywhere as an offence. The learned Doctor seems to have forgotten for the moment that about a hundred years before the Dhvanyāloka Vāmana expressly tells us that he wrote the sūtras as well as the vṛtti. Hemacandra does the same. We have at the end of the Kauṭilīya the well-known words 'svayam-eva Viṣṇuguptaś-cakāra sūtram ca bhāṣyam ca'. So it is clear that there is no prohibition against an author saying that he himself composed the sūtra and the vṛtti, even when he speaks of himself in the third person in the vṛtti. Why should a stranger (like Abhinava) be prevented from saying that the author of the kārikās and vṛtti thereon is different or the same as the case may be ? The two learned Doctors make a fetish of the argument derived from what is said against 'utsūtra-vyākhyāna' and on this very slight foundation have advanced strange propositions. It passes my understanding how Dr. Krishnamoorthy arrived at the following conclusion (I. H. Q. vol. 24 at p. 187) 'Nor can we look for any internal evidence embodied either in the original text or in the gloss purporting or alluding to personal identity since such a procedure would definitely go against the rule of the game' (this is copied from Dr. Mookerjee quoted above). *Hence the only reliable evidence which can prove the difference* of the authors will be extra-textual testimony". I repudiate these propositions as entirely baseless and unwarranted. It is for scholars to say whether they will accept these '*rules of the game*', which, in my opinion, are non-existent.

'Utsūtravyākhyāna' was condemned mostly in grammar, where the perfection of Pāṇini's work made people resent attempts to add to Pāṇini's sūtras by *adhyāhāra* and the like.[1] But it will be quite clear to anyone who has read the bhāṣyas, vṛttis and vārtikas on many sūtra works that commentators, while paying lip service to the theory of the condemnation of utsūtra-vyākhyāna, have added enormously even to what can be regarded by the utmost stretch of the imagination as implications of sūtras. Works callad bhāṣyas have no higher privileges than those called vṛttis. Śaṅkarācārya's famous bhāṣya on the Bṛhadāraṇyaka is called a vṛtti.[2] The Śāba-

1. Compare शिशुपालवध II. 112 'अनुत्सूत्रपदन्यासा'.
2. Compare सुरेश्वर who in his बृ. उ. भाष्यवार्तिक Intro. verse 2

rabhāṣya (on Jaimini I. 3. 4, IV. 1. 2) and Kumārila's Tantravārtika (I. 3. 5-7, I. 3, 8-9) sometimes give as many as three interpretations of the *same sūtra or adhikaraṇa*. It is impossible to hold that the sūtras were intended by the author of the sūtras to have three meanings. The पूर्वमीमांसासूत्र contains no sūtra on आत्मास्तित्व and Śabara enters on that question in great detail. The पञ्चपादिका of पद्मपाद remarks on this विधिवृत्तमीमांसाभाष्यकारोऽपि उत्सूत्रमेवात्मसिद्धौ पराकान्तवान् (p. 148 of the Madras Govt. mss. Library ed.). Similarly, Dr. K. Krishnamoorthy on p. 185 refers to the dictum of Kullūka that ācāryas do not speak about their views in the first person but in the third person. There is nothing in this. I showed long ago from Medhātithi's bhāṣya on Manu I. 4 (H. of Dh. vol. I. p. 90) which Kullūka merely repeats that this is the practice of ācāryas. But this is not invariably so, as Yāj. I. 56 will show. Dr. Krishnamoorthy further relies on what Dr. K. C. Pandey says in his work on 'Abhinavagupta' pp. 134 ff., who puts forward the practice in Kashmir that the same person wrote sūtras or kārikās and a commentary. Hardly any one would dispute this (at least I do not). But all this is irrelevant. The question is not whether the same writer could have written a vṛtti on his own kārikās, but whether in this particular case he actually did so and whether passages of the Locana accept the identity or whether they lead to the inference of non-identity. Dr. Krishnamoorthy (pp. 187 ff.) follows Dr. Mookerjee in the propositions about exegetical etiquette. We are not dealing here with the two works of the same author, but with the remarks of a commentator like Abhinava who had before him a work of kārikās and a vṛtti thereon. There is nothing in exegetical rules of any kind to prevent the commentator from indicating that the kārikākāra and vṛttikāra are identical or different. Kumārilabhaṭṭa, a great commentator and author of the Tantravārtika, expressly tells us that several sūtras of Jaimini have no substance in them or are meaningless.[1] He combats the positon

---

says: 'यां काण्वोपनिषच्छलेन सकलाम्नायार्थसंशोधिनीं सञ्चक्रुर्गुरवोऽनुवृत्तगुरवो वृत्तिं सतां शान्तये ।'.

1. अतः परं षट्सूत्राणि भाष्यकारेण न लिखितानि । तत्र व्याख्यातारो विवदन्ते । केचिदाहुर्विस्मृतानि ।...फल्गुत्वादुपेक्षितानीत्यन्ये । अनार्षेयत्वादित्यपरे । वृत्त्यन्तरकारैस्तु सर्वैर्व्याख्यातानि । सन्ति च जैमिनेरेवंप्रकाराण्यनत्यन्तसारभूतानि सूत्राणि । तन्त्रवार्तिक after जै. III. 4. 9 p. 895 (Ānan. ed.),

'sūtreṣveva hi tatsarvam yadvṛttau yacca vārtike' (on Jaimini II. 3 16). The following quotation explains in what cases it is the *duty* of the वृत्तिकार to make additions and in what cases he should avoid saying that words have to be understood in the सूत्र.[1] That quotation makes it clear that whatever is necessary for helping the pupil or reader to understand the subject may be done by the वृत्तिकार. All that was meant by the fact of 'utsūtravyākhyāna' not being allowed was that, as long as possible, a commentator should not put forward words as being understood in a sūtra. But otherwise the commentator was free to say that the sūtra is not clear and that it does not mention the subject of discussion (as Śabara does on Jaimini II. 3. 16 विशये प्रायदर्शनात्) or to say that the sūtrakāra held a certain view ignoring a certain Upaniṣad passage (as done by Śaṅkara on Vedāntasūtra III. 4. 18). Even the merest tyro can see that every bhāṣya or vṛtti adds vastly to what the plain meaning of the sūtra is and introduces topics far beyond what the sūtra expresses or implies. To take one glaring example, the sūtra 'अंशो नानाव्यपदेशात्' (वेदान्तसूत्र II. 3. 43) is explained by Śaṅkarācārya as अंश इव; while several other commentators take the sutra as it is without adding any word and criticize Śaṅkarācārya for the result of his taking such liberties in order to make the meaning of the sūtra square with his philosophy of the Absolute. Dr. Pandey in his work on 'Abhinava' p.

---

1. सूत्रेष्वेव हि सत्सर्वं (तत्सर्वं ?) यद्वृत्तौ यच्च वार्तिके। सूत्रं योनिरिहार्थानां सर्वं सूत्रे प्रतिष्ठितम्॥ इति ये वदन्ति तान्प्रत्युच्यते। न किंचित्साधनमप्रदर्शितविषयं स्वार्थं साधयति। सूत्रकारेण चेह हेतुमात्रमुपात्तम्। न चार्थप्रकरणादिभिरप्युदाहरणप्रतिज्ञासंशयहेतूनामन्यतममुपलभ्यते। तस्मादगमके सूत्रे सति अवश्यं दोष-प्रतिसमाधानार्थं वृत्तिकारादिभिर्यतितव्यम्। सत्येव सम्भवेऽध्याहारादिवर्जनमुक्तम्। **सर्वथा शिष्यप्रज्ञासंस्कारे सूत्रकारादीनां प्रवर्तमानानां येनैव तदनुगुणं यत्कृतं तदेव ग्रहीतव्यं नासद्ग्रहः कर्तव्यः।** इदं सूत्रकारेण नोपात्तमिदं वृत्तिकारेणैतत्प्रदर्शनार्थमेतद्वर्णयन्ति।. Dr. Mookerjee (B. C. Law vol. I at p. 180) merely refers to Nāgeśa quoting the first half of the kārikā cited above in this note. He should have gone to the Tantravārtika where this is quoted not as Kumārila's own view but of others, which he rejects. The न्यायसुधा (p. 932 of Ch. S. Series) explains the words सर्वथा शिष्य...नासद्ग्रहः कर्तव्यः as follows: भाष्यं व्याचष्टे सर्वथेति। युक्तिगम्येऽर्थे पुरुषविशेषस्यानादरणीयत्वाद्युक्तियुक्तं यद्वृत्तिकारादिभिरुक्तं तत्सूत्रकारानुपात्तत्वान्न ग्राह्यमित्यसदाग्रहो न कार्य इत्याशयः।'

133 admits 'here we might add that though there is considerable expansion, revision and modification of the views of the *kārikā* in the *vṛtti*, yet all that is of the nature of an addition to clear the ideas of the former, for that is the one purpose that the commentary is intended to serve'. Dr. Krishnamoorthy also admits this (I. H. Q. vol. 24 p. 301).

But if the vṛtti is composed by the author of the kārikās himself, then the edge of the reproach of 'utsūtravyākhyāna' is altogether blunted. He can very well say 'my sūtra is brief and I am expanding its meaning for the sake of clear grasp of the subject'. Or he may say in the vṛtti that what he stated in the sūtra in due only to his following old writers and that his own real opinion is different. I may give one or two striking examples. The अलं. सं. (p. 109) defines अर्थान्तरन्यास as 'सामान्यविशेषभावकार्यकारणभावाभ्यां निर्दिष्टप्रकृतसमर्थनमर्थान्तरन्यासः' and काव्यलिङ्ग as 'हेतोर्वाक्यपदार्थता काव्यलिङ्गम्'। (p. 143). But on p. 148 the सर्वस्व observes in the वृत्ति 'ततश्च सामान्यविशेषभावोऽर्थान्तरन्यासस्य विषयः, यत्पुनरर्थान्तरन्यासस्य कार्यकारणगतत्वेन समर्थकत्वमुक्तं तदुक्तलक्षणकाव्यलिङ्गमनाश्रित्य। तद्विषयत्वेन लक्षणान्तरस्यौद्भटैरनाश्रितत्वात्।' &c. The सर्वस्व practically admits in the वृत्ति that he defined अर्थान्तरन्यास without adverting to his own definition of काव्यलिङ्ग (in the सूत्र.). That is here the वृत्तिकार gives up the position taken by himself in the sūtra. मम्मट defines काव्य as तददोषौ॰ according to the older rhetoricians, though he is a staunch advocate of the ध्वनि theory. If a वृत्तिकार can himself give up what he stated in the sūtra without any breach of any supposed rule of etiquette, much more therefore does it follow that a stranger commentator explaining a sūtra and vṛtti by the same author is not tramelled by any rule of exegesis about stating anything about the sūtra and vṛtti and is not bound to keep the sūtrakāra and vṛttikāra in watertight compartments. I request Dr. Pandey, Dr. Mookerjee and Dr. Krishnamoorthy to produce eight (or even a lesser number of instances of clear apparent opposition of the views of the vṛttikāra and kārikākāra (where the author of both is the same and where he belongs to the 9th or 10th century) and the commentator is a different person altogether and brings out the opposition. They have said that in Kashmir it was a practice in the 9th century for the same man to write kārikās and explanatory commentary thereon. So it should not be difficult for them to give such instances from the commentator of a work containing both कारिकाs and वृत्ति by the same author. Dr. Pandey (in 'Abhinavagupta' p. 135) refers to the fact that the great Utpaladeva, the *paramaguru* of Abhinava, himself wrote a vṛtti and a ṭīkā on his own ईश्वरप्रत्यभिज्ञासूत्र (in the form of Kārikās) and states that Abhinava in his com. called Vimarśinī does not expressly mention (on p. 22 of the विमर्शिनी) that the वृत्तिकार and टीकाकार quoted by the विमर्शिनी are the same person and thereby might lead a person ignorant of the truth to hold that the two (वृत्तिकार and टीकाकार) are different persons. I believe that this is cited by Dr. Pandey as an argument by analogy for establishing the identity of the कारिकाकार and the वृत्तिकार (in the ध्वन्यालोक). Not only is this analogy worthless, but it will rather indicate that Abhinavagupta did not hold the view that the कारिकाकार (of ध्व०) was identical with the वृत्तिकार and it further demolishes all the strange arguments about the supposed exegetical etiquette advanced by Dr. Mookerjee and Dr. Krishnamoorthy. In the Introductory verse 5 at p. 3 (of the विमर्शिनी) अभिनवगुप्त expressly states that on the Pratyabhiñā-sūtras (the kārikās) the *author himself* (Utpaladeva) wrote a *vṛtti* in which he explained only the purport and a ṭīkā in which he discussed the doctrines of the kārikās (वृत्त्या तात्पर्यं टीकया तद्विचारः सूत्रेष्वेतेषु ग्रन्थकारेण दृब्धम् ।). Nothing could be clearer than this. No exegetical etiquette stood in the way of Abhinavagupta against telling his readers about the identity of the kārikākāra and vṛttikāra. Applying this to the Dhvanyāloka, one may naturally ask : why did not the लोचन of अभिनवगुप्त expressly state in the beginning of his commentary (as he does in the विमर्शिनी) that the kārikākāra and vṛttikāra were identical and why does he keep silence about this identity and leave students to surmises and arguments based on his words sown broadcast in his Locana ? Then there is another point. Having once expressly stated that the kārikās, vṛtti and ṭīkā were all composed by Utpaladeva, why should he have every now and then trotted forth the fact of identity ? अभिनव thought that those who cared to understand Kashmir Pratyabhijña Philosophy would be a few but earnest and careful students and would always bear in mind what he had stated in the very beginning of his commentary. He could not and did not anticipate how writers of theses in the 20th century would handle his works and words. Dr. Krishnamoorthy blindly picks up (in I.H.Q. vol. 24 at p.186) the example cited by Dr. Pandey and does not care to read in the original the work on which Dr. Pandey relies in order to see whether the latter's arguments are sound and whether they are of any value whatever on the question in hand.

Out of the several striking passages mentioned by me Dr. Bhattacārya emphasizes the one p. 149 (old ed. p. 121) where the वृत्ति has the expression यतश्च on which the लोचन remarks 'उक्तमेव ध्वनिस्वरूपं तदाभासविवेकहेतुतया कारिकारोऽनुवदतीत्यभिप्रायेण वृत्तिकृदुपस्कारं ददाति। यतश्चेति'. One cannot understand why on the theory of identity the लोचन should have employed these words stating that the वृत्तिकार adds a supplement or embellishment (उपस्कार) to what the कारिकाकार (i. e. to himself, on the theory of identity) says.

Some capital is sought to be made by M. M. Kuppuswami Sastri (p. 11 in उपलोचन) and by Dr. Pandey (in his 'Abhinavagupta' pp. 135-136) of the apparent absence of a maṅgala Śloka at the beginning of the kārikās and of the presence of a maṅgala in the vṛtti. Several replies can be offered as against this. In the first place, the practice about a maṅgala at the beginning of each work is not observed invariably by all early writers. So far as I know, there is no maṅgala at the beginning of Śabara's bhāṣya on Jaimini or at the beginning of Śaṅkarācārya's bhāṣya on the Vedāntasūtras, or in Vātsyāyana's bhāṣya on the Nyāyasūtra, or in उद्योतकर's न्यायवार्तिक or in मण्डनमिश्र's विधिविवेक (to take only eminent early writers). Where the same author composes the sūtras or kārikās and the vṛtti, the practice varies. Vāmana has apparently no maṅgala in his sūtras but he has one at the beginning of his vṛtti. Mammaṭa has maṅgala kārikā at the beginning of the Kāvyaprakāśa, but none in the vṛtti. Udbhaṭa commences his work on Alaṅkāra without any maṅgala. The Alaṅkārasarvasva has no maṅgala in the sūtras, but has one only in the vṛtti. Hemacandra has a maṅgala both at the beginning of his sūtras and in his vṛtti, Alaṅkāracūḍāmaṇi. Further, no particular form is prescribed. Pāṇini is supposed to have performed maṅgala by employing the word 'vṛddhi' at the beginning of his first sūtra and the Mahābhāṣya says that the word सिद्ध was employed in the वार्तिक 'सिद्धे शब्दार्थसम्बन्धे' for the same purpose. In the same way, the words काव्यस्यात्मा at the beginning of the कारिकाs may well serve as a maṅgala by invoking Dhvani as Śabda-Brahma or Sarasvatī that has two functions viz. kavi and sahṛdaya (sarasvatyāstattvam kavisahṛdayākhyam vijayatāt, as the Locana puts it).

Dr. K. Krishnamoorthy (in Annals of B.O.R.I. vol. 28 at p. 194) quotes the three passages from Mukula and Pratīhārendurāja that I set out in my last edition and then remarks 'these evidences are quite insufficient to prove the hypothesis that a circle of *sahṛadayas* first gave currency to the theory of Dhvani' and argues that '*sahṛadayaiḥ*' can be taken as standing for the author of Dhvanyāloka also. It must be remembered, however, that I never said that a circle of सहृदयs composed कारिकाs. But on p. 195 he seems to be mystified why Mukula and Pratīhārendurāja should give such respect to an author who belongs to a rival school of thought and winds up 'Thus though incidentally आनन्दवर्धन may also be meant by the expression it is not exclusively applicable to him. It primarily refers to the whole class of critics that preceded आनन्द०.'

The general practice seems to be that ancient authors were mentioned in the singular while those that were elderly contemporaries or flourished just a little before the writer are mentioned in the plural. For example, Mammaṭa mentions Bharata (an ancient *muni*), Rudraṭa (from whom he quotes probably more verses than from any other single author) and Dhvanikāra in the singular, while he refers to Abhinava a commentator of Bharata and of the Dhvanyāloka in the plural. Śaṅkarācārya refers to Bhagavān Upavarṣa and Ācārya Śabara in the singular. For this reason Mukula who as will be shown below was almost a younger contemporary of Ānanda spoke of the latter's teacher (if he was called Sahṛdaya) in the plural. The Dhvanyāloka itself pays great honour to Udbhaṭa and others from whom it entirely differed as to the soul of poetry (as in the vṛtti on II. 27 'तत्रभवद्भिरुद्भटादिभिः'), since Udbhaṭa was very near in time. I cannot accept the hypothesis of Dr. Krishnamoorthy that there was a circle of sahṛdayas who first gave currency to the theory of dhvani. Such revolutionary theories are not embodied in kārikās by a *circle* of people, but only by a single gifted author. The words of Mukula ध्वने.....नूतनतयोपदर्शितस्य should leave no doubt in an unbiassed mind that the reference is to a work recently produced. प्रतीहारेन्दुराज, being a pupil of Mukula, followed his master in employing the plural सहृदयैः.

The word काव्यजीवितभूत: employed by him pointedly refers to the first Kārikā 'काव्यस्यात्मा'.

The three[1] passages mentioned by Dr. Krishnamoorthy on pp. 182-183 can be explained in various ways. In the first place, the कारिकाs become part of the वृत्ति which explains them. The word व्याख्याय and निरूप्य refer to the वृत्तिकार as the agent of these actions and the word आह itself refers to him because the वृत्तिकार begins the discussion of असंलक्ष्यक्रमव्यंग्य in the first case by citing and explaining the कारिका 'यस्तु' (III. 2). The same remarks apply to the words of the लोचन on p. 275 'एवं व्यंग्यस्वरूपं' &c. In the second place, it is not an invariable rule that the agent of the *lyabanta* and of the principal verb in the sentence should be the same. Even great poets like Kālidāsa and Bhāravi do not observe this rule, as in रघुवंश I. 77(अवजानासि मां यस्मादतस्ते न भविष्यति। मत्प्रसूतिमनाराध्य प्रजेति त्वां शशाप सा ॥)[2] and in किरातार्जुनीय III. 21. In the third place, the two passages do not vividly and forcibly emphasize the identity as the non-identity is brought out very forcibly by the eight passages quoted by me (on pp. 165-166). Lastly, it has to be remembered that the कारिकाकार and वृत्तिकार had come to be identified, as shown later on, even before अभिनवगुप्त. So अभिनव did not harp every now and then upon the difference between the two. That a commentator often takes over the words from the original work and incorporates them among his own remarks (even by using the first person) may be illustrated from several commentaries. To take one instance from the Vedāntasūtras, I extract the following from Śaṅkara's bhāṣya on III. 4. 47 (सहकार्यन्तरविधि: पक्षेण तृतीयं तद्वतो विध्यादिवत्) 'तस्माद्ब्राह्मण इति प्रशंसावादस्तथैवाथ मुनिरित्यपि भवितुमर्हति समाननिर्देशत्वादिति। एवं प्राप्ते ब्रूमः—सहकार्यन्तरविधिरिति'. I may cite another example from the लोचन itself (p. 22) 'अथोच्यते दृष्टैव झडिति तात्पर्यप्रतिपत्तिः किमत्र कुर्मः इति तदिदं वयमपि नाङ्गीकुर्मः। यद्वक्ष्यामः– 'तद्वत्सचेतसां सोऽर्थो वाच्यार्थविमुखात्मनाम्। बुद्धौ तत्त्वावभासिन्यां झटित्येवावभासते॥'. This is कारिका I. 12.

1. Two of the passages are:

(a) एवं कारिकां व्याख्याय तदसंगृहीतमलक्ष्यक्रमव्यङ्ग्यं प्रपञ्चयितुमाह यस्त्विति। लोचन p. 159.

(b) एवं व्यंग्यस्वरूपं निरूप्य सर्वथा यत्तच्छून्यं तत्र का वार्तेति निरूपयितुमाह प्रधानेत्यादिना कारिकाद्वयेन। लोचन p. 275 (old ed. pp. 219-220).

2. आराधनस्य राजा कर्ता भवनस्य प्रजेति।

As regards the quotations from the अभिनवभारती (quoted in the note below) which seem to regard आनन्दवर्धन as the author of the kārikās and the vṛtti we have to remember several facts. Abhinava's teacher in the exposition of the Dhvanyāloka was Indurāja (whose explanations he implicitly follows as stated in Locana pp. 44, 227); the अभिनवभारती was composed sometime after the लोचन (as the passages in the footnote expressly state).[1] His teacher in the Nāṭyaśāstra was a different one viz. Bhaṭṭa Tota who was the author of a work called Kāvyakautuka on which Abhinava wrote a vivaraṇa.[2] For भट्टतोत and the great respect paid to him by अभिनव० and for following his views in preference to those of others, vide the 3rd introductory verse to अ. भा. ('सद्विप्रतोतवदनोदितनाट्यवेदतत्त्वार्थमर्थिजनवाञ्छितसिद्धिहेतोः । माहेश्वराभिनवगुप्तपदप्रतिष्ठः संक्षिप्तवृत्तिविधिना विशदीकरोति ॥) and pp. 3, 292-93, 310 of vol. I., pp. 67, 216, 395, 423, 440-441 of vol. II. of the अ. भा. and pp. 78 (six verses of Bhaṭṭa

---

1. अभिनवगुप्त in his commentary on भरत (chap. 7 vol. I. p. 341) refers to his commentary on ध्वन्यालोक as सहृदयालोकलोचन; 'स्वशब्दानाभिधेयत्वं हि रसादीनां ध्वनिकारादिभिर्दर्शितम् । तच्च मदीयादेव तद्विवरणात्सहृदयालोकलोचनादवधारणीयमिह तु यथावसरं वक्ष्यत एव'. Again on भरत 16. 5 vol. II. pp. 299-300 अभिनवगुप्त says "एतमेवार्थं सम्यगानन्दवर्धनाचार्योऽपि विविच्य न्यरूपयत् । 'ध्वन्यात्मभूते०' (ध्व. II. 21) इत्युक्त्वा क्रमेण 'विवक्षा तत्परत्वेन०' (ध्व. II. 22) इत्यादिना ग्रन्थसन्दर्भेण सोदाहरणेन । तच्चास्माभिः सहृदयालोकलोचने तद्विवरणे विस्तरतो व्याख्यातमिति". As shown below the work was called सहृदयहृदयालोक by राघवभट्ट and in the colophons of certain mss. That was probably its original name and it meant 'the light of or on the heart or meaning of sahṛdaya'. This would be an additional argument for postulating सहृदय as the name of the author of the कारिकाs. In course of time हृदय came to be dropped and the work was called simply सहृदयालोक as the quotations from the अ. भा. show. आलोक is used in the sense of 'light' by the कारिका I. 9 (आलोकार्थी यथा दीपशिखायां यत्नवाञ्जनः) and in the sense of 'proper knowledge or understanding' in कारिका II. 14 (बुद्धिरासादितालोका सर्वत्रैव भविष्यति), where the लोचन explains 'आसादितः आलोकः अवगमः सम्यग्व्युत्पत्तिर्यया' (p. 84).

2. This was composed by अभिनव even before the लोचन; vide p. 221 'स चास्मदुपाध्यायभट्टतौतेन काव्यकौतुके, अस्माभिश्च तद्विवरणे बहुतरकृतनिर्णयः &c.'

Tota on rasa, abhinaya &c are quoted), 82 (द्विजवरतोतनिरूपितसन्ध्यध्यायार्थतत्त्वघटनेयम्। अभिनवगुप्तेन कृता शिवचरणाम्भोजमधुपेन॥) of vol. III. of अ. भा. The reference to उपाध्यायाः (in अ. भा. vol. III. pp. 3, 10, 19, 47, 163) and to उपाध्यायपादाः on p. 71 (2 verses quoted) of vol. III. of अ. भा. are meant for भट्टतोत. Therefore, it is possible that Abhinava in the अ. भा. simply states the views of his teacher Tota about the authorship of the kārikās and vṛtti. The fact that almost all writers who come long after the Dhvanyāloka (as shown by myself) identify the Kārikākāra and Vṛttikāra is not of great moment, if even a single writer contemporary with or immediately coming after it states to the contrary and if there are other cogent reasons for holding the opposite view. Truth is not governed by mere majorities or is not necessarily in accord with what majorities believe.

Dr. Mookerjee charges me with having failed to pay proper attention to the word सता in the passage quoted a few lines below and himself translates the words as 'by me, in the capacity of a vṛttikāra'. If one has already made up one's mind that the authors of kārikā and vṛtti are identical, then only this translation is proper. But it begs the whole question. There is no word for 'capacity,'. The literal translation is 'by me who am vṛttikāra'. But if one's mind is open and one reads the whole passage up to संमतमेव, a totally different conclusion has to be arrived at as shewn above and everything including 'satā' is quite explicable. The वृत्तिकार according to लोचन means to say : 'I being (सता) a वृत्तिकार expounded at length the two major divisions of ध्वनि; I have not, in doing so, drawn purely on my own imagination (reading उत्सूत्र) but what I have said is implicit in the words of the कारिकाकार'. Let us examine how both Dr. Mookerjee (in B. C. Law vol. I. p. 184 n. 7) and Dr. Krishnamoorthy (I. H. Q. 24 pp. 188-189) lay great emphasis on the words of Locana in explaining the vṛtti at the beginning of ध्व. II. 1 (एवमवि...ध्वनिर्द्विप्रकारः प्रकाशितः). The लोचन as they quote it from the Banaras edition (p. 165) runs 'मया वृत्तिकारेण सतेति भावः। न चैतन्मयोत्सूत्रमुक्तमपि तु कारिकाकाराभिप्रायेणेत्याह तत्रेति।...भवति मूलतो द्विभेदत्वं कारिकाकारस्यापि संमतमेवेति भावः।.' I do not know on what mss. the Banaras edition is based. Mss. or their sources or dates are nowhere mentioned in that edition. But in the first sentence the K. M. edition (p. 73 of 1935 ed.) omits the important word उत्सूत्रं and the editors who rely on three mss. do not note that anyone of the mss. had the word उत्सूत्रम्. I have already dealt with the inferences to be drawn from the use of the word अभिप्रायेण and संमतमेव in the वृत्ति (pp. 165 and 167 above). Dr. Mookerjee relies upon a passage of the वृत्ति introducing the third उद्द्योत (B. C. Law vol. I. pp. 185-186) and enters upon a discussion of the words of the Locana referring to Candrikākāra. This has to be very carefully scrutinized. Later on I shall quote several passages from the Locana in which a previous commentator called चन्द्रिकाकार, who belonged to the same family as Abhinava's and who must have preceded him by at least a generation or two, is criticized or mentioned. On p. 150 the लोचन summarises laconically the views of the चन्द्रिकाकार about the construction of certain words of the वृत्ति. At the beginning of the third Uddyota the वृत्ति reads 'एवं व्यङ्ग्यमुखेनैव ध्वनेः प्रदर्शिते सप्रभेदे स्वरूपे पुनर्व्यञ्जकमुखेन तत्प्रकाश्यते' and then follows the कारिका 'अविवक्षितवाच्यस्य.' The लोचन passage is (p. 150) 'यस्तु व्याचष्टे व्यङ्ग्यानां वस्त्वलङ्काररसानां मुखेन इति स एवं प्रष्टव्यः। एतत्तावत् त्रिभेदत्वं न कारिकाकारेण कृतं वृत्तिकारेण तु दर्शितम्। न चेदानीं वृत्तिकारो भेदप्रकटनं करोति। ततश्चेदं कृतमिदं क्रियते इति कर्तृभेदे का सङ्गतिः। न चैतावता सकलप्राक्तनग्रन्थसङ्गतिः कृता भवति। अविवक्षितवाच्यादीनामपि प्रकाराणां दर्शितत्वादित्यलं निजपूर्वजसगोत्रैः साकं विवादेन.' It appears that the चन्द्रिका explained the words of the vṛtti (एवं व्यङ्ग्यमुखेनैव) by saying that the vyaṅgya was dilated upon under the three categories viz. वस्तु, अलङ्कार and रस (and then it went on to show the सङ्गति of what preceded with what is to come in the kārikās of the third Uddyota). The Locana objects to this explanation of व्यङ्ग्यमुखेन and asks a question : 'These three categories were propounded by the वृत्तिकार and not by the कारिकाकार. Further, the vṛttikāra does not propound this division into three now and here; when (as you hold) the authors of the कारिका and of the वृत्ति are different, what is the use of showing the सङ्गति by saying this has been done (by the वृत्तिकार) and this is being done (by the कारिकाकार in 3rd उद्योत)? There can be no सङ्गति when the वृत्तिकार says one thing about which the कारिकाकार is silent'. Then लोचन finds further faults in that explanation. To me it appears clear, on the strength of this passage, that the चन्द्रिकाकार held the view of non-identity and the लोचन asserts that no question of सङ्गति arises on the explanation given by the चन्द्रिका of the words व्यंग्यमुखेन. Unless the चन्द्रिका is recovered no one can be *certain* of the meaning. Whether the लोचन.

held the same view is not so clear. But the explanation of the लोचन is so framed that even if the authors of the कारिका and of the वृत्ति were different, it would hold good. Dr. Mookerjee (B. C. Law vol. I. pp. 185-186) thinks that लोचन is petulant and not logically consistent nor correct; while Dr. Krishnamoorthy (I. H. Q. vol. 24 pp. 189-190) for once disagrees with Dr. Mookerjee about the interpretation of this passage. I leave the two Doctors to settle their differences. I have given my own interpretation. It is for scholars to decide what the correct interpretation of the attitude of the चन्द्रिकाकार as reported by the लोचन is. Dr. Mookerjee has given up recently in 'Indian Culture' vol. 12 (pp. 57-60) his own explanation of कर्तृभेदे का सङ्गतिः and puts forward another explanation in which कर्तृ means only grammatical agent of an action and not 'author of a book' as he once proposed. It is unnecessary to comment on this new explanation. He does not know his own mind.

One of the most cogent arguments against the theory of identity is furnished by the large number of what are called in the vṛtti 'Parikaraślokas' on pp. 40, 159 (three ślokas), 169, 182, 203 (four),[1] 'saṅgrahaślokas' on pp. 106 (4 verses), 280 (two verses) and saṅkṣepaślokas pp. 53-54, 90, 305. Besides these, there is a verse quoted in the वृत्ति with the words तदयमत्र परमार्थः on ध्व. III. 10-14 and five verses quoted by the वृत्ति with the words तदिदमुक्तं (p. 277) and तदिदमुच्यते p. 278 (the first two being expressly ascribed to the वृत्तिकार himself by लोचन and one out of the group of the three on p. 278 being ascribed to आनन्दवर्धन in the अभिनवभारती).[2] Thus there are over twenty-five verses quoted in the vṛtti itself, all of which are the composition of आनन्दवर्धन. Some of these verses are striking and pregnant with meaning and far better than several kārikās. A few of them are set out below.[3] If the author of both was the same

1. For explanation of परिकरश्लोक, vide लोचन p. 40 quoted below.

2. Vide pp. 7-8 above about these verses.

3. विच्छित्तिशोभिनैकेन भूषणेनेव कामिनी । पदद्योत्येन सुकवेर्ध्वनिना भाति भारती ॥ a परिकरश्लोक on p. 159; अव्युत्पत्तिकृतो दोषः शक्त्या संव्रियते कवेः । यस्त्वशक्तिकृतस्तस्य स झटित्यवभासते ॥ परिकरश्लोक p. 169 (q. by राजशेखर in काव्यमी. p. 16); अनौचित्यादृते नान्यद्रसभङ्गस्य कारणम् । प्रसिद्धौचित्यबन्धस्तु रसस्योपनिषत्परा ॥ (cited as परमार्थ on p. 180 and quoted

why did he relegate these verses to a subordinate position in the वृत्ति and not give them a place in the कारिकाs ? No satisfactory explanation for this is forthcoming from anyone of the three Doctors who are for the theory of identity. Does Mammaṭa who traversed a much vaster field than the Dhvanyāloka in 142 कारिकाs anywhere give परिकरश्लोकs or संग्रहश्लोकs in the वृत्ति ? The only explanation vouchsafed by Dr. Krishnamoorthy (I. H. Q. vol. 24 at p. 301) is that it is possible that आनन्द० wrote the kārikās first, taught them to his students and that after some intervening time composed the vṛtti. This is a most lame explanation. Even supposing that the kārikās were written first and the vṛtti many years later, what prevented the author of the kārikās from including the ślokas (called परिकर and संग्रह) in the kārikās when making the whole work available for the benefit of all ? The obvious reason is that the वृत्तिकार being different from the कारिकाकार, the former did not like to foist his own verses upon another.

Reliance is placed on the following words in the Locana that introduce the words तथा च that precede the कारिका II. 26 (शब्दार्थशक्त्या वा०) 'प्रक्रान्तप्रकारद्वयोपसंहारं तृतीयप्रकारसूचनं चैकेनैव यत्नेन करोमीत्याशयेन साधारणमवतरणपदं प्रक्षिपति वृत्तिकृत् तथा चेति' (p. 126). This is of no use for proving identity. As stated above the कारिका becomes part of the वृत्ति. Here the Locana says that the कारिका II. 26 mentions only two varieties and the वृत्ति adds a third. This may be availed of by those who oppose identity for showing that the वृत्तिकार is different from the कारिकाकार. If there is identity why are not the three mentioned in the kārikā itself and why does the वृत्ति become guilty of उत्सूत्रव्याख्यान about which Dr. Mookerjee and Dr. Krishnamoorthy have made such fuss ? Similar explanations can be given about the passages on pp. 82-83, 85, 105, 223 which pages are merely mentioned by Dr. Pandey without any discussion. Dr. Pandey (in 'Abhinavagupta' p. 137) asks a question whether the Locana is a commentary on the vṛtti only or on the kārikā and vṛtti

---

by व्यक्तिविवेक I. p. 31, काव्यप्र. VII. 82, p. 445 Vā.); अपारे काव्यसंसारे कविरेव प्रजापतिः। यथास्मै रोचते विश्वं तथेदं परिवर्तते ॥ शृङ्गारी चेत्कविः काव्ये जातं रसमयं जगत्। स एव वीतरागश्चेन्नीरसं सर्वमेव तत् ॥ quoted on p. 278 with the words तथा चेदमुच्यते, the 2nd being cited as आनन्दवर्धन's by अ. भा. vol. I. p. 295.

together. He thinks that this will be a sort of dilemma to those who oppose the theory of identity of authorship. In the first place, the proper answer depends on the question as to who is meant by the word ग्रन्थकृत् or ग्रन्थकार occurring in the Locana. That question has been already dealt with above (pp. 168-169). In the second place, the 2nd Introductory verse of the Locana expressly states that what is explained by the Locana is 'Kāvyāloka'. The Locana starts with the explanation of the maṅgala verse of the vṛtti. It does not explain the first kārikā word by word, but states that the first sentence (ādivākya) is 'Kāvyasyātmā' &c. and at once begins to explain the first words of the *vṛtti* 'budhaiḥ kāvyatattva-vidbhiḥ &c.'. It follows that the Locana is concerned with the vrtti and the kārikās come in for explanation only as they are part of the vṛtti by being explained at length in it. If anywhere the vṛtti is very brief (as on I. 3 and 6) the Locana explains some of the words of the kārikā.[1] The Locana also states that a certain kārikā being of the nature of a saṅgraha-śloka is not explained in the vṛtti.[2] The colophons are not parts of the work. They often differ in the several mss, some calling the work ध्वन्यालोक, others सहृदयालोक, and still others describing it (in the लोचन) as सहृदयालोकनाम्नि काव्यालङ्कारे. The first verse out of the two at the end of the Locana on the first Uddyota and on the third makes it clear that Locana is required for Āloka, which properly applies to the vṛtti, the kārikās being merely called ध्वनिकारिका or ध्वनि. The penultimate verse at the end of the vṛtti suggests that the vṛtti was called Kāvyāloka[3] and the last verse (tad-vyākarot &c. quoted below p. 191) expressly states that Ānanda explained the essence of real poetry in that work. I do not dwell upon passages in

1. There are more than one hundred kārikās in the first three Uddyotas. Dr. Pandey will not be able to cite a dozen kārikās that are directly explained in the Locana. He only cites I. 3 and 6.

2. On IV. 4 the लोचन is यदि वा उच्यते संग्रहश्लोकोयमिति भावः। अत एवास्य श्लोकस्य वृत्तिग्रन्थे व्याख्यानं न कृतम् (vide Dr. De in Journal of Dept. of Letters, Calcutta Un. vol. IX.).

3. Mark the words काव्याख्येऽखिलसौख्यधाम्नि विबुधोद्याने ध्वनिर्दर्शितः।. विबुधाः means 'gods' and also 'काव्यतत्त्वविदः'.

the Locana which speak of vṛttikāra adding words by way of *upaskāra* and which are relied upon by some of those who are for non-identity. Nor is it necessary to dwell on the breaking up of kārikās into smaller portions. But one thing is remarkable. If the kārikās and vṛtti were from the same hand the breaking up of kārikās and interspersing portions of vṛtti should have been uniform.[1] But even so early as the Locana it was noted that there is no such uniformity in this respect, some mss. of the vṛtti reading the kārikās in pieces and others reading them as wholes. Dr. Krishnamoorthy (I. H. Q. vol. 24 p. 300), while trying to explain away the splitting up of kārikās by the example of Mammaṭa, has not said a word about the discrepancy in the mss. noted so early by the Locana as the 10th century A. D.[2] I have replied to most of the important points put forward by those who are for identity.

It is not possible for restrictions of space to refute each and every point (however insignificant it may be) made by the opponents of the theory of non-identity. But one or two insignificant matters must be cleared up. Dr. Krishnamoorthy ridicules[3] as absurd my suggestions (I. H. Q. vol. 24 p. 184 n. 17) on p. LX. of the last edition 'The penultimate verse at the end of the 4th उद्योत (काव्याख्ये०) leads one to infer that काव्य formed part of the name of the original work (or was itself its name) on which आनन्दवर्धन commented (probobly it was called काव्यध्वनि or simply काव्य or ध्वनि)'. But Dr. K. himself concedes that the name काव्यध्वनि is possible. I hope he knows that the work is called काव्यालोक as in Dr. De's edition of 4th उद्द्योत of

---

1. On कारिका II. 32-33 the लोचन notes about 'तासामेवालं-कृतीनाम्' (in the वृत्ति) and पुन: also 'तासामेवालङ्कृतीनामित्ययं **पठिष्यमाण**-कारिकोपस्कार:। पुनरिति कारिकामध्ये उपस्कार:।; again on IV. 9-10 लोचन says 'शक्तीनामित्यन्तत: कारिकयोर्मध्योपस्कार:'.

2. On संवादो ह्यन्य० (IV. 12) लोचन remarks : एषा खण्डीकृत्य वृत्तौ पठिता; on आत्मनोन्यस्य सद्भावे (IV. 14) the लोचन says 'इति कारिका वृत्तौ खण्डीकृत्य पठिता। केषुचित् पुस्तकेषु कारिका अखण्डिता एव दृश्यन्ते।' (J. of Dept. of Letters, Cal. Un. vol. IX. at p. 39). Kārikā IV. 16 also was split up by some according to the लोचन.

3. The learned Doctor remarks 'It is *nothing short of absurd to urge* seriously *that a work on literary criticism* was itself *designated as kāvya or dhvani*'.

लोचन in J. of Dept. of Letters, Cal. Un. vol. IX. p. 42. That the work was called ध्वनि is clear from राजशेखर's verse (ध्वनिनातिगभीरेण) quoted later on and from the fact that many writers speak of आनन्दवर्धन as ध्वनिकार or-कृत् (author of ध्वनि), and from certain colophons. So my statements about the possible names of the work are borne out or admitted. The work was called ध्वनि, also ध्वन्यालोक, काव्यालोक, सहृदयालोक and सहृदयहृदयालोक. Why were the two names ध्वन्यालोक and काव्यालोक given to the work? काव्यालोक would mean only 'a peep into kāvya or light or comprehension of kāvya'. Therefore, there is nothing *absurd* in suggesting that, just as ध्वनि was the name of the work also called ध्वन्यालोक, so the word काव्य might have been a concise way of referring to काव्यालोक. Dr. Krishnamoorthy is fond of dubbing others' arguments as absurd (vide what he says about Mr. Goda Verma on p. 305 of I. H. Q. vol. 24). But he does not see what strange (not to say 'absurd' by way of imitating him) propositions he has advanced as discussed above on 'utsūtra-vyākhyāna'. Besides, the learned writer adduces no evidence except the words 'kavyasyātmā dhvanir' for branding Dr. Verma's arguments as the 'height of absurdity'. Dr. Mookerjee (B. C. Law vol. 10 pp. 189-190) and following him Dr. Krishnamoorthy (I. H. Q. vol. 24 p. 193) place much reliance on the remarks of Locana about the penultimate verse in the vṛtti : नित्याक्लिष्टरसाश्रयोचितगुणालङ्कारशोभाभृतोर्यस्मादस्तु समीहितं सुकृतिभिः सर्वं समासाद्यते । काव्याख्येऽखिलसौख्यधाम्नि विबुधोद्याने ध्वनिर्दर्शितः सोऽयं कल्पतरूपमानमहिमा भोग्योऽस्तु भव्यात्मनाम् ॥. In the first place, the verse is read as given above in all the three editions available to me and not as इत्यक्लिष्ट.[1] In the 2nd place, even on the theory of non-identity the लोचन could very well explain the word इति in the वृत्ति as meaning 'by the exposition given in the कारिका and वृत्ति'. One fails to understand how these words prove identity. Dr. Mookerjee thinks (B. C. Law vol. I. p. 190) that all lingering doubts about the identity of the authors of the कारिकाs and of the वृत्ति are completely dispelled by the last verse

1. The लोचन on this is 'इतीति कारिकातद्वृत्तिनिरूपणप्रकारेणेत्यर्थः' in the Kasi S. Series edition p. 551. In the text printed by Dr. De (Journal, Dept. of Letters, Calcutta Un. vol. IX. at p. 40) the reading is इतीति कारिकातद्वृत्तिनिरूपणेनेत्यर्थः. Most mss. at B. O. R. I. read नित्याक्लिष्ट०.

of the वृत्ति which is set out below.[1] Dr. Krishnamoorthy (I. H. Q. 24 pp. 193-194) borrows wholesale the translation of Dr. Mookerjee, which is not quite accurate. There are no corresponding words in the original verse (of K. M.) which can be rendered as 'for all ages'. Even taking the reading of Dr. De the meaning would be 'dormant for long'. The reasoning of both the Doctors does not appeal to me. आनन्द० does not claim anything more than having explained what the essence of real poetry is. The word 'vyākarot' is important. The meaning of that word is made clear by the kārikā I. 3 'तत्र वाच्यः प्रसिद्धो यः प्रकारैरुपमादिभिः । बहुधा व्याकृतः सोन्यैः काव्यलक्ष्मविधायिभिः ॥'. Vide also III. 47. आनन्द० states he explained the essence of true poetry. How that sentence establishes that he was the author of the kārikās also is not clear to me. The kārikā (III. 47) says that the essence of poetry declared in the kārikās was dimly perceived by its predecessors who being unable to explain it clearly set forth the doctrine of the *rītis*.[2] The last verse simply echoes the words of the कारिका III. 47 just as the words मे मीतिः in कारिका II. 5 are explained as मामकीनः पक्षः in वृत्ति. The वृत्ति is like the भाष्य of शङ्कर on the Vedāntasūtra. The sūtrakāra is a great man and Śaṅkara is equally great (or some would say even greater). So the kārikākāra briefly described the essence of poetry, which Ānanda explained at great length. Dr. Krishnamoorthy has not put a correct interpretation on the words मामकीनः पक्षः in the वृत्ति on II. 5 p. 86 (I. H. Q. vol. 24 p. 300). Dr. Satkari Mookerjee (B. C. Law vol. I. p. 191) and Dr. Krishnamoorthy (I H. Q. vol. 24, p. 194) try to clinch their arguments by referring to certain passages of the वृत्ति and लोचन on pp. 79, 85, 102, 104 and 105, which correspond, it appears, to pp. 96, 103, 124, 127, 128 (of the edition

---

1. सत्काव्यतत्त्वविषयं स्फुरितप्रसुप्तकल्पं &c. Dr. De (in Journal of Dept. of Letters, vol.IX. p. 41) reads 'सत्काव्यतत्त्वनयवर्त्म चिरप्रसुप्त०. Dr. M. translates 'आनन्द०, whose name is widely known, has explicitly brought out for the edification of men of taste the real essence of true poetry which lay dormant for all ages in the minds of even men of mature intellect.'

2. अस्फुटस्फुरितं काव्यतत्त्वमेतद्यथोदितम् । अशक्नुवद्भिर्व्याकर्तुं रीतयः संप्रवर्तिताः ॥ ध्व. III. 47. व्याकर्तुं is explained by the लोचन as प्रतिपादयितुम्.

1935 used in the present edition of the History of Poetics by me. They did not escape me as those learned writers state. In fact in my Intro. to साहित्य० I had myself referred to some of those passages. No detailed statement of my views thereon is necessary, as, in my opinion, those passages are either not against the theory of non-identity or are quite explicable on that theory. So also the words इयत्पुनरुच्यते एव in the वृत्ति on p. 131 explained by लोचन as 'अस्माभिरिति वाक्यशेषः' are to be explained in the same way as done above on p. 169 (citing शाङ्करभाष्य) and as shedding no clear light on the question of identity. When the लोचन says (on p. 14) 'आनन्दवर्धन इति च ग्रन्थकृतो नाम। तेन स एवानन्दवर्धनाचार्य एतच्छास्त्रद्वारेण सहृदयहृदयेषु प्रतिष्ठां...लभताम्', Dr. Mookerjee argues (B. C. Law vol. I p. 189) that such high praise is not deserved by a mere वृत्तिकार, if he were not also kārikākāra. In the first place, the Locana does not expressly designate आनन्द as शास्त्रकार. All that it says is (literally) 'through this śāstra as the door Ānanda may secure a firm place in the hearts of sahṛdayas.' In the 2nd place, Śaṅkaracārya wrote only a vṛtti on the Bṛ. Up. and a bhāṣya on the Vedāntasūtra and Patañjali wrote only a com. on the Vārtikas, but no one would grudge high praise being bestowed on both of them on account of the fact of their having expounded Advaita Vedānta and Sanskrit grammar respectively. So there is hardly anything in this argument. I may bring to the notice of Dr. Mookerjee that, though Pāṇini is the author of a perfect sūtra, Pātañjali's authority is regarded as greater than even that of Paṇini by later Sanskrit grammarians. Vide what the Kaumudī says on the sūtra 'na bahuvrīhau'[1]. If the author of the kārikās be different from that of the vṛtti and one had to make a choice between the two as to who should be called Śāstrakāra *par excellence* there is hardly any doubt that most scholars would bestow the palm of superiority on the Vṛttikāra.

Dr. Mookerjee is not at all right in thinking that the Locana alludes to Kuntaka (B. C. Law vol. I. p. 183). There is no evidence worth the name to prove this or even to make

1. न बहुव्रीहौ। पा. I. 1. 29; सि. कौ. 'बहुव्रीहौ चिकीर्षिते सर्वनामसंज्ञा न स्यात्। त्वकं पिता यस्य स त्वत्कपितृक इति। भाष्यकारस्तु त्वत्कपितृक मत्कपितृक इति रूपे इष्टापत्तिं कृत्वैतत्सूत्रं प्रत्याचख्यौ। यथोत्तरं मुनीनां प्रामाण्यम्।'.

the inference very probable. Nor is Dr. Mookerjee correct in what he says about Jayantabhaṭṭa (*ibid.* p. 192). The words of the न्यायमञ्जरी are : 'यमन्यः पण्डितंमन्यः प्रपेदे कंचन ध्वनिम् । विधेर्निषेधावगतिर्विधिबुद्धिर्निषेधतः ॥ यथा—मम धम्मिअ वीसत्थो मा स्म पान्थ गृहं विश । मानान्तरपरिच्छेद्यवस्तुरूपोपदेशिनाम् । शब्दानामेव सामर्थ्यं तत्र तत्र तथा तथा । अथवा नेदृशी चर्चा कविभिः सह शोभते ॥' (Vizianagaram ed. p. 48). The words of Dr. Mookerjee 'the doctrine of Dhvani is refuted which has been propounded by a fellow who considered himself a real scholar' do not accurately render the first half. The half line and the following lines really mean "a wise-acre *resorted* to or *adopted* a certain (doctrine called) dhvani, (according to which) there may be a suggestion of prohibition from words that (apparently) allow a certain act to be done or there is the suggestion of some act being allowed to be done (from words) that express a prohibition, as in 'bhama dhammia' &c." This is a pointed reference to the words of the वृत्ति (in ध्व०) 'स हि कदाचिद्वाच्ये विधिरूपे प्रतिषेधरूपः । यथा मम धम्मिअ०, कचिद्वाच्ये प्रतिषेधरूपे विधिरूपो यथा । अत्ता एत्थ०, (pp. 19, 24). The word 'prapede' cannot mean 'propounded'. It can only mean 'resorted to, took refuge, or adopted.'[1] This quotation would recoil on Dr. Mookerjee. The words of Jayanta would mean 'there was already a doctrine of ध्वनि, which was adopted by a man who posed as a scholar &c.' That would lead to this that ध्वनि already existed (in a work or in kārikās) and the vṛttikāra only adopted it. There is a further hit in Jayanta's words vix. 'what is the use of arguing with poets' ? The plural is satirical. The vṛttikāra (of ध्वन्यालोक) was a poet and is spoken of as कविरानन्दवर्धनः in the राजत० (quoted below). Jayanta says 'the writer (of वृत्ति) is a mere poet and not an acute logician or philosopher; there is no use in arguing with such a man'. जयन्तवृत्तिकार was almost a contemporary of आनन्दवर्धन, since his son अभिनन्द in his कादम्बरीकथासार states that जयन्त was the great-grandson of शक्तिस्वामिन्, minister of king मुक्तापीड of कर्कोटवंश.

Mr. Goda Verma in New I. A. vol. V. pp. 265-272 has brought forward certain matters of contradiction between the kārikās and the vṛtti and Dr. Krishnamoorthy (I. H. Q. vol. 24,

---

1. Compare रघुवंश VI. 17 'नरेन्द्रमार्गाट्ट इव प्रपेदे विवर्णभावं स स भूमिपालः' or राजशेखर 'ततः प्रपेदे भुवि भर्तृमेण्ठताम्' or श्वेताश्वतरोपनिषद् VI. 18 'मुमुक्षुर्वै शरणमहं प्रपद्ये'.

300-311, at p. 305 tries to meet Mr. Verma's arguments. I do not think that it is necessary for me to go into these matters at length. Though I do not agree with everything that Mr. Verma says, some of the points that he has made are arresting and worthy of consideration. For example, (a) on the कारिका I. 4 (प्रतीयमानं पुनरन्यदेव वस्त्वस्ति वाणीषु महाकवीनाम् । यत्तत्प्रसिद्धावयवातिरिक्तं विभाति लावण्यमिवाङ्गनासु ॥) the वृत्ति gives two explanations of प्रसिद्ध 'यत्तत्सहृदयहृदयसुप्रसिद्धं प्रसिद्धेभ्योऽलङ्कृतेभ्यः प्रतीतेभ्यो वावयवेभ्यो व्यतिरिक्तत्वेन प्रकाशते &c.(the लोचन says प्रसिद्धशब्दस्य सर्वप्रतीतत्वमलङ्कृतत्वं चार्थः). In the very preceding kārikā I. 3 (तत्र वाच्यः प्रसिद्धो यः &c.) the word प्रसिद्ध is employed in the sense of 'well-known to all people'. If the author of कारिका and वृत्ति were the same he should have in the वृत्ति stuck to one meaning in succeeding verses; (b) कारिका II. 11 is 'समर्पकत्वं काव्यस्य यत्तु सर्वरसान्प्रति । स प्रसादो गुणो ज्ञेयः सर्वसाधारणक्रियः ॥'. The preceding kārikās (II. 9-10) state that the guṅa *mādhurya* is specially suited to विप्रलम्भश्रृङ्गार and करुण and the guṅa *ojas* sets off Raudra, Vīra and Adbhuta. Kārikā II. 11 states that *prasāda* is a guṇa common to all rasas. The word सर्वसाधारणक्रियः is explained in the वृत्ति as 'सर्वरससाधारणो गुणः सर्वरचनासाधारणश्च'. The context and the expression सर्वरसान् प्रति in the kārikā itself clearly convey that सर्व in सर्वसाधारणक्रियः must refer only to सर्वरस. Hencc the second explanation (सर्वरचनासाधारण) is out of place and (to use the language of which Doctor Mookerjee has made a fetish) is उत्सूत्रव्याख्यान; (c) कारिका III. 19 (last half) is 'रसस्य स्याद्विरोधाय वृत्त्यनौचित्यमेव च ॥.' The vṛtti gives three meanings to the word वृत्ति viz. व्यवहार (तथा वृत्तेर्व्यवहारस्य यदनौचित्यं तदपि रसभङ्गहेतुरेव । यथा नायकं प्रति नायिकायाः कस्याश्चिदुचिताङ्गभङ्गिमन्तरेण स्वयं सम्भोगाभिलाषकथने), कैशिक्यादिवृत्तिs (known from भरत) or उपनागरिकादिवृत्ति. Out of these at the most the last two may be accepted as meant in the कारिका, looking to कारिकाs III. 33 and 48. These are matters worthy of consideration. I pass over the other points of Mr. Verma.

Before proceeding further a few remarks have to be made about the name of the work. In the colophons of the work, it is often called सहृदयालोक[1] or सहृदयहृदयालोक or काव्यालोक or काव्या-

1. Vide Des. cat of Govt. mss library at BORI, Poona, vol. XII pp. 209, 214, 215 mss. No. 254 & 256 & 255 of 1875-76 pp. 209-215) where the colophons are : इत्यानन्दवर्धनाचार्यविरचिते सहृदयहृदयालोके. ..उद्योतः. राघवभट्ट in his com. on शाकुन्तल says 'यदुक्तं राजानकानन्दवर्धनैः सहृदयहृदयालोके...निबन्धनम् ॥" pp. 133-134.

लङ्कार and ध्वनि also. Vide Cat. of. Govt. mss. at B. O. R. I. vol. XII p. 215, 216 for these names. The third introductory verse of the लोचन (यत्किञ्चिदप्यनुरणन् स्फुटयामि काव्यालोकं सुलोचननियोजनया जनस्य) seems to suggest that the author of the लोचन called the work काव्यालोक also. The second verse at the end of लोचन printed in Journal of Department of Letters, Calcutta vol. IX p. 42 is आनन्दवर्धनविवेकविकासिकाव्यालोकार्थतत्त्वघटनादनुमेयसारम् ।. This suggests that the work of आनन्दवर्धन was called काव्यालोक. अभिनव himself calls it सहृदयालोक in the अभिनवभारती quoted above p. 179. The penultimate verse at the end of the 4th उद्योत (काव्याख्येऽखिलसौख्यधाम्नि विबुधोद्याने ध्वनिर्दर्शितः) leads one to infer that काव्य formed part of the name of the original work (or was itself the name) on which आनन्दवर्धन commented (probably it was called काव्यध्वनि or simply काव्य or ध्वनि). ध्वनिकारिका III. 53 (वृत्तयोपि प्रकाशन्ते ज्ञातेऽस्मिन् काव्यलक्षणे) speaks of the कारिकाs as काव्यलक्षण. It is therefore proper that the वृत्ति is called काव्यालोक or ध्वन्यालोक. But it is not so easy to say why the work should have been styled सहृदयालोक. Prof. Sovani (JRAS 1910 pp. 164-167) made the plausible conjecture that सहृदय was the name of the author of the कारिकाs. He relied upon the name सहृदयालोक and on the words of the लोचन in the 2nd introductory stanza (सरस्वत्यास्तत्त्वं कविसहृदयाख्यं विजयताद्). It may ultimately turn out that Prof. Sovani is right, but the reasons assigned by him are quite meagre and more substantial evidence ought to be adduced for the purpose. If आलोक is the name of a work (as in the case of प्रदीप, प्रकाश) it seems natural to argue that सहृदय is the name of a *work* and *not of an author*. So it is difficult to make सहृदयालोक yield by itself सहृदय as the name of the *author* of the कारिकाs. The words 'सरस्व.... विजयताद्' may, for ought we know, contain a veiled allusion to सहृदय as the name of the author of the कारिकाs. But the words clearly mean that the real essence of सरस्वती is poets (कवि) and men of taste (सहृदय, literary *critics*). The last verse of the ध्वन्यालोक would seem to suggest that आनन्दवर्धन claimed for himself the position of the expounder of the real essence of poetry which lay almost dormant though alive (lit. throbbing) in mature minds (सत्काव्यतत्त्वविषयं स्फुरितप्रसुप्तकल्पं मनःसु परिपक्वधियां यदासीत्। तद्व्याकरोत्सहृदयोदयलाभहेतोरानन्दवर्धन इति प्रथिताभिधानः ॥).

The evidence so far advanced for holding that सहृदय was the author of the *kārikās* is quite inadequate. But there is more evidence, which as far as my knowledge goes, had not been relied upon by scholars before I wrote in 1923. The अभिधावृत्तिमातृका, which was composed about a hundred years earlier than the लोचन, distinctly says that ध्वनि, which had been propounded as a new doctrine by the respected सहृदय, does fall within the sphere of लक्षणा 'लक्षणामार्गावगाहित्वं तु ध्वनेः सहृदयैर्नूतनतयोपवर्णितस्य विद्यत इति दिशमुन्मीलयितुमिदमत्रोक्तम्' p. 21. So also on p. 19 मुकुल says 'तथाहि तत्र विवक्षितान्यपरता सहृदयैः काव्यवर्त्मनि निरूपिता'. This clearly shows that when मुकुल wrote (about 900-925 A. D.) ध्वनि was a new doctrine and that सहृदय propounded it. Similarly, प्रतीहारेन्दुराज, the pupil of मुकुल, says 'ननु यत्र काव्ये सहृदयहृदयाह्लादिनः प्रधानभूतस्य स्वशब्दव्यापारास्पृष्टत्वेन प्रतीयमानैकरूपस्यार्थस्य सद्भावस्तत्र तथाविधार्थाभिव्यक्तिहेतुः काव्यजीवितभूतः कैश्चित्सहृदयैर्ध्वनिर्नाम व्यञ्जकत्वभेदात्मा काव्यधर्मोऽभिहितः' (p. 79). These passages, particularly the first two, make it very probable that सहृदय was the name of the author who propounded the theory of ध्वनि or (more probably) was the title given to him by his admirers.

As to the identity of the author of the *kārikās* with आनन्दवर्धन, a perplexing difficulty arises. राजशेखर in his काव्यमी० (p. 16) says 'प्रतिभाव्युत्पत्त्योः प्रतिभा श्रेयसी इत्यानन्दः । सा हि कवेरव्युत्पत्तिकृतं दोषमशेषमाच्छादयति । तत्राह—अव्युत्पत्तिकृतो दोषः शक्त्या संव्रियते कवेः । यस्त्वशक्तिकृतस्तस्य झगित्येवावभासते ॥' (p. 16). The verse quoted as आनन्द's is a परिकरश्लोक in ध्व०. (p. 179); so by about 900 to 925 A. D.) it was well-known that आनन्दवर्धन was the author of the वृत्ति in the ध्व०. But this has no bearing on identity. A verse ascribed to राजशेखर in जह्लण's सूक्तिमुक्तावली (p. 46 of G. O. S. ed.) speaks of आनन्दवर्धन as one who established the true essence of poetry by means of (the work) ध्वनि 'ध्वनिनातिगभीरेण काव्यतत्त्वनिवेशिना । आनन्दवर्धनः कस्य नासीदानन्दवर्धनः ॥'. प्रतीहारेन्दुराज, after the passage quoted above about सहृदय, gives it as his opinion that ध्वनि is included among the *alaṅkāras* and proceeds to examine the threefold division of ध्वनि into वस्तु, अलङ्कार and रस and tries to show that the examples of these given in the ध्व० are merely examples of अलङ्कारs (pp. 79-85). In these pages occur passages which show that he attributed the वृत्ति also to सहृदय; for example, ('तथाहि प्रतीयमानैकरूपस्य वस्तुनस्त्रैविध्यं तैरुक्तं (तैः = सहृदयैः) वस्तुमात्रालङ्काररसादिभेदेन तत्र वस्तुमात्रं तावत्प्रतीयते यथा चक्राभिघातप्रसभाज्ञयैव'; *vide*, ध्व. p. 109 for this illustration; (2) "वाच्यशक्त्याश्रयं (व्यञ्जकत्वं) तु रसादिवस्तुमात्रालङ्काराभिव्यक्तिहेतुत्वात्त्रिविधम् । तत्र यत्तावद्वाचकशक्त्याश्रयं व्यङ्ग्यभूतालङ्कारैकनियतं शब्दशक्तिमूलानुरणनरूपव्यङ्ग्यतया सहृदयैर्व्यञ्जकत्वमुक्तं 'सर्वैकशरणमक्षयम्' इत्यादौ, तत्र शब्दशक्त्या ये प्रतीयन्ते विरोधादयोलङ्कारास्तत्संस्कृतस्वभावं

वाच्यमवगम्यते । अतस्तत्र वाच्यस्य विवक्षैव" (p. 83); on this passage it is to be noted that the verse सर्वैक० is cited *as his own* by आनन्दवर्धन (p. 123) which is attributed to सहृदय by प्रतीहारेन्दुराज; (3) अत एव च सहृदयैर्यत्र वाच्यस्य विवक्षितत्वं तत्रैव वस्त्वलङ्कारयोः प्रतीयमानयोर्वाच्येन सह क्रमव्यवहारः प्रवर्तितोऽर्थशक्तिमूलानुरणनरूपव्यङ्ग्यो ध्वनिरित्युक्तं न तु वाच्यविवक्षायामपि (? वाच्या०) । यत्र च वाच्यस्याविवक्षा पूर्वमुक्ता रामोस्मीति सुवर्णपुष्पामिति च तत्र वयमधिकारापेतप्रस्तुतार्थानुबन्धिवस्तूपनिबन्धादप्रस्तुतप्रशंसाभेदत्वमेव न्याय्यं मन्यामहे' (p. 84). Both the verses रामोस्मि and सुवर्णपुष्पां are cited as examples of अविवक्षितवाच्यध्वनि (p. 75 and p. 58 respectively of the ध्व०). The words of प्रतीहारेन्दुराज lead to the conclusion that he attributed both कारिका and वृत्ति to सहृदय. The words यत्र वाच्यस्य...ध्वनिरित्युक्तं in passage 3 refer to p. 119 of ध्व०.

The वक्रोक्तिजीवित cites (II. example 25) ताला जाअन्ति गुणा... कमलाइँ (ध्व० p. 76) as an example of रूढिशब्दवक्रता (it is आनन्द's own verse) and remarks 'ध्वनिकारेण व्यङ्ग्यव्यञ्जकभावोऽत्र सुतरां समर्थितः किं पौनरुक्त्येन.' So the वक्रोक्तिजीवित speaks of आनन्दo as ध्वनिकार.

Coming to महिमभट्ट, a writer who was almost a contemporary of the author of the लोचन, we find that he makes no distinction between the author of the कारिकाs and the वृत्ति. On p. 1 he quotes the कारिका 'यत्रार्थः शब्दो वा' etc. (ध्व. p. 38) as ध्वनिकार's, while on p. 11 he quotes several passages from the वृत्ति as ध्वनिकार's (viz, the passage "तथा चाह ध्वनिकारः "साररूपो ह्यर्थः" is from p. 239 of ध्व.; the passage पुनः स एवाह न हि व्यंग्ये प्रतीयमाने वाच्यबुद्धिर्दूरीभवति, occurs on p. 236 of the ध्व०; again 'न हि विभावानुभावव्यभिचारिण एव' etc. occurs on p. 227 of ध्व०). On p. 16 of the व्यक्तिविवेक we read 'अथार्थशब्देनोभयमपि सङ्गृहीतं तस्योभयार्थविषयत्वेनेष्टत्वात् । यदाह—अर्थः सहृदयश्लाघ्यः...स्मृतौ (ध्वनिकारिका I. 2) इति । सत्यम् । किन्तु तमर्थमिति तच्छब्देनानन्तर्यात् प्रतीयमानस्यार्थस्य परामर्शे सति पारिशेष्याद्यर्थो वाच्यविशेष इति स्वयं विवृतत्वाच्चार्थशब्दो वाच्यविषय एव विज्ञायते'. It will be noticed that the व्यक्तिविवेक clearly states that the वृत्ति 'यत्रार्थो वाच्यविशेषः' etc., on the *kārikā* यत्रार्थः शब्दो वा etc. (ध्व. p. 38) belongs to the author of कारिकाs. So also pp. 29 and 34 of the व्यक्तिविवेक will show that he designated the author of the ध्वनिकारिकाs and of the वृत्ति also as ध्वनिकार. The औचित्यविचारचर्चा of क्षेमेन्द्र (on कारिका 18) quotes the कारिका (ध्व०, III. 24) 'विरोधी वाविरोधी वा रसोऽङ्गिनि रसान्तरे ।...विरोधिता ॥' as आनन्दवर्धन's. हेमचन्द्र (विवेक p. 26) ascribes the कारिका 'प्रतीयमानं पुनरन्यदेव' &c., (ध्व. I. 4) to आनन्दवर्धन, while on pp. 113 and 235 (of काव्यानुशासन) he ascribes the कारिकाs III. 30 and 39 to ध्वनिकार. The साहित्यदर्पण quotes the first कारिका and II. 12 as from ध्वनिकार or ध्वनिकृत् and also ascribes the वृत्ति (viz. the words

नहि कवेरितिवृत्तमात्रनिर्वाहेण &c. on p. 148 of ध्व०) to ध्वनिकार. No useful perpose will be served by referring to later writers, when comparatively early writers who were not separated from the ध्वन्यालोक by more than a century or two hold conflicting opinions as to the identity of the कारिकाकार and the वृत्तिकार.

It is difficult to give a decisive opinion in the midst of the conflict of views between certain passages of the लोचन itself read with मुकुल on the one hand and महिमभट्ट and क्षेमेन्द्र on the other. The चन्द्रिका (which as we shall see later on was a commentary on the ध्वन्यालोक written before the लोचन) and the हृदयदर्पण of भट्टनायक (which strongly criticized ध्व.) would in all probability throw some light on this question; but unfortunately these works have not yet been discovered. The passage of the लोचन (pp. 150-51) however quoted above if rightly interpreted, seems to show that the चन्द्रिका also regarded the कारिकाकार and वृत्तिकार as distinct. At present I feel inclined to hold (though with hesitation) that मुकुल and some passages of लोचन are right and that कुन्तक, महिमभट्ट, क्षेमेन्द्र and a host of other writers had not the correct tradition before them. It seems that सहृदय was either the name or the title of the कारिकाकार and that आनन्दवर्धन was his pupil and was very closely associated with him. This would serve to explain the confusion of authorship that arose within a short time. Faint indications of this relationship may be traced in the ध्वन्यालोक itself. The word सहृदयमनःप्रीतये in the first कारिका is explained in the वृत्ति as 'रामायणमहाभारतप्रभृतिनि लक्ष्ये सर्वत्र प्रसिद्धव्यवहारं लक्षयतां सहृदयानामानन्दो मनसि लभतां प्रतिष्ठामिति प्रकाश्यते.' It will be noticed that the word प्रीति is purposely rendered by the double-meaning word आनन्द (pleasure and the author आनन्द०). The whole sentence may have two meanings 'may pleasure find room in the hearts of the men of taste &c.' and 'may आनन्द (the author) secure regard in the heart of the (respected) सहृदय who defined (the nature of ध्वनि) to be found in the रामायण &c.' Similarly, the words सहृदयोदयलाभहेतोः in the last verse of the वृत्ति may be explained as 'for the sake of the benefit viz, the appearance of men of correct literary taste' or 'for the sake of securiug the rise (of the fame) of सहृदय' (the author). The word सहृदय (as well as its synonym सचेतस्) occurs scores of times in the कारिकाs, वृत्ति and लोचन. For example, *vide* कारिकाs I. 1 and 2, II. 14, III. 40; ध्व० pp. 3, 8, 9, 12, 17, 40, 71, 97, 102, 197, 198 etc; लोचन pp.

3, 7, 13, 14, 26, 28, 68, 254. The ध्वन्यालोक (p. 198) holds a discussion about the meaning of सहृदयत्व and the लोचन defines सहृदय as 'येषां काव्यानुशीलनाभ्यासवशाद्विशदीभूते मनोमुकुरे वर्णनीयतन्मयीभवनयोग्यता ते हृदयसंवादभाजः सहृदयाः' (p. 13) and again (at p. 68) 'हृदयसंवादापरपर्यायसहृदयत्वपरवशीकृततया etc.' हेमचन्द्र in his विवेक (p. 3) merely copies the words of the लोचन. It is to be noted that the लोचन speaks of आनन्दवर्धन as 'सहृदयचक्रवर्ती खल्वयं ग्रन्थकृदिति भावः' (p. 14). One may hazard the conjecture that it was due to the profuse use of the word सहृदय in the ध्वन्यालोक and to making the सहृदय the final court of appeal in all matters of literary appreciation that the founder of the ध्वनि theory earned the epithet सहृदय (*par excellence*).

Apart from the use of the word सहृदय or सचेतस् in the रामायण (अयोध्या 13. 22) and कालिदास (सचेतसः कस्य मनो न दूयते in कुमारसम्भव V. 48) in a general sense (viz. one who has a feeling or sympathetic heart), the word सहृदय in the technical sense occurs more than a hundred years before आनन्दवर्धन in वामन's काव्यालङ्कारसूत्रवृत्ति (I. 2. 21 where the following is one of two verses quoted with the caption "तथाचाहुः —'वचसि यमधिगम्य स्यन्दते वाचकश्रीर्वितथमपि तथात्वं यत्र वस्तु प्रयाति । उदयति हि स तादृक् क्वापि वैदर्भरीतौ सहृदयहृदयानां रञ्जकः कोपि पाकः ॥". Therefore, the emergence of the word सहृदय in a technical sense must be placed long before वामन. There is nothing unusual in a person being called by a word that has a general sense (such as सहृदय) as we have authors in the अलङ्कारशास्त्र itself named मेधाविन्, दण्डिन्, धनिक and so on. Dr. Krishnamoorthy (in Annals B. O. R. I. vol. 28 at p. 190 n. 1) tries to explain away the occurrence of the word सहृदय in Vāmana's work by saying that he was a contemporary of the new critics (whom he postulates without any sound reason). Further, he does not prove when and where those critics flourished. I do not understand what Dr. Krishnamoorthy means when he says 'But Vāmana was a Kashmirian who was *perhaps* a contemporary of the new critics ; hence Vāmana's usage does not alter the position.' Vāmana merely quotes a predecessor, who may have flourished for aught we know several hundred years before Vāmana. Hence the position about the use of the word sahṛdaya in a technical sense will be very much altered, Ānandavardhana's work cannot be placed earlier than about 875 to 900 A. D. Vāmana flourished between 775-810 A. D. And the author of that verse flourished before वामन. How much earlier one cannot say. So it is not possible that the unnamed predecessor of वामन borrowed the ideology of आनन्दवर्धन or his master (if he had one for teaching him the canons of literary appreciation). On the theory of identity both the kārikās and vrtti belong to the same period (875-900) and as आनन्द॰ does not expressly acknowledge a master who guided his steps, there is nothing to show that a circle of *literary critics* of the type of आनन्द॰ existed before him.

The question about the name of the author of the kārikās is entirely separate from the question of the identity of the author of the kārikās and of the vṛtti. A scholar accepting non-identity of authorship may yet argue that the name of the kārikākāra is not known. The late Prof. Sovani suggested that Sahṛdaya was the name of the Kārikākāra and I adduced more evidence in support of that view than Prof. Sovani had put forward. I do not profess that I have completely proved my hypothesis. The remarks of Mukula cited by me above indicate that Sahṛadaya was in the opinion of Mukula the author of the kārikās or of the whole work and according to Pratīhārendurāja, of the whole work. Now I have drawn attention to the fact that the work was called सहृदयहृदयालोक by राघवभट्ट and in some colophons. We have further to notice that in his comment on the very first verse of the Nāṭyaśāstra, Abhinavagupta mentions Bhaṭṭa-Nāyaka and his work called सहृदयदर्पण.[1] This raises the important question whether Bhaṭṭanāyaka's work was called सहृदयदर्पण or हृदयदर्पण. In the लोचन the work[2] is quoted as हृदयदर्पण (pp. 32, 76). When the व्यक्तिविवेक says in Intro. verse 4 (सहसा यशोभिसर्तुं समुद्यताऽदृष्टदर्पणा मम धीः) the commentator explains 'दर्पणो हृदयदर्पणाख्यो ध्वनिध्वंसग्रन्थोपि'. Most of the Mss. of the लोचन at the B. O. R. I. read हृदयदर्पणे. It looks to me more likely that the work was called सहृदयदर्पण which makes far better sense than हृदयदर्पण and which might convey two meanings also, viz. 'mirror of the

1. भट्टनायकस्तु ब्रह्मणा परमात्मना यदुदाहृतं...इति व्याख्यानं सहृदयदर्पणे पर्यगृहीत्। अ. भा. vol. I. pp. 4-5.

2. एतदेवोक्तं हृदयदर्पणे यावत्पूर्णो न चैतेन तावन्नैवैवम्। तेन यदाह भट्टनायकः 'शब्दप्राधान्यमाश्रित्य॰'। p. 32; तेनैतन्निरवकाशं यदुक्तं हृदयदर्पणे सर्वत्र तर्हि काव्यव्यवहारः स्यादिति। p. 32; यत्तु हृदयदर्पणे उक्तं 'हहा हेति संरम्भार्थोयं चमत्कारः' इति। p. 76.

ideas of men of literary appreciation' or 'mirror that will show Sahṛdaya (in his true light)'. The अभिनवभारती (vol. I. p. 173) states: अत एव सहृदयाः स्मरन्ति 'वध (स) म चूडामणिश्रा.' The text of the verse is corrupt, but there is hardly any doubt that सहृदयाः here stands for an author. The कौमुदी of उदयोत्तुङ्ग gives several explanations of the last pāda of the मङ्गल to the लोचन 'सरस्वत्यास्तत्त्वं कविसहृदयाख्यं विजयते', one of which is as follows: 'यदि वा कविशब्देन सर्वेपि कवयः सहृदया गृहीताः **सहृदयशब्देनानन्दवर्धनाचार्यः** ततश्च देवतात्मत्वे गुरुनमस्कारोपि अनुसंहितो भवति ।'. This shows that to the कौमुदी the idea of holding that Sahṛdaya was a proper name did not appear far-fetched. There is one more reference which is interesting and would have some bearing on the question of the author of the कारिकाs and वृत्ति. The व्यक्तिविवेक at the beginning of the 2nd विमर्श (Tri. ed./p. 37) remarks: इह खलु द्विविधमनौचित्यमुक्तमर्थविषयं शब्दविषयं च । तत्र विभावानुभावव्यभिचारिणामयथायथं रसेषु यो विनियोगस्तन्मात्रलक्षणमेकमङ्गमार्यैरेवोक्तमिति नेह प्रतन्यते ।'. On this the com. (of रुय्यक) remarks "उक्तमिति सहृदयैः । अन्तरङ्गमिति साक्षाद्रसविषयत्वात् । आर्यैरिति ध्वनिकारप्रभृतिभिरिति । तदुक्तं 'अनौचित्या...परा' ॥ इत्यादिना ।". It may be noted that ध्वनिकारिका III. 10 is विभावभावानुभवसञ्चार्यौचित्यचारुणः । विधिः कथाशरीरस्य वृत्तस्योत्प्रेक्षितस्य वा ॥'. So the words उक्तमिति सहृदयैः refer to this कारिका. The verse अनौचित्यादृते occurs in the वृत्ति on p. 180 explaining the ध्वनिकारिका III. 10. So here at least the commentator ascribes the कारिका to सहृदय and the वृत्ति to ध्वनिकार. Dr. Mookerjee has again come forward to the attack in 'Indian Culture' vol. 12 pp. 57-60. But he has advanced hardly any new arguments which would require any fresh reply. He has, however, indulged in two remarks which I cannot allow to pass unchallenged. On p. 60 he is pleased to observe 'I am categorically definite that *all right thinking men* will be convinced that the theory of dual authorship of the Dhvanyāloka is a *canard and a figment of misconception* due to lack of careful appraisal of the rules of exegesis. I am definite that the problem is *set at rest finally and once for all*' (Italics are mine here and below). I ask all scholars to mark the abusive epithets in the first sentence. Abuse of one's opponents or of their arguments is held by all discerning judges to be a sure sign of the weakness of the case put up by one who indulges in abuse and vituperation. I may assure Dr. Mookerjee that several persons can use far more abusive language than he has indulged in, but that is not the way of a true scholar who is in pursuit of the truth. The second sentence shows a lamentable mentality. Dr. Mokerjee desires to silence all opponents by his *ipse dixit* and has been so bold as to assume the role of an *advocate* and also of *a judge* in his own cause. Whether a question in issue has finally been decided and set at rest is not for Dr. Mookerjee but for independent scholars to decide. Similarly, Dr. Krishnamoorthy shows how far he has balanced judgment in the following remark: 'there *is not a single piece of* evidence to support firmly the theory of dual authorship (I. H. Q. vol. 24 p. 307). He has proved to his own satisfaction that he is right. I leave him to enjoy that satisfaction. It is for discerning Sanskrit scholars to judge him finally and properly.

Additional arguments for asserting that the theory of ध्वनि in poetry had been propounded before आनन्दवर्धन may be set out. आनन्द॰ quotes (on p. 10) a verse which the लोचन ascribes to मनोरथ, a contemporary of आनन्द॰, in which the theory of ध्वनि is ridiculed 'काव्यं तद्ध्वनिना समन्वितमिति प्रीत्या प्रशंसञ्जडो नो विद्मोभिदधाति किं सुमतिना पृष्टः स्वरूपं ध्वनेः ॥'. Vide राजतर॰ (IV. 497) for मनोरथ and others and IV. 671 मानी मनोरथो मन्त्री परं परिजहार तम्. This refers to मनोरथs avoiding the voluptury ललितापीड who succeeded king जयापीड. The सुभा॰ (No. 51, 58, 440) quotes verses of a मनोरथ. If this मनोरथ is identical with the मनोरथ who flourished in the reign of जयापीड and ललितापीड the ध्वनिकारिकाs were composed between 800-825. Parhaps the लोचन is slightly wrong in making आनन्द॰ a contemporary of मनोरथ.

The लोचन while commenting on the words 'परम्परया समाम्नातः' in the ध्वन्यालोक says that before the ध्वन्यालोक there existed no work dealing with the theory of ध्वनि 'विनापि विशिष्टपुस्तकेषु विवेचनादित्यभिप्रायः' (p. 4). The ध्वन्यालोक makes it clear that the theory of ध्वनि and its nomenclature were suggested by the स्फोट theory of the grammarians 'प्रथमे हि विद्वांसो वैयाकरणाः । व्याकरणमूलत्वात्सर्वविद्यानाम् । ते च श्रूयमाणेषु वर्णेषु ध्वनिरिति व्यवहरन्ति । तथैवान्यैस्तन्मतानुसारिभिः सूरिभिः काव्यतत्त्वार्थदर्शिभिर्वाच्यवाचकसंमिश्रः शब्दात्मा काव्यमिति व्यपदेश्यो व्यञ्जकत्वसाम्याद् ध्वनिरित्युक्तः ।' (ध्व॰ pp. 55-56) and again on p. 249 'परिनिश्चितनिरपभ्रंशशब्दब्रह्मणां विपश्चितां मतमाश्रित्यैव प्रवृत्तोयं ध्वनिव्यवहार इति तैः सह किं विरोधाविरोधौ चिन्त्येते ।'. The स्फोट theory is probably older than पाणिनि who mentions a predecessor स्फोटायन in 'अवङ् स्फोटायनस्य' पा. VI. 1. 123. The वाक्यपदीय at great length propounds the doctrine of स्फोट (I. 44 ff). The ध्वन्यालोक says that the object of writing the book is not merely to establish by polemics that ध्वनि exists, but it is to show that the true function and purpose of poetry is व्यङ्ग्य which may take the form of रस etc. and to show that if the poet regards mere narration of events as his principal function, he is liable to commit serious breaches of good taste 'अत एव चेतिवृत्तमात्रवर्णनप्राधान्येऽङ्गाङ्गिभावरहितभावनिबन्धेन च कवीनामेवंविधानि स्खलितानि भवन्तीति रसादिरूपव्यङ्ग्यतात्पर्यमेवैषां युक्तमिति यत्नोऽस्माभिरारब्धो न ध्वनिप्रतिपादनमात्राभिनिवेशेन' (p. 201-202).

On going over all the arguments for and against the identity or non-identity of authorship I cannot help suspecting that, soon after Ānandavardhana, those who believed in identity tried to tamper with the text of the ध्वन्यालोक in various ways such as introducing the spurious verse इति काव्यार्थ...विस्मार्यः (after III. 9 on p. 178), reading इत्यक्लिष्ट for नित्याक्लिष्ट०, the splitting up of kārikās and sc on.

It is impossible to convey an adequate idea of the contents of the ध्वन्यालोक in a few lines. The following is a bare outline. In the first उद्द्योत, the author refers to the different views about ध्वनि, some holding that it does not exist, some saying that it is included under लक्षणा, others holding that ध्वनि cannot be defined and is beyond the province of words but can at the most be relished by the man of taste; there are two senses in poetry, expressed (वाच्य) and implied (प्रतीयमान); the वाच्य sense in the form of figures of speech is well-known; the प्रतीयमान is like personal charm in the case of beautiful ladies (which is distinct from the body and the limbs); प्रतीयमान is of three kinds, वस्तु, अलङ्कार and रस and there are many subdivisons of these three; this प्रतीयमान sense is not understood by those who merely know grammar and lexicons, but only by those who know the essence of poetry; the प्रतीयमान sense is the principal thing in poetry; when the व्यंग्य sense is the most prominent, it is ध्वनिकाव्य; in figures like समासोक्ति, आक्षेप, पर्यायोक्त and others, though there is a प्रतीयमान sense, the वाच्य sense is the most prominent and hence they are not ध्वनि; ध्वनि is of two kinds अविवक्षितवाच्य (in which the expressed sense is not intended to be conveyed or taken literally and विवक्षितान्यपरवाच्य (where the वाच्य sense is intended to be conveyed and also suggests another sense). ध्वनि is not identical with भक्ति (लक्षणा); nor is ध्वनि

incapable of being defined and illustrated. In the 2nd उद्योत he subdivides अविवक्षितवाच्य into अर्थान्तरसंक्रमित and अत्यन्ततिरस्कृतवाच्य and cites instances of each; the instances of the two respectively are 'तदा जायन्ते गुणा यदा ते सहृदयैर्गृह्यन्ते । रविकिरणानुगृहीतानि भवन्ति कमलानि कमलानि ॥' (here the 2nd कमलानि is अर्थान्तरसं०) and रविसंक्रान्तसौभाग्यस्तुषारावृतमण्डलः । निःश्वासान्ध इवादर्शश्चन्द्रमा न प्रकाशते ॥' (here the word अन्ध is अत्यन्ततिरस्कृतवाच्य); he divides विवक्षितान्यपरवाच्य into असंलक्ष्यक्रमव्यङ्ग्य and संलक्ष्यक्रमव्यंग्य; असंल० is constituted by रस, भाव, रसाभास, भावाभास and भावप्रशम, when these occupy the principal position; where रस, भाव and others are subordinate and the principal purport of the passage is different, there occur the figures रसवद् &c; difference between *guṇas* and *alaṅkāras*; remarks on the three *guṇas* माधुर्य, ओजस् and प्रसाद; अनुप्रास and यमक are not very desirable in शृङ्गार; illustrations of such figures as रूपक, पर्यायोक्त as subsidiary and favourable to the evolution of शृङ्गाररस; subdivision of संलक्ष्यक्रम into शब्दशक्तिमूल and अर्थशक्तिमूल, the former occurs where by the power of words an अलङ्कार is suggested (and not expressed), while in श्लेष two meanings are directly conveyed by the words themselves; examples of श्लेष and शब्दशक्तिमूलध्वनि; definition and elucidation of अर्थशक्तिमूल (an example is 'एवं वादिनि देवर्षौ पार्श्वे पितुरधोमुखी। लीलाकमलपत्राणि गणयामास पार्वती ।' where the व्यभिचारिभाव लज्जा is suggested); difference between अर्थशक्तिमूल and असंलक्ष्यक्रमव्यंग्य (the latter occurs where रस is relished by the express mention of विभावs, अनुभावs and व्यभिचारभावs); subdivision of अर्थशक्तिमूल into वस्तु and अलङ्कार, the former being प्रौढोक्तिनिष्पन्न[1] and स्वतःसम्भवी; examples of अलङ्कारध्वनि. III. In the second उद्योत the sub-divisions of ध्वनि were based upon व्यंग्य, in the third उद्योत sub-divisions are made from the point of view of the व्यञ्जक; अविवक्षितवाच्य (in its two varieties) is पदप्रकाश्य (an example is कः सन्नद्धे विरहविधुरां त्वय्युपेक्षेत जायां) or वाक्यप्रकाश्य (as in या निशा सर्वभूतानां तस्यां जागर्ति संयमी); the same two varieties occur in the संलक्ष्यक्रमव्यंग्य division of विवक्षितान्यपरवाच्य; असंलक्ष्यक्रम is helped by वर्ण, पद, वाच्य, सङ्घटना and प्रबन्ध; three kinds of सङ्घटना (असमासा, मध्यमसमासा and दीर्घसमासा); the relation of सङ्घटना[2] to गुणs; सङ्घटना depends upon

---

1. Vide Mr. A. K. Subramania Aiyer's article on 'Praudhokti in Alaṅkāra-śāstra' in J. O. R., Madras, vol. 16 pp. 20-31.

2. Vide a brief article on सङ्घटना in New I. A. vol. VII. pp. 76-78.

its appropriateness to speaker, the sense, the subject, the *rasa*; how *rasa* is manifested, how it is to be sustained, the figures favourable to the various *rasas*; the plot and its relation to *rasa*; illustration of the fact that असंलक्ष्यक्रम is conveyed even by particular declensions, conjugations, कृत् and तद्धित affixes, compounds etc.; what things are opposed (विरोधिनः) to the proper evolution of *rasa*; one रस should be the principal one in a composition and others should be ancillary to it; discussion of the difference between वाच्य and गम्य sense; difference between गुणवृत्ति and व्यंग्य; व्यंग्यव्यञ्जकभाव is not the same as अनुमान; a second variety of काव्य called गुणीभूतव्यंग्य (where, though there is a व्यंग्य sense, the expressed sense is charming); examples of गुणीभूतव्यंग्य ; the third variety of काव्य is चित्र, which is of two kinds, शब्दचित्र (such as यमक) and वाच्यचित्र (such as the figures उत्प्रेक्षा etc.); the third variety of काव्य occurs when the poet has no intention to convey a suggested sense or to evolve *rasa* etc; by the combination of these three varieties of काव्य numerous sub-varieties arise; the *rītis* and *vṛttis* (कैशिकी etc. and उपनागरिका etc.). IV The प्रतिभा of poets presents ever fresh aspects in the domain of ध्वनि and गुणीभूतव्यङ्ग्यकाव्य; the same thought, when made to glow by the poet's imagination, appears new; the poet should concentrate upon one *rasa* as the main purport of his work; in the रामायण, करुण is the main *rasa* and in the महाभारत, which is both शास्त्र and काव्य, शान्त *rasa* is the principal one intended by the poet; the province of poetry is unlimited in spite of the fact that hundreds of poets have composed works for centuries; the thoughts of inspired poets may bear a certain correspoudence; the resemblance between the works of two poets may be like that of बिम्ब and प्रतिबिम्ब, or between a thing and its picture, or between two human beings; the first two kinds of resemblance should be avoided, but the third is charming.

Besides the रामायण and the महाभारत (the अनुक्रमणी, गीता, गृध्रगोमायुसंवाद of which are quoted) the following are among the authors and works mentioned by name:—अर्जुनचरित (a महाकाव्य by आनन्द० pp. 183, 218), अमरुक, उद्भट (116, 131), कादम्बरी, कालिदास, तापसवत्सराज (a drama), धर्मकीर्ति, नागानन्द, भट्टबाण, भरत, भामह (46, 259), मधुमथनविजय, रत्नावली, रामाभ्युदय, विषमबाणलीला (a work by आनन्द० in Prakrit), वेणीसंहार, सर्वसेन (author of हरिविजय in Prakrit), सातवाहन (as having gone to नागलोक, 179), सेतुकाव्य, हरिविजय, हरिवंश (as composed by कृष्णद्वैपायन and placed at the end of the

महाभारत, 300), हर्षचरित; quotations are taken from the गाथासप्तशती, मनोरथ, the शाकुन्तल and other works of कालिदास, शिशुपालवध, सूर्यशतक; he frequently quotes his own verses (in Sanskrit and Prakrit) as illustrations (123 two verses, 134, 136, 284, 303, 306); he gives here and there a few verses called परिकरश्लोक (vide above p. 182); this expression is explained by लोचन (p. 40) 'परिकरार्थं कारिकार्थस्याधिकावापं कर्तुं श्लोकः परिकरश्लोकः' *i.e.* a verse that explained and expanded the sense of a कारिका (discussed in the वृत्ति). For the meaning of परिकर compare 'व्याकरणस्य शरीरं परिनिष्ठितशास्त्रकार्यमेतावत्। शिष्टः परिकरबन्धः क्रियतेस्य ग्रन्थकारेण ॥' (Peterson on ms. of काशिका JBBRAS vol. 16 extra No. p. 29). On p. 277 he introduces two verses with the words 'तदिदमुक्तं' on which the लोचन remarks 'मयैवेत्यर्थः'. On p. 292 he quotes a verse with the words तदिदमुक्तं on which the लोचन says 'उक्तमिति संग्रहार्थं मयैवेत्यर्थः'. On p. 278 we have two well-known verses 'अपारे काव्यसंसारे' etc. and 'शृङ्गारी चेत्कविः' introduced by the words तथा चेदमुच्यते (discussed above pp. 7-8). On p. 280 he gives two verses that summarise the preceding discussion with the words तदयमत्र संग्रहः.

The date of आनन्दवर्धन can be settled with great precision. The राज० says 'मुक्ताकणः शिवस्वामी कविरानन्दवर्धनः। प्रथां रत्नाकरश्चागात्साम्राज्येवन्तिवर्मणः ॥' (V. 34). This shows that आनन्दवर्धन attained fame as a poet in the reign of अवन्तिवर्मन् of Kashmir (855-883 A. D.). This date agrees well with what we know from other sources. He quotes उद्भट and so is later than 800 A. D.; while he is quoted by राजशेखर (about 900-925 A. D.). Therefore, the period of this literary activity would lie between 860-890 A. D. रत्नाकर is the author of the महाकाव्य हरविजय, which was composed by him, as he says, in the reign of बालबृहस्पति. Numerous verses are quoted by the सुभा० from a poet called शिवस्वामी. We are told by the लोचन that मनोरथ was one of the contemporaries of आनन्द० (vide above p. 198). Besides the अर्जुनचरित, the ध्वन्यालोक and the विषमबाणलीला, आनन्द० wrote after the ध्वन्यालोक a work on the धर्मोत्तमा, a commentary on the (प्रमाण) विनिश्चय (of धर्मकीर्ति). 'यत्त्वनिर्देश्यत्वं सर्वलक्षणविषये बौद्धानां प्रसिद्धं तत्तन्मतपरीक्षायां ग्रन्थान्तरे निरूपयिष्यामः' (p. 292), on which the लोचन remarks 'विनिश्चयटीकायां धर्मोत्तमायां या विवृतिरमुना ग्रन्थकृता कृता तत्रैव तद्व्याख्यातम्'. In 'History of Indian Logic' (pp. 329-331) Dr. Vidyābhushan assigns 847 A. D. as the date of the धर्मोत्तमा of धर्मोत्तर on प्रमाणविनिश्चय. The original (of धर्मोत्तमा) is lost, but there is a Tibetan translation. आनन्द० also composed the देवीशतक which is full of यमक, भाषाश्लेष, गोमूत्रिका and other चित्रबन्धs. From verse 101 of देवीशतक it appears that he was the son of नोण and wrote the work after the विषमबाणलीला and the अर्जुनचरित 'येनानन्दकथायां त्रिदशानन्दे च लालिता वाणी। तेन सुदुष्करमेतत्स्तोत्रं देव्याः कृतं भक्त्या ॥'. हेमचन्द्र also in his काव्यानुशासनविवेक (p. 225) states that आनन्दवर्धन was son of नोण. The देवीशतक was commented upon by कय्यट, son of चन्द्रादित्य and grandson of वल्लभदेव, in 4078 गतकलि (i.e. 977 A.D.) in the reign of king भीमगुप्त.[1]

The commentary of अभिनवगुप्त is variously designated in the mss. as सहृदयालोकलोचन or ध्वन्यालोकलोचन or काव्यालोकलोचन; the name of the commentary is लोचन and not आलोचन as some suppose. At the end of the first and the third उद्द्योत we have the verse 'किं लोचनं विनालोको भाति चन्द्रिकयापि हि। तेनाभिनवगुप्तोत्र लोचनोन्मीलनं व्यधात् ॥'; later writers like विश्वनाथ cite him as लोचनकार. The commentary of अभिनवगुप्त occupies in the Alaṅkāra literature a position analogous to that of पतञ्जलि's महाभाष्य in grammar or Śaṅkarācārya's bhāṣya on the Vedāntasūtras. अभिनवगुप्त was a profound philosopher, an acute critic and a great poet. His commentary is sometimes more erudite and difficult than the text. Here and there he discusses various reading in the कारिकाs and the वृत्ति (vide p. 180, कारिका III. 46 on p. 290). Among the authors and the works quoted by him (besides those in the ध्वन्यालोक) in the लोचन are:—इन्दुराज (frequently quoted), उत्पल (p. 35 as his परमगुरु), कादम्बरीकथासार of भट्टजयन्तक[2] (p.176),

1. Vide Journal (No. IX) of the Department of Letters, Calcutta University, which contains the comment of अभिनवगुप्त on the 4th उद्द्योत edited by Dr. Sushil Kumar De from two mss. at Madras. From this it appears that आनन्द० wrote a work called तत्त्वालोक in which he discussed the relation of शास्त्रनय and काव्यनय and that the verse उदिह० cited on p. 297 (of ध्व०) as his was composed in the सैन्धवभाषा. On the words in the वृत्ति (p. 300) 'मोक्षलक्षण एवैकः परः पुरुषार्थः शास्त्रनये काव्यनये च तृष्णाक्षयसुखपरिपोषलक्षणः शान्तो रसो महाभारतस्याङ्गित्वेन विवक्षित इति सुप्रतिपादितम्' the लोचन states 'शास्त्रनय इति। तत्रास्वादयोगाभावे पुरुषार्थ इत्ययमेव व्यपदेश सोदरः, चमत्कारयोगे तु रसव्यपदेश इति भावः। एतच्च ग्रन्थकारेण तत्त्वालोके वितत्योक्तम् ।'.

2. In the कादम्बरीकथासार (K. M. Series) the author is said to be अभिनन्द, son of जयन्तवृत्तिकार. In the Intro. verses to

काव्यकौतुक (231) of भट्टतौत, कुमारिलभट्ट (234), चन्द्रिकाकार (221), तन्त्रालोक (23), तापसवत्सराज (an analysis of its six Acts, on pp. 186-187), भट्टतौत (34), दण्डी (175), प्रभाकरदर्शन (234), भर्तृहरि (author of वाक्यपदीय, p. 55), भागुरि, मनोरथ, विवरणकृत्, यशोवर्म (author of रामाभ्युदय), वत्सराजचरित, वामन, स्वप्नवासवदत्ता (a drama), हृदयदर्पण (32 twice, 76). He frequently quoted his own verses (43, 48, 51, 91, 114, 143, 223). Some of these verses are said to be from his own स्तोत्र (pp. 91, 223). He tells us that he wrote a commentary (विवरण) on the काव्यकौतुक of his teacher तौत (p. 221). He wrote the लोचन after the तन्त्रालोक (p. 23).

अभिनवगुप्त was a very prolific writer. For an account of his parents, teachers and works, vide below section 21. In the introduction to the लोचन he refers to भट्टेन्दुराज as his teacher and quotes very frequently the verses of भट्टेन्दुराज as illustrations (29, 51, 142, 197. 259, 279). On pp. 29, 51, 142 he is cited simply as भट्टेन्दुराज and on pp. 51 and 142 as अस्मदुपाध्याय-भट्टेन्दुराज. The quotations show that भट्टेन्दुराज composed poems in both Sanskrit and Prakrit. The last is a Prakrit गाथा. That भट्टेन्दुराज was not only a poet but also a critic follows from the words of the लोचन (p. 197) 'यथा वास्मदुपाध्यायस्य विद्वत्कविसहृदयचक्रवर्तिनो भट्टेन्दुराजस्य' where he highly eulogises इन्दुराज as supreme amongst learned men, poets and men of taste. In his commentary on the भगवद्गीता (Buhler's K. report) p. 80 and p. CXLVIII) he tells us that his *guru* भट्टेन्दुराज belonged to the कात्यायनगोत्र, that the latter's grandfather was सौचुक and father भूतिराज. In several places the लोचन quotes the views of his *guru* or उपाध्याय on the words of the ध्वन्यालोक or examples cited therein. On the introductory verse स्वेच्छाकेसरिणः of the ध्वन्यालोक, the लोचन (p. 3

कादम्बरीकथासार we have a pedigree. शक्तिस्वामिन् who was a councillor of king मुक्तापीड of कर्कोट dynasty—his son कल्याणस्वामिन्—his son चन्द्र—son जयन्त—son अभिनन्द. From राजत. IV. 43 it appears that ललितादित्य was another name of मुक्तापीड, who ruled Kashmir from 700 to 736 A. D. अभिनन्द was 5th in descent from शक्तिस्वामिन् and so allowing about 120 years for four generations अभिनन्द should have flourished about 820-850 A. D. Why अभिनव mentions जयन्तक as the author and not अभिनन्द is not clear. Probably it is a slip or जयन्तक means 'son of जयन्त' or जयन्तक was written by scribes for जयन्तपुत्रक. The तिलकमञ्जरी of धनपाल (about 1000 A. D.) praises अभिनन्द in Intro. verse 33.

says 'एवं वस्त्वलङ्काररसभेदेन त्रिधा ध्वनिरत्र श्लोकेऽस्मद्गुरुभिर्व्याख्यातः'; 'सर्वथालङ्कारादिषु व्यङ्ग्यं वाच्ये गुणीभवतीति नः साध्यमित्यत्राशयोऽत्र ग्रन्थेऽस्मद्गुरुभिर्निरूपितः' (p. 44); 'अस्मद्गुरवस्त्वाहुः—अत्रोच्यते इत्यनेनेदमुच्यते etc.' (p. 227; 'अस्मदुपाध्यायास्तु इयन्तमानि पुष्पाणि अमुके गृहाण गृहाणेत्युच्चैस्तारस्वरेणादरातिशयार्थं प्रयच्छता' (p. 267, on the verse 'प्रयच्छतोच्चैः कुसुमानि मानिनी', where the explanation of लोचन is different). These quotations show that his teacher had explained the ध्वन्यालोक either orally to अभिनवगुप्त or in some commentary.

The question arises whether भट्टेन्दुराज is identical with प्रतीहारेन्दुराज, commentator of उद्भट. We do not know the parentage of the latter. But we know this that the latter did not approve of the theory of ध्वनि and included ध्वनिकाव्य under *alaṅkāras*; while भट्टेन्दुराज seems to have approved of it and explained the ध्वन्यालोक to अभिनवगुप्त. This circumstance by itself is not enough to hold that the two were different. There is nothing to prevent a teacher from expounding the views of a work from which he himself differs. There are other circumstances such as the non-employment of the title प्रतीहार to उपाध्याय इन्दुराज by अभिनव anywhere, that would have to be carefully considered in arriving at a decision. प्रतीहारेन्दुराज was a कौङ्कण and had come to काश्मीर for study. The word प्रतिहार or प्रतीहार indicates a high office. बृहस्पति quoted by विश्वरूप on या. I. 307 says 'कुलाढ्य उद्युक्तो मृदुरुदात्तः समरचित्तः शूरोऽनुरक्तोऽभेद्यः पत्तिविशेषज्ञ इङ्गिताकारकुशलः प्रतीहारः स्यात्'. शान्तिपर्व 85. 28-29, विष्णुधर्मोत्तर II. 24. 12 and शुक्रनीति II. 121-122 also give definitions. In the Valabhi grant of Dhruvasena I. dated in the Valabhi year 206 (525-26 A. D.) the *dūtaka* of the grant is Pratihāra Mammaka (E. I. vol. XI. pp. 105-9). For the form प्रतीहार, vide Vasantagadh inscription of Varmalāta (E. I. vol. IX. p. 187-192), the Candrāvatī plate of Candradeva of Kanoj in संवत् 1148 (E. I. IX. at p. 305) and राजत० V. 151. So प्रतीहारेन्दुराज was a high officer in Kashmir and probably prefixed that word to his name to distinguish himself from other Indurājas. Besides, he might possibly have been proud of the distinctions he secured in a country like Kashmīr, very distant from Koṅkaṇa from which he originally came. Though भट्टेन्दुराज and प्रतीहारेन्दुराज were both of them well versed in Alaṅkāraśāstra and flourished nearly at the same time, they must be regarded as distinct. It is possible that प्रतीहारेन्दुराज flourished a little earlier than इन्दुराज or was at least an elder contemporary of इन्दुराज. We shall see later on that the अभिधावृत्तिमातृका of मुकुल, son of कल्लट, has to be assigned to the period 900-925 A. D. प्रतीहारेन्दुराज was a pupil of मुकुल and in the verse at the end of his commentary on Udbhaṭa's work bestows the highest praise on मुकुल, from the tenor of which it appears very likely that मुकुल was alive when the commentary on उद्भट's work was written. So प्रतीहारेन्दुराज's commentary should be assigned to the period 920-950 A. D. We shall see later on that Abhinavagupta's literary activity lies between 980-1020 A. D. Therefore his *guru* Indurāja would have to be placed somewhere between 960-990 A. D. Abhinavagupta nowhere speaks of प्रतीहारेन्दुराज nor of मुकुल. If प्रतीहारेन्दु॰ was identical with इन्दुराज, we should expect to find some references to his teacher's teacher मुकुल, as in the case of उत्पलदेव who was Abhinava's teacher's teacher. Besides, we do not find प्रतीहारेन्दुराज quoting any verse of his own in his commentary which is of considerable extent. He seems to have been only a literary critic and not a poet, while Indurāja was not only a great literary critic but is spoken of as a great poet in the same breath with Vālmīki, Vyāsa, and Kālidāsa in the अ. भा. vol. II. p. 293 'न हि सर्वो वाल्मीकिर्व्यासः कालिदासो भट्टेन्दुराजो वा' and vol. I. p. 287 'अनुभावप्राधान्यं यथा—शुद्धसारस्वतप्रवाहपवित्रसकलवाङ्मयमहार्णवपूर्णभावसम्पादनाद्द्विजराजस्येन्दुराजस्य'. Dr. K. C. Pandey in his work on 'Abhinavagupta' (pp. 74 and 142) holds the two to be identical, but that view is based on very slender grounds. No scholar has yet explained why इन्दुराज the teacher of अभिनव in Poetics is nowhere mentioned by him as प्रतीहारेन्दुराज, which is the way in which the commentator of Udbhaṭa refers to himself, nor has anyone adverted to the meaning of प्रतीहार given by me above. For the present I must say that the evidence for the identity of the two इन्दुराजs is almost nil (except the name itself). इन्दुराज[1] the teacher of अभिनव, was the son of श्रीभूतिराज and grandson of सौचुक of the कात्यायनगोत्र, while we know nothing about the ancestors of प्रतीहारेन्दुराज. So Indurāja was a teacher of Abhinavagupta not only in Poetics, but also in the doctrines of the Gītā. It is, however, noteworthy that समुद्रबन्ध on the अलङ्कारसर्वस्व (p. 130 Trivendrum ed.) seems to identify the two by

1. At the beginning of his commentary on the भगवद्गीता (Nirn. edition with eight com.) अभिनव says : भट्टेन्दुराजादाम्नायं विविच्य च चिरं धिया। कृतोऽभिनवगुप्तेन सोयं गीतार्थसंग्रहः ॥ verse 6.

calling प्रतीहारेन्दुराज by the name भट्टेन्दुराज 'भट्टेन्दुराजेन प्रीणितप्रणयीत्यादि अप्रस्तुतप्रशंसोदाहरणे...भट्टोद्भटग्रन्थे...व्याख्यातम्'; *vide* p. 34 of the अलङ्कारसारसंग्रहलघुवृत्ति for the verse प्रीणितप्रणयि० which is भामह III. 30. भट्टतौत or भट्टतोत was another teacher of अभिनवगुप्त (लोचन pp. 34, 221) who wrote the work called काव्यकौतुक on which अभिनवगुप्त wrote a commentary (विवरण). At the end of chap. 19 of the नाट्यशास्त्र (GOS) अ. भा. (vol. III) says द्विजवरतोतनिरूपित-सन्ध्यध्यायार्थतत्त्वघटनेयम्। अभिनवगुप्तेन कृता शिवचरणाम्भोजमधुपेन ॥. The लोचन refers to उत्पल as the परमगुरु of अभिनवगुप्त (p. 35), who wrote on the प्रत्यभिज्ञाशास्त्र.

Before the लोचन, there existed a commentary on the ध्वन्यालोक called चन्द्रिका, which was composed by some one who belonged to the same family to which अभिनवगुप्त belonged. The लोचन cites it in many places and strongly condemns it: 'चन्द्रिकाकारस्तु पठितमनुपठतीति न्यायेन गजनिमीलिकया व्याचचक्षे तस्य तस्य शब्दस्य फलं तदा फलं वाच्यव्यङ्ग्यप्रतीत्यात्मकं तस्य घटना निष्पादना यतोऽनन्यसाध्या शब्दव्यापारैकजन्येति। न चात्रार्थसतत्त्वं व्याख्यानेन किञ्चिदुत्पश्याम इत्यलं पूर्ववंश्यैः सह विवादेन बहुना' (लोचन p. 231); 'आधिकारिकत्वेन तु शान्तो रसो निबद्धव्य इति चन्द्रिकाकारः। तच्चेहास्माभिर्न पर्यालोचितम्। प्रसङ्गान्तरात्' (लो० p. 221). This view is quoted by the काव्यप्रकाशसङ्केत of माणिक्य० (p. 101 Mysore ed.) and by सोमेश्वर. The verse किं लोचनं विनालोको भाति चन्द्रिकयापि हि' (at the end of the 1st and 3rd उद्द्योतs) contains a pun on the three words आलोक, चन्द्रिका (moonlight and the com. on the ध्वन्यालोक) and लोचन. The लोचन in several other places quotes the explanation of the ध्वन्यालोक by a previous commentator and adds words to the effect 'इत्यलं पूर्ववंश्यैः सह विवादेन.' For example, p. 150-51 'यस्तु व्याचष्टे...त्यलं निजपूर्वजसगोत्रैः साकं विवादेन,' p. 216-17 'अन्यस्तु व्याचष्टे-एतच्चापेक्षिकमित्यादिग्रन्थो...इत्यलं पूर्ववंश्यैः सह बहुना संलापेन, p. 269 यत्तु (यस्तु ?) त्रिष्वपि श्लोकेषु प्रतीयमानस्यैव रसाङ्गत्वं व्याचष्टे स्म स देवं विक्रीय तद्यात्रोत्सवमकार्षीत्।...इत्यलं पूर्ववंश्यैः सह विवादेन. The चन्द्रिका is referred to in the व्यक्तिविवेक also (5th intro. verse) 'ध्वनिवर्त्मन्यतिगहने स्खलितं वाण्याः पदे पदे सुलभम्। रभसेन यत्प्रवृत्ता प्रकाशकं चन्द्रिकाद्यदृष्ट्वैव ॥'. Therefore the चन्द्रिका must have been composed between 900-950 A. D.

On the first उद्योत of the लोचन a commentary called Kaumudī by उदयोत्तुङ्ग (from केरल) has been published at Madras (1944) edited with some verses of his own called उपलोचन by the late Mahāmahopādhyāya Prof. Kuppuswami and two of his pupils. This is a late but a learned commentary. I understand that the commentary (Kaumudī) on the remaining

Uddyotas has not yet been found. The author of the Kaumudī also wrote मयूरसन्देश which was published by Dr. Kunhan Raja who is himself a descendant of the author. Vide Prof. K. R. Pisharoti in Journal of Ganganath Jha Institute, vol. I. p. 445-452. Prof. Pisharoti shows that उदयोत्तुङ्ग was alive about 1480 A. D. and came of a princely family. The author of the कौमुदी quotes his own verses on pp. 227, 234, 261 &c.

The ध्वनिगाथापञ्जिका of रत्नाकर (see Govt. collection of mss. at B. O. R. I., cat. vol. XII. No. 182) explains the Prākrit verses occurring in the ध्व०. The रत्नाकर is probably later than लोचन as the former's explanations agree almost word for word with those given by the Locana. In the colophon he is styled काश्मीरकाचार्य. It would be almost impossible to hold that लोचन borrows from him. The verse on p. 133 चन्दमऊ...करइ गरूई is quoted but not explained in ध्व. गा. प. (folio 4a) and the corrupt verse on p. 297 (उदिह०) is not cited nor explained. In some cases ध्व. गा. गा. प, (folio 7a) helps in restoring the प्राकृत text and its *chāyā* as on p. 192 (the प्राकृत verses अत्ता वच्च बालअ०). There are 46 Prākrit verses quoted in the Dhvanyāloka out of which 20 have not been yet traced. In several other places the लोचन refers (in the words अन्यः, कश्चित् &c) to the explanations and comments of the passages of the ध्वन्यालोक or the illustrations cited therein, but dose not name the author nor does it add the words इत्यलं पूर्ववंश्यैः सह विवादेन. The views quoted are likely to be those of चन्द्रिका in some cases and of भट्टनायक in others, vide pp. 8, 23 (यस्तु ध्वनिव्याख्यानोद्यतस्तात्पर्यशक्तिमेव...स नास्माकं हृदयमावर्जयति), 42 (यस्तु व्याचष्टे...स प्रकृतार्थमेव ग्रन्थार्थमत्यजत्), 151, 180, 217, which are cases where probably the चन्द्रिका is referred to, while p. 69 (यत्तु वाक्यभेदः स्यादिति केनचिदुक्तं तदनभिज्ञतया), 248, 259 seem to refer to the views of independent writers like भट्टनायक, मीमांसकs and others.

16 The काव्यमीमांसा of राजशेखर. This work has been published in the Gaikwal Oriental Series (3rd edition of 1934 with a learned Introduction by C. D. Dalal, Pandit R. A. Sastry and K. S. Ramswami Sastry and there is another edition with a Hindi translation by Pandit Kedaraśarmā published by the बिहारराष्ट्रभाषापरिषद् in 1954, which does not clearly state on what mss. material it is based and in the Chowkhamba S. series with a modern commentary. This is a unique work, but it does not directly concern itself with the exposition of *rasas*,

guṇas or *alaṅkāras*, and it is rather in the nature of a practical handbook for poets. It is divided into 18 chapters. The following is a brief analysis of the contents. I, शास्त्रसंग्रह, narrates how instruction in काव्यमीमांसा was imparted by Śiva to Brahmā and others (64 in all) and how from Brahmā through a succession of teachers and pupils the 18 sections of the काव्यमीमांसा were dealt with by 18 different writers (vide p. 1 above), how राजशेखर of the यायावरीय family summarized the views of sages. II शास्त्रनिर्देश—वाङ्मय is of two kinds शास्त्र and काव्य; शास्त्र is अपौरुषेय and पौरुषेय; the four Vedas, 4 उपवेद्s (vide above p. 18 note), six *aṅgas* (and their subjects); यायावरीय thinks that अलङ्कार is the seventh *aṅga*; पौरुषशास्त्र is constituted by the पुराणs, आन्वीक्षिकी, the two मीमांसाs, 18 स्मृतिs, the number of विद्यास्थानs, 14 or 18 is the number of विद्याs according to various authorities, यायावरीय calls काव्य the 15th विद्यास्थान; meaning of such words as सूत्र, भाष्य, वृत्ति, पद्धति, टीका, समीक्षा, पञ्जिका, कारिका etc.; different views about the number of विद्याs and राज० thinks that साहित्य is the 5th विद्या. III. काव्यपुरुषोत्पत्ति; a mythical account of the birth of काव्यपुरुष from सरस्वती; काव्यपुरुष is described as 'शब्दार्थौ ते शरीरं, संस्कृतं मुखं, प्राकृतं बाहुः, जघनमपभ्रंशः, पैशाचं पादौ, उरो मिश्रम् । समः प्रसन्नो मधुर उदार ओजस्वी चासि । उक्तिचणं च ते वचो, रस आत्मा, रोमाणि च्छन्दांसि, प्रश्नोत्तरप्रवह्लिकादिकं च वाक्केलिः, अनुप्रासोपमादयश्च त्वामलङ्कुर्वन्ति ।' (p. 6), marriage of काव्यपुरुष with साहित्यविद्यावधू at the city of वत्सगुल्म (probably modern Basim in Berar); the definitions of प्रवृत्ति, वृत्ति and रीति; IV पदवाक्यविवेक;—what are the essential requisites to become a poet? यायावरीय said शक्ति was the only काव्यहेतु and gave rise to प्रतिभा and व्युत्पत्ति; while others said that the aid of समाधि (concentration) and अभ्यास was required; various classifications of poets; V काव्यपाककल्प—meaning of व्युत्पत्ति, शास्त्रकवि, काव्यकवि and उभयकवि and their sub-divisions; the ten stages (अवस्था) of a poet, the various meanings of the term पाक; VI पदवाक्यविवेक—the five वृत्तिs of शब्द, सुप्, समास, तद्धित, कृत् and तिङ्; definition of वाक्य; its threefold expressive power वैभक्त, शाक्त, शाक्तिविभक्तिमय; ten kinds of वाक्य; definition of काव्य as 'गुणवदलङ्कृतं च वाक्यमेव काव्यम्'; VII पाठप्रतिष्ठा—the appropriate languge and style for gods, Apsarases, पिशाचs &c; the three रीतिs वैदर्भी, गौडीया and पाञ्चाली; काकु of two kinds and their sub-divisions with illustrations, the intonation of various peoples in India and the different languages they employ;[1] VIII काव्यार्थयोनयः—the sources

1. For example, he speaks about लाट, काश्मीर and पाञ्चाल

of the subject matter of काव्य are 12, श्रुति, स्मृति, इतिहास, पुराण, प्रमाणविद्या (मीमांसा and तर्कशास्त्र), समयविद्या, राजसिद्धान्तत्रयी (अर्थशास्त्र, नाट्यशास्त्र, कामशास्त्र), लोक, विरचना (कविमनीषानिर्मितं कथातन्त्रमर्थमात्रं वा विरचना) and प्रकीर्णक; यायावरीय adds four more; IX अर्थव्याप्ति—the subject of description may be दिव्य, दिव्यमानुष, मानुष, पातालीय, मर्त्यपातालीय, दिव्यपातालीय and दिव्यमर्त्यपातालीय; whatever the location may be the subject must be रसवत् (p. 45 रसवत एव निबन्धो युक्तो न नीरसस्येति आपराजितिः ... आमिति यायावरीयः), the subject of description may be in an isolated verse or in a प्रबन्ध, each of which is of five kinds; X कविचर्या and राजचर्या—काव्यविद्याs (नामधातुपारायण, अभिधानकोश, छन्दोविचिति and अलङ्कार), 64 कलाs are the उपविद्याs, काव्यमातरः (देशवार्ता, विदग्धवाद, लोकयात्रा, विद्वद्गोष्ठी etc.), purity of body, speech and thought necessary for a poet; the house of a poet, his attendants and writing materials, how a poet should divide the whole day into eight parts and the duties appropriate to each of the eight parts, women also may write poetry, assembly hall to be erected by kings for examining poets, in large towns assemblies to be formed for testing those learned in the शास्त्रs and काव्य; XI-XIII—how far a poet can appropriate a predecessor's words and thoughts; XIV-XVI about कविसमय (conventions) with reference to countries, trees, plants, flowers, etc. about intangible things (as a smile which is said to be white); XVII देशविभाग— the various countries, rivers, mountains in the four quarters of India and the products peculiar to each; the colour of the complexion of verious peoples; XVIII कालविभाग—the seasons, the winds, flowers, birds and actions appropriate to variuos seasons.

It will be seen that this work is a mine of information on numerous matters. It appears that the printed काव्यमीमांसा is only a fragment of what the author contemplated (e. g. on p. 11 it says—तमौपनिषदिके वक्ष्यामः). The अलङ्कारशेखर at the end of the 11th मरीचि quotes two verses from राजशेखर which are not found in the काव्यमी०, one of which is 'अलङ्कारशिरोरत्नं सर्वस्वं काव्यसम्पदाम्। उपमा कविवंशस्य मातैवेति मतिर्मम ॥'. The work is written somewhat after the अर्थशास्त्र of कौटिल्य and the style is vigorous,

---

poets as follows : पठन्ति लटभं लाटाः प्राकृतं संस्कृतद्विषः। जिह्वया ललितोल्लापलब्धसौन्दर्यमुद्रया ॥ शारदायाः प्रसादेन काश्मीरः सुकविर्जनः। कर्णाटे गुडूचीगण्डूषस्तेषां पाठक्रमः किमु ॥...पाञ्चालमण्डलभुवां सुभगः कवीनां श्रोत्रे मधु क्षरति किंचन काव्यपाठः ॥ काव्यमी० VII. p. 34.

though sometimes ponderous. He quotes numerous verses from ancient authors. Among the works drawn upon are those of कालिदास, अमरुशतक, किरातार्जुनीय, कादम्बरी, मालतीमाधव, वेणीसंहार, शिशुपालवध, सूर्यशतक, हयग्रीववध, his own works. He quotes the opinions of numerous writers on Alaṅkāra, some of whom are known from his work alone, *viz.* अवन्तिसुन्दरी, आनन्द, आपराजिति, उद्भट, उद्भट, कालिदास, द्रौहिणि, पाल्यकीर्ति, भरत, मङ्गल, रुद्रट, वाक्पतिराज, वामन, श्यामदेव, सुरानन्द. He cites (about 18 times) certain views as those of the ācāryas (pp. 3, 9, 13, 16, 20, 23, 30, &c.). It is not possible to say who are meant but he generally dissents from the आचार्यs, as does कौटिल्य. He quotes his own views as those of यायावरीयः. The काव्यमीमांसा has not been frequently quoted in later works on साहित्य. हेमचन्द्र (काव्यानुशासन pp. 126-130 and 130-135) and वाग्भट borrowed from him very largely, particularly chapters 17-18. The काव्यप्रकाशसङ्केत of माणिक्य० (p. 308 Mysore ed.) quotes the words 'अभिप्रायवान्पाठधर्मः काकुः स नालङ्कारी स्यादिति यायावरीयः' (which occur in the काव्यमी० p. 31). हेमचन्द्र (p. 235 काव्यानु०) and सोमेश्वर also quote these words. He gives some striking historical and literary information. He tells us that मेधाविरुद्र and कुमारदास were poets that were blind from birth (p. 12), that certain kings such as शिशुनाग in मगध, कुविन्द in शूरसेन, सातवाहन in कुन्तल and साहसाङ्क in उज्जयिनी respectively made rules that in their palaces eight letters that were difficult to utter were not to be employed, that harsh conjunct consonants were to be avoided, that only Prakrit was to be employed or only Sanskrit (p. 50); that वासुदेव, सातवाहन, शूद्रक and साहसाङ्क were great patrons of learning and that in उज्जयिनी the poets कालिदास, मेण्ठ, अमर, रूपसूर (?), भारवि, हरिचन्द्र, चन्द्रगुप्त, were examined and in पाटलिपुत्र, उपवर्ष, वर्ष, पाणिनि, पिङ्गल, व्याडि, वररुचि, and पतञ्जलि were tested (p. 55). He is very fond of the Prākrits (pp. 34, 51) and speaks of the languages in different countries (p. 51, where पैशाची is said to prevail in अवन्ती, पारियात्र and दशपुर).

About his personal history राजशेखर gives far more information than most Sanskrit poets do. His ancestors appear to have hailed from महाराष्ट्र. In the बालरामायण and the विद्धशालभञ्जिका it is stated that he was the 4th in descent from अकालजलद[1]

1. तदामुष्यायणस्य महाराष्ट्रचूडामणेरकालजलदस्य चतुर्थो दौर्दुकिः शीलवतीसूनुरुपाध्यायश्रीराजशेखर इत्यपर्याप्तं बहुमानेन । बालरामायण I. 13; in

the crest-jewel of Mahārāṣṭra, that he was the son of शीलवती and of दुर्दुक (or दुहिक). In the बालरामायण I. 13 we are told that in his family (which was called यायावरकुल) were born great men such as अकालजलद, सुरानन्द, तरल, कविराज and several others. In the बालरामायण (I. 16) and बालभारत (I. 12) the same verse occurs, in which he claims to have been वाल्मीकि, मेण्ठ and भवभूति in his former lives.[1] He is spoken of as the son of a great minister in the Prastāvanā of the Bālabhārata drama, otherwise called Pracaṇḍapāṇḍava, (उक्तं हि तेनैव महामन्त्रिपुत्रेण 'यशः प्रसूते विपदो क्वचिद् यशांसि दुग्धे मलिनं प्रमार्ष्टि। I. 9). His wife was अवन्तिसुन्दरी who came from the Cāhuāṇa (modern Cavāṇ) family. She was an accomplished lady and her views are quoted by her husband in the काव्यमीमांसा (on pp. 20, 46, 57). It was at her desire that the Prākrit drama (described as Saṭṭaka) कर्पूरमञ्जरी was represented on the stage.[2] In the बालरामायण (I. 12) reference is made to his six works.[3] Therefore, it is clear that the बालरामायण was composed by him when he was somewhat mature in years. In the कर्पूरमञ्जरी it is stated that अपराजित, author of मृगाङ्कलेखा, spoke of him as बालकवि, कविराज and the teacher of king निर्भर and that in this way he attained eminent[4] positions one after another. At the end of the first chapter (p. 2) he describes himself as यायावरीय राजशेखर and states that he summarized the views of sages and expounded the काव्यमीमांसा for the benefit of poets. Hence, there can be no doubt that the काव्यमीमांसा was composed by the same man that composed the four dra-

---

the विद्ध० (I. प्रस्तावना) we have 'यायावरेण दौहिकिना कविराजशेखरेण विरचिताया विद्धशालभञ्जिकानामनाटिकायाः' and 'किमात्थ तदकालजलदस्य प्रणप्तुः &c.'

1. बभूव वल्मीकभवः कविः पुरा ततः प्रपेदे भुवि भर्तृमेण्ठताम्। स्थितः पुनर्यो भवभूतिरेखया स वर्तते संप्रति राजशेखरः॥ बालरा. I. 16; बालभारत I. 12.

2. चाहुआणकुलमउलिमालिआ राजसेहरकइन्दगेहिणी। भत्तुणो किदिमवन्तिसुन्दरी सा पउंजइदु मेदमिच्छदि॥ कर्पूरमञ्जरी I. 10 (of Dr. Ghosh's edition).

3. यद्वस्ति स्वस्ति तुभ्यं भव पठनरुचिर्विद्धि नः षट् प्रबन्धान्। 3rd *pāda* in बालरा. I. 12 (K. M. ed.).

4. बालकइ कइराअो णिब्भरराअस्स तह उवज्झाओ। इइ जस्स परेहिँ परम्पराय माहप्पमारूढं॥ कर्पूर० I. 8. According to his own statements in the काव्यमी. p. 19 कविराज is higher in status than even a महाकवि.

mas. It is also clear from the कर्पूरमञ्जरी I. 5 and the reply in the next line that he was the *guru* of king Mahendrapāla[1] and the very first sentence of the बालरामायण and a line before बालभारत I. 6 show that those dramas were staged before an assembly of learned men in the court of Mahendrapāla at महोदय.[2] The Bālabhārata (I. 7) speaks of king Mahīpāla and the following prose passage states that the king was the son of निर्भयनरेन्द्र and that he was sovereign of Āryāvarta (India north of Narmadā or Vindhya) and that Mahendrapāla was a pupil of राजशेखर (बालभारत I. 11). Hence it is clear that राजशेखर's family left महाराष्ट्र and that राजशेखर came to महोदय (i. e. modern Kanoj) and was the guru or Upādhyāya of the kings निर्भय (or महेन्द्रपाल) and his son महीपाल. राजशेखर knew many languages and was very fond of Prākrits. In the कर्पूरमञ्जरी he is spoken of as सर्वभाषाचतुर (one line before I. 7) and a verse of his is quoted by the attendant of the stage manager to the effect that any language may do for a kāvya which consists in being a striking mode of speech, the meaning being the same and the (Prākrit) words being merely modifications (of Sanskrit). He is fond of repeating the same verse in two dramas : e. g. बालरामायण I. 18 (आपन्नार्तिहरः०) is the same as बालभारत I. 11 and बालरामायण I. 20 (प्रथयति०) is the same as बालभारत I. 14. The काव्यमीमांसा (p. 94 तत्रापि महोदयं मूलमवधीकृत्येति यायावरीयः) lays down that directions of countries are to be measured from महोदय. In two verses his ancestor अकालजलद was praised, which are quoted in the सूक्तिमुक्तावलि.[3] The verse said to have been written by शङ्करवर्मन्

1. विद्धशाल० I. 6 also says 'रघुकुलतिलको महेन्द्रपालः सकलकलानिलयः स यस्य शिष्यः ॥'.

2. महोदय is generally held to be कान्यकुब्ज (Kanoj). Vide E. I. vol. VII pp. 23, 30 and 43 where राष्ट्रकूट king इन्द्र III is said to have devastated महोदय or Kanoj; but in the Barah Copper-plate of भोजदेव (Gurjara Pratīhāra king) dated *saṁvat* 893 (836 A. D.) महोदय seems to be spoken of as a स्कन्धावार (camp) and कान्यकुब्ज is separately mentioned in the same record (E. I. vol. 19 at p. 17). Vide J. R. A. S. for 1908 pp. 765-793 for the history of Kanoj by Vincent Smith and Bilhari stone Inscription of Cedi rulers (E. I. vol. I. pp. 251-270).

3. अकालजलदेन्दोः सा हृद्या वदनचन्द्रिका । नित्यं कविचकोरैर्या पीयते न च हीयते ॥ अकालजलदश्लोकैश्चित्रमात्मकृतैरिव । जातः कादम्बरीरामो नाटके प्रवरः कविः ॥ सूक्तिमु. p. 46, verses 83-84. In the 2nd verse it is

about राजशेखर is quoted by the earliest anthologies.[1] It appears that सुरानन्द who is mentioned as a member of his family by राजशेखर had migrated to the kingdom of Cedi (त्रिपुरी or modern Tewar, six miles from Jubbulpore).[2] Hence it is probable that from Mahārāṣṭra सुरानन्द went to Central India and that Rājaśekhara pushed further north. This laudatory verse about सुरानन्द and another about तरल are ascribed, along with about thirty others, to Rājaśekhara in the anthologies.[3] Most probably they are the composition of the author of the काव्यमीमांसा. Being at the court of Kanoj राजशेखर shows great partiality for महोदय, for पाञ्चाल poets and for the dress of the ladies of Mahodaya (vide काव्यमी. p. 8 वेषं नमस्यत महोदयसुन्दरीणाम्; बालरामायण X. 86 'पञ्चालास्तव पश्चिमेन त इमे वामा गिरां भाजनाः...यमुनां त्रिस्रोतसं चान्तरा ॥'). He seems to have also been familiar with Lāṭadeśa (country round about Surat), its language, the speech of its people and the charm of the ladies. It is interesting to note that the काव्यमी. (p. 93) includes under दक्षिणापथ (which is stated to be beyond Māhiṣmatī) the countries of महाराष्ट्र, माहिषक, अश्मक, विदर्भ, कुन्तल, क्रथकैशिक, सूर्पारक, वानवासक, नाशिक्य, कौङ्कण &c. कुन्तल is the country from modern Belgaum to Bellary (E. I. 14 p. 265, E. I. 15 p. 32, I. A. vol. 8 at p. 17 'the country between the Kṛṣṇā and Verṇā'). Aśmaka (North Khandesh), विदर्भ (Berar) कौङ्कण being separately mentioned, महाराष्ट्र must be held according to Rājaśekhara to be roughly the present महाराष्ट्र from Nasik to Belgaum excluding Koṅkaṇa. Vide Prof. V. V. Mirashi in I.

---

said that कादम्बरीराम plagiarised the verses of अकालजलद and took them in his drama.

1. पातुं कर्णरसायनं रचयितुं वाचः सतां संमतां व्युत्पत्तिं परमामवाप्तुमवधिं लब्धुं रसस्रोतसः। भोक्तुं स्वादुफलं च जीविततरोर्यद्यस्ति ते कौतुकं तद्भ्रातः शृणु राजशेखरकवेः सूक्तीः सुधास्यन्दिनीः॥ विद्धशाल॰ I. 7 and बालरामायण I. 17, quoted in सदुक्तिकर्णामृत V. 27. 3 p. 296 and सूक्तिमु. p. 48.

2. नदीनां मेकलसुता नृपाणां रणविग्रहः। कवीनां च सुरानन्दश्चेदिमण्डलमण्डनम्॥ यायावरकुलश्रेणेर्मुक्तायष्टेश्च मण्डनम्। सुवर्णबन्धरुचिरस्तरलस्तरलो यथा॥ सूक्तिमु. p. 47 verses 88-89. The view of सुरानन्द is quoted on p. 75 of काव्यमी. and also a verse.

3. They were probably placed at the beginning of the हरविलासकाव्य. In any case anthologies from the 12th century onward quote them as Rājaśekhara's. Vide Introduction to कवीन्द्रवचनसमुच्चय ed. by Dr. F. W. Thomas pp. 80-92 for the verses in praise of poets named therein.

H. Q. vol. 22 pp. 309-315 for अश्मक and कुन्तल. It is clear that the four plays कर्पूरमञ्जरी, बालभारत (only two Acts are edited in the K. M. series), बालरामायण, विद्धशालभञ्जिका are the works of राजशेखर, the काव्यमीमांसा being another work. He wrote also a महाकाव्य called हरविलास mentioned by हेमचन्द्र (काव्यानुशासन pp. 334-335) who quotes a verse therefrom and states 'स्वनामाङ्किता यथा राजशेखरस्य हरविलासे'.

No work of his wife अवन्तिसुन्दरी has come down. हेमचन्द्र in his देशीनाममाला quotes three Prākrit verses of अवन्तिसुन्दरी (one on I. 81 and two on I. 157). On p. 46 the काव्यमी० quotes an opinion of अवन्तिसुन्दरी and a Sanskrit verse (वस्तुस्वभावोऽत्र०).

One important question is whether राजशेखर was a ब्राह्मण or a क्षत्रिय. The name राजशेखर (राजा चन्द्रः शेखरे यस्य) means शिव (चन्द्रशेखर being given by Amara as a synonym of शिव). He was said to be उपाध्याय or गुरु of two kings of Kanoj. There is no total prohibition against a kṣatriya's being a teacher. Yet it is very unlikely that in the 9th or 10th century two kings made a kṣatriya their उपाध्याय. The word यायावर, which occurs 34 times in काव्यमी०, also is important. For its meaning, vide H. of Dh. vol. II. pp. 641-642 and footnotes. यायावर means a brāhmana who leads a very plain life, does not accept gifts, does not accumulate wealth &c. Vide the Mitākṣarā on Yāj. I. 128. A क्षत्रिय family could hardly have ever been called यायावर. Similarly, an उपाध्याय is, acc. to मनु. II. 141, विष्णुधर्मसूत्र (29. 2), शङ्खस्मृति (3. 2) one who teaches the Veda or Vedāṅgas for his livelihood. Vide H. of Dh. vol. II. pp. 322-324, 361. The only circumstance which raises a doubt (particularly in minds of writers in modern times) is the fact that his wife appears to have come from a kṣatriya family. But *anuloma* marriages were allowed in ancient and medieval India. Medhātithi, who belonged probably to the same period as Rājaśekhara, allowed a brāhmana to adopt a kṣatriya boy (H. of Dh. vol. III. p. 675). Vide History of Dharmaśāstra vol. II. pp. 50-58, 448-450 for *anuloma* marriages. Hence it should be held that राजशेखर was a brāhmaṇa. Dr. Hultzsch in I. A. vol. 34 pp. 177-180 holds that राजशेखर was only a teacher of fine arts. But that does not seem to be quite accurate if we look to the primary meaning of the words उपाध्याय and यायावर.[1]

---

1. Dr. M. Ghosh (Intro. to कर्पूरमञ्जरी p. 69, ed. of 1948)

The date of राजशेखर does not present much difficulty. He quotes रुद्रट's काव्यालङ्कार (on काव्यमी. p. 31), आनन्दवर्धन's वृत्ति (on p. 16) and the school of Udbhaṭa (pp. 22, 44) and the school of Vāmana (pp. 14, 20); hence he is certainly later then 875 A. D. The Yaśastilaka, composed in 959-960 A. D., mentions in the 4th आश्वास (K. M. ed. part II. p. 113) numerous poets of whom राजशेखर is one. The तिलकमञ्जरी of धनपाल composed about 1000 A. D. praises the poetic passages of यायावर (समाधिगुणशालिन्यः प्रसन्नपरिपक्त्रिमाः। यायावरकवेर्वाचो मुनीनामिव वृत्तयः ॥ verse 33). Soḍḍhala, author of उदयसुन्दरीकथा (8th उच्छ्वास p. 558), praises राज० ('यायावरः प्राज्ञवरो गुणज्ञैराशंसितः सूरिसमाजवर्यैः'). Soḍḍhala composed his work between 1026-1050 A. D. (vide Intro.). So राजशे० flourished before 950 A. D. Here Inscriptions come to our help. The Siyadoni stone inscription (E. I. vol. I. pp. 162-179) refers to संवत् 960 (903-4 A. D.) and a king ०पालदेव (p. 173) of महोदय (p. 178, line 40) and I. A. vol. 16 pp. 175-178 the Asni Inscription of महीपाल (dated विक्रमसंवत् 974, 917 A. D.) speaks of a king महीपाल who succeeded महिषपालदेव. They are taken by Dr. Fleet to refer to महीपाल and his predecessor निर्भयनरेन्द्र. The result is that राजशेखर flourished towards the end of the 9th century A.D. and the first quarter of the 10th. This is further corroborated by the fact that अभिनवगुप्त expressly mentions the कर्पूरमञ्जरी of राजशेखर 'तथाहि शृङ्गाररसे सातिशयोपगिनी प्राकृतभाषेति सट्टकः कर्पूरमञ्जर्याख्यो राजशेखरेण तन्मय एव निबद्धः' (on chap. 19 verse 130 p. 72 of vol. III. of GOS ed. of नाट्यशास्त्र). The बालरामायण is mentioned by name on भरत 16. 39 (vol. II. p. 320 G.O.S. ed.) by अभिनवगुप्त. Vide p. 50 above where it is shown that a verse attributed to लोल्लट by हेमचन्द्र is quoted by the काव्यमी. (p. 45) as आपराजिति's. The Bilhari stone Inscription of युवराजदेव II, the ruler of Cedi (E. I. vol. I. p. 251) contains a verse at the end in praise of Rājaśekhara 'सुश्लिष्टबन्धघटनाविस्मितकविराजशेखरस्तुत्या। अस्तामियमाकल्पं कृतिश्च कीर्तिश्च पूर्वा च ॥' (at p. 262). The date is effaced, but the editor of the Inscription conjectures from the script and the contents that it belongs to the 10th century. This Inscription has been re-edited by Prof. V. V. Mirashi in C. I. I. vol. IV pp. 204-224, the verse occurring on p. 215.

---

is not prepared to hold that राजशेखर was a ब्राह्मण. He does not pay sufficient attention to the ancient smṛti meaning of यायावर and to the word यायावरकुल.

On p. 98 of काव्यमी. राजशे० states that those who desire further information about countries[1] may refer to his भुवनकोश. It is not necessary to suppose that भुवनकोश was a distinct work of राजशेखर. On p. 2 he sets out the subjects of his first अधिकरण, the last of which is भुवनकोश. But in the present text of the काव्यमी. (1st अधिकरण) the treatment of भुवनकोश is wanting. Hence on p. 98 he probably refers to the last part of the 1st अधिकरण and not to a distinct work as the editor (p. XV Intro. of the edition of 1924) holds though Dr. De. (H. S. P. vol. I p. 123) holds that the reference is to another work of his.

It is not possible to say how many works राजशेखर wrote. The बालरा. (as stated above) refers to six works having been already composed (probably including itself). As the काव्यमी. (p. 38) quotes the verse शमव्यायामाभ्यां (which occurs in बालरा. I. 24), the verse मूलं बालकवीरुधां which occurs in विद्धशालभञ्जिका (IV 5), the verse ये सीमन्तित० (p. 71 found in बालभारत (I. 2), it may be presumed that the काव्यमीमांसा was composed after these plays. Vide Prof. Mirashi's views in his paper 'The chronological order of Rājaśekhara's works' in Prof. Pathak Commemoration vol. (1934) pp. 359-366, which Dr. Manomohan Ghosh follows (71-72 of Intro. to कर्पूरमञ्जरी ed. of 1948). Though I do not agree with all the conclusions of Prof. Mirashi, yet as this subject is not relevant here, I do not enter into any discussion.

The following important authors and works are quoted in the काव्यमीमांसा : अवन्तिसुन्दरी, आनन्द, आपराजिति, औद्भटाः, कालिदास, कुमारदास, कौटिल्य (p. 4.), पाल्यकीर्ति (p. 46), भरत, मङ्गल, मेघठ, मेधाविरुद्र (p. 12), रुद्रट, वररुचि, वाक्पतिराज[2] (p. 62), वामनीयाः, श्यामदेव (pp. 11, 13, 17). Several authors and works such as भामह (I. 7. on p. 90), काव्यादर्श (I. 70 on काव्यमी. p. 82, II. 99 on काव्यमी. p. 24) are quoted though not named. For further information on राजशेखर and his works, the following may be consulted. Prof. V. S. Apte's book on 'Rājaśekhara, his life and writings' (1886 A. D.), Dr. Sten Konow's 'Karpūramañjari' part III. and Dr. Manomohan Ghosh's Introduction to his edition of the Karpūramañjari, Sir C. V. Kumarswami Sastriar's article on

---

1. इत्थं देशविभागो मुद्रामात्रेण सूत्रितः सुधियाम् । यस्तु जिगीषत्यधिकं पश्यतु मद्भुवनकोशमसौ ॥

2. This is the author of the Prākrit poem Gauḍavaho.

Rājaśekhara in J. O. R., Madras, vol. 7 pp. 25-32 (on date), Festgabe Jacobi pp. 169-179 (by Nobel), J. I. H. for 1930 vol. IX. pp. 119-131 (paper by Prof. Dasaratha Sharma on 'gleanings from Rājaśekhara's works' emphasizing laxity of morals and the influence of the Kaula system in the times of Rājaśekhara.

17 The अभिधावृत्तिमातृका of मुकुलभट्ट (Nir. Press, 1916). This work deserves a passing notice. This is a work containing 15 *kārikās* with वृत्ति thereon by the author himself. It deals with the two senses of words viz. मुख्य and लाक्षणिक and gives a detailed treatment of लक्षणा (its sub-divisions and examples). Later works like the काव्यप्रकाश base there treatment of लक्षणा on this work. He quotes or refers to उद्भट (definition of उत्प्रेक्षा), कुमारिलभट्ट, ध्वन्यालोक, भर्तृमित्र (a मीमांसा writer), महाभाष्य, विज्जिका (the verse दृष्टिं हे प्रतिवेशिनि०), वाक्यपदीय, शबरस्वामी. He was the son of भट्टकल्लट and the teacher of प्रतीहारेन्दुराज. भट्टकल्लट flourished in the reign of अवन्तिवर्मन् (855-883 A.D.) 'अनुग्रहाय लोकानां भट्टाः श्रीकल्लटादयः । अवन्तिवर्मणः काले सिद्धा भुवमवातरन् ॥' राजतर० V. 66.[1] He is frequently quoted in the काव्यप्रकाशसङ्केत of माणिक्यचन्द्र. It follows that the अभिधावृत्तिमातृका should be assigned to the period 900-925 A. D.

18 The काव्यकौतुक of भट्टतौत (or तोत). We know that भट्टतौत was the *guru* of अभिनवगुप्त (लोचन p. 34) and that he wrote a work called काव्यकौतुक on which अभिनवगुप्त wrote a विवरण (लोचन p. 221). In the introductory 4th verse of his commentary on the Nāṭyaśāstra अभिनवगुप्त states that Tota expounded to him the Nāṭyaveda (सद्विप्रतोतवदनोदितनाट्यवेद-तत्त्वार्थमर्थिजनवाञ्छितसिद्धिहेतोः । माहेश्वराभिनवगुप्तपदप्रतिष्ठः संक्षिप्तवृत्तिविधिना विशदीकरोति ॥). Again

---

1. The word 'siddha' indicates that Kallaṭa must have been a man of mature years before he could have attained mystic experience and yogic powers in the times of Avantivarman. He is connected with the Spanda branch of Kashmir Śaivism. It may be assumed that Kallaṭa was on old man about 890 A. D. Therefore his son Mukula may be held to have flourished in the last qnarter of the 9th century and the first two decades of the 10th. Vide p. 192 above on प्रतीहारेन्दुराज, the pupil of मुकुल. माणिक्यचन्द्र who wrote his commentary called सङ्केत on the काव्यप्रकाश in 1159-60 A. D. mentions Mukula and his अभिधा(वृत्ति)मातृका by name (pp. 32, 38 of Mysore ed.).

at the end of the 19th chap. of Nāṭyaśastra he states that the principles of the chapter on the *sandhis* were explained to him by Ṭota, the best of *dvijas*. Vide above p. 20 for the verse). One of his doctrines was that शान्तरस was at the head of all *rasas* as it led on to मोक्ष. 'मोक्षफलत्वेन चायं (शान्तो रसः) परमपुरुषार्थनिष्ठत्वात्सर्व-रसेभ्यः प्रधानतमः । स चायमस्मदुपाध्यायभट्टतौतेन काव्यकौतुके अस्माभिश्च तद्वि-वरणे बहुतरकृतनिर्णयः पूर्वपक्षसिद्धान्त इत्यलं बहुना' (लोचन p. 221 on कारिका III. 26). There is another doctrine which the लोचन (on p. 184) ascribes to Abhinava's Upādhyāya (i. e. तोत) 'प्रीत्यात्मा च रसस्तदेव नाट्यं नाट्य एव च वेद इत्यस्मदुपाध्यायः'. A few notices of the काव्यकौतुक of तोत may be stated here from the अभिनवभारती. On the words of भरत (नाट्य० VI. 36. G. O. S.) 'तस्मान्नाट्यरसाः स्मृताः' अभिनवगुप्त remarks: 'रससमुदायो हि नाट्यम् । न नाट्य एव च रसा काव्येपि नाट्यायमान एव रसः, काव्यार्थविषये हि प्रत्यक्षकल्पसंवेदनोदये रसोदय इत्युपा-ध्यायाः । तदाहुः काव्यकौतुके-प्रयोगत्वमनापन्ने काव्ये नास्वादसम्भवः । इति । वर्णनो-त्कलिकाभोगप्रौढोक्त्या सम्यगर्पिताः । उद्यानकान्ताचन्द्राद्या भावाः प्रत्यक्षवत्स्फुटाः ॥ इति ।' vol. I. pp. 291-92. This means that when the poet by his wonderful power of delineation makes the reader feel that the objects described are as if present before his eyes, then only *rasa* is realized by the reader of a poem. On p. 223 of vol. I (of नाट्य०) reference is made to the verse in the काव्यकौतुक enumerating *rasas* (यत्तूपाध्यायैः काव्यकौतुके रसोद्देशपरे श्लोके निरूपितं etc.). On vol. I p. 187 reference is made to Tota's explanation of भरत IV. 281 (G. O. S. ed.). On the verse of भरत (in VI. 51 p. 310 G. O. S.) a half verse in quoted to the effect that when *karuṇa* is not subordinate to *vipralambha* (the love of separated lovers), then it is possible to find it in all beings (तदुक्तमस्मदुपा-ध्यायभट्टतोतेन—स्वातन्त्र्येण प्रवृत्तौ तु सर्वप्राणिषु सम्भवः ।). On नाट्यधर्मी (भरत 13. 14, G. O. S.) a verse of his teacher is quoted: 'यथोक्तमुपा-ध्यायैः—यदत्रास्ति न तत्रास्य कवेर्वर्णनमर्हति । यत्रासम्भवि तत्र स्यात्सम्भव्यत्र तु धर्मतः ॥' vol. II. p. 216. This verse and one more verse are quoted by अभिनव on the 19th chap. (p. 71 of the GOS vol. III). On भरत chap. 15 last verse, अभिनव quotes a verse which requires even great poets not to forget the due order of the steps to be taken for making the play effective (स एव क्रम इत्युपाध्यायाः । यदाहुः । महाकवीनां पदवीमुपात्तामारुरुक्षताम् । नासंस्मृत्य पदस्पर्शं सम्पत्सोपान-पद्धतिः ॥ इत्यादि । vol. II. pp. 292). On p. 78 (of GOS ed. vol. III.) अभिनव remarks that *rasa* is a store of strikingness and charm that is entirely out of the common run and quotes six verses of Tota in support (about वाच्याभिनय), the last two of which are corrupt. On p. 153 chap. 22) a half verse of तोत is quoted न चालङ्कृतीनामत्र (?) लक्षणं महदाश्रयमिति (vol. III GOS). On नाट्यशास्त्र 31. 513-520 (Ch. ed.) a half verse is quoted to the effect that there is no restriction about employing a particular language in a poem or as to the characters in a play, but in the context the language meant is Saindhavī (i. e. the dialect of Sindhudeśa). 'यत्र भाषानियमो नोक्तस्तत्र प्राथम्यात्संस्कृतैव, यथेच्छमित्यन्ये, स्त्रीपुंभावाश्रयत्वात् प्राकृतभाषैवेत्यपरे, सैन्धव्येव प्रकरणादिति भट्टतोतः । यदाह काव्यकौतुके—न भाषानियमः पात्रे काव्ये स्यात्सैन्धवीमिति ।' (p. 503 of B. O. R. I. transcript). On p. 345 of B. O. R. I. transcript काव्यकौतुक view is referred to; on p. 355 of transcript (B. O. R. I.) 'तथा च भट्टतोतेनोक्तम्—कामावस्था न शृङ्गारः कश्चिदासां तदक्षता ।'. On p. 497 (B. O. R. I. transcript) there is a corrupt passage which is important : 'तथा च डोम्बिकासु स एवार्थः प्रधानभूत इति चूडामणौ स्पष्टमेवोक्तम् । चोरिश्रमि ... तथा च चिरन्तन्तेयं. . . (gap) दयप्रवादं पएडमचूडामणिश्रा इति । तदेतद्भट्टतोतेन काव्यकौतुके वितत्य दर्शितम् । (in chap. 31 verse 478 of Ch. ed.). The words पएडमचूडामणिश्रा remind one of similar words quoted on p. 197 above.

In numerous places Abhinava mentions the views of his teacher with the words उपाध्यायाः or गुरवः as in GOS vol. I pp. 3, 107, 207, 275, vol. II. pp. 67, 386, 395, 423, 440, 441 and vol. III. pp. 3, 10, 19, 47, 71 (उपाध्यायपादाः), 163. There is no doubt that Tota exercised a profound influence on Abhinava and through him on the theory of *rasa*. From the several quotations cited above it appears that the काव्यकौतुक was mostly in verse (if not entirely), dealt with the theory of Poetry in general and *rasa* in particular and that it also explained relevant passages of the Nāṭyaśāstra, though it cannot be said in the preseent state of our knowledge that it was a regular commentary thereon. On ch. 16. 4 (about 36 लक्षणs) अ. भा. remarks 'पठितोद्देशक्रमस्तु अस्मदुपाध्यायपरम्परागत :,' thereby making it clear that भट्टतोत was the representative of a school of the interpretation of the Nāṭyaśāstra.

It will be shown later on that Abhinavagupta's literary activity lies between 980-1020 A. D. So his teacher's activity may be placed between 950-980. Another doctrine that तोत held was that the poet, the hero (of a poem) and the (sympathetic) reader pass though the same experience 'नायकस्य कवेः श्रोतुः समानोनुभवस्ततः' (लोचन p. 34). The औचित्य० of क्षेमेन्द्र (on कारिका

35) attributes to him the well-known definition of प्रतिभा 'प्रज्ञा नवनवोन्मेषशालिनी प्रतिभा मता'. The काव्यकौतुक of तोत and its विवरण by अभिनव have not yet been discovered. They would be of great use in solving problems of identity and in tracing all the stages of the doctrines of Poetics in the several schools. हेमचन्द्र (काव्यानु. p. 316) quotes three verses from भट्टतोत 'नानृषिः कविरित्युक्तमृषिश्च किल दर्शनात् । विचित्रभावधर्मांशतत्त्वप्रख्या च दर्शनम् ॥ स तत्त्वदर्शनादेव शास्त्रेषु पठितः कविः । दर्शनाद्वर्णनाच्चाथ रूढा लोके कविश्रुतिः ॥ तथाहि दर्शने स्वच्छे नित्येप्यादिकवेर्मुनिः (नेः ?) । नोदिता कविता लोके यावज्जाता न वर्णना ॥'. सोमेश्वर (in his टीका on काव्यप्र. I folio 2 b) quotes these verses. The काव्यप्रकाशसङ्केत (of माणिक्य) ascribes the following to काव्यकौतुक 'प्रज्ञा...प्रतिभा मता । तदनुप्राणनाजीवद्वर्णनानिपुणः कविः । तस्य कर्म स्मृतं काव्यं' (p. 7 Mysore ed.). This is quoted by हेमचन्द्र (काव्यानु. p. 3) also without name; the व्यक्तिविवेकव्याख्या (p. 13) also says "अनेन कवेः काव्यमिति काव्यकौतुकविहितां काव्यस्य शब्दव्युत्पत्तिं कविमूलकाव्यत्वप्रतिपादिकां दर्शयति । तत्र ह्युक्तं 'तस्य कर्म स्मृतं काव्यम्' इति ॥." It may be noted that the कामधेनु on वामन's सूत्र ascribes these to भामह. हेमचन्द्र (विवेक p. 59) tells us that भट्टतौत was against the view of शङ्कुक 'अनुकरणरूपो रसः'. So also माणिक्यचन्द्र (p. 69), सोमेश्वर and अभिनवभारती vol. I. p. 37 say the same.

19 The **हृदयदर्पण** of **भट्टनायक**. भट्टनायक is one of the four writers whose interpretations of the *sūtra* of Bharata 'विभावानुभावव्यभिचारिसंयोगाद्रसनिष्पत्तिः' are quoted in the काव्यप्रकाश (IV. 90 Vā). His view of रस is: (1) न ताटस्थ्येन नात्मगतत्वेन रसः प्रतीयते नोत्पद्यते नाभिव्यज्यते अपि तु काव्ये नाट्ये चाभिधातो द्वितीयेन विभावादिसाधारणीकरणात्मना भावकत्वव्यापारेण भाव्यमानः स्थायी सत्त्वोद्रेकप्रकाशानन्दमयसंविद्विश्रान्तिसतत्त्वेन भोगेन भुज्यत इति भट्टनायकः । काव्यप्र. IV. p. 90 (Vā). Vide लोचन pp. 82-83 for a more detailed statemant of the views of भट्टनायक about रस. According to him, there are three functions of the words of a poem or drama, अभिधा, भावना, भोगीकृति (or रसचर्वणा or भोग).[1] The first is common to शास्त्र also. By the second function (भावना), the विभाव s (like सीता &c.) are presented to the reader or spectator stripped of their individual existence and only in a general or impersonal way (as chaste and charming womanhood &c.). The third function leads to the ultimate

1. लोचन p. 82 summareses his views as follows: प्रतीयते नोत्पद्यते नाभिव्यज्यते काव्येन रसः । किं त्वन्यशब्दवैलक्षण्यं काव्यात्मनः शब्दस्य त्र्यंशताप्रसादात् । तत्राभिधायकत्वं वाच्यविषयम्, भावकत्वं रसादिविषयम्', भोक्तृत्वं सहृदयविषयमिति त्रयोंऽशभूता व्यापाराः ।

experience of the reader or spectator (which, like ब्रह्मानन्द, is स्वसंवेद्य and not capable of being defined in words); that experience for the moment makes the सहृदय reader or spectator forget all else and makes him one with the subject presented. अभिनवभारती vol. I p. 279, हेमचन्द्र (विवेक p. 61) and जयरथ (अलं. स. वि. p. 11) quote the following verses on this point : (2) 'अभिधा भावना चान्या तद्भोगीकृतिरेव च। अभिधाधामतां याते शब्दार्थालङ्कृती ततः॥ भावनाभाव्य एषोपि शृङ्गारादिगणो मतः। तद्भोगीकृतिरूपेण व्याप्यते सिद्धिमान्नरः॥'. जयरथ adds one half verse (दृश्यमानाथवा मोक्षे यात्यक्तत्वमियं स्फुटम्). That he was the author of the हृदयदर्पण follows from several circumstances. The लोचन quotes certain verses of भट्टनायक in which he distinguishss between शास्त्र and आख्यान on the one hand and काव्य on the other : (3) 'शब्दप्राधान्यमाश्रित्य तत्र शास्त्रं पृथग्विदुः। अर्थतत्त्वेन युक्तं तु वदन्त्याख्यानमेतयोः। द्वयोर्गुणत्वे व्यापारप्राधान्ये काव्यगीर्भवेत्॥' (p. 32) and अ. भा. vol. II. p. 298. These verses are quoted from the हृदयदर्पण by हेमचन्द्र (काव्यानु. pp. 3-4). माणिक्यचन्द्र on का. प्र. (संकेत p. 6) quotes these verses. The अलङ्कारसर्वस्व (pp. 10-11) summarizes the views of भट्टनायक 'भट्टनायकेन तु व्यङ्ग्यव्यापारस्य प्रौढोक्त्याभ्युपगतस्य काव्यांशत्वं ब्रुवता न्यग्भावितशब्दार्थस्वरूपस्य व्यापारस्यैव प्राधान्यमुक्तम्। तत्राप्यभिधाभावकत्वलक्षणव्यापारद्वयोत्तीर्णो रसचर्वणात्मा भोगापरपर्यायो व्यापारः प्राधान्येन विश्रान्तिस्थानतयाङ्गीकृतः'. With reference to this view, जयरथ speaks of भट्टनायक as हृदयदर्पणकार (p. 15). महिमभट्ट says that he composed the व्यक्तिविवेक to secure fame (of demolishing the ध्वन्यालोक) without looking at the दर्पण (the हृदयदर्पण) 'सहसा यशोभिसर्तुं समुद्यतादृष्टदर्पणा मम धीः। स्वालङ्कारविकल्पप्रकल्पने वेत्ति कथमिवावद्यम्॥' (p. 1, अभिसर्तुं means also to approach as an अभिसारिका' and दर्पण also means 'mirror'). The commentary on this explains 'दर्पणो हृदयदर्पणाख्यो ध्वनिध्वंसग्रंथोपि'. The com. on व्यक्तिविवेक (p. 13) quotes a half verse from the हृदयदर्पण-तत्कर्ता च कविः प्रोक्तो भेदेपि हि तदस्ति यत्।' इति काव्यमूलं कवित्वं प्रतिपादितम्. It follows that भट्टनायक wrote the हृदयदर्पण for demolishing the theory of ध्वनि. The लोचन (p. 23) refers to the adverse criticism of भट्टनायक on the illustration भम धम्मिअ (ध्व. p. 19). and then twits him by saying 'किं च वस्तुध्वनिं दूषयता रसध्वनिस्तदनुग्राहकः समर्थ्यत इति सुष्ठुतरां ध्वनिध्वंसोयम्' (लोचन p. 23). The principal point on which he differs from the ध्वन्यालोक is that he regards ध्वनि as transcending definition and as purely स्वसंवेद्य. So he was a follower of those of whom the ध्वनिकारिका says 'केचिद्वाचां स्थितमविषये तत्त्वमूचुस्तदीयम्' or as the ध्व० says 'केचित्पुनर्लक्षणकरणशालीनबुद्धयो ध्वनेस्तत्त्वं गिरामगोचरं सहृदयहृदयसंवेद्यमेव समाख्यातवन्तः' (p. 12). According to him रसचर्वणा (or भोगकृत्व) is the soul of poetry and he is not prepared to admit ध्वनि in general as the soul of poetry. 'ध्वनिर्नामापरो योपि व्यापारो व्यञ्जनात्मकः । तस्य सिद्धेपि भेदे स्यात्काव्यांशत्वं न रूपिता ॥' (लोचन pp. 14 and 19; जयरथ p. 10). The लोचन refers to the views of भट्टनायक and हृदयदर्पण very frequently and generally for condemnation. Besides the references given above *vide* लोचन p. 14 ('काव्ये रसयिता सर्वो न बोद्धा न नियोगभाक्'), pp. 24-25 (on the verse 'अत्ता एत्थ' in ध्व. p. 24), p. 32 (एतदेवोक्तं हृदयदर्पणे 'यावत्पूर्णो न त्वेतेन तावन्नैवैवम् इति), 32 (आत्मसद्भावेपि कश्चिदेव जीवव्यवहार इत्युक्तं प्रागेव। तेनैतन्निरवकाशं यदुक्तं हृदयदर्पणे-सर्वत्र तर्हि काव्यव्यवहारः स्यात् इति), 34 (यदाह भट्टनायकः-वाग्धेनुर्दुग्ध एकं हि रसं यद्बालतृष्णया । तेन नास्य समः स स्याद्दुह्यते योगिभिर्हि यः), 39 (तेन यद्भट्टनायकेन द्विवचनं दूषितं तद्गजनिमीलिकयैव); the reference here is to the form व्यङ्क्तः in ध्वनिकारिका I. 13 and this passage of the लोचन has been criticized in the व्यक्तिविवेक (p. 19); 77 (भट्टनायकेन तु यदुक्तं-इवशब्दयोगाद्गौणताप्यत्र न काचित्-तच्छ्लोकार्थमपरामृश्यon निश्वासान्ध इवादर्शः); this is with reference to the verse निश्वासान्ध इवादर्शः (from रामायण); p. 76 यत्तु हृदयदर्पणे उक्तम्—हहा हेति संरम्भार्थोयं चमत्कार इति (on the verse स्निग्धश्यामल० in ध्व. p. 74-75). From these quotations it will be clear that the हृदयदर्पण was a work in verse and prose composed for establishing a theory of Poetics and for controverting the position of the ध्वन्यालोक. माणिक्यचन्द्र gives two verses characterising लोल्लट, शङ्कुक and नायक quoted above on pp. 50-51 but the सङ्केत p. 147 (in Ānan. ed.) has some different readings. Whether the work was originally called सहृदयदर्पण, vide above pp. 196-7.

In the edition of 1923 I could not make use of the अभिनवभारती, no part of which had then been published. On pp. 4-5 of the अभिनवभारती vol. I. is set out the view of भट्टनायक on the first verse of the नाट्यशास्त्र 'नाट्यशास्त्रं प्रवक्ष्यामि ब्रह्मणा यदुदाहृतम्' which comes to this that this world of name and from (नामरूप) is a means of helping one on the road of the highest goal of man (viz. मोक्ष) and that this verse suggests the idea of Śāntarasa and then quotes the following verse from the सहृदयदर्पण of भट्टनायक viz. नमस्त्रैलोक्यनिर्माणकवये शम्भवे यतः । प्रतिक्षणं जगन्नाट्यप्रयोगरसिको जनः ॥. This appears to have been the first verse of the सहृदयदर्पण (or हृदयदर्पण). The late Prof. V. V. Sovani thought that the work of भट्टनायक was a commentary on the Nāṭyāśāstra (vide Dr. Bhandarkar Commemoration volume p. 390). But this does not seem to be right. The quotations cited above from भट्टनायक establish that the latter was concerned to show that ध्वनि means *rasa* only, that the Dhvanikāra is wrong in postulating वस्तुध्वनि and अलङ्कारध्वनि, that the principle of *rasa* apprehension cannot be explained in words and that the explanation of such verses as भम धम्मिअ and अत्ता एत्थ given by the ध्वन्यालोक (p. 19 and p. 24) are not correct. Thus the हृदयदर्पण dealt with रस and in explaining it had naturally to deal with Bharata's sūtra 'विभावानुभाव॰'. The अभिनवभारती very rarely puts forward the interpretations of नायक on the verses of Bharata as it does in the case of उद्भट or लोल्लट or शङ्कुक (vide pp. 48-52 above). On the chapter on सिद्धिलक्षण (27th at p. 305 of अ. भा. in G. O. S. vol. III) अभिनव quotes the following from भट्टनायक 'प्रधाने सिद्धिभागेस्य प्रयोगाङ्गत्वमागताः। गेयादयस्तथैवैते त्रैधैनं (?) त्युपयोगिनः। सोपानपदपङ्क्त्या च सा च मोक्षस्पृगात्मिका।'. Then on page 309 again नायक is quoted and ridiculed as a prosaic follower of जैमिनि 'यत्तु भट्टनायकेनोक्तं सिद्धेरपि नटादेरङ्गत्वं अजन्यास्तत्पक्षेयमिति तेन नाट्याङ्गता समर्थिता फलं च पुरुषार्थत्वादिति केवलं जैमिनिरनुसृत इत्यलमनेन।'. For 'फलं च पुरुषार्थत्वात्', vide पूर्वमीमांसासूत्र III. 1. 5. In the लोचन also (pp. 76-77) in rejecting the view of भट्टनायक on the verse निःश्वासान्ध इवादर्शश्चन्द्रमा न प्रकाशते his interpretation is ridiculed as follows: न च...कल्पना युक्ता। जैमिनिसूत्रे ह्येवं योज्यते न काव्येपीत्यलम्. It appears from these references that भट्टनायक was a मीमांसक or at least relied on मीमांसा rules in his work. भट्टनायक's approach to the theory of रसचर्वणा or भोग reminds one of the सांख्य doctrine that पुरुष is only भोक्ता and not कर्ता (i. e. is quite passive and not active). The mention of सत्त्वोद्रेक in the passage about मम्मट's resume of भट्टनायक's theory also tends to show that he leant on the सांख्य doctrine of the three *guṇas* of सत्त्व, रजस् and तमस्. I am of the opinion that भट्टनायक was not a regular commentator of the नाट्यशास्त्र as उद्भट and शङ्कुक were. His main differences from the ध्वन्यालोक have been pointed out above. Bhaṭṭa-Nāyaka held that kāvya is different from शास्त्र and आख्यान in this that काव्य depended solely on कविव्यापार, that काव्य gives आनन्द to all, while शास्त्र gives injunctions and आख्यान (इतिहासपुराण) gives information.

भट्टनायक flourished after the ध्वन्यालोक and before the लोचन i. e. between 900 and 1000 A. D. From the somewhat bitter and personal attacks that the लोचन makes it appears likely that he was nearer to the times of the लोचन than to those of the ध्वन्यालोक. If he was a contemporary of अभिनवगुप्त or only slightly older, then भट्टनायक, the author of the हृदयदर्पण, cannot be identified with the भट्टनायक mentioned in the राजतरङ्गिणी 'द्विजस्तयोर्नायकाख्यो गौरीशश्वशुरसद्मनोः। चातुर्विद्यः कृतस्तेन वाग्देवीकुलमन्दिरम् ॥' (V. 59). This refers to the time of शङ्करवर्मन् (883-902 A. D.). It is difficult to decide positively one way or other, but I am inclined to hold that the two are not identical and that भट्टनायक flourished between 935-985. Vide J. O. R., Madras vol. I. pp. 267-276 for 'Fragments of Bhaṭṭanāyaka' collected by Mr. T. R. Chintamani and Journal of Bombay Un. vol. 17 part 2 pp. 267-276 for भट्टनायक's criticism of ध्वन्यालोक and for Bhaṭṭa-Nāyaka's theory of Rasa. The verse कौटानुविद्ध० quoted in the साहित्यदर्पण I is ascribed to the हृदयदर्पण by प्रभाकर in his रसप्रदीप (p. 3 Tri. ed.). The work of भट्टनायक would be of great value for the theories of kāvya, rasa and dhvani and as it was available to प्रभाकर towards the end of the 16th century, it is quite possible that, if a vigorous search were made, a ms. of his work may yet be discovered.

20 The वक्रोक्तिजीवित of कुन्तक. This work had been known for many years only through quotations and references in other Alaṅkara works, such as the अलं. स०, साहित्यदर्पण. Through the kindness of Dr. Belvalkar I was able to secure a transcript of a ms. of the work recently discovered in Madras. That transcript was used in my edition of 1923. Dr. De published the first two उन्मेष in 1923, which are used in this edition. Subsequently in 1928 he brought out another edition but I could not get a copy of it. The ms. made use of here is No. 114 of 1919-24 at the B. O. R. I. described in Cat. vol. XII No. 256 pp. 300–2.

The work consists of three parts, कारिकाs, वृत्ति, and examples, almost all of which are taken from previous authors. It is divided into four उन्मेषs. The transcript breaks off in the fourth, but it seems that the work did not extend much beyond where the transcript breaks off. That कुन्तक is the author of the whole of the work and that the entire work containing कारिकाs, वृत्ति and examples was called वक्रोक्तिजीवित follows from several considerations. It appears that कुन्तक meant the Kārikās alone to be called काव्यालङ्कार as the Kārika[1] of the first उन्मेष states : लोकोत्तरचमत्कारकारिवैचित्र्यसिद्धये । काव्यस्यायमलङ्कारः

1. An excellent edition of the four Unmeṣas of the Vakroktijīvita, with a modern Hindi commentary by Ācarya Viśveśvara and exhaustive Introduction in Hindi has been

कोप्यपूर्वो विधीयते ॥. The वृत्ति on this says ननु च सन्ति चिरन्तनास्तदलंकारास्तत्किमर्थमित्याह—अपूर्वः तद्व्यतिरिक्तार्थाभिधायी ।···कोपि अलौकिकः सातिशयः । लोको···सिद्धये-असामान्याह्लादविधायिविचित्रभावसम्पत्तये । यद्यपि सन्ति शतशः काव्यालङ्कारास्तथापि न कुतश्चिदप्येवंविधवैचित्र्यसिद्धिः ।. It may be noticed that the works of भामह, उद्भट and रुद्रट were called काव्यालङ्कारs. Though the कारिकाs thus appear to have been meant to be called काव्यालङ्कार, the whole work has been referred to by later writers as वक्रोक्तिजीवित. The वृत्ति is quite clear on this point : तदयमर्थः । ग्रन्थस्यास्य अलङ्कार इत्यभिधानम्, उपमादिप्रमेयजातमभिधेयम्, उक्तरूपवैचित्र्यसिद्धिः प्रयोजनमिति ।'. The व्यक्तिविवेक (p. 28) quotes the words 'शब्दार्थौ सहितौ. . .कारिणि (which is वक्रोक्तिजीवित I. 8 p. 7), says that certain people who regard themselves as सहृदय assert that वक्रोक्ति is the soul of poetry and then (on p. 37) quotes the verse संरम्भः करिकीट० (which is quoted in the वक्रोक्तिजीवित I. p. 17 as an example of an excellent काव्य) and finds several faults in that verse and winds up by saying (p. 58) 'काव्यकाञ्चनकषाश्ममानिना कुन्तकेन निजकाव्यलक्ष्मणि । यस्य सर्वनिरवद्यतोदिता श्लोक एष स निदर्शितो मया ॥'. This shows that the *definition* (लक्ष्म) and the citation of examples are कुन्तक's according to महिमभट्ट (who was not far removed in time from the वक्रोक्ति०). The टीका on the व्यक्ति० (p. 16) says 'अयं श्लोको वक्रोक्तिजीविते वितत्य व्याख्यात इति तत एवावधार्यः'. So according to the टीका also, the वृत्ति and the examples formed part of the वक्रोक्तिजीवित. The एकावली (p. 51) says 'एतेन यत्र कुन्तकेन भक्तावन्तर्भावितो ध्वनिस्तदपि प्रत्याख्यातम्'. सोमेश्वर in his commentary on the काव्यप्र० (61 b and 67a) quotes two verses of कुत्तक (?कुन्तक) the first of which is found in the printed वक्रोक्ति० (कारिका I. 31. p. 48) and the 2nd is quoted below.[1] The काव्यप्रकाशसङ्केत of माणिक्य० says on the verse 'तरन्तीवाङ्गानि स्खलदमललावण्यजलधौ' इत्यत्र सादृश्योपचारमूले यथा चोपचारस्तथा वक्रोक्तिजीवितग्रंथाज्ज्ञेयः' (p. 40-41). This verse is cited as an example of उपचारवक्रता in the वक्रोक्ति० (II. p. 99) with the remark 'अत्र चेतनपदार्थसम्भविसादृश्योपचारात् तारुण्यतरलतद्गात्रायां तरणमुत्प्रेक्षितम् ।'. The colophons at the end of the first and second उन्मेष are respectively 'इति राजानककुन्तल (क ?) विरचिते वक्रोक्तिजीविते काव्यालङ्कारे प्रथमोन्मेषः' and 'इति श्रीकुन्तलविरचिते वक्रोक्तिजीविते

published recently by Dr. Nagendra of the Delhi University. There are, however, many misprints and it is not clear on what mss. or editions the text is based.

1. सोमेश्वर (folio 67a) सुकुमारेति यत्कुन्तकः 'सन्ति तत्र त्रयो मार्गाः कविप्रस्थानहेतवः । सुकुमारो विचित्रश्च मध्यमश्चोभयात्मकः ॥'.

द्वितीय उन्मेषः'. As the work is not generally studied, a somewhat detailed analysis is given below.

The first उन्मेष begins 'वन्दे कवीन्द्रवक्त्रेन्दुलास्यमन्दिरनर्तकीम् । देवीं सूक्तिपरिस्पन्दसुन्दराभिनयोज्ज्वलाम् ॥ वाचो विषयनैयत्यमुत्पादयितुमुच्यते । आदिवाक्ये-भिधानादि निर्मितेर्मानसूत्रवत् ॥ लोकोत्तरचमत्कारकारिवैचित्र्यसिद्धये । काव्यस्या-यमलङ्कारः कोऽप्यपूर्वो विधीयते ॥ धर्मादिसाधनोपायः सुकुमारक्रमोदितः । काव्य-बन्धोभिजातानां हृदयाह्लादकारकः ॥ (after two more verses) the वृत्ति goes on कटुकौषधवच्छास्त्रमविद्याव्याधिनाशनम् । आह्लाद्यमृतवत्काव्यमविवेकगदापहम् ॥ आयत्यां च तदात्वे च रसनिष्यन्दसुन्दरम् । येन सम्पद्यते काव्यं तदिदानीं विचार्यते ॥ (I. 7) अलङ्कृतिरलङ्कारमुपोद्धृत्य (र उपो?) विवेच्यते । तदुपायतया तत्त्वं सालङ्कारस्य काव्यता ॥'. It will be noticed that he gives the प्रयोजन of काव्य like भामह I. 2 (धर्मार्थ...काव्यनिबन्धनम्) and calls his work काव्या-लङ्कार. The वृत्ति begins 'जगत्त्रितयवैचित्र्यचित्रकर्मविधायिनम् । शिवं शक्तिपरि-स्पन्दमात्रोपकरणं नुमः ॥...साहित्यार्थसुधासिन्धोः सारमुन्मीलयाम्यहम् ॥ येन द्वितयमप्येतत्तत्त्वनिर्मितिलक्षणम् । तद्विदामद्भुतामोदं चमत्कारं विधास्यति ॥'. Following भामह (I. 16 शब्दार्थौ सहितौ काव्यं) he defines काव्य as शब्दार्थौ सहितौ वक्रकविव्यापारशालिनि । बन्धे व्यवस्थितौ काव्यं तद्विदाह्लादकारिणि ॥' (quoted in व्यक्ति० p. 28 and by समुद्रबन्ध p. 8) i. e. words and senses that contain a certain striking turn of ideas due to the poet's imagination and fancy constitute काव्य. His position is that सालङ्कृत *śabda* and *artha* constitute काव्य and it is not proper to say that अलङ्कारs belong to काव्य (as this mode of speech suggests that काव्य may exist without them). In order to attain the position of काव्य, the composition must be 'वक्रताविचित्रगुणालङ्कार-संपदां परस्परस्पर्धाधिरोहः' (p. 10). He gives as an example of काव्य the verse (on p. 10) ततोरुणपरिस्पन्दमन्दीकृतवपुः शशी । दध्रे कामपरिक्षाम-कामिनीगण्डपाण्डुताम् ॥ (quoted in the काव्यप्र. IX). Then he comes to the part वक्रोक्ति plays (कारिकाs I. 10-11) 'शब्दो विवक्षिता-र्थैकवाचकोन्येषु सत्स्वपि । अर्थः सहृदयाह्लादकारी स्वस्पन्दसुन्दरः ॥ उभावेतावलङ्कार्यौ तयोः पुनरलङ्कृतिः । वक्रोक्तिरेव वैदग्ध्यभङ्गीभणितिरुच्यते ॥'(last quoted by जयरथ p. 9). वक्रोक्ति is a striking mode of speech differing from and transcending the ordinary everyday mode of speaking about a thing (and hence called वक्रोक्ति); it is speech that charms by the skill of the poet. The वृत्ति explains 'वक्रोक्तिः प्रसिद्धाभिधानव्य-तिरेकिणी विचित्रैवाभिधा वैदग्ध्यं कविकर्मकौशलं तस्य भङ्गी विच्छित्तिः तया भणितिः (p. 21). He cites तामभ्यगच्छत् (रघु. 14. 70) and सद्यः पुरीपरिसरे (in बालरा. 6. 34.) respectively as examples of poetry that is सहृदया-ह्लादकारि and not so (and points out how the latter verse will become charming by a change of words). He ridicules those who regard स्वभावोक्ति as an अलङ्कार and says that when in a so-called स्वभावोक्ति other figures occur, there will always be सङ्कर or संसृष्टि; अलङ्कारकृतां येषां स्वभावोक्तिरलङ्कृतिः अलङ्कार्यतया तेषां किमन्यदवतिष्ठते ॥ ...स्पष्टे सर्वत्र संसृष्टिरस्पष्टे सङ्करस्ततः' (कारिकाs I. 12 and 16). The साहित्य of शब्द and अर्थ is explained in the वृत्ति as 'तत्र वाचकस्य वाच्यान्तरेण साहित्यमभिप्रेतम्' and negatives the साहित्य of वाचक with वाच्यान्तर and of वाच्य with वाचकान्तर. 'शब्दार्थौ सहितावेव प्रतीतौ स्फुरतः सदा ।...साहित्यमनयोः शोभाशालितां प्रति काप्यसौ । अन्यूनानतिरिक्तत्वमनोहारिण्यवस्थितिः ॥ (कारिका I. 17 and 18). Then the वृत्ति proceeds p. 26) मार्गानुगुण्यसुभगो माधुर्यादिगुणोदयः । अलङ्करणविन्यासो वक्रतातिशयान्वितः ॥ वृत्त्यौचित्यमनोहारि रसानां परिपोषणम् । स्पर्धया विद्यते यत्र यथास्वमुभयोरपि ॥ सा काप्यवस्थितिस्तद्विदाह्लादैकनिबन्धनम् । पदादिवाक्परिस्पन्दसारः साहित्यमुच्यते ॥' (these are quoted in साहित्यमीमांसा p. 14 Tri. ed.). वक्रता is explained as 'वक्रत्वं प्रसिद्धप्रस्थानव्यतिरेकि वैचित्र्यम्' (p. 27 on कारिका I. 19). Then he enumerates six varieties of कविव्यापारवक्रत्व°, viz. वर्णविन्यासवक्रत्व, पदपूर्वार्धव°, प्रत्ययव°, वाक्यव°, प्रकरणव°, प्रबन्धव° वर्णविन्यासवक्रत्वं, पदपूर्वार्धवक्रता । वक्रतायाः परोऽप्यस्ति प्रकारः प्रत्ययाश्रयः ॥ वाक्यस्य वक्रभावोऽन्यो भिद्यते यः सहस्रधा । यत्रालङ्कारवर्गोऽसौ सर्वोऽप्यन्तर्भविष्यति (this verse is quoted by समुद्रबन्ध p. 9) ॥ वक्रभावः प्रकरणे प्रबन्धेऽप्यस्ति यादृशः । उच्यते सहजाहार्यसौकुमार्यमनोहारः ॥' (कारिका I. 20-22). पदपूर्वार्ध means पदस्य सुबन्तस्य तिङन्तस्य वा पूर्वार्धं प्रातिपदिकं धातुर्वा (p. 28). He briefly mentions the varieties of these and cites examples. His position is that वक्रोक्ति is the soul of poetry[1] (i. e. it is वक्रोक्ति that breathes life into poetry, makes it poetry, without it काव्य cannot exist), but वक्रोक्ति itself is not possible unless the poet possesses the necessary fancy and imagination (therefore कविव्यापार is प्रधान in काव्य). Vide p. 55 also. About वैचित्र्य he says 'विचित्रो यत्र वक्रोक्तिवैचित्र्यं जीवितायते । परिस्फुरति यस्यान्तः सा काप्यतिशयाभिधा ॥' (कारिका I. 27 p. 45), the first half being quoted by जयरथ (p. 8). He then speaks of certain गुणs of वैचित्र्य viz. माधुर्य, प्रसाद (rare use of compounds and well-connected sentences), लावण्य, आभिजात्य. लावण्य and आभिजात्य are defined as 'अत्रालुप्तविसर्गान्तैः पदैः प्रोतैः परस्परम् । ह्रस्वैः संयोगपूर्वैश्च लावण्यमतिरिच्यते (quoted by सोमेश्वर, folio 11b) ॥ यन्नातिकोमलच्छायं नातिकाठिन्यमुद्वहत् । आभिजात्यं मनोहारि तदत्र प्रौढिनिर्मितम् ॥' (कारिकाs I. 31-32 pp. 48-49). Examples of all

1. This follows from what is stated in the वृत्ति (p. 27) 'शरीरं जीवितेनेव स्फुरितेनेव जीवितम् । विना निर्जीवतां येन वाक्यं याति विपश्चिताम् ॥ यस्मात्किमपि सौभाग्यं तद्विदामेव गोचरम् । सरस्वती समभ्येति तदिदानीं विचार्यते ॥'. This कविव्यापारवक्रत्व is जीवित.

these are cited. किं तारुण्यतरोः (साहित्यद० X example of सन्देह) illustrates माधुर्य as causing वैचित्र्य. An example of लावण्य is 'श्वासोत्कम्पतरङ्गिणि स्तनतटे धौताञ्जनश्यामलाः कीर्यन्ते कणशः कृशाङ्गि किममी बाष्पाम्भसां बिन्दवः। किं चाकुञ्चितकण्ठरोधकुटिलाः कर्णामृतस्यन्दिनो हुङ्काराः कलपञ्चमप्रणयिनस्त्रुट्यन्ति निर्यान्ति च ॥' (p. 48). He speaks of three मार्गs, वैचित्र्यमार्ग, सुकुमारमार्ग and सौकुमार्यवैचित्र्यसंवलितमार्ग. The last is called मध्यममार्ग; 'मार्गोऽसौ मध्यमो नाम नानारुचिमनोहरः। स्पर्धया यत्र वर्तन्ते मार्गद्वितयसम्पदः॥' (कारिका I. 35 p. 50). The edition of Dr. Nagendra contains a few additional kārikās, vṛtti and examples about माधुर्य, प्रसाद and other guṇas which are not noticed here. And it also contains in the first उन्मेष kārikās on *aucitya* and *saubhāgya*.

The 2nd उन्मेष starts with the explanation and elucidation of वर्णविन्यासवक्रत्व. He defines it as 'एको द्वौ बहवो वर्णा बध्यमानाः पुनः पुनः। स्वल्पान्तरास्त्रिधा सोक्ता वर्णविन्यासवक्रता ॥ वर्गान्तयोगिनः स्पर्शा द्विरुक्तास्तलनादयः। रेफादिभिश्च संयुक्ताः प्रस्तुतौचित्यशोभिनः॥' (II. 1-2 pp. 60-61). It will be noticed that वर्णविन्यासवक्रता is practically the same as the अनुप्रास of the ancient आलङ्कारिकs. An example (of एकस्य द्वयोर्बहूनां च) is भग्नैलावल्लरीकास्तरलितकदलीस्तम्बताम्बूलजम्बूजम्बीरास्तालतालीतरलतरलतालासिका यस्य जहुः। वेल्लत्कल्लोलहेला विसकलनजडाः कूलकुञ्जेषु सिन्धोः सेनासीमन्तिनीनामनवरतरताभ्यासतन्द्रीं समीराः ॥'. The verse प्रथममरुणच्छायस्तावत्ततः कनकप्रभः (cited in the काव्यप्र. VI. p. 260 Vā.) is an example of वर्णविन्यासव०. He does not like, however, that too many *alaṅkāras* should be heaped up in one verse 'अलङ्कारस्य कवयो यत्रालङ्करणान्तरम्। असन्तुष्टा निबध्नन्ति हारादेर्मणिबन्धवत्॥ नातिनिर्बन्धविहिता नाप्यपेशलभूषिता। पूर्वावृत्तपरित्यागनूतनावर्तनोज्ज्वला ॥' (first verse is quoted in व्यक्तिविवेकटीका pp. 43-44 and it is stated that वक्रोक्तिजीवित finds fault with it). He says that the उपनागरिका and other वृत्तिs of the ancients (*vide* उद्भट I) are the same as वर्णविन्यासवक्रता 'वर्णच्छायानुसारेण गुणमार्गानुवर्तिनी। वृत्तिवैचित्र्ययुक्तेति सैव प्रोक्ता चिरन्तनैः' ॥ (II. 5 p. 66). यमक also is a kind of वर्णविन्यासव० 'यमकं नाम कोऽप्यस्याः प्रकारः परिदृश्यते। स तु शोभान्तराभावादिह नातिप्रतन्यते ॥' (II. 7 p. 67). Then he comes to the several varieties of पदपूर्वार्धवक्रता, viz. रूढिवैचित्र्यवक्रता (रूढि means रूढिप्रधानाः शब्दाः) 'यत्र रूढेरसम्भाव्यधर्माध्यारोपगर्भता। सद्धर्मातिशयारोपगर्भत्वं वा प्रतीयते ॥ लोकोत्तरतिरस्कारश्लाघ्योत्कर्षाभिधित्सया। वाच्यस्य सोच्यते कापि रूढिवैचित्र्यवक्रता ॥' (कारिका II. 8-9 p. 68). There are two varieties of रूढिवै०, as the first verse shows. Examples (of the first variety) are the word कमलानि in ताला जायन्ति quoted above (from ध्व० p. 76) and the word रामः in स्निग्ध० (ध्व० 75). Example of the 2nd variety of रूढिवै० (विद्यमानधर्मा-

तिशयवाच्याध्यारोपगर्भत्व) are : ततः प्रहस्याह पुनः पुरन्दरं (रघु. III. 51, the word रघुं) and रामोसौ भुवनेषु (quoted in the काव्यप्र. IV p. 182). Another variety of पदपूर्वार्धं॰ is पर्यायवक्रता (पर्यायप्रधानः शब्दः पर्यायः) 'अभिधेयान्तरतमस्तस्यातिशयपोषकः । रम्यच्छायान्तरस्पर्शात्तदलङ्कर्तुमीश्वरः ॥ स्वयं विशेषणेनापि स्वच्छायोत्कर्षपेशलः । पर्यायस्तेन वैचित्र्यं ॥' (II. 11-12 p. 72). An example is नाभियोक्तुमनृतत्वमिष्यसे कस्तपस्विविशिखेषु चादरः । सन्ति भूभृति हि नः शराः परे ये पराक्रमवसूनि वज्रिणः ॥ (here the word इन्द्रस्य for वज्रिणः would not convey the same force and charm). Another and a very important variety of पदपूर्वार्धं॰ is उपचारवक्रता 'यत्र दूरान्तरेऽन्यस्मात् सामान्यमुपचर्यते । लेशेनापि भवत्कांचिद् वक्तुमुद्रिक्तवृत्तिताम् ॥ यन्मूला सरसोल्लेखा रूपकादिरलङ्कृतिः । उपचारप्रधानासौ वक्रता काचिदुच्यते ॥' (कारिका II. 13-14 p. 80, both quoted by जयरथ p. 10). Examples of उपचारवक्रता are स्निग्धश्यामल॰, गच्छन्तीनां रमणवसतिं (पूर्वमेघ 38) and 'गअणं च मत्तमेहं' (the first and last being cited in the ध्व. as examples of अर्थान्तरसंक्रमितवाच्य and अत्यन्ततिरस्कृतवाच्य respectively). It is therefore that the अलं. स. (p. 10) in summarising the view of the वक्रोक्तिजीवितकार says 'उपचारवक्रतादिभिः समस्तो ध्वनिप्रपञ्चः स्वीकृतः' and जयरथ after saying that the verse गअणं च मत्तमेहं is cited as an example by the वक्रोक्तिजीवितकार remarks 'अत्र मदनिरहङ्कारत्वे औपचारिके इति उपचारवक्रतादीनामपि ग्रहणम्'. As remarked by Jayaratha the वक्रोक्तिजीवितकार was to be included among those who regarded ध्वनि as भाक्त. भाक्त (in ध्व॰) is derived from भक्ति which is the same as लक्षणा or गुणवृत्ति and is used by आनन्दवर्धन in the sense of 'something associated with भक्ति or लक्षणा'. The words of जयरथ (p. 9) on अलं. स. are 'इदानीं यदप्यन्यैरस्यभक्त्यन्तर्भूतत्वमुक्तं तदपि दर्शयितुमाह-वक्रोक्तिजीवितकारः पुनर्वैदग्ध्यभङ्गीभणितिस्वभावां बहुविधां वक्रोक्तिमेव & c.; vide Dr. Haradatta Sharma on the meaning of उपचार in Poona Orientalist vol. I. p. 26 ff. and the author's notes to साहित्यदर्पण pp. 59-60. Two other varieties are विशेषणवक्रता and संवृतिवक्रता 'विशेषणस्य माहात्म्यात् क्रियायाः कारकस्य वा । यत्रोल्लसति लावण्यं सा विशेषणवक्रता ॥ यत्र संव्रियते वस्तु वैचित्र्यस्य विवक्षया । सर्वनामादिभिः कैश्चित्सोक्ता संवृतिवक्रता ॥' (II. 15-16 p. 83 and p. 85). Examples of the two are (respectively) शुचिशीतलचन्द्रिकाप्लुताश्चिरनिःशब्दमनोहरा दिशः । प्रशमस्य मनोभवस्य वा हृदि तस्याप्यथ हेतुतां ययुः ॥ and निवार्यतामालि किमप्ययं बटुः (कुमार॰ V. 83). He remarks अत्र...भगवदपभाषणं च न कीर्तनीयतामर्हतीति संवरणेन रमणीयतां नीतम् ।. Then he speaks of various other varieties of पदपूर्वार्धव॰ such as वृत्तिवैचित्र्यवक्रता (वृत्ति is fivefold कृत्, तद्धित, समास, एकशेष, सन्नन्त), भाववैचित्र्यव॰, लिङ्गवैचित्र्यव॰, कर्त्रन्तरविचित्रता, क्रियावैचित्र्यव॰, कालवै॰, कारकवै॰, संख्या॰, पुरुष॰, उपग्रह॰. An example of लिङ्ग॰ is 'त्वं रक्षसा भीरु यतोपनीता तं मार्गमेताः कृपया लता मे' &c.' (रघु. 13. 24 where लताः

for वृत्ताः is very charming); of संख्यावक्रता is 'वयं तत्त्वान्वेषान्मधुकर &c. शाकुन्तल I; उपग्रह[1] is explained as 'धातूनां लक्षणानुसारेण नियतपदाश्रयः प्रयोगः पूर्वाचार्याणामुपग्रहशब्दाभिधेयतया प्रसिद्धः' and an example of उपग्रह-वक्रता is 'तस्यापरेष्वपि मृगेषु शरान्मुमुक्षोः कर्णान्तमेत्य बिभिदे निबिडोपि मुष्टिः। (रघु. 9. 58, अत्र बिभिदे भिद्यते स्म स्वयमेवेति कर्मकर्तृकत्व आत्मनेपदमतिचमत्कारकारि).

In the third उन्मेष the author comes to the discussion of वाक्यवैचित्र्यवक्रता. In connection with this he speaks of वस्तुवक्रता. The वस्तु may be सहज or आहार्य (कविशक्तिव्युत्पत्तिपरिपाकप्रौढ). In this उन्मेष and the next it is very difficult to construct the original कारिकाs from the वृत्ति (in which they are imbedded and are not given in full). 'उदारस्वपरिस्पन्दसुन्दरत्वेन वर्णनम्। वस्तुनो वक्रशब्दैकगोचरत्वेन वक्रता ॥'. He quotes here the verse अपारे काव्यसंसारे... परिवर्तते (ध्व. p. 278), for which see above pp. 7-8. The verse अस्याः सर्गविधौ (विक्रमोर्वशीय I. 10) is cited as an example in which सहज and आहार्य are both skilfully combined. He gives directions here as to how sentient and other objects can be used in a poem to yield charming results and how to lend charm to poetry by nourishing appropriate रस, भावs etc. The verse तिष्ठेत्कोपवशात् (विक्र. IV. 9) is cited (folio 99) as an excellent example of विप्रलम्भ and the lamentations of वत्सराज (in तापसवत्सराज 2nd Act) as examples of करुण (folio 100). 'चूताङ्कुरास्वाद' etc.' (कुमार III. 32 and 'इदमसुलभवस्तु' (विक्रमो० II. 6) are examples where चेतनस्वरूप is रसोद्दीपनसामर्थ्यबन्धुर (बन्धुरं हृदयहारि) and अचेतनानां स्वरूपं रसोद्दीपनसामर्थ्यबन्धुरम्. Incidentally he launches upon a discussion as to whether रसवद्, प्रेयः, ऊर्जस्वि, समाहित, उदात्त are alaṅkāras and decides that they are not alaṅkāras but अलङ्कार्य (folio 104) 'अलङ्कारो न रसवद...। स्वरूपादतिरिक्तस्यापरस्याप्रतिभासनात् ॥...ऊर्जस्व्युदात्ताभिधयोः पौर्वापर्यप्रणीतयोः। अलङ्करणयोस्तद्वद्भूषणत्वं न विद्यते ॥'. He criticizes the various definitions of रसवत् such as 'रसवद्दर्शितस्पष्टशृङ्गारादिरसं यथा' (भामह III. 6), 'रसवद्रससंश्रयात्,' 'रसवद्रसपेशलम्' (काव्या० II. 275). His words are दर्शिताः स्पष्टाः अस्पष्टाश्च शृङ्गारादयो यत्रेति व्याख्याने काव्यव्यतिरिक्तो न कश्चिदन्यः समासार्थभूतः स लक्ष्यते योसावलङ्कारः।...(folio 106) यदपि रसवद्रससंश्रयाद् इति कैश्चिल्लक्षणमकारि तदपि न सम्यक् समाधेयतामधितिष्ठति। तथाहि रसः संश्रयो यस्यासौ रससंश्रयः तस्मात्कारणादयं रसवदलङ्कारः सम्पद्यते। तथापि वक्तव्यमेव कोसौ रसव्यतिरेकवृत्तिरन्यः पदार्थः। काव्यमेवेति चेत्तदपि पूर्वमेव प्रत्युक्तम्। तस्य स्वात्मेति

---

1. उपग्रह means परस्मैपद or आत्मनेपद; compare महाभाष्य 'तिङभिहितेन भावेन कालपुरुषोपग्रहा अभिव्यज्यन्ते कृदभिहितेन पुनर्न व्यज्यन्ते' (Kielhorn ed. II. p. 57 on पा. III. I. 67).

क्रियाविरोधादलङ्कारत्वानुपपत्तेः ।...रसपेशलमिति पाठे न किञ्चिदत्रातिरिच्यते।'. He cited (on folio 107-108) the verse quoted by ध्व. p. 93 viz, तन्वी मेघ० and तरङ्गभ्रूभङ्गा (ed. p. 92) discusses them and quotes ध्व. कारिका II. 5 (प्रधानेऽन्यत्र० as that of अभियुक्तs folio 109). He considers the examples of रसवदलङ्कार given by ध्व. pp. 87-88 (किं हास्येन) and क्षिप्तो० (ध्व० p. 89) and rejects the views of the ध्व. (folios 109-110). He criticizes the definitions and examples of प्रेयः and ऊर्जस्वि given by उद्भट, भामह and दण्डी. According to him proper examples of रसवदलङ्कार (in a different sense, रसेन वर्तते तुल्यं) would be (folio 122-123) 'उपोढरागेण विलोलतारकं' (cited in ध्व० p. 41), चलापाङ्गां दृष्टिं (शाकुन्तल I. 21), ऐन्द्रं धनुः' (cited in अलं. स. p. 92 and साहित्य० X). He finds fault with the threefold division of दीपक given by भामह and after citing भामह's three examples (folios 124-125) approves of the addition (अन्तर्गतोपमाधर्माः) in the definition of दीपक made by उद्भट (whom he designates अभियुक्ततरैः on folio 125). His own example of a proper दीपक is 'असारं संसारं...विधातुं व्यवसितः' (मालतीमाधव V; अत्र विधातुं व्यवसितः कर्ता संसारादीनामसारत्वप्रभृतीन्धर्मानुद्योतयन् दीपकालङ्कारमवाप्तवान् on folio 127). He goes on examining many other figures and elucidates them in his own way, such as रूपक, अप्रस्तुतप्रशंसा, पर्यायोक्त, व्याजस्तुति, उत्प्रेक्षा, अतिशयोक्ति and about 20 more figures. He quotes the लिम्पतीव verse (folio 140) as an example of उत्प्रेक्षा, and remarks 'अत्र दण्डिना विहितमिति न पुनर्विधीयते'. On परिवृत्ति he cites the example 'शस्त्रप्रहारं ददता भुजेन तव भूभुजाम् । चिरार्जितं हृतं तेषां यशः कुमुदपाण्डुरम् ॥' (काव्या. II. 356) with the words 'तथा च लक्षणकारेणात्रैवोदाहरणं दर्शितम्'. On folio 161 he quotes ध्वनिकारिका I. 13 and also the verse व्याख्यारोषतनुं (ध्व. p. 117), which is आनन्दवर्धन's own verse. He remarks at the beginning of the 4th उन्मेष 'एवं सकलसाहित्यसर्वस्वकल्पवाक्यवक्रताप्रकारप्रकाशनान्तरमवसरप्राप्तं etc.'

In the 4th उन्मेष he gives the treatment of प्रकरणवक्रता and प्रबन्धवक्रता. As examples of प्रकरणवक्रता he cites several verses from रघुवंश (5th *sarga*, such as किं वस्तु विद्वन् गुरवे प्रदेयं, यावद्यते साधयितुं त्वदर्थं) with the remark 'कुबेरं प्रतिसामन्तसम्भावनया जयाध्यवसायः कामपि सहृदयाह्लादकारितां प्रतिपद्यते' (folio 179). Similarly, the introduction of the curse of Durvāsas in the शाकुन्तल is a charming example of प्रकरणवक्रता. Another example is the मृगयाप्रकरण in the रघुवंश on which he dwells at great lengh and remarks 'दशरथेन राज्ञा स्थविरान्धतपस्विबालवधो व्यधीयतेति एकवाक्यशक्यप्रतिपादनः पुनरयमप्यर्थः परमार्थसरससरस्वतीसर्वस्वायमानप्रतिभाविधानकलेशेन तादृश्या प्रकरणविच्छित्त्या विस्फारितश्चेतनचमत्कारकरणतामधितिष्ठति (folio 190)'. 'प्रधानवस्तुनिष्पत्त्यै वस्त्वन्तरवि-

चित्रता । यत्रोल्लसति सोल्लेखा सापराप्यस्य वक्रता ॥' (अस्य प्रकरणस्य). The episode introduced with the words ततः प्रविशति रज्जुहस्तः पुरुषः (6th Act of मुद्राराक्षस) is an instance of प्रकरणवक्रता. प्रबन्धवक्रता is defined as (folio 203) 'इतिवृत्तान्यथावृत्तरससम्पदपेक्षया । रसान्तरेण रम्येण यत्र निर्वहणं भवेत् ॥ तस्या एव कथामूर्तेरामूलोन्मीलितश्रियः । विनेयानन्दनिष्पत्त्यै सा प्रबन्धस्य वक्रता ॥'. The रामायण and the महाभारत are examples 'रामायणमहाभारतयोश्च शान्ताङ्गित्वं पूर्वसूरिभिरेव निरूपितम् ।' folio 204 (probably a reference to ध्वन्यालोक pp. 298-300). Another variety of प्रबन्धवक्रता is 'त्रैलोक्याभिनवोल्लेखनायकोत्कर्षपोषिणा । इतिहासैकदेशेन प्रबन्धस्य समापनम् ॥ तदुत्तरकथावर्तिविरसत्वजिहासया । कुर्वीत यत्र सुकविः सा विचित्रास्य वक्रता ॥'. An example is the किरातार्जुनीय. He says that great poets show their imagination in the very names with which they christen their works (आस्तां वस्तुषु वैदग्ध्यं काव्ये काममपि वक्रताम् । प्रधानसंविधानाङ्कनाम्नापि कुरुते कविः ॥) and instances (folio 208) अभिज्ञानशाकुन्तल, मुद्राराक्षस, प्रतिमानिरुद्ध, मायापुष्पक, कृत्यारावण etc. as instances. But there is no such charm in the names of certain works such as हयग्रीववध, शिशुपालवध, पाण्डवाभ्युदय, रामानन्द, रामचरित &c. It is genius that makes all the difference, though the plot may be the same (folio 209) 'कथोन्मेषे समानेपि वपुषीव निजैर्गुणैः । प्रबन्धाः प्राणिन इव भासन्ते हि पृथक् पृथक् ॥'.

The वक्रोक्तिजीवित denies the independent existeuce of ध्वनि or व्यङ्ग्य as the soul of poetry and tries to include it under its all-pervading वक्रोक्ति. It therefore makes the soul of poetry to consist of something that is strikingly different from pue above what is ordinary. The emphasis is mainly laid by Kuntaka on कविव्यापार and secondarily on the aesthetic pleasure that the man of taste enjoys from poetry or drama.

According to Jayaratha and the Ekāvalī[1] (p. 51) the Vakroktijīvita was included among those who belong to the भक्त्यादि school referred to in the first kārikā of the Dhvanyāloka (भाक्तमाहुस्तमन्ये). But this is not accurate, as the discussion about the Vakrokti school in the 2nd part will show.

In the colophons to the *unmeṣas* of the ms. the author is spoken of as राजानककुन्तलक. But in the verse from the व्यक्तिविवेक quoted above (p. 216 काव्यकाञ्चन०) the name is given as कुन्तक. Gopāla in his com. on the काव्यप्रकाश (Intro. vers. 2) indicates

1. एतेन अत्र कुन्तकेन भक्तावन्तर्भावितो ध्वनिस्तदपि प्रत्याख्यातम् । एकावली p. 51 (B. S. S. ed.); इदानीं यदप्यन्यैरस्य भक्त्यन्तर्भूतत्वमुक्तं तदपि दर्शयितुमाह वक्रोक्तीत्यादि । जयरथ p. 8.

that the name should be कुन्तक 'वक्रानुरञ्जनीमुक्ति चञ्चूमिव मुखे वहन् । कुन्तकः क्रीडति सुखं कीर्तिस्फटिकपञ्जरे ॥' (कुन्तक means a small spear and can be compared to the beak of a parrot, but कुन्तल meaning hair cannot be so compared).

The वक्रोक्तिजीवित is a work of great value and deserves to be rescued from the oblivion into which it has fallen. Whatever one may think of his central theory that वक्रोक्ति is the soul of poetry and of the somewhat quaint nomenclature adopted by the author, the work shows originality, great literary acumen and is full of charming ideas. He is at one with भट्टतोत in saying that it is the poet's own genius that is the source of good poetry. His choice of examples is very judicious and he casts his net over a wide area. In the analysis given above I have referred to well-known examples for saving space; but no reader should entertain the impression that he very largly quotes Kālidāsa only. The work contains over five hundred examples. The *kārikās* are composed in a smooth, limpid style and the वृत्ति generally shows very high qualities of a grand literary style, which is rhythmic and melodious. He very profusely quotes भामह and दण्डी and to a lesser extent उद्भट and tries to weld together the figures of speech with his own theory of वक्रोक्ति. He does not slavishly follow anyone of his predecessors and criticizes them all, though he admires आनन्दवर्धन, भामह and दण्डी. For example, he finds fault with भामह's three kinds of दीपक and with his way of dealing with the figure ऊर्जस्वि 'कैश्चिदुदाहरणमेव व्यक्तत्वाल्लक्षणं मन्यमानैस्तदेव प्रदर्शितम् । यथा—ऊर्जस्वि कर्णेन यथा पार्थाय पुनरागतः ।' etc. (भामह III. 7). He finds fault with those who regard आशीः as an अलङ्कार (दण्डी does so). About रुद्रट's well-known verses भण तरुणि रमणमन्दिर० and अनणुरणन्मणिमेखलं (रुद्रट II. 22-23) he remarks (p. 7 Dr. De's ed.) 'प्रतिभादारिद्र्यदैन्यादतिस्वल्पसुभाषितेन कविना वर्णसावर्ण्यरम्यतामात्रमत्रोदितं न पुनर्वाच्यवैचित्र्यकणिका काचिदस्तीति' and says that the verses are ग्राम्य. He quotes the first verse 'स्वेच्छाकेसरिणः . . . नखाः' of आनन्दवर्धन's वृत्ति as a fine example of क्रियावैचित्र्य. He names a very large number of works. Among the authors and works quoted are :—उत्तररामचरित, उदात्तराघव (in which लक्ष्मण is represented as pursuing मारीचमृग), उद्भट, कालिदास (as composing *kāvyas* which possess सहजसौकुमार्य), किरातार्जुनीय, कुमारसम्भव, कृत्यारावण, छलितराम, तापसवत्सराज (a drama in which करुण is more charming in each succeeding Act), दण्डी, ध्वनिकार, नागानन्द, पाण्डवाभ्युदय, पुष्पदूषितक, प्रतिमानिरुद्ध, बालरामायण, भट्टबाण, भरत,

भवभूति, भामह, मञ्जीर (as a poet of the मध्यममार्ग), महाभारत, मातृगुप्त (as a poet of the मध्यममार्ग), मायापुष्पक, मालती०, मुद्राराक्ष०, मेघ०, रघु०, राजशेखर, रामचरित, रामानन्द, रामाभ्युदय, रामायण, रुद्रट, विक्रमो०, वीरचरित, वेणीसंहार, शाकुन्तल, शिशुपालवध, सर्वसेन (as a poet of the सुकुमारमार्ग), सेतुप्रबन्ध (a drama), हयग्रीववध, हर्षचरित (in which there are numerous charming descriptions of moonrise). The transcript in various places points out that there are large gaps (अत्र ग्रंथपातः). Here and there certain *kārikās* (in all eight) occur which are styled अन्तरश्लोक (in some cases अनन्त०), which expression occurs in the व्यक्तिविवेक also (pp. 46.54. 55, etc.) and is explained by हेमचन्द्र (विवेक p. 392) as अन्तरे मध्ये वक्तव्यशेषाभिधायकौ श्लोकौ अन्तरश्लोकौ'. One verse on p. 101 (of Dr. De's edition) is styled संग्रहश्लोक. There is no परिकरश्लोक. As the वक्रोक्तिजीवित quotes the ध्वनिकार, रुद्रट and the बालरामायण of राजशेखर it is later than the first quarter of the 10th century. Therefore जयरथ is right when he says 'यद्यपि वक्रोक्तिजीवितहृदयदर्पणकारावपि ध्वनिकारानन्तरभाविनावेव तथापि तौ चिरन्तनमतानुयायिनावेवेति तन्मतं etc.' अलं. स. वि. (p. 15). The वक्रोक्तिजीवित is quoted and criticized by महिमभट्ट in his व्यक्तिविवेक (pp. 28, 37, 58) and its views are summarised by the अलङ्कारसर्वस्व and many verses from it are cited in the साहित्यमीमांसा. महिमभट्ट's manner of referring to the वक्रोक्तिजीवित (p. 28 सहृदयमानिनः केचिदाचक्षते) implies that कुन्तक was his contemporary or only slightly older. He refers to the लोचनकार in a similar strain (व्यक्तिविवेक p. 19 अत्र केचिद्विद्वन्मानिनः...यदाहुः). It is further noteworthy that the लोचन contains no reference to the वक्रोक्तिजीवित and कुन्तक does not refer to अभिनवगुप्त. Hence he was probably a contemporary of the लोचनकार also. Dr. P. C. Lahiri in 'Indian Culture' vol. III. 530-534 on Lakṣaṇas in Abhinavabhāratī and in 'Concept of Rīti and Guṇa' pp. 17-20 holds that Abhinavagupta's treatment of Lakṣaṇas is influenced by the वक्रोक्ति० and that अभिनव knew Kuntaka's work. Dr. Mookerjee in B. C. Law vol. I. at p. 183 says the same thing. On the other hand, Dr. Sankaran in 'the Theory of Rasa and Dhvani' pp. 119-120, while admitting that in the whole of the वक्रोक्तिजीवित there is no reference to the लोचन or अभिनवभारती, sets out passeges from Kuntaka and Abhinava which bear remarkably close resemblance and holds that there is a strong presumption in favour of the view that Abhinava was distinctly aware of the conception of *vakratā* according to the school represented by Kuntaka and possibly of the Vakroktijīvita also. If the whole work was before

Abhinava when he composed the Locana and the अभिनवभारती, it is unlikely that he would have allowed its views to be left uncriticized at length, when he severely handles Bhaṭṭa Nāyaka and others. Dr. Raghavan (in J. O. R., Madras vol. VI. pp. 218-222 and 'Indian Culture' vol. III. p. 756) holds that there is not evidence enough to enable us to speak definitely about Abhinava's indebtedness to Kuntaka. I agree with the views of Dr. Sankaran and Dr. Raghavan that the evidence is too meagre to enable one to pronounce a definite opinion on Abhinava's indebtedness to (or awareness of) Kuntaka. Dr. Haradatta Śarma contributes a paper on Kuntaka's conception of Guṇas in I. H. Q. vol. 8 pp. 257-266.

21 अभिनवगुप्त–Abhinavagupta is one of the most remarkable personalities of medieval India. He was a man of very acute intellect and was an encyclopoedic scholar. He had taken all knowledge for his province. Numerous works are attributed to him. From several of his works we get a tolerably full account of his ancestors, his parents, his other relatives, his several *gurus* and his works. At the end of his commentary on the परात्रिंशिका which is a dialogue between Bhairava (Śiva,) and Bhairavī (Śakti) in 35 ślokas, and at the end of ईश्वरप्रत्यभिज्ञाविवृतिविमर्शिनी, अभिनवगुप्त gives a brief account of his ancestors (in No. 18 of the Kashmir S. Series, pp. 278-280 and in No. 65, p. 405). He states that his remote ancestor अत्रिगुप्त at first resided in Antarvedi (the Doab between the Ganges and the Jumna), came to Kashmir at the instance of king ललितादित्य of Kashmir (for this last, vide Dr. Pandey's 'Abhinavagupta' Appendix A, p. 337, which quotes a passage from the 37th आह्निक of तन्त्रालोक). राजत. (IV. 660 and 673) shows that ललितापीड ruled for twelve years after जयापीड from 783 to 795 A. D. In the family of Atrigupta was born Varāhagupta, whose son was Cukhala, a great devotee of Śiva, whose son was Abhinavagupta[1].

1. The name of the father is variously written or printed, either as चुखल (in परात्रिंशिकातत्त्वविवरण) or as चुखुल or चुखुलक (as in तन्त्रालोक, Kashmir S. S. vol. XXIII, I. 12 'स चुखुलको दिश्यादिष्टं मे गुरुरुत्तमः') or as विचुलक (in Buhler's Kashmir Report p. CLV) or as दुःखल (in अभिनवभारती, G. O. S. vol. II. p. 117). In vol. III. of अ. भा. (G. O. S.) at the end of chap. 27 the father's name is सुखल and नृसिंहगुप्त also. Some of these must be

The father's name was really नृसिंहगुप्त, but चुखल was his well-known name. On the first verse of the तन्त्रालोक (**विमलकला-श्रयाभिनवसृष्टिमहा भरिततनुश्च जननी पञ्चमुखगुप्तरुचिर्जनकः** ।), जयरथ explains the double meanings of the words in thick type, states that the father was called नरसिंहगुप्त and the mother of अभिनवगुप्त was called विमला or विमलकला, that अभिनवगुप्त was what is designated as योगिनीभूः, since he was born of such spiritually high personages as his parents and was therefore peculiarly qualified to compose a work containing a summary of all the Āgama works on त्रिकशास्त्र (pp. 14-15 of जयरथ's विवेक on तन्त्रालोक I. 1). अभिनवगुप्त further states that he composed his commentary on परात्रिंशिका for the benefit of his younger brother मनोरथगुप्त, a ब्राह्मण named कर्ण who was son of वल्लभ minister of king यशस्कर[1] of Kashmir and one रामदेव who was proficient in grammar, Tarka and Mīmāṅsā. Similarly, his मालिनीविजयवार्तिक was composed at the frequent requests of his good pupils कर्ण and मन्द्र. In the अभिनवभारती (vol. I p. 297) he quotes a verse of his uncle वामनगुप्त on हास्याभास (G. O. S. ed. chap. 6-45) p. 297 of the Nāṭyaśāstra. Abhinavagupta mentions that his father's maternal grand-father was a famous man named Yasorāga 'इति षोडशमध्यार्यं ग्रन्थनिर्ग्रन्थिकं व्यधात् । यशोराशेर्यशोरागनाम्नो दौहित्रदेहजः ॥'. The fact that Abhinava feels pride in naming him and also states that he was famous would indicate that that relative must have attained eminence in some branch of learning or must have held some high position. But at present we know nothing about यशोराग.

---

mistakes due to not deciphering the script properly. At the beginning of मालिनीविजयवार्तिक (Kashmir S. S. No. 31) अभिनवगुप्त says : गुरुभ्योपि गरीयांसं युक्तं श्रीचुखलाभिधम् । वन्दे यत्कृतसंस्कारः स्थितोस्मि गलितग्रहः ॥ verse 5; नृसिंहगुप्तायतिनेत्थमत्र वृत्तिस्वरूपं प्रकटं व्यधायि । यत्त-त्रिनेत्रेण हृदन्तरात्मस्वरूपमेव प्रकटं व्यधायि ॥ verse at the of the अ. भा. chap. 20 on वृत्तिs (p. 107 of vol. III of अ. भा. in G. O. S.). On p. 14 of तन्त्रालोक I. 1 (No. 23) जयरथ states 'अस्य हि ग्रन्थकृतः श्रीनरसिंह-गुप्तविमलाख्यौ पितरौ इति गुरवः'. Vide also Dr. Raghavan on 'writers quoted in Abhinavabhārati' J. O. R., Madras, vol. VI. at p. 153 for नरसिंहगुप्त and विमला as अभिनवगुप्त's parents and for अभिनव being an अवतार of परमशिव.

1. From राजत. VI. 2-99 it appears that यशस्कर ruled for nine years from 939-948 A. D.

अभिनवगुप्त, it appears, remained celibate all his life, was extremely devoted to Śiva and studied at the feet of several teachers in order to develop his intellect and knowledge.[1] His works fall into several groups. One group concerns his work on the Tantras. The तन्त्रालोक is the most voluminous work of his that deals with Tantric Āgamas enumerated in तन्त्रालोक I. 18 (Kashmir S. Series vol. XXII. p. 35) as दशाष्टादशवस्वष्टभिन्नं[1] यच्छासनं विभोः। तत्सारं त्रिकशास्त्रं हि तत्सारं मालिनीमतम् ॥'. To this group belong his मालिनीविजयवार्तिक (written by him in the eastern part of प्रवरपुर in Kashmir), परात्रिंशिकाविवरण, तन्त्रालोकसार &c.

The 2nd group consists of his स्तोत्रs such as भैरवस्तव and क्रमस्तोत्र and certain small tracts such as बोधपञ्चदशिका (Kashmir S. S. No. 14). A third group is constituted by his works on Poetics and Dramaturgy, which have been already mentioned above. His teacher in Poetics was Indurāja[3] and in dramaturgy Tota.[4] In these two branches his two works viz. लोचन

---

1. ईश्वरप्रत्यभिज्ञाविवृतिविमर्शिनी (Kashmir S. S. No 65, 1943 A. D.) says at end (p. 405) 'तज्जन्मदेहपदभाक्पदवाक्यमानसंस्कारसंस्कृतमतिः परमेशशक्तिः। सामर्थ्यतः शिवपदाम्बुजभक्तिभागी दारात्मजप्रभृतिबन्धुकथामनाप्तः ॥ नानागुरुप्रवरपादनिपातजातसंवित्सरोरुहविकासनिवेशितश्रीः ॥ verses 2 and 3.

2. This means 10, 18 and 64 (these last divided into eight groups of eight each). The तन्त्रालोक says 'whoever always studies closely these 37 āhnikas would himself become Bhairava' I. 214-215).

3. At the end of the लोचन on the 4th उद्योत of ध्व. (published by Dr. De in J. of Letters, Cal. Un., vol. IX. p. 42) two teachers viz. सिद्धिचेल and इन्दुराज are mentioned (श्रीसिद्धिचेलचरणाब्जपरागपूते भट्टेन्दुराजमतिसंस्कृतबुद्धिलेशः।). The teacher सिद्धिचेल is not mentioned anywhere else in the लोचन or अ. भा. It is possible that we have to read 'परागपूत-भट्टेन्दुराज०, which would mean 'भट्टेन्दुराज was purified by the pollen from the lotus of the feet of सिद्धिचेल' i. e. सिद्धिचेल was the guru of भट्टेन्दुराज.

4. Abhinavagupta bestowed great labour in consulting numerous mss. of the Nāṭyśāstra and then found that there were two recensions on several sections such as the names and definition of *lakṣaṇa*, the definitions of metres and the arrangement of the sections on guṇas and doṣas. Vide p. 13 above

and अभिनवभारती are monuments of learning, critical insight, literary grace and style. He has been followed by all subsequent eminent writers on these two subjects, except महिमभट्ट. Vide Prof. S. P. Bhattācārya's paper on the impress of Kashmsr Śaivism on Alaṅkāraśāstra in J. O. I (Baroda) vol. I pp. 245-252. He holds that such alaṅkāras as Smaraṇa, Pariṇāma, Ullekha are due to Śaivadarśana. I regard this as far-fetched.

The fourth group of his works concerns the philosophy of the monistic Śaivism of Kashmir (or Pratyabhijnāśāstra). In his ईश्वरप्रत्यभिज्ञाविमर्शिनी (I. 1. 2-5) he gives the गुरुपरम्परा as follows : त्र्यम्बक was the founder, in whose family was born सोमानन्दनाथ (who called his system शिवदृष्टि and expounded it). उत्पल, son of उदयाकर, was a pupil of सोमानन्दनाथ and composed the प्रत्यभिज्ञासूत्र in 190 कारिकाs and himself wrote a वृत्ति and a टीका thereon (vide p. 175 above); his pupil was लक्ष्मणगुप्त whose pupil was अभिनवगुप्त.[1] No work of लक्ष्मणगुप्त has so far been recovered. At the end of the ईश्वरप्रत्यभिज्ञाविवृतिविमर्शिनी verse 3rd states 'श्रीशाम्भवदटितलक्ष्मणगुप्तपादसत्योपदर्शितशिवाद्वयवाददृप्तः ॥' Kashmir S. S. No. 65). This means that the philosophy of

where passages concerning the first two matters have been set out. In the 2nd passage quoted there Abhinava expressly states that he follows the tradition that was handed down to him by his guru (Tota). As regards guṇas and doṣas he remarks (on नाट्यशास्त्र 16. 87 अतः परं प्रवक्ष्यामि काव्यदोषान्गुणांस्तथा। vol. II. p. 331 G. O. S.) 'केषुचित्पुस्तकेषु चैतद्ग्रंथः पश्चाद् दृश्यते, बाहुल्येन प्रथमं दृश्यते इति तथैव व्याचक्ष्महे ।' We have seen above how but for his elaborate commentary on the नाट्यशास्त्र we would have been in the dark about the vast literature on dramaturgy that once existed. अभिनवगुप्त in his great regard for poetry and dramaturgy boldly says (vol. III. p. 74 of GOS) 'रामायणेपि तथा वर्णितमिति चेत्किमतः । वेदेपि तथा वर्ण्यतां न वयमतो बिभीमः । स हि भागः काव्यं यत्र यत्र रसोभिष्यन्दी वर्ण्य इत्युक्तमसकृत् ।'.

1. उत्पल is mentioned in the लोचन (p. 30 K. M. ed.) as परमगुरु of अभिनव० and a verse of his is quoted. The ईश्वरप्रत्यभिज्ञाविमर्शिनी (Kashmir S. S. vol. XXII) states at the beginning that उत्पल propounded the प्रत्यभिज्ञाशास्त्र 'श्रीसोमानन्दनाथस्य विज्ञानप्रतिबिम्बकम् । अनुत्तरानन्यसाक्षि पुमर्थोपायमभ्यधात् । ईश्वरप्रत्यभिज्ञाख्यं यः शास्त्रं यत्सुनिर्मलम् । तत्प्रशिष्यः करोम्येतां तत्सूत्रविवृतिं लघुम् ।' verses 2-4.

Śaiva monism was systematized by the Śāstrakāra (Utpala ?) and was correctly expounded by लक्ष्मणगुप्तपाद. In the मालिनीविजयवार्तिक[1] Abhinavagupta highly praises his *guru* Lakṣmaṇagupta. As regards अभिनवगुप्त himself he wrote two very important works on the प्रत्यभिज्ञाशास्त्र viz. ईश्वरप्रतिभिज्ञाविमर्शिनी (also called लघुवृत्ति) on उत्पलदेव's प्रत्यभिज्ञाकारिका and ईश्वरप्रत्यभिज्ञाविवृतिविमर्शिनी (also called बृहतीवृत्ति) on उत्पलदेव's टीका on his own प्रत्यभिज्ञाकारिका.

The *guru—paramparā* to his study of the Tantras was as follows : सुमतिनाथ—सोमदेव—शम्भुनाथ—अभिनवगुप्त. Vide जयरथ on तन्त्रालोक vol. I. p. 236, तन्त्रालोक 1st आह्निक verses 13 and 21 and तन्त्रसार (3rd Intro. verse about शम्भुनाथ.).

In his eager search for knowladge Abhinavagupta states that he resorted to teachers of *tarka* (Nyāya and Vaiśeṣika systems), and of Bauddha, Ārhata and Vaiṣṇava doctrines.[2] Abhinavagupta was proficient in yogic practices, he believed that he had realized the Highest Reality (Śiva) and was inspired by Śiva to proclaim an easy way of Release out of compassion for less favoured people struggling to find spiritual enlightenment and peace. Even after having become blessed, for the sake of others he wrote works.[3] At the end of the प्रत्यभिज्ञाविमर्शिनी[4] Abhinava says that he has opened an easy and new way which former great teachers declared in the 'Śivadṛṣṭi'; a man planting his feet on this path becomes perfect and one with Śiva. At the end of his परमार्थसार (verse

1. तद्दृष्टिसंसृतिच्छेदिप्रत्यभिज्ञोपदेशिनः । श्रीमल्लक्ष्मणगुप्तस्य गुरोर्विजयते वचः । verse 8.

2. अहमप्यत एवाधःशास्त्रदृष्टिकुतूहलात् । तार्किकश्रौतबौद्धार्हद्वैष्णवादीनसेविषि ॥ तन्त्रालोक, 13 आह्निक verses 345-346; vol. VIII. p. 206 of Kashmir S. S.

3. शिवस्मृतिकृतार्थोऽपि परार्थं दुःखलात्मजः (चुखलात्मजः ?) । अ. भा. vol. II. p. 117; इति यज्ज्ञेयसतत्त्वं दर्श्यते तच्छिवाज्ञया । मया स्वसंवित्सत्तर्कपतिशास्त्रत्रिकक्रमात् ॥ तन्त्रालोक 1st आह्निक verse 106. स्वसंवित् स्वानुभवः सत्तर्को युक्तिः पतिशास्त्रं भेदप्रधानं शैवं त्रिकं परादिशक्तित्रयाभिधायकं शास्त्रं क्रमः चतुष्टयार्थः (जयरथ's विवेक).

4. इति प्रकटितो मया सुघट एष मार्गो नवो महागुरुभिरुच्यते स्म शिवदृष्टिशास्त्रे यथा । तदत्र निदधत्पदं भुवनकर्तृतामात्मनो विभाव्य शिवतामयीमनिशमाविशन् सिद्धयति ॥ ईश्वरप्रत्यभिज्ञाविमर्शिनी vol. 2 p. 271 No. 33 of Kashmir S. S.).

105) he declares that in one hundred Āryās he has summarized the very secret essence and adds that he, Abhinavagupta, has received light by dwelling on the feet of Śiva.[1] In the 13th Āhnika, verse 215, he enumerates the five signs of a man that has attained the highest spiritual eminence viz. सुनिश्चला रुद्रभक्ति, मन्त्रसिद्धि, सर्वतत्त्ववशित्व, कृत्यसम्पत्, (i. e. प्रारब्धकार्यनिष्पत्ति), कवित्व and सर्वशास्त्रार्थवेत्तृत्व and जयरथ in his commentary on it (vol. 8 p. 137, No. 47 of Kashmir S. S.) remarks that it was well-known that all these signs had manifested themselves in अभिनव and quotes a verse of his teacher in support. In commenting on the concluding verse of Pratyabhijñā-kārikā (जनस्यायत्नसिद्ध्यर्थमुदयाकरसूनुना । ईश्वरप्रत्यभिज्ञेयमुत्पलेनोपपादिता ॥ Kashmir S. S. vol. 33 p. 276) Abhinavagupta boldly states that this Pratyabhijñā philosophy is meant for all men whatever, without any reference to caste or the like.[2]

It is far beyond the scope of this work to set out or discuss the tenets of Kashmir monistic Śaivism or its literature. Those who desire to secure further information on these matters should read Mr. J. C. Chatterji's very careful and pioneer work on 'Kashmir Śaivism' (in 1914) and Dr. K. C. Pandey's excellent dissertation,[3] on 'Abhinavagupta; an Historical and Philosophical study in Chowkhamba Sanskrit studies vol. I.; Dr. 'Bhandarkar's Vaishṇavism and Śaivism' pp. 129-131.[4]

The tradition in Kashmir says that Abhinavagupta accompanied by 1200 disciples entered a cave repeating the

1. The word 'शिवचरणस्मरणदीप्तेन' (of परमार्थसार verse 105) is explained by योगेश्वर as 'उपदेष्टुः समाविष्टमहेश्वरस्वभावोऽनेन वाक्येनोक्तः स्यात्'.

2. यस्य कस्यचिज्जन्तोरिति नात्र जात्याद्यपेक्षा काचित् इति सर्वोपकारित्वमुक्तम् । ई. प्र. वि. vol. II. p. 276.

3. Though I have had to criticize some opinions of Dr. Pandey I quite appreciate his great industry in putting together all about Abhinavagupta, his works and the monistic Śaiva philosophy. I am sorry that he was misled by Mr. Kavi's method of editing the अभिनवभारती into thinking that नान्यदेव was quoted by अभिनव and needlessly expended pp. 121—125 of his thesis. He missed the note of Mr. Kavi on अ. भा. vol. I .p. 253.

4. On p. 130 there is apparently a slip, where उदयाकर is mentioned as the pupil of सोमानन्द (not उत्पल).

Bhairavastotra and was seen no more (vide J. R. A. S. for 1910 p. 1334 at p. 1336 n. 1). Dr. Grierson states there that the cave is shown at Bīrū, ancient Bahurūpa, 13 miles to the south-west of Śrīnagar.

The question of the date of Abhinavagupta does not present any difficulty. At the end of his ईश्वरप्रत्यभिज्ञाविवृतिविमर्शिनी (Kashmir S. S. No. 65) there occurs the following statement about the date of its composition (verse 15 on p. 407) 'इति नवतितमेऽस्मिन् वत्सरेन्त्ये युगांशे तिथिशशिजलधिस्थे मार्गशीर्षावसाने । जगति विहित-बोधामीश्वरप्रत्यभिज्ञां व्यवृणुत परिपूर्णां प्रेरितः शम्भुपादैः ॥'. This means that the commentary was completed in the year 4115 of the Kali age when the Laukika year[1] (in Kashmir) was 90 at the end of Mārgaśīrṣa i. e. in 1014 A. D. At the end of Bhairavastava he states the date as follows: वसुरसपौषे कृष्णदशम्यामभिनवगुप्तः स्तवमिममकरोत् । येन विभुर्भवमरुसन्तापं शमयति झटिति जनस्य दयालुः ॥' (vide Buhler's Kashmir Report p. CLXII). The भैरवस्तव was composed in 68 of the लौकिक era (22 years before the composition of the ईश्वरप्रत्यभिज्ञाविवृतिविमर्शिनी) i. e. in 992-3 A. D. The Kramastota was composed in 66 of the Laukika era. i. e. exactly 24 years before his great commentary ईश्वर° (षट्षष्टिनामके वर्षे नवम्यामसितेऽह्नि । मयाभिनवगुप्तेन मार्गशीर्षे स्तुतः शिवः ॥ vide p. 412 in Dr. Pandey's 'Abhinavagupta'). These three dates range from 990-1 A. D. to 1014-15 A. D. The तन्त्रालोक a voluminous work (29 āhnikas of which out of 37 occupy eleven volumes in the Kashmir S. S.) was composed before the लोचन, which latter in its turn was followed by another voluminous work viz. the अभिनवभारती on भरत's नाट्यशास्त्र. Besides these he composed other works.[2] Therefore, it would not be

1. For the 'lokakāla' or 'laukika vatsara', vide Buhler's Kashmir Report pp. 59-60 and Stein's Intro. to राजतरङ्गिणी. This era called also Saptarṣi era began in 25 of the Kaliyuga era. It is even now current in Kashmir and generally the centuries are omited in referring to it i. e. the year 4090 (= 4115 of Kaliyuga era) is mentioned by अभिनवगुप्त himself as 90. Vide E. I. vol. XX No. 1441-1445 p. 197 for inscriptions dated in the Saptarṣi or Laukika era..

2. Vide for the works of अभिनवगुप्त, Intro. p. 15 (for books on Śaivism) to परात्रिंशिकाविवरण (Kashmir S. S. No. 18). Dr. K. C. Pandey on 'Abhinavagupta' pp. 122-124, Dr. Raghavan in J. O. R., Madras, vol. 14 pp. 318-328, New Cat. Cat. vol. I. pp. 224-226.

quite wrong to assume that Abhinavagupta's literary activity must have extended over 35 or 40 years i. e. from about 980 A. D. to about 1020 A. D. If we suppose that his first works (among which the तन्त्रालोक is one) must have been written when he was about or over 30 years of age, Abhinavagupta was probably born about 950 A. D. These dates receive strong corroboration from several considerations. अभिनव° wrote his commentary on परात्रिंशिका for his pupil कर्ण, son of a minister of यशस्कर who died in 948 A. D. This son must have been old enough to understand the doctrines of Tantra. So he must have been 25 or 30 years old at the time of his request and if कर्ण was born about 960 to the former minister of यशस्कर the परात्रिंशिकाविवरण might have been composed about 980 A. D. क्षेमेन्द्र mentions at the end of his बृहत्कथामञ्जरी and भारतमञ्जरी that he learnt *Sāhitya* from Abhinavagupta.[1] We know that क्षेमेन्द्र wrote his समयमातृका[2] in 1050 A. D. and his दशावतारचरित in 1066 A. D. He was also a voluminous writer. So his literary activity would have to be placed between 1030-1070 A. D. It appears, therefore, that क्षेमेन्द्र came in contact with अभिनव° towards the close of the latter's life.

22 The दशरूप (or दशरूपक) of धनञ्जय. This work with the commentary called अवलोक by धनिक has been published several times, i. e. by F. E. Hall (B. I. Series) in 1865, by Haas (New York, 1912) with transliterated text, notes and a valuable Introduction and by the Nir. Press. Here references are made to Nir. Press, 4th edition (1941). As Dr. Hall remarked and Dr. Rāghavan in his 'Sṛṅgāraprakāśa part I pp. 188-190 says, there is a good deal of variance in the mss. of the Daśarūpa

---

1. श्रुत्वाभिनवगुप्ताख्यात्साहित्यं बोधवारिधेः । आचार्यशेखरमणेर्विद्याविवृतिकारिणः ॥ बृहत्कथाम°, उपसंहार verse 37, भारतमञ्जरी concluding verse 8 (here the halves are transposed).

2. The समयमातृका (concluding verses 2 and 4) states that it was composed in the 25th year of Laukika era in the reign of king Ananta, while the दशावतारचरित (verse 5 at end) says that it was composed in the 41st year of the Laukika era in the reign of king कलश of काश्मीर. अनन्त ruled from 1028 to 1063 A. D., when he abdicated in favour of his son कलश who was a king (for some years only in name) from 1063 to 1089 A. D.

wit 'Avaloka', which suggests interpolations. The दशरूप deserves to be referred to here because it contains a treatment of the *rasa* theory. Otherwise it is a work dealing with dramaturgy alone and not with the several topics of Poetics. The work contains about 300 *kārikās* and is divided into four प्रकाशs. Bharata in chap. 20 verses 1-2 (Ch. ed.=18th chapter in K. M. ed.) states that he will set out the ten kinds of plays together with their names, their actions, their representation on the stage. The ten principal varieties of drames are नाटक, प्रकरण, अङ्क, व्यायोग, भाण, समवकार, वीथी, प्रहसन, डिम, ईहामृग. Out of these नाटक and प्रकरण are most important and serve as the pattern (prakṛti) on which the remaining kinds and other kinds of plays (such as the नाटिका described by Bharata himself in chap. 20 verses 62-63) are constructed. The work is called दशरूप or दशरूपक because it is concerned with the representation of ten principal kinds of plays (called rūpakas). Bharata employs kāvya and nāṭya as synonyms.[1] Vāmana states that among poetic compositions, the ten rūpakas are superior[2] (काव्या. सू. I. 3. 30). The view of Tota identifying *rasa* with *nāṭya* has been already quoted (p. 219). Three works stand pre-eminent in the treatment of dramaturgy in Sanskrit viz. भरतनाट्यशास्त्र, दशरूप[3] (with अवलोक) and the साहित्यदर्पण. In the Udepur

---

1. Vide नाट्यशास्त्र 16. 169 काव्यबन्धास्तु कर्तव्याः षट्त्रिंशल्लक्षणान्विताः ।; 'षट्त्रिंशल्लक्षणान्येवं काव्यबन्धेषु निर्दिशेत् । 17. 5; also 17. 42 and 121.

2. अवस्थानुकृतिर्नाट्यं रूपं दृश्यतयोच्यते । रूपकं तत्समारोपाद् दशधैव रसाश्रयम् ॥ दशरूप I. 7. This means that नाट्य is called रूप because it is something to be seen (just as रूप i. e. the form of a body is seen) and it is called रूपक because while it is being represented the actors have for the time being superimposed upon them the actions and situations of other men (viz. the hero राम and the like). Vide for a discussion on the meaning of दशरूपक J. O. R., Madras, for 1933 p. 277-290 (Dr. Raghavan).

3. The last verse of the work is : विष्णोः सुतेनापि धनञ्जयेन विद्वन्मनोरागनिबन्धहेतुः । आविष्कृतं मुञ्जमहीशगोष्ठीवैदग्ध्यभाजा दशरूपमेतत् ॥. This goes to show that दशरूप is the proper name of the work. The Colophons at the end of the commentary describe it as दशरूपावलोक composed by धनिक son of विष्णु. Hall notes in his Preface (p. 3) that one of the mss. of the *Avaloka* speaks of

Praśasti of the kings of Malwa edited by Buhler (E. I. vol. I pp. 222-238) and in the Nagpur Praśasti of the same line of kings (E. I. II pp. 180-194 edited by Kielhorn) the following pedigree of the Paramāra kings is given. परमार—descendant उपेन्द्र—वैरिसिंह I —सीयक I—वाक्पति I—वैरिसिंह II—हर्ष—son वाक्पति II—सिन्धुराज brother of the preceding—भोज son of सिन्धु०—उदयादित्य relative of भोज[1]—लक्ष्मदेव and नरवर्मदेव. वाक्पतिराज was also called मुञ्ज and उत्पलराज, while सिन्धुराज was called नवसाहसाङ्क and कुमारनारायण. The नवसाहसाङ्कचरित of पद्मगुप्त *alias* परिमल states in (XI. 101-102) that सिन्धुराज younger brother of वाक्पतिराज was called नवसाहसाङ्क. The तिलकमञ्जरी of धनपाल also gives briefly the pedigree as वैरिसिंह—सीयक alias श्रीहर्ष—sons वाक्पतिराज and सिन्धुराज—son भोज of सिन्धुराज.

The first प्रकाश after bowing to गणेश, विष्णु, भरत and सरस्वती speaks of the ten kinds of *rūpakas*, नृत्य and नृत्त, लास्य, ताण्डव, the five *sandhis* and their *aṅgas*, definition of विष्कम्भ, चूलिका, अङ्कास्य, अङ्कावतार, प्रवेशक etc. The 2nd speaks of several kinds of heroes (नायक) and heroines (नायिका), their charcteristics, their friends, the four *vṛttis* and their *aṅgas*. The third gives practical directions as to how to begin a nāṭaka,[2] about the prologue, about the various requisites that constitute the ten kinds of *rūpakas*. The fourth deals with the *rasa* theory in all its details. The commentary of धनिक is a learned one and

---

धनिक as an officer of उत्पलराज. Buhler on Udepur Praśasti (E. I. vol. I. at p. 227) states that धनिक was the महासाध्यपाल of उत्पलराज (i. e. वाक्पति). मुञ्ज and वाक्पतिराज are the same since the same verse is attributed by धनिक to मुञ्ज and also to वाक्पतिराज and since the Nagpur praśasti (E. I. vol. II. p. 184 verse 23) speaks of मुञ्ज as the son of सीयक and does not mention वाक्पतिराज. The नवसाहसाङ्कचरित XI. 93 speaks of him as कविमित्र, 'अतीते विक्रमादित्ये गतेस्तं सातवाहने । कविमित्रे विशश्राम यस्मिन् देवी सरस्वती ॥'.

1. The Nagpur Praśasti of *saṁvat* 1161 (1104-5 A.D.) in E. I. vol. II. 180 at p. 185 (verse 32) states 'तस्मिन्वासवबन्धुतामुपगते राज्ये च कुल्याकुले मग्नस्वामिनि तस्य बन्धुरुदयादित्योभवद्भूपतिः ।'.

2. The दशरूप expressly states that Nāṭaka is the pattern on which other varieties of plays are to be modelled 'प्रकृतित्वादथान्येषां भूयोरसपरिग्रहात्। सम्पूर्णलक्षणत्वाच्च पूर्वं नाटकमुच्यते ॥' III. 1.

is full of quotations. Over 330 verses are quoted, including about twenty verses of धनिक himself, some of which are in Prākrit (two on II. 34 and one on II. 37). We learn from धनिक's comment (on IV. 37) that he wrote a work called काव्यनिर्णय from which he quotes seven verses. He seems to have held views somewhat similar to those of भट्टनायक, when he says (on IV. 37) 'न रसादीनां काव्येन सह व्यङ्ग्यव्यञ्जकभावः किं तर्हि भाव्यभावकसम्बन्धः। काव्यं हि भावकम्। भाव्या रसादयः'। The दशरूप says that for the plot the poet should turn to the रामायण and the बृहत्कथा (I. 68). For want of space all the works quoted by धनिक are not set out here. Of special interest are his quotations from वाक्पतिराजदेव *alias* मुञ्ज (the verse प्रणयकुपितां being attributed once to वाक्पति॰ and again to मुञ्ज on IV. 58 and 60), पद्मगुप्त (under II. 40 'चित्रवर्तिन्यपि नृपे' नवसाहसाङ्क॰, VI. 42), the विद्धशालभञ्जिका I. 31 (सुधाबद्धग्रासैरुपवन॰ on IV. 53), कर्पूरमञ्जरी (रअणा चअणा I. 22. under दशरूप III. 15).

धनञ्जय, the author of कारिकाs, was son of विष्णु and a member of the *sabhā* of king Muñja; while धनिक also was the son of विष्णु and therefore seems to have been the brother of धनञ्जय. The कारिकाs were composed in the time of Muñja. In order to fix the date of the दशरूप we have to see when Munja alias Vākpatirāja flourished. In the paper of Buhler and Zachariae on the नवसाहसाङ्कचरित (translated in I. A. vol. XXXVI pp. 149-172) there is an account of Vākpatirāja alias Muñja (pp. 168-170). In I. A. vol. VI pp. 51-52 there is an inscription of वाक्पतिराज dated संवत् 1031 (974 A. D.) which records a grant of lands to Vasantācārya, son of धनिकपण्डित who hailed from अहिच्छत्र. In I. A. vol. XIV pp. 159-161 there is a copperplate grant of वाक्पतिराज in संवत् 1036 (979 A. D.) which records the gift of a village to the goddess Bhaṭṭeśvarī at Ujjayinī. It is stated that Muñja was defeated, captured and beheaded by Tailapa II (I. A. 36 at p. 170). अमितगति author of सुभाषितरत्नसन्दोह composed it in संवत् 1050 (993-94 A. D.) during the reign of king Muñja and as Tailapa II. died before or in *śake* 919 (997-98 A. D.), it follows that वाक्पतिराज alias मुञ्ज was killed between 993-4 to 997 (*ibid.*). Thus Muñja was on the throne of Malva from at least 974 A. D. Therefore, the दशरूप must have been composed between 974 to 996 A. D. Whether the धनिकपण्डित whose son वसन्ताचार्य was the donee in I. A. vol, VI. pp. 51-52 in 974 A. D. is to be identified with धनिक the commentator of दशरूप is a difficult question. Whatever may be the case, the दशरूप was composed in the last quarter of the 10th century. But it appears that the commentary was written a little later. सिन्धुराज alias नवसाहसाङ्क succeeded वाक्पतिराज (मुञ्ज) and the नवसाहसाङ्कचरित (a महाकाव्य) was composed by पद्मगुप्त (alias परिमल) at the command of सिन्धुराज.[1] For an account of सिन्धुराज, vide I. A. vol. 36 pp. 170-172. As धनिक quotes a verse from the नवसाहसाङ्कचरित the commentary must have been composed not earlier than 1000 A. D. and if we identify धनिक with the धनिकपण्डित of the I. A. vol. VI (as Dr. Ganguly in his History p. 285 does) it would have to be held that धनिक was a very old man (about 80 or so) when he wrote the अवलोक.

Vide Dr. D. C. Ganguly's 'History of the Paramāra dynasty' for वाक्पतिराज and सिन्धुराज (pp. 45-81). The verse दशरूप I. 6 (आनन्दनिस्यन्दिषु रूपकेषु व्युत्पत्तिमात्रं फलमल्पबुद्धिः । योपीतिहासादिवदाह साधुस्तस्मै नमः स्वादुपराङ्मुखाय) seems to ridicule भामह I. 2.

There is a commentary by नृसिंह on धनिक's अवलोक (vide Bulletin of London School of O. Studies, vol. IV. at p. 280). He has also commented on the सरस्वतीकण्ठाभरण of भोज. There is a very valuable commentary on the Daśarūpaka by Bahurūpamiśra, for an account of which vide Dr. Raghavan in J. O. R., Madras, vol. VIII. pp. 321-334 and Dr. Raghavan informs me that a post-graduate student has prepared for publication a critical edition of the Daśarūpaka with Bahurūpa's commentary.

Some scholars regarded धनञ्जय and धनिक as identical but that is wrong. Vide for a discussion of this problem Dr. De's H. S. P. vol. I. pp. 131-134. The दशरूप and its commentary अवलोक were probably composed before अभिनव० wrote the अभिनवभारती. The earliest datable work of अभिनवगुप्त is the क्रमस्तोत्र composed in 990 A. D. It has been shown above that the दशरूप was composed between 974-996 A. D. and the commentary of धनिक was composed not before 1000 A. D.

---

1. Vide नवसा० I. 9 नैते कवीन्द्राः कति काव्यबन्धे तदेष राज्ञा किमहं नियुक्तः। and the closing verse 'यच्चापलं किमपि मन्दधिया मयैवमाख्यत्रितं नरपते नवसाहसाङ्क । आज्ञैव हेतुरिह ते शयनीकृतोग्रराजन्यमौलिकुसुमा न कवित्वदर्पः ॥'.

Therefore, धनञ्जय and धनिक were contemporaries of अभिनवगुप्त. At all events the two works do not refer to each other, though they differ in several important respects. The most striking points of difference are: (1) The दशरूप does not regard शान्त as a proper *rasa* in dramaturgy and does not recognize शम as a स्थायिभाव of शान्त 'रत्युत्साहजुगुप्साः क्रोधो हासः स्मयो भयं शोकः। शममपि केचित्प्राहुः पुष्टिर्नाट्येषु नैतस्य॥' दशरूप IV. 35, on which धनिक after stating several views remarks 'सर्वथा नाटकादावभिनयात्मनि स्थायित्वमस्माभिः निषिध्यते। तस्य समस्तव्यापारप्रविलयरूपस्याभिनयायोगात्।'. अभिनवगुप्त on the other hand looks upon शान्त as the ninth and the most important rasa (अ. भा. vol. I. p. 340) (2) धनञ्जय as interpreted by धनिक (on दशरूप IV. 37-39) is opposed to the theory of the ध्वन्यालोक, holds that *rasa* is not suggested by *kāvya* and that it is experienced or enjoyed by the spectator or reader: 'अतो न रसादीनां काव्येन सह व्यङ्ग्यव्यञ्जकभावः। किं तर्हि भाव्यभावकसम्बन्धः। काव्यं हि भावकं भाव्या रसादयः। ते हि स्वतो भवन्त एव भावकेषु विशिष्टविभावादिमता काव्येन भाव्यन्ते।' धनिक on IV. 37. In this he follows भट्टनायक. Vide New I. A. vol. VI. pp. 272-282 (Dr. K. C. Pandey) for धनञ्जय and अभिनवगुप्त.

23 The व्यक्तिविवेक of राजानकमहिमभट्ट. This work has been published in the Trivandrum Series (1909) with a commentary that breaks off in the middle of the 2nd विमर्श. महिमभट्ट wrote the work for demolishing the theory of dhvani propounded by the ध्वन्यालोक. He controverts the position of the ध्वन्यालोक that there is a third function of words called व्यञ्जना (besides अभिधा and लक्षणा) and that the suggested sense is conveyed by this process. His own position is that words have a single power (अभिधा), that the suggested sense (प्रतीयमान) is conveyed by the expressed sense through the process of inference (अनुमान) and that word and sense are not व्यञ्जक. He does not dispute that the soul of poetry is *rasa* etc. (as the ध्वन्यालोक would say) "वाच्यस्तदनुमितो वा यत्रार्थोऽर्थान्तरं प्रकाशयति। सम्बन्धतः कुतश्चित्सा काव्यानुमितिरित्युक्ता॥ इति। एतच्चानुमानस्यैव लक्षणं नान्यस्य। यदुक्तं 'त्रिरूपलिङ्गाख्यानं परार्थानुमानम्' इति। केवलं संज्ञाभेदः। काव्यस्यात्मनि संज्ञिनि रसादिरूपे न कस्यचिद्विमतिः। संज्ञायां सा केवलमेषापि व्यक्त्ययोगतोऽस्य कुतः॥" (व्यक्ति० p. 22); the last verse is: 'प्राणभूता ध्वनेर्व्यक्तिरिति सैव विवेचिता। यस्त्वन्यत्तत्र विमितिः प्रायो नास्तीत्युपेक्षितम्।'. जयरथ on अलं. स. (p. 15) quotes the verse वाच्यस्तदनुमितो वा०, as from व्यक्तिविवेक. It is not to be supposed that महिमभट्ट was the first to advance this

theory. The ध्वन्यालोक anticipates the theory and tries to meet it (vide pp. 251-254) 'अस्त्यभिसन्धानावसरे व्यञ्जकत्वं शब्दानां गमकत्वं तच्च लिङ्गत्वमतश्च व्यङ्ग्यप्रतीतिर्लिङ्गिप्रतीतिरेवेति लिङ्गलिङ्गिभाव एव तेषां व्यङ्ग्यव्यञ्जकभावो नापरः कश्चित् ।...न पुनरयं परमार्थो यद् व्यञ्जकत्वं लिङ्गत्वमेव सर्वत्र व्यङ्ग्यप्रतीतिश्च लिङ्गिप्रतीतिरेवेति ।...काव्यविषये च व्यङ्ग्यप्रतीतीनां सत्यासत्यनिरूपणस्याप्रयोजकत्वमेवेति तत्र प्रमाणान्तरव्यापारपरीक्षोपहासायैव संपद्यते । तस्माल्लिङ्गिप्रतीतिरेव सर्वत्र व्यङ्ग्यप्रतीतिरिति न शक्यते वक्तुम्.' The व्यक्तिविवेक elaborates the arguments of those who relied upon भक्ति (गुणवृत्ति i. e. उपचार and लक्षणा) and regarded व्यञ्जकत्व as identical with it (vide ध्व० pp. 59, 67 तस्मादन्यो ध्वनिरन्या च गुणवृत्तिः). शङ्कुक also was अनुमितिवादिन् acc. to मल्लिनाथ's तरल pp. 85, 191-197. The view of महिमभट्ट is severely criticized by the अलं. स. (pp. 15-16), the एकावली and other later writers.[1] The एकावली says : 'यत्पुनरनुमानतो नातिरिच्यते ध्वनिरित्याचष्ट महिमभट्टस्तदपि पलालायमानम् (i. e. निःसारम्) । अनुमानस्य चाङ्गं व्याप्तिः' and then it is established that there can be no invariable concomitance between शब्दार्थौ, साधन or हेतु and ध्वनि (साध्य).

The व्यक्तिविवेक is divided into three विमर्शs. महिम० states his प्रतिज्ञा in the first verse 'अनुमानान्तर्भावं सर्वस्यैव ध्वनेः प्रकाशयितुम् । व्यक्तिविवेकं कुरुते प्रणम्य महिमा परां वाचम् ॥'. In the first विमर्श he starts by quoting the definition of ध्वनि ('यत्रार्थः शब्दो वा' ध्वनिकारिका I. 13), finds several faults with it and says that the definition, if properly considered, applies to अनुमान. The first objection is that the qualification उपसर्जनीकृतात्मत्व should not have been mentioned in connection with the word अर्थ. The second objection is that the word शब्द should not occur in the लक्षण, as a शब्द has no व्यापार except अभिधा. Then he finds fault with the word वा. He quarrels with the word विशेष in काव्यविशेष, as according to ध्वनिकार himself, all काव्य must have रस as its soul (ध्व. p. 31). He says that सूरिभिः (ध्व०. I. 13) in the definition is unnecessary. In all he finds ten faults 'अर्थस्यवि शिष्टत्वं शब्दः सविशेषणस्तदः पुंस्त्वम् । द्विवचनवाशब्दौ च व्यक्तिर्ध्वनिनाम काव्यवैशिष्ट्यम ॥ वचनं च कथनकर्तुः कथिता ध्वनिलक्षणीति दश दोषा; ।' (pp. 21-22). His

1. The early commentators such as माणिक्यचन्द्र and सोमेश्वर do not expressly refer the passage in the काव्यप्रकाश V (beginning with ननु वाच्यादसम्बद्धं तावन्न प्रतीयते pp. 252-254 of वामनाचार्य's ed.) to महिमभट्ट; but गोविन्दठक्कुर and other comparatively later ones do so). Therefore it is somewhat doubtful whether the Kāvya-prakāśa is actually criticizing the Vyaktiviveka.

own position is 'सर्वं एव हि शाब्दो व्यवहारः साध्यसाधनभावगर्भतया प्रायेणानुमानरूपोऽभ्युपगन्तव्यः, तस्य परप्रवृत्तिनिवृत्तिनिबन्धनत्वात् तयोश्च सम्प्रत्ययासम्प्रत्ययात्मनोरन्यथाकर्तुमशक्यत्वतः ।' (p. 3) and 'अर्थोपि द्विविधो वाच्योनुमेयश्च । तत्र शब्दव्यापारविषयो वाच्यः । स एव मुख्य उच्यते ।...तत एव तदनुमितादा लिङ्गभूतायदर्थान्तरमनुमीयते सोनुमेयः । स च त्रिविधः, वस्तुमात्रमलङ्कारा रसादयश्चेति । तत्राद्यौ वाच्यावपि सम्भवतः । अन्यस्त्वनुमेय एवेति वक्ष्यते' (p. 7). So it will be noticed that, according to his view, शब्द has only two senses वाच्य and अनुमेय; the लक्षणा of other writers will be included under अनुमान. He says that in such verses as 'सुवर्णपुष्पां पृथिवीं चिन्वन्ति पुरुषास्त्रयः (example of अविवक्षितवाच्यध्वनि in ध्व. p. 58), 'पत्युः शिरश्चन्द्रकलामनेन' (ध्व. p. 267), 'एवं वादिनि देवर्षौ (ध्व० p. 124), the suggested sense is really inferred 'अत्र हि सर्वत्र सुलभा विभूतयः शूरादीनामित्ययमर्थोऽनुमीयत इत्येतद्वितनिष्यते' (व्यक्ति० p, 9). As वाच्य sense and प्रतीयमान sense stand in the relation of लिङ्ग and लिङ्गिन् the process is अनुमान 'वाच्यप्रतीयमानयोर्वर्ण्यमाणक्रमेण लिङ्गलिङ्गिभावस्य समर्थनात् सर्वस्यैव ध्वनेरनुमानान्तर्भावः समन्वितो भवति तस्य च तदपेक्षया महाविषयत्वात्' (व्यक्ति० p. 12) and he relies upon ध्वनिकार's own words that the principal sense intended appears more charming when it is suggested (i. e. is left to be gathered from the words) 'साररूपो ह्यर्थः स्वशब्दानभिधेयत्वेन प्रकाशितः सुतरां शोभामावहति' (ध्व० p. 300). He says that in many of the instances of ध्वनि cited in the ध्वन्यालोक the ultimate व्यङ्ग्य sense is not suggested by the expressed sense but between the two one or more inferences intervene (as in 'वाणिअअ हत्थिदन्ता' ध्व० p. 157). In गौर्वाहीकः, the ultimate sense is arrived at by अनुमान; as the two cannot in reality be identical, one comes to the conclusion that they possess similar qualities 'तस्मादयं वाहीकादौ गवादिसाधर्म्यावगमः स तत्त्वारोपान्यथानुपपत्तिपरिकल्पितोऽनुमानस्यैव विषयः न शब्दव्यापारस्येति स्थितम्' (p. 24). The same reasoning the व्यक्ति० applies to गङ्गायां घोषः. It asserts, by using ध्वनिकारिकाs themselves with a slight turn of expression, that ध्वनि is identical with भक्ति 'भक्त्या बिभर्ति चैकत्वं रूपाभेदादयं ध्वनिः । न च नाव्याप्त्यतिव्याप्त्योरभावाल्लक्ष्यते तया ॥ सुवर्णपुष्पामित्यादौ न चाव्याप्तिः प्रसज्यते । यतः पदार्थवाक्यार्थभेदाद् भक्तिर्द्विधोदिता ॥ अतस्मिंस्तत्समारोपो भक्तेर्लक्षणमिष्यते । अर्थान्तरप्रतीत्यर्थः प्रकारः सोपि शस्यते ॥' (व्यक्ति० p. 26; compare ध्वनिका० I. 17 pp. 59-61). He opposes (pp. 27-28) the views of those who think that there is a single pervasive power of words which conveys what is called the वाच्य sense and the implied sense and who rely upon the instance of an arrow. He controverts the position of the वक्रोक्तिजीवित (कारिका I. 7-8 शब्दार्थौ सहितौ वक्र०) and says that if what is conveyed by the striking mode of speech adopted by the poet is different from the plain expressed sense, then वक्रोक्ति also is included like ध्वनि under अनुमान (p. 28). He denies that words have any other power than अभिधा 'नापि शब्दस्याभिधाव्यतिरेकेण व्यापारान्तरमुपपद्यते येनार्थान्तरं प्रत्याययेत्, व्यक्तेरनुपपत्तेः सम्बन्धान्तरस्य चासिद्धेः' (p. 29). He ridicules the ध्वनिकार for not giving a definition of *kāvya* in general and for dilating upon the two varieties of it, ध्वनि and गुणीभूतव्यङ्ग्य, in the absence of a general definition 'किं च काव्यस्य स्वरूपं व्युत्पादयितुकामेन मतिमता तल्लक्षणमेव सामान्येनाख्यातव्यम् ...यत्तु तदनाख्यायैव तयोः प्रधानेतरभावकल्पनेन प्रकारद्वयमुक्तं तदप्रयोजकमेव ।' (p. 32). He finds fault (p. 35) with the two terms अविवक्षितवाच्य and विवक्षितान्यपरवाच्य, says that examples of the former are like the examples of भक्ति (अग्निर्माणवकः) and that the term विवक्षितान्य° contains a contradiction (if a thing is विवक्षित i. e. प्रधान, it cannot be अन्यपर).

In the second विमर्श, he considers अनौचित्य (impropriety or incongruity). It is of two kinds, अर्थविषय and शब्दविषय. The अन्तरङ्ग अनौचित्य consists in the improper employment of विभावs, अनुभावs and व्यभिचारिभावs in the manifestation of रस and has been explained by former writer (such as आनन्द°). The बहिरङ्ग (formal) impropriety falls under five faults, विधेयाविमर्श, प्रक्रमभेद, क्रमभेद, पौनरुक्त्य and वाच्यावचन. The whole of the second विमर्श (pp. 37-112) is concerned with the explanation and exemplification of these five faults amidst several digressions. The first fault विधेयाविमर्श is treated of in pp. 37-58. He takes the verse 'संरम्भः करिकीटमेघशकलोद्देशेन सिंहस्य यः सर्वस्यैव स जातिमात्रनियतो हेवाकलेशः किल । इत्याशाद्विरदक्षयाम्बुदघटाबन्धेप्यसंरब्धवान् योसौ कुत्र चमत्कृतेरतिशयं यात्वम्बिकाकेसरी' cited in the वक्रोक्तिजीवित (I. p. 17) as a faultless piece of poetry and shows that it contains three cases of विधेयाविमर्श. The first is that the compound (नञ्समास) असंरब्धवान् is improper, the second is that the relative pronoun in योसौ has no corresponding demonstrative pronoun (सः) in the verse, and the third is that the compound अम्बिकाकेसरी is improper, as the word अम्बिका, being a member of a compound, is subordinate and the sense also is therefore subordinate and not at once perceived as principal (while Ambikā is really the principal object of adoration to the poet). He suggests (on p. 57) how the verse should be read to avoid these faults. His position on this point of विधेयाविमर्श is briefly put in these words 'तदिदमत्र तात्पर्यं यत् कथंचिदपि प्रधानतया विवक्षितं न तन्नियमेनेतरेण सह

समासमर्हतीति । इतरश्च विशेष्यमन्यद्वास्तु न तत्र नियमः ।' (p. 52). He gives numerous examples where this rule is followed or violated by the greatest poets and in cases of violation of the rule suggests how the verses should be composed. Examples where the rule is followed are 'सूर्याचन्द्रमसौ यस्य मातामहपितामहौ ।' (विक्रमो. IV. 38); उपपन्नं ननु शिवं सप्तस्वङ्गेषु यस्य मे । दैवीनां मानुषीणां च &c. (रघु. I. 60); अङ्गराज, सेनापते, द्रोणोपहासिन् etc. (वेणी॰ III.); 'रामस्य पाणिरसि दुर्वहगर्भखिन्न॰' (उत्तरराम. II). Opposite examples are 'आसमुद्रक्षितीशानाम्' (रघु. I. which should be आ समुद्रात्); पृथ्वि स्थिरा भव...देवः करोति हरकार्मुकमाततज्यम्' (बालरामा. I. 48 cited in साहित्यद॰ under अर्थान्तर॰), where the reading 'देवो धनुः पुररिपोर्विद-धात्यधिज्यम् would be better (as the most important point is that it is Hara's bow). प्रक्रमभेद is dealt with on pp. 58-66. 'प्रक्रमभेदोपि शब्दानौचित्यमेव । स हि यथाप्रक्रममेकरसप्रवृत्तायाः प्रतिपत्तिप्रतीतेस्खलनात् इव परिस्खलनखेददायी रसभङ्गाय पर्यवस्यति ।...स चायमनन्तप्रकारः सम्भवति प्रकृतिप्रत्ययपर्यायादीनां तद्विषयभावाभिमतानामानन्त्यात् (p. 58) and 'यथोद्देशं हि प्रतिनिर्देशोस्य विषयः (p. 59). Examples of the fault are 'ते हिमा...सिद्धं चास्मै निवेद्यार्थं तद्विसृष्टाः खमुद्ययुः ॥' (कुमार॰ 6. 24, अस्मै requires a similar pronoun in place of तत्); 'उदन्वच्छिन्ना भूः स च निधिरपां योजनशतं' भर्तृहरि (मिता भूः पत्यापां स च पतिरपां &c. whould be better); 'गाहन्तां महिषा' (शाकुन्तल II. 6, the active forms गाहन्तां, अभ्यस्यतु and लभतां require the same form in the third पाद and therefore 'कुर्वन्स्वस्तभियो वराहततयो मुस्ता॰' is better). Yet कर्तृप्रक्रमभेद (i. e. the use of the third person for the second or first) is not a fault, but a गुण e. g. 'अयं जनः प्रष्टुमनास्तपोधने' (for अहं in कुमार॰ V.). क्रमभेद is treated of in pp. 66-69. An example is 'कला च सा कान्तिमती कलावतस्त्वमस्य लोकस्य च नेत्रकौमुदी' (कुमार॰ V. 71, where the second च should be after त्वम्). पौनरुक्त्य is dealth with on pp. 69-84. शब्दपुनरुक्तत्व is not a fault if the senses of the words are different (as in हसति हसति स्वामिन्युच्चै रुदत्यपि रोदिति) where हसति is 3rd per. present as also loc. sing of pr. p. and even if the sense of the repeated word be the same there is no fault (but it is an ornament called लाटानुप्रास) if the purport is different (e. g. 'वक्षायन्ते नदीनां सितकुसुमधराः शक्रसङ्काशकाशाः काशाभा भान्ति तासां नवपुलिनगताः श्रीनदीहंस हंसाः ।' quoted in वामनीयवृत्ति IV. I. 10). Examples of (आर्थ) पौनरुक्त्य are 'बिसकिसलयच्छेदपाथेयवन्तः' (मेघ॰), 'त्वगुत्तरासङ्गवतीमधीतिनीम्' (कुमार॰ V. 16), where the affix वत् is superfluous as the same sense can be had by means of a बहुव्रीहि; one word इव after गेयस्य is said to be superfluous (p. 72) in वर्णैः कतिपयैरेव ग्रथितस्य स्वरैरिव । अनन्ता वाङ्मयस्याहो गेयस्येव विचित्रता ॥

and he proposes a better reading as गेयस्य वाङ्मयस्याहो अपर्यन्ता विचित्रता ॥; 'सहसा विदधीत न क्रियाँ' (किराता० II. 30) is वाक्यार्थविषयपौनरुक्त्य, as the second half contains the same proposition as 'अविवेकः परमापदां पदं'); 'यदा यदा हि धर्मस्य' (गीता 4. 7) also exemplifies पुनरुक्तत्व, as अभ्युत्थानमधर्मस्य is the same os धर्मस्य ग्लानिः. His position on the point of पुनरुक्त is 'न च सामर्थ्यसिद्धेर्थे शब्दप्रयोगमाद्रियन्ते सत्कवयः' (p. 77) and 'सा (प्रतीतिः) च यावद्भिरुपजायते तावतामेव प्रयोगो युक्तो नातिरिक्तानाम्' (p. 78), on which the commentary justly observes that poetry is not व्याकरणसूत्र ('न हीदं वाक्यं लक्षणशास्त्रं येन मात्रालाघवं चिन्त्यते । तत्रापि वा न नियमेन लाघवमाश्रितं महद्भिः' p. 44). Where there is a special sense intended there is no पौनरुक्त्य as in कुर्यां हरस्यापि पिनाकपाणेः' (कुमार० III. 10). The fifth fault वाच्यावचन is treated of in pp. 84-109. An example is 'कमलमनम्भसि कमले कुवलये etc' (here the 2nd word कमल should have been expressed by a सर्वनाम 'तस्मिंश्च कुवलये'). He says 'यत्रान्यस्यालङ्कारस्य विषयेऽलङ्कारान्तरनिबन्धः सोपि वाच्यावचनं दोषः' (p. 86) and instances 'भैरवाचार्यस्तु दूरादेव दृष्ट्वा राजानं शशिनमिव जलनिधिश्चचाल' (हर्षचरित III. para 20, here राजानं would also mean शशिनं and this is a proper subject for श्लेष and not उपमा as the poet has done). His position about श्लेष is 'तस्मादर्थान्तरव्यक्तिहेतौ कस्मिंश्च नासति । यः श्लेषबन्धनिर्बन्धः क्लेशायैव कवेरसौ ॥' (p. 89) and that the piling up of श्लेषs for their own sake and for no other purpose is वाच्यावचन. He finds this fault (on p 95) in the verse (सर्वैकशरणमक्षयमधीशं which is आनन्दवर्धन's own and cited in ध्व० p. 123). He finds this fault in many of the instances of शब्दशक्तिमूलध्वनि cited by the ध्वन्यालोक. He winds up by saying that even great poets did not perceive these faults and instances उमावृषाङ्कौ शरजन्मना यथा (रघु. 3. 23) as vitiated by पौनरुक्त्य, प्रक्रमभेद and अवाच्यवचन and there are faults in काव्यस्यात्मा ध्वनिरिति (the first ध्वनिकारिका). In the last there is प्रक्रमभेद as इति should be placed after आत्मा; there is also पौनरुक्त्य, as बुधैः and पूर्वं need not have been mentioned (as समाम्नात itself expresses past tense). Several more faults are found and then he proposes to read the कारिका differently (p. 112) to avoid most of these faults and then states his position briefly but firmly. व्यक्ति० p. 112 states how the first verse of ध्वन्यालोक should be read: तेन वरमयमत्र पाठः श्रेयानल्पदोषत्वात् । काव्यस्यात्मेत्यमलमतिभिर्यो ध्वनिर्नाम गीतस्तस्याभावं जगदुरपरे भक्तिरित्येवमन्ये । केचिद्वाचामविषय इति प्रस्फुरत्तत्त्वमन्तस्तेन ब्रूमः सहृदयजनप्रीतये तत्स्वरूपम् ॥. इति।...तस्मात्स्थितमेतद्यथा शब्दस्याभिधानमन्तरेण न व्यापारान्तरं सम्भवतीति। गमयन्त्यर्थमुखेन हि सुसिद्धवचनादयोऽपरानर्थान् । तेन ध्वनिलक्षमविधौ । शब्दग्रहणं विफलमेव ॥ इति सङ्ग्रहार्या ।

In the third विमर्श he takes about forty examples cited by the ध्वन्यालोक and shows that they are really cases of अनुमान. For example, the verse भम धम्मिअ (ध्व. p. 19) contains nothing but अनुमान 'केवलं योसौ भ्रमणविधौ हेतुभावेन दृप्तपञ्चाननव्यापारस्तत्रोपात्तः स एव विमृश्यमानः परम्परया धार्मिकस्य तन्निषेधे पर्यवस्यति तयोर्बाध्यबाधकभावेनावस्थानात्' (p. 113). As regards *rasas* he says that their apprehension also comes under अनुमान 'यापि विभावादिभ्यो रसादीनां प्रतीतिः सानुमान एवान्तर्भावमर्हति । विभावानुभावव्यभिचारिप्रतीतिर्हि रसादिप्रतीतेः साधनमिष्यते' (p. 119) and concludes by saying 'तदेवं सर्वस्यैव ध्वनेरनुमानान्तर्भावाभ्युपगमः श्रेयानिति ।' (p. 137).

महिमभट्ट was a Kashmirian as the title राजानक indicates. His father was श्रीधैर्य and he was the pupil of श्यामल, a great poet. क्षेमेन्द्र in his सुवृत्ततिलक and औचित्य॰ quotes verses from a श्यामल and so does सुभाषितावलि (No. 2292). A श्यामिलक is the author of a भाण called पादताडितक (vide श्र. भा. vol. I. p. 178), which has been edited by Mr. Kavi. महिमभट्ट wrote the work for his grandsons, who were the sons of भीम. The latter was probably his son-in-law 'आधातुं व्युत्पत्तिं नप्तॄणां क्षेमयोगभाजानाम् । सद्यः प्रथितनयानां भीमस्यामितगुणस्य तनयानाम् ॥'. 'The word क्षेमयोगभाजानाम् is probably double-meaning and क्षेम, योग and भाज (?) were probably the names of the grandsons. If they were his son's sons he could have used the word पौत्राणां without spoiling the metre. He wrote another work called तत्त्वोक्तिकोश on Poetics 'इत्यादि प्रतिभातत्त्वमस्माभिरुपपादितम् । शास्त्रे तत्त्वोक्तिकोशाख्ये इति नेह प्रपञ्चितम् ॥' (p. 108). His work is one of the masterpieces of the Alaṅkāra Literature and deserves to be saved from the unmerited oblivion in which it has fallen. His work contains brilliant arguments and exhibits great erudition, logical acumen, fastidious criticism and deep insight. Among later Alaṅkāra writers he found no follower and being pitted against the famous आनन्दवर्धन, he does not receive his due. Though he tries to disarm all critisism against his boldness in finding fault with great poets by saying 'स्वकृतिष्वयन्त्रितः कथमनुशिष्यादन्यमयमिति न वाच्यम् । वारयति भिषगपथ्यादितरान् स्वयमाचरन्नपि ॥' (p. 37), yet he seems to have been proud and self-confident e. g. p. 97 'अत्रोदाहरणप्रत्युदाहरणप्रतीत्योर्यदन्तरं तन्मतिमतामेवावभासते, अन्येषां तु शपथप्रत्ययमेव'; p. 109 'ता एता दोषजातयो महाकवीनामपि दुर्लक्षा इत्यवसीयन्ते'. He seems to have followed शङ्कुक in regarding even *rasa* as inferred. His views are quoted at length and severely criticized in the साहित्यदर्पण (under V. 4). *Vide* also एकावली

p. 32. He very often quotes the views of पाणिनि as thsoe of the आचार्य (p. 55), he enters upon a learned discussion about पर्युदास and प्रसज्यप्रतिषेध (on pp. 38-39), very often quotes others' views with the words तदुक्तं, यदाहुः (pp. 6, 7, 82, 121). Often he gives verses styled संग्रहश्लोक or संग्रहार्या,[1] which summarise the discussion that precedes them; *vide* (pp. 6, 14, 18, 22-23, 26, 32, 34-35, 56 etc.). They are in all 146, of which five are आर्याs. Some of these contain the पूर्वपक्ष and the उत्तरपक्ष on a topic (e. g. pp. 124-125). All these संग्रहश्लोकs seem to be his own. In other cases he gives verses that are called अन्तरश्लोक or अन्तरार्या (pp. 28, 39, 46. 54, 85-86, 97, 109, 110, 136). The संग्रहश्लोकs summarise a preceding discussion, while अन्तरश्लोकs seem to be verses that add to the discussion. In one case (on p. 97) the अन्तरश्लोकs seem to be not his own (viz. the two verses 'अनुवाद्यमनुक्त्वैव न विधेयमुदीरयेत्', 'विधेयोद्देश्यभावोय"). He cites कारिकाs dealing with Alaṅkāra topics which are styled neither संग्रहश्लोक nor अन्तरश्लोक (pp. 74, 76, 77, 108). They may be his own composition; He profusely quotes from the works of कालिदास, from भरत, भारवि, the ध्वन्यालोक. He also quotes उत्तरराम°, उद्भट, चन्द्रिका (Intro. verse 5), बालरामायण (pp. 40, 50), भट्टट, भामह, माघ, रत्नावलि, लोचन, वक्रोक्तिजीवित, वामन, वेणीसंहार, विद्धशालभञ्जिका (p. 85), हर्षचरित and refers to हृदयदर्पण (Intro. verse 4). As the views of the व्यक्तिविवेक are summarised by the अलङ्कारसर्वस्व it is earlier than about 1100 A. D. and as it quotes the बालरामायण and विद्धशालभञ्जिका and criticizes the वक्रोक्तिजीवित and the लोचन (p. 19, where a passage from लोचन on p. 38-39 is quoted) he is later than 1020 A. D. It is supposed by सरस्वतीतीर्थ, गोविन्दठक्कुर and other commentators of the काव्यप्रकाश that मम्मट in the 5th उल्लास combats the view of the व्यक्तिविवेक though he does not name the latter. The passage of the काव्यप्रकाश (V. p. 252 beginning with ननु वाच्यादसम्बद्धं तावन्न प्रतीयते quoted above on p. 219n closely resembles the व्यक्तिविवेक (pp. 15 and 111). Further,

1. On p. 98 there are three संग्रहश्लोकs of which the first (येन यस्याभिसम्बन्धो दूरस्थेनापि तेन सः। पदानामसमासानामानन्तर्यमकारणम् ॥) appears to be a quotation. The तन्त्रवार्तिक on जै. III. 1. 27 states 'दूरस्थत्वादशक्योऽस्योपसंहार इति चेद् न। यस्य येनार्थसम्बन्ध इति न्यायात्'। p. 744 (Ānan. ed.). The editor gives the whole verse as 'यस्य येनार्थसम्बन्धो दूरस्थेनापि तस्य सः। अर्थतो ह्यसमर्थानामानन्तर्यमकारणम् ॥'. The अभिनवभारती vol. I. p. 210 mentions this न्याय 'तथापि यस्य येनार्थसम्बन्ध इत्यर्थक्रम आदर्तव्यो न शाब्द इति'.

in the 7th उल्लास the काव्यप्रकाश seems to follow the व्यक्तिविवेक very closely in pointing out *doṣas*. If this is the case as appears very likely, then महिमभट्ट flourished between 1020 and 1050 A. D. Even supposing that the reference by मम्मट to व्यक्तिविवेक is doubtful, he must be deemed to have flourished between 1020 to 1100 A. D. गोपाल in his com. on काव्यप्र. has a verse on महिमभट्ट.[1]

The commentary as published is unfortunately incomplete (i. e. only on the first two विमर्श s). The author's name is not given. But he appears to have been the same as the author of the वृत्ति in the अलङ्कारसर्वस्व. On p. 44 the commentator says that he wrote हर्षचरितवार्तिक and on p. 32 that he wrote साहित्यमीमांसा and नाटकमीमांसा, while the author of the अलङ्कारसर्वस्ववृत्ति (p. 77) refers to them as his own works. जयरथ (p. 13) ascribes a commentary on the व्यक्तिविवेक to the author of the अलङ्कारसर्वस्व (वृत्ति) 'व्यक्तिविवेकविचारे हि मयैवैतद्दितत्य निर्णीतमिति भाव:'. The commentary is a very learned one, but his standpoint being different from that of the व्यक्तिविवेक (as he is a staunch follower of the ध्वन्यालोक) he frequently takes महिमभट्ट to task. On the third introductory verse (ध्वनिकारस्य वचोविवेचनं न:) he remarks 'यथास्थितपाठे तु ध्वनिकारस्येति वच:शब्दान्वितमिष्यमाणं प्राधान्याद्विवेचनशब्दान्वितं प्रतीयते । एतच्चास्य साहित्यविचारदुर्निरूपकस्य प्रमुख एव स्खलितमिति महान् प्रमाद:'. The commentator pulls him up very frequently for his pride e. g. p. 41 'तदेतदस्य विश्वमगणनीयं मन्यमानस्य स्वात्मन: सर्वोत्कर्षशालिताख्यापनमिति'; vide p. 44 also. But the commentator is prepared to give the author his due; *vide* pp. 15 and 16 (where he calls him महामति). The commentator gives संग्रहश्लोकs of his own (on p. 3, which contains a reply to a verse of the text and p. 12 which contains a reply to a verse on p. 14 of the text). Older commentators seem to be referred to in the word केचित् (on p. 32). On p. 20 he quotes the well-known verse 'हेम्नो (हेम्नां) भारशतानि' about हर्ष and बाण and another verse about भर्तृमेण्ठ. He refers to a work called बृहती (p. 45) which he contemplated writing. He quotes भट्टपाद, दण्डी (दाण्डो ग्रथ: p. 47), a वार्तिक of धर्मकीर्ति (p. 34), उद्भट, ध्वनिकार, वक्रोक्तिजीवित, वामन, परिमल (p. 53), सहृदय, सौगता: (in Sanskrit p. 41). He discusses readings of the text (pp. 33, 35, 51 about an interpolation). As he is identical with the author of the

1. 'रसामृतनदीमग्ने ध्वनिकारे महागुरौ । अनुमायापि महिमा काव्यगोष्ठीं न मुञ्चति ॥' (p. 3).

वृत्ति in the अलं. स. he flourished about 1135-1145 A.D. For the mention of a com. called तिलकरत्न on the व्यक्तिविवेक caused to be written by a king named चामुण्डसिंह on the banks of the river Sarayū, vide Prof. S. R. Bhandarkar's Report on the Search for mss. in Rājputana and Central India for 1904-5 and 1905-6, pp. 39-40 and 85-87.

24. The सरस्वतीकण्ठाभरण and शृङ्गारप्रकाश of भोज. The first work has been published several times (e.g. by Mr. Borooah, at Benares in 1887 and in the K. M. series 1934). In these pages reference is made to the K. M. edition of 1934 with the com. of रत्नेश्वर composed under king रामसिंह (on परिच्छेदs I-III) and of जगद्धर (on IV). The सरस्वतीकण्ठाभरण is a voluminous work, but it is more or less a compilation. It is divided into five परिच्छेदs. The first speaks of काव्यप्रयोजन, काव्यलक्षण, काव्यभेद, 16 *doṣas* of *pada*, 16 of वाक्य and 16 of वाक्यार्थ, the 24 गुणs of शब्द and the same number in वाक्यार्थ; in the second परि० the author treats of 24 शब्दालङ्कारs such as जाति, रीति, वृत्ति, छाया, मुद्रा, गुम्फना, शय्या, यमक, श्लेष, प्रहेलिका; in the third he defines and illustrates 24 अर्थालङ्कारs, जाति, विभावना, हेतु, अहेतु, सूक्ष्म, उत्तर, विरोध, सम्भव, अन्योन्य, परिवृत्ति, निदर्शन, भेद, समाहित, भ्रान्ति, वितर्क, मीलित, स्मृति, भाव, प्रत्यक्ष, अनुमान, उपमान, आगम, अर्थापत्ति and अभाव; in the fourth परि० he dwells upon 24 figures of both शब्द and अर्थ viz. उपमा, रूपक, साम्य, संशय, अपह्नुति, समाधि, समासोक्ति, उत्प्रेक्षा, अप्रस्तुतप्रशंसा, तुल्ययोगिता, लेश (the same as व्याजस्तुति), सहोक्ति, समुच्चय, आक्षेप, अर्थान्तरन्यास, विशेषोक्ति, परिकर, दीपक, क्रम, पर्याय, अतिशयोक्ति, श्लेष, भाविक, संसृष्टि; in the fifth he treats of *rasas*, *bhāvas*, heroes and heroines and their subdivisions and characteristics, the five *sandhis*, मुख, प्रतिमुख etc., the four *vṛttis* भारती etc. In all there are 643 कारिकाs, some of which are taken bodily from the काव्यादर्श, ध्वन्यालोक and other works. For example, कारिकाs V. 5-6 are the same as काव्यादर्श I. 21-22, कारिका V. 3 (शृङ्गारी चेत्कविः) occurs (in ध्व. p. 278). The first कारिका in the 5th परिच्छेद (रसोऽभिमानोऽहङ्कारः शृङ्गार इति गीयते) bears a close resemblance to certain verses of the अग्निपुराण, (338. 1-4) quoted above on p. 8. Similarly, सर. क. II. 2, 39, 75 are much the same as the अग्निपुराण 341. 18-19, 21 and 342. 10. Dr. De in J. R. A. S. 1923 pp. 537-549 holds that भोज borrows from the Agnipurāṇa. I demur to his conclusion. He is wrong as to the verse शृङ्गारी चेत् found both in सर. क. V. 3 and अग्निपु. 338. 11, as shown above on pp. 7-8.

The सरस्वतीकण्ठाभरण quotes profusely from Daṇḍin's

Kāvyādarśa, about two hundred verses being borrowed from the latter. भामह is very rarely drawn upon (e. g. the definition of प्रसाद from भामह II. 3 occurs as सर. क. I. 129). The सरस्वतीकण्ठाभरण quotes over 1500 examples from former poets and therefore is valuable for the chronology of Sanskrit literature. But, as much earlier works like the काव्यालङ्कारसूत्रवृत्ति of वामन, the ध्वन्यालोक and लोचन have become available to all, its importance is now much less than in the days of Aufrecht. It draws upon कालिदास and भवभूति at every step. Besides the above it quotes अभिधानमाला, कादम्बरी, कामशास्त्र, छलितराम, जैमिनि, तापसवत्सराज, ध्वन्यालोक, बाण, भट्टि, भरत, भामह, भारवि, महाभारत, रत्नावलि, राजशेखर, रामायण, रुद्रट, विक्रान्तशूद्रक (a drama), वेणीसंहार, शिशुपालवध. Though several verses are quoted in the सर. क. which also occur in the com. of Dhanika on दशरूप, it cannot be said with certainty that Bhoja took the verses from the Avaloka (as Dr. De does in H. S. P. vol. I. p. 145). It is quite possible that Bhoja took them from works to which both धनिक and he had access. But there is one verse which धनिक claims as his own (under दशरूप IV. 72 यथा च ममैव—लक्ष्मीपयोधरोत्सङ्गकुङ्कुमारुणितो हरेः । बलिरेष स येनास्य भिक्षापात्रीकृतः करः ॥), which is quoted in the सर. क. (IV. verse 98 p. 462 as an example of अन्योक्ति). In several respects his views are peculiar. There is a certain symmetrical arrangement in everything that भोज treats of, as in the sixteen *doṣas* and 24 figures of शब्द, अर्थ and उभय, the six varieties of रीति, वृत्ति, मुद्रा etc. He stands almost alone in regarding उपमा, आक्षेप, समासोक्ति, अपह्नुति and several others as figures of both *śabda* and *artha*. In this he probably follows the Agnipurāṇa (*vide* chap. 344) or some other prior work. He looks upon *rīti* as शब्दालङ्कार and enumerates six *rītis* वैदर्भी, पाञ्चाली, गौडीया, आवन्तिका, लाटीया and मागधी. He raised all the six *pramāṇas* of Jaimini to the status of figures of speech. Although, following old writers, he speaks of eight *rasas*, from the way in which he treats of them, it seems that he looked upon Śṛṅgāra as the only *rasa*. This accords well with what we are told by the Ekāvali (p. 98) that in the शृङ्गारप्रकाश composed by 'the king' a single *rasa* alone has been admitted (राजा तु शृङ्गारमेकमेव शृङ्गारप्रकाशे रसमुररीचकार, on which the तरल says 'भोजराजमतमाह राजा त्विति'). In the रत्नापण also (p. 221) कुमारस्वामी quotes the same view from the शृङ्गारप्रकाश 'शृङ्गार एक एव रस इति शृङ्गारप्रकाशकारः'. The भावप्रकाशन (pp. 12, 213, 219, 242, 245, 251) mentions the views of the शृङ्गार-

प्रकाश and भोज on matters of नाट्यशास्त्र. The मन्दारमरन्दचम्पू (5th बिन्दु p. 107) says 'अथ भोजनृपादीनां मतमत्र प्रकाश्यते । रसो वै स इति श्रुत्या रस एकः प्रकीर्तितः ॥ अतो रसः स्याच्छृङ्गार एक एवेतरे तु न । धर्मार्थकाममोक्षाख्यभेदेन स चतुर्विधः ॥'. Another very peculiar view is that he looks upon even *guṇa* and *rasa* as *alaṅkāras.* He quotes the words of दण्डी 'काव्यशोभाकरान् धर्मान्' (काव्यादर्श II. 1-2) and then remarks 'तत्र काव्यशोभाकरानित्यनेन श्लेषोपमावद्गुणरसभावतदाभासप्रशमादीनप्युपगृह्णाति' (5th परि॰p. 704). Some of these peculiar views have been referred to by comparatively early writers. The का. प्र. सङ्केत of माणिक्य॰ frequently refers to भोज and कण्ठाभरण (e. g. p. 300, 332, 338, 339). On p. 469 it says 'श्रीभोजेन जैमिन्युक्तषट्प्रमाणानि सम्भवश्चालङ्कारतयोक्तानि'. हेमचन्द्र (in काव्यानुशासनविवेक p. 295) says 'जातिगतिरीतिवृत्तिच्छाया...शय्यापीति वाक्ये...सम्भवप्रत्यक्षागमोपमानार्थापत्त्यभावलक्षणाश्चार्थालङ्कारा ये भोजराजेन प्रतिपादिताः' etc.; जयरथ (pp. 244-45) says that भोज treats of only संसृष्टि (and not of सङ्कर).

When I published the History of Alaṅkāra Literature in 1923 I had no access to the शृङ्गारप्रकाश of भोज. Since then Dr. Raghavan has published his studies in Śṛṅgārprakāśa (vol. I parts 1 and 2 pp. 1-542). The शृङ्गारप्रकाश is a very voluminous work, larger than any work on Sanskrit Poetics. No part of the original is yet published except three prakāśas (22nd, 23rd and 24th) that were published in 1926 under the auspices of His Holiness Śrī Yatirājasvāmin of Melcote, a short chapter XI in Dr. A. Sankaran's work on 'Theories of Rasa and Dhvani', and extracts from it are given by Dr. Raghavan on pp. 513-542 in part 2 of his vol. I. on 'Bhoja's Śṛṅgāraprakāśa.' In these circumstances I shall content myself by giving here a brief summary of the contents based on pp. 10-11 and 13-69 of Dr. Raghavan's work and the Sanskrit Summary given in the Introduction to the three प्रकाशs already printed.[1] In the mss. there are gaps in many places. The whole of chapter 26 is lost and so are portions of chapters 25 and 27 (Dr. Raghavan p. 3). The शृङ्गारप्रकाश deals with both Poetics and Dramaturgy just as the साहित्यदर्पण and the प्रतापरुद्रयशोभूषण do later on. The शृङ्गारप्रकाश defines kāvya as शब्दार्थौ सहितौ काव्यम् (which was the view of भामह I. 16) and propounds that शृङ्गार identified with अभिमान and अहङ्कार is the only *rasa* in the higher sense. The contents

1. Recently, prakāśa's 1-8 have been edited by Śri G. R. Joyser for International Academy of S. Research, Mysore, 1955.

of the 36 chapters (prakāśas) of the शृङ्गारप्रकाश are: 1 Definitions of *kāvya*, *śabda* and *artha*, 12 functions of each; 2 प्रातिपदिक, its divisions and sub-divisions; 3 meaning of पद and वाक्य and their varieties; 4 The 12 varieties of अर्थ viz. क्रिया, काल, कारक &c.; 5 The meaning of उपाधि; 6 meaning of विभक्ति; 7 the several powers of a word viz. अभिधा, विवक्षा, तात्पर्य &c.; 8 the powers of words in connection with other words viz. व्यपेक्षा, सामर्थ्य &c.; 9 avoidance of दोषs and securing of गुणs in काव्य; 10 अलङ्कारs of शब्द, अर्थ and उभय; 11 *Rasa*; 12 Dramas and their 64 features: 13 *Rati*, mokṣa-śṛṅgāra, dharmaśṛṅgāra, vṛttis, ritis; 14 हर्ष and 48 भावs; 15 the आलम्बनविभावs of रति; 16 उद्दीपनविभावs of रति; 17 अनुभावs; 18 delineation of धर्मशृङ्गार; 19 अर्थशृङ्गार; 20 कामशृङ्गार; 21 मोक्षशृङ्गार, नायक-नायिकाविभाग and नायकनायिकागुणाः; 22 अनुराग (ordinary love); 23 विप्रलम्भ and सम्भोगशृङ्गार; 24 विप्रलम्भ; 25 पूर्वानुरागविप्रलम्भ; 26 wanting; 27 अभियोगविधि; 28 दूतीविशेषदूतकर्मोपवर्णन; 29 दूतप्रेषण, सन्देशदान &c.; 30 मानस्वरूप; 31 प्रवासोपवर्णन; 32 करुणरसविनिर्णय; 33 सम्भोगस्वरूप; 34 प्रथमानुरागानन्तरसम्भोग; 35 मानप्रवासकरुणानन्तरसम्भोग; 36 चतसृणां सम्भोगावस्थानां वर्णनम्.

Not having read the शृङ्गारप्रकाश in the original (except the three printed prakāśas) I am not in a position to say how many verses it contains. But they must be several thousands. In the three printed prakāśas alone there are 467 quotations, out of which 251 are in Prakrit. In the 22nd prakāśa the Prakrit quotations are three-fourths of the total verses quoted therein. A good edition of the whole of the शृङ्गारप्रकाश is sure to be of immense importance for the chronology of literary works, for the Prakrits and for the correct readings of many verses and above all for the unique theory of one *rasa*.

Numerous works are ascribed to भोज. He seems to have written on धर्मशास्त्र and is quoted by the मिताक्षरा (generally as धारेश्वर) and the दायभाग. In the राजमार्तण्ड (a commentary on the योगसूत्र) we read 'शब्दानामनुशासनं विदधता पातञ्जले कुर्वता वृत्तिं राजमृगाङ्कसंज्ञकमपि व्यातन्वता वैद्यके। वाक्चेतोवपुषां मलः फणभृतां भर्त्रेव येनोद्धृतस्तस्य श्रीरणरङ्गमल्लनृपतेर्वाचो जयन्त्युज्ज्वलाः॥' (verse 4 Intro.). His astronomical work, the करण called राजमृगाङ्क, was probably composed in 1042-43. A. D. as it takes for its initial date the *śaka* year 964.[1] Dr. Bhandarkar ('Early History of the Deccan' p. 60)

1. शाको वेदतुनन्दोनो रविघ्नो माससंयुतः। अधो देवान्वितो दिस्थखिवेदप्तसंयोद्धृतः॥ राजमृगाङ्क (D. C. ms. No. 105 of 1873-74, verse 2).

came to the conclusion that भोज flourished in the first half of the 11th century. Dr. Buhler (Intro. to विक्रमाङ्कदेवचरित pp. 19-25) holds that भोज flourished somewhat later then that date. His reasons were principally two. The राजतर० (VII. 259) says 'स च भोजनरेन्द्रश्च दानोत्कर्षेण विश्रुतौ। सूरी तस्मिन्क्षणे तुल्यौ द्वावास्तां कविबान्धवौ ॥'. This passage according to Dr. Buhler refers to the period after 1062 A. D. when कलश had been crowned king of Kashmir. The second reason is that the सरस्वतीकण्ठाभरण quotes a verse from the चौरपञ्चाशिका which, according to Buhler, is the work of Bilhṇa. Buhler laid too much emphasis on the words तस्मिन् क्षणे in the राज०. Moreover, a gloss refers the word सः to अनन्त. Further, the authorship of the चौरपञ्चाशिका is not beyond the pale of discussion. According to the भोजप्रबन्ध, there was a prophecy that Bhoja would reign for 55 years. Bhoja's uncle Muñja was slain by Tailapa between 994 and 997 A. D. and Muñja was succeeded by his brother सिन्धुराज or सिन्धुल also styled नवसाहसाङ्क. An inscription of जयसिंह the successor of भोज dated संवत् 1112 (1055-56) A.D.) settles this dispute about the date of भोज (*vide* E. I. vol. III. pp. 46-50 Mandhata plate of जयसिंह of धारा.). It shows that भोज could not have been living beyond 1054 A. D. Bhoja had a very long reign. Other certain dates are those of his grants such as I. A. vol. VI. p. 53 (संवत् 1078). The नवसाहसाङ्कचरित was written by order of king सिन्धुराज and speaks of his invasions. So सिन्धुराज must have reigned for some years. Therefore it must be held that भोज came to the throne about 1005 and not earlier. The सरस्वतीकण्ठाभरण and शृङ्गारप्रकाश must have been composed between 1005-1054, probably towards the close of Bhoja's career i. e. between 1030-1050 A. D. The सरस्वती० contains a verse in praise of मुञ्ज 'सौजन्याम्बुनिधे...श्रीमन्मुञ्ज किमित्ययं जनमुपस्रष्टुं दृशा नार्हसि ॥' (1st परि० कारिका 71 p. 60). The Dhar प्रशस्ति speaks of अर्जुनवर्म (whose dates are 1211, 1213 and 1215 A. D.) as a descendant and *avatāra* of भोज (E. I. vol. VIII. p. 96). The story about Muñja's cruel treatment of Sindhurāja and Bhoja set forth in the Bhojaprabandha and in Merutunga's Prabandha-cintāmaṇi (pp. 32-36 of Tawney's translation) and the statement that Vākpatirāja was immediately succeeded by Bhoja must be treated as mere legendary trash in view of the fact that several inscriptions (such as the Banswara plate, E. I. XI. p. 181 dated संवत् 1076, the Betma plate dated the same year in E. I. vol. XVIII p. 320, Mandhata plate of जयसिंह of धारा dated संवत् 1112, the plate dated संवत् 1079 in I. H. Q. vol. 8 pp. 305-315 and the Ujjain plate dated *saṁvat* 1078, I. A. 6 p. 53 speak of Sindhurāja as succeeding Vākpatirāja with the usual titles of परमभट्टारक—महाराजाधिराज—परमेश्वर. Bhoja suffered from a long illness and died in the midst of wars with Bhīma, king of Gujarat and Kalacuri Karṇa, king of Tripurī (प्रबन्धचिन्तामणि; Tawney's tr. p. 4). The सुकृतसङ्कीर्तन (II. 16-18) narrates Bhoja's defeat by king Bhīma and the Vadnagar praśasti of कुमारपाल (1151 A. D.) in E. I. vol. I. p. 293 at p. 297 speaks of Dhārā being devastated by the cavalry of Bhīma. This unhappy state of भोज is referred to in the Nagpur Praśasti (E. I. vol. II. pp. 180-191 verse 32). Vide Dr. Ganguly's 'History of the Paramāra dynasty' pp. 82-122 for Bhoja and J. I. H. vol. VI. pp. 79-87 for the chronology of the Paramāras of Malva (Mr. Diskalkar). Bhoja was one of the most illustrious kings of ancient and medieval India. He was justly famed as a great patron of poets and literature, as a great builder of temples and as a literary man of no mean achievements. His has been a name to conjure with. The Udepur praśasti of the kings of Malva (E. I. vol. I. p. 222 at p. 235 very finely hits off Bhoja's achievements in a single verse 'साधितं विहितं दत्तं ज्ञातं तद्यन्न केनचित् । किमन्यत्कविराजस्य श्रीभोजस्य प्रशस्यते ॥' (he achieved, he laid down, he donated and knew what was not (achieved &c.) by anyone else; what further encomium can be passed on the glorious Bhoja, the poet-king (or prince of poets)? The राजत० quoted above speaks of him as कविबान्धव. The सर. कण्ठा. II. verse 239 (on कारिका 99) contains a reference to भोज himself 'जयजयजय श्रीमन्भोज प्रभाति विभावरी वदवदवद श्रव्यं). विद्वन्निदं ह्यवधीयते । शृणुशृणुशृणु स्वद्वत्सूर्योऽनु रज्यति मण्डलं नहिनहिनहि क्ष्मामार्तण्डः क्षणेन विरज्यते ॥'

Bhoja is credited with having composed 84 works on almost all sciences of medieval India by Ājada quoted by Dr. Raghavan in note 2 on p. 5. Dr. Raghavan appears to treat with ridicule those who hold that these works cannot all be the compositions of Bhoja and that several of them must have been composed by those whom Bhoja patronized (pp. 5-6 of Raghavan's vol. I). The analogy of Prof. Keith whom Dr. Raghavan cites has no application and carries no conviction. Prof. Keith was a university Professor not burdened with much teaching work nor with the cares of Government nor with constant wars as king Bhoja was. Besides, the number of all Keith's works is hardly one-fourth of what Bhoja is credited with and several of Keith's books are small manuals. Bhoja waged protracted wars with neighbouring kings viz. those of Karṇāṭa, of Gujarat and Cedi and also with Turuṣkas (vide Udepur Praśasti in E. I. vol. I. pp. 230-232). The विक्रमाङ्कदेवचरित I. 91 says 'प्रमारपृथ्वीपतिकीर्तिधारां धारामुदारां कवलीचकार' (vide Buhler's Intro. on p. 23). The last years of Bhoja were unhappy as stated above.

Some of Bhojas's works are very voluminous. He wrote सरस्वतीकण्ठाभरण (on Poetics and also on Grammar). His समराङ्गणसूत्रधार (about 7000 verses) has been published in the G. O.S. His work on grammar (सरस्वतीकण्ठाभरण) has been published in the Madras Un. S. Series (1937) and also in Tri. S. Series. In धर्मशास्त्र he appears to have composed several works such as भूपालकृत्यसमुच्चय (m. in कृत्यरत्नाकर pp. 499), भुजबलभीम (quoted in रघुनन्दन's तिथितत्त्व, संस्कारतत्त्व, श्राद्धतत्त्व), the राजमार्तण्ड (quoted in आह्निकतत्त्व). The present author edited from three mss. 286 verses (out of the 1462 of the Rājamārtaṇḍa) on tithis, vratas and utsavas in ABORI vol. XXXVI parts III-IV pp. 306-339. Vide the present author's paper on 'Bhoja and his works on Dharmaśāstra and astrology' in JOR (Madras) vol. 23 pp. 94-127. His युक्तिकल्पतरु has been published at Calcutta by Dr. N. N. Law (1917) and the तत्त्वप्रकाश in the Tri. S. Series. Besides the huge work called शृङ्गारप्रकाश he wrote a कथा called शृङ्गारमञ्जरी (vide Annals of Venkateshwar O. Institute, vol. II pp. 459-60 and Buhler's reference in E. I. vol. I. pp. 231-232). He wrote राजमार्तण्ड (on medicine in 418 verses published by Vaidya Jadawji, 1924) and a com. of the same name on the योगसूत्र of पतञ्जलि (published in Kashi S. Series with five other commentaries).

The commentary on the सर. क. is called रत्नदर्पण and was composed by महामहोपाध्याय रत्नेश्वर at the instance of king रामसिंहदेव (of Tirhut). He seems to have flourished in the 14th century. The commentary on the first three परिच्छेदs only has been published. The commentary is a learned one and quotes आनन्दवर्धन, the काव्यप्रकाश, चन्द्रगोमिन्, राजशेखर, रुद्रट, लोचनकार, शृङ्गारप्रकाश. He tells us that he wrote a commentary on the काव्यप्रकाश. On the verse 'हा तो जोज्जलदेउ नैव मदनः साक्षादयं भूतले' (1st परि०

कारिका 118, pp. 110-111) the commentator remarks 'हा तो' are Marathi words meaning 'अयं सः'. There are other commentators who are passed over here.

25 औचित्यविचारचर्चा and कविकण्ठाभरण of क्षेमेन्द्र. क्षेमेन्द्र, a Kashmirian, was a voluminous writer and wrote on a variety of subjects. He wrote the भारतमञ्जरी, the बृहत्कथामञ्जरी and about forty other works. The राजत० (I. 13) refers to his नृपावलि (राजावलि) which has not yet been found. His contribution to Poetics was meagre and he did not exert any appreciable influence over the Alaṅkāraśāstra. In his सुवृत्ततिलक (divided into three विन्यास's) he makes very interesting remarks upon metres, gives directions as to their employment and points out in what metre certain poets excelled e. g. अभिनन्द in अनुष्टुभ्, पाणिनि in उपजाति, भारवि in वंशस्थ, कालिदास in मन्दाक्रान्ता, रत्नाकर in वसन्ततिलक, भवभूति in शिखरिणी, राजशेखर in शार्दूलविक्रीडित. His औचित्यविचारचर्चा (K. M. ed. of 1929) contains *kārikās* with his own *vṛtti* and illustrations taken from numerous authors and works (including his own). His position is that औचित्य (appropriateness) is the essence of *rasa*, 'औचित्यस्य चमत्कारकारिणश्चारुचर्वणे। रसजीवितभूतस्य विचारं कुरुतेऽधुना' (कारिका 3) and defines औचित्य as 'उचितं प्राहुराचार्याः सदृशं किल यस्य यत्। उचितस्य च यो भावस्तदौचित्यं प्रचक्षते॥' (7). Then he illustrates औचित्य in connection with पद, वाक्य, प्रबन्धार्थ, गुण (such as ओजः), अलङ्कार, रस, क्रिया, कारक, लिङ्ग, वचन, उपसर्ग, काल, देश and several other matters. His method is to give an appropriate example on each topic and also to cite an inappropriate one. In the औचित्य० he simply developes what the ध्वन्यालोक had laid down (in III. 7-14 and pp. 174-186) and which the ध्व० had summarised in the verse 'अनौचित्यादृते नान्यद्रसभङ्गस्य कारणम्। प्रसिद्धौचित्यबन्धस्तु रसस्योपनिषत्परा॥' (p. 180).[1] For want of space the numerous authors and works quoted by him are not given here. He quotes परिमल, the कुन्तेश्वरदौत्य of कालिदास, गौडकुम्भकार, भट्टमल्लट, भट्टतौत and his own *guru* भट्टगङ्गक.[2] In the

1. In the वक्रोक्तिजीवित also it is stated (in कारिकाs I. 37 and 38, pp. 52-54 of Dr. De's ed.) that औचित्य is a quality common to all the three *mārgas* mentioned by it. यत्र वक्तुः प्रमातुर्वा वाच्यं शोभातिशायिना। आच्छाद्यते स्वभावेन तदप्यौचित्यमुच्यते॥ I. 31. रघुवंश 5. 15 and किरातार्जुनीय 8. 6 are cited as examples of this verse.

2. There is a com. called सहृदयतोषिणी on the औचित्यविचारचर्चा published at Madras in 1906. Vide Dr. De's H. S. P. vol.

औचित्य० he refers to a work of his own called कविकर्णिकाकाव्यालङ्कार which is not yet found. Whether this is a different work from the कविकण्ठाभरण is doubtful. His कविकण्ठाभरण (K. M. ed. of 1937) is divided into five *sandhis* and has 55 *kārikās*, the subjects of which are respectively 'तत्राकवेः कवित्वाप्तिः शिक्षा प्राप्तगिरः कवेः । चमत्कृतिश्च शिक्षाप्तौ गुणदोषोद्गतिस्ततः ॥ पश्चात्परिचयप्राप्तिरित्येते पञ्च सन्धयः ।' (I. 3-4). He divides pupils into three kinds and poets into छायोपजीवी, पदकोपजीवी, पादोपजीवी, सकलोपजीवी, भुवनोपजीव्य, and gives certain directions to poets about the गुणs and *doṣas* of काव्य and the study of व्याकरण, तर्क, नाट्य. In कविकण्ठाभरण III. 2 he speaks of ten kinds of चमत्कार (strikingness, रसास्वाद, विस्मय or वक्रत्व). His own works referred to in the two books are अवसरसार, अमृततरङ्ग (काव्य), कनकजानकी, कविकर्णिका, चतुर्वर्गसंग्रह, चित्रभारतनाटक, देशोपदेश, नीतिलता, पद्यकादम्बरी, बौद्धावदानकल्पलता, मुक्तावलीकाव्य, मुनिमतमीमांसा, ललितरत्नमाला, लावण्यवती (काव्य), वात्स्यायनसूत्रसार, विनयवल्ली, शशिवंश. In the सुवृत्ततिलक he quotes a verse of कलश and in the कविकण्ठा० (5th सन्धि) the ललिताभिधानमहाकाव्य of his pupil भट्टोदयसिंह and quotes a verse of his pupil राजपुत्रलक्ष्मणादित्य. क्षेमेन्द्र was the son of प्रकाशेन्द्र and grandson of सिन्धु. His family was very rich and his father's benefactions were on a lavish scale.[1] He wrote many of his works at the instance of one रामयशस्. In the बृहत्कथामञ्जरी he tells us that he learnt साहित्य at the feet of अभिनवगुप्त 'श्रुत्वाभिनवगुप्ताख्यात् साहित्यं बोधवारिधेः ।'. He was originally a शैव but was converted to the वैष्णव faith in later life by सोमाचार्य. He calls himself व्यासदास in almost all works. He wrote his समयमातृका in 25th लौकिककाल *i. e.* 1050 A. D. and the दशावतारचरित in 41 लौकिक era (i. e. 4141) when कलश was ruling (*i. e.* 1066 A. D.). The औचित्य० and the कवि० were composed by him in the time of king अनन्त ('तस्य श्रीमदनन्तराजनृपतेः काले किलायं कृतः' औचित्य० and 'राज्ये श्रीमदनन्तराजनृपतेः काव्योदयोयं कृतः' कवि०. King Ananta ruled in Kashmir from 1028 to 1063 A. D. and crowned his son कलश in 1063.

I. p. 142. Vide Dr. Raghavan on the 'History of aucitya', J. O. R., Madras, vol. VI, pp. 111-134 and 135-162.

1. At the end of the दशावतारचरित verse 2 is : 'कश्मीरेषु बभूव सिन्धुरधिकः सिन्धोश्च निम्नाशयः प्राप्तस्तस्य गुणप्रकर्षयशसः पुत्रः प्रकाशेन्द्रताम् । विप्रेन्द्रप्रतिपादितान्नदानधनभूगोसहस्रकृष्णाजिनैः प्रख्यातातिशयस्य तस्य तनयः क्षेमेन्द्रनामाभवत् ॥'. At the end of the भारतमञ्जरी (K. M. ed. pp. 849-850 verses 3-5) क्षेमेन्द्र specifies some of the great benefactions of his father and a few ones at the end of the औचित्यविचारचर्चा.

अनन्त died in 1081 A. D. at the age of 61. The words of क्षेमेन्द्र lead one to suppose that the two works were written while अनन्त was actually reigning. Therefore, क्षेमेन्द्र wrote the two works before 1063 A. D. and his literary activity lay in the 2nd and 3rd quarters of the 11th century. As he was a pupil of अभिनव० whose literary activity lay between 980-1020, क्षेमेन्द्र must have been born about 990 A. D. and died sometime after 1066 A. D. For further information about his works *vide* Buhler's Kashmir Report (pp. 45-48), JBBRAS vol. 16 (extra No. pp. 5-9) and vol. 16 pp. 167-179 (Peterson on the औचित्य०), Dr. De in H. S. P. vol. I pp. 142-143, Dr. Suryakānta's exhaustive paper in Poona Orientalist vol. 17 for 1952 pp. 1. 220 for Kṣemendra's life and works and translation of his औचित्यविचारचर्चा, कविकण्ठाभरण, and सुवृत्ततिलक. .

26 The काव्यप्रकाश of मम्मट. This far-famed work has been published several times. Here it is the edition with the बालबोधिनी of वामनाचार्य (5th edition of 1933) that is referred to; it was originally published in the B. S. series. In the *alaṅkāra* literature the काव्यप्रकाश occupies a unique position. It sums up in itself all the activities that had been going on for centuries in the field of Poetics; while it becomes itself a fountain-head from which fresh streams of doctrines issue forth. Like the शारीरकभाष्य in Vedānta or the महाभाष्य in grammar, the काव्यप्रकाश becomes a starting point for future exegesis and expansion. The great merit of the work is that it combines fulness of treatment with conciseness. In 143 *kārikās* (often called *sūtras*[1]) the whole field of Poetics is traversed. The work is divided into ten *ullāsas* and comprises as usual three parts, the कारिकाs, the वृत्ति and the examples, all of which are taken from other works (except probably a few simple examples under उपमा, व्यतिरेक &c.). The contents of the work are:—I, the purpose of काव्य, काव्यहेतु, the definition of काव्य, its sub-divisions into उत्तम (where the suggested sense far excels the वाच्य sense), मध्यम and अधम; II. word is वाचक, लाक्षणिक and व्यञ्जक and sense also is वाच्य, लक्ष्य and व्यङ्ग्य; some maintain a fourth sense called तात्पर्यार्थ; explanation of these terms and the sub-divisions of

1. The संप्रदायप्रकाशिनी of श्रीविद्याचक्रवर्तिन् (Tri. ed.) speaks of the कारिकाs as सूत्रs (vide pp. 7, 81); चण्डीदास also in his com. calls the 'कारिकाकार सूत्रकृत्' (p. 88).

लक्षणा and व्यञ्जना; III. how all kinds of senses may be व्यञ्जक and how the function in such cases is व्यञ्जना; IV. the two varieties of ध्वनि viz. अविवक्षितवाच्य and विवक्षितान्यपरवाच्य and their sub-divisions, the nature of *rasa*, of स्थायिभावs, of विभावs and व्यभिचारिभावs; various theories about *rasa*; V. the second variety of काव्य viz. गुणीभूतव्यङ्ग्य and its eight sub-divisions: VI. third kind of काव्य called चित्र (or अधम) and its two varieties, शब्दचित्र and अर्थचित्र; VII. the *doṣas* of पद, वाक्य, अर्थ and of *rasa* and how in some cases what is generally a *doṣa* may lend charm; VIII. distinction between *guṇas* and *alaṅkāras* and the position that there are only three *guṇas* माधुर्य, ओजस् and प्रसाद; definitions of these; other *guṇas* are included under these or are really the absence of *doṣas*; the combination of certain letters is conducive to these *guṇas*; IX. the figures of *śabda*, viz. वक्रोक्ति (two varieties, श्लेष and काकु), अनुप्रास (छेकानु० and वृत्त्यनु०) and the three वृत्तिs (उपनागरिका, परुषा and कोमला which were designated वैदर्भी, गौडी and पाञ्चाली *ritis* by Vāmana and others), लाटानुप्रास, यमक (with its numerous varieties), श्लेष, चित्र (its varieties such as खड्गबन्ध, मुरजबन्ध), पुनरुक्तवदाभास; X. sixty-one अलङ्कारs of sense; the *doṣas* of अलङ्कार are included under the *doṣas* treated in the 7th उल्लास.

It will have been noticed how मम्मट deals with all topics of Poetics except dramaturgy. He casts his net over a wide area. He quotes about 620 verses from other authors to illustrate his teachings. For want of space it is not possible to set out in detail all the authors and works from which quotations are taken. The following are mentioned by name:—आचार्याभिनवगुप्त, कालिदास, कामशास्त्र, उद्भट, ध्वनिकार or ध्वनिकृत्, बाण, भट्टनायक, भरत, महाभाष्यकार, मयूर, रुद्रट, लोल्लट, वाक्यपदीय, शङ्कुक, श्रीहर्ष. Among those which are not named are the following:—the works of कालिदास and भवभूति, अमरुशतक, कर्पूरमञ्जरी, कुट्टनीमत, चण्डीशतक, नवसाहसाङ्कचरित, नागानन्द, बालरामायण, भट्टि, भर्तृहरि, भल्लट, भामह, भास, माघ, रत्नावली, राघवानन्द, विज्जका, विद्धशालभञ्जिका, विष्णुपुराण, वेणीसंहार, हयग्रीववध, हरविजय. Thought much of मम्मट's treatment is based upon the works of his predecessors, such as the ध्वन्यालोक, उद्भट, भामह, रुद्रट (from whose work about 30 verses are quoted), वामन, अभिनवगुप्त, yet he is a man of independent views and his respect for these ancient authorities does not preclude him from criticizing them when occasion demands. For example, he strongly criticizes (in 9th उल्लास pp. 516-527) भट्टोद्भट for the latter's view about

श्लेष. He finds fault (towards the end of the 7th उल्लास, pp. 448-449) with the remarks of the ध्वन्यालोक on the verse सत्यं मनोरमा रामाः सत्यं रम्या विभूतयः। किं तु मत्ताङ्गनापाङ्गभङ्गलोलं हि जीवितम्॥ (ध्व० p. 224), which say that the first half begins with the विभावs of शृङ्गार and the latter half culminates in शान्त and yet there is no विरोध, as this mode of treatment is adopted for inducing the instructed to be ready to receive instruction and for lending charm to the verse. Though मम्मट borrows several verses from रुद्रट, he differs from the latter on several occasions. For example, मम्मट's remark on समुच्चय (धुनोति चासिं तनुते च कीर्तिमित्यादेः, कृपाणपाणिश्च भवान्रणक्षितौ। ससाधुवादाश्च सुराः सुरालये इत्यादेश्च दर्शनात्, 'व्यधिकरणे' इति, 'एकस्मिन् देशे' इति च न वाच्यम्। p. 691) are directed against रुद्रट's words 'व्यधिकरणे वा यस्मिन्गुणक्रिये' &c. (VII. 27); similarly, his words on कारणमाला ('हेतुमता सह हेतोरभिधानमभेदतो हेतुः' इति हेत्वलङ्कारो न लक्षितः...'अविरलकमलविकासः...कालः' इत्यत्र काव्यरूपतां कोमलानुप्रासमहिम्नैव समाम्नासिषुर्न पुनर्हेत्वलङ्कारकल्पनया pp. 706-707) refer to रुद्रट's definition of हेतु and his example thereof (VII. 82-83). So also the *dictum* under अनुमान 'साध्यसाधनयोः पौर्वापर्यविकल्पे न किञ्चिद्वैचित्र्यमिति न तथा दर्शितम्' (p. 698) has in view रुद्रट VII. 56. He criticizes (in the 8th उल्लास pp. 471-72) वामन's distinction between *guṇas* and *alaṅkāras* (काव्यशोभायाः कर्तारो धर्मा गुणाः। तदतिशयहेतवस्त्वलङ्काराः। काव्या. सू. III. I. 1-2). Similarly, he finds fault with वामन's explanation of ओजः as प्रौढि 'पदार्थे वाक्यरचनं वाक्यार्थे च पदाभिधा। प्रौढिर्व्याससमासौ च साभिप्रायत्वमस्य च॥ इति या प्रौढिरोज इत्युक्तं तद्वैचित्र्यमात्रं न गुणः, तदभावेपि काव्यव्यवहारप्रवृत्तेः' (VIII उल्लास pp. 480-81). वामन says: 'अर्थस्य प्रौढिरोजः' (काव्या. सू. III. 2. 2) and quotes the verse पदार्थे० in the वृत्ति. Thought he quotes three verses from भामह (I. 13-15) in the sixth उल्लास and the famous verse of भामह (II. 85 सैषा सर्वैव वक्रोक्तिरनयार्थो विभाव्यते।...कोलङ्कारोनया विना॥) in the 10th उल्लास (under विशेष p. 744), yet he appears to find fault with भामह (श्रव्यं नातिसमस्तार्थं काव्यं मधुरमिष्यते। II. 3) when he says (8th उल्लास p. 474) 'आह्लादकत्वं माधुर्यं शृङ्गारे द्रुतिकारणम्।...श्रव्यत्वं पुनरोजःप्रसादयोरपि'. मम्मट does not scruple to find fault with the greatest of poets, e. g. he says that in मृदुपवनविभिन्नो (विक्रमो० 4. 22) there is the fault अमङ्गलाश्लील, in दिवाकराद्रक्षति (कुमार० I. 12) there is अनुचितार्थता, in अतिथिं नाम (रघु 17. 1) there is भग्नप्रक्रमदोष, in गाहन्तां महिषा (शाकुन्तल II. 6) also there is भग्नप्रक्रम, in वपुर्विरूपाक्षमलक्ष्यजन्मता (कुमार० V. 72) there is अविमृष्टविधेयांशदोष.

Several later commentators affirm that the *kārikās* are the work of भरत and that मम्मट only commented on them (i. e.

he is only a वृत्तिकार). The साहित्यकौमुदी of विद्याभूषण says 'सूत्राणां भरतमुनीशवर्णितानां वृत्तीनां मितवपुषां कृतौ ममास्याम् ।' (2nd Intro. verse) and at the end we have 'मम्मटाद्युक्तिमाश्रित्य मितां साहित्यकौमुदीम् । वृत्तिं भरतसूत्राणां श्रीविद्याभूषणो व्यधात् ॥'. Vide Peterson's 2nd Report pp. 10-11. Similarly, महेश्वर (Jivanand's edition p. 3) says that भरत is the author of the कारिकाs in the काव्यप्रकाश. जयराम in his तिलक first puts forward the view that भरत is the author of the कारिकाs and then comes to the conclusion that the author of the कारिकाs and of the वृत्ति is the same (vide Peterson's 2nd Report, p. 107). The main grounds on which this theory is based are three; (I) some of the कारिकाs are identical with verses of the नाट्यशास्त्र e.g. the कारिकाs 'शृङ्गारहास्य...स्मृताः', 'रतिर्हासश्च', 'निर्वेदग्लानि...नामतः' (in the 4th उल्लास) are नाट्यशास्त्र VI. 15, 17, 18-21-VI. 19-22 of GOS. ed. vol. I; (II) the वृत्ति on the first कारिका is 'ग्रन्थारम्भे विघ्नविघाताय समुचितेष्टदेवतां ग्रन्थकृत्परामृशति. This use of the third person shows that the कारिकाकार is a different person from the author of the वृत्ति. (III) There is a difference of opinion between the कारिका 'समस्तवस्तुविषयं श्रौता आरोपिता यदा' (10th उल्लास) and the वृत्ति thereon 'बहुवचनमविवक्षितम्. If the कारिकाs had been the work of the वृत्तिकार, it is argued, the कारिकाकार would have said 'श्रौतावारोपितौ यदि'. All these arguments will be found on ex ımination to be extremely weak. Only a few out of the 143 कारिकाs are found in the नाट्यशास्त्र [1] मम्मट probably incorporated the कारिकाs on *rasas* etc. because he could not convey the ideas more oncisely and because by his time भरत's work had attained the premier place in the matter of *rasa*. It will be found that there are other *kārikās* which are adapted almost *verbatim* from other works e. g. the कारिका 'कर्णावतंसादिपदे कर्णादिध्वनिनिर्मितिः । संनिधानादिबोधार्थम्' (VII उल्लास p. 406) is an adaptation of वामन's *sūtra* 'कर्णावतंसश्रवणकुण्डलशिरःशेखरेषु कर्णादिनिर्देशः सन्निधेः' (II. 2. 14) and the verse 'कर्णावतंसादिपदे॰' is quoted on वामन II. 1, 19; कारिका 'ये रसस्याङ्गिनो धर्माः' etc. and उपकुर्वन्ति तं सन्तं येऽङ्गद्वारेण जातुचित्' (8th उल्लास, pp. 462, 464) closely follow ध्वनिकारिका (II. 7) 'तमर्थमवलम्बन्ते येऽङ्गिनं ते गुणाः स्मृताः । अङ्गाश्रितास्त्वलङ्कारा मन्तव्याः कटकादिवत् ॥'. As regards the use of the third person in

1. जयराम in his तिलक remarks 'कारिकाणां भरतसंहितायां कासांचिद्दर्शनं न दोषाय प्रामाण्यज्ञापनार्थं कचित्तासां लिखनात् ।' (Peterson's 2nd Report p. 107). About ग्रन्थकृत् he says: ग्रन्थकृदित्यादिना निर्देशस्तु धीरोदात्तत्वस्य सङ्गोपनाय.

पराभ्युपगति, the truth lies exactly the other way. Ancient writers regarded it as too dogmatic to express their opinions in the first person. Vide notes to the साहित्यदर्पण on आचक्षते (p. 1), where मेधातिथि and कुल्लूक are quoted. There is really no divergence between the कारिका 'समस्त...यदा' and the वृत्ति. The point of the वृत्ति has been missed altogether. In the *kārikā* the plural is employed to lay down a general proposition. In a समस्तवस्तुविषयरूपक, there will generally be *many* आरोप्यमाणs; and hence the plural आरोपिताः has been used. The वृत्ति also begins the explanation in the same way 'आरोपविषया इवारोप्यमाणा यदा &c'. In the words बहु...चित्तम् the वृत्ति calls attention to a special case, which may perhaps be overlooked. Even if the आरोप्यमाणs be two there may be समस्तवस्तुविषयरूपक. This case is not clearly referred to by the *kārikā* (which uses the plural) and is therefore brought out in the वृत्ति.

There are positive grounds for asserting that the कारिकाs and वृत्ति are both the work of मम्मट. (I) मम्मट nowhere conveys in an unmistakable manner that he is commenting on another's work. There is no separate मङ्गल in the वृत्ति. If the वृत्ति had been composed by one person and the कारिकाs by another, there should have been a separate मङ्गल in the वृत्ति as there is one at the beginning of the कारिकाs. (II) Upon the कारिकाs कारणान्यथ कार्याणि, &c. (in the 4th उल्लास) the वृत्ति says 'तदुक्तं भरतेन विभावानुभाव०'. If भरत had been the author of the कारिकाs in the काव्यप्रकाश, the वृत्तिकार would more naturally have said 'तदुक्तमनेनैवान्यत्र' or 'तदुक्तं कारिकाकृतान्यत्र etc.'. (III) We have the कारिका 'साङ्गमेतन्निरङ्गं तु शुद्धं माला तु पूर्ववत्'. Here the कारिका refers to मालारूपक and adds that it is similar to the former (i. e. मालोपमा). But मालोपमा has been spoken of only in the वृत्ति. Therefore, this clearly indicates that the कारिकाs and the वृत्ति are the compositions of the same hand.[1] (IV) None of the early commenta-

1. On माला तु पूर्ववत् a great deal has been written. Vide I. A. vol. 47 p. 23 (Zimmermann), Annals of B. O. R. I. vol. 6. pp. 50-54 (Prof. Divekar), Annals of B. O. R. I. vol. 8 pp. 419-424 (Dr. De replies to Prof. Divekar); Z.D.M.G. 67 p. 35 (Nobel). Dr. Divekar's objection is that माला तु पूर्ववत् in the कारिका cannot refer to मालोपमा mentioned in the वृत्ति, because a good many other kārikās have intervened and he takes पूर्ववत् to refer to साङ्ग. But there are serious objections to

tors such as माणिक्यचन्द्र, जयन्त, सरस्वतीतीर्थ, सोमेश्वर makes any distinction between the author of the कारिकाs and of the वृत्ति. On the other hand, there are both early and later writers who distinctly ascribe the कारिकाs and वृत्ति to the same author. हेमचन्द्र says (in com. on काव्यानुशासन p. 4) 'एवमानन्दयशश्चतुर्वर्गोपायव्युत्पत्तीनां काव्यप्रयोजनतामसाधारणीं प्रतिपाद्य यत्कैश्चित श्रीहर्षादेर्धावकादीनामिव धनं...नर्थनिवारणं प्रयोजनत्रयमुपन्यस्तम्'. It will be noticed that this passage ascribes the कारिका 'काव्यं यशसे etc.' and the वृत्ति thereon to the same person (viz. मम्मट). Similarly, हेमचन्द्र (com. on काव्यानुशासन p. 109) says 'यथाह मम्मटः-अगूढमपरस्याङ्ग etc. (which is उल्लास V. 1-2). Here हेमचन्द्र (who wrote his काव्यानु॰ within about 50 years of मम्मट) distinctly ascribes the कारिकाs to मम्मट. जयरथ applies the term काव्यप्रकाशकृत् without distinction to the author of the कारिकाs and of the वृत्ति (vide pp. 102, 137, 150, 199). The प्रतापरुद्रीय speaks of the कारिकाs as काव्यप्रकाश (vide pp. 6. 90, 225, 236). The चित्रमीमांसा (p. 80) ascribes a कारिका (definition of उत्प्रेक्षा) and an example thereon to काव्यप्रकाशिकाकार. The रसगङ्गाधर (p. 30) ascribes the कारिकाs to मम्मटभट्ट. जयराम (in his तिलक), भीमसेन in सुधा सागर (p. 4. Ch. S. S.), गोपाल in साहित्यचूडामणि (p. 4, Tri. ed.), and कमलाकरभट्ट say that the कारिकाकार and वृत्तिकार are the same person. Therefore, मम्मट must be held to be the author of the *kārikās* also.

We find at the end of the काव्यप्रकाश a verse which has been interpreted in two ways even by the earliest comentators, viz. 'इत्येष मार्गो विदुषां विभिन्नोप्यभिन्नरूपः प्रतिभासते यत् । न तद्विचित्रं यदमुत्र सम्यग्विनिर्मिता सङ्घटनैव हेतुः ॥'. The earliest known commentator माणिक्यचन्द्र remarks 'अथ चायं ग्रन्थोऽन्येनारब्धोऽपरेण च समर्थित इति द्विखण्डोपि सङ्घटनावशादखण्डायते'. The काव्यप्रकाशसङ्केत (Peterson's 2nd Report p. 13 and Cal. O. J. vol. II ed. by Prof. S. P. Bhattacharya) says: 'एतेन महामतीनां प्रसरणहेतुरेष ग्रन्थो ग्रन्थकृतानेन कथमाप्यसमाप्तत्वादपरेण च पूरितावशेषत्वात् द्विखण्डोपि etc. सोमेश्वर also says "अथ च सुधियां विकासहेतुर्ग्रन्थोयं कथंचिदपूर्णत्वादन्येन पूरितशेष इति द्विखण्डोपि &c." The काव्यप्रकाशनिदर्शन of राजानकानन्द (written in 1665 A. D.) tells us that मम्मट composed the work up to परिकर and the rest was completed by अलक 'यदुक्तं—कृतः श्रीमम्मटाचार्यवर्यैः परिकरावधिः । प्रबन्धः पूरितः शेषो विधायालकसूरिणा ॥ अन्येनाप्युक्तम्-काव्यप्रकाशदशकोपि निबन्धकृद्भ्यां द्वाभ्यां कृतोपि कृतिनां रसतत्त्वलाभः। etc.' (*vide* JBBRAS vol. 16 extra

Prof. Divekar's suggestion as stated by Dr. De and दूरान्वय is not a serious matter as the न्याय quoted above (p. 255 n. 1) 'यस्य येनार्थसम्बन्धो......आनन्तर्यमकारणम्' shows.

No. 23). The colophons at the end of the first and 10th chap. of the काव्यप्रकाशसङ्केत are 'इति श्रीमद्राजानकामल्लमम्मटरुचकविरचिते निजग्रन्थ-काव्यप्रकाशसङ्केते प्रथम उल्लास:' and 'कृती राजानकमम्मटालकरुचकानाम्' (vide Peterson's 2nd Report p. 14). A ms. of the काव्यप्रकाश dated संवत् 1215 (i. e. 1158 A. D.) described by prof. S. R. Bhandarkar (Report on tour for 1905-6 p. 79) has the colophon 'कृती राजानकमम्मटालकयो:'. This joint authorship of the काव्यप्रकाश is referred to by अर्जुनवर्मदेव in his commentary on the अमरुशतक. He says (on verse 30 of K. M. ed. भवतु विदितं p. 29) 'यथोदाहृतं दोष-निर्णये मम्मटालकाभ्यां प्रसादे वर्तस्व etc. (vide काव्यप्र. p. 438). In another place (on verse 72 of अमरु 'लीलातामरसाहतो°' p. 55) he remarks 'अत्र केचिद्राद्युपदेन जुगुप्साश्लीलमिति दोषमाचक्षते...तदा वाग्देवतादेश इति व्यवसितव्य एवासौ। किं तु द्वावेकमयीवरलब्धप्रसादौ काव्यप्रकाशकारौ प्रायेण दोषदृष्टी etc.' For the verse लीलाताम°, vide काव्यप्रकाश (p. 278). अर्जुनवर्मदेव was 13th in succession from भोज of धारा and his inscriptions range from 1211 to 1216 A. D. Therefore, in about a hundrad and fifty years मम्मट came to be regarded as an *avatāra* of सरस्वती. It further follows from the words of अर्जुन° that अलक had a hand not only in the 10th but also in the 7th उल्लास. It is probable that having known by tradition that अलक was associated with the composition of the काव्यप्रकाश, अर्जुन° ascribes to him the authorship of the whole work. Dr. H. R. Divekar (in JRAS 1927 pp. 505-520) puts forward certain grounds and holds that मम्मट composed only the kārikās up to the figure called Parikara and the remaining kārikās and the whole of the vṛtti were composed by Alaka. His reasons are in some cases subjective and all af them are unconvincing. Most mss. read the name as अलक, but Dr. Stein remarks 'In order to complete the case for अल्लट as the name of the continuator of the Kāvyaprakāśa, it suffices for me to point out that this form of the name is the only one known to the tradition of the Kashmirian *pandits*, to whom the double authorship of the Kāvyaprakāśa is otherwise perfectly familiar' (*vide* Cat. of Jammu mss. p. XXIII-XXVI). Col. Jacob, therefore, thinks that अलट is the correct form and not अलक (JRAS for 1897 p. 282). I would attach more importance to ancient mss. than to the traditions of modern *pandits* (one of the mss. which gives the name as अलक is so old as 1158 A. D.). Vide Gode, vol. I. pp. 234-238 where the colophon of the mss. is dated संवत् 1215 आश्विन सुदि १४ बुध (i. e. Wednesday 8th October 1158) and says 'कृती राजानकमम्मटालकयोः ।...अणहिल्लपाटके...शाकम्भरिभूपाल-श्री-कुमारपालदेव—कल्याणविजय &c.' कुमारपाल ruled from 1142 to 1173 A. D. अलक would be as good a Kashmirian name as अल्लट or अलट. We have such well-known Kashmirian names as कुन्तक, शङ्कुक, लल्लुक, मङ्खक that end in क, to match with रुद्रट, मम्मट, कल्लट, भल्लट etc. Vide my note in I. A. for 1911 p. 209 on the subject.[1] The सम्प्रदायप्रकाशिनी of विद्याचक्रवर्तिन् (Tri. ed.) says on the last verse इत्येष० 'मन्मथग्रन्थशेषं परिपूरितवतोयमलर्कस्य स्वापेद्यः श्लोकः' (part II p. 449).

Whether the अलकदत्त ((styled सान्धिविग्रहिक by जोनराज), who imparted instruction in Poetics to कल्याण (probably कल्हण, the author of the राजतर०), as said in the श्रीकण्ठचरित of मङ्ख (25. 78-80), is identical with this अलक, it is difficult to say.

About the personal history of मम्मट we know practically nothing. भीमसेन in his सुधासागर (Ch. S. S.) says that मम्मट was the elder brother of both कैयट (author of महाभाष्यप्रदीप) and उवट (author of भाष्य on ऋक्प्रातिशाख्य), that he was the son of जैयट and, though born in Kashmir, studied at Benares and taught his brothers. But this account furnished by an author who wrote six senturies after मम्मट (in 1672-73 A. D.) seems to be more or less fanciful and based probably on the similarity of sounds in the three names. We know from उवट's भाष्य on the ऋक्प्रातिशाख्य that he was a son of वज्रट (and not of जैयट) and a native of आनन्दपुर. उवट wrote his वाजसनेयसंहिताभाष्य while भोज was reigning (भोजे राज्यं प्रशासति). There is therefore nothing improbable in

---

1. In Z. D. M. G. vol. 66 pp. 477-490 on 'two authors of the Kāvyaprakāśa' Sukthankar shows that the portion after परिकर in काव्यप्रकाश X follows रुद्रट very closely, while the portion up to परिकर does not and that in the latter part of Ullāsa X six examples are cited from the नवसाहसाङ्कचरित while not one is cited from that poem in the first part of काव्यप्र. X. One curious coincidence may be noted. In I. A. vol. 58 for 1929 p. 161 there is an inscription of the time of Allaṭa, king of Mewar, dated in *saṁvat* 1010 wherein one मम्मट is referred to as अमात्य. Hence it follows that these names were not restricted to Kashmir. In the Harsha stone Ins. of चाहमान विग्रहराज (E. I. vol. II. p. 116 at p. 122) about 970 A.D. a पाशुपत named भल्लट alias भावरक्ष occurs.

मम्मट being a brother of उवट, but he cannot then be the brother of कैयट, whose father was जैयट. The Kashmirian *pandits* say that मम्मट was the maternal uncle of श्रीहर्ष, the author of the नैषधीय (Buhler's K. Report p. 68). मम्मट was a man of great erudition and vast reading. He seems to have been a profound student of grammar also. He quotes the महाभाष्य and the वाक्यपदीय, places the divisions of उपमा on a grammatical basis, takes क्रिया in the sense of हेतु (in the definition of विभावना), follows the views of grammarians about the सङ्केत of words (जात्यादि:), speaks of the grammarians as learned men *par excellence*. He wrote another work called शब्दव्यापारविचार (published by Nirṇaya-sāgar Press). In that work he discusses in greater detail the subject of his 2nd उल्लास (viz. अभिधा and लक्षणा). He was styled राजानक, which is a title borne by Kashmirian brāhmaṇas even now. It means 'almost a king'. *Vide* राजतर० (VI. 261) 'राज्ञी कृतश्रभावेन सापि मन्त्रिसभान्तरे। तमाजुहाव निर्द्रोहं स्वयं राजानकाख्यया ॥'. मम्मट became the most popular writer on Poetics throughout India, as the large number of commentaries (about 75 yet discovered) testifies.

मम्मट quotes अभिनवगुप्त (who was still living in 1015 A. D.) and नवसाहसाङ्कचरित (composed about 1005 A. D.). He also refers to the liberality of भोज to learned men (यद्विद्वद्भवनेषु भोजनृपतेस्तत्त्यागलीलायितं on उदात्त). Even if this verse was composed during भोज's life-time, it must have been composed towards the latter part of his life, as it would take some years before his fame spread abroad. It was shown above that भोज could not have ruled beyond 1054 A. D. Hence the काव्यप्रकाश is not most probably earliar then 1050 A. D. हेमचन्द्र wrote his काव्यानुशासन about 1143 A. D. and mentions मम्मट (vide p. 271 above). The काव्यप्रकाश was commented upon by माणिक्यचन्द्र in his सङ्केत in संवत् 1216 (*i.e.* 1159-1160 A.D.) and a ms. of the work is dated संवत् 1215 (*i.e.* 1158). Vide Prof. Gode in J. O. R., Madras, vol. 13 p. 49 about the date of the ms. It will be established below that the अलङ्कारसर्वस्व refers to the काव्यप्रकाश and the काव्यप्रकाशसङ्केत refers to previous commentaries on the काव्यप्रकाश (pp. 3 and 5 of text in Cal. O. J. vol. II). Therefore, the काव्यप्रकाश was composed at all events before 1100 A. D. Hence the date of the काव्यप्रकाश lies between 1050 and 1100 A. D.

Among the numerous commentaries, those of माणिक्यचन्द्र,

सोमेश्वर, सरस्वतीतीर्थ and जयन्त deserve special mention as being amongst the earliest ones. The काव्यप्रकाशसङ्केत of रुचक was edited by Prof. S. P. Bhattacharya in the Calcutta Oriental Journal vol. II. pp. 1-75 with valuable English notes and the com. on 10th Ullāsa by Prof. Sukthankar at the end of his edition of a part of the काव्यप्रकाश. The com. (called प्रदीप) of गोविन्दठक्कुर is a very learned one. He flourished probably in the 15th century. Except the Bhagavadgītā there is hardly any other work in classical Sanskrit that has so many commentaries[1] on it.

27 The अलङ्कारसर्वस्व of रुय्यक. This is a standard work on figures of speech. The author is a staunch advocate of the *dhvani* school and briefly summarises the views of Bhāmaha, Udbhaṭa, Rudraṭa, Vāmana, the वक्रोक्तिजीवित, व्यक्तिविवेक and ध्वनिकार on the essence of Poetry. He then deals with पुनरुक्तवदाभास, छेकानुप्रास, वृत्त्यनुप्रास, यमक, लाटानुप्रास, चित्र and about 75 figures of अर्थ beginning with उपमा. He defines more figures than मम्मट and his treatment (in the 86 sūtras and the वृत्ति thereon) is generally more elaborate than that of the latter. The edition here referred to is the K. M. one of 1939 A. D. He adds a few figures such as परिणाम, रसवत्, प्रेयः, ऊर्जस्वि, समाहित, भावोदय, भावसन्धि and भावशबल to those defined by मम्मट and gives two altogether new figures, viz. विकल्प (pp. 198-200, as he himself says 'पूर्वैरकृतविवेकोऽत्र दर्शित इत्यवगन्तव्यम्') and विचित्र (pp. 168-169, about which जयरथ says 'एतद्धि ग्रन्थकृतैवाभिनवत्वेनोक्तम्). My notes to the साहित्यदर्पण will show how विश्वनाथ was indebted to the अलङ्कारसर्वस्व and received inspiration from it. The same may be said of the एकावली, कुवलयानन्द and other works. The work is divided into three parts; first come the *sūtras* (in prose) defining the figures, then the *vṛtti* and the examples, all of which are cited from previous works. Among the authors and works quoted or referred to the following deserve attention:—

1. कमलाकर (who wrote the निर्णयसिन्धु in 1612 A. D.) says in his टीका on the काव्यप्रकाश 'काव्यप्रकाशे टिप्पण्यः सहस्रं सन्ति यद्यपि। तास्वस्त्यस्या विशेषो यः पण्डितैः सोऽवधार्यताम्॥ (D. C. ms. No. 429 of 1895-1900 described in Govt. mss. at B. O. R. I. cat. vol. XII. p. 129). महेश्वर in his भावार्थचिन्तामणि remarks 'काव्यप्रकाशस्य कृता गृहे गृहे टीका तथाप्येष तथैव दुर्गमः। सुखेन विज्ञातुमिमं य ईहते धीरः स एतां निपुणं विलोकताम्॥'.

अलङ्कारमञ्जरी (p. 18), उद्भट, बिल्हण's विक्रमाङ्कदेवचरित (p. 150, two verses I. 11-12), भामह (228), वामन (p. 160), श्रीकण्ठस्तव (p. 23 four verses quoted), श्रीकण्ठचरित of मङ्ख, हरिश्चन्द्रचरित (p. 130). He frequently cites the views of उद्भट (pp. 156, 219, 239, 256) and जयरथ (p. 158) tells us that the author of the सर्वस्व generally follows the views of राजानकतिलक who wrote a work called उद्भट-विवेक or—विचार (pp. 146, 257). In one place (p. 151) he differs from the ध्वन्यालोक (p. 136) in not regarding the verse 'स वक्तुमखिलाञ्शक्तो हयग्रीवाश्रितान्गुणान्। योऽम्बुकुम्भैः परिच्छेदं कर्तुं शक्तो महोदधेः।' as an example of आक्षेपध्वनि. He finds fault with the लोचन (52) for citing 'किं वृत्तान्तैः परगृहगतैः' &c. as an example of व्याजस्तुति (p. 144). The अलं. स. quotes the काव्यप्रकाश in several places and also criticises the latter. For example, the सर्वस्व (p. 136) cites the verse 'राजन्राजसुता न पाठयति मां देव्योपि तूष्णीं स्थिताः...चित्रस्थानवलोक्य शून्यवलभावेकैकमाभाषते' as an example of पर्यायोक्त and remarks 'अन्ये तु दण्डयात्रोद्यतं त्वां बुद्ध्वा त्वदरयः पलाय्य गता इति कारणरूपस्यैवार्थस्य प्रस्तुतत्वात्कार्यरूपोर्थोऽप्रस्तुत एव राजशुकवृत्तान्तस्याप्रस्तुतत्वात्प्रस्तुतार्थं प्रति स्वात्मानं समर्पयतीत्यप्रस्तुतप्रशंसैवात्र न्याय्येति वर्णयन्ति'. The काव्यप्रकाश cites the verse as an instance of अप्रस्तुतप्रशंसा and makes the same remarks as in 'अन्ये तु etc'. The सर्वस्व (p. 130) quotes the verse 'अलङ्कारोऽथ वस्त्वेव शब्दाद्यत्रावभासते। प्रधानत्वेन स ज्ञेयः शब्दशक्त्युद्भवो द्विधा ॥' as a न्याय. This is a कारिका of the काव्यप्र. (4th उल्लास p. 128). On p. 230 the सर्वस्व says "अत एव 'प्रत्यक्षा एव ('इव' in समुद्रबन्ध) यत्रार्थाः क्रियन्ते भूतभाविनः। तद्भाविकम्' इत्येवमन्यैर्भाविकलक्षणमकारि"; this is the definition of भाविक in the काव्यप्र०. On p. 250 the सर्वस्व says 'शब्दालङ्कारसङ्करस्तु कैश्चिदुदाहृतो यथा—राजति तटीयमभिहत...सारा वनदा। अत्र यमकानुलोमप्रतिलोमयोः शब्दालङ्कारयोः परस्परापेक्षत्वेनाङ्गाङ्गिसङ्कर इति। एतत्तु न सम्यगावर्जकम्। शब्दालङ्कारयोः शब्दवदुपकार्योपकारकत्वाभावेनाङ्गाङ्गिभावाभावात्। शब्दालङ्कारसंसृष्टिस्त्वत्र श्रेयसी'. The काव्यप्र. cites the verse राजति तटी० as an example of शब्दालङ्कारसङ्कर (with the words 'अत्र यमकमनुलोमप्रतिलोमश्च चित्रभेदः पादद्वयगते परस्परापेक्षे' p. 759. On p. 255 the सर्वस्व remarks 'अत एव व्यवस्थितत्वमन्यानुभाषितमप्रयोजनकम्'; this clearly refers to the words of the कारिका 'स्फुटमेकत्र विषये शब्दार्थालङ्कृतिद्वयम्। व्यवस्थितं च (काव्यप्र. X. p. 765). On p. 256 the सर्वस्व asserts that आश्रयाश्रयिभाव is the determining principle as to whether a particular अलङ्कार is शब्दालङ्कार or अर्थालङ्कार (लोकवदाश्रयाश्रयिभावश्च तत्तदलङ्कारनिबन्धनम्। अन्वयव्यतिरेकौ तु तत्कार्यत्वे प्रयोजकौ) and not अन्वयव्यतिरेकौ; while मम्मट takes the opposite view; similarly, on p. 4 the सर्वस्व quotes 'स्वसिद्धये पराक्षेपः etc.' which occurs in the काव्यप्र. (II. p. 43). It may be conceded that the quotation by रुय्यक of कारिकाs that occur in the काव्यप्रकाश is not conclusive as to the priority of the काव्यप्र. over रुय्यक; for, some of the कारिकाs in the काव्यप्र. are borrowed from others. Still, there are other passages from the वृत्ति in the काव्यप्र. quoted above, which are conclusive on this point. Vide also विमर्शिनी (pp. 189, 204). It is further to be noted that the definitions of several अलङ्कारs are the same in both काव्यप्र. and अलं. स. e. g. चित्र, काव्यलिङ्ग, व्याजोक्ति, उत्तर, मीलित, समाधि and that about 76 illustrations are the same in the 10th उल्लास of मम्मट and in the सर्वस्व.

About the authorship of the वृत्ति in the अलङ्कारसर्वस्व a very perplexing question arises. In the K. M. edition the first verse reads 'निजालङ्कारसूत्राणां वृत्त्या तात्पर्यमुच्यते ॥'. जयरथ who flourished within about 75 years of रुय्यक commented upon the words निजालङ्कार &c.; hence according to him रुय्यक is the author of the वृत्ति also. Later writers also regard रुचक (or रुय्यक) as the author of the वृत्ति. For example, the रत्नापण says 'तदुक्तं रुचकेन पक्षार्थाश्रयापि धर्मविषये श्लिष्टशब्दहेतुका क्वचिद्दृश्यते' (p. 393: this occurs on p. 72 of सर्वस्व): 'न चेदं विषमाद्भेदेन्तर्भवति । इह हि स्वनिषेधो वैपरीत्यं गमयति विषमे तु व्यत्यय इति भेदस्य रुचकेनोक्तत्वात्' (p. 425; this is सर्वस्व p. 168); काव्यग्रहणं तर्कवैलक्षण्यार्थम् । तेन व्याप्तिपक्षधर्मतादयो न क्रियन्ते इति रुचकः' (p. 448; this is on p. 181 of सर्वस्व); चित्रमीमांसा (p. 72) 'ये तु उद्भिन्नवस्तुनिगूहनं व्याजोक्तिः...तेषामिहापि व्याजोक्तिरेव नापह्नुतिरिति रुचकादयः' (vide अलं. स. p. 219). But a ms. described in Burnell's Tanjore cat. (p. 54) reads the first verse as गुर्वलङ्कारसूत्राणां वृत्त्या०. The Trivandrum edition of the सर्वस्व with the commentary of समुद्रबन्ध reads the first verse similarly and adds at the end of the work the verse 'इति मङ्खुको वितेने काश्मीरक्षितिपसान्धिविग्रहिकः । सुकविमुखालङ्कारं तदिदमलङ्कारसर्वस्वम् ॥'. The com. of समुद्रबन्ध ends with the words 'मङ्खुकनिबन्धविवृतौ विहितायामिह समुद्रबन्धेन' and in several other places (p. 2 कदाचिन्मङ्खुकोपज्ञं and p. 4 'व्यक्तिविवेककाराभिमतस्त्वनुमानपक्षः... मङ्खुकस्य पूर्वपक्षत्वेनाप्यनभिमत इत्याहुः') ascribes the *vṛtti* to मङ्खुक. मङ्खुक is an incorrect form of मङ्खक. We know from the श्रीकण्ठचरित (25. 26-30) of मङ्ख that रुय्यक was the teacher of मङ्ख or मङ्खक (III. 63 and 72 for the form मङ्खक and I. 56 for मङ्ख) and the राजतरङ्गिणी says that मङ्खक was made minister for peace and war by king जयसिंह of काश्मीर 'सान्धिविग्रहिको मङ्खकाख्योलङ्कारसोदरः । स मठस्याभवत्स्रष्ठः श्रीकण्ठस्य प्रतिष्ठया ॥' (VIII. 3354). *Vide* श्रीकण्ठचरित III. 66 also. Therefore, it appears that a tradition arose in southern India that मङ्खक had a hand in the अलङ्कारसर्वस्व. For several reasons this tradition must be discarded. Except समुद्रबन्ध,

hardly any writer ascribes the वृत्ति to मङ्खक.[1] On the contrary, even such south Indian writers as कुमारस्वामी (vide रत्नापण pp. 393, 396, 425, 448) and जगन्नाथ (pp. 251, 342-43, 352, 482) ascribe both the *sūtras* and the *vṛtti* to the same author. Besides जयरथ, who was himself a very learned Kashmirian and flourished in the first quarter of the 13 century, distinctly ascribes the *vṛtti* to the author of the *sūtras*. समुद्रबन्ध wrote about 1300 A. D. and is much later than जयरथ. It is probable that मङ्खक, who was a pupil of रुय्यक, took great pains to spread the fame of his master's work and in editing it afresh made some additions. It is probably in this way that a few verses from the श्रीकण्ठचरित of मङ्ख (II. 49 on p. 25, and V. 23, VI. 16 and X. 10 on pp. 114-115) got into the अलं. स. (i. e. the master appears to quote from his pupil's work). That the वृत्ति came to be ascribed to मङ्खक is probably due to the fact that quotations from the श्रीकण्ठचरित occur in it. That unauthorised additions and alterations were made in the *vṛtti* is attested by जयरथ who frequenely complains about the corruptions that crept into the text and about the tampering with the text itself (vide pp. 63, 85, 137, 158, 160); vide also JOR (Madras) vol. XXVI (1956-57) pp. 40-52 for papers on the 'authorship of the Alaṅkāra-sarvasva' by Mr. S. Venkitasubramonia Iyer, and pp. 53-54 (of the same) by Dr. V. Raghavan.

According to the colophon[2] of a ms. of the सहृदयलीला, रुचक is another name of रुय्यक, who was the son of राजानकतिलक (*vide* Pischel's Intro. to शृङ्गारतिलक pp. 28-29). जयरथ is positive (p. 130) that the काव्यप्रकाशसङ्केत (ascribed to रुचक) was the work of the author of the अलङ्कारसर्वस्व. This statement coming from a Kashmirian writer who flourished within less than a century of the सर्वस्व is very valuable and should be accepted. The काव्यप्रकाशसङ्केत itself says that the author learnt poetics under तिलक (vide p. 139 note above). Later writers frequently use

1. But the following passage from the चित्रमीमांसा (p. 10) is noteworthy 'किं तु श्लेषस्यालङ्कारान्तरविविक्तविषयाभावेन निरवकाशतया बलवत्त्वेन...श्लेष एव नोपमेति मङ्खकादिभिरभ्युपेयते'. Vide p. 126 of सर्वस्व for this view.

2. The colophon runs 'कृतिः श्रीविपश्चिद्वरराजानकतिलकात्मजश्रीमदालङ्कारिकसमाजाग्रगण्यश्रीराजानकरुय्यकस्य राजानकरुचकापरनाम्नोऽलङ्कारसर्वस्वकृतः ।'

the form रुचक (vide रत्नापण pp. 393, 396)· Instead of the name अलङ्कारसर्वस्व many writers use the shorter form सर्वस्व (रत्नापण pp. 424, 449, 452, रसगङ्गाधर pp. 220, 227 355, चित्रमीमांसा p. 98). The *sūtras* as well as the *vrtti* are often referred to as अलङ्कारसर्वस्व or सर्वस्व; *vide* एकावलीतरल (pp. 136, 146, 237), प्रतापरुद्र॰ p. 291, रत्नापण (pp. 341,452). The अलं. स. was translated into German by Jacobi in Z. D. M. G. vol. 62.

Besides the अलङ्कारसर्वस्व, रुय्यक wrote the following works:— 1, अलङ्कारानुसारिणी (mentioned by जयरथ on pp. 44, 73, 76); 2, काव्यप्रकाशसङ्केत (p. 130 of विमर्शिनी); 3, नाटकमीमांसा; 4, व्यक्तिविवेकविचार; 5, श्रीकण्ठस्तव (vide अलं. स. p. 23 'उदाहरणं मदीये श्रीकण्ठस्तवे'); 6, सहृदयलीला; 7, साहित्यमीमांसा; 8, हर्षचरितवार्तिक. About the last two the अलं. स. says (p· 77) 'एषा (उत्प्रेक्षा) च समस्तोपमाप्रतिपादकविषयेपि हर्षचरितवार्तिके साहित्यमीमांसायां च तेषु तेषु प्रदेशेषूदाहृता । इह तु ग्रन्थविस्तरभयान्न प्रपञ्चिता'. जयरथ (p. 16) distinctly ascribes the com. on the व्यक्तिविवेक to रुय्यक 'वाच्यस्य प्रतीयमानेन तादात्म्यतदुत्पत्त्यभावादि नेह प्रतन्यत इति व्यक्तिविवेकविचारे हि मयैवैतद्वितत्य निर्णीतमिति भावः'. The com. on the व्यक्तिविवेक (Trivandrum ed. p. 44) claims the हर्षचरितवार्तिक as a work of the author 'एतदस्माभिर्हर्षचरितवार्तिके विस्तृत्य प्रतिपादितम्'. Vide p. 50 also for the same statement. In the same work (p. 32) the नाटकमीमांसा and साहित्यमीमांसा are said to be the author's works. Aufrecht (C. C. p. 32 b) says that the अलंकारानुसारिणी is a commentary on the सोमपालविलास of जह्लण, relying upon the remarks of रत्नकण्ठ (1681 A. D.) on स्तुतिकुसुमाञ्जलि (VIII. 19 तथाहि कविवरजह्लणकृते सोमपालविलासे ...अस्यार्थः श्रीराजनकरुचकविरचितायामलङ्कारानुसारिण्यां etc.). But the remarks of जयरथ show that the अलङ्कारानुसारिणी was an independent work on अलङ्कार, containing a dissertation on the 48 varieties of प्रतीयमानोत्प्रेक्षा, on मालारूपक etc. A mere commentary on another work is hardly likely to contain such dissertations. The व्यक्तिविवेकविचार (p. 45) shows that the author contemplated writing a work called बृहती. This last, if actually completed, whould be his tenth work. The सहृदयलीला (published in K. M. series and by Pischel at Kiel in 1886) is a brief work divided into four उल्लेख called गुण, अलङ्कार, जीवित and परिकर. The first उल्लेख describes the ten *guṇas*, रूप, वर्ण, प्रभा etc. of charming ladies; the 2nd speaks of the various kinds of ornaments (of gold, pearl, stones) etc., unguents, flowers worn by women; the third speaks of youth, that is the very essence of charm; and the last briefly refers to the paraphernalia that sets off beauty to advantage.

In the Tri. S. Series a work callad साहित्यमीमांसा was published in 1934, the edition being based on a single ms. although a fragment of another ms. from Tanjore was also available for comparison. The editor points out that in several places there are gaps and lacunae. The work is a large one. It is in the form of kārikās, a vṛtti in prose and illustrations. Unfortunately the name of the author is not given either at the beginning or at the end. About six hundred verses are quoted from numerous sources in this work, out of which one hundred are prākrit. It is divided into eight prakaraṇas, the first and last being very brief (about two printed pages each). A brief summary is given here. I. Salutation of vācya and vācaka (which stand for Para and Apara Brahma), enumeration of the topics to be discussed in the work viz. eight topics of वृत्ति, विवक्षा, तात्पर्य, प्रविभाग, व्यपेक्षा, सामर्थ्य, अन्वय, ऐकार्थ्य (these eight are called साहित्य); 4 topics that set off साहित्य (i. e. साहित्यपरिष्कार) viz. दोषत्याग, गुणाधान, अलङ्कारयोग and रसान्वय; four kinds of कवि viz. सत्कवि, विदग्धकवि, अरोचकिकवि, सतृणाभ्यवहारककवि; three kinds of रसिक viz. उत्तम, मध्यम, अधम (i. e. सात्त्विक, राजस and तामस); II. definition of वृत्ति (as पदानां व्यापारः), which is three-fold मुख्या, लक्षणा, गौणी; definitions of these three; definitions of विवक्षा, प्रविभाग (into प्रकृति and प्रत्यय, वाक्य, महावाक्य), व्यपेक्षा (आकांक्षा), सामर्थ्य (भेद, संसर्ग and उभय), अन्वय (परस्परग्रथन), ऐकार्थ्य (एकवाक्यता) and their examples; these eight constitute साहित्य (साहित्य is language and grammar and not poetics), difference between साहित्य and काव्य (the latter is साहित्य with four परिष्कारs, दोषत्याग &c.); III. *Doṣas*, six of पद viz. अप्रयुक्त, ग्राम्य, असमर्थ, अनर्थक, साधारण, प्रसिद्धार्थ (?); विरुद्ध of various kinds is defined and illustrated (there is loss of a page or two); IV Guṇas of काव्य, शब्दगुणs being बाह्य and अर्थगुणs being आभ्यन्तर; ten गुणs (श्लेष प्रसादः समता माधुर्यं सुकुमारता । अर्थव्यक्तिरुदारत्वमोजः कान्तिसमाधयः ॥)[1]; their definitions and illustrations; V defininition of अलङ्कार (काव्ये शोभाकरान् धर्मानलङ्कारान्प्रचक्षते ।, which is काव्यादर्श II. 1); difference between गुणs and अलङ्कारs; अलङ्कारs of शब्द are अनुप्रास, क्रम, श्लेष, मुद्रा, दीपक, युक्ति, पठिती, गुम्फना, चित्र, यमक; their definitions and examples; लाटानुप्रास; the three वृत्तिs called परुषा, उपनागरिका and कोमला; अलङ्कारs of अर्थ are उपमा, रूपक, उत्प्रेक्षा, व्यतिरेक, विभावना, अपह्नुति, भ्रम, साम्य, संशय, सङ्कर; definitions and illustrations; other अलङ्कारs are

1. This very verse is काव्यादर्श I. 41.

included in these or are to be dealt with under वक्रोक्ति; VI[1] Rasa, its causes (bija), nature, co-operating elements (सहकारि) and whatever else is useful for the elucidation of *Rasa* are dealt with here; भावs are प्रधान and अप्रधान; प्रधानभावs are the eight called स्थायिनः, अप्रधानभावs are बाह्य (eight called सात्त्विक) and 33 आभ्यन्तर (called व्यभिचारिणः); enumeration of these, their definitions and examples; *Rasa* expounded; eight rasas enumerated by the ancients; Śānta rasa enumerated by some, its स्थायिभाव being धृति; some add three more rasas; शृङ्गार of two sorts सम्भोग and विप्रलम्भ; difference between विप्रलम्भ and करुण; other rasas; the four रीतिs वैदर्भी, आवन्ती, पाञ्चाली, गौडी and their appropriateness to the several rasas; the *rītis* लाटी and मागधिका resemble these four; the वृत्तिs कैशिकी, भारती, सात्वती and आरभटी and their employment in the several rasas; संस्कृत and प्राकृत and अपभ्रंश; twenty modes of वक्रोक्ति; समासोक्ति, अप्रस्तुतप्रशंसा, सहोक्ति and several others are varieties of वक्रोक्ति; there is वक्रत्व in ध्वनि, वर्ण, पद (पूर्वार्ध and प्रत्यय), वाक्य, प्रकरण and प्रबन्ध; enumeration of the 36 लक्षणs and illustrations of[2] the first three of them; VII The fourfold equipment of the poet (श्रमः सर्वकलावीक्षा नियोगस्तस्य शीलनम् । स क्लेशः करणोद्योगः प्रतिभा भास्वती मतिः । प्रज्ञा नवनवोन्मेषशालिनी प्रतिभेति वा ।); कवि is four kinds, सत्कवि who wields वैदर्भी style (such as वाल्मीकि and कालिदास), विदग्धकवि who is bent on वक्रोक्ति (such as व्यास and बाण), अरोचकिकवि who sticks to अर्थालङ्कारs (such as माघ and भारवि), सतृणाभ्यवहारककवि who writes in the Gauḍī style and is after श्लेष, चित्र and यमक (such as शिवभद्र);[3] conventions (कविसमयs); certain directions to poets such as not employing words like खलु, बत, हन्त at the beginning of a पाद, a short vowel at the end of a pāda being generally regarded as *guru*

---

1. The 6th and 7th प्रकरणs are the longest, covering pp. 54-118 and 119-159 respectively.

2. The first 7 verses of chapter 16 of the नाट्यशास्त्र (G. O. S. edition) in which the लक्षणs are enumerated in the उपजाति metre are quoted here and the illustrations are the same that the अभिनवभारती gives.

3. वामन (I. 2. 1-3) speaks of कविs as अरोचकिनः and सतृणाभ्यवहारिणः. Vide काव्यमीमांसा p. 14 for a discussion about these two and the addition of two more मत्सरिणः and तत्त्वाभिनिवेशिनः by राजशेखर.

though not always[1] (like वामन V. I. 3-5); some examples of words employed in the Veda, in Pāṇini, Vārtika and Bhāṣya, Nirukta, sūtras, smṛtis that are to be employed by poets; the usage of śiṣṭas like Kālidāsa and Bāṇa is to be followed; modes of address for characters in dramas; characteristic descriptions of the ladies of several countries and their complexions; *pravṛttis* called आवन्त्य, दाक्षिणात्य, पौरस्त्य and ओढ्रमागध; various festivals and sports of different countries and in different seasons; the six pramāṇas; VIII. The reader who relishes kāvya secures the highest pleasure (ईदृशं भावयन् काव्यं रसिकः परमं सुखम् । प्राप्नोति कालवैषम्याद्गुणतश्चिविधोपि सन् ॥); the Veda (in Ṛg. X. 71. 2 सक्तुमिव०) and the Uttararāmacarita (आविर्भूतज्योतिषां IV. 18) state that the most auspicious glory resides in the words of poets and unparallelled pleasure is the reward of revolving the meaning of a good poem in the mind.

Among the authors and works expressly named are अक्षपाद, अनर्घराघव, उत्तररामचरित, कादम्बरी, कालिदास, कात्यायन (p. 108), जैमिनि, धनदत्त (p. 94), बाण, भगवदज्जुक (p. 72), भवभूति (p. 54 भवभूतिः श्मशानाङ्के जगाद रसिकप्रभुः), भामह (p. 89), भारवि, भोजराज, महावीरचरित, माघ, मालतीमाधव, वक्रोक्तिकार (p. 117), वामन (p. 32), वाल्मीकि, विन्ध्यवासिन् (p. 43), वेणीसंहार, व्यास, शिवभद्र (p. 120). Among those not named are the following; more than a dozen definitions and illustrations are quoted from the काव्यादर्श. Similarly, about a dozen definitions and examples are quoted from उद्भट's अलङ्कारसारसंग्रह. After quoting the first two verses of उद्भट's work the commentary of प्रतीहारेन्दुराज also is quoted 'पुनरुक्त...कैश्चिदुपाहृता इति पठित्वा एवमाचार्या व्याचक्षते अत्रालङ्कारा...र्थालङ्कारता—इति' (p. 39). On p. 54 the verse विरुद्धैरविरु...णाकरः is quoted from दशरूप (IV. 34). On p. 51 two verses and a half (अपह्नुतिर०...कथ्यते) are quoted from the सरस्वतीकण्ठाभरण (IV. 41-43) and on p. 87 is quoted the कारिका 'वैदर्भादिकृतः पन्थाः' which is सर. क. II. 27. Eight verses on p. 137 are quoted from the तन्त्रवार्तिक of कुमारिल (pp. 259-260, व्याकरणाधिकरण). On pp. 145-146 are quoted three verses about the dress of the ladies of Gauḍa, Mahodaya and Avanti which occur in राजशेखर's काव्यमीमांसा (pp. 8-9). The most important thing is that the काव्यप्रकाश is quoted twice viz. I. 3 (शक्तिर्निपु-

1. Many of these such as न कर्मधारयः कार्यो बहुव्रीहिप्रतीतिदः । सम्भाव्यस्य निषेधे च द्वौ निषेधावुदाहृतौ (p. 128) are like वामन's in V. I. 7 and 9.

यता॰) on p. 119 and the passage of the वृत्ति in the 2nd उल्लास (p. 26 Vāmanācārya) 'आकांक्षासंनिधि...समुल्लसति' is quoted on p. 85. The वक्रोक्तिजीवित appears to have exerted a great influence over the साहित्यमीमांसा. The verse शब्दार्थौ सहितावेव (वक्रोक्ति॰ I. 17 p. 24) and the illustration ततोरुण॰ are both quoted on p. 13. On pp. 14-15 nine verses are quoted from the वक्रोक्तिजीवित. On p. 117 the verses speaking of the six kinds of वक्रत्व are quoted from the वक्रोक्तिजीवित (I. 19-21), the same examples are cited (on p. 116) and the words 'एतदेव वर्णविन्यासवक्रत्वं चिरन्तनेष्वनुप्रास इति प्रसिद्धं' (वक्रोक्ति॰ p. 28) are quoted in सा. मी. (p. 117 एतदेव... प्रसिद्धमिति व्याख्यातम्); many verses are quoted as from आचार्याः on pp. 21-25, 75, 85, 86, 94. Vide Dr. Rāghavan on 'Śṛṅgāraprakāśa' vol. I. pp. 88-103, who shows that the साहित्यमीमांसा follows the शृङ्गारप्रकाश, though it differs from it in some respects. He also doubts (pp. 99-100) whether it is the work of रुय्यक.

The most important characteristics of the साहित्यमीमांसा are two, viz. that it does not speak of the व्यञ्जना function of words at all, but of तात्पर्यवृत्ति whieh gives rise to the realization of *rasa* (अपदार्थोऽपि वाक्यार्थो रसस्तात्पर्यवृत्तितः। p. 85). Secondly, it treats of only a few अर्थालङ्कारs and includes such figures as समासोक्ति, अप्रस्तुतप्रशंसा, सहोक्ति under वक्रत्व. It does not appear to accept the theory of the शृङ्गारप्रकाश when it says 'विशिष्टादृष्टजन्मन आत्मगुणोद्भूतिहेतोरनादिवासनारूपस्याहङ्कारस्य च रसत्वमैक्यं च निषिद्धमस्माभिः। न तु कूटस्थात्मस्वरूपस्यानन्दस्यैकरूपस्य भेदो वक्तुं न शक्यते इत्यादि।' (p. 161).

The above characteristics of the साहित्यमीमांसा create a difficulty. A साहित्यमीमांसा was the work of रुय्यक author of the अलङ्कारसर्वस्व, as stated by himself. The सर्वस्व was a staunch advocate of the ध्वनि theory and the व्यञ्जना function, as stated on p. 16 (अस्ति तावद् व्यङ्ग्यनिष्ठो व्यञ्जनाव्यापारः). It also enumerates about 75 अर्थालङ्कारs beginning with उपमा and including समासोक्ति, अप्रस्तुतप्रशंसा, रसवद्, ऊर्जस्वि, प्रेयः. The only way in which this contradiction between the same author's view-point in two works can be explained is by supposing that the साहित्यमीमांसा was composed by him when the author was comparatively young and under the influence of the वक्रोक्तिजीवित, while the अलङ्कारसर्वस्व was composed when he was of mature intellect and had come completely under the influence of the ध्वन्यालोक and अभिनवगुप्त. If this explanation be not accepted it would have to be held that the साहित्यमीमांसा in the Tri. S. Series is not the work of the author of the Alaṅkārasarvasva, but of some one else. I must say that this latter alternative is not very likely, though not quite impossible. The अलं. स. (p. 159) quotes as an example of अनुक्तनिमित्ता विभावना the verse 'अङ्गलेखामकाश्मीरसमालम्भनपिञ्जराम् । अनलक्तकताम्राभामोष्ठलेखां च बिभ्रतीम् ।' which is उद्भट's example of विभावना (p. 38 of काव्यालङ्कार०). The K. M. सर्वस्व mentions four views about the alaṅkāra in this verse. जयरथ (p. 160) states that the text of सर्वस्व has been tampered with here, that the author of सर्वस्व, when he cites this verse in the साहित्यमीमांसा and comments on it, refers to two views only 'ग्रन्थकृतापि साहित्यमीमांसायामेतच्छ्लोकविवृतौ पक्षद्वयमेवोक्तम् । लेखकैश्चास्य ग्रन्थस्य प्रतिपदमेव विपर्यासः कृतः ।'. In the साहित्यमीमांसा this verse is cited on p. 47 after setting out Udbhaṭa's definition of विभावना and it then remarks : 'अङ्गलेखा...बिभ्रतीम्' इत्यादिः संपाद्य न पिञ्जरत्वाद्युपमानेन स्वाभाविकस्य पिञ्जरत्वादेरुपमेयस्याभेदाध्यवसायोऽतिशयोक्त्या द्रष्टव्यः ।." Therefore, is appears that the printed साहित्यमीमांसा is the साहित्यमीमांसा which जयरथ knew as composed by रुय्यक. The प्रतापरुद्रयशोभूषण (p. 11) mentions the view of a साहित्यमीमांसा as follows : प्रपञ्चितं साहित्यमीमांसायाम् । नायकगुणग्रथिताः सूक्तिस्रजः सुकृतिनामाकल्पमाकल्पन्ति—इति. I have not been able to trace this in the साहित्यमीमांसा (Tri. ed.),

The date of रुय्यक can be easily determined. He quotes from the विक्रमाङ्कदेवचरित (composed about 1085 according to Buhler) and criticizes the व्यक्तिविवेक and the काव्यप्रकाश. Therefore the सर्वस्व is later than 1100 A. D. He was teacher of मङ्खक,[1] whose elder brother was the सान्धिविग्रहिक of जयसिंह of Kashmir (1128-1149 A. D.), as stated in श्रीकण्ठचरित 25. 66. मङ्ख's श्रीकण्ठचरित was composed according to Buhler (K. Report p. 50) between 1135-1145 A, D. Therefore, if the quotations from the श्रीकण्ठचरित were originally part of the वृत्ति, the सर्वस्व was composed about 1150 A. D. The सर्वस्व cites (p. 118) the verse असमाप्तजिगीषस्य, which occurs in the राजतर० (IV. 441), but it is quoted also in अभिनवभारती vol. I. p. 305, and therefore no chronological conclusion should be drawn from this, Dr. De

1. In श्रीकण्ठचरित 25. 15 मङ्ख states shat his elder brother लङ्कक held a meeting of learned men from time to time and verses 48ff state the names of about 30 men before whom the श्रीकण्ठचरित was read ont, among, whom were सुहल and तेजकण्ठ Ambassadors to Kashmir court from king गोविन्दचन्द्र of Kanoj and अपरादित्य ruler of कोङ्कण. Verses 29-30 highly praise रुय्यक as गुरु.

is wrong in thinking that सर्वस्व borrows from राजतर. (vide J. R. A. S. 1927 at p. 474). The काव्यप्रकाशसङ्केत of माणिक्यचन्द्र (composed in 1159-60) refers to the अलं. स. several times (pp. 321, 355 Mysore ed.). Therefore the अलं. स. was composed sometime between 1135-1150 A. D. *Vide* Z. D. M. G. 62 p. 289.

A few words must be said about the commentators of the अलं. स. जयरथ's commentary; designated विमर्शिनी, is a learned one and is very frequently quoted and criticized by जगन्नाथ (pp. 325, 337, 352, 380, 387, 414, 418). Among the authors and works quoted by him are अनङ्गलेखा, अलङ्कारभाष्यकार (pp. 44, 106, 217), अलङ्कारवार्तिक (p. 71), अलङ्कारसार (pp. 88, 97, 171, 172), अलङ्कारानुसारिणी, उद्भटविवेक or-विचार, काव्यप्रकाश, काव्यप्रकाशसङ्केत (p. 130), तिलक, पृथ्वीराजविजय (p. 82), प्रत्यभिज्ञा, भोजदेव (pp. 154, 244), मम्मट, राजतर० (pp. 243-244 twelve verses describing ललितादित्य quoted containing pure *upamās*), रुद्रट, लोचनकार (p. 144), वक्रोक्तिजीवितकार (p. 188). He frequently discusses readings (pp. 26, 47, 63, 158, 215 etc.). He criticizes रुय्यक also (pp. 89, 137). He refers to previous commentators of the सर्वस्व as अन्यैः (p. 5). He wrote another work called विवेक (a com. on the तन्त्रालोक of अभिनवगुप्त), at the end of which he gives his pedigree at great length (*vide* Buhler's Kashmir Report p. 98 and CXLVIII-CXLX). His great-grand-father's brother was a minister of king उच्चल (1101-1111 A. D.) and his father शृङ्गार was a minister of राजराज or राजदेव (1203-1226 A. D.). जयरथ learnt vidyās from शङ्खधर and सुभटदत्त gave him दीक्षा. जयरथ's younger brother जयद्रथ wrote the हरचरितचिन्तामणि (in 32 cantos, published in K. M. series). Therefore, he flourished in the first quarter of the 13th century. This is corroborated by the fact that he mentions पृथ्वीराजविजय which speaks of the exploits of the great Chohan king पृथ्वीराज (captured in 1193 A. D.). The com. of समुद्रबन्ध (published in T. S. S. 1926) is not so learned and so copious as that of जयरथ. It was composed at the court of रविवर्मा (of यदुवंश) king of कोलम्ब in केरल (Malabar). This king is said to have been born in 1265 A. D. The com. quotes verses in honour of रविवर्मा (pp. 12, 13, 54, 196 &c.), discusses various readings (p. 52) and complains of the loss of illustrations from रुय्यक's work (p. 117) and refers to the explanations of other commentators of the सर्वस्व (pp. 88, 132, 227). He states that there are five views about the special feature of

काव्य.[1] A third commentary called सञ्जीविनी composed by विद्याचक्रवर्तिन् is quoted by मल्लिनाथ in his तरल (pp. 31, 221), in the रत्नापण (pp.54,319,377, 387 &c.) and in चित्रमीमांसा (pp.7,74). That commentary contained verses summarising the distinctions between figures (e. g. between रूपक and परिणाम). Dr. Raghavan informs me that a postgraduate student of his has prepared for the Press a critical edition of the अलं. स. with the commentary of विद्याचक्रवर्तिन्.

28 The वाग्भटालङ्कार of वाग्भट. This work with the commentary of सिंहदेवगणि has been published in the K. M. series (1933). There are two वाग्भट's in अलङ्कारशास्त्र. This is the first. The work is not an elaborate treatise. It is divided into five परिच्छेदs, which contain 260 verses. Most of the verses are in the Anuṣṭubh metre, a few, particularly at the end of each परिच्छेद, being composed in other metres. There is a single passage in prose for illustrating ओजोगुण (III. 14). The passage in समराजिरस्फुरदरिनरेशकरिनिकरशिरःसरससिन्दूरपूरपरिचयेनेवारुणितकरतलो देवः. The first परिच्छेद defines काव्य, gives प्रतिभा as the source of काव्य and defines प्रतिभा, व्युत्पत्ति and अभ्यास, speaks of the favourable circumstances for the out-turn of poetry and the conventions to be observed by poets. The second परि० says that '*kāvya* may be composed in four languages, संस्कृत, प्राकृत, अपभ्रंश and भूतभाषा, divides काव्य into metrical (छन्दोनिबद्ध) and non-metrical, into पद्य, गद्य and मिश्र and then defines and illustrates eight *doṣas* of *pada* and of *vākya* and the *doṣas* of *artha*. The third परि० defines and illustrates the ten *guṇas*. The fourth परि० treats of four *alaṅkāras* of *śadha* viz. चित्र, वक्रोक्ति, अनुप्रास and यमक and their varieties and 35 *alaṅkāras* of sense and the two styles वैदर्भी and गौडीया. The fifth परि० is concerned with the treatment of nine *rasas*, the different kinds of नायक and नायिका and kindred topics.

The author was a Jain. His name occurs as बाहड or वाहड (in Prakrit) and he seems to have been the son of सोम and was a minister. On the verse बंभण्डसुत्तिसंपुड-मुत्तिअमणिणो पहासमूह व्व ।

---

1. The five pakṣas are: first the Alaṅkara school of Udbhaṭa and others, 2nd of Vāmana (the rīti school), the third of वक्रोक्तिजीवित, 4th of भट्टनायक and 5th of आनन्दवर्धन. Vide समुद्रबन्ध p. 4. The अनुमानपक्ष of व्यक्तिविवेक is unworthy of serious consideration acc. to the वृत्ति in अलं. स.

सिरिबाहडत्ति तणओ आसि बुहो तस्स सोमस्स (IV. 148 p. 72), the com. remarks 'इदानीं ग्रन्थकार इदमलङ्कारकर्तृत्वख्यापनाय वाग्भटाभिधस्य महाकवेर्महामात्यस्य तन्नाम गाथयैकया निदर्शयति'. All the examples cited in the work appear to be the author's own. A few examples are in Prākrit (e. g. IV. 49, 53, 54, 74, 78, 106, 107, 148). He cited (as pointed out by Col. Jacob, JRAS 1897 p. 309) six verses which occur in the नेमिनिर्वाणमहाकाव्य, the author of which is a वाग्भट. On the verse ककाकुकक्ककेकाङ्ककेकिकोकैककुः कक: । अकुकौकः काककाक्क कक्काकुकुककाङ्कुः ॥ (IV. 12), the com. remarks 'ककाकु इत्येष श्लोक एकव्यञ्जनो नेमिनिर्वाणमहाकाव्ये राजीमतीपरित्यागाधिकारे समुद्रवर्णनरूपो ज्ञेयः'. But this verse is not found in the printed नेमिनिर्वाण (K. M. series), though नेमिनिर्वाण VII. 50 is cited by वाग्भट in काव्यालङ्कार as an example of महायमक. It appears that the same वाग्भट was the author of both works. In the verses cited as illustrations king जयसिंह (चालुक्य) of Anhilvad, son of कर्ण, figures very frequently. For example, 'इन्द्रेण किं यदि स कर्णनरेन्द्रसूनुरैरावणेन किमहो यदि तद्द्विपेन्द्रः । दम्भोलिनाप्यलमलं यदि तत्प्रतापः स्वर्गोप्ययं ननु मुधा यदि तत्पुरी सा ॥' (IV. 76); जगदात्मकीर्तिशुभ्रंजनयन्नुद्दामधामदोःपरिघः । जयति प्रतापपूषा जयसिंहः क्ष्माभृदधिनाथः (IV. 45); अणहिल्लपाटकं पुरमवनिपतिः कर्णदेवनृपसूनुः । श्रीकलशनामधेयः करी च रत्नानि जगतीह ॥' (IV. 132). *Vide* also IV. 81, 85, the former of which (आः स्यन्दनध्वजधृतोद्धुरताम्रचूडः श्रीकर्णदेवनृपसूनुरयं रणाग्रे) shows that the Anhilvad Chālukyas had the figure of a cock on their banner. जयसिंह reigned from 1093 A. D. to 1143 A. D. *Vide* I. A. vol. 6 p. 180 (at p. 213 the pedigree of the चालुक्यs of Anhilwad with dates is set forth by Buhler) and E. I. vol. I. p. 293 for the Vaḍnagar प्रशस्ति of कुमारपाल's reign. The editors of the K. M. series show from the प्रभावकचरित्र of प्रभाचन्द्र (p. 205) that वाग्भट was living in *saṁvat* 1179 and 1213 (i. e. 1123 and 1156 A. D.). Therefore, वाग्भट flourished in the first half of the 12th century and his काव्यालङ्कार was written between 1125-1143 A. D. There are several commentaries besides that of सिंहदेवगणि such as those of जिनवर्धनसूरि, of गणेश, क्षेमहंसगणि, राजहंसोपाध्याय.

29 The काव्यानुशासन of हेमचन्द्र. This work, together with the author's own commentary, has been published in the KM series. The references here are to that edition. There is another edition in two volumes (in महावीरजैनविद्यालय series, containing text, Introduction pp. I—CCCXXX by Mr. R. C. Parikh and notes by Prof. R. B. Athavle (pp. 1-276). The work is divided as usual into three parts, *sūtras* (in prose), explanation and

examples. It appears that the *sūtras* constitute the काव्यानुशासन and the वृत्ति explaining the *sūtras* is styled अलङ्कारचूडामणि and the commentary, which in some places is extremely meagre and explains the वृत्ति and adds some examples, is styled विवेक, as the introductory verse shows (विवरीतुं क्वचिद्दृब्धं नवं सन्दर्भितुं क्वचित्। काव्यानुशासनस्यायं विवेकः प्रवितन्यते ॥). The work is divided into eight अध्यायs. The first deals with the purposes of काव्य, the *hetu* (cause) of kāvya (viz. प्रतिभा), the aids to प्रतिभा, viz. व्युत्पत्ति, अभ्यास; definition of काव्य; the nature of शब्द and अर्थ, meanings of मुख्यार्थ, गौणार्थ, लक्ष्यार्थ and व्यंग्यार्थ. The second chapter deals with *rasas*, *sthāyibhāvas*, व्यभिचारिभावs, सात्त्विकभावs. The third treats of *doṣas* of word, sentence, *artha* and *rasas*. The fourth is concerned with *guṇas* which are three, माधुर्य, ओजस् and प्रसाद and the letters that help on these. The fifth speaks of six figures of *śabda*, अनुप्रास, यमक, चित्र, श्लेष, वक्रोक्ति, पुनरुक्ताभास. The 6th discourses upon 29 figures of sense. He includes संसृष्टि under सङ्कर, so defines दीपक as to include तुल्ययोगिता in it, defines a figure परिवृत्ति which contains the पर्याय and परिवृत्ति (of मम्मट), omits all those figures that have a touch of *rasa*, bhāva &c. in them (viz. रसवत्, प्रेयः, ऊर्जस्वि, समाहित) and passes over अनन्वय, उपमेयोपमा (as varieties of उपमा), includes under निदर्शन the figures प्रतिवस्तूपमा, दृष्टान्त and निदर्शना (of others). He used the names जाति and अन्योक्ति for स्वभावोक्ति and अप्रस्तुतप्रशंसा. On pp. 292-294 he explains why he does not define some of the above figures. The 7th chap. treats of the characteristics and kinds of नायक and नायिका. The 8th gives the divisions of काव्य into प्रेक्ष्य and श्रव्य and their sub-divisions and their characteristics.

The काव्यानुशासन is a compilation[1] and exhibits hardly

---

1. Mr. Vishnupada Bhattacharji takes objection (in 'Indian Culture' vol. XIII pp. 218-224) to my statement that the काव्यानुशासन is a compilation and has hardly any originality. He points out that हेमचन्द्र demurs to Mammata's view that *artha* (wealth) is one of the rewards of writing poetry, that हेमचन्द्र differs from मुकुल and मम्मट and holds that लक्षणा is not based on रूढि or प्रयोजन but on प्रयोजन alone, that he differs (on p. 46) from ध्वनिकार who divides अर्थशक्तिमूलध्वनि into three varieties viz. स्वतःसम्भवी, कविप्रौढोक्तिनिष्पन्न and कविनिबद्धवक्तृप्रौढोक्ति०, that मम्मट gives पुंस्त्वादपि प्रविचलेत् as an example of श्लेषमूलाप्रस्तुतप्रशंसा, while

any originality. It borrows wholesale from the काव्यमीमांसा of राजशेखर, the काव्यप्रकाश, the ध्वन्यालोक and from अभिनवगुप्त's works. For example, compare pp. 8-10 of हेमचन्द्र with काव्यमीमांसा p. 56, pp. 11-16 of हेमचन्द्र with pp. 42-54 of the काव्यमीमांसा and pp. 122-123 of हेमचन्द्र with pp. 42-44 of the काव्यमीमांसा. He expressly states that he bases his views upon those of अभिनवगुप्त and भरत 'साधारणीभावना च विभावादिभिरिति श्रीमानभिनवगुप्ताचार्यः। एतन्मतमेव चास्माभिरुपजीवितं वेदितव्यम् (p. 66 of विवेक); 'तेऽस्माभिर्भरतमतानुसारिभिरुपेक्षिताः' (p. 316 of काव्यानु०). The one merit of his work is that in the वृत्ति and the commentary he cites about 1500 examples from various authors. He, however, exercised very little influence over later rhetoricians and is scarcely ever quoted (except in the रत्नापण pp. 46, 75, 224, 233, 259, 279, 299). He wrote the काव्यानुशासन after his great grammatical work (शब्दानुशासन), सिद्धहेमचन्द्र. He wrote also छन्दोनुशासन, द्व्याश्रयकाव्य, अभिधानचिन्तामणि, देशीनाममाला, त्रिषष्टिशलाकापुरुषचरित, योगशास्त्र. Vide for his life and works Mr. R.C. Parikh's Introduction pp. CCLIII-CCCXXX. Among the authors and works (too numerous to be set out at length) referred to by him the following deserve to be noted:—अवन्तिसुन्दरी, उपाहरण, दण्डी, भट्टतोत, भट्टनायक, पञ्चशिखशूद्रककथा, भामहविवरण, भोजराज, मम्मट, मङ्गल, मायुराज, यायावरीय, रावणविजय, वामन, शाक्याचार्यराहुल (p. 316), हरविलास of राजशेखर, हरिप्रबोध, हृदयदर्पण. The कीर्तिकौमुदी I. 18 praises him as follows : 'सदा हृदि वहेम श्रीहेमसूरेः सरस्वतीम्। सुवत्या शब्दरत्नानि ताम्रपर्णी जिता यया॥'.

हेमचन्द्र is the brightest star in the galaxy of Jain writers. He was a voluminous writer and wrote on numerous branches of study. Materials for the life of हेमचन्द्र are supplied by the कुमारपालप्रतिबोध of सोमप्रभ (composed in संवत् 1241, 1185 A.D.), the प्रभावकचरित of प्रभाचन्द्र (composed in संवत् 1334, 1277 A. D. and

---

हेमचन्द्र says it is an example of शब्दशक्तिमूलध्वनि, that ध्वनिकार does not point out the mistakes of great poets in violating the principles about the introduction of figures of speech among *rasas,* while हेमचन्द्र does so. Even accepting all these, they can hardly entitle the काव्यानुशासन to any claim for originality. Such points of difference are found among several other authors also. It should be noted that recently Sri Trilokanath Jha in J. of Bihar Research Society, vol. XLIII parts 1-2, 1957 pp. 22-23 contributes an exhaustive article on 'Indebtedness of Hemachandra to the author of the Vyaktiviveka, and agrees with my view about Hemachandra's काव्यानुशासन.

published in the Singhi Jain Granthamālā), the प्रबन्धचिन्तामणि of मेरुतुङ्ग (composed in संवत् 1364, 1307, A. D. and translated by Tawney) and the प्रबन्धकोश of राजशेखर pp. 46-54 (written in संवत् 1405, 1348 A. D. and published in the Singhi Jain Series). The प्रभावकचरित (pp. 183-212) gives at some length an account of the life of हेमचन्द्र, who was born at Dhandhukā of Moḍh Bania parents named चाच or चाचिग and पाहिनी. हेमचन्द्र's original name was चङ्गदेव. The four important dates concerning हेमचन्द्र are given by the प्रभावकचरित (p. 212) as follows: He was born on the Full-Moon day of Kārtika in संवत् 1145 (1088 A. D.), he was initiated in संवत् 1150 (1093 A. D.), he became a *sūri* or आचार्य in saṁvat 1166 (1109 A. D.) and died at the age of 84 in संवत् 1229 (1173 A. D.). हेमचन्द्र's *guru* was देवचन्द्र. Forbes in his 'Rāsmālā' gives an account of the two kings Siddharāja and Kumārapāla with whom हेमचन्द्र was connected (vol. I. pp. 165-197 of the Oxford Press ed. of 1924). Buhler's monograph 'Uber das Leben des Jaina Mönches Hemacandra' (1889) is complete and authentic, except in a few unimportant particulars. This German work was translated into English by Dr. Manilal Patel and published in the Singhi Jain Series in 1936. From the fact that हेमचन्द्र (on p. 109) mentions मम्मट by name and quotes from काव्यप्रकाश a verse and a half (V. 1-2) and from the fact that he wrote the काव्यानुशासन after the शब्दानुशासन and makes no mention of कुमारपाल in the काव्यानुशासन it may be said that he composed it about 1140 A. D. जयसिंह सिद्धराज at whose bidding he composed शब्दानुशासन reigned from 1093 to 1143 A. D. and कुमारपाल his successor from 1143 to 1172 A. D. Mr. R. C. Parikh holds that the काव्यानुशासन was composed between 1136-1143 A. D. (Intro. p. CCLXII).

30 The चन्द्रालोक of जयदेव. This has been printed several times in India. The Gujarati Press edition with the com. Ramā of वैद्यनाथ पायगुण्ड has been used for purposes of this note. The चन्द्रालोक is an elementary treatise on Poetics written in the Anuṣṭubh metre. The author gives his own examples as do भामह and दण्डी. The work is divided into ten मयूखs and contains about 350 verses. The style is lucid and easy, the language is flowing and sonorous, and the work is admirably adapted to the needs of beginners. The contents are:—I. the definition of काव्य, the *hetu* of काव्य (viz. प्रतिभा aided by श्रुत and अभ्यास), the threefold division of words into रूढ, यौगिक and

योगरूढ; II *doṣas* of शब्द, अर्थ, वाक्य etc.; III. some devices which poets adopt to heighten the charm of their works, such as निर्वचन (exemplified in ईदृशैश्चरितैर्जाने सत्यं दोषाकरो भवान्); IV ten *guṇas*; V figures af शब्द, अनुप्रास (छेका०, वृत्त्यनु०, लाटानु०), पुनरुक्ताभास, यमक, चित्र and one hundred figures of sense; in the midst of the 5th मयूख, at the beginning of अर्थालङ्कारs there is a fresh मङ्गल; VI *rasas*, *bhāvas*, the three *rītis* गौडी, लाटी and पाञ्चाली and the five वृत्तिs (मधुरा, प्रौढा, परुषा, ललिता and भद्रा); VII व्यञ्जना and divisions of ध्वनि (as in the ध्वन्यालोक); VIII the divisions of गुणीभूतव्यङ्ग्य; IX लक्षणा; X अभिधा. The several editions differ to some extent in the number of verses.

The author was also styled पीयूषवर्ष (shower of nectar) as the work itself shows 'चन्द्रालोकममुं स्वयं वितनुते पीयूषवर्षः कृती' (I. 2); 'अनेनासावाद्यः सुकविजयदेवेन रचिते चिरं चन्द्रालोके सुखयतु मयूखः सुमनसः ॥' (I. 16). The राकागम, com. on the चन्द्रालोक, by गागाभट्ट expressly says 'जयदेवस्यैव पीयूषवर्ष इति नामान्तरम्' on the verse 6 at the end of the चन्द्रालोक in the Chowkhambha S. Series. जयदेव was the son of महादेव and सुमित्रा (महादेवः सत्रप्रमुखमखविद्यैकचतुरः सुमित्रा तद्भक्तिप्रणिहितमतिर्यस्य पितरौ । I. 16). जयदेव, the author of the drama प्रसन्नराघव, was also the son of महादेव and सुमित्रा (vide प्रसन्न० I. 14 and 15). From the प्रसन्नराघव it appears that he was a great logician also (ननु अयं प्रमाणप्रवीणोपि श्रूयते । ...सूत्रधारः-येषां कोमलकाव्यकौशलकलालीलावती भारती तेषां कर्कशतर्कवक्रवचनोद्गारेपि किं हीयते ॥ I. 18). This जयदेव is different from the जयदेव that was the author of the गीतगोविन्द, as the latter was the son of भोजदेव and रामादेवी and was an inhabitant of किन्दुबिल्व in the Birbhum district of Bengal (while जयदेव पीयूषवर्ष seems to have been a native of विदर्भ and not of Bengal). The author of the चन्द्रालोक is probably to be identified with जयदेव named पक्षधर, author of the मणयालोक (a work on logic).

The date of the चन्द्रालोक cannot be fixed with certainty. The चन्द्रालोक mentions no author by name. But in the verse 'अङ्गीकरोति यः काव्यं शब्दार्थावनलङ्कृती । असौ न मन्यते कस्मादनुष्णमनलं कृती ॥' (I. 8), there is clearly a reference to the काव्यप्रकाशकारिका (तददोषौ शब्दार्थौ सगुणावनलङ्कृती पुनः क्वापि). We saw above (p. 275) that the अलङ्कारसर्वस्व was the first to define the two figures विचित्र and विकल्प. The चन्द्रालोक defines both these figures and almost in the same words as the सर्वस्व ('तुल्यबलविरोधो विकल्पः' अलं. स. p. 198; 'विकल्पस्तुल्यबलयोर्विरोधश्चातुरीयुतः' चन्द्रालोक V. 96; 'स्वविपरीतफलनिष्पत्तये प्रयत्नो विचित्रम्' अलं. स. p. 168; विचित्रं चेत्प्रयत्नः स्याद्विपरीतफलप्रदः ।

चन्द्रालोक V. 82)[1] The चन्द्रालोक defines and exemplifies about 100 figures. This shows that the author is one of the later writers on *alaṅkāra*. The number of *alaṅkāras* defined is in favour of a late date. मम्मट defines only 61 figures of sense, the सर्वस्व about 75. Hence the चन्द्रालोक is much later than the अलं. स. and cannot be much earlier than about 1200 A. D. A verse of the प्रसन्नराघव (कदली कदली &c. I. 37) is quoted in the साहित्यदर्पण (under IV. 3). A few verses of the प्रसन्नराघव are quoted in the शार्ङ्गधरपद्धति (dated 1363 A. D.) viz. Nos 164 (प्रसन्न० 1. 9), 3520 (1. 33), 3557 (2. 22), 3626 (7. 59), 3631 (7. 60). Therefore, जयदेव must have flourished before 1250 A. D. Hence the चन्द्रालोक is to be placed between 1200 and 1250 A. D. The अलङ्कारशेखर of केशवमिश्र (p. 17) speaks of a poet जयदेवपण्डित who vanquished by his logical subtlety the *pandits* at the court of the king of उत्कल. This probably refers to the author of the चन्द्रालोक. The कुवलयानन्द has a verse at the end 'चन्द्रालोको विजयतां शरदागमसम्भवः । हृद्यः कुवलयानन्दो यत्प्रसादादभूदयम् ॥. The three words in thick type have two meanings each. वैद्यनाथ explains that शरदागम is the original work on which the चन्द्रालोक is based. But this is wrong. शरदागम is the name of a com. on the चन्द्रालोक by प्रद्योतनभट्टाचार्य patronized by वीरभद्र, a Bundella prince (*vide* the com. published in the Kashi S. Series in 1929). This प्रद्योतन wrote a commentary on the कामसूत्र in 1557 A. D. The कुवलयानन्द expressly states that it incorporates the definitions and examples of the चन्द्रालोक on अर्थालङ्कारs (vide under अप्पय्यदीक्षित below).

31. The एकावली of विद्याधर. This work with the commentary, तरल of मल्लिनाथ, has been edited by Mr. Trivedi in the B. S. series. The work contains three parts, the *kārikās*, the *vṛtti* and the examples. The peculiarity of this work is that all the examples are composed by विद्याधर himself and contain panegyrics of his patron, king नरसिंह of उत्कल (or Orissa). He himself says (Intro. verse 7) 'एष विद्याधरस्तेषु कान्तासंमितलक्षणम् । करोमि नरसिंहस्य चाटुश्लोकानुदाहरन् ॥'. विद्याधर notes (in I. 4-6) that शास्त्र is of three kinds viz. शब्दप्रधान (called प्रभुसंमित), अर्थप्रधान (called

---

1. It is noteworthy that in some editions of the चन्द्रालोक such as Jivananda's the definitions of विकल्प and विचित्र are 'विरोधे तुल्यबलयोर्विकल्पालङ्कृतिर्मता' and 'विचित्रं तत्प्रयत्नश्चेद्विपरीतफलेच्छया'. The definition in the Gujarati Press edition is that of the साहित्यदर्पण.

मित्रसंमित, such as इतिहास i. e. महाभारत) &c.) and ध्वनिप्रधान (called कान्तासंमित). In this respect it resembles the प्रतापरुद्रयशोभूषण, the नञ्जराजयशोभूषण, the रघुनाथभूपालीय and the अलङ्कारमञ्जूषा. The work is divided into eight उन्मेषs, the subjects of which are :— I the *hetu* of काव्य (प्रतिभा, बहुशास्त्रदर्शिता and अभ्यास), definition of काव्य, discussion of the views of भामह, महिमभट्ट and others; II. word is वाचक, लाक्षणिक and व्यञ्जक and discussion of the three powers, अभिधा, लक्षणा and व्यञ्जना; III. sub-divisions of ध्वनि; IV. treatment of गुणीभूतव्यङ्ग्य; V. *guṇas* (three) and three *rītis*; VI: *doṣas*; VII *alaṅkāras* of *śabda*; VIII *alaṅkāras* of sense. In the first उन्मेष, विद्याधर is a thorough—going follower of the ध्वन्यालोक. His work is based on the काव्यप्रकाश and the अलङ्कारसर्वस्व. In the treatment of *alaṅkāras* he prefers the सर्वस्व to the काव्यप्रकाश e. g. he defines the figures परिणाम, उल्लेख, विचित्र and विकल्प almost in the same words as the सर्वस्व, which do not occur in the काव्यप्रकाश at all. Among others he names the following:—अभिनवगुप्त, अलङ्कारसर्वस्व, काव्यप्रकाश, विह्लण, भोज, महिमभट्ट, वामन, श्रीहर्ष, हम्मीर, हरिहर and अर्जुन, and quotes from दशरूप, नैषधीय, राजशेखर. He wrote another work केलिरहस्य on Erotics; vide Trivedi's Intro. pp. XV- XVI.

Mr. Trivedi (in his Introduction) collects all the data for arriving at the age in which विद्याधर flourished and comes to the conclusion (p. XXIII) that he was patronised either by केसरिनरसिंह (1282-1307) or प्रतापनरसिंह (1307-1327 A. D.). The Intro. verse 11 mentions the poet हरिहर and king अर्जुन (*i.e.* अर्जुनवर्मदेव), for whose dates vide p. 272 above. Therefore एकावली is later than the first half of 13th century. The रसार्णवसुधाकर of शिङ्गभूपाल (about 1330 A. D.) refers to the एकावली 'उत्कलाधिपतेः शृङ्गाररसाभिमानिनो नरसिंहदेवस्य चित्तमनुवर्तमानेन विद्याधरेण कविना बाढमभ्यन्तरीकृतोसि। एवं खलु समर्थितमेकावल्यामनेन' (p. 206 of Trivandrum ed.) and on pp. 258 and 277 शिङ्गभूपाल quotes प्रसन्नराघव; therefore the एकावली must have been composed between 1285-1325 A. D.

The तरल is a model commentary. It is from the pen of the famous commentator of the *mahākāvyas*. मल्लि० flourished probably at the end of the 14th century and in the beginning of the 15th century. Vide Trivedi's Intro. pp. XXIV-XXX for the life and works of मल्लिनाथ.

32. The प्रतापरुद्रयशोभूषण of विद्यानाथ. An excellent edition of this work, with the commentary called रत्नापण by कुमारस्वामिन् son of मल्लिनाथ, was brought out by Mr. Trivedi in the B. S.

series (in 1909). Another edition of the work with रत्नापण was brought out in Madras in 1914 (which reached the third ed. in 1950). This work is very popular in Southern India. The work contains three parts, *kārikās*, *vṛtti* and illustrations. All the examples are composed in honour of the काकतीय king of Telaṅgaṇa, प्रतापरुद्रदेव (also called वीररुद्र or रुद्र), whose capital was एकशिला (Orangal or Warangal) 'प्रतापरुद्रदेवस्य गुणानाश्रित्य निर्मितः। अलङ्कारप्रबन्धोयं सन्तः कर्णोत्सवोस्तु वः ॥' I. 9. In this respect it resembles the एकावली. The work has 9 प्रकरणs on नायक, काव्य, नाटक, रस, दोष, गुण, शब्दालङ्कार, अर्थालङ्कार, मिश्रालङ्कार. Among others the following are named:—अनर्घराघव, अभिनयदर्पण, अलङ्कारसर्वस्व, उद्भट, काव्यप्रकाश, दण्डिन्, दशरूपक, बालरामायण, भरत, भामह, भोज, रुद्रभट्ट, शृङ्गारतिलक, साहित्यमीमांसा. In the third प्रकरण, while illustrating the requirements of a नाटक, he exhibits a model drama called प्रतापरुद्रकल्याण (on p. 139-218). He follows in general the काव्यप्रकाश but prefers the अलङ्कारसर्वस्व to मम्मट in the matter of figures. He defines the figures परिणाम, उल्लेख, विचित्र, and विकल्प, which are passed over by मम्मट and his definition of विकल्प (विरोधस्तुल्यबलयोर्विकल्पालङ्कृतिर्मता p. 456) is almost the same as that of the चन्द्रालोक. प्रतापरुद्रदेव was the son of महादेव and मुम्मुडि or मुम्मुडम्बा, who was the daughter of रुद्राम्बा. This रुद्राम्बा was known as रुद्र and ruled at एकशिला after her father गणपति. प्रतापरुद्रदेव is said to have routed सेवण of the यादव family (i. e. रामदेव of देवगिरि, 1271-1309 A. D.). From this fact and the information supplied by epigraphic records it followes that प्रतापरुद्रदेव ruled in the last quarter of the 13th and the first quarter of the 14th century and was captured in 1323 A. D. by Muhammad Tughlak's armies. Therefore, the प्रतापरुद्रयशोभूषण was composed in the first quarter of the 14th century.[1]

1. The pedigree of the काकतीय dynasty is as follows : (1) Betma—(2) Proda or Prola—(3) Rudra,—(4) Mahadeva brother of (3)—(5) Gaṇapati or Gaṇapa son of (4)—daughter Gaṇapāmbā married Beta; another daughter of Gaṇapati was Rudrāmbā also styled Rudradeva who ruled as king, she is the 6th king—(7) Prātāparudradeva was the daughter's son of Rudrā. Vide the Yenamadala Inscription of Gaṇapāmbā (E. I. vol. III. p. 94), the Arulala Perumal Inscription of the time of Pratāparudra dated śaka 1238 (1316-17 A. D.), the Malkapuram stone Inscription of रुद्रदेव (*i. e.* रुद्राम्बा) dated saka 1183 *i. e.* 1261-62 A. D. (J. of Andhra H. R. S. vol. IV.

The रत्नापण of कुमारस्वामिन् is a good commentary, though inferior to the तरल of मल्लिनाथ. He quotes a host of writers, among whom the following deserve to be noted—अलङ्कारचूडामणि, एकावली, एकावलीतरल, कविकल्पद्रुम, गोपाल, चक्रवर्तिन् (author of अलङ्कारसर्वस्वसञ्जीविनी), दशरूपक, नरहरि, नाटकप्रकाश, पञ्चपादिका, पदमञ्जरी, भट्टमल्ल, भावप्रकाश, भोजराज, महिमभट्ट, मानसोल्लास, रसनिरूपण (of नरहरि), रसमञ्जरी, रसार्णव, रुचक, वसन्तराजीय, विदग्धमुखमण्डन, विद्याधर, शारदातनय, शिङ्गभूपाल, शृङ्गारप्रकाश, सञ्जीविनी, साहित्यचिन्तामणि, साहित्यदर्पण, हेमचन्द्र. Another com. रत्नशाण is incomplete and refers to रत्नापण.

33. The काव्यानुशासन of वाग्भट. This वाग्भट is वाग्भट II, This work has been published in 1915 in the K. M. series together with the commentary अलङ्कारतिलक composed by the author himself. The work consists of sūtras in prose, वृत्ति and examples mostly borrowed. The work is divided into five अध्यायs. The main part is in the form of *sūtras* in prose and the explanation and all illustrations occur in the commentary. The first अध्याय dwells upon the प्रयोजन of काव्य, the *hetu* of *kāvya* (viz. प्रतिभा aided by व्युत्पत्ति and अभ्यास) and the definitions of these; conventions of poets; definition of *kāvya* and its divisions गद्य, पद्य and मिश्र; definitions of महाकाव्य, आख्यायिका, कथा, चम्पू, मिश्रकाव्य (the ten रूपकs and गेयs). The second chapter deals with the 16 *doṣas* of पद and वाक्य, 14 *doṣas* of sense, speaks of the ten *guṇas* according to Daṇḍin and Vāmana, but gives as its opinion that the *guṇas* are really three, माधुर्य, ओजस्, and प्रसाद; and mentions the *rītis*, वैदर्भी, गौडीया and पाञ्चाली. The third chap. defines 63 *alaṅkāras* of sense, of which the following deserve mention as being somewhat rare : अन्य, अपर, पूर्व, लेश, पिहित, मत, उभयन्यास, भाव, and आशीः. The fourth chap. treats of six *alaṅkāras* of *śabda*, चित्र, श्लेष, अनुप्रास, वक्रोक्ति, यमक, पुनरुक्तवदाभास, and their varieties. The fifth chapter dilates upon the nine *rasas*, विभावs, अनुभावs, व्यभिचारिभावs, the varieties of नायक and नायिका, the ten stages of love and the *doṣas* of *rasas*. The author was a Jain. He mentions the country of मेदपाट (Mewad) and the towns of राहडपुर and नलोटकपुर. He was the son of नेमिकुमार and is to be distinguished from वाग्भट I who was the author of वाग्भटालङ्कार, as he himself mentions the latter 'दण्डिवामनवाग्भटादि-

p. 47), 'Indian Culture' vol. III. pp. 465-475; J. of Andhra H. R. S. vol. III. pp. 111-118 on 'some interesting facts about the Kākatīyas' by Mr. M. Rama Rao. काकती is the name of दुर्गा. The काकतीय rulers were śūdras and śaivas.

प्रणीता दश काव्यगुणाः । वयं तु माधुर्यौजःप्रसादलक्षणांस्त्रीनेव गुणान्मन्यामहे' (काव्यानुशासनवृत्ति p. 31). In his commentary (pp. 3-5) he gives long lists of countries, rivers, plants and products peculiar to each. He seems to have written a महाकाव्य named ऋषभदेवचरित (p. 15) and a work on metrics styled छन्दोनुशासन (p. 20). A verse (on p. 58) addressed to वाग्भट (i. e. probably the author himself) is quoted in the com. and another in which नेमिकुमार is addressed occurs on p. 32 (गायन्ति रासकविधाविह मेदपाटनार्योऽधुनापि तव नेमिकुमार कीर्तिम् ॥). Among the authors and works quoted by him are अब्धिमथन (अपभ्रंशनिबद्ध p. 15), आनन्दवर्धन, काव्यप्रकाश (p. 29), चन्द्रप्रभकाव्य, त्रिविक्रम (p. 20), दमयन्ती (p. 19), नेमिनिर्वाण (p. 16), बालरामायण (p. 67), भीमकाव्य (in ग्राम्यभाषा p. 15), राजीमतीपरित्याग, लीलावती (पद्यमयीकथा p. 18), वासवदत्ता (चम्पू p. 19), विष्णुविजय, शीता (a poetess p. 20), शृङ्गारतिलक (pp. 61 and 63 the verses अस्माकं सखि and गाढालिङ्गन०). There is no originality in the work. He largely borrows from the काव्यमीमांसा of राजशेखर, the काव्यप्रकाश and other works and quotes examples contained in other works e. g. he quotes under यमक the verse रम्भारामा० which is वाग्भटालङ्कार IV. 30 and नेमिनिर्वाणकाव्य VII. 50.

A ms. of the काव्यानुशासन (Eggeling's cat. No. 1157) is dated संवत् 1515 (1458-59 A. D.). He mentions the काव्यप्रकाश and वाग्भट. Therefore he is later than 1150 A.D. He probably flourished in the 14th century.

34. The साहित्यदर्पण of विश्वनाथ. Beyond a few scraps of information gathered from his own works, we know very little about the personal history of Viśvanātha. He come of a brāhmaṇa family that had distinguished itself by learning. His great-great-grand-father was Nārāyaṇa, who appears to have been a learned man and to have written a work on Rhetoric.[1] His father was Chandraśekhara, who was a poet

---

1. 'तत्प्राणत्वं चास्मद्वृद्धप्रपितामहसहृदयगोष्ठीगरिष्ठकविपण्डितमुख्यश्रीमन्नारायणपादैरुक्तम् ।' S. D. III. 2-3; but in his Kāvyaprakāśadarpaṇa, Viśvanātha says that Nārāyaṇa was his grandfather "यदाहुः श्रीकलिङ्गभूमण्डलाखण्डलमहाराजाधिराजश्रीनरसिंहदेवसभायां धर्मदत्तं स्थगयन्त...... अस्मत्पितामहश्रीमन्नारायणदासपादाः" Intro. to K. P. p. 25 (Vā.). Two explanations are possible; I Nārāyaṇa was really the great-great-grand-father and is referred to as the grand-father for the sake of brevity; II The two Nārāyaṇas were distinct, one being the grand-son of the other. In India, a grandson often bears the name of his grand-father.

and scholar. His verses are often quoted by Viśvanātha (pp. 108, 122, 178, 182 &c. Nirn. ed, of 1922). Viśvanātha mentions by name two works of his father, viz. the Puṣpamālā (on VI. 25) and Bhāṣārṇava which dealt with the characteristics of Sanskrit, Śaurasenī, Mahārāṣṭrī and other Prākrit dialects. As Viśvanātha explains certain Sanskrit expressions by Uriya equivalents in his commentary on the Kāvyaprakāśa, he appears to have been an inhabitant of Orissa.[1] The father of Viśvanātha and Viśvanātha himself appear to have held some important office at the court of a king, probably of Kaliṅga. Both of them are styled Sāndhivigrahika-Mahāpātra. Viśvanātha was a Vaiṣṇava as is made clear by the colophon[2] at the end of the first Pariccheda and the last verse of the Sāhityadarpaṇa.[3] He was a poet and quotes his own verses in Sanskrit and Prakrit at every step, when illustrating the canons of Rhetoric. He composed a number of works, besides the Sāhityadarpaṇa, of which the following are mentioned in the latter:—I. a *mahākāvya* in Sanskrit, called Rāghava-vilāsa (under III. 222-224); II Kuvalayāśvacarita, a *kāvya* in Prakrit (III. 149); Prabhāvatī-pariṇaya, a Nāṭikā (III (58); IV Chandrakalā, another Nāṭikā (III. 96); V Praśastiratnāvalī, a Karambhaka in sixteen languages (VI. 337). After composing the Sāhityadarpaṇa, he wrote two other works, a *kāvya* called Narasiṁha-vijaya[4] and a commentary on the Kāvyaprakāśa called Kāvyaprakāśa-darpaṇa (see Intro. to K. P. p. 25, Vā,). Caṇḍīdāsa, who wrote a commentary on the Kāvyprakāśā, was the younger brother of Viśvanātha's grand-father.[5]

The question of Viśvanātha's date does not present much difficulty. There are certain data, which fortunately for us, fix within very narrow limits his chronological position.

---

1. See Vāmanācharya's Introduction to K. P. p. 25 'वैपरीत्यं रुचिं कुर्विति पाठः, अत्र चिङ्कुपदं काश्मीरादिभाषायामश्लीलार्थबोधकम्, उत्कलादिभाषायां घृतवाडकद्रव इत्यादि ।'

2. 'श्रीमन्नारायणचरणारविन्दमधुव्रत etc.' Note the words 'काव्याद्धर्मप्राप्तिर्भगवन्नारायणचरणारविन्दस्तवादिना' p. 1.

3. यावत्प्रसन्नेन्दुनिभानना श्रीर्नारायणस्याङ्कमलङ्करोति ।.

4. अनन्तदास quotes a verse on p. 9 with the words यथा मम तातपादानां विजयनरसिंहे.

5. 'अस्मत्पितामहानुजकविपण्डितमुख्यश्रीचण्डीदासपादानां तु खण्डरसनाम्ना' VII. 31.

A ms. of the Sāhityadarpaṇa deposited at Jammu[1] is dated in the Vikrama year 1440, *i. e.* approximately 1384 A.D. From this it may be safely concluded that the Sāhityadarpaṇa was composed at some time earlier than 1384 A. D. Viśvanatha quotes a verse which speaks of a Mohammadon king named Allauddin.[2] We saw above that Viśvanātha came from Orissa. The king referred to in the verse is certainly Sultan[3] Allauddin Khilji, whose favourite general Malik Kafur invaded the Deccan, seized Warangal and carried his victorious arms as far as Cape Comorin. Allauddin, it is said, was poisoned in 1316 A. D. Supposing that the verse in which Allauddin is mentioned by name was written in his life-time, the Sāhityadarpaṇa cannot be said to have been composed at a date earlier than 1300 A. D. From these two circumstances it follows that the Sāhityadarpaṇa was composed at some time between 1300 A. D. and 1384 A. D.

There is a good deal of evidence, both internal and external, that confirms this conclusion.

I The internal evidence is a follows:—(a) Viśvanātha quotes a verse from the Gītagovinda of Jayadeva.[4] Tradition makes Jayadeva, along with Govardhana, Śaraṇa, Umāpati and Kavirāja, a protege of Lakṣmaṇa-sena whose inscription at Gayā is dated in saṁvat 1173 or 1116 A. D.[5] Jayadeva himself mentions Govardhana and others as his contemporaries.[6] We may say that Jayadeva flourished in the first half of the 12th century.

---

1. See Dr. Stein's Catalogue of mss. at Jammu under the heading Alaṅkārśāstra p. 64.

2. सन्धौ सर्वस्वहरणं विग्रहे प्राणनिग्रहः ।
अलावदीननृपतौ न सन्धिर्न च विग्रहः ॥ IV. 14, p. 244 Nir. ed.

3. The word Sultan, it should be noted, occurs under the Sanskritized from सुरत्राण in the साहित्यदर्पण, 'गङ्गाम्भसि सुरत्राण तव निःशाननिस्वनः ।' p. 30 of our text (under) उत्प्रेक्षा).

4. 'हृदि बिसलताहारो नायं' etc. p. 29 of our text (under निश्चय). This verse is ascribed to Jayadeva in the Subhāshitāvali also.

5. Buhler's Kashmir Report p. 64.

6. वाचः पल्लवयत्युमापतिधरः सन्दर्भशुद्धिं गिरां जानीते जयदेव एव शरणः श्लाघ्यो दुरूहद्रुते । शृङ्गारोत्तरसत्प्रमेयवचनैराचार्यगोवर्धनः स्पर्धी कोऽपि न विश्रुतः श्रुतधरो धोयी कविक्ष्मापतिः ॥ 4th verse of thc Gītagovinda.

(b) विश्वनाथ quotes a verse (कदली कदली &c. under IV. 3) from the प्रसन्नराघव (I. 37) of जयदेव who flourished between 1200 and 1250 A. D. We have pointed out in our notes to साहित्यदर्पण that Viśvanātha often quotes[1] verbatim from the Alaṅkārrasarvasva of Ruyyaka and in some places even criticizes it. We know that Ruyyaka was the teacher[2] of Maṅkha, author of Śrīkaṇṭhacarita. In the 25th *sarga* of the Śrīkaṇṭhacarita Maṅkha tells us that he showed his work to an assembly of learned men in the house of his elder brother Alaṅkāra[3] who was minister[4] of king Jayasiṁha of Kashmir (1129-1150 A. D.). The Śrīkaṇṭhacarita was composed about 1140 A. D. at an advanced age. A good deal of time must have elapsed before Ruyyaka's work attained such popularity as to be the guide of a writer from Orissa.

(c) Viśvanātha quotes some verses from the Naiṣadhīyacarita of Śrīharṣa.[5] The date of Śrīharṣa has been for a long time a subject of discussion among scholars. Śrīharṣa tells us that he was patronized by a king of Kānyakubja.[6] Rājaśekhara in his Prabandhakośa written in saṁvat 1405 informs us that Śrīharṣa was the son of Hīra, who was a minister of Jayantacandra of Kāśī. It is probable that this Jayantachandra is the same as the Jayacandra that was a king of Kanauj. One of the earliest inscriptions of Jayachandra is dated in saṁvat 1223.[7] Buhler referred the composition of

1. See e. g. pp. 41, 42, 60 of the text and the notes thereon.

2. तं श्रीरुय्यकमालोक्य स प्रियं गुरुमग्रहीत् ।
सौहार्दप्रश्रयरसस्रोतःसम्भेदमज्जनम् ॥ श्रीकण्ठ. XXV. 30.

3. मदग्रजन्मनः श्रीमल्लङ्ककस्य सभागृहम् । तेध्यासते च विस्रब्धाः सारसा इव मानसम् ॥ XXV. 15. लङ्कक must have been another name of अलङ्कार. In the third *sarga* Maṅkha tells us that he was the last of four brothers, the other three being शृङ्गार, भृङ्ग and अलङ्कार (verse 45, 53, 56).

4. एकं श्रीजयसिंहपार्थिवपतिं काश्मीरमीनध्वजं
तस्योपासितसन्धिविग्रहमलङ्कारं द्वितीयं स्तुमः । श्रीकण्ठ० XXV. 61.

5. हनूमदाद्यैः etc. (p. 31), धन्यासि वैदर्भि etc. (p. 36) which are respectively नैषधीय IX. 123 and III. 116.

6. 'ताम्बूलद्वयमासनं च लभते यः कान्यकुब्जेश्वरात्' etc. last verse of the Naiṣadhīya.

7. J. B. B. R. A. S. vol. X. p. 31 ff.

the Naiṣadhīya to some date between 1167 A.D. and 1174 A. D. Gadādhara, a commentator of the Naiṣadhīya, makes Śrīharṣa a protege of Govindachandra of Vārāṇasī.[1] Maṅkha informs us that a king of Kānyakubja, named Govindachandra, sent an ambassador to Jayasiṁha, king of Kashmir.[2] It is not unlikely that this is the same as the king mentioned by Gadādhara. Vārāṇasī and Kānyakubja may have both been the capitals of the king, or the king may have conquered Vārāṇasī after coming to the throne of Kanauj. There is another line of reasoning which leads us approximately to the sama date as the above. Śrīharṣa wrote the Khaṇḍanakhaṇḍakhādya[3] in which he ridicules Udayana by twisting a verse of the latter.[4] उदयन wrote his लक्षणावली in śake 906 i. e. 984--5 A. D. 'तर्काम्बराङ्कप्रमितेष्वतीतेषु शकान्ततः । वर्षेषूदयनश्चक्रे सुबोधां लक्षणावलीम् ॥'.

(d) Caṇḍīdāsa, a commentator of the Kāvyaprakāśa, was the younger brother of Viśvanātha's grand-father. It has been shown (p. 274) that the काव्यप्रकाश was composed between 1050 and 1100 A. D. Caṇḍīdāśa is not one of the oldest commentators of the Kāvyaprakāśa and Viśvanātha is removed by two generations from him. Prof. Bhattacharya in his edition of काव्यप्रकाशसङ्केत in Cal. O. J. vol. II. p. 10 (note) finds fault with me for saying (on p. 73 of my Notes) that in the words मान्य and उपजीव्य the reference is to रुय्यक. He says that विश्वनाथ refers in these words to चण्डीदास's दीपिका. But I am not at all wrong. He admits that the words set out in the साहित्यदर्पण are not found in the दीपिका. I gave two meanings of that passage : (1) विश्वनाथ rebukes रुय्यक for going against मम्मट who is both मान्य

1. See Prof. S. R. Bhandarkar's Report on his second tour for 1904-5 pp. 43, 87.

2. अन्यः स सुहलस्तेन ततोऽवन्द्यत पण्डितः ।
दूतो गोविन्दचन्द्रस्य कान्यकुब्जस्य भूभुजः ॥ श्रीकण्ठ० XXV. 102.

3. 'षष्ठः खण्डनखण्डतोऽपि सहजात्क्षोदक्षमे तन्महाकाव्येऽयं व्यगमन्नलस्य चरिते सर्गो निसर्गोज्ज्वलः ॥' at the end of the sixth *sarga* of the Nai.

4. See Preface to Nyāyakusumāñjali, p. 15. Udayana's verse is 'शङ्का चेदनुमास्त्येव न चेच्छङ्का ततस्तराम् । व्याघातावधिराशङ्का तर्कः शङ्कावधिर्मतः ॥' 3rd स्तबक, 7th verse p. 382 of न्यायकुसुमाञ्जली, on which Śrīharṣa retorts 'तस्मादस्माभिरप्यस्मिन्नर्थे न खलु दुष्पठा । त्वद्गाथैवान्यथाकारमक्षराणि कियन्त्यपि । व्याघातो यदि शङ्कास्ति न चेच्छङ्का ततस्तराम् । व्याघातावधिराशङ्का तर्कः शङ्कावधिः कुतः ॥'.

and उपजीव्य to रुय्यक, or (2) he would not further criticize रुय्यक who is मान्य and उप०.

(e) Viśvanātha quotes the words of a writer called Dharmadatta,[1] who was a contemporary of Nārāyaṇa, the grand-father (great-great-grand-father ?) of Viśvanātha and was vanquished by him in the court of king Narasiṁha of Kaliṅga. Whether Nārāyaṇa was the grandfather or great-great-grand-father of Viśvanātha would not make much difference. Many kings of Kaliṅga bore the name Narasiṁha. Besides, there is a good deal of confusion about the dates of their accession.[2] As a ms. of the Sāhityadarpaṇa is dated in 1384 A. D. Narasiṁha IV is not certainly the king at whose court Nārayaṇa lived, because Narasiṁha IV came to the throne at some time between 1373 A. D. and 1411 A. D. Narasiṁha III also is out of question, as the date of his accession is somewhere between 1328 A. D. and 1361 A. D. It is likely that Narasiṁha II is the king referred to. The date of his accession falls between 1270 A. D. and 1303 A. D.; he is also styled Kavipriya in his inscriptions, which makes it probable that he patronized many learned men. If Nārāyaṇa was really the great-great-grand-father of Viśvanātha, then the king may have been Narasiṁha I, the date of whose accession is somewhere near 1253 A. D.

II. The external evidence is as follows:—(f) The Sāhityadarpaṇa is twice mentioned by name in the Ratnāpaṇa[3] of Kumārasvāmin, a commentary of the Pratāparudrīya. Kumārasvāmin is the son of the famous commentator Mallinātha, who is believed by all competent authorities to have flourished in the 15th century.[4]

---

1. तदाह: धर्मदत्तः स्वग्रन्थे 'रसे सारश्चमत्कारः सर्वत्राप्यनुभूयते । तच्चमत्कारसारत्वे सर्वत्राप्यद्भुतो रसः । तस्मादद्भुतमेवाह कृती नारायणो रसम् ॥' on S. D. III. 2-3.

2. See Dr. Bhandarkar's Note on the kings of Kaliṅga in the Introduction to Mr. Trivedi's edition of the Ekāvalī.

3. See pp. 245, 248 of the प्रतापरुद्रयशोभूषण. The quotations are the definitions of the व्यभिचारिभावs मद and मोह, which occur in the S. D (III. 146-47 and 150).

4. See Dr. Bhandarkar's Preface to the Mālatīmādhava and Mr. Trivedi's Introduction (pp. XXIV-XXV) to the Bhaṭṭikāvya.

(h) Govinda Ṭhakkura in his Kāvyaprakāśa-pradīpa quotes the criticism of Viśvanātha on Mammaṭa's definition of *kāvya* and Viśvanātha's definition of *kāvya* without actually naming him.[1] Govinda is earlier than 1600 A. D., as he is mentioned by Kamalākarabhaṭṭa, who wrote a commentary on the Kāvyaprakāśa and finished the Nirṇayasindhu in 1612 A. D.[2]

From the foregoing, we see that Viśvanātha refers to a number of writers who flourished in the 12th century A. D. and is in his turn referred to by writers belonging to the 15th and 16th centuries. The date above assigned to Viśvanātha, viz. between 1300-1380 A. D., is thus confirmed by unimpeachable and independent testimony.

In the first *pari.* after the customary *maṅgala,* the author speaks of the fruits of poetry, discusses the definitions of *kāvya* proposed by different writers and at last gives his own definition and illustrates it. In the second *pari.* after defining a sentence and a word, the author deals at great length with three powers of a word. In the third *pari.* a full disquisition on *rasas, bhāvas* and other cognate topics is given. The fourth *pari.* exhaustively deals with the two divisions of *kāvya,* viz. ध्वनि and गुणीभूतव्यङ्ग्य and their sub-divisions. In the fifth, the author establishes the existence of the *vyañjanāvṛtti* and refutes the arguments of those who deny its existence. In the sixth a full and complete treatment of the science of dramaturgy is given. The 7th deals with the *doṣas* of *kāvya.* The 8th speaks of the three *guṇas* of *kāvya* and shows that the *guṇas* spoken of by others are either included in the three mentioned by Viśvanātha or are no *guṇas* at all. In the 9th, the author dilates upon the styles of composition, which are four वैदर्भी, गौडी, पाञ्चाली and लाटी. In the 10th, both शब्दालङ्कारs and अर्थालङ्कारs are dealt with.

In the galaxy of Sanskrit rhetoricians Viśvanātha is a

---

1. अर्वाचीनास्तु "यथोक्तस्य काव्यलक्षणत्वे काव्यपदं निर्विषयं प्रविरलविषयं वा स्यात्। दोषाणां दुर्वारत्वात्। तस्मात् 'वाक्यं रसात्मकं काव्यम्' इति तल्लक्षणम्। तथा च दुष्टेऽपि रसान्वये काव्यत्वमस्त्येव। परं त्वपकर्षमात्रम्। तदुक्तम् 'कीटानुविद्धरत्नादि' इत्यादि। एवं चालङ्कारादिसत्त्वे उत्कर्षमात्रम्। नीरसे तु चित्रादौ काव्यव्यवहारो गौणः" इत्याहुः। प्रदीप p. 13 (Nir.)

2. वसुऋतुऋतुभूमिते गतेब्दे नरपतिविक्रमतोऽथ याति रौद्रे। तपसि शिवतिथौ समापितोऽयं रघुपतिपादसरोरुहेऽर्पितश्च ॥.

star of the second magnitude only. Beside the brilliance of Ānandavardhana, Mammaṭa and Jagannātha his light appears dim. Still the work of Viśvanātha has some merits of its own. Its greatest merit is that it presents in the compass of a single work, a full and complete treatment of the science of rhetoric in all its branches. Most Sanskrit writers on Sāhitya, such as Daṇḍin[1], Mammaṭa and Jagannātha, leave out the treatment of dramaturgy. The साहित्यदर्पण, however, contains a thorough disquisition on the technicalities of the dramatic art and forms, together with the Nāṭyaśāstra of Bharata and the Daśarūpa of धनञ्जय, a triumvirate in the domain of the Sanskrit drama. Another merit of the work is that it is written in a simple and flowing style. The reader is often hampered in going over the Kāvyaprakāśa of Mammaṭa by the author's studied efforts at brevity. Jagannātha frightens the student by his flowery language, his subtle reasoning and his scathing criticisms of his predecessors. Viśvanātha, although he displays here and there a love for hair-splitting, is generally clear in expression. He is, however, more or less a compiler and not an original writer. In the notes to the साहित्यदर्पण we have pointed out in detail to what extent he borrows from the अलं. स.[2] Sometimes his judgment seems to forsake him and he follows slavishly the Sarvasva.[3] He does not appear to have bestowed much time and pains upon the selection of examples. Out of about 250 quotations occurring in परिच्छेदs I, II and X he borrows no less than 85 from the Dhvanyāloka, the Kāvyaprakāśa or the Sarvasva and quotes about 20 verses of his own. He is not happy in the innovations that he introduces[4] and is sometimes wrong in what he says.[5] In spite of these blemishes, his work forms an easy and suitable introduction to Sanskrit *sāhitya*. Vide an article on

1. Daṇḍin says 'मिश्राणि नाटकादीनि तेषामन्यत्र विस्तरः ।' K. D. I. 31; Bhāmaha says 'नाटकं द्विपदीशम्यारासकस्कन्धकादि यत् । उक्तं तदभिनेयार्थमुक्तोन्यैस्तस्य विस्तरः ॥' I. 24.

2. See p. 187, 209, 216, 310 etc.

3. Vide e. g. the treatment of परिणाम, व्यतिरेक and अर्थान्तरन्यास.

4. For example, vide निश्चय pp. 138-141 and अनुकूल pp. 230-231 of my notes on साहित्यदर्पण.

5. Vide remarks on pp. 100, 125, 213, 243, of the notes.

Viśvanātha Kavirāja and his references to forgotten Alaṅkāra writers by Prof. S.P. Bhattachārya in JOI (Baroda) vol. III. pp. 357-365.

To judge from the number of commentaries, Viśvanātha's work seems not to have enjoyed much popularity except perhaps in Bengal. From the various report's on the search for mss. it appears that there exist five commentaries.[1] That of Rāmacaraṇa is printed in the Nir. edition. The commentary, though useful in its own way, is not so learned or helpful as the Pradīpa or the Uddyota. It seldom gives the sources of the verses quoted in illustration or explanations of them. It very rarely compares the author's definitions with those of other writers. It commits serious mistakes in certain cases.[2] Mr. Motilal Banarasidas of Lahore published in 1938 A. D. an edition of the साहित्यदर्पण with two commentaries, viz. the विज्ञप्रिया of महेश्वरभट्ट and the लोचन of अनन्तदास, son of विश्वनाथ himself. The लोचन is brief, but learned and to the point. The विज्ञप्रिया is an extensive and learned commentary. महेश्वर commented on the काव्यप्रकाश also. He flourished about the middle of the 17th century. Recently the Kāśī-sanskrita-granthmālā (2nd ed. in 1955) published the whole of the Sāhityadarpaṇa with a modern sanskrit commentary called Lakṣmī by ācārya Kṛṣṇamohana Śāstri, and Dr. Satyavrata Sinha has brought out an edition (1957) with a Hindī commentary in the Vidyābhavana-granthamālā (Banaras).

35 The रसमञ्जरी and रसतरङ्गिणी of भानुदत्त. The first work has been published with two commentaries (in the Banaras S. Series) and the second by P. Regnaud in 'La Rhetorique Sanskrite' pp. 43-66 and by the Venkateśwar press, Bombay. The रसतरङ्गिणी is divided into eight तरङ्गs; I मङ्गल in honour of कृष्ण, definitions, and sub-divisions of भाव, स्थायिभाव; II definition and divisions of विभाव; III अनुभावs (such as कटाक्ष); IV the eight सात्त्विकभावs (स्तम्भ, स्वेद, रोमाञ्च &c.); V व्यभिचारिभावs; VI *Rasas* and detailed treatment of शृङ्गार; VII हास्य and other *rasas*; VIII three kinds of दृष्टि, viz. that due to

1. Viz. that of अनन्तदास, a ms. of which is dated in 1626 A. D.; that of रामचरण written in 1700 A. D., that of मथुरानाथ शुक्ल, the प्रभा of गोपीनाथ and विज्ञप्रिया of महेश्वर.

2. Vide notes on निश्चय (p. 139), विशेष (pp. 255-257), भाविक (pp. 307-308).

स्थायिभावs (eight kinds), that due to व्यभिचारिभावs (20 kinds), that due to the rasas (eight kinds) and illustration of some of them; how some rasas spring from others and opposition among them. The रसमञ्जरी is a somewhat smaller treatise than the रसतर० and their topics are somewhat different. The रसमञ्जरी deals with नायिकाs and their varieties (about two-thirds of the work are taken up by this subject), the सखी of the नायिका, दूती, नायकs (in शृङ्गार) and their varieties, the friends of the नायक (viz. पीठमर्द, विट, चेट, विदूषक), the eight सात्त्विकगुणs (स्तम्भ &c.), two varieties of शृङ्गार and ten stages of विप्रलम्भ. In both works all the examples except in a few cases where the author indicates to the contrary are the author's own as he says 'अवगाहस्व वाग्देवि दिव्यां रसतरङ्गिणीम् । अस्मत्पद्यान पद्येन रचय श्रुतिभूषणम् ॥' (रसत० 8. 29) and पद्येन स्वीकृतेन तेन कविना श्रीभानुना योजिता (last verse of रसमञ्जरी). In the रसत०, भरत is very frequently quoted and also author's father (pp. 16, 81, 141, 168). In both he quotes from the अमरुशतक the पाद 'ताम्बूलाहरणच्छलेन० of verse 18 in रसत० V. p. 109 and verse 35 प्रस्थानं वलयैः कृतं in रसमञ्जरी p. 183 (which is noted as प्राचीनग्रन्थलेखन). For the रसमञ्जरी the edition in the Benares S. Series is used. In both works the author refers to पूर्वाचार्य (रसत० 175), प्राचीनलिखित (रसम० p. 43), पूर्वग्रन्थकारसंमति (रसत० p. 168), प्राचीनसंमति (रसत० pp. 170, 182). In the रसत० he mentions the रसरत्नदीपिका (p. 20) and शृङ्गारतिलक (p. 68). The रसमञ्जरी was composed before रसत० (p. 130). He quotes in the रसत० 177) as प्राचीनग्रन्थ the verse 'अनौचित्यादृते नान्यद्रसभङ्गस्य कारणम् । प्रसिद्धौचित्यबद्धस्तु रसस्योपनिषत् परा' ॥ which is very similar to a verse in ध्व० (p. 180) and व्यक्तिविवेक (p. 31).

In the रसमञ्जरी he tells us that his father was गणेश्वर and his country was विदेह watered by the Ganges (तातो यस्य गणेश्वरो कविकुलालङ्कारचूडामणिर्देशो यस्य विदेहभूः सुरसरित्कल्लोलकिर्मीरिता, last verse). Some mss. read विदर्भभूः, which does not agree with the word सुर...रिता that follows. In Burnell's Tanjore Cat. भानुदत्त is styled मैथिल. In Eggeling's Cat. of India Office mss. vol. III. No. 1211 p. 353 a ms. of the Rasamañjarī dated संवत् 1780 ascribes it to मैथिलश्रीगणनाथसन्मिश्र०

The two published commentaries on the रसमञ्जरी are the व्यङ्ग्यार्थकौमुदी of अनन्तपण्डित, son of त्र्यम्बक, composed in 1635 A. D. at पुण्यस्तम्भ (modern Puṇtāmbeṁ) on the गोदावरी, and प्रकाश by नागेशभट्ट son of शिवभट्ट in the first half of the 18th century.

A lyrical poem called गीतगौरीश or गीतगौरीपति is ascribed

to भानुदत्त, which is an imitation of the गीतगोविन्द. It describes the affection of Gaurī for Śiva in ten cantos. It specifies how the verses (in groups of eight) are to be sung to certain melodies (such as Āsāvarī, Karṇāṭaka, Kedāra, Bhūpāla, Bhairavī, Mālava). Vide Eggeling's Cat. of India Office mss. vol. VII. pp. 1443-45 No. 3847. This work was published in the ग्रन्थरत्नमाला in Bombay in 1887 but I could not get a copy of it. The गीतगौरीश appears to be the work of the author of the रसमञ्जरी and रसतरङ्गिणी. Another work named कुमारभार्गवीय described in Eggeling's Cat. vol. VII pp. 1540-41 speaks of Kārtikeya. It is in twelve उच्छ्वास in mixed prose and verse. There the author's pedigree is given as follows : रत्नेश्वर-सुरेश्वर-विश्वनाथ-रविनाथ-भवनाथ-महादेव-गणपति-भानुदत्त. Introductory verse 18 ascribes the वार्तिक on Vedānta to सुरेश्वर, the ancestor of भानुदत्त. But this is certainly wrong; सुरेश्वर wrote his वार्तिक in the 9th century and it is not possible to hold that सुरेश्वर who was only 7th in ascent from भानुदत्त (including the latter) could have flourished in the 9th century.

Dr. Har Dutta Śarma (in Annals of B. O. R. I. vol. 17 pp. 243-258) shows that in some of the later anthologies such as the पद्यरचना, सुभाषितहारावलि and रसिकजीवन verses from रसमञ्जरी and रसत० are ascribed to भानुकर, that भानुकर and भानुदत्त are the same, that as भानुदत्त says in his रसत० V. p. 73 (क्षोणीपर्यटनं श्रमाय विहितं...कुज्ञानेन मया प्रयागनगरे नाराधि नारायणः ॥), he wandered over several parts of India and that भानुकर being patronized by वीरभानु, he should be placed at the beginning of the 16th century. Dr. De in the same vol. (pp. 297-98) does not accept the identity of भानुकर and भानुदत्त and I also hold that the evidence for identifying the two is not satisfactory and is meagre. Dr. Raghavan (in Annals of B. O. R. I. vol. XVIII. pp. 85-86) states that the ascriptions of authorship in onthologies should not be much relied on and that a verse quoted in रसिकजीवन and relied upon by Dr. Har Dutta Sarma (on p. 257 of vol. 17 of Annals B. O. R. I.) is really a verse in the बालभारत (I. 28) of राजशेखर. We have seen (pp. 148-150) what a mess the anthologies make about रुद्रट and रुद्रभट्ट. Prof. Devasthali in New I. A. vol. VII. pp. 111-117 examines several questions connected with भानुदत्त and he concludes that भानुदत्त is certainly the author of six works, viz. रसत०, रसम०, अलङ्कारतिलक, गीतगौरीश, कुमारभार्गवीय and चित्रचन्द्रिका (mentioned in अलङ्कारतिलक as his work but no ms. of it is yet found) and that a ms. of शृङ्गारदीपिका not being available as yet, it cannot be said with certainty that it is भानुदत्त's work. He further establishes that भानुदत्त was a Maithila and argues that as the शार्ङ्गधरपद्धति (which was composed about 1363 A. D.) does not mention any verse of भानुदत्त, the latter must be held to be later than that work. The argument from silence is never a satisfactory one. We must have positive evidence about भानुदत्त and about the ancestors of भानुकर.

As भानुदत्त mentions the सरस्वतीकण्ठाभरण, the काव्यप्रकाश and the गीतगोविन्द, he is certainly not earlier than about 1250 A. D. In Stein's Cat. of Jammu mss. the date of a commentary on the रसमञ्जरी called विकास (or विलास) by गोपाल, son of नृसिंह, was given as 1484. Stein committed two mistakes; the date was really 1494 and he took it as referring to the संवत् era, but the mention of Aṅgiras as the name of the year establishes that it was a *śaka* year (vide Prof. S. R. Bhandarkar's Report for 1904-6 p. 36 and Prof. Gode in Annals of B. O. R. I. vol. 16 pp. 145-147). Thus the ms. is dated in 1572 A. D. The रत्नापण (p. 280) quotes the view of रसमञ्जरी as follows: 'नायकयोर्निमित्ततो विप्रयोगः प्रणयमानापरपर्यायो विरहविप्रलम्भ इत्यर्थः। रसमञ्जर्यां परस्परमाक्षोल्लङ्घनं प्रणयमान इति'. It is not necessary to take this as a quotation. It is quite possible that this is a summary of the views of the रसमञ्जरी which on pp. 42-44 (of the Benares S. Series, 1904) contains similar views. Therefore भानुदत्त flourished after 1250 and before 1500 A. D. In 1923 I had put forward the conjecture that भानुदत्त was the son of गणेश्वर, who was the uncle of चण्डेश्वर and minister of a king of Mithilā. If we look to the pedigree of भानुदत्त given above from the कुमारभार्गवीय and compare it with that of गणेश्वर given in my H. of Dh. vol. I. p. 371 note 889, it would appear that this conjecture cannot be supported. In Mitra's Notices vol. IX. No. 3115 (pp. 194-5) the commentary परिमल on रसमञ्जरी by शेषचिन्तामणि, son of नृसिंह, is described and at the end of the colophon occurs the date संवत् 1609 (i. e. 1552-3 A. D.). There is nothing to show that this is the date of the composition of the commentary. It may be the date of the copying of the com. In Dr. Bhandarkar's Report on mss. for 1883-84 (pp. 365-66) the colophon is somewhat different and the date is altogether absent. Dr. Har Dutta Sharma has changed his views from time to time (vide p. 248 of Annals of B. O. R. I. vol. 17) and at one time he held that Nizam mentioned as praised by भानुकर (according to late anthologies) is a king of the Nizamshahi dynasty and now he thinks (*ibid* p. 254) that he is Nizamkhan of the Lodi dynasty. Further verses ascribed to भानुकर praise Sher Shah (1540-1545 A. D.). So if भानुकर and भानुदत्त are identical भानुदत्त flourished about 1540 A. D. This is an almost impossible date. If a com. on रसमञ्जरी was copied in 1552-53 and भानुदत्त flourished about 1540, then the रसमञ्जरी, its commentary and a copy of the latter would have only a period of ten or 15 years. It appears that भानुदत्त was married to a sister of मिसरुमिश्र, author of विवादचन्द्र (vide Patna University Journal vol. III. No. 1 and 2, a paper by Pandit Ramanatha Jha). In my H. of Dh. vol. I. p. 399 I have shown that मिसरुमिश्र must be assigned to the middle of the 15th century. Therefore भानुदत्त also must be deemed to belong to a period not later than that date by more than a few years. The रसमञ्जरी (Benares ed. p. 232, verse 121) is 'भेदो वाचि दृशोर्जलं कुचतटे स्वेदः प्रकम्पोऽधरे पाण्डुर्गण्डतटी वपुः पुलकितं लीनं मनस्तिष्ठति। आलस्यं नयनश्रियश्चरणयोः स्तम्भः समुज्जृम्भते तत्किं राजपथे निजामधरणीपालोऽयमालोकितः ॥'. There is here a reference to a Moslem ruler निजाम. The व्यङ्ग्यार्थकौमुदी explains that he was king of देवगिरि. If one looks at Duff's Chronology of India, there are at least a dozen rulers between 1400 to 1550 A. D. who were called निजाम and who ruled in the Deccan or Central India and other places. Therefore, it is difficult to say what Moslem king is referred to by the रसमञ्जरी. Dr. Har Dutta Śarma (in I. H. Q. vol. X pp. 478 ff) relies on this that some anthologies mention भानुकर and quote some verses as his in which निजाम, वीरभानु and कृष्ण are mentioned. At present no great writer named भानुकर is known. Therefore Dr. Śarma and others identify भानुदत्त and भानुकर. But I cannot admit that this is legitimate. We do not know all poets that flourished through the centuries. Besides, भानुदत्त may be shortend into भानु, just as भीमसेन is mentioned as भीम. There is so far as I know no instance of men like हरदत्त, रुद्रदत्त, रुचिदत्त being referred to anywhere as हरकर, रुद्रकर or रुचिकर. Therefore, it is doubtful whether भानुदत्त and भानुकर are identical. In the रसपारिजात[1] edited

1. The रसपारिजात is a work of भानुदत्त, wherein are collected about a thousand verses of भानुदत्त himself and his father

by Pandit Badarinath Jha verses of भानुदत्त and his father alone are included and in some of them verses of भानुदत्त addressed to निजामशाह, कृष्ण and वीरभानु are quoted. But this may only prove that भानुदत्त had the patronage of these three.

Recently, Prof. G. V. Devasthali has published a work called अलङ्कारतिलक of भानुदत्त (based on three mss.) in J. B. B. R. A. S. (New Series) vol. 23 pp. 57-82 and vol. 24-25 pp. 93-120. It is divided into five परिच्छेदs. It is in mixed prose and verse. The illustrations are the author's own or of his father who is frequently quoted (pp. 60, 61, 62, 94, 95 &c.). The contents are : परिच्छेद I : after Maṅgala in honour of वाराहावतार and reference to himself as भानुसत्कवि, he states that rasas are the soul, kāvya is the body, *gati, rīti, vṛtti*, absence of *doṣas*, guṇas and alaṅkāras are the indriyas, *vyutpatti* is prāṇa and *abhyāsa* is mind; three kinds of *kāvya, uttama, madhyama, adhama*; kāvya is of four kinds acc. to language, संस्कृत, प्राकृत, अपभ्रंश, मिश्र; *śabda*, and *artha* are kāvya and *rīti* is a characteristic (धर्म) of kāvya; 6 rītis; वृत्तिs कैशिकी &c. II discussion about दोषs, doṣas of पद, वाक्य, वाक्यार्थ; III guṇas of three kinds बाह्य, आन्तर and वैशेषिक; बाह्यगुणs are of शब्द and आन्तर of अर्थ; 24 guṇas, श्लेष &c. IV Definition of अलङ्कार (औपाधिकप्रकर्षहेतुरलङ्कारः); six अलङ्कारs of शब्द, वक्रोक्ति, अनुप्रास, यमक, श्लेष, चित्र, पुनरुक्तवदाभास acc. to काव्यप्रकाश and गति, रीति, वृत्ति, छाया &c. in addition acc. to कण्ठाभरण; V अर्थालङ्कारs, in all 71. भानुदत्त closely follows the सरस्वतीकण्ठाभरण in the matter of the number of वृत्तिs, the दोषs of पद, वाक्य and वाक्यार्थ and in other matters. Among the authors and works quoted are :

गणपति, divided into ten chapters called पल्लवs. In the 2nd and 3rd पल्लवs there are 89 verses of which 80 are those of भानुदत्त himself in which king Nijam Shah or simply Nijam is praised in 14 verses, वीरभान in five verses, king कृष्ण in two and king संग्रामसाहि in only one. Dr. De thought that Nizamshah was the first founder king of Ahmednagar, while Pandit Ramanath Jha thinks (Journal, Patna University vol. III cited above) that he is the 2nd king of that dynasty and कृष्ण is the Krishnadeva Raya of Vijayanagar who ascended the throne in 1509 A. D. and reigned up till 1530. These are all conjectures and the only solid basis is that भानुदत्त had married a sister of मिसरुमिश्र. Therefore भानुदत्त must have lived between 1450 to 1500 A. D.

कण्ठाभरण (सरस्वतीकण्ठाभरण of भोज), काव्यप्रकाश, गीतगोविन्द (vol. 24 p. 94), चित्रचन्द्रिका (his own work, vol. 24 p. 96), दण्डी (vol. 23 p. 58 and p. 79 called दण्डीकार), भरत, वामन. He does not mention the name of his father or does not give any other information about himself. At the end he says : 'विबुधा पद्यसूत्रेण गुम्फितालङ्कृतिर्मया । सूत्रभङ्गो यथा न स्यादेतस्याः कलयेत्तथा ॥'. This indicates that the illustrative verses are his own.

36 The भक्तिरसामृतसिन्धु and उज्ज्वलनीलमणि of रूपगोस्वामिन्. The great Vaiṣṇava movement inspired by Śrī Caitanya (1486-1533 A. D.) produced an erotico-mystical technique. Dr. De in 'The Vaiṣṇava faith and movement in Bengal' (1942, Calcutta) furnishes an exhaustive and well-documented treatment of this movement. Our concern with that movement is due to the fact that रूपगोस्वामी was inspired to write the above works to place the doctrine of *bhakti* concentrated on Kṛṣṇa into the garb and phraseology of the *rasa* theory. Religious hankerings and spiritual mysticism are here clothed in the language and ideology of earthly love and passion. It is impossible to give even a brief account of these two works within the limited space that I can afford. I shall content myself by giving a very brief outline of the उज्ज्वलनीलमणि. Those who want further information may read the original works and the analysis of the भक्तिरसामृतसिन्धु and उज्ज्वलनीलमणि furnished in the abovementioned work by Dr. De at pp. 126-153 and pp. 153-167 respectively and the paper 'Bhaktirasaśāstra in Bengal Vaiṣṇavism' (by Dr. De) in I. H. Q. vol. VIII pp. 643-688.

The उज्ज्वलनीलमणि[1] has been published in the K. M. Series (1932) with two commentaries, viz. लोचनरोचनी of जीवगोस्वामी,

---

1. The last verse is : अयमुज्ज्वलनीलमणिर्गहनमहाघोषसागरप्रभवः । भजतु तव मकरकुण्डलपरिसरसेवौचितीं देव ॥. It says that it may reach the ears of Śrīkṛṣṇa who dwelt in the ocean-like Nandavraja. The word उज्ज्वलनीलमणि applies to the work and also to श्रीकृष्ण who is शृङ्गार incarnate and who is described as घननील. उज्ज्वलः शृङ्गाररसः एव नीलमणिः. गहन···प्रभवः also suggests that the work उज्ज्वलनीलमणि arose out of the previous work भक्तिरसामृतसिन्धु. जीवगोस्वामी in his com. on Intro.. verse 2 makes it clear that even when the उज्ज्वलनीलमणि is meant to expound शृङ्गार explicitly in relation to श्रीकृष्ण, it is not meant that is should be laid

the nephew of रूपगोस्वामी (son of रूप's younger brother वल्लभ) and the आनन्दचन्द्रिका of विश्वनाथचक्रवर्तिन् composed at वृन्दावन in śaka 1618. The first verse is : नामाकृष्टरसज्ञः शीलेनोद्दीपयन् सदानन्दम् । निजरूपोत्सवदायी सनातनात्मा प्रभुर्जयति ॥ (the word सनातन applies to श्रीकृष्ण as well as to सनातन the elder brother of रूप). The 2nd verse says that in the previous work (भक्तिरसामृतसिन्धु) भक्तिरस (which is the chief among rasas called शान्तप्रीतिप्रेयोवत्सलोज्ज्वलनामसु) was briefly dealt with because of its esoteric character but is dealt with at length in the उज्ज्वल०. भक्तिरस has मधुरारति as the स्थायिभाव and is called मधुर when it reaches the position of aesthetic enjoyment through the विभाव &c. (वक्ष्यमाणैर्विभावाद्यैः स्वाद्यतां मधुरा रतिः । नीता भक्तिरसः प्रोक्तो मधुराख्यो मनीषिभिः ॥). भरत in his नाट्यशास्त्र VI p. 73 (G.O.S. ed. VI after verse 50 pp. 301-2) says 'शृङ्गारो नाम रतिस्थायिभावप्रभव उज्ज्वलवेषात्मकः। यथा यत् किञ्चिल्लोके शुचि मेध्यं दर्शनीयं वा तच्छृङ्गारेणानुमीयते (णोपमीयते) । यस्तावदुज्ज्वलवेषः स शृङ्गारवानित्युच्यते ।...तदेवमेव गुर्वाचारसिद्धो हृद्योज्ज्वलवेषात्मकः शृङ्गारो रसः ।'. The उज्ज्वलनीलमणि in स्थायिभावप्रकरण verses 54-55 (on p. 417 of 2nd ed.) states that six *bhāvas* स्नेह, मान, प्रणय, राग, अनुराग, महाभाव are playful manifiestations of love (प्रेम) and compares them to the sugarcane stalks, the juice extracted from them, jaggery, sugar, white sugar and candied sugar, all of which are different stages of the products of sugarcane (बीजमिक्षुः स च रसः स गुडः खण्ड एव सः । स शर्करा सिता सा च सा यथा स्यात्सितोपला । अतः प्रेमविलासाः स्युर्भावाः स्नेहादयस्तु षट् ॥). Whatever is pure, holy, and attractive to the eye in the world is inferred to be (or compared to) Śṛṅgāra, which has as its chief element attractive and brilliant

---

bare anywhere and before anybody like other works 'पुरा संक्षेपेणोदितत्वे हेतुरतिरहस्यत्वादिति निवृत्तानां लौकिकादुज्ज्वलाख्यरसात्तत्साम्यम् ।......तथा भागवते ये केचित् तस्मिन् बहुमानिनोपि तात्पर्यालोचनायां न चतुरास्तैरपि दुरूहोऽयं रस इति तेभ्योऽपि गोप्य एव कार्यः किमुत विषयिभ्य इति रहस्यमेवात्र मुख्यो हेतुरिति भावः । अत्र तु विस्तरेण वचने हेतुः रहस्यत्वादित्येव । कालदेशपात्रविशेषसम्बन्धेन रहस्यत्वं प्राप्येत्यर्थः । ल्यब्लोपे पञ्चमी स्यात् । यदा पृथगित्यनेनैव रहस्य इति व्यज्यते । तस्माद्ग्रन्थान्तरवद्यत्र कुत्रचिन्नायं प्रकाशनीय इत्युपदिष्टम् ।'. रूप says, quoting भागवत, that the husbands of the Vraja women thought that their wives were by their sides and did not feel jealousy about Kṛṣṇa 'न जातु व्रजदेवीनां पतिभिः सह सङ्गमः । तथाहि श्रीदशमे । नासूयन्खलु कृष्णाय मोहितास्तस्य मायया । मन्यमानाः स्वपार्श्वस्थान्स्वान्स्वान् दारान्व्रजौकसः ॥' (I. 31 pp. 58-59). This last verse is भागवत 10th स्कन्ध, पूर्वार्ध, chap. 33. 38.

appearance and attire. In this rasa, the आलम्बनविभावs are Kṛṣṇa (as the विषय of मधुरारति) and his loves (वल्लभाs) who are the आश्रय of मधुरारति; the qualities of Kṛṣṇa (his charm, physical and mental youth, agreeable speech &c.), his actions and his decorations are the exciting (उद्दीपनविभावs) circumstances; the well-known four kinds of hero (नायक viz. धीरोदात्त, धीरोद्धत्त, धीरललित, धीरप्रशान्त) have further two varieties पति (as of रुक्मिणी and सत्यभामा) and उपपति (as of the women of *vraja*); the four varieties are again either पूर्णतम, पूर्णतर and पूर्ण; each of these (पति and उपपति) is of four kinds viz. अनुकूल, दक्षिण, शठ and धृष्ट; definitions and illustrations of all these varieties, qualities, actions &c. (अनुकूलपति being राम and अनुकूल-उपपति being कृष्ण in relation to राधा); so नायकs are of 96 varieties; the nāyaka's friends are five, viz. चेट, विट, विदूषक, पीठमर्द, प्रियनर्मसख; their definitions and examples[1]; the beloved of Hari is of two kinds, svakīyā and parakīyā; the first were 16108 wives of Hari residing in Dvārakā, out of these eight viz. रुक्मिणी, सत्या, जाम्बवती, अर्कनन्दिनी, शैब्या, भद्रा, कौशल्या, माद्री were the principal ones; parakīyās are of two kinds viz. kanyā (maidens) and परोढा (married to another), that were mostly resident in Vraja; the paroḍhā nāyikās were of three kinds, viz. साधनपरा, देवी, नित्यप्रिया; साधनपराs are again of two kinds यौथिक्यः and अयौथिक्यः; the first are those

1. रूपगोस्वामी says that what is called illicit and secret love and is ordinarily condemned is the highest pinnacle of śṛṅgāra and that the condemnation applies only to ordinary mortals and not to a completely perfect avatāra (Kṛṣṇa) who took to an incarnation to give a taste of mystic love to his devotees 'अत्रैव परमोत्कर्षः शृङ्गारस्य प्रतिष्ठितः। तथा च मुनिः। बहु वार्यते यतः खलु यत्र प्रच्छन्नकामुकत्वं च। या च मिथो दुर्लभता सा परमा मन्मथस्य रतिः॥ लघुत्वमत्र यत्प्रोक्तं तत्तु प्राकृतनायके। न कृष्णे रसनिर्यासस्वादार्थमवतारिणि॥ उज्ज्वल० I. 16-18 pp. 14-15. The भागवत (X. 33. 30-31) states 'धर्मव्यतिक्रमो दृष्ट ईश्वराणां च साहसम्। तेजीयसां न दोषाय वह्नेः सर्वभुजो यथा॥ नैतत्समाचरेज्जातु मनसापि ह्यनीश्वरः। विनश्यत्याचरन्मौढ्याद्यथा रुद्रोऽब्धिजं विषम्॥'. The उज्ज्वलनीलमणि quoting श्रीमद्भागवत gives the following warning: वर्तितव्यं शमिच्छद्भिर्भक्तवन्न तु कृष्णवत्। इत्येवं भक्तिशास्त्राणां तात्पर्यस्य विनिर्णयः॥ रामादिवद्वर्तितव्यं न क्वचिद्रावणादिवत्। इत्येष मुक्तिधर्मादिपराणां नय इष्यते॥'. But this advice is, I am afraid, too much for common people. The words 'रामादिवद्वर्तितव्यं न रावणादिवदित्युपदेशं च' in the काव्यप्रकाश I (p. 10) are probably taken from the भागवत.

that work in a group; they are of two kinds, *muni* and *upaniṣads*; अयौथिक्य: were of two kinds, प्राचीन and नव; देवीs were those goddesses that were born on the earth along with कृष्ण; राधा and चन्द्रावली were among नित्यप्रियाs; and enumeration of the guṇas of Rādhā and their illustrations; five kinds of सखी; स्वकीया and परकीया are each of three kinds viz. मुग्धा, मध्या and प्रगल्भा; their definitions and illustrations; sub-divisions of these; all nāyikās are again of eight kinds viz. अभिसारिका, वासकसज्जा, उत्कण्ठिता, खण्डिता, विप्रलब्धा, कलहान्तरिता, प्रोषितपतिका, स्वाधीनभर्तृका, their definitions and examples; further sub-divisions; in all 360 kinds of नायिका; दूतीs of two kinds स्वयंदूती and आप्तदूती; their sub-divisions and characteristics; सखीs and their qualities and characteristics; the उद्दीपनविभावs, viz. the guṇas (मानस, वाचिक, कायिक) of Hari and his *priyās* and their elucidation; their names, actions, decorations, things in contact with them (such as flute, song, *nirmālya*, basil plant), *anubhāvas*; 20 guṇas due to sattva, bhāva, hāva, helā (three aṅgaja), seven (śobhā, kānti &c.) that are natural and] without effort and ten that are svabhāvaja (līlā, vilāsa, &c.); the sāttvikabhāvas, stambha (due to fear, wonder, grief, anger), perspiration &c.; thirty-three vyabhīcāribhāvas, such as *nirveda, glāni* &c.; explanation of śṛṅgāra called मधुरारति; firm रति is called प्रेमा, which has six aspects viz. स्नेह, मान, प्रणय, राग, अनुराग, भाव, just as from the same sugarcane one can get juice, गुड, खण्ड, शर्करा, सिता, सितोपला; subdivisions of प्रेमा; शृङ्गार is of two kinds. विप्रलम्भ and सम्भोग; the latter is of two kinds, मुख्य and गौण and sub-divisions of these two.

The उज्ज्वलनीलमणि is distinguished from many other works on Poetics in two ways, viz. it treats exhaustively of *Bhaktirasa* and all the illustrations relate to Kṛṣṇa, his devotees and their moods and doings.

Rūpagosvāmin also composed a work on dramaturgy called नाटकचन्द्रिका. At the beginning of his work he states that he followed Bharata and Rasasudhākara and rejected the dicta of the Sāhityadarpaṇa as they were opposed to those of Bharata. It is divided into eight sections. It contains the usual topics of the general characteristics of a drama, the Nāyaka, other topics of a drama such as nāndī, sandhis, patākā, viṣkambhaka, bhāṣās, vṛttis and their adaptation to the several rasas. Most of the numerous examples are taken from Vaiṣṇava works. For an analysis of the contents, vide Mitra's

Notices, vol. IX No. 3160, pp. 40-41. The पद्यावलि of रूप has been edited by Dr. De in the Dacca University Publications Series.

A few words must be said about the personal history of रूपगोस्वामी and जीवगोस्वामी. सनातन, his younger brother रूप and जीव (son of the youngest brother वल्लभ or अनुपम) are the most prominent of the *gosvāmins* of Vṛndāvana. Their family was originally a Karṇāta brāhmaṇa[1] family that migrated to Bengal at the end of the 14th century. सनातन, रूप and जीव fell heart and soul in the bhakti movement of Caitanya, otherwise called Gaurāṅga. रूप systematized the भक्तिरसशास्त्र in the भक्तिरसामृतसिन्धु and उज्ज्वलनीलमणि, while जीव specially dealt with the metaphysics of the Caitanya movement. Vide Aufrecht's cat. I p. 533, Dr. De's 'Vaiṣṇava faith and movement in Bengal' pp. 113-114 for the works of Rūpa and pp. 116-118 of the latter for the works of Jīva. Among the authors and works named in the उज्ज्वलनीलमणि the following may be noted: उद्धवसन्देश (pp. 115, 126, 181, 291, &c.), कर्णामृत (p. 602), क्रमदीपिका (p. 425), गीतगोविन्द (pp. 140, 199, 215 &c.), छन्दोमञ्जरी, जगन्नाथवल्लभ (p. 525, a प्राकृत verse), दशरूपक, दानकेलिकौमुदी (a drama pp. 198, 272, 283 &c.), पद्मपुराण, पद्यावलि (his own work frequently quoted), भरत (quoted several times), भागवत (particularly 10th skandha frequently cited), मुक्ताचरित (p. 318), मुनि (i. e. भरत pp. 14, 40

---

1. M. T. Kennedy in his 'Caitanya movement' (Oxford Un. Press, 1925, pp. 45-46) states that when Caitanya set out for Brindavan he met at Rāmkelī two remarkable men, who were originally Maratha brāhmaṇas of princely descent, whose ancestors had migrated to Bengal and who had adopted the faith of Islam and had risen to be high officials in the Muhammedan court at Gaur. They were at once drawn to Caitanya and became the followers of Caitanya who gave them the names of Sanātana and Rūpa. These men played a leading part in the Caitanya movement. Dr. De in 'Early History of the Vaiṣṇava faith &c.' p. 73 n. 2 scouts the idea that Sanātana and Rūpa had embraced the faith of Islam and states that there is no evidence for holding so. But the evidence to the contrary that he brings forward is not very satisfactory nor conclusive.

&c.), रससुधाकर[1] (pp. 282, 296 &c.), रुक्मिणीस्वयंवर (p. 333), रुद्र[2] (p. 54), ललितमाधव[3] (a drama in 10 Acts, very frequently quoted), वामनपुराण (p. 65), विदग्धमाधव (a नाटक in 7 Acts printed in K. M. Series, most frequently quoted), विष्णुगुप्तसंहिता (p. 54), विष्णुपुराण (p. 352), सप्तशती, हंसदूत (p. 232), हरिवंश.

As regards the dates of रूप and जीव there is not much difficulty. रूप's दानकेलिकौमुदी was written in 1495 A. D. The verse at the end of the विदग्धमाधवनाटक (in 7 Acts) states that it was composed in saṁvat 1589 (i. e. 1532-3 A. D.) 'नन्दसिन्धुरबाणेन्दुसंख्ये संवत्सरे गते । विदग्धमाधवं नाम नाटकं गोकुले कृतम् ॥ (K. M. ed.). Mitra (Notices, vol. IX No. 3159) notes that his उत्कलिकामञ्जरी was composed in 1550 A.D. (शाके 1471). भक्तिरसामृतसिन्धु is expressly dated śaka 1463 (1541-42 A. D.). The उज्ज्वल° was composed after this. See Dr. Stein, Jammu Cat. p. 222. These dates show that रूप had at least 55 year's literary activity. Dr. De (in the work cited above p. 121) states that both सनातन and रूप were alive in 1554 A. D. and died in the same year at the interval of a few months. So the life of रूप extended from about 1470 A. D. to 1554 A. D. There are two different traditions about the birth date of जीव, either śaka 1435 (1513-4 A. D.) or 1445 (1523-24 A. D.). The माधवमहोत्सव of जीव was composed in 1555 A. D. and his गोपालचम्पू bears the dates 1589 and 1592 A. D. Vide Dr. De's work cited above pp. 119-122 for the dates of सनातन, रूप and जीव.

37 The अलङ्कारशेखर of केशवमिश्र. The work has been published in the K. M. series. The work is divided into three parts, कारिकाs, वृत्ति and examples. The author himself tells us that the कारिकाs are the work of शौद्धोदनि 'अलङ्कारविद्यासूत्रकारो भगवा-

---

1. The रससुधाकर is the same as the रसार्णवसुधाकर of Śiṅgabhūpāla (Tri. ed.). The verse अलोलैरनुमीयते° cited from रससुधाकर by उज्ज्वल° (p. 282) occurs in रसार्णवसु° (I. p. 45) and the two verses दुरासदे° and वर्षासु तासु° on p. 296 of उज्ज्वल° occur in रसार्णवसु. on pp. 45 and 47 respectively. Dr. De (HSP, vol. I. p. 256) was in doubt whether रससुधाकर was रसार्णवसुधाकर.

2. The verse from रुद्र 'वामता दुर्लभत्वं च......परममायुधम्' quoted in उज्ज्वल° p. 54 occurs in the शृङ्गारतिलक (Pischel's ed.) II. 41, p. 52.

3. See Eggeling's Cat. vol. VII p. 1592 No. 4179 for a description of ललितमाधव.

ब्छौद्धोदनिः परमकारुणिकः स्वशास्त्रे प्रवर्तयिष्यन्प्रथमं काव्यस्वरूपमाह (p. 2); 'श्रुतमेवान्यथाकारमक्षराणि कियन्त्यपि । काव्यालङ्कारविधायां शौद्धोदनिरसूत्रयत् ।। (p. 83). Whether शौद्धोदनि is the name of an author or whether the कारिकाs were composed by some Buddhist writer and were subsequently ascribed to शौद्धोदनि (a name of भगवान् बुद्ध) cannot be determined. The work very largely draws upon the काव्यादर्श, काव्यमीमांसा, the ध्वन्यालोक, the काव्यप्रकाश, वाग्भटालङ्कार, भोजराज and quotes श्रीपाद (an otherwise unknown author on *alaṅkāra*) very frequently. The work is divided into 8 रत्नs and 22 मरीचिs (rays) the subjects of which are—1, definition of काव्य as 'रसादिमद्वाक्य' and its *hetu*, प्रतिभा etc.; 2, three रीतिs (वैदर्भी, गौडी and मागधी), उक्ति and मुद्रा with their varieties; 3, the three functions of a word viz. शक्ति, लक्षणा and व्यञ्जना; 4, eight *doṣas* of पद; 5, twelve *doṣas* of वाक्य; 6, eight *doṣas* of अर्थ; 7, the five *guṇas* of शब्द, संक्षिप्तत्व, उदात्तत्व, प्रसाद, उक्ति and समाधि; 8, four *guṇas* of sense, भाविकत्व, सुशब्दत्व, पर्यायोक्ति and सुधर्मिता; 9, in some cases the above *doṣas* become *guṇaṣ* and are called वैशेषिकगुणs or are not faults; 10, eight अलङ्कारs of शब्द, viz. चित्र, वक्रोक्ति, अनुप्रास, गूढ, श्लेष, प्रहेलिका, प्रश्नोत्तर and यमक; 11, only fourteen *alaṅkāraṣ* of sense and no more viz. उपमा, रूपक, उत्प्रेक्षा, समासोक्ति, अपह्नुति, समाहित, स्वभाव, विरोध, सार, दीपक, सहोक्ति, अन्यदेशत्व (i. e. असङ्गति of मम्मट), विशेषोक्ति and विभावना are enumerated and ten varieties of उपमा are illustrated; 12, sub-divisions of रूपक; 13, other figures (such as उत्प्रेक्षा and समासोक्ति) defined and illustrated; the उपमानs of a damsel and of her complexion, hair, forehead, eyebrows etc.; 14, how poets should describe the physical characteristics of the heroes of their works; 15, words that convey सादृश्य, conventions of poets; 16, the topics to be described such as king, queen, country, town, city, river etc. and the peculiar characteristics of each that should be dwelt upon; 17, the colours of various objects in nature; 18, words that convey numerals from one to thousand, certain tricks of words such as गतागत, संस्कृत-प्राकृतैक्यता (i. e. भाषासम); 19, समस्यापूरण; 20, रस is the soul of poetry, the nine *rasas*, the sub-divisions of नायक and नायिका, the different भावs; 21, the *doṣas* of रस; 22, what letters are favourable to each *rasa*.

The कारिकाs of शौद्धोदनि appear to have been composed after the 11th century. He defines *kāvya* as a sentence containing *rasas* etc. (p. 2) and says that *rasa* is the soul of poetry (p. 6). On p. 83 शौद्धोदनि refers to महिमभट्ट the author of the

व्यक्तिविवेक and his treatment bears close resemblance to वाग्भटालङ्कार (compare p. 27 with वाग्भटा० p. 28). The अलङ्कारशेखर mentions among others the following works and authors:— कविकल्पलता (p. 48, as following श्रीपाद), गोवर्धन (frequently quoted pp. 17, 29, 37, 43, 49 &c.), भार्गवसर्वस्व (p. 24), भोजराज (p. 7), महिमा (p. 81, the verse अनौचित्यादृते which occurs in ध्व० p. 145 and also in व्यक्तिविवेक), राजशेखर (pp. 32, 67), श्रीपाद (frequently quoted, pp. 4, 5, 23, 27, 32, 72, 83 &c.), श्रीहर्ष (p. 41). The author tells us that before the अलङ्कारशेखर he composed seven works for the benefit of poets (3rd Intro. verse). Out of these he mentions two works अलङ्कारसर्वस्व (pp, 9, 38) and काव्यरत्न (p. 72). The word वाक्यरत्ने (on p. 12) seems to be a mistake for काव्यरत्ने.

केशवमिश्र tells us in the Introduction and at the end that he wrote the अलङ्कारशेखर at the instance of king माणिक्यचन्द्र son of धर्मचन्द्र. This धर्मचन्द्र was son of रामचन्द्र, a scion of the family of सुशर्मा, who routed a Kābila (Afgan) king of Delhi. According to Cunningham (Arch. Survey of India vol. V. p. 160) माणिक्यचन्द्र, king of Kangra, succeeded धर्मचन्द्र in 1563 A. D. and ruled for about ten years. Hence the अलङ्कारशेखर was composed in the latter half of the 16th century.

38 अप्पय्यदीक्षित. This versatile and prolific writer, who is credited with the authorship of over one hundred works, contributed at least three works on Poetics. In the वृत्तिवार्तिक, which is divided into two परिच्छेद्स as printed, he treats at length of the two functions of words, viz. अभिधा (of three sorts रूढि, योग and योगरूढि) and लक्षणा (first divided into शुद्धा and गौणी each of which is again sub-divided into निरूढ and फल and their sub-divisions). His second work कुवलयानन्द is an elementary treatise on अलङ्कारs. It generally adopts the definitions and examples of the चन्द्रालोक 'येषां चन्द्रालोके दृश्यन्ते लक्ष्यलक्षणश्लोकाः । प्रायस्त एव तेषामितरेषां त्वभिनवा विरच्यन्ते ॥' (verse 5) and he wrote the work by order of king वेङ्कटपति 'अमुं कुवलयानन्दमकरोदप्पदीक्षितः । नियोगाद्वेङ्कटपतेर्निरुपाधिकृपानिधेः ॥' In the कुवलयानन्द he adds his own comments and cites examples from other authors also. To the hundred figures of the चन्द्रालोक, he adds 15 separate ones. In some editions of the कुवलयानन्द (e. g. Nir. edition of 1910) some शब्दालङ्कारs are interpolated from चिरञ्जीवभट्टाचार्य's काव्यविलास. His third work, the चित्रमीमांसा, is a more solid performance. His method is to give a *kārikā* at first and then discuss in prose the views

of others and to refute them where necessary. He first of all briefly treats the division of काव्य into ध्वनि, गुणीभूतव्यङ्ग्य and चित्र, and says that, as शब्दचित्र is generaly void of charm, he will treats of अर्थचित्र alone. He then takes up उपमा and points out how twenty-two figures are based thereon. Unfortunately the printed edition (K. M. series) breaks off in the midst of अतिशयोक्ति (the figures treated of being उपमा, उपमेयोपमा, अनन्वय, स्मरण, रूपक, परिणाम, ससन्देह, भ्रान्तिमान्, उल्लेख, अपह्नुति, उत्प्रेक्षा, अतिशयोक्ति) and a verse at the end says that the चित्रमीमांसा, though mutilated, causes delight like the digit of the moon or like Aruṇa 'अप्यर्धचित्रमीमांसा न मुदे कस्य मांसला । अनूरुरिव घर्मांशोरर्धेन्दुरिव धूर्जटेः ॥'. The printed चित्रमीमांसाखण्डन of जगन्नाथ goes only as far as अपह्नुति. That he contemplated writing on more figures follows from his words 'अधिकं निदर्शनालङ्कारप्रकरणे चिन्तयिष्यते' (चित्र० p. 131); while in the कुवलयानन्द (at end of श्लेष) he says '(एतद्विवेचनं तु चित्रमीमांसायां द्रष्टव्यम्', on which वैद्यनाथ remarks 'यद्यप्युत्प्रेक्षाग्रन्थानन्तरं चित्रमीमांसा न क्वापि दृश्यते'. This shows that we have now a little more of it than वैद्यनाथ could secure. It appears that Appayya wrote also a work called लक्षणरत्नावलि in which he defined technical dramatic words like नान्दी, सूत्रधार, पूर्वरङ्ग, प्रस्तावना, Vide J. O. R. Modras, vol. IV. pp. 242-244.

The name of the author is written in various ways, अप्पदीक्षित, अप्पयदी० and अप्पय्यदीक्षित. For the form अप्पय, *vide* रसगङ्गाधर p. 218. The third Intro. verse in the चित्रमीमांसाखण्डन gives it as अप्पय्य (and the metre requires it to be so 'सूक्ष्मं विभाव्य मयका समुदीरितानामप्पय्यदीक्षितकृताविह दूषणानाम् ।') and रसग० (p. 120) has that form also. The verse at the end of the कुवलयानन्द (अमुं... दीक्षितः) shows the form अप्पदीक्षित and रसग० (pp. 209, 226, 249, 254, &c.) has that form also. अप्पय्यदीक्षित is very severely criticized by जगन्नाथ and on the devoted head of the दीक्षित he heaps the choicest abuse (such as दीर्घश्रवस् at रसग. p. 239, द्रविडपुङ्गव p. 420). He was of the भारद्वाजगोत्र and a Tamil brāhmaṇa and Śaiva. His position as an Advaitin devotee of शिव may be understood from the following verses at the beginning of his 'शिवादित्यमणिदीपिका "यद्यप्यद्वैत एव श्रुतिशिखरगिरामागमानां च निष्ठा ।...प्रत्नैराचार्यरत्नैरपि परिजगृहे शङ्कराद्यैस्तदेव ॥ तथाप्यनुग्रहादेव तरुणेन्दुशिखामणेः । अद्वैतवासना पुंसामाविर्भवति नान्यथा ॥ (Hultzsch's Report II. at p. 100). That he wrote one hundred works is stated by नीलकण्ठविजय (I. 44) composed in 1637 A. D.

As अप्पय्यदीक्षित quoted the एकावली, the प्रतापरुद्रयशोभूषण and the

अलङ्कारसर्वस्वसञ्जीविनी, he is later than the 14th century. There is a great deal of controversy about the exact period of Appayya. The generally accepted dates are 1554 A. D. to 1626 A. D. Vide E. I. vol. XII. p. 340 (plate of Śri Rangaraya II dated śaka 1499). It records that at the request of Śevappa Nāyaka, the first prince of the Nāyaka dynasty of Tanjore, the विजयनगर emperor श्रीरङ्गदेवराय granted the village of Arumolimaṅgalam to the Madhva pontiff Vijayīndratīrtha, who before he became a sannyāsin, was a friend of the celebrated Appayya. On p. 345 the editors quote the following from the com. of शिवानन्दयति on the आत्मार्पणस्तुति of अप्पय्य—वीणातत्त्वश्वसंख्यालसितकलिसमाभाक्प्रमादी च वर्षे कन्यामासे तु कृष्णप्रथमतिथियुते-प्युत्तरप्रोष्ठपादे । कन्यालग्नेऽह्निकन्यापतिरमितदयासेवधिर्वैदिकेषु श्रीगौर्यै प्राग् यथाह स्म समजनि विरिञ्चीशपुर्यां कलेशः ॥ लग्ने रवीन्दुसुतयोर्मकरे च मान्यौ मीने शशिन्यथ वृषे रविजे च राहौ । चापे गुरौ क्षितिसुते मिथुने तुलायां शुक्रे शिखिन्यलिगते शुभलग्न एवम् ॥. This gives the horoscope of अप्पय्य and states that he was born in कलि 4654. The editors of the plates further note that acc. to the शिवलीलार्णवकाव्य of नीलकण्ठदीक्षित (grandson of अप्पय्य's younger brother Āccān) अप्पय्य lived for 72 years and composed one hundred works (I. 6 कालेन शम्भुः किल तावतापि कलाश्चतुष्षष्टिमिताः प्रणिन्ये । द्वासप्ततिं प्राप्य समाः प्रबन्धाञ्छतं व्यधादप्पयदीक्षितेन्द्रः ॥). This date is very seriously challenged by Mr. Y. Mahalinga Sastri (in J. O. R. Madras vol. III. pp. 140-160) who says that the horoscope set out above in two verses was forged by Appaya's biographers and that if we take into account the kings mentioned by अप्पय्य in his several works, viz. Chinna Timma, Chinna Bomma and Veṅkaṭa, the proper dates of Appayya should be 1520 A. D. to 1593 A. D. He relies (*ibid* p. 141-149) on an inscription in the temple of Kālakaṇṭheśvara at Adaiyapālam, the birth-dlace and ancestral abode of Appayya, dated śaka 1504 (1582 A. D.), which mentions Appayya, son of Raṅgarāja and his patron Chinna Bomma and the fact that he wrote 100 works. This establishes, acc. to Mr. Sastri, that in 1582 A.D. Appayya must have been an old man. It is possible to argue that some one put up that inscription long after the death of Appayya, and may ask what guarantee there is that it was inscribed during Appayya's own life and, if it be said that a horoscope was forged, there is nothing to prevent an inscription being antedated when Appayya's fame had spread far and wide. If अप्पय्य was dead in 1593 as Mr.

Sastri contends, it becomes very difficult to explain several matters. We shall see later on that Jagannātha's literary activity lies between 1620-1665 A. D. He heaps personal abuse on Appayya, which can be explained more satisfactorily on the hypothesis of the two being contemporaries for some years, Appayya being much older than Jagannâtha. This cannot be explained away by saying that Jagannātha hated all Draviḍas. Besides नीलकण्ठदीक्षित wrote his नीलकण्ठविजयचम्पू in गतकलि 4738 i. e. 1637 A. D. Tradition says that when he was 12 years old he was blessed by the aged Appayya who was the elder brother of Āccān, the grand-father of नीलकण्ठ. That makes the usually accepted dates of Appayya more probable. Besides, there is an Inscription of Veṅkaṭa I dated śaka 1523 i. e. 1601-2 A. D. (E. I. vol. IV. pp. 269-271). Chinna Bomma was prince of Velur (or Vellore) and his son Liṅgama Nāyaka was a contemporary of Veṅkaṭa I, Vide E. I. vol. IV. p. 269 at p. 271. Therefore, it follows that Appayya first enjoyed the patronage of Chinna Bomma and then of Veṅkaṭa. I am not prepared to place implicit reliance on the inscription referred to by Mr. Sastri and would still stick to the generally accepted dates of 1554-1626 A. D. It is possible that Appayya may have been born a little earlier than 1554 A. D. But it is difficult to hold that he was born in 1520 A. D. and died in 1593 A. D. as Mr. Mahaliṅga Sastri, a descendant of Appayya himself, contends on the strength of the single inscription mentioned above. For an account of अप्पय्य's life, family, pedigree and works, vide Sanskrit Intro. to यादवाभ्युदय vol. II pp. XV ff. According to the remarks in चित्रमीमांसा (K. M. ed. p. 63) वक्षःस्थलाचार्य was his ancestor (सन्देहालङ्कारध्वनिर्यथा अस्मत्कुलकूटस्थ-वक्षःस्थलाचार्यकृते वरदराजवसन्तोत्सवे·कांचित्काञ्चनगौराङ्गीं...वक्षःस्थलमवैक्षत ॥). According to some, आचार्य (or आचान्) दीक्षित, grand-father of अप्पय्य was called वक्षःस्थलाचार्य. Acc. to another account वक्षःस्थल was the great-grand-father of अप्पय्य. Āccān had from his 2nd wife several sons of whom रङ्गराज was the eldest. His sons were अप्पय्य and आचान्. The यात्राप्रबन्ध of समरपुङ्गवदीक्षित (II. 86) states that the author learnt under Appayya and that रङ्गराजाध्वरि was patronized by king चिन्नबोम (II. 95). Vide Sanskrit Intro. to यादवाभ्युदय pp. XXIII-XXVII for 54 works attributed to अप्पय्य; and Introduction to अप्पय्यदीक्षित's शिवाद्वैतनिर्णय edited and translated by Prof. S. S. Suryanarayana Sastri

(Madras University, 1929) pp. 9-15, where a list collected from several sources is given. Many of the works are lost. In Hultzsch's Report on South Indian Sanskrit mss. vol. II. pp. 90-100 an extract from the शिवादित्यमणिदीपिका of अप्पय्य is set out, wherein अप्पय्य speaks of आचार्यदीक्षित and रङ्गराज as his grandfather and father respectively and the colophon states that he was urged to write the work by king चिन्नबोम्म. This last was the son of चिन्नवीर and father of लिङ्गमनायक. These three chiefs are mentioned in the Vilāpāka grant of *śaka* 1523 (I. A. vol. XIII, p. 127 note 17 and E. I. vol. IV. p. 269). The inscriptions of चिन्नबोम्म of Velūr are dated *śaka* 1471 and 1488 (vide South Indian Ins. vol. I. p. 69 and p. 84). Veṅkaṭa I of Pennakoṇḍa urged अप्पय्य to compose the कुवलयानन्द and the former's inscriptions range from *śaka* 1508 to 1535 (E. I. vol. III. p. 238 Table) i. e. 1586 to 1613 A. D. Dr. Raghavan (in Proceeding of the 10th Session of the All India O. Conference pp. 176-180) shows that there were three persons named Appayya in the same family in three generations. This circumstance has naturally caused some confusion.

39 The रसगङ्गाधर of जगन्नाथ. This work together with the commentary called मर्मप्रकाश by नागेशभट्ट has been edited in the K. M. series. This is a standard work on poetics, particularly on *alaṅkāras*. The रसगङ्गाधर stands next only to the ध्वन्यालोक and the काव्यप्रकाश in the field of Poetics. Though a modern writer he has a wonderful command over classical Sanskrit. He cites his own examples, as he proudly says in रसग. p. 3. 'निर्माय नूतनमुदाहरणानुरूपं काव्यं मयात्र निहितं न परस्य किञ्चित्। किं सेव्यते सुमनसां मनसापि गन्धः कस्तूरिकाजननशक्तिभृता मृगेण ॥'. His verses are composed in an easy, flowing and graceful style and exhibit great poetic talent. His method is first to define a topic, then to discuss it and elucidate it by citing his own examples and to comment on the views of his predecessors. His prose is characterised by a lucid and vigorous style and displays great critical acumen. He is always independent in his views and boldly criticizes on occasions esteemed ancient writers, e. g. ध्वन्यालोक (for regarding the verse प्राप्तश्रीः as an example of रूपकध्वनि, p. 247), मम्मट (pp. 5, 229, 324), अलङ्कारसर्वस्व (pp. 251, 269, 301, 342 &c.), साहित्यदर्पण (p. 7). His criticism displays great sanity of judgment, maintains a high level of brilliant polemics and acuteness and is generally couched in courteous language

(except when dealing with the views of Appayya). The justice of his criticism has to be acknowledged in most cases. जगन्नाथ was a poet of great creative genius and also possessed the faculty of aesthetic appreciation in an eminent degree (i. e. he was a कवि as well as a सहृदय). Jagannātha was very proud and confident of his great command over classical Sanskrit. He could write verses that were full of pathos or joy as the mood of his mind dictated and he could make the sound an echo to the sense. At the end of the भामिनीविलास he says 'धुर्यैरपि माधुर्यैर्द्राक्षाक्षीरेक्षुमाक्षिकसुधानाम्। वन्द्यैव माधुरीयं पण्डितराजस्य कवितायाः॥'.

The work is a very bulky one and it is impossible to convey even a vague idea of its contents by a mere outline. It is the K. M. edition that is referred to here. In the first आनन he begins by defining *kāvya* as 'रमणीयार्थप्रतिपादकः शब्दः काव्यम्', examines the definitions of काव्य given by others, asserts that *pratibhā* alone is the source of *kāvya,* divides काव्य into four varieties उत्तमोत्तम, उत्तम, मध्यम, अधम; explains *rasas, bhāvas* and kindred topics; speaks of the different views about *guṇas* being three or ten; explains भाव, रसाभास, भावोदय &c. The 2nd आनन treats of the divisions of ध्वनि; of संयोग, विप्रयोग and other determining circumstances; discusses अभिधा and लक्षणा and their varieties; उपमा and other figures of speech (70 in all). The work breaks off in the midst of the figure उत्तर and the com. of नागेश who flourished only about 50 years after जगन्नाथ extends only up to that figure. It is not to be supposed that जगन्नाथ passed away in the midst of the task of composing the रसगङ्गाधर because from the 2nd introductory verse to his चित्रमीमांसाखण्डन it appears that he wrote the latter after the former 'रसगङ्गाधरे चित्रमीमांसायां मयोदिताः। ये दोषास्तेत्र संक्षिप्य कथ्यन्ते विदुषां मुदे॥'. In the चित्रमीमांसाखण्डन (p. 12) he says 'विशेषस्तु उदाहरणालङ्कारप्रकरणे रसगङ्गाधरादवसेयः'. But in the extant रसगङ्गाधर there are no remarks on the figure उदाहरण. The following are the well-known works of जगन्नाथ : (1) रसगङ्गाधर and (2) चित्रमीमांसाखण्डन in Poetics; (3) मनोरमाकुचमर्दनं[1] (or -मर्दिनी) in grammar against the प्रौढमनोरमा of

1. Jagannātha's temper was roused by the fact that Bhaṭṭoji, a pupil of शेषश्रीकृष्ण, attacked his guru in his मनोरमा. Therefore, at the beginning of the मनोरमाकुचमर्दिनी Jagannātha pours the phials of his wrath on Bhaṭṭoji by calling the latter *gurudruh* (traitor to his *guru*) and delivers his own diatribe against the Dīkṣita in the somewhat indecent but striking

भट्टोजिदीक्षित, which is a com. on the सि. कौ.; (4-8) five लहरिs (mentioned in रसग. p. 109 called सुधा, अमृत about the river यमुना in 10 शार्दूलविक्रीडित verses in K. M. series, लक्ष्मी (41 verses), करुणा (60 verses in वियोगिनी and other metres[1] in K. M. series), गङ्गा or पीयूष (in 52 शिखरिणी verses); (9) जगदाभरण (in praise of Dara Shukoh), (10) आसफविलास (about Nabob Asafkhan, who died in 1641 A. D.); (11) प्राणाभरण (in praise of प्राणनारायण, prince of कामरूप or कमता in Assam in 51 verses in different metres;[2] (12) भामिनीविलास (in four समुल्लासs on अन्योक्ति, शृङ्गार, करुण and शान्ति); (13) यमुनावर्णनचम्पू (quoted in रसगङ्गाधर pp. 19 and 128).

The रसगङ्गाधर quotes verses from many of his other works such as from the गङ्गालहरि (समृद्धं सौभाग्यं॰ p. 243, समुत्पत्तिः p. 491), from the भामिनीविलास (दिगन्ते श्रूयन्ते॰ p. 402, पुरा सरसि॰ p. 403).

For detailed information about Jagannātha, his date, his poetry and literary criticism, his works and the like, vide Mr. V. A. Ramswami Śāstri's contributions in Journal, Annamalai University, vol. II pp. 201-208, vol. III pp. 106-116, 229-244, vol. IV pp. 149-158, 262-274. These contributions were corrected and supplemented by the learned Pandit and issued as a separate work in 32 pages 'Jagannātha Paṇḍit' in 1942 at Annamalingara.

जगन्नाथ was a Tailaṅga brāhmaṇa of the आन्ध्रवेंगिनाडि family. He was the son of पेरुभट्ट (or पेरमभट्ट)[3] and learnt at the feet of his own father and also of शेषवीरेश्वर. पेरुभट्ट was the pupil of ज्ञानेन्द्रभिक्षु in अद्वैत, of महेन्द्र in न्याय and वैशेषिक, of खण्डदेव in पूर्वमीमांसा at Benares, of वीरेश्वर surnamed शेष in grammar (Intro. verses 2 and 3 of रस॰). It appears that the title of पण्डितराज was conferred

---

name मनोरमाकुचमर्दिनी. Vide Calcutta Oriental Journal vol. III. No. 3 pp. 41-51 for a statement of जगन्नाथ's criticism of Bhaṭṭoji.

1. Some of these are found in the भामिनीविलास and the रसगङ्गा॰ (e. g. वाचा निर्मलया on p. 66).

2. प्राणनारायण was a feudatory of the Mogul Emperor and died in 1666 A. D.

3. At the end of his प्राणाभरण we have the following verse : तैलङ्गान्वयमङ्गलालयमहालक्ष्मीदयालालितः श्रीमत्पेरमभट्टसूनुरनिशं विद्वल्लाटंतपः। सन्तुष्टः कमताधिपस्य कवितामाकर्ण्य तद्वर्णनं श्रीमत्पण्डितराज—पण्डितजगन्नाथो व्यधासीदिदम्॥. In the रसगङ्गाधर (Intro. verses) the father is called पेरुभट्ट. He probably migrated to Assam during the tumultuous times when there was fratricidal war between the sons of Shah Jahan.

upon जगन्नाथ by Emperor Shah Jahan. In the भामिनीविलास he states that he passed his youth under the Delhi emperor (दिल्लीवल्लभपाणिपल्लवतले नीतं नवीनं वयः). He bewails over the death of Āsaf (in the आसफविलास), probably the favourite Khan Khanan of Shah Jahan, who died in 1641 A. D. and praises Dārā, the son of Shah Jahan, in his जगदाभरण. Vide the verses सुधेव वाणी (on. p. 166 of रस०) and युक्तं तु याते (p. 457) for आसफ० and the verse भूमीनाथ शहाबदीन for Shah Jahan (p. 210). A ms. of the चित्रमीमांसाखण्डन is dated *saṁvat* 1709 (i. e. 1652-53 A. D.). Therefore, both the रसगङ्गाधर and चित्रमीमांसाखण्डन were composed before 1650 and after 1641 A. D. and they are the products of a mature mind. Therefore, the literary activity of जगन्नाथ lies between 1620 and 1665 A. D.

The same date of Jagannātha can be arrived at from another point of view. जगन्नाथ wrote the मनोरमाकुचमर्दिनी for criticizing the प्रौढमनोरमा of Bhaṭṭoji Dīkṣita on the सिद्धान्तकौमुदी. A ms. of the प्रौढमनोरमा at the B. O. R. I. (No. 657 of 1883-84 of D. C. Collection) is dated *saṁvat* 1713 (i. e. 1656-7 A.D.) and a ms. of शब्दकौस्तुभ is dated 1633 A. D. नृसिंहाश्रम, teacher of भट्टोजि, composed his तत्त्वविवेक in 1547 A. D., while Bhaṭṭoji's pupil नीलकण्ठशुक्ल wrote his शब्दशोभा in 1637 A. D. Therefore, भट्टोजि's literary activity may be placed somewhere between 1580 and 1630 A. D. भट्टोजि must be held to be about one generation earlier then जगन्नाथ, as the former was a pupil of शेषकृष्ण, while पेरुभट्ट and जगन्नाथ were pupils of शेषवीरेश्वर, son of शेषकृष्ण. Vide Prof. P. K. Gode in Annals of the Venkatesh Oriental Institute at Tirupati, vol. I. part 2 pp. 117-127 and his paper on 'Varadarāja and his works' in P. V. Kane Festschrift pp. 188-199.

The story about Jagannātha's *liason* with a *yavana* damsel called Lavaṅgī (in such verses as यवनी नवनीत०) appears to be a myth spread by those who were offended by the biting tongue (or rather pen) of Jagannātha. Similarly, the story that old Appayya met Jagannātha at Benares and addressed to him the verse (which occurs in the रसग. p. 421 'किं निःशङ्कं शेषे...जननी जागर्ति जाह्नवी निकटे ॥' is without any warrant, as अप्पय्य never left South India in his old age (Gode, vol. II pp. 460 ff).

नागेश is a very learned author and wrote commentaries on several Śāstras, his special *forte* being व्याकरण and धर्मशास्त्र. He is removed by about two generations from जगन्नाथ, as the following pedigrees will show, and flourished in the first quarter of the 18th century. A ms. of Nāgeśa's com. on the Rasamañjarī is dated *saṁvat* 1769 Māgha (i. e. February 1713 A. D.). Vide Eggeling's Cat. vol. III pp. 355-356 and H. of Dh. vol. I pp. 453-456. In Poetics itself he wrote commentaries on the following works: मर्मप्रकाश on रसगङ्गाधर, उद्योत on भट्टगोविन्द's प्रदीप on काव्यप्रकाश; उदाहरणदीपिका on मम्मट's काव्यप्रकाश; प्रकाश on रसमञ्जरी of भानुदत्त; अलङ्कारसुधा and विषमपदव्याख्यान-षट्पदानन्द on कुवलयानन्द; टीका on रसतरङ्गिणी.

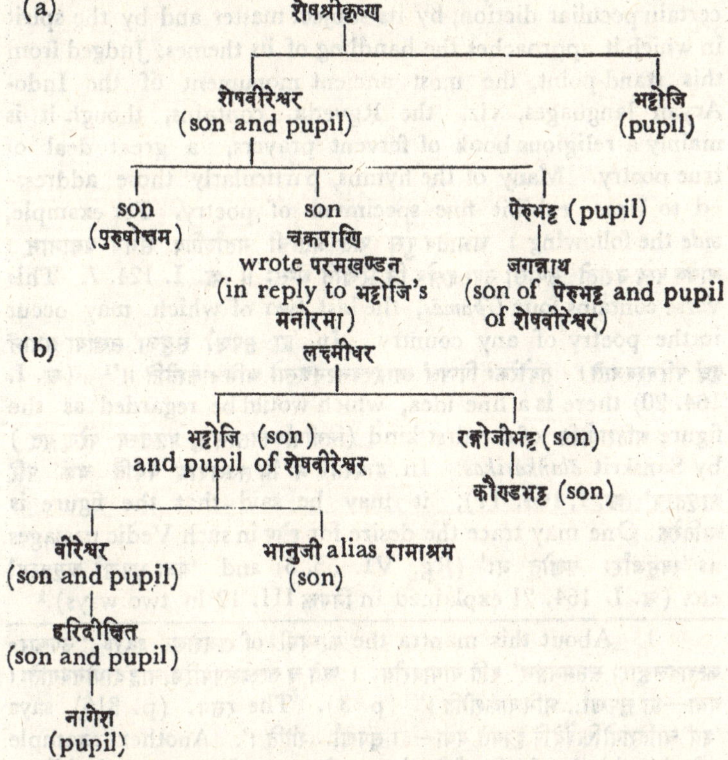

For the शेष family of Benares, vide I. A. for 1912 p. 245-253. There is great divergence of views about the descendants of Bhaṭṭoji among scholars; but I believe that the pedigree given by me is correct as far as it goes.

Jagannātha is the last great writer on Sanskrit Poetics. Therefore, it is proper to bring this part of the subject to a close at this stage.

PART II

The origin and growth of Poetics

1. Early poetic efforts. It is extremely difficult to give an accurate definition of poetry and try to distinguish it from other forms of literature. But true poetry (leaving aside the question whether a work clothed in prose is poetry or not) is distinguished at least by three things, viz. by a certain peculiar diction, by its subject matter and by the spirit in which it approaches the handling of its themes. Judged from this stand-point, the most ancient monument of the Indo-Aryan languages, viz. the Ṛgveda, contains, though it is mainly a religious book of fervent prayers, a great deal of true poetry. Many of the hymns, particularly those addressed to Uṣas, exhibit fine specimens of poetry. For example, *vide* the following : अभ्रातेव पुंस एति प्रतीची गर्तारुगिव सनये धनानाम् । जायेव पत्य उशती सुवासा उषा हस्रेव नि रिणीते अप्सः ॥ ऋ. I. 124. 7. This verse contains four *Upamās*, the last two of which may occur in the poetry of any country. In 'द्वा सुपर्णा सयुजा सखाया समानं वृक्षं परिषस्वजाते। तयोरेकः पिप्पलं स्वाद्वत्त्यनश्नन्नन्यो अभिचाकशीति ॥'[1] (ऋ. I. 164. 20) there is a fine idea, which would be regarded as the figure अतिशयोक्ति of the first kind (निगीर्याध्यवसानं तु प्रकृतस्य परेण यत्) by Sanskrit *ālaṅkārikas*. In 'द्वादशारं न हि तज्जराय वर्वर्ति चक्रं परि द्यामृतस्य' (ऋ. I. 164. 11), it may be said that the figure is व्यतिरेक. One may trace the desire for श्लेष in such Vedic passages as 'स्वसुर्जारः शृणोतु नः' (Ṛg. VI. 55. 5) and 'यत्रा सुपर्णा अमृतस्य' etc. (ऋ. I. 164. 21 explained in निरुक्त III. 12 in two ways).[2]

---

1. About this mantra the काव्यमी. of राजशेखर says "उपकारकत्वादलङ्कारः सप्तममङ्गम्' इति यायावरीयः । ऋते च तत्स्वरूपपरिज्ञानाद्वेदार्थानवगतिः। यथा—द्वा सुपर्णा...अभिचाकशीति ।" (p. 3). The रसग. (p. 316) says 'इयं चातिशयोक्तिर्वेदेपि दृश्यते यथा—द्वा सुपर्णा...शीति ।'. Another example of this kind of अतिशयोक्ति is चत्वारि शृङ्गा त्रयो अस्य पादा द्वे शीर्षे सप्त हस्तासो अस्य । त्रिधा बद्धो वृषभो रोरवीति महो देवो मर्त्यां आ विवेश ॥ ऋ. IV. 58. 3, explained in निरुक्त 13. 7 and in the महाभाष्य (vol. I. p. 3); in ऋ. X. 63. 10 (=वाज. सं. 21. 6) यज्ञ or द्युलोक is spoken of in terms of a नौका.

2. In the शतपथब्राह्मण we find that there is a pun on the words हित (placed, beneficial) and वर्ष (year and rainy season)

In Ṛg. X. 146. 1 (अरण्यान्यरण्यान्यसौ या प्रेव नश्यसि । कथा ग्रामं न पृच्छसि न त्वा भीरिव विदन्तीइं ॥) there is उत्प्रेक्षा, which resembles the one in लिम्पतीव तमोऽङ्गानि० discussed by the काव्यादर्श (vide p. 88 above) and in Ṛg. II. 35. 13 (सो अपां नपादनभिम्लातवर्णोऽन्यस्येवेह तन्वा विवेष) also there is a fine उत्प्रेक्षा.

Prof. Charu Deva Sastri in his valuable paper on 'Bhartṛhari and the Vākyapadīya' (Proceedings, 5th All India O. Conference pp. 630-655) points out at p. 650 that भर्तृहरि in his महाभाष्यटीका states that one and the same object can be compared to itself (which is the figure अनन्वय) in the following कारिका 'दस्युहेन्द्र इवेत्येतदैन्द्रे मन्त्रे प्रयुज्यते । अन्यत्र दृष्टकर्मेन्द्रो यथेत्यस्मिन् विवक्षितो॥'. Prof. Charu Deva sets out the mantra as 'इन्द्र इव सुपरस्तुयसे इन्द्र इव दस्युहा भव क्षेत्राणि सृज', but does not state whence it is taken. The मन्त्र means 'O Indra, you are praised like Indra,[1] may you be killer of *dasyus* like Indra, create fields for us.'

Dr. De (in H. S. P. vol. I. p. 341) says 'Undue emphasis appears to have been laid on the use of poetic figures in Vedic Literature by Kane in I. A. XLI, 1912, p. 120f.'. He is wrong. I put forward my thesis rather briefly and modestly. Therefore, I am obliged to elaborate it here. In the first place, reference must be made to the dialogues in the Ṛgveda, some of which are highly poetic and imaginative and all of which must be regarded as precursors of the later classical dramas. The following dialogues may be referred to: Ṛg. III. 33 (Viśvāmitra and the rivers); X 10 (Yama and Yamī), X. 108 (Saramā and Paṇis); I. 165 and 170 (Indra, Maruts and Agastya); I. 179 (Agastya and Lopāmudrā and pupil); IV. 18 (Indra, Aditi and Vāmadeva); IV. 42 (Indra and Varuṇa); VII. 33 (Vasiṣṭha, his sons and Indra); VIII. 100 (Nema Bhārgava and Indra); X. 28 (Indra and wife of Vasukra); X. 51-53 (Gods and Agni); X. 86 (Indra, Indrāṇī and Vṛṣākapi). Some of these are obscure or enigmatic and one or two like X. 86 are almost unintelligible. Ṛg. X. 119 in a monologue (in which the poet fancies that Indra being intoxicated with Soma offerings muses to himself). Similarly, Ṛg. I. 24 is a soliloquy of

in I. 3. 1. 25 and II. 2. 3. 7 (S. B. E. vol. 12 pp. 77, 315) respectively and on महिषी (crowned queen, she-buffalo) in VI. 5. 3. 1 (S. B. E. vol. 41 p. 235).

1. This मन्त्र is found in मैत्रायणीसंहिता IV. 12. 73 as 'इन्द्र इव दस्युहा भवापः क्षेत्राणि संजय ।'.

Śunaḥśepa whose story is developed in the Ait. Br. Beautiful similes are found by the hundred in the Ṛg. Vide Prof. H. D. Velankar's exhaustive treatment of similes in the 4th and 5th Maṇḍalas of the Ṛg. in J.B.B.R.A.S. vol. 14 pp. 1-47 and vol. 16 pp. 1-42, 'Figures of speech in the Ṛgveda' Annals of B.O. R.I. vol. 17 pp. 61-83 (translated from A. Bergaigne's Article) and pp. 259-288 by Mr. A. Venkatasubbiah; Abel Bergaigne's 'La Syntaxe des comparaisons Vediques' (1886) translated in Annals B.O.R.I. vol. XVI pp. 232-261 by Mr. A. Venkatasubbiah, 'Figures of speech in Ṛgveda' by Mr. P. S. Sastri in Annals B.O.R.I. vol. 28 pp. 34-64. The Ṛgvedic poets not only indulge in such figures of speech as Upamā, Atiśayokti and Rūpaka (as in Ṛg. III. 27. 15, IX. 64. 1 वृषा सोमः), but they appear to have had some ideas about a theory of poetics, as the following brief statement will show. They are fond of the repetition of the same letters or words which create an appearance of what is called *anuprāsa* in later times, e.g. रक्षाणो अग्ने तव रक्षणेभी रारक्षाणः (IV. 3. 14), प्रतार्यग्ने प्रतरं न आयुः (IV. 12. 6), अब्जा गोजा ऋतजा अद्रिजा ऋतम् (IV. 40. 5), वयमग्ने वनुयाम त्वोता वसूयवो (V. 3. 6); repetition of the same word at the beginning of several *pādas* in IV. 23. 3-5 or in several pādas as in Ṛg. IV. 40. 5 हंसः शुचिषद् वसुरन्तरिक्षसद्धोता वेदिषदतिथिर्दुरोणसत्'; Ṛg. V. 27. 4) ददृचा सनिं यते ददन्मेधामृतायते) and V. 76. 2 दिवाभिपित्वेऽवसा गमिष्ठा प्रत्यवर्तिं दाशुषे शंभविष्ठा); the last two seem to be efforts at यमक. The sage often says that he brings to the god a new and forceful verse, a product of his speech (प्र तव्यसीं नव्यसीं धीतिमग्नये वाचो मतिं सहसः सूनवे भरे । Ṛg. I. 143. 1). An interesting verse is Ṛg. X. 71. 2 सक्तुमिव तितउना पुनन्तो यत्र धीरा मनसा वाचमक्रत । अत्रा सखायः सख्यानि जानते भद्रैषां लक्ष्मीर्निहिताधि वाचि ॥ 'When men of wisdom create by their intellect verse (lit. speech) after winnowing (words) as barley grains are sifted by means of a winnowing basket, then men of equal knowledge understand (recognize) meaning (contained in the verse); in their verses (speech) blessed glory is enshrined, (resides).[1] This makes it clear that a distinction is here made between ordinary speech and poetic speech, that poets have to pick and choose their words and that poetry leads on to bliss and glory. Ṛg. X. 125 is a sublime hymn to Vāk (put in the

1. This verse is explained in the Nirukta IV. 10 and in the महाभाष्य (vol. I. p. 4) at the beginning. It is also quoted in the साहित्यमीमांसा (p. 161). Vide above p. 271.

mouth of Vāk herself) wherein the power of speech is most effectively and picturesquely described. One half verse may be quoted here 'यं कामये तं तमुग्रं कृणोमि तं ब्रह्माणं तमृषिं तं सुमेधाम् ॥'. Ṛg. X. 71. 4 (उत त्वः पश्यन्न ददर्श वाचमुत त्वः शृण्वन्न शृणोत्येनाम् । उतो त्वस्मै तन्वं विसस्रे जायेव पत्य उशती सुवासाः ॥) is another verse which is explained both in the Nir. I. 19 and in the महाभाष्य (vol. I. p. 4) and which marks the difference between the man who does not understand the greatness of speech and him who looks more to the inner meaning of speech than to the nice words in which it may be clothed. The word 'kāvya' (poem) occurs several times in the Ṛgveda; e. g. III. I. 17 is आ देवानामभवः केतुरग्ने मन्द्रो विश्वानि काव्यानि विद्वान् ॥ 'Agni! thou art the banner of the gods and knowest all poems); vide also III. 1. 18 for 'अग्निर्विश्वानि काव्यानि विद्वान्; IV. 3. 16 (nivacanā kavaye kāvyanyasaṁsiṣam); in Ṛg. VI. 11. 3 'मधु च्छन्दो भनति रेभ इष्टौ (the singer utters in the sacrifice a sweet verse); VIII. 3. 15 'उदुत्ये मधुमत्तमा गिरः स्तोमास ईरते' (those men send forth songs of praise, that are most sweet words); the word गाथा (a verse that is sung) also often occurs in the Ṛgveda; e. g. VIII. 6. 43 'तं गाथया पुराण्या पुनानमभ्यनूषत' (with an ancient gāthā they send forth a laud towards Soma that is being washed); vide also X. 85. 6. These passages show that poems with sweet words were highly valued in those very ancient times and, though no theory of Poetics could be stated to have been evolved, the germs of it were there. The शतपथब्रा. I. 2. 5. 16 emphasizes the same points of female beauty as later classical Sanskrit poets do (एवमेव हि योषां प्रशंसन्ति पृथुश्रोणीर्विमृष्टान्तरांसा मध्ये संग्राह्येति). This much will suffice for the different aspects of Poetry in general. As regards dramas and dramatic representation the following points have to be noted. A dramatic representation has generally four aspects viz. the dialogue, songs, music and dance. All these elements were developed in Vedic Literature. Dialogues have been already referred to. Then there were the ब्रह्मोद्य (questions and answers) as in वाज. सं. 23. 9-12 and 45-62 explained in शतपथब्राह्मण XIII. 2. 6. 9-17 and XIII. 5. 2. 12-21 (S. B. E. vol. 44 pp. 314-316 and pp. 388-90). Vide also तै. सं. VII 4. 18 and तै. ब्रा. III. 9. 5. In Vedic ritual there were several incidentes that partook of the nature of the drama. First, there is a dialogue between the Adhvaryu and the vendor of Soma (vide H. of Dh. vol. II. p. 1143 and notes). Then in the

Mahāvrata which is the penultimate day in a Sattra, there is a mock fight between a brāhmaṇa and a śūdra for a white circular skin that symbolizes the sun, and it is so arranged that it ends in a victory for the *ārya*. Vide H. of Dh. vol. II. p. 1244. In the same rite there was beating of drums, chanting of hymns by the priests whose wives acted as choristers and played on several musical intruments, and servants and maids danced with water jars on their heads and sang songs in which cows were lauded (*ibid.* pp. 1244-45). Compare for this Tai. S. VII. 5. 10. In the Aśvamedha, after the horse was sacrificed, there was an exchange of obscene abuse between the hotṛ priest and the crowned queen and the brahmā priest and the favourite wife of the king (vide H. of Dh. vol. II. pp. 1234-35). In the Aśvamedha a brāhmaṇa and a rājanya were engaged in playing on the lute everyday for one year and they sang three songs each composed by themselves, the brāhmaṇa's songs saying[1] 'you donated this, you performed such and such a sacrifice,' while the gāthās of the Rājanya stated 'you fought this war, you won this battle'. Vide H. of Dh. vol. II. p. 1231. The Śat. Br. refers to the Uttaramandrā tune of the Viṇā. Several musical instruments are mentioned such as दुन्दुभि (Ṛg. I. 28. 5, VI. 47. 29, Vāj. S. 29. 55-56), गर्गर (Ṛg. VII. 69. 9), वाण (Ṛg. IX. 50. 1, IX. 97. 8, X 32. 4, Tai. S. VII. 5. 9. 2 वाणः शततन्तुर्भवति). Persons playing on वीणा, तूणव, दुन्दुभि and blowing a conch are mentioned in वाज. सं. 30. 19 and तै. ब्रा. III. 4. 13. Ṛg. I. 92. 4 compares Uṣas to a female dancer (नृतू) that puts ornaments on her body and bares her breast (अधि पेशांसि वपते नृतूरिवापोर्णुते वक्ष उस्रेव बर्जहम् ।). Dancing is referred to in Ṛg. X. 94. 4-5. The Vāj. S. (30. 6) in its symbolical पुरुषमेध consigns the सूत to नृत्त and the शैलूष to गीत; compare तै. ब्रा. III. 4. 2 (where it is exactly the opposite viz. गीताय सूतं नृत्ताय शैलूषम्). The Ait. Ār. III. 2. 5 speaks of the several parts of a वीणा which was covered in a hairy skin cover. The कौषी. ब्रा. 29. 5 says त्रिवृद्वै शिल्पं नृत्यं गीतं वादितमिति. Therefore, it follows that even the earlier period of Vedic Literature knew dramatic spectacles of a religious character.

1. अयजतेत्यददादिति ब्राह्मणो गायति...अयुध्यतेत्यमुं संग्राममजयदिति राजन्यो...तिस्रोऽन्यो गाथा गायति तिस्रोऽन्यः ।...शतपथब्रा. XIII. 1. 5. 6.; तस्यै प्रयाजेषु तायमानेषु ब्राह्मणो वीणागाथी दक्षिणत उत्तरमन्द्रामुदाघ्नंस्तिस्रः स्वयं संभृता गाथा गायति...। शतपथ XIII. 4. 2. 8.

Western scholars such as Schroeder, Windisch, Oldenberg, Pischel, Konow have evolved various theories about the origin of the Sanskrit drama, all of which are criticized by Prof. A. B. Keith in S. D. pp. 13-27. The Nāṭyaśāstra of Bharata shows its consciousness that the classical Sanskrit drama has its roots deep down in the Vedic age when भरत states (in नाट्यशास्त्र I. 17 Ch. ed. and in G. O. S. ed. also) that पाठ्य (recitation and dialogue), गीत, अभिनय and रस were taken from the ऋग्वेद, सामवेद, यजुर्वेद and आथर्वणवेद respectively (vide p. 29 above).

In the Baud. Gṛ. I. 4. 5 (Mysore ed.) and in the Hir. Gṛ. I. 24. 6 we come across the following verse which refers to Cakravāka birds that are symbols of tender conjugal love and concord in classical Sanskrit 'चाक्रवाकं संवननं यन्नदीभ्य उदाहृतम् । यद्दिव्यौ देवगन्धर्वौ तेन संवनिनौ स्वः ॥' (the husband says this to the wife on the 4th night after monthly illness starts). Vide S. B. E. vol. 30 p. 198 for Hir. Gṛ. and H. of Dh. vol. II. p. 224 on सीमन्तोन्नयन for references to other गृह्य sūtras.

The Upaniṣads also, though they are devoted to the pursuit of philosophical truth, contain highly poetic passages e. g. 'धनुर्गृहीत्वौपनिषदं महास्त्रं शरं ह्युपासानिशितं संधयीत । आयम्य तद्भावगतेन चेतसा लक्ष्यं तदेवाक्षरं सोम्य विद्धि ॥'' मुण्डकोपनि. II. 2. 3. Similarly, the verse 'आत्मानं रथिनं विद्धि शरीरं रथमेव तु' (कठोपनिषद् I. 3. 3) contains a good रूपक and the verses 'इन्द्रियेभ्यः परा ह्यर्था अर्थेभ्यश्च परं मनः ।...... पुरुषः परः ।' contain the figure सार. Vide H. of Dh. vol. II. pp. 1231-1233 for the recitation of narratives called पारिप्लव for one year in अश्वमेध and Śat. Br. XIII. 4. 3 (SBE. vol. 44 pp. 360-371). In the ऐत. ब्रा. (VII. 18. 10=33. 6) the story of शुनःशेप is called शौनःशेपाख्यान, which the *hotṛ* priest was to recite to the king in the Rājasūya sacrifice. In ऐत. ब्रा. (III. 25. 1= 13. 1) there is mention of सौपर्णाख्यान.

2 Coming to later days, there is ample evidence to show that centuries before the Christian era poetry of a high order had been composed. It is accepted almost by all scholars that the Mahābhārata in its extant form cannot be placed later than the 2nd century A. D. and that a large portion of it may be at least as old as 500 B.C. Similarly, the रामायण has been assigned to the 4th century B. C. by some scholars (Dr. Keith in JRAS 1915 p. 320), while others (like Dr. Jacobi) would place it as far back as 600 B. C. These two epics contain highly poetical passages. Many passages are quoted from the महाभारत in the

ध्वन्यालोक (pp. 153 where the verse या निशा सर्वभूतानां is quoted and p. 299 where 'भगवान् वासुदेवश्च कीर्त्यतेऽत्र सनातनः' आदिपर्व chap. I. 256 is quoted) and in the काव्यप्रकाश (4th उल्लास p. 169 the गृध्रगोमायुसंवाद in शान्तिपर्व 153)[1] and a few from the रामायण are mentioned (e. g. in ध्व० p. 76 रविसंक्रान्त० which is अरण्य० 22. 13), The महाभारत is more of a धर्मशास्त्र than a काव्य, though, as the work itself asserts in no mood of vanity, it has inspired many poets ('इतिहासोत्तमादस्माज्जायन्ते कविबुद्धयः' आदिपर्व 2. 385 and 'इदं कविवरैः सर्वैराख्यानमुपजीव्यते' आदि. 2 389). The रामायण is truly a *kāvya* in its main purpose, its form and contents.[2] It abounds in elaborate descriptions and flights of fancy. For example, the highly poetical description of the sea (हसन्तमिव फेनौघैर्नृत्यन्तमिव चोर्मिभिः) in the युद्धकाण्ड (4. 115 ff), the imaginative description of the sky in सुन्दरकाण्ड (57. 1-4) and the elaborate रूपक in अयोध्याकाण्ड (69. 28 ff), may be referred to in this connection. The दशरूप (I. 68)advises the authors of dramas to draw upon the रामायण and the बृहत्कथा for their plots. The quotation 'अक्रूरो ददते मणिम्' in the निरुक्त (II. 2) seems to be taken from some secular poetic work. The *sūtra* of Pāṇini (अधिकृत्य कृते ग्रन्थे IV. 3. 87) and the following sūtra indicate the existence of secular works before Pāṇini's day which may have been poetic. नमिसाधु on रुद्रट (II. 8) tells us that पाणिनि wrote a महाकाव्य called पातालविजय and then quotes one verse and a portion of another from that work. राजशेखर[3] attributes the composition of the *kāvya* जाम्बवतीजय to

1. गृध्रगोमायुसंवाद in शान्तिपर्व 153 verses 11, 12, 19, 65 (=cr. ed. chap. 149, verses 8, 9, 15, 60) are quoted in the काव्यप्रकाश as an example of प्रबन्धनिष्ठध्वनि. On 'या निशा' etc. the ध्व. remarks (p. 154) 'अनेन हि वाक्येन निशार्थो न जागरणार्थः कश्चिद्विवक्षितः किं तर्हि तत्त्वज्ञानावहितत्वमतत्त्वपराङ्मुखत्वं च मुनेः प्रतिपाद्यत इति तिरस्कृतवाच्यस्यास्य व्यञ्जकत्वम्'.

2. बालकाण्ड 2. 15 is the famous verse मा निषाद ... मोहितम्; 2. 18 is शोकार्तस्य प्रवृत्तो मे श्लोको भवतु नान्यथा; 40-41 'समाक्षरैश्चतुर्भिर्यः पादैर्गीतो महर्षिणा ।। सोनुव्याहरणाद्भूयः शोकः श्लोकत्वमागतः ।.' Thus the बालकाण्ड states the origin of the classical Sanskrit śloka and also contains the germs of the *rasa* theory. The रघुवंश (14. 70) श्लोकत्वमापद्यत यस्य शोकः) echoes the words of the बालकाण्ड and so does ध्व. I. 5 p. 31 'काव्यस्यात्मा स एवार्थस्तथा चादिकवेः पुरा । क्रौञ्चद्वन्द्ववियोगोत्थः शोकः श्लोकत्वमागतः' and then the ध्व० (p. 32) quotes the verse 'मा निषाद०'.

3. स्वस्ति पाणिनये तस्मै यस्य रुद्रप्रसादतः । आदौ व्याकरणं काव्यमनु जाम्बवतीजयः ॥ राजशेखर quoted in सूक्तिमु० p. 42. Vide कवीन्द्र० Intro. pp. 51-53 for collecting together all the verses attributed to

the grammarian पाणिनि (Peterson's 4th Report LXXVI). The सुवृत्ततिलक (III. 30) says that पाणिनि excelled in the composition of the उपजाति metre. Many verses ascribed to पाणिनि in the anthologies (*vide* Peterson's preface to सुभाषितावलि p. 58 out of which the verse उपोढरागेण० is ascribed to पाणिनि in सदुक्ति० p. 58, सूक्तिमु० p. 260 and शार्ङ्ग० No. 3634 and occurs in the ध्व० p. 35, without name) and the verse ऐन्द्रं धनुः is ascribed to पाणिनि in सुभा. (No. 1815) and occurs in काव्या. सू. of वामन (IV. 3. 27) and व्यक्तिविवेक p. 75. A *vārtika* on अधिकृत्य कृते ग्रन्थे viz. लुबाख्यायिकाभ्यो बहुलम्) shows that the class of composition known as आख्यायिका existed long before पतञ्जलि. The latter speaks of a *kāvya* composed by वररुचि ('यत्तेन कृतं न च तेन प्रोक्तं [1]वाररुचं काव्यं जालूकाः श्लोकाः' महाभाष्य vol. II. p. 315). On pp. 2-3 पतञ्जलि refers to certain ślokas called भ्राजs from which he quotes one verse 'यस्तु प्रयुंक्ते' and explains it at length on which कैयट says that they were composed by कात्यायन. Vide काव्यमी. pp. 25-27. पतञ्जलि, while commenting on the वार्तिक 'लुबाख्यायिकाभ्यो बहुलम्' mentions by name three works of the आख्यायिका class, viz. वासवदत्ता, सुमनोत्तरा[2] and भैमरथी (महाभाष्य vol. II. p. 313; see also p. 284).

पाणिनि in the several anthologies. Two questions arise: (1) Whether Pāṇini the poet is identical with Pāṇini the grammarian and (2) whether the names पातालविजय (in नमिसाधु on रुद्रट II. 8) and जाम्बवतीजय refer to the same work. On the first question opinion is divided. I think that we should rather adopt the cautious attitude so finely put by Peterson in his Intro. to सुभा० p. 58 (note). In H. I. Q. vol. 13 pp. 167-171 Mr. Krishnadeva Upadhyaya shows that the दुर्घटवृत्ति of शरणदेव composed in *śaka* 1095 (1173 A. D.) quotes three verses (not mentioned anywhere else, two of which are Upajātis and one अनुष्टुभ्) from the 2nd, 5th and 18th cantos respectively of the जाम्बवतीविजय.

1. राजशेखर quoted in the सूक्ति.मु. p. 43 says 'यथार्थता कथं नाम्नि मा भूद्वररुचेरिह । व्यधत्त कण्ठाभरणं यः सदा रोहणप्रियः ॥'. Vide Peterson's Intro. to सुभा. pp. 108-109 for verses attributed to वररुचि in the anthologies.

2. For the story of सुमन, a rich merchant of Rājagṛha, and his wife उत्तरा, vide 'Poona Orientalist' vol. 7 pp. 197-200. पतञ्जलि mentions the word सौमनोत्तरिकः (one who studies the आख्यायिका सुमनोत्तरा) in vol. II. p. 284 on पाणिनि IV. 2.60

He refers to two works dealing with the death of Kaṁsa and the humiliation of Bali and dramatic representations of these themes (vol. II. p. 34 and p. 36).[1] In another passage he makes a reference to the wives of actors 'व्यञ्जनानि पुनर्नटभार्याविद्भवन्ति। नटानां स्त्रियो रङ्गं गता यो यः पृच्छति कस्य यूयं कस्य यूयमिति तं तं तव तवेत्याहुः' (vol. III. p. 7). The महाभाष्य contains many quotations from the works of poets that went before it, some of which possess poetic charm, e.g. 'असि द्वितीयोनुससार पाण्डवम्' and 'सङ्कर्षणद्वितीयस्य बलं कृष्णस्य वर्धताम्' (vol. I. p. 426); जघान कंसं किल वासुदेवः (vol. II. p. 119); जनार्दनस्त्वात्मचतुर्थ एव (vol. III. p. 143): प्रियां मयूरः प्रतिनर्नृतीति and यद्वत्त्वं नरवर नर्नृतीषि हृष्टः (vol. III. p. 338); एति जीवन्तमानन्दः (vol. I. p. 277); वरतनु संप्रवदन्ति कुक्कुटाः[2] (vol. I. p.283). The verse[3] एति etc. occurs in the युद्धकाण्ड (129. 2 where it is called लौकिकीगाथा). On the sūtra रसादिभ्यश्च (पा. V. 2. 95) the Mahābhāṣya gives the example रसिको नटः (vol. II. p. 394), thereby indicating that there were even then in the air some ideas about the relation of *rasas* to actors. In the days of the महाभाष्य also the face of a charming young woman was compared to the moon, since he cites the example चन्द्रमुखी देवदत्ता (vol. I. p. 397) and remarks that though the moon has many good points what is conveyed here is प्रियदर्शनता. On 'उपमानानि सामान्यवचनैः' पा. II. 1. 55 we have 'चन्द्रमुखी देवदत्तेति बहवश्चन्द्रे गुणा या चासौ प्रियदर्शनता सा गम्यते (महा-

1. महाभाष्य says 'इह तु कथं वर्तमानकालता कंसं घातयति बलिं बन्धयतीति चिरहते कंसे चिरबद्धे च बलौ। अत्रापि युक्ता। कथम्। ये तावदेते शोभनिका नामैते प्रत्यक्षं कंसं घातयन्ति प्रत्यक्षं च बलिं बन्धयन्तीति। चित्रेषु कथम्।...ग्रन्थिकेषु कथम्। यत्र शब्दगडुमात्रं लक्ष्यते। तेऽपि तेषामुत्पत्तिप्रभृत्या विनाशादृद्धीर्व्याचक्षाणाः सतो बुद्धिविषयान् प्रकाशयन्ति'। vol. II. p. 36. This refers to three separate matters. शोभनिक (explained by कैयट as कंसाद्यनुकारिणां नटानां व्याख्यानोपाध्यायाः) represent the killing of कंस; pictures paint these incidents and thirdly poets compose works describing their actions. पतञ्जलि says that some of the actors have their faces coloured red and others black.

2. In औचित्यविचारचर्चा (कारिका 24) क्षेमेन्द्र quotes as कुमारदास's the verse 'अयि विजहीहि दृढोपगूहनं त्यज नवसङ्गमभीरु वल्लभम्। अरुणकरोद्गम एष वर्तते वरतनु संप्रवदन्ति कुक्कुटाः॥', where the महाभाष्य quotation is taken up as if for समस्यापूरण. The verse अयि विजहीहि occurs as an example of शब्दालङ्कारगति under सर. क. II. 26. p. 151.

3. Vide I. A. vol. 14 pp. 326 ff and Indische Studien vol. XII pp. 293-496.

भाष्य). The महाभाष्य also says 'यदारम्भका रङ्गं गच्छन्ति नटस्य श्रोष्यामः ग्रन्थिकस्य श्रोष्यामः' (vol. I. p. 329 on 'आख्यातोपयोगे' पा. I. 4. 29).[1] This example clearly shows that पतञ्जलि here refers to actors who deliver dramatic dialogues on the stage (रङ्ग), and not to any shows concerned with pantomimes. On पा. II. 4. 77 (vol. I. p. 495,) the महाभाष्य cites 'अगासीन्नटः' showing thereby that a नट also sang. Why the same meaning should not be taken in the case of Pāṇini's sūtra 'पाराशर्यशिलालिभ्यां भिक्षुनटसूत्रयोः' (IV. 3. 110) is not clear to me. Western scholars like Keith obstinately and persistently refuse to hold that the Naṭasūtra referred to by Pāṇini is some work on actors and dramaturgy (vide 'Sanskrit Drama' pp. 31, 291) but that all that Pāṇini meant are rules on pantomimes. No works dealing with pantomimes alone have been discovered so far.

In I. H. Q. vol. 17 pp. 196-206 Dr. Wijesekera cites evidence from ancient Buddhist works for the early existence of drama. At. p. 197 he quotes a passage from the गामणिसंयुत्त (IV. p. 306) wherein a नटगामणि (the leader of naṭas) asks the Blessed One 'योऽसो नटो रंगमज्झे समज्जमज्झे सच्चालिकेन जनं हासेति रमेति &c.' (that naṭa who on the stage or in an arena makes people laugh and delights them by a mixture of truth and falsehood). On p. 200 he quotes from the Dialogues of Buddha a passage where नृत्य, गीत, वादित, प्रेक्षा, आख्यान and शोभानगरक are mentioned. The preceding brief discussion shows that from at least 500 B. C. to 100 B. C. a great deal of poetical material of a secular character had been accumulated in classical Sanskrit. This must have naturally led to speculations about the functions and objects of poetry, the classification of different kinds of poetry and literary works like आख्यायिका, the enunciation of rules about the standard form of certain classes of composition, in short, to attempts, more or less crude, to establish a theory of Poetics and literary criticism. From this time forward the two processes, viz. composition of secular poetry and the elaboration of rules, must have proceeded hand in hand.

3. **Early beginnings of Poetics.** Epigraphic records of the 2nd century A.D. and onwards show that before that period a theory of Poetics had been evolved. *Vide* on this part of the

---

1. उपयोग means नियमपूर्वकविद्यास्वीकारः. In such a case the आख्याता (i. e. वक्ता) is put in the ablative as in उपाध्यायादधीते.

subject and in general for the development of Poetics my articles in I. A. for 1912 pp. 124-128 and pp. 201-208 and on the epigraphic material in Buhler's essay 'Die Indische Inschriften etc.' (translated by Prof. Ghate in I. A. for 1913 pp. 29, 137, 172, 188, 230, 243). In 'seven Brāhmī Inscriptions from Mathurā' E. I. vol. 24 pp. 199 ff. Prof. Lüders says that in one of them occurs a verse in the भुजङ्गविजृम्भित metre and that therefore it must be conceded that *Kāvya* poetry was fully developed before 1st century B.C. The Inscription of रुद्रदामन् at Junagad (dated 150 A.D.) sheds very great light on the stage Poetics had reached by that time. Vide ASWI vol. II p. 128 and E. I. vol. VIII. p. 36 for the inscription. The preserved portion contains only two verbs, it is written in prose with long compounds, it is full of alliteration and other tricks with words. A brief quotation will convey an idea of the nature of the inscription: सर्वक्षत्राविष्कृतवीरशब्दजातोत्सेकाविधेयानां यौधेयानां प्रसह्योत्सादकेन... शब्दार्थगान्धर्वन्यायाद्यानां विद्यानां महतीनां पारणधारणविज्ञानप्रयोगावाप्तविपुलकीर्तिना... स्फुटलघुमधुरचित्रकान्तशब्दसमयोदारालङ्कृतगद्यपद्य...यमभिगतमहाक्षत्रपनाम्ना नरेन्द्रकन्यास्वयंवरानेकमाल्यप्राप्तदाम्ना महाक्षत्रपेण रुद्रदाम्ना (p. 44). This shows that in or before the second century A. D. काव्य had been divided into गद्य and पद्य, that some of the *guṇas* that figure in later works had been already named (*vide* स्फुट,[1] मधुर, कान्त, उदार, which correspond to प्रसाद, माधुर्य, कान्ति and उदारता of the काव्यादर्श), both गद्य and पद्य were required to be अलङ्कृत (that is endowed with figures of speech). The नाट्यशास्त्र 17. 102, 106, 107 (K. M. ed. 16. 103, 107-108 and GOS. ed. 16. 104, 110, 112), define माधुर्य, उदात्त, कान्त. The composer of this inscription was evidently trying to come up to the standard of a good poet laid down in the works on Poetics of his day and therefore this inscription represents at least a mediocre attempt at what a *kāvya* was in those days required to be. The Nasik Inscription of Siri Pulumāyi, which is somewhat earlier than that of रुद्रदामन्, though in Prakrit, exhibits the same traits (Bombay Gazetteer vol. 16 p. 550 and E. I. vol. 8 p. 60 No. 2). In the first two centuries of the Christian era both

---

1. कौटिल्य II. 10 p. 71 (शासनाधिकर) says अर्थक्रमः, सम्बन्धः, परिपूर्णता माधुर्यमौदार्यं स्पष्टत्वमिति लेखसम्पत् and defines the last three as 'सुखोपनीतचार्वर्थशब्दाभिधानं माधुर्यम्। अग्राम्यशब्दाभिधानमौदार्यम्। प्रतीतशब्दप्रयोगः स्पष्टत्वमिति'. Compare वामन's काव्या. सू. III. 2. 11, 13, 14 of which अग्राम्यत्वमुदारता is very close to कौ.

Sanskrit and Prakrit inscriptions were engraved and followed the same pattern of literary style. The Ayodhyā Śuṅga Inscription of धन (देव or भूति), who was the sixth from Senāpati Puṣyamitra is in Sanskrit (E. I. vol. 20 p. 54) and the Inscription of रुद्रदामन् has been cited above already. The Inscription of Khāravela (referred to above on p. 19 and n 3) is in Prākrit, shows all the traits of the Ins. of रुद्रदामन् and mentions गन्धर्ववेद, नट, गीत, वादित्र and उत्सवसमाज. A quotation from it and one from the Nasik Ins. in the 19th year of Siri Pulumāyi are given below.[1] It will be noticed that they are full of alliteration, the language is forcible and sonorous and there are long compounds, which were the essence of prose according to somewhat later works like the काव्यादर्श (ओजः समासभूयस्त्वमेतद्गद्यस्य जीवितम् । I. 80) which dictum was probably based on older prose works now lost that were imitated by the writers of the early inscriptions in Sanskrit and Prakrit. Vide for other comparatively old Sanskrit Inscriptions, Dr. R. C. Majumdar's 'Ancient Indian Colonies in the Far East' (vol. 1, book III. p. 1, the Vo-Chanh Rock Inscription from Champā in Sanskrit of the 2nd or 3rd century A. D. containing two वसन्ततिलका verses), I. H. Q. vol. 16 p. 484 (Dr. G. Coedés), vol. 17 pp. 107-110 (Dr. D. C. Sarkar for same as to date); the Pikira grant of Pallava king सिंहवर्मन्, son of युवमहाराज विष्णुगोप and grandson of महाराजस्कन्दवर्मन् II in Sanskrit prose with long compounds. An inscription of the 4th century A. D. contains a panegyric of the great Emperor समुद्रगुप्त by हरिषेण (*vide* Fleet's Gupta Inscriptions, No. 1 p. 8). The prose of this प्रशस्ति rivals the style of Bāṇa. This प्रशस्ति tells us that 'the title कविराज has been applied to समुद्रगुप्त on account of the composition of many *kāvyas* that were the source of inspiration to learned men'. A

---

1. महाराजेन...पसथसुभलखनेन चतुरन्तलुठितगुणोपहितेन कलिङ्गाधिपतिना सिरिखारवेलेन...ततो लेखरूपगणनाववहारविधिविसारदेन सवविजावदातेन नववसानि योवराजं पसासितं......सवपासण्डपूजको सवदेवायतनसंखारकारको अपतिहतचकिवाहिनिबलो चकधुरगतचको...राजा खारवेलसिरि । E. I. vol. 20 at pp. 79-80; Nasik Ins. No. 2 in Bombay Gazetteer vol. 16 at p. 550 and E. I. vol. 8 at p. 60 'राजरञो गोतमिपुतस हिमवतमदरपवतसमसारस...सवराजलोकमडलपतिगहीतसासनस...दिवसकरविबोधितकमलविमलसदिसवदनस...पटिपुणचदमडलससिरीकपियदसनस...सुविभततिवगदेसकालस पोरजननिविसेससमसुखदुखस...सकयवनपल्हवनिसूदनस धमोपचितकरविनियोगकरस &c.'

brief quotation will be helpful : 'कृपणदीनानाथातुरजनोद्धरणसमन्त्रदीक्षा-ग्युपगतमनसः समिद्धस्य विग्रहवतो लोकानुग्रहस्य धनदवरुणेन्द्रान्तकसमस्य स्वभुजबलविजितानेकनरपतिविभवप्रत्यर्पणनित्यव्यापृतायुक्तपुरुषस्य निशितविदग्धमतिगान्धर्वललितैर्व्रीडितत्रिदशपतिगुरुतुम्बुरुनारदादेर्विद्वज्जनोपजीव्यानेककाव्यक्रियाभिः प्रतिष्ठितकविराजशब्दस्य etc.' These inscriptions therefore show that long before the 4th century, Poetics had made a good deal of progress. There are other indications of great antiquity that point in the same direction. The निघण्टु (III. 13) collects twelve phrases from the Ṛgveda and calls them उपमा (such as इदमिव, इदं यथा, अग्निर्न, तद्वत्). The निरुक्त, while commenting on this part of the निघण्टु cites a scientific definition of उपमा from गार्ग्य, a predecessor of यास्क, and remarks that in the Ṛgveda a superior object is sometimes compared with an inferior one (though the general rule is that the उपमान is superior to or more well-known than the उपमेय) 'अथात उपमा यदतत्तत्सदृशमिति गार्ग्यस्तदासां कर्म ज्यायसा वा गुणेन प्रख्याततमेन वा कनीयांसं वाप्रख्यातं वोपमिमीतेऽथापि कनीयसा ज्यायांसम्' (III. 13). The निरुक्त then cites Ṛg. X. 4. 6 (तनूत्यजेव तस्करा वनर्गू &c., where the arms are compared to desperate thieves) and Ṛg. X. 40. 2 (कुह स्विद्दोषा कुह वस्तोरश्विना &c., where the Aśvins are compared to the *levir* having intercourse with his brother's widow). यास्क foreshadows the later distinction between पूर्णा and लुप्ता simile in the words 'लुप्तोपमान्यर्थोपमानीत्याचक्षते' (निरुक्त III. 18). A complete *Upamā* has four constituent elements, उपमान, उपमेय (or उपमित), the common property (सामान्य) and the word expressive of the relation (such as इव, तुल्य). Long before Pāṇini these technical words had become fixed in the language. The followsng sūtras will make this clear : 'उपमानानि सामान्यवचनैः' and 'उपमितं व्याघ्रादिभिः सामान्याप्रयोगे' (पा. II. 1. 55-56); तुल्यार्थैरतुलोपमाभ्यां तृतीयान्यतरस्याम्' पा. II. 3. 72; 'उपमानादाचारे' पा. III. 1. 10 (क्यच् स्यात्); 'तेन तुल्यं क्रिया चेद्वतिः । तत्र तस्येव' पा. V. 1. 115-16. Pāṇini refers to the *Naṭasūtras* composed by Śilālin and कृशाश्व ('पाराशर्यशिलालिभ्यां भिक्षुनटसूत्रयोः' and 'कर्मन्द-कृशाश्वादिनिः' IV. 3. 110-111). There is nothing left to show what these contained, but if they were to deserve the high-sounding designation of a *sūtra*, it is not unlikely that they gave (however crudely) instruction as to what the business of an actor was, how he could work upon the emotions of the audience (i. e. in short some theory of *rasa*). The Vedānta-sūtras name two *alaṅkāras* viz. उपमा and रूपक ('अत एव चोपमा सूर्यकादिवत्' III. 2. 18 and 'आनुमानिकमप्येकेषां शरीररूपकविन्यस्तगृहीतेर्दर्श-

यति च' I. 4. 1). The बुद्धचरित of अश्वघोष (not later than 3rd century, as it was translated into Chinese about 414-421 A. D. and probably of the 1st or 2nd century A. D.) was composed at a time when some theory of poetics had already been in vogue. Each canto has at the end a verse or verses in a different metre. The author is very much after alliteration (I. 14, 15; V. 26), employs such a frightful jingle as हरितुरगतुरङ्गवत्तुरङ्गः (V.87) and is very fond of यथासंख्य (V. 42 and IX. 16). The बुद्धचरित III. 51 employs the word रसान्तरम्. Similar remarks apply to Aśvaghoṣa's another Mahākāvya, the Saundarananda. In X. 2 there is अनुप्रास and in X. 11 there is यमक 'चलत्कदम्बे हिमवन्नितम्बे तरौ प्रलम्बे चमरो ललम्बे ।'. Compare नाट्यशास्त्र 17. 84 (हली बली लली &.); the same verse is K. M. ed. 16.85 and GOS. vol. II chap. 16. 84 p. 330. Prof. H. Lüders published in 1911 fragments of a drama of Aśvaghoṣa called सारिपुत्रप्रकरण which had nine Acts. That shows that ancient dramas on which the rules of the नाट्यशास्त्र were most probably based were lost or forgotten when later dramas like those of भास and कालिदास took the field. Sabhāparva 11. 36 speaks of नाटकs 'नाटका विविधा काव्याः कथाख्यायिककारिकाः'. अश्वघोष uses the technical words हाव and भाव ('भावज्ञानेन हावेन चातुर्याद्रूपसम्पदा । बुद्ध० IV. 12). Vide नाट्य० 24. 8-10 for भाव and हाव. नाट्यशास्त्र (GOS. ed. vol. III.) chap. 22. 6-8 are : देहात्मकं भवेत्सत्त्वं सत्त्वाद्भावः समुत्थितः । भावात्समुत्थितो हावो हावाद्धेला समुत्थिता ॥ वागङ्गमुखरागैश्च सत्त्वेनाभिनयेन च । कवेरन्तर्गतं भावं भावयन्भाव उच्यते ॥. It was shown above (p. 47) that the नाट्यशास्त्र must have been composed not later than 300 A. D. It contains a full exposition of the *rasa* theory, of dramaturgy and of four figures of speech and *gunas*. कालिदास is fond of अनुप्रास and employs यमक in रघुवंश IX. Bhāravi (who is mentioned in the Aihole Inscription) cannot be placed later than about 580-590 A.D. and in the 15th sarga of Kirātārjunīya exemplifies such चित्रबन्धs as गोमूत्रिका (verse 12), सर्वतोभद्र (25), एकाक्षर (verse 14 in which the only consonant that occurs is न्), different kinds of यमकs (verses 35, 37, 52), a verse with three applications (45).

1. In the 15th sarga of the किरातार्जुनीय we have एकाक्षरपाद in verse 5, एकाक्षर in all pādas in verse 14, सर्वतोभद्र and various kinds of यमकs and verse 45 has three meanings. It has been shown above (pp. 119-20) that भारवि flourished about 580-590 A. D. at the latest.

Subandhu in his वासवदत्ता alludes in various places to topics of Poetics. He boasts of his skill in weaving a web of puns on each syllable (प्रत्यक्षर—श्लेषमयप्रबन्धविन्यासवैदग्ध्यनिधिर्निबन्धम्.), speaks of वक्रोक्ति, of the soul of poetry, of the composition of an excellent poet in which the expletives तु and हि do not occur and which is divided into long sections and contains Vaktra metre ('अग्रहेयापि काव्यजीवज्ञेन' pp. 113-114 of Hall's ed., 'सत्कविकाव्यबन्ध इवानवद्यतुहिनिपातः' p. 134, 'दीर्घोच्छ्वासरचनाकुलं सुश्लेषवक्त्रघटनापटु सत्कविवचनमिव' p. 184). He speaks of शृङ्खलाबन्ध, उत्प्रेक्षा and आक्षेप (p. 136) and on p. 41 we have a मालादीपक 'यस्य समरभुवि भुजदण्डेन कोदण्डं कोदण्डेन शरा...आसादितम्' and यमक on p. 53 and pp. 203-14. In the Intro. to Harṣacarita by the present author (pp. 11-12, 1918 A. D.) it was held that Subandhu was probably earlier than Bāṇa. He still sticks to that view. In P. O. vol. XI pp. 29ff. it is shown that जिनभद्र in विशेषावश्यकभाष्य refers to वासवदत्ता and तरङ्गवती and that according to an ancient ms. that work of जिनभद्र was finished at Valabhi in śaka 531 (609 A.D.) when king Silāditya was reigning. It is most probable that जिनभद्र is referring to the वासवदत्ता of सुबन्धु. If so, सुबन्धु cannot be later than the last quarter of the 6th century A. D. बाण speaks of such puzzles as अक्षरच्युतक, मात्राच्युतक, बिन्दुमती, प्रहेलिका &c.; he knew the difference made between कथा and आख्यायिका (उच्छ्वासान्तेप्यखिन्नास्ते येषां वक्त्रे सरस्वती । कथमाख्यायिकाकाराः, हर्षचरित Intro. verse 10)[1], he speaks of श्लेष, उत्प्रेक्षा, उपमा, दीपक, जाति (हरन्ति कं नोज्ज्वलदीपकोपमैः &c. in कादम्बरी) and श्लेषप्रायमुदीच्येषु...उत्प्रेक्षा दाक्षिणात्येषु गौडेष्वक्षरडम्बरः ॥ in the हर्षचरित), he extols a prince as the source or fountain of the ambrosial *rasas* of *kāvyas* ('आगमः काव्यामृतरसानाम्' कादम्बरी 1st para). Thus by 600 A. D., we find that numerous figures

1. Vide p. 107 above for Bāṇa's words saying that the कादम्बरी was a कथा and हर्षचरित was an आख्यायिका. It is strange that Dr. De (in H. S. P. vol. I. p. 67) remarks 'Bāṇa designates his Harṣacarita as a Kathā and his Kādambarī as Ākhyāyikā.' There is either a slip of the pen here or Dr. De has altogether forgotten the last Intro. verse of the कादम्बरी 'द्विजेन...धिया निबद्धेयमतिद्वयी कथा' and Bāṇa's son's words 'याते दिवं पितरि तद्वचसैव सार्धं विच्छेदमाप भुवि यस्तु कथाप्रबन्धः ।' and verse 6 'क्षिप्ता कथानुघटनाय मयापि वाणी'. The 19th Intro. verse to the हर्षचरित is 'तथापि नृपतेर्भक्त्या...करोम्याख्यायिकाम्भोधौ जिह्वाप्लवनचापलम् ॥'. Nothing could be clearer than this.

had been defined, rules had been laid down for the guidance of poets and various classes of composition such as कथा and आख्यायिका had distinctive forms. Works dealing with Poetics are extant that were composed about the time of (or a little later than) Bāṇa (such as those of दण्डी and भामह).

4. The name of the Śāstra. The earlier works on Poetics are generally designated Kāvyālaṅkāra, e.g. the works of भामह, वामन and रुद्रट. These works were so called probably because *alaṅkāras* played the most prominent part in the treatment of poetics in them (following the maxim प्राधान्येन व्यपदेशा भवन्ति). वामन in his काव्या. सू. tells us that the word अलङ्कार is used in two senses, viz. (I) a thing of beauty and (II) a figure of speech (अलङ्क्रियते अनेन). According to him it follows that a work on Poetics is called काव्यालङ्कार because it points out and explains the things of beauty in a *kāvya*, which make us prize the latter 'काव्यं ग्राह्यमलङ्कारात् । सौन्दर्यमलङ्कारः । काव्या. सू. I. 1. 1-2 (वृत्ति—अलङ्कृतिलङ्कारः । करणव्युत्पत्त्या पुनरलङ्कारशब्दोऽयमुपमादिषु वर्तते ।). The कामधेनु remarks : योऽयमलङ्कारः काव्यग्रहणहेतुत्वेन उपन्यस्यते तद्व्युत्पादकत्वाच्छास्त्रमपि अलङ्कारनाम्ना व्यपदिश्यत इति शास्त्रस्यालङ्कारत्वेन प्रसिद्धिः प्रतिष्ठिता स्यादिति सूचयितुमयं विन्यासः कृतः काव्यं ग्राह्यमलङ्कारादिति. This is more or less scholastic. Even in those early works that are not designated as अलङ्कार, figures of speech loom very large as in the काव्यादर्श of Daṇḍin, three fourths of which is taken up by the explanation and elucidation of figures of speech (of *śabda* and *artha*). The काव्यादर्श says 'यथासामर्थ्यमस्माभिः क्रियते काव्यलक्षणम् ॥" (I. 2). The ध्व. (pp. 11 and 13) speaks of writers on Poetics as काव्यलक्षणविधायिनः. Though in I. 1 भामह calls his work काव्यालङ्कार, at the end (VI. 64) he says 'अवलोक्य मतानि सत्कवीनामवगम्य स्वधिया च काव्यलक्ष्म ।.' The ध्व० also (in I. 3) speaks of काव्यलक्ष्मविधायिभिः (as having explained Upamā and other figures of expressed sense). Another name for Poetics is *sāhitya*. This word seems to have been used in early works in three different but allied senses, though in modern times it is generally employed for Poetics. In the verse साहित्यसङ्गीतकलाविहीनः the word साहित्य appears to have been used in the sense of काव्य. In the verse साहित्यपाथोनिधिमन्थनोत्थं कर्णामृतं रक्षत हे कवीन्द्राः (बिह्लण's विक्रमाङ्कदेवचरित I. 11), it will be noticed that साहित्य means 'literature in general' and *kāvya* is said to arise like nectar from the ocean of साहित्य (i.e. काव्य is the quintessence of साहित्य). प्रतीहारेन्दुराज eulogising his teacher मुकुल and his proficiency in the मीमांसा and other *śāstras* speaks of

him as 'साहित्यश्रीमुरारेः. Here obviously the word साहित्य stands for साहित्यशास्त्र (as in the case of मीमांसा, व्याकरण and तर्क that precede the word साहित्यश्रीमुरारेः). मुकुल in the explanation of the *kārikā* पदवाक्यप्रमाणेषु तदेतत्प्रतिबिम्बितम् । यो योजयति साहित्ये तस्य वाणी प्रसीदति ॥' अभिधावृत्ति॰ p. 22) remarks 'व्याकरणमीमांसातर्कसाहित्यात्मकेषु चतुर्षु शास्त्रेषूपयोगात्'. राजशेखर (काव्यमी. p. 4) says 'पञ्चमी साहित्यविद्येति यायावरीयः । सा हि चतसृणामपि विद्यानां निष्यन्दः ।'. मङ्खक says 'विना न साहित्यविदाऽपरत्र गुणः कथञ्चित्प्रथते कवीनाम् ।' श्रीकण्ठचरित II. 12). These passages establish that sometime before 900 A.D. (when राजशेखर flourished) the word साहित्य came to be used in the sense of 'the science of Poetics'. How much earlier it was employed in that sense it is difficult to say. The word साहित्य seems to be derived from सहित (meaning 'together'). When poetry came to be defined as 'शब्दार्थौ सहितौ काव्यं,' the science of poetic critisism that propounded this definition was naturally called साहित्य. राजशेखर gives this etymology "शब्दार्थयोर्यथावत्सहभावेन विद्या साहित्यविद्या' (काव्यमी. p. 5). Similarly, the व्यक्तिविवेकटीका (p. 36) remarks 'न च काव्ये शास्त्रादिवदर्थप्रतीत्यर्थं शब्दमात्रं प्रयुज्यते सहितयोः शब्दार्थयोस्तत्र प्रयोगात् । साहित्यं तुल्यकक्षत्वेनान्यूनातिरिक्तत्वम् ।'. भामह says 'शब्दार्थौ सहितौ काव्यं' (I. 16) and the वक्रोक्तिजीवित (I. 8 and 17 quoted above on p. 227) does the same. The शिशुपालवध says 'शब्दार्थौ सत्कविरिव द्वयं विद्वानपेक्षते' (II. 86). In order to constitute real काव्य, the साहित्य of शब्द and अर्थ is required to possess peculiar charm. This will be discussed later. Therefore the use of the word साहित्य arose probably after the 7th or 8th century A. D. In J. O. R., Madras, vol. IX. pp. 128-134, in 'Some concepts of Alaṅkāra-śāstra' pp. 264-267 Dr. Raghavan puts forward the theory that, before the days of दण्डी and भामह, क्रियाकल्प was the name of Sanskrit Poetics. He relies upon the list of 64 कलाs mentioned in वात्स्यायन's कामसूत्र and upon the words in the रामायण, उत्तरकाण्ड chap. 94. 7 (क्रियाकल्पविदश्चैव तथा काव्यविदो जनान्). There is absolutely no proof that the chapter 94 is a genuine part of the रामायण, but Dr. Raghavan holds without hardly any objective evidence that that chapter is genuine or an old part of the epic. Granting for argument that the उत्तरकाण्ड passage is genuine, it does not prove that the *śāstra* was called क्रियाकल्प. काव्यविद् by itself might mean 'he who knows the science of Poetics'; compare साहित्यविदा quoted above. So क्रियाकल्पविदः may have to be construed otherwise. Further, in an appropriate context क्रिया may mean काव्यक्रिया and क्रियाकल्प may mean the *procedure* of how a काव्य was to be composed and not the whole शास्त्र of Poetics. The word कल्प apart from its technical meaning of 'śrauta sacrifices' (as in कल्पसूत्र) simply means 'procedure'. The word क्रिया by itself means also rites on and after death as in विष्णुपुराण III. 13. 34 (पूर्वाः क्रिया मध्यमाश्च तथा चैवोत्तराः क्रियाः ।). There are many works called क्रियापद्धति which deal only with rites on death and after death (e. g. D. C. ms. No. 118 of 1879-80, 207 of 1884-87, 156 of 1880-81, 99 of 1884-86). If क्रिया by itself (apart from the context) meant (before भामह and दण्डी) काव्य, why was it necessary to say काव्यक्रियाभिः in समुद्रगुप्तप्रशस्ति quoted above and in नाट्यशास्त्र 22. 23 (मया काव्यक्रियाहेतोः प्रक्षिप्ता द्रुहिणाज्ञया) ? This verse occurs in K. M. ed. 20, 23 and in GOS. ed. 20. 24 vol. III. p. 90 where अ. भा. explains 'काव्यस्य क्रिया काव्यरूपतापादनं तदेव हेतुः ततः' In the कामसूत्र I. 3. 16 sixty-four kalās are enumerated which maidens had to learn secretly (अभ्यासप्रयोज्यांश्च चातुःषष्टिकान्योगान् कन्या रहस्येकाकिन्यभ्यसेत् । कामसूत्र I. 3. 14) and which were to be learnt by वेश्याs also (काम. I. 3. 20). In that list occur the following 'संपाठ्यं मानसी काव्यक्रिया, अभिधानकोषः छन्दोज्ञानम्, क्रियाकल्पः, छलितकयोगाः.' It would be noticed that unmarried girls and courtezans were to learn along with गीत, वाद्य, नृत्य, आलेख्य the kalās mentioned above which would suffice for their own education and for attracting worthy husbands or lovers. I do not know whether in any serious work on Aesthetics in Sanskrit साहित्यशास्त्र has been or would be called a कला. All that is meant in the कामसूत्र is that the unmarried girls were to be given some guidance in composing (probably amorous) poetic pieces. As the word काव्यक्रिया is very near, it mentions simply क्रियाकल्प and (not काव्यक्रियाकल्प). कालिदास himself employs क्रिया elsewhere in the sense of 'rite' (कुतो धर्मक्रियाविघ्नः) and 'intellectual attainments' as in 'शिष्टा क्रिया कस्यचिद्' in मालविका० I. In the सौन्दरनन्द I. 55 we read 'समाजैरुत्सवैर्दायैः क्रियाविधिभिरेव च । अलंचक्रुरलंवीर्यास्ते जगद्धाम तत्पुरम् ॥'. It is not possible to hold here that the city was decked with काव्यालङ्कारशास्त्रs, but here क्रियाविधि means the performance of religious rites. Dr. Raghavan relies on ललितविस्तर p. 156 of Lefman's edition where the word क्रियाकल्प occurs. But he begs the whole question there. In the ललितविस्तर passage[1] (B. I. ed.)

1. ललितविस्तर pp. 178-179 'लिपिमुद्रा-गणना...अक्षक्रीडायां काव्यव्याकरणे ग्रन्थरचिते रूपे रूपकर्मणि...वीणायां वाद्यनृत्ये गीतपठिते...लास्ये नाट्ये...

about 90 matters in which बोधिसत्त्व became proficient are enumerated. In the context where क्रियाकल्प is sandwiched between Vedāṅgas and several other lores, क्रियाकल्प can only mean श्राद्धकल्प, particularly when the word यज्ञकल्प precedes. Dr. Raghavan himself points out that the काव्यादर्श employs the word क्रियाविधि (in I. 9). Then, as Daṇḍin refers to what former writers did for the व्युत्पत्ति of people, why does Dr. Raghavan not say that क्रियाविधि was the name of the शास्त्र ? For reasons of space I do not pursue this matter much further. I do not accept the new name for the शास्त्र which he propounds as used in olden times. It has further to be noted that five great commentators of the भागवतपुराण X. 45. 36 have the reading (in the list of 64 कलाs) क्रियाविकल्प instead of क्रियाकल्प. Thus the whole edifice of क्रियाकल्प being the ancient name of the science of Poetics is raised on rather slippery foundations, viz. a doubtful reading क्रियाकल्प. श्रीधर expressaly states that his enumeration is based on शैवतन्त्र (and not on the कामसूत्र). The *kalās* have been variously given from ancient times. The कामसूत्र itself (I. 3.17) states that पाञ्चाल (बाभ्रव्य) proclaimed another set of 64 kalās. The कामसूत्र states (I. 3. 17-18) 'पाञ्चालिकी च चतुःषष्टिरपरा। तस्याः प्रयोगाननन्ववेत्य सांप्रयोगिके वक्ष्यामः।'. Here the meaning of कला is different, as it means 'different modes of sexual enjoyment'. सांप्रयोगिक is the 2nd अधिकरण of कामसूत्र. Vide 'तदाभ्रीषु प्रायेणेति संवेशनप्रकारा बाभ्रवीयाः' II. 6 21. कामसूत्र I. 1. 10 mentions a work of पाञ्चाल बाभ्रव्य in 7 अधिकरणs on कामशास्त्र. Vide I. H. Q. vol. VIII pp. 542-548 for different lists of kalās (Prof. Chintaharan Chakravarti), I. H. Q. vol. V. pp. 88 ff (Dr. Acharya), J.R. A. S. 1914 p. 355, the कलाविलास of क्षेमेन्द्र who furnishes two different lists in the 4th and 10th (verse 40) cantos. The नाट्यशास्त्र appears to presuppose 64 kalās (34. 44, 35. 60). In the वासवदत्ता (p. 140 of Hall's ed.) there is a reference to 64 कलाs.

5 The topics of the अलङ्कारशास्त्र. The next question is to consider the problems with which the science of Poetics grapples. In part I when describing the contents of several works these topics have been more or less indicated as regards each individual work. Here all these topics will be brought

---

निर्घण्टौ निगमे पुराणे इतिहासे वेदे व्याकरणे निरुक्ते शिक्षायां छन्दसि यज्ञकल्पे ज्योतिषि सांख्ये योगे क्रियाकल्पे वैशेषिके वैशिके अर्थविद्यायां बार्हस्पत्ये' &c.

together and their connection with each other will be briefly pointed out. The first problem of Poetics is to declare what poetry can do for us and for the poet also (i.e. to enumerate the प्रयोजनs of काव्य). Then the *śāstra* has to consider the essential qualities that constitute the equipment of a poet (i. e. काव्यहेतु has to be considered). A definition of *kāvya* is attempted. In defining a *kāvya*, reference is generally made to *śabda* and *artha* and one has also to say what constitutes the soul or the essence of *kāvya* (which makes काव्य what it is). It is here (about the soul of poetry) that the greatest divergence of view prevails. As *śabda* and *artha* are necessary for *kāvya*, the various powers of word and its relation to *artha* have to be discussed. This leads to the topic of the three वृत्तिs, अभिधा, लक्षणा and व्यञ्जना and their sub-divisions and the three kinds of *artha*, वाच्य, लक्ष्य and व्यङ्ग्य. The critic has to give the several divisions of *kāvya* from different stand-points, viz. into गद्य, पद्य and मिश्र (according to the external form), into the best, mediocre and inferior *kāvya* according to the predominance or otherwise of the most essential things in a *kāvya*, into दृश्य and श्रव्य, into संस्कृत, प्राकृत etc. (according to the language employed) and so on. The division into दृश्य and श्रव्य opens up the vast field of dramaturgy. Certain *guṇas* must always be present. As to their number (3, 10, 24 etc.) great difference of opinion prevails. As allied to this subject of *guṇas*, the various dictions (*rītis*) have to be considered. A *kāvya* must be free from blemishes and therefore the *doṣas* of *pada*, *vākya*, *artha*, *rasa* etc. have to be discussed. Lastly, certain embellishments of *kāvya* (either of *śabda*, *artha* or of both) are dealt with. Certain works on Poetics go beyond this and lay down practical rules (as to the conventions to be observed by poets) and give information of an encyclopaedic character (e. g. about geography, about flora and fauna etc.).

It is by no means to be supposed that all or even many works on Poetics attempt the treatment of all these topics. The works on Poetics fall into several groups. (I) Some like the साहित्यदर्पण and the प्रतापरुद्रयशोभूषण traverse the whole field of Poetics (including dramaturgy). (II) Most of the well-known works on Poetics confine themselves to the topics indicated above except dramaturgy e. g. the काव्यादर्श, the काव्यालङ्कार-सूत्र of वामन, काव्यालङ्कारs of भामह, रुद्रट and वाग्भट, the काव्यप्रकाश,

रसगङ्गाधर etc. In the present book also it has not been possible for reasons of space to include a full account of the works on dramaturgy except in a few cases (where the *rasa* theory is concerned). (III) Some works treat of only dramaturgy and the theory of *rasa*, such as the नाट्यशास्त्र, the दशरूपक. (IV) Many works are concerned with *alaṅkaras* alone e. g. अलङ्कारसारसंग्रह, अलङ्कारसर्वस्व, कुवलयानन्द, चित्रमीमांसा. (V) A few are concerned with the exposition of some special theory of poetics, *viz.* the ध्वन्यालोक on the ध्वनि theory, the वक्रोक्तिजीवित, व्यक्तिविवेक. (VI) Some works deal only with the powers of words, *viz.* अभिधा etc. such as the अभिधावृत्तिमातृका, वृत्तिवार्तिक, शब्दव्यापारविचार. (VII) A few deal only with the theory of *rasa* (without treating of dramaturgy) such as the शृङ्गारतिलक, रसतरङ्गिणी. (VIII) Several dilate upon only some special matters such as the रसमञ्जरी (where नायिकाs and their sub-divisions and other kindred topics are discussed). The यशस्तिलक vol. 1 p. 479 (3rd आश्वास verse 274, Nir. ed.) quotes 'त्रिमूलकं द्विधोत्थानं पञ्चशाखं चतुश्छदम् । योऽर्गं वेत्ति नवच्छायं दशभूमिं स काव्यकृत् ॥'. त्रिमूलकं-लोको वेदोऽध्यात्मं (compare व्यक्तिविवेक on p. 7 and p. 35 n 2 above); द्विधोत्थानं refers to शब्दार्थौ, पञ्चशाखं to five वृत्तिs, परुषा, उपनागरिका, ग्राम्या &c.; चतुश्छदं refers to four रीतिs; अर्ग=वृत्तं; नवच्छायं=नवरसपूर्णं दशभूमिं दशगुणकम्.

The ध्व. p. 278 quotes a verse to the effect that a good poet presents without any hindrance at his own will things that are without *cetanā* as *acetana* and *vice versa* (भावानचेतनानपि चेतनवच्चेतनानचेतनवत् । व्यवहारयति यथेष्टं सुकविः काव्ये स्वतन्त्रतया ॥).

The अग्निपुराण makes a profound observation that poets are rare and that even among poets 'śakti' (imagination) is rarer still (नरत्वं दुर्लभं लोके विद्या तत्र सुदुर्लभा । कवित्वं दुर्लभं तत्र शक्तिस्तत्र सुदुर्लभा ॥ अग्नि० chap. 337. 3-4)

6 The purpose of Poetry (काव्यप्रयोजन). Poetry is an art and its immediate purpose and aim are the giving of delight, of aesthetic pleasure. This has been recognised by Sanskrit critics from very ancient times. The नाट्यशास्त्र says that the dramatic art was promulgated by Bharata as a pleasure-giving device for all people 'क्रीडनीयकमिच्छामो दृश्यं श्रव्यं च यद्भवेत्' and 'वेदविद्येतिहासानामाख्यानपरिकल्पनम् । विनोदजननं लोके नाट्यमेतद्भविष्यति ॥' नाट्य. I. 11 and 116-7 (=K. M. ed. I. 11 and 120 and GOS. vol. I. pp. 9 and 45, chap. I. 11 and 123); 'तथापि प्रीतिरेव प्रधानं...प्राधान्येनानन्द एवोक्तः' लोचन p. 14 and प्रीत्यात्मा च रसस्त-

देव नाट्यं नाट्य एव च वेद इत्यस्मदुपाध्यायः' लोचन p. 114; 'सकलप्रयोजनमौलिभूतं समनन्तरमेव रसास्वादनसमुद्भूतं विगलितवेद्यान्तरमानन्दं' काव्यप्र. I. Several other purposes that are served by poetry are enumerated by the works on Poetics. Some of them are benefits derived by the poet himself, while others are reaped by the reader. They are (from the reader's point of view); I delight, solace; II instruction in knowledge of religion, morality and philosophy; III. proficiency in the arts and ways of the world. To the poet also poetry brings fame and wealth. The नाट्यशास्त्र says that to minds that are afflicted by the sorrows and worries of this world, नाट्य would bring relief and solace 'दुःखार्तानां श्रमार्तानां शोकार्तानां तपस्विनाम्। विश्रामजननं लोके नाट्यमेतद्भविष्यति ॥' (I. 111-12). भामह says 'धर्मार्थकाममोक्षेषु वैचक्षण्यं कलासु च। प्रीतिं करोति कीर्तिं च साधुकाव्यनिबन्धनम् ॥' I. 2; सर. क. I. 2 निर्दोषं गुणवत्काव्यमलङ्कारैरलङ्कृतम्। रसान्वितं कविः कुर्वन् कीर्तिं प्रीतिं च विन्दति; वामन says 'काव्यं सद्दृष्टादृष्टार्थं प्रीतिकीर्तिहेतुत्वात्' I. 1. 5; 'काव्यं यशसेऽर्थकृते व्यवहारविदे शिवेतरक्षतये। सद्यः परनिर्वृतये कान्तासंमिततयोपदेशयुजे ॥' काव्यप्र. I; this mentions 6 purposes viz. fame, wealth, knowledge of the ways of the world, removal of ills, highest delight, sweet instruction. Delight of a high spiritual order is the chief end of poetry. Instruction, moralizing, cleverness in arts are only by-products, secondary results of poetry. The Daśarūpaka (I. 6) ridicules भामह and others who speak of व्युत्पत्ति or knowledge of पुरुषार्थs as the purpose of poetry. Similarly, the view of भामह (V. 3 quoted on p. 76) saying that Poetry is like a dose of honey inducing persons to take a bitter medicine has a parallel in western theories of Aesthetics that explained that poetry was 'the pleasant taste which hid the Aloes and Rhubarb of wholesome things' as Prof. E. F. Carritt says in his 'the Theory of Beauty' p. 43 (5th ed. of 1949). That Aesthetics would influence life (though indirectly) is emphasized by Mammaṭa in the words 'रामादिवद्वर्तितव्यं &c. हेमचन्द्र (p. 2) accepts only three of these 'काव्यमानन्दाय यशसे कान्तातुल्यतयोपदेशाय च' and says that one may or may not get wealth from काव्य and the other purposes can be secured by other means; *vide* रुद्रट I. 4, 8-13, 21 and XII. 1 'ननु काव्येन क्रियते सरसानामवगमश्चतुर्वर्गे। लघु मृदु च नीरसेभ्यस्ते हि त्रस्यन्ति शास्त्रेभ्यः ॥'. Poetry however, does not (or should not) directly teach religion, philosophy or morality, but only indirectly and impliedly as said by मम्मट 'कान्तेव सरसतापादनेनाभिमुखीकृत्य रामादिवद्वर्तितव्यं न रावणा-

दिवदित्युपदेशं...करोतीति'. *Vide* my notes on साहित्यद० p. 4. Most of the works on Poetics more or less echo the words quoted above. Vide उज्ज्वलनीलमणि pp. 55-56 quoting भागवत X 'वर्तितव्यं शमिच्छद्भिर्भक्तवन्न तु कृष्णवत । इत्येवं भक्तिशास्त्राणां तात्पर्यस्य विनिर्णयः । रामादिवद् वर्तितव्यं न क्वचिद्रावणादिवत् ।'. The word प्रीति (among प्रयोजनs) mentioned by भामह, वामन, सर. क. may be construed with the poet also. The poet finds supreme delight in creating an artistic poem. The words सद्यः परनिर्वृतये of मम्मट (immediate higher and delightful experience) are more definite and appropriate. Even an early writer like Aśvaghoṣa states that whatever else he included in his work other then relevant to the subject of Mokṣa was included because of the rules of poetics in the same way as a bitter medicine is mixed with honey in order that it may be pleasant to drink (Saundarananda 18.63 यन्मोक्षात्कृतमन्यदत्र हि मया तत्काव्यधर्मात्कृतं पातुं तिक्तमिवौषधं मधुयुतं हृद्यं कथं स्यादिति).

7 The equipment of the poet (काव्यहेतु). Most of the writers on Poetics lay down that the things essential to the making of a true poet are three, प्रतिभा (Imagination), व्युत्पत्तिः (culture) and अभ्यास (constant practice). नैसर्गिकी च प्रतिभा श्रुतं च बहु निर्मलम् । अमन्दश्चाभियोगोऽस्याः कारणं काव्यसम्पदः ॥' काव्यादर्श I. 103; 'काव्यं तु जायते जातु कस्यचित्प्रतिभावतः ।...शब्दाभिधेये विज्ञाय कृत्वा तद्विदुपासनाम् । विलोक्यान्यनिबन्धांश्च कार्यः काव्यक्रियादरः ॥' भामह I. 5 and 10; 'त्रितयमिदं व्याप्रियते शक्तिर्व्युत्पत्तिरभ्यासः ॥' रुद्रट I. 14; 'शक्तिर्निपुणता लोकशास्त्रकाव्याद्यवेक्षणात् । काव्यज्ञशिक्षयाभ्यास इति हेतुस्तदुद्भवे ॥' काव्यप्र. I. 8; *vide* also एकावली I. 12; वाग्भटालङ्कार I. 3; अलङ्कारशेखर (p. 4). There were other writers who regarded *pratibhā* as the sole equipment required for the making of a genuine poet. राजशेखर says 'सा (शक्तिः) केवलं काव्ये हेतुरिति यायावरीयः' (p. 11); 'प्रतिभैव च कवीनां काव्यकरणकारणम् । व्युत्पत्त्यभ्यासौ तस्या एव संस्कारकारकौ न तु काव्यहेतू' अलङ्कारतिलक of वाग्भट (p.2); तस्य च 'कारणं कविगता केवला प्रतिभा' रसगङ्गाधर p. 8. प्रतिभा is that power whereby the poet sees the subjects of his poem as steeped in beauty and gives to his readers in apt language a vivid picture of the beauty he has seen. It is a power whereby the poet not only calls up in his reader's heart the impressions of faded experiences, but whereby he presents ever new, wonderful and charming combinations and relations of things never before experienced or thought by the ordinary man. A poet is one who is a seer, a prophet, who sees visions and possesses the additional gift of conveying to others less fortunate through the medium of language the visions he has

or the dreams he dreams. The following definitions of प्रतिभा will make this clear. 'प्रज्ञा नवनवोन्मेषशालिनी प्रतिभा मता...वर्णनानिपुणः कविः' भट्टतौत in काव्यकौतुक (vide p. 221 above); 'प्रतिभा अपूर्ववस्तुनिर्माणक्षमा प्रज्ञा तस्या विशेषो रसावेशवैशद्यसौन्दर्यकाव्यनिर्माणक्षमत्वं' and शक्तिः प्रतिभानं वर्णनीयवस्तुविषयनूतनोल्लेखशालित्वम्' लोचन pp. 34 and 164: अपारे काव्यसंसारे कविरेव प्रजापतिः । यथास्मै रोचते विश्वं तथेदं परिवर्तते ॥' (ध्व. p. 278); प्रसन्नपदनव्यार्थयुक्त्युद्बोधविधायिनी । स्फुरन्ती सत्कवेर्बुद्धिः प्रतिभा सर्वतोमुखी ॥' वाग्भटालङ्कार I. 4; vide also वामन's वृत्ति on I. 3. 16 'कवित्वबीजं प्रतिभानम्'; रुद्रट I. 15-16; the *prakrit* verse अतहट्ठिए[1] वि तहसंठिए व्व हिअअम्मि जा णिवेसेइ । अत्थविसेसे सा जअइ विकडकविगोअरा वाणी ॥' quoted in ध्व. p.296; राजशेखर p. 11 and भट्टतौत (p. 221 above) refer to this two-fold gift of the poet, of seeing visions of striking beauty (विचित्र... प्रख्या) and of conveying to others through appropriate language the visions he sees. Generally most great poets in Sanskrit did not endeavour to state explicitly any moral purpose as the aim of their works. They were more concerned with a happy ending to their dramas and with creating an atmosphere of ideas and bliss by their poems than with explicitly stated moral endings or ends. Their dominant mood was delight and they exhibited it mostly on the plane of normal relations, passions, affections and even prejudices of men and women. For restrictions of space I cannot go deeper into the nature of प्रतिभा.[2] It means 'that mental faculty which presents ever fresh flashes or coruscations of ideas' (with उन्मेष) or 'ever fresh

---

1. (छाया) अतथास्थितानपि तथासंस्थितानिव हृदये या निवेशयति । अर्थविशेषान् सा जयति विकटकविगोचरा वाणी ॥. The idea is : वाणीप्रसादादेव कविगोचरो वर्णनीयार्थो विकटो निःसीमा संपद्यते ।

2. It is usual to translate प्रतिभा by 'imagination'. It is better to translate प्रतिभा as (inborn) 'creative faculty'. I. A. Richards defines 'Imagination' (on p. 242) basing his remarks on Coleridge as follows : That synthetic and magic power reveals itself in the balance or reconcilation of opposite or discordant qualities, the sense of novelty and freshness with old and familiar objects, a more than usual state of emotion with more than usual order. But that word has six meanings, according to R. A. Richards' 'Principles of Literary criticism (ed. of 1925 pp. 239-243, chap. XXXII). Coleridge made a distinction between 'Imagination' and 'Fancy'. Others do not make that distinction.

delineations or pictures of the matters to be described' (with उल्लेख). In defining प्रतिभा (or प्रतिभान) or शक्ति the word प्रज्ञा is used. A distinction is made between स्मृति, मति and प्रज्ञा; e. g. त्रिधा च सा (बुद्धिः) स्मृतिः मतिः प्रज्ञेति । अतिक्रान्तस्यार्थस्य स्मर्त्री स्मृतिः वर्तमानस्य मन्त्री मतिः अनागतस्य प्रज्ञात्री प्रज्ञा सा त्रिप्रकारापि कवीनामुपकर्त्री ।' काव्यमी. p. 10. The संप्रदायप्रकाशिनी (on काव्यप्र., Tri. ed.) gives the following śloka 'स्मृतिर्व्यतीतविषया मतिरागामिगोचरा । बुद्धिस्तात्कालिकी ज्ञेया प्रज्ञा त्रैकालिकी मता ॥' (p. 13). Pratibhā is said to be सहजा (natural) and उत्पाद्या (cultivated) by रुद्रट (I. 16) and उत्पाद्या and औपाधिकी (due to external agencies like mantras, the grace of God) by हेमचन्द्र (काव्यानु. p. 4-5). Old writers like Daṇḍin held that *pratibhā* (in a poet) was natural (नैसर्गिकी च प्रतिभा, quoted on p. 348). Rudraṭa (I. 16), Hemachandra (p. 4) and others say that व्युत्पत्ति and अभ्यास polish, brighten and sharpen *pratibhā*. The ध्व० (p. 169) makes it clear that if a poet has शक्ति (i. e. प्रतिभा), it conceals the defects that may arise from lack of व्युत्पत्ति, but if a poet is deficient in प्रतिभा and has only व्युत्पत्ति, the defects in his composition are noticed at once (अव्युत्पत्तिकृतो दोषः शक्त्या संव्रियते कवेः । यस्त्वशक्तिकृतो दोषः स झटित्यवभासते ॥ ध्व. p. 169). The important question is : how does a man become possessed of प्रतिभा ? It appears that early writers held that प्रतिभा was the outcome of *saṁskāras* (impressions) made on the soul in countless births (e. g. काव्यादर्श I· 104 न विद्यते यद्यपि पूर्ववासना; काव्यमी. I. p. 12 'जन्मान्तरसंस्कारापेक्षिणी सहजा'; वामन I. 3. 16 वृत्ति 'कवित्वबीजं जन्मान्तरागतसंस्कारविशेषः कश्चित्'; अ. भा. vol. I. p. 346 कवेः वर्णनानिपुणस्य यः अन्तर्गतोऽनादिप्राक्तनसंस्कारप्रतिभानमयः &c.). The रसगङ्गाधर (pp. 8-9) does not accept the theory that प्रतिभा is invariably due to अदृष्ट. The काव्यमी. (pp. 12-14) brings out this idea by stating that *pratibhā* is of two kinds viz. कारयित्री (creative) and भावयित्री (appreciative): पृथगेव हि कवित्वाद्भावकत्वं भावकत्वाच्च कवित्वं । स्वरूपभेदाद्विषयभेदाच्च । काव्यमी. p. 14. The काव्यमी. p. 11) distinguishes between शक्ति and व्युत्पत्ति and states that शक्ति alone is the cause of poetry. शक्तिकर्तृके प्रतिभाव्युत्पत्तिकर्मणी । शक्तस्य प्रतिभाति शक्तश्च व्युत्पद्यते । या शब्दग्राममर्थसार्थमलङ्कारतन्त्रमुक्तिमार्गमन्यदपि तथाविधमधिहृदयं प्रतिभासयति सा प्रतिभा । अप्रतिभस्य पदार्थसार्थः परोक्ष इव । प्रतिभावतः पुनरपश्यतोऽपि प्रत्यक्ष इव ।'. रुद्रट I. 15 says : मनसि सदा सुसमाधिनि विस्फुरणमनेकधाभिधेयस्य । अक्लिष्टानि पदानि च विभान्ति यस्यामसौ शक्तिः ॥' (Śakti is that whereby in a mind that is free from distractions subjects of description always flash and words that are perspicuous shine forth). The लोचन on ध्व. I. 6 (saying that Sarasvatī manifests in great poets special imagination which is uncommon) remarks that the speciality of a great poet's imagination consists in the ability to produce poetry that is endowed with beauty and clarity due to the onrush of emotional thrill in the heart.

Vide Annals B. O. R. I. vol. V for M. M. Gopinath Kaviraja's learned article on 'the doctrine of Pratibhā in Indian Philosophy', I. H. Q. vol. 13 pp. 58-84 on 'Imagination in Indian Poetics' (by Prof. T. N. Shrikantayya).

It has to be remembered that even the reader of the best poetry must have a modicum of imagination and culture in order to enjoy aesthetically the poet's outpourings, as said in 'नायकस्य कवेः श्रोतुः समानोनुभवस्ततः' (लोचन cited above on p. 220) or 'न जायते तदास्वादो विना रत्यादिवासनाम्' साहित्यदर्पण III. 9.

व्युत्पत्ति dose not present much difficulty. There is theoretically no subject which the poet may not handle and therefore a certain modicum of culture is necessary for him if he is to appeal to the hearts of his contemporaries and to future generations. The नाट्यशास्त्र says 'न तज्ज्ञानं' 21, 122 quoted above on p. 35 n2; 'छन्दोव्याकरणकलालोकस्थितिपदपदार्थविज्ञानात् । युक्तायुक्तविवेको व्युत्पत्तिरियं समासेन ॥' रुद्रट I. 18, हेमचन्द्र p. 5 'लोकशास्त्रकाव्येषु निपुणता व्युत्पत्तिः'. काव्यमी. 5th chap. which contains very useful information about शास्त्रकवि, काव्यकवि and उभयकवि and their sub-divisions (p. 17) states ten stages of कवित्व (p. 19). The सुवृत्ततिलक of क्षेमेन्द्र (K. M. ed.) has another division of Literature in general : शास्त्रं काव्यं शास्त्रकाव्यं काव्यशास्त्रं च भेदतः । काव्यं विशिष्टशब्दार्थसाहित्यसदलङ्कृति । शास्त्रकाव्यं चतुर्वर्गप्रायं सर्वोपदेशकृत् । तत्र केवलशास्त्रेपि केचित्काव्यं प्रयुञ्जते ॥ 2-4. An example of शास्त्रकाव्य is भट्टिकाव्य. The Pāli texts also have such divisions of poets. The Aṅguttara Nikāya speaks of four kinds of *kavi* viz. चिन्ताकवि, सुतकवि (श्रुतकवि), अत्थकवि and पटिभानकवि (vol. II. p. 230 of Pāli Texts Society's ed.) and the commentary मनोरथपूरणी (vol. III. p. 211) explains 'यो चिन्तेत्वा काव्यं करोति स चिन्ताकवि नाम यो सुत्वा करोति अयं सुतकवि नाम यो एकमत्थं निस्साय करोति अयं अत्थकवि । यो तं खणं येव वंगीसथेरो विय अत्तनो पटिभानेन करोति अयं पटिभानकवि नाम'. The साहित्यमीमांसा (Tri. ed.) mentions four ingredients in the making of a poct viz. श्रम, नियोग, क्लेश, प्रतिभा (vide p. 281 above for quotation).

On this subject of 'the making of the Sanskrit poet' *vide* Dr. Thomas in Bhandarkar Commemoration vol. pp. 375-376 and Prof. Kalicharan Shastri on 'Requisites of a poet' in

Journal of Dept. of Letters, Cal. Un., vol. XXVI pp. 1-31. A true poet's work cannot be described in nobler or more sublime language than what the ध्वन्यालोक[1] says about it, viz. that the poet is a Creator in the boundless world of poetry, that the Universe appears to assume that form which he is pleased to give to it, that whatever *rasa* (either love or pathos or heroism) he puts into his poem the world becomes immersed therein and that if he himself becomes devoid of *rasa* then all follow suit. The Vyaktiviveka also employs equally sublime language about the poet's *pratibhā*, which, he says, is the intellect of the poet that has become absorbed in selecting words and sense appropriate to the *rasa* he wants to evolve, that (प्रज्ञा) rises after touching for a moment the Real Essence (viz. the Highest Spirit) and that *pratibhā* is the third eye of the Divine (Śiva), whereby the poet perceives the shape of things, past, present and future.

8 The definition of poetry (काव्यलक्षण). Numerous definitions of *kāvya* have been offered by several writers; many of these definitions are affected by the author's view about the essence of poetry. Some of the definitions are no more than mere descriptions. The definitions of a few writers, particularly early ones, treat शब्द and अर्थ as equally prominent, while others give more prominence to शब्द; some give a definition of काव्य which is more difficult than the thing to be defined (such as that of विश्वनाथ 'वाक्यं रसात्मकं काव्यं'). An attempt will be made to group together some of these definitions. The following lay equel emphasis on शब्द and अर्थ 'शब्दार्थौ सहितौ काव्यं' (भामह I. 16; vide also I. 11 and 13 for काव्य being निर्दोष and सालङ्कार); 'ननु शब्दार्थौ काव्यं' रुद्रट III. 1; 'शब्दार्थौ सहितौ वक्र०' वक्रोक्तिजीवित (p. 227 above); 'तददोषौ शब्दार्थौ सगुणावनलङ्कृती पुनः क्वापि' मम्मट; गुणालङ्कारसहितौ शब्दार्थौ दोषवर्जितौ ।... काव्यं काव्यविदो विदुः ॥ प्रतापरुद्रीय०; 'शब्दार्थौ निर्दोषौ सगुणौ प्रायः सालङ्कारौ काव्यम्' काव्यानु० of वाग्भट p. 14; 'अदोषौ सगुणौ सालङ्कारौ च शब्दार्थौ काव्यम्' हेमचन्द्र p. 16; vide वामन's वृत्ति on I. 1. I. Other writers lay more emphasis on शब्द. 'तैः शरीरं च काव्यानामलङ्काराश्च दर्शिताः । शरीरं तावदिष्टार्थव्यवच्छिन्ना पदावली ॥'

1. अपारे काव्यसंसारे कविरेव प्रजापतिः । यथास्मै रोचते विश्वं तथेदं परिवर्तते ॥ शृङ्गारी चेत्कविः काव्ये जातं रसमयं जगत् । स एव वीतरागश्चेन्नीरसं सर्वमेव तत् ॥ ध्व. p. 278, quoted on p. 183 n3 above; रसानुगुणशब्दार्थचिन्तास्तिमितचेतसः । क्षणं स्वरूपस्पर्शोत्था प्रज्ञैव प्रतिभा कवेः ॥ सा हि चक्षुर्भगवतस्तृतीयमिति गीयते । येन साक्षात्करोत्येष भावांस्त्रैकाल्यवर्तिनः ॥ व्यक्तिविवेक p. 108.

काव्यादर्श I. 10; इष्टार्थव्यवच्छिन्ना पदावली । काव्यं स्फुटदलङ्कारं गुणवद्दोषवर्जितम् ॥' अग्निपुराण 336. 6-7; 'रमणीयार्थप्रतिपादकः शब्दः काव्यम्' रसगङ्गा॰ (p. 4); *vide* also चन्द्रालोक (I. 7). On the whole Jagannātha's definition is preferable, as it avoids all reference to debatable points and ध्व. I p. 8 also gives a similar definition in one place viz. 'सहृदयहृदयाह्लादिशब्दार्थमयत्वमेव काव्यलक्षणम्'. These latter definitions emphasize one of the aspects of poetry, viz. that, though poetry may employ the words of the current language, it differs from the everyday speech of people in the choice of words, in the diction that it employs which is chosen with an eye to beauty. But these definitions are very defective in one respect. If, as Daṇḍin says, words are the body of poetry, it may be asked (to continue that metaphor): 'what is the soul of Poetry ?' To this question various answers have been given by several schools.[1] The रस school of भरत made रस the soul of poetry (dramatic), while the school of आनन्दवर्धन (called the ध्वनि school) extends the conception underlying the *rasa* theory and lays down that व्यंग्य sense is the soul of

1. Some scholars object to the use of the word 'schools'. Their argument is: all extant writers were aware of रस, गुण, रीति, अलङ्कार and were not opposed to rasa or guṇa or alaṅkāra. But this is not a correct statement of the position. There are four or five elements in high poetry. Bharata, Daṇḍin, Bhāmaha, Vāmana, and others knew all this. But the question is; what is the soul or essence of poetry (applying metaphorically to poetry the image of body, limbs and soul) ? Here it is quite clear that the authors differ as to the *soul of Poetry* e.g. Vāmana says 'rītirātmā kāvyasya', Dhvanikāra says 'kāvyasyātmā dhvaniriti' and vide also his remarks quoted on p. 166 above. The Vakroktijīvitakāra denies the independent existence of ध्वनि or व्यंग्य as the soul of poetry and includes the latter under its all-embracing Vakrokti. In each of these the emphasis is on a different matter. The case is analogous to that of the Vedānta schools of Śaṅkara, Bhāskara, Rāmānuja, Madhva and Vallabha. All these admit the authority of the Upaniṣads and Vedāntasūtra and also admit the existence of Brahma, Jīva and the world but they differ on the relation of these to each other. Therefore, they are treated as different schools. The same holds good as to the different schools of Sanskrit Poetics.

poetry. Some of the definitions dominated by the *rasa* school and ध्वनि school are 'आस्वादजीवातुः पदसन्दर्भः काव्यम्' चण्डीदास in काव्यप्रकाशदीपिका (p. 13); काव्यं रसादिमद्वाक्यं श्रुतं सुखविशेषकृत्' शौद्धोदनि in अलङ्काररशेखर (p. 2); 'वाक्यं रसात्मकं काव्यं' साहित्यदर्पण; निर्दोषं गुणवत्काव्यमलङ्कारैरलङ्कृतम्। रसान्वितं कविः कुर्वन्कीर्ति प्रीतिं च विन्दति ॥' सरस्वती०. On account of the limitaions of space imposed in this work it is impossible to refer to the criticisms passed on these definitions. *Vide* my notes to साहित्यदर्पण pp. 5-30 for some of them. In order to understand the relative positions of रस, ध्वनि, गुण, अलङ्कार, रीति in the theory of Poetics, the different schools or rather theories must be enumerated and their doctrines briefly stated. The principal theories in chronological order of the extant works are those of *rasa*, of *alaṅkāra*, of *rīti*, of *dhvani*, of *vakrokti*. Vide ध्वन्यालोक pp. 5-12 where the author refers to three schools, one totally denying the existence of ध्वनि, the 2nd saying that what is called ध्वनि is included under भक्ति (i.e. उपचार or लक्षणा) and the third asserting that ध्वनि is not capable of scientific treatment but can only be experienced by the mind of the man of literary taste (सहृदयहृदयसंवेद्य). In the first class (ध्वन्यभाववादिनः) again three sub-schools are pointed out slightly differing from each other (*vide* लोचन p. 4). समुद्रबन्ध speaks of five schools in a somewhat different manner 'इह विशिष्टौ शब्दार्थौ काव्यम्। तयोश्च वैशिष्ट्यं धर्ममुखेन व्यापारमुखेन व्यङ्ग्यमुखेन वेति त्रयः पक्षाः। आद्येप्यलङ्कारतो गुणतो वेति द्वैविध्यम्। द्वितीयेपि भणितिवैचित्र्येण भोगकृत्त्वेन वेति द्वैविध्यम्। इति पञ्चसु पक्षेष्वाद्य उद्भटादिभिरङ्गीकृतः, द्वितीयो वामनेन, तृतीयो वक्रोक्तिजीवितकारेण, चतुर्थो भट्टनायकेन, पञ्चम आनन्दवर्धनेन।' (p. 4). It is to be noted here that समुद्रबन्ध does not mention the *rasa* theory of भरत; while भट्टनायक is really an adherent of the *rasa* school, though his method of explaining it is peculiar (vide pp. 221-23). He did not follow the ध्वनिकार in his treatment of the functions of words as explained above. Besides these, the view of महिमभट्ट that all ध्वनि is included under अनुमान stands by itself, but as he had no followers, he need not be considered as the founder of a school. The वक्रोक्तिजीवितकार also had hardly any followers and there was no school and further the meaning of वक्रोक्ति has changed from time to time. जयरथ in his विमर्शिनी quotes two verses (p. 9) in which twelve different theories opposed to the *dhvani* theory are enumerated 'तात्पर्यशक्तिरभिधा लक्षणानुमिती द्विधा। अर्थापत्तिः क्वचित्तन्त्रं समासोक्त्याद्यलङ्कृतिः॥ रसस्य कार्यता भोगो व्यापारान्तरबाधनम्। द्वादशेत्थं ध्वनेरस्य स्थिता विप्रतिपत्तयः॥'. But he points out that, as said in the ध्वनिकारिका (काव्य-

स्यात्मा etc.), three theories opposed to that of ध्वनि are principal. *Vide* Prof. Sovani's learned paper in the Bhandarkar Com. vol. pp. 383 ff on the 'pre-*dhvani* schools of *alaṅkāra*'. It may not be strictly accurate to employ the word school for the several पक्ष (theories) about what constitutes the soul of kāvya. But, since that word has been frequently employed by many of those who have written on the subject of Sanskrit poetics and since even as early as Rājaśekhara's Kāvyamīmāṁsā the views of Vāmanīyas (the followers of or school of Vāmana) and of Audbhaṭas are mentioned (vide pp. 14, 20 for वामनीयाः and pp. 22, 44 for औद्भटाः), the word 'school' may still be retained for the theories of *rasa*, *alaṅkāra* and *dhvani*. The A. B. (GOS. vol. I. p. 266) also refers to the views of Audbhaṭas on Nāṭyaśāstra VI. 10. Vide 'definition of poetry or Kāvya' in JOR (Madras vol. III. pp. 85-100, 170-180, 199-223, 331-348 and vol. IV. 45-56 by Pandit D. T. Tatacharya.

9 The Rasa School. So far as the extant litereture goes, the earliest exponent of this school is the Nāṭyśāstra of Bharata. But is should not be supposed that speculations about *rasa* were not put forward before the Nāṭyśāstra. It has already been shown that many verses called 'ānuvaṁśya' and several Āryā verses had been composed before the current नाट्य० took shape and were incorporated in the extant Nāṭyaśāstra (vide p. 17 above). The Nāṭyaśāstra was composed with an eye to dramatic representation and it has been seen (p. 210) that *kāvya* and *nāṭya* are regarded as synonyms (chap. 16. 169, 17. 5 &c.). The रस theory is set down at great length in the अभिनवभारती (GOS vol. I. pp. 274-295 and to a lesser extent in ध्व. and लोचन pp. 54-72 and pp. 182 ff. अभिनवगुप्त who was himself a great critic and poet and who comments both on the ध्वन्यालोक and the नाट्यशास्त्र says (on नाट्यरसाः स्मृताः in नाट्य० VI. G. O. S. p. 291): नाट्यात्समुदायरूपाद्रसाः, यदि वा नाट्यमेव रसाः। रससमुदायो हि नाट्यम्। न नाट्य एव च रसाः काव्येपि. The rest of the passage is quoted on p. 219 above and अभिनव० proceeds 'काव्यं तावन्मुख्यतो दशरूपकात्मकमेव। ...तत्र ये स्वभावतो निर्मलमुकुरहृदयास्त एव संसारोचितक्रोधमोहाभिलाषपरवशमनसो न भवन्ति तेषां तथाविधदशरूपकाकर्णनसमये साधारणरसनात्मकचर्वणग्राह्यो रससञ्चयो नाट्यलक्षणः स्फुट एव। ये त्वतथाभूतास्तेषां प्रत्यक्षोचिततथाविधचर्वणालाभाय नटादिप्रक्रिया स्वगतक्रोधशोकादिसङ्कटहृदयग्रन्थिभञ्जनाय गीतादिप्रक्रिया च मुनिना विरचिता। सर्वानुग्राहकं हि शास्त्रमिति न्यायात्तेन नाट्य एव रसा न लोके इत्यर्थः। काव्यं च नाट्यमेव।' vol. I. p. 292.

रस primarily means 'taste' or 'flavour' or 'savour', or 'relish' but metaphorically it means 'the emotional experience of beauty in poetry and drama'. Mammaṭa speaks of the poet's work as 'hlādaikamayī' (comprising pleasure or delight alone). It thus emphasizes the effect of poetry on the reader. Sanskrit writers also were aware of the fact that literature can be divided into two classes as De Quincey said viz. 'literature of knowledge' and 'literature of power'. The former teaches while the latter moves. The two kinds may be often mixed up in the same work but it is possible to keep them entirely separate. Literary criticism, whether in Sanskrit works or elsewhere, is mainly concerned with works of the second of the two classes mentioned above. No question of being right or wrong arises as regards the 2nd class of literature, which mainly comprises Poetry, Drama and Fiction. There is a distinction between intuitive consiousness and consiousness arrived at by reasoning. ध्व० (on p. 253) makes the position clear that no question of being right or wrong arises as to the suggested sense of poetry 'काव्यविषये च व्यङ्ग्यप्रतीतीनां सत्यासत्यनिरूपणस्याप्रयोजकत्वमेवेति तत्र प्रमाणान्तरव्यापारपरीक्षा उपहासायैव संपद्यते'. The relation of *rasas* to poetry in general was not systematically dealt with till the Dhvanyāloka was composed. But it would not be correct to say that writers on Poetics were not at all cognisant of the employment of or importance of *rasas*. The Kāvyādarśa I. 62 says 'कामं सर्वोप्यलङ्कारो रसमर्थे निषिञ्चति। तथाप्यग्राम्यतैवैनं भारं वहति भूयसा॥'. In II. 280-292 the काव्यादर्श describes how the figure रसवद् is dependent on one of the eight rasas and they further show that Daṇḍin was quite aware of the difference between स्थायिभाव and रस. Vide काव्यादर्श I. 51, 64 also. Bhāmaha III. 6 (रसवद् दर्शितस्पष्टशृङ्गारादिरसं यथा।) shows that he was aware of rasas, but did not treat them as the most essential element in poetry. He says in I. 21 that a mahākāvya should be endowed with rasas (युक्तं लोकस्वभावेन रसैश्च विविधैः पृथक्). वामन also says 'दीप्तरसत्वं कान्तिः।' III. 2. 24. Both Daṇḍin (I. 31) and Bhāmaha (I. 24) leave out of account dramas (which they regard as a kind of kāvya) and refer the curious reader to other works for rules about them. It appears that in ancient times poems and dramas ordinarily were looked upon as separate compartments. Writers on Poetics did not at first include a treatment of rasas in their works. रुद्रट is the first extant writer to treat of *rasa* in a work called काव्यालङ्कार. The शिशुपालवध 14.50 (composed about a hundred years before रुद्रट) speaks of *rasas* in connection with dramas.[1] Even in Bharata's Nāṭyaśāstra, rasa is not the principal subject treated of, but it is dealt with therein because of its relation to dramatic representation. The business of the drama was to evolve *rasa* in the spectator by means of the four kinds of *abhinaya*.[2] The नाट्यशास्त्र says that without *rasa* nothing can be done in drama (नहि रसादृते कश्चिदर्थः प्रवर्तते । नाट्यशास्त्र G. O. S. vol. I. p. 274) and the अ. भा. remarks that one *rasa* runs like a thread in a dramatic representation (एक एव तावत्परमार्थतो रसः सूत्रस्थानीयत्वेन रूपके प्रतिभाति । अ. भा. vol. I. p. 273). In the नाट्यशास्त्र the largest portion is devoted to matters specially concerning the dramatist and the actor, while the analysis of the emotional effect desired to be produced and actually produced on the audience is dealt with mainly in chapters 6 and 7. It may be noted here that according to the काव्यमीमांसा p. 1 (quoted on p. 1 above) Bharata dealt with *rūpakas* and Nandikeśvara with *rasas*. But the present Nāṭyaśastra deals with both these subjects and no ancient work of Nandikeśvara on *rasas* has come down to us. In my last edition I said that the theory of *rasa* has a semi-physiological and semi-psychological basis and that it tries to explain how human feelings and emotions are worked upon and roused by drama and poetry. But I did not go into the psychological basis. I should like here to indicate briefly the psychological aspect of the theory.

I have neither the time nor space nor ability to discuss the varying views of modern Psychologists. Psychologists are not agreed on many points. I shall set out very briefly what psychologists like MacDougall say. In 'The Energies of men'

---

1. स्वादयन्रसमनेकसंस्कृतप्राकृतैरकृतपात्रसङ्करैः । भावशुद्धिविहितैर्मुदं जनो नाटकैरिव बभार भोजनैः ॥ शिशुपालवध 14. 50.

2. The four kinds of अभिनय are आङ्गिक (concerning the movements of the head, face, the hands and other limbs of the body, described in chap. 8-13 of the Nāṭyaśāstra), वाचिक (in chapters 15-22, dealing with metres, lakṣaṇas, figures of speech, plot, the vṛttis), आहार्य (dress, ornaments &c. in chap. 23), सात्त्विक (horripilation, tears, *bhāva*, *hāva* &c. in chap. 24).

(1932) chap. VII pp. 97-98 he sets out a long list of eighteen innate propensities of human beings. Dr. R. J. S. McDowall in 'Sane Psychology' (1944) shortens MacDougall's list to fourteen instincts and sets them out together with their attendant emotions as follows (pp. 20-21).

	Instinct.	Attendant emotion.
(1)	Escape from danger	Fear
(2)	Combat	Anger
(3)	Repugnance	Disgust
(4)	Parental protection of the young	Parental feeling
(5)	Curiosity	Adventure
(6)	Self—assertion	Superiority
(7)	Self—abasement	Subjection
(8)	Cry of distress	Helplessness
(9)	Sex	Sexual desire
(10)	Herd	Loneliness
(11)	Food seeking	Appetite
(12)	Hoarding	Feeling of ownership
(13)	Construction	Feeling of creativeness
(14)	Laughter	Amusement

We shall now turn to the analysis Bharata and his followers make about the effect produced on the minds of the spectators when they see a drama. It should be remembered that they had only a limited objective before them and were not concerned with any perfect or all-round system of psychology concerning man from his primitive stage or from childhood onwards. They knew that the representation of a drama appealed only to two senses, viz. the eye and the ear (क्रीडनीयकमिच्छामो दृश्यं श्रव्यं च यद्भवेत् । नाट्य. I. 11). This was the physiological basis. Among those arts that appeal through the eye are included dancing (नृत्य) and acting, ornaments, painting; the arts of hearing include oratory and repetition of poetic stanzas (पाठ्य), singing and music in general. They knew that a dramatic representation gave delight to the audience even when in the drama presented there were some sad episodes. In ordinary life pity and fear do not give rise to pleasure or repose but the pity and fear felt by the representation on the stage of a tragic event differ in their effects. They therefore described and analysed the nature of the aesthetic pleasure derived and relished by appreciative men and women. Aesthetic pleasure or delight is one (*rasa* is really one)[1]; but as in the case of speech, where senses are derived from sentences and sentences are split up into words and letters, so they held that the pleasurable feeling, experience (संवेदन or अनुभूति) or effect could be distinguished as of eight sorts viz. relating to sex (sṛṅgāra), hāsya[2] &c. It would not be proper to say that the *rasa* theorists held that all men had only eight or nine instincts and that, as compared to the findings of modern psychologists, they were wrong in recognizing शोक and one or two others as fundamental, innate or basic propensities. Their theory was that as the effect of the representation of a drama the audience went through an experience that was packed full of delight, that there was no question of pain in that experience, that the experience appeared various owing to the impressions of love, sorrow and other propensities lying dormant in the mind, which were roused by the several kinds of *abhinaya*. The अ. भा. says 'अस्मन्मते तु संवेदनमेवानन्दघनमास्वाद्यते तत्र का दुःखाशङ्का केवलं तस्यैव चित्रताकरणे रतिशोकादिवासनाव्यापारस्तदुद्बोधने चाभिनयादिव्यापारः ।' (vol. I. p. 293 on VI. 37).[3] The poetic theory at its best was that

---

1. The अभिनवभारती compares रस to स्फोट. 'तेन रस एव नाट्यं यस्य व्युत्पत्तिः फलमित्युच्यते । तथा च रसादृते इत्यत्र (नाट्यशास्त्र ६, ३४) एकवचनोपपत्तिः । ततश्च मुख्यभूतान्महारसात्स्फोटदृशीवासत्यानि वा, अन्विताभिधानदृशीवोपायात्मकानि सत्यानि वा, अभिहितान्वयदृशीव तत्समुदायरूपाणि वा रसान्तराणि भागाभिनिवेशदृष्टानि रूप्यन्ते ।' on VI. 16, vol. I. p. 269.

2. The भावप्रकाशन II. p. 46 says that रस is सामाजिकाश्रय and that aesthetic relish is of eight kinds. 'यतोऽष्टधा मनोवृत्तिः सभ्यानां नाट्यकर्मणि । अष्टावेवानुभूयन्ते तासक्तास्तै रसाः पृथक् ॥ सामाजिकैस्तु रस्यन्ते यस्मात्तस्माद्रसाः स्मृताः ।. Vide also pp. 58-59 of भावप्रकाशन particularly 'वर्धिताः स्थायिनो भावा नायकादिसमाश्रयाः । अनुकारतया नाट्ये क्रियमाणा नटादिषु । रसतां प्रतिपद्यन्ते सामाजिकमनःसु ते । संस्कारैः प्राक्तनैस्तैश्च रस्यन्ते यततो रसाः ॥'. The दशरूप (IV. 38-39) says the same thing. The लोचन (p. 23) says that in order that suggested sense (or *rasa*) may be relished there must be co-operation between the speaker (poet or dramatist) and the hearer 'वक्तृप्रतिपत्तृप्रतिभासहकारित्वं हि अस्माभिर्द्योतनस्य प्राणत्वेनोक्तम्'.

3. There was no unanimity on this point. The नाट्यदर्पण (pp. 158-159) elaborates the theory that rasa has a touch of

nothing was ugly in the world and that everything was beautiful when the dramatist or poet by his imaginative creation and the spectator or reader by imaginative centemplation expresses or visualises to himself the idealised circumstances delineated in the drama or poem. This is explicitly stated by the नाट्यशास्त्र 21. 122 in the words न तज्ज्ञानं &c quoted in note 2 on p. 35 and by भामह in V. 4.

There are several works that expound the theory of *rasa* realization such as the नाट्यशास्त्र VI-VII with the commentary of अभिनव०, the सरस्वतीकण्ठाभरण V, शृङ्गारप्रकाश, दशरूप, शृङ्गारतिलक, भावप्रकाशन, रसतरङ्गिणी. It is not possible to describe in detail what all these works say and to mark out the points of difference among some of them. Bharata's text being the earliest one I shall rely on that text and the अभिनवभारती thereon and briefly set forth the several interpretations of that sūtra. The pivot round which the whole rasa system revolves

---

sorrow in it. The शृ. प्र. also said 'रसा हि सुखदुःखावस्थारूपाः' (Dr. Raghavan's 'Number of rasas' p. 155). Most writers, however, hold that all relishing of *rasa* due to dramatic representation is pleasurable. It is no doubt true that when an actor is seen weeping on the stage some at least among the audience find their eyes moist. The साहित्यदर्पण III. 8 explains 'अश्रुपातादयस्तद्वद्द्रुतत्वाच्चेतसो मताः'. The लोचन (on p. 18) puts the doctrine as follows 'यस्तु स्वप्नेपि न स्वशब्दवाच्यो न लौकिकव्यवहारपतितः, किंतु शब्दसमर्प्यमाणहृदयसंवादसुन्दर-विभावानुभावसमुदित-प्राङ्निविष्टरत्यादिवासनानुरागसुकुमारस्वसंविदानन्दचर्वणव्यापाररसनीयरूपो रसः।'. Vide also अ. भा. vol. I. p. 290 'सामाजिकानां हि हर्षैकफलं नाट्यं न शोकादिफलम्।'. The नाट्यदर्पण passage is : स्थायी भावः श्रितोत्कर्षो विभावव्यभिचारिभिः। स्पष्टानुभावनिश्चेयः सुखदुःखात्मको रसः...यत्पुनः सर्वरसानां सुखात्मकत्वमुच्यते तत्प्रतीतबाधितम्। pp. 158-159. Some of the works say that when one is relishing *rasa* all other cognitions disappear from the mind for the moment and the state of aesthetic enjoyment is like ब्रह्मानन्द, which state lasts as long as विभाव s and the other *bhāvas* continue to operate. Compare काव्यप्रकाश IV. p. 92 'सामाजिकानां वासनात्मतया स्थितः स्थायी रत्यादिकः...चर्व्यमाणैकताप्राणो विभावादिजीवितावधिः...पुर इव परिस्फुरन्...अन्यत्सर्वमिव तिरोदधद् ब्रह्मास्वादमिवानुभावयन् अलौकिकचमत्कारकारी शृङ्गारादिको रसः'. Compare साहित्यदर्पण III. 2-3 for similar words. As regards there being a mixture of pain in *rasa*, the साहित्यदर्पण remarks III. 4-5 'करुणादावपि रसे जायते यत्परं सुखम्। सचेतसामनुभवः प्रमाणं तत्र केवलम्। किं च तेषु यदा दुःखं न कोपि स्यात्तदुन्मुखः।'.

is the passage 'विभावानुभावव्यभिचारिसंयोगाद्रसनिष्पत्तिः' (नाट्यशास्त्र VI. p. 274 G. O. S.). Two matters have to be noted in relation to this sūtra : (1) the word स्थायि does not occur in it and (2) it is somewhat vague, particularly as to the import of the two words संयोग and निष्पत्ति. There are four interpretations of this sūtra respectively made by लोल्लट, शङ्कुक, नायक and अभिनवगुप्त and the रसगङ्गाधर (p. 28) speaks of eight varying interpretations.

The original works of लोल्लट, शङ्कुक and नायक are not yet found and we have to rely upon the summaries of their doctrines furnished by their adverse critics such as अभिनवगुप्त and मम्मट. These four views are respectively labelled उत्पत्तिवाद, अनुमितिवाद, भुक्तिवाद and अभिव्यक्तिवाद (of अभिनव०, मम्मट and most others). Before briefly stating the interpretations of these ancient writers, we must first understand the ideas underlying the technical words employed in the *rasasūtra*. There are certain permanent and dominant propensities or basic moods in the minds of all theatre-going people or readers of poetry which are ordinarily dormant, but when appropriate stimuli such as dialogues, songs, acting and music in case of drama, and mere words in the case of a poem are employed, they are roused and evolve a pleasurable state of the mind of the spectator or reader. These permanent moods are called स्थायिभाव. Bharata (VII. vol. I pp. 350-351) illustrates why these moods are called स्थायि. Though a king and his servants are all possessed of similar limbs and physical endowments, one man is called the king and others wait upon him, so one mood is called स्थायि and others associated with it are called विभाव, अनुभाव and व्यभिचारि and the स्थायिभाव so accompanied attains the position of रस (the aesthetic pleasure or relish). 'यथा नरेन्द्रो बहुजनपरिवारोपि सन्स एव नाम लभते नान्यः सुमहानपि पुरुषः । तथा विभावानुभावव्यभिचारिपरिवृतः स्थायी भावो रसनाम लभते । भवति चात्र श्लोकः । यथा नराणां नृपतिः शिष्याणां च यथा गुरुः । एवं हि सर्वभावानां भावः स्थायी महानिह ॥' नाट्यशास्त्र K. M. ed. chap. VII. 8 and G. O. S. ed., VII. pp. 350-51. The दशरूप (IV. 34) deseribes स्थायिभाव from another stand-point, viz. स्थायिभाव is like the ocean which may be now and then disturbed by other भावs but always retains its own position; so स्थायिभाव is that dominant mood which is not broken up altogether by other bhāvas and makes the other bhāvas subordinate to itself. The permanent or dominant moods that may be aroused by a dramatic representation and brought to a state of pleasurable relish are eight रति (love), हास (gaiety or laughter), शोक, क्रोध, उत्साह (energy or vigour), भय, जुगुप्सा (repugnance) and विस्मय. Some add a ninth स्थायिभाव viz. शम. The resultant aesthetic enjoyment and pleasure are called *rasa*. Bharata (VI. vol. I. pp. 288-291) explains why this aesthetic pleasure is called *rasa*. Just as persons who partake of food prepared with many condiments (such as jaggery, curds, cardamom, camphor, *marica*) taste many flavours and feel pleasure and delight, so spectators relish स्थायिभावs suggested by various bhāvas, acting, recitation &c. and enjoy delight and therefore are called नाट्यरसs. The word रस in ordinary life has many senses viz. mercury, sweetness and other flavours (मधुराम्ललवणकटुकषायतिक्तभेदात्), essence, strong liking, decoction, exuded juice, one of the bodily dhātus (अ. भा. vol. I. p. 289), but in काव्य and नाट्य it has another meaning derived by metapher from the idea of tasting or relishing (रसनाद्रसत्वमेषां मधुरादीनामिवोक्तमाचार्यैः। रुद्रट XII. 4). विभावानुभावसात्त्विकव्यभिचारिभावैरुपनीयमानः परिपूर्णः स्थायिभावो रस्यमानो रसः। रसतर. VI. The रसतरङ्गिणी says 'चरमसमयपर्यन्तस्थायित्वादस्य स्थायित्वव्यपदेशः'. अनुभाव is defined as अनुभावो विकारस्तु भावसंसूचनात्मकः। दशरूप IV. 3, on which धनिक says 'स्थायिभावाननुभावयन्तः सामाजिकान् सभ्रूविक्षेपकटाक्षादयो रसपोषकारिणोऽनुभावाः'. Eight of the अनुभावs are called सात्त्विकभावs : 'पृथग्भावा भवन्त्येतेऽनुभावत्वेपि सात्त्विकाः। सत्त्वादेव समुत्पत्तेस्तच्च तद्भावभावनम्। स्तम्भप्रलयरोमाञ्चाः स्वेदो वैवर्ण्यवेपथू। अश्रु वैस्वर्यमित्यष्टौ स्तम्भोस्मिन् निष्क्रियाङ्गता। प्रलयो नष्टसंज्ञत्वं शेषाः सुव्यक्तलक्षणाः॥ दशरूप IV. 4-6. There is a difference of opinion as to why they are called सात्त्विक. Acc. to दशरूप, सत्त्व means a 'sympathetic heart' and सात्त्विक means 'सत्त्वेन निर्वृत्त' ; vide साहित्यदर्पण III. 134 for a similar view; but the रसतर॰ IV says सत्त्वं जीवशरीरं तस्य धर्माः सात्त्विकाः। इत्थं च शरीरभावाः स्तम्भादयः सात्त्विका भावा इत्यभिधीयन्ते।. About the भावs which are 49 (as noted below) नाट्यशास्त्र says: नानाभिनयसम्बद्धान्भावयन्ति रसानिमान्। यस्मात्तस्मादमी भावा विज्ञेया नाट्ययोक्तृभिः॥ न भावहीनोस्ति रसो न भावो रसवर्जितः। परस्परकृता सिद्धिस्तयोरभिनये भवेत्। व्यञ्जनौषधिसंयोगो यथान्नं स्वादुतां नयेत्। एवं भावा रसाश्चैव भावयन्ति परस्परम्॥ 6. 34, 36-37. It should be noted that the word स्थायि does not occur in the sūtra. Love manifests itself in relation to a man and woman i. e. it depends upon these and when the mood of love is to be roused it is furthered by such exciting causes as moonrise, spring, flowers, bower &c. These two viz. the fundamental determining elements of love (man and woman) and the exciting elements are called विभावs[1] (the former being called आलम्बनवि० and the latter उद्दीपनवि०). Such external manifestations as movements of the eye and eye-brows, glances, smiling face convey the working of the emotion of love and hence are called अनुभावs. There are many fleeting or secondary moods that are common to several dominant moods and serve the purpose of completely manifesting the permanent mood, such as निर्वेद (despondency), ग्लानि (*ennui* or fatigue), शङ्का. These may help to completely manifest the permanent moods of रति and शोक. These are called सञ्चारि or व्यभिचारि भावs. They are 33 and भरत in vol. I pp. 356 ff. describes them at length (विविधमाभिमुख्येन रसेषु चरन्तीति व्यभिचारिणः). The dominant moods रति, हास, शोक, when fully roused by means of appropriate विभावs, अनुभावs, व्यभिचारिभावs attain to the condition of शृङ्गार, हास्य and करुण *rasas*. It is to be noted that the dramatist does not put down any labels that in a particular composition there is शृङ्गार or करुण. He simply refers to the appropriate विभावs (hero and heroine and exciting circumstances), the ensuants (such as glances) and the accessory moods and leaves the spectator or reader to enjoy the aesthetic pleasure resulting from such description. It is therefore that

1 The नाट्यशास्त्र (VI. vol. I pp. 347-348) explains विभाव as विज्ञान and says that विभाव is nothiug but कारण or निमित्त or हेतु. The विभावs are so called because many matters (viz. स्थायिभावs and व्यभिचारिभावs that depend upon अभिनय of two kinds viz. वाचिक and आङ्गिक) are specially understood from them (वागाद्योऽभिनया येषां स्थायिव्यभिचारिणां ते वागाद्यभिनयसहिता विभाव्यन्ते विशिष्टतया ज्ञायन्ते यैस्ते विभावाः। अ. भा.). For अनुभाव, vide दशरूप IV. 3 quoted above. The भावs are 49 viz. 8 स्थायिभावs, 33 व्यभिचारिभावs and eight सात्त्विकभावs. The last are स्तम्भ (immobility due to fear, anger &c.), स्वेद, रोमाञ्च, स्वरभङ्ग, वेपथु, वैवर्ण्य, अश्रु, प्रलय. प्रलय means 'सुखदुःखाभ्यां चेष्टाज्ञाननिराकृतिः' साहित्यदर्पण III. 139) i. e. loss of activity and consciousness due to happiness or sorrow. It may be noted that विभावs and अनुभावs (other than सात्त्विक भावs) are not included among the 49 bhāvas and that even those that are called स्थायिभावs may become व्यभिचारिभावs under certain circumstances e. g. when शृङ्गार is the predominant रस, रति is स्थायिभाव and if हास is described as an incident in that composition it becomes सञ्चारिभाव, though हास is enumerated as one of the स्थायिभावs.

the *rasas* are said to be only suggested (and not expressed). Conversely, even if an author expressly said that there was शृङ्गार or करुण *rasa* in a particular piece, still there would be no aesthetic enjoyment of that *rasa* in case the appropriate elements were wanting. Rasa is out of the ordinary, can be understood only by सहृदयs and the only proof of its existence is the चर्वणा or आस्वाद which a सहृदय has. For a detailed description of the *rasa* theory in all its parts, vide नाट्यशास्त्र (VI and VII chap.), दशरूप (4th prakāśa), साहित्यदर्पण (III) and Rasataraṅgiṇī. The eight *rasas* are शृङ्गार, हास्य, करुण, रौद्र, वीर, भयानक, बीभत्स, and अद्‌भुत (vide नाट्य. VI. 15, pp. 268-269, G.O.S. ed. and K. M. ed. VI. 16). Some added a ninth *rasa* (शान्त).

We may apply the theory of *rasa* to the ādikāvya viz. Rāmāyaṇa. It is narrated in the Bālakāṇḍa that the sage Vālmīki saw a hunter killing one out of a pair of amorous krauñca birds. The parting of the loving pair by violent means, the fall and death of the female bird are the vibhāvas of karuṇa-rasa and the lamentation and piercing cry of anguish uttered by the surviving male partner are the anubhāvas of *karuṇa*; these powerfully moved the dormant mood of sympathy and pathos in Vālmīki's heart, for a moment it beat in unison with the sorrow of the bird (तन्मयीभाव) and there was an overflow of that powerful feeling in the form of the measured verse 'मा निषाद प्रतिष्ठां त्वमगमः शाश्वतीः समाः'. It should not be thought that the sage was plunged into grief (शोक) in the popular sense. The word शोक in रघुवंश XIV. 70 and ध्व० quoted above (on p. 332 n. 2) is used in the dramatic sense (viz. as the स्थायिभाव)[1]. The sage was not occupied with his own

1. The words of the ध्व० 'काव्यस्य स एवार्थः सारभूतः संनिहितसहचरीविरहकातरक्रौञ्चाक्रन्दजनितशोक एव श्लोकतया परिणतः' (p.32) and of the लोचन क्रौञ्चद्वन्द्ववियोगेन सहचरीहननोद्‌भूतेन साहचर्यध्वंसनेनोत्थितः (p. 317) create a serious difficulty. All editions of the रामायण make the hunter kill the male bird and it is the female that laments. The ध्व. and लोचन had, it is clear, a reading before them which made the female die by the arrow. Not only so, the काव्यमी. of राजशेखर (p. 7) reads 'निषादनिहतसहचरीकं क्रौञ्चयुवानं करुणक्रेङ्कारया गिरा क्रन्दन्तमुदीक्ष्य' &c. and supports the above interpretation of the ध्व० given by me. The late M. M. Prof. Kuppuswami in his उपलोचन on कौमुदी explains 'निहतः सहचरीविरहकातरः क्रौञ्चः' &c. But

sorrow felt for the poor bird, but with the whole objective episode that stirred his heart and that led to the outburst (viz. मा निषाद प्र०). The situation as idealized by the sage's vision due to his sensitive nature and imagination gave rise to the poetic outburst, when the poet is completely full of the transcendental (*alaukika*) mental experience of an emotional idealized situation, then poetry gushes out from him, as the Locana p. 32 puts it (यावत्पूर्णो न चैतेन तावन्नैवैवमिति). Not every reader of a poem can appreciate or experience the emotional appeal of that poem. The reader also must possess sufficient mental equipment and visualize in his own mind the situation as expressed by the poet. This is what is meant by Tota quoted from the Locana at p. 220 above (नायकस्य कवेः श्रोतुः समानोनुभवस्ततः). The poet cannot communicate to every *reader* the emotional situation depicted in the poem. He can only awaken in the

---

this is not satisfactory. The word in ध्व० is संनिहित and not निहत; besides the लोचन has 'सहचरीहनन'. Supposing that निहत is the correct reading, we expect सहचरीविरहकातरनिहतक्रौञ्च, as he must have been कातर before he was shot when the male gave out a cry in the pangs of death. Why should the क्रौञ्च male be ०विरहकातर after being निहत ? Further, the verse is indicative of Rāma's life. When सीता was carried away by रावण, she was as if dead to him and it is राम that laments (as भवभूति says अपि ग्रावा रोदिति about राम's condition). So क्रौञ्चीहनन corresponds with सीतापहरण and क्रौञ्चाक्रन्द with Rāma's lamentations. And the काव्यमी. is quite clear. Recently Prof. G. H. Bhatt (in J. O. I., Baroda, vol. IX part 2 pp. 148-151) contributes a paper on this episode and prefers to read निहतसहचरीविरहकातर-क्रौञ्चाक्रन्दजनितः in ध्व० and explains the composition in a peculiar way viz. निहतश्च सहचरीविरहकातरश्च निहत...... कातरः स चासौ क्रौञ्चश्च क्रौञ्च्याः आक्रन्दश्च & c. This is a strange way of dissolving the compound. This interpretation gives a topsyturvy order. The क्रौञ्च must have been first कातर and then killed and so we expect सहचरीविरहकातरनिहत & c. Prof. Bhatt connects the आक्रन्द with the सहचरी. The straightforward and usual construction would be to connect आक्रन्द with क्रौञ्च that immediatly precedes. The reference he makes to preceding verses does not impress me. When once the theory was espoused that it was the male that was killed, then suitable verses could have been easily interpolated.

man of taste (sahṛdaya) an emotional state similar to what he depicts in the poem. There must be a close correspondence between the poet's impulses conveyed by his choice of words and possible impulses in the reader.

Numerous books and papers have been written on the theory of *rasa.* I can do nothing more than mention some of the most prominent ones. Vide Dr. De in HSP vol. II pp. 21-32, 135-174 and in 'the theory of Rasa' in Mookerjee Silver Jubilee commemoration volume III pp. 207-253; Dr. A. Sankaran in 'Theories of Rasa and Dhvani', particularly pp. 15-17, 91-117; Dr. Raghavan on 'Śṛṅgāraprakāśa' vol. I part 2 pp. 418-542; 'Indian Aesthetics' by Dr. K. C. Pandey (1950); 'a criticai survey of Indian Aesthetics' Journal of Ganganath Jha Institute vol. III pp. 379-426; 'Psychological Basis of Alaṅkāra Literature' by Prof. S. P. Bhattacharya in Mookerjee Silver Jubilee C. volume III pp. 661-682; 'Rasa doctrine' by Mr. P. S. Naidu in Journal of Annamalai University vol. X pp. 1-12; 'Psychology of Beauty' by Dr. B. L. Atreya in J. of Benares H. Un. vol. VI pp. 43-55; 'Concept of sthāyibhāva' by Prof. Wadekar in Annals of B. O. R. I. vol. 24 pp. 207-214; 'Psychology of Rasa theory' by Prof. K. N. Watve in Annals of B. O. R. I. Silver Jubilee vol. 26 pp. 669-677; 'Philosophy of Aesthetic pleasure' by Pancapagesa Sastri, Annamalai University, 1940; 'Rasa cult in the Caitanyacaritāmṛta' in Asutosh Mookerjee S. J. vol. III Orientalia part 3 pp. 368-388; 'Cornerstone of Rasa idealogy' by Prof. S. P. Bhattacharya in Pro. of All India O. Con., 13th Session pp. 253-267; 'The Ālaṅkārikas and the semantics of suggestion' by N. Bala Subrahmanya in Journal of Mysore University, vol. XVI No. 1; 'Psychologic studies in Rasa' by Dr. Rakesa Gupta (Aligarh, 1950); 'Art Experience' by Prof. M. Hiriyanna in volume of comparative studies presented to Dr. Radhakrishnan on his 60th birthday pp. 176-188; 'Aesthetic experience according to Abhinavagupta' by Raniero Gnoli, Rome, 1956; 'The critical and comparative study of Indian Aesth·tics' J. G. J. R. I. vol. XV parts 3 and 4 pp. 187-132 by Shri H. L. Sharma; 'Comparative Aesthetics' vol. I on 'Indian Aesthetics' 2nd edition (1959) by Dr. K. C. Pandey.

Important questions arise about शान्तरस and about the number of rasas. Dr. Raghavan dealt with these two topics in J. O. R., Madras, vol. X pp. 1-10, 97-114, 240-250 and vol. XI pp. 12-21, 77-115, 269-284 and in a separate book 'Number of Rasas' (1940) in which are included his contributions in the J.O.R. Madras. Vide pp. 12-13 above where this question about शान्तरस is discussed. From the Vikramorvaśīya II. 18 and the काव्यादर्श II. 392 and the text of भरत (VI. 15-16) it follows that there were originally only eight *rasas*. As उद्भट (IV. 5) and the विष्णुधर्मोत्तरपुराण (p. 68 above) mention nine *rasas* it follows that शान्तरस was certainly included from about the 7th century. The भावप्रकाशन p. 47 states that it was वासुकि who first recognized शान्तरस. Some hold that शान्त may be a रस in poetry but not in dramas; vide दशरूप IV 35 (शममपि केचित्प्राहुः पुष्टिर्नाट्येषु नैतस्य) and भावप्रकाशन p. 47 (नाटकादिनिबन्धे तु तपश्चरणवस्तुनि। अभिनेतुमशक्यत्वात्तद्वाक्यार्थपदार्थयोः। सामाजिकानां मनसि रसः शान्तो न जायते ॥). The reasons why it was said that शान्त should not be recognized in a drama were many. One can hardly say that any big audience can be influenced to relish शान्तरस. The very atmosphere of dramatic representation with its songs, music and make-up is rather antagonistic to the development of a mood of शम (tranquility and self-effacement). In a mere poem Śāntarasa may be evolved by reading it in a quiet and secluded spot. The ध्व० (4th उद्योत pp. 298-300) after a lengthy examination shows that in the Mahābhārata शान्तरस is intended to be the most predominant and करुण is the most predominant rasa in the रामायण. It is not impossible to perform on the stage a drama such as the प्रबोधचन्द्रोदय but the audience may be sparse. If नाट्य is defined (by दशरूप I. 7) as अवस्थानुकृतिः (imitative representation of various conditions), there is no theoretical reason why *śāntarasa* cannot be represented on the stage by clever actors with appropriate settings. Abhinavagupta went to the other extreme and propounded the view that शान्त was the greatest रस because of its relation to मोक्ष, the highest goal of human life, and because all poetic pleasure is अलौकिक and like ब्रह्मास्वाद. Vide अ. भा. vol. I. p. 340 'सर्वरसानां शान्तप्राय एवास्वादः'. Acc. to अभिनव and धनञ्जय, शम is the स्थायिभाव of शान्त, वैराग्य and संसारभीरुता are विभावs, मोक्षशास्त्रचिन्ता is अनुभाव, निर्वेद, मति, धृति, स्मृति are व्यभिचारिभाव. Acc. to मम्मट (IV 35. निर्वेदस्थायिभावोस्ति शान्तोपि नवमो रसः) and सङ्गीतरत्नाकर the स्थायिभाव of शान्त is निर्वेद, while others put forward जुगुप्सा or उत्साह as the स्थायिभाव (सङ्गीतर. verse 1374). On pp. 92-106 of his work 'The number of rasas' Dr. Raghavan furnishes a corrected text of the section on शान्तरस from the अभिनवभारती. Vide p. 207 above for the view of the चन्द्रिका on शान्त viz. आधिकारिकत्वेन शान्तो रसो न निबद्धव्यः. We saw above that रुद्रट mentions a 10th रस called प्रेयान्. The अ. भा. (vol. I pp. 341-42) states that other *rasas* were put forward by some viz. स्नेह (आर्द्रता as स्थायिभाव), लौल्य and भक्ति and explains that स्नेह is nothing but रति and उत्साह, लौल्य would be included under हास or रति and भक्ति under रति. As देवादिविषयरति was called भाव (रतिर्देवादिविषया व्यभिचारी तथाञ्जितः। भावः प्रोक्तः-काव्यप्र. IV. 35) and not शृङ्गार, others put forward भक्ति as a separate रस. The सङ्गीतरत्नाकर (verses 1370-71, VII. p. 815) says : the नट is like a vessel (पात्र) in which some liquid is kept. As the vessel does not taste the liquid, so the actor does not relish the rasa that is being evolved and further states that some put foreward भक्ति (श्रद्धा as स्थायिभाव), स्नेह and लौल्य as three rasas; but it rejects these. The ध्वन्यालोक[1] says that शान्त and शृङ्गार both pervade the drama called नागानन्द, that तृष्णाक्षयसुख is the स्थायिभाव of शान्त, quotes a verse from the Mahābhārata in support and remarks that even granting for argument that all men have not the experience of तृष्णाक्षयसुख that does not matter. The Locana refers to the words of the नाट्यशास्त्र that in नाट्य are shown sometimes *drama*, sport, wealth and also *śama* sometimes (त्रैलोक्यस्यास्य सर्वस्य नाट्यं भावानुकीर्तनम्। क्वचिद्धर्मः क्वचित्क्रीडा क्वचिदर्थः क्वचिच्छमः॥ I. 104). It further says that śama is suggested, though all may not like it. But, this last is not the test. Śṛṅgāra also may not be liked by some people such as those who are वीतराग (who have subdued all passions) but this does not mean that शृङ्गार is not a rasa. Some said that if śama is held to be the sthāyibhāva of *śānta*, then, as the actor does not possess that quality of śama, *śānta* cannot be a *rasa* in *nāṭya*. The reply of the सङ्गीतरत्नाकर is quoted below.[2]

---

1. शान्तश्च तृष्णाक्षयसुखस्य यः परिपोषस्तल्लक्षणो रसः प्रतीयते। तथा चोक्तम्। यच्च कामसुखं लोके यच्च दिव्यं महत्सुखम्। तृष्णाक्षयसुखस्यैते नार्हतः षोडशीं कलाम्॥ यदि नाम सर्वजनानुभवगोचरता तस्य नास्ति नैतावतासावलोकसामान्यमहानुभाव-चित्तवृत्तिविशेषवत् प्रतिक्षेप्तुं शक्यः। ध्व. (III. pp. 219-220). The verse यच्च० is शान्तिपर्व 175. 35=वायुपुराण 93. 101.

2. शान्तस्य शमसाध्यत्वान्नटे च तदसम्भवात्। अष्टावेव रसा नाट्येष्विति केचिदचूचुदन्। तदचारु यतः कंचिन्न रसं स्वदते नटः। सामाजिकास्तु लिहते रसान् पात्रं नटो मतः॥ संगीतरत्नाकर VII. p. 815 verses 1370-71. The words

The actor does not himself relish what the spectator is to relish. When the actor pretends to feel fear or anger, he does not feel those sentiments in reality.

We saw above (p. 248) that Bhoja developed in the Śṛṅgāraprakāśa the theory (adumbrated in S. K. A.) that *rasa* is only one, that poetry is beautiful because of its presence, that the one *rasa* may be called śṛṅgāra and is identified with अभिमान and अहङ्कार, that it pervades the soul of man owing to the impressions made on the soul in many births and that it is the one cause from which spring many good characteristics of the soul (रसोभिमानोहङ्कारः शृङ्गार इति गीयते। योर्थस्तस्यान्वयात् काव्यं कमनीयत्वमश्नुते॥ विशिष्टादृष्टजन्मायं जन्मिनामन्तरात्मसु। आत्मसम्यग्गुणोद्भूतेरेको हेतुः प्रकाशते॥ सर. क. V. 1-2). What Bhoja means by शृङ्गार being identified with अहङ्कार is practically the same as holding that *rasa* realization is आनन्दमय and ब्रह्मास्वाद-सहोदर. When Bhoja says that śṛṅgāra is the only *rasa* he gives a different and philosophic significance to that word from what it ordinarily has viz. the love of man and woman. He keeps the two meanings apart. Those who want to understand Bhoja's point of view should read pp. 435-513 of Dr. Raghavan's work on the Śṛṅgāraprakāśa (vol. I part 2). Vide 'Number of rasas' by Dr. Raghavan pp. 92-106 (=Abhinavabhāratī vol. I. pp. 333-342) for a corrected text of A. B. on शान्तरस.

There were some writers who held that *adbhuta* (wonderful) was the only *rasa*. The साहित्यदर्पण (III. 2-3) states that his great-great-grand-father Nārāyaṇa held that *camatkāra* or *vismaya* was the essence of *rasa* and quotes what धर्मदत्त says in his work (vide p. 289 n. 3).

Dr. De in his paper on 'the theory of Rasa' contributed to the Sir Asutosh Mookerjee Silver Jubilee vol. III (pp. 240-253) gave the text of Abhinavagupta's commentary on the *rasasūtra* in chap. VI of the नाट्यशास्त्र (corresponding to vol. I pp. 274-288). It is in these pages that the views of लोल्लट, शङ्कुक, नायक and अभिनवगुप्त are set out at length. It is impossible in the space that I can afford to expound in detail

---

अष्टावेव...नटः are quoted by जगन्नाथ (रसग. p. 30), who accepts शान्त as 9th रस. The अ. भा. (vol. I. p. 292) says 'नटे तर्हि किमास्वादनोपायः। अत एव पात्रमित्युच्यते। नहि पात्रे मद्यास्वादोपि तदुपायकः।'.

the views of these writers and the objections raised against them. I shall briefly indicate the special characteristics of the theory of early writers on the question of *rasa* realization. The important questions are : 'where does *rasa* reside',[1] 'what the nature of *rasa* is' and 'how it is evolved and realized'. Briefly put, Lollaṭa's view is as follows: *Rasa* in the primary sense belongs to the hero, Rāma etc. (i. e. Rāma loves Sītā and the dramatist describes this love in appropriate words). The spectator ascribes to the actor, on account of the latter's clever acting, the same mental attitude that belonged to Rāma and the spectator's apprehension of imputed love in the actor brings to him delight. This is the meaning of the words विभावा...रसनिष्पत्तिः. This view does not treat of *rasa* as a matter of the spectator's aesthetic appreciation of the inner meaning of the representation. All that Lollaṭa means is that the spectator is delighted by the fact that the actor cleverly represents by his acting that he is Rāma himself, feels the same love that the historic or legendary person (Rāma) felt towards the heroine. The spectator is charmed by this. The view of Lollaṭa is not very clearly expressed by अभिनवगुप्त or by मम्मट (तेन स्थाय्येव विभावानुभावादिभिरुपचितो रसः। स्थायी भवत्यनुपचितः। स चोभयोरपि मुख्यया वृत्त्या रामादावनुकार्येऽनुकर्तरि च नटे रामादिरूपतानुसन्धानबलादिति। अ. भा. vol. I p. 274; रसस्वरूप एव तावद्विप्रतिपत्तयः प्रतिवादिनाम्। तथा हि पूर्वावस्थायां यः स्थायी स एव व्यभिचारिसम्पातादिना प्राप्तपरिपोषोऽनुकार्यंगत एव रसः। लोचन p. 83; नटे तु तुल्यरूपतानुसन्धानवशादारोप्यमाणः सामाजिकानां चमत्कारहेतुः। प्रदीप p. 74 on काव्यप्र. 4. 5-6). Here real रस (शृङ्गार) is produced in राम and therefore this view is called उत्पत्तिवाद. शङ्कुक thinks that *rasa* is a matter of inference. The actor who has been well trained in the art of gesticulation cleverly simulates the actions of real heroes and the spectator apprehends for the moment the actor as non-different from the real hero and infers love (of Rāma etc.) from the अनुभावs, व्यभिचारिभावs presented by the actor and mentally contemplates such love and relishes it. Here *rasa* is no doubt spoken of in rela-

1. It should be noted that as said by Tota (p. 211 above) the original hero, the dramatist or the poet who composes his work and the spectator or reader pass through the same experience. The actor is only simulating but some writers say that there is nothing to prevent the actor also from relishiag *rasa*.

tion to the spectator; but it is said to be a matter of inference due to clever imitation (अनुकरणरूपो रसः). It would be noticed that Śaṅkuka speaks of *rasa* from the standpoint of the spectator. It is his view that *rasa* is inferred by the spectator. The स्थायिभाव in the original hero is inferred to exist in the actor (though not actually existing in him) on account of *vibhāvas* cleverly represented by him in his acting, so as to give rise to the notion that the actor experiences feelings identical with those of the hero and makes the spectator forget for the time being the difference between the actors and the characters they represent. This inferred mood possesses peculiar charm entirely different from ordinary perceptions and inferences. Hence the realisation of *rasa* by the spectator is a logical inference. This view is elaborated and criticized in several pages of the अभिनवभारती (vol. I pp. 274-278). Numerous objections are raised against it. But the important one is that it is direct apprehension that produces strikingness and not mere inference (एतदप्यहृदयग्राहि यतः प्रत्यक्षमेव ज्ञानं सचमत्कारम्, नानुमित्यादिरिति लोकप्रसिद्धिमवधूयान्यथा कल्पने मानाभावः। प्रदीप p. 77 on काव्यप्र. IV. 4-5). For the view of भट्टनायक, vide above pp. 212-213. भट्टनायक denies that *rasa* is a matter of inference; nor does he accept the view that *rasa* is manifested as something relished by the spectator. He looks upon रसास्वाद as in the same category with परब्रह्मसाक्षात्कार. As परब्रह्म is आनन्दमय, so is the apprehension of *rasa*. He held that besides *abhidhā* there were two more powers of word viz. भावकत्वव्यापार and भोग or भोगीकृति. By the first the *vibhāvas* like Rāma and Sītā are represented to the audience or reader stripped of their individual aspects (साधारणीकरण or साधारणगुणयोग) and the sentiment of love is aroused in the mind and then the audience or reader enjoys a thrill which is आनन्दमय, is different from ordinary experience (अनुभव) or recollection (स्मृति) and is like परब्रह्मास्वाद. The अ. भा. (नाट्यशास्त्र vol. I pp. 278-279) remarks:. 'तस्मात्काव्ये दोषाभावगुणालङ्कारमयत्वलक्षणेन, नाट्ये चतुर्विधाभिनयरूपेण, निबिडनिजमोहसङ्कटतानिवारणकारिणा विभावादिसाधारणीकरणात्मना अभिधातो द्वितीयेनांशेन भावकत्वव्यापारेण भाव्यमानो रसोऽनुभवस्मृत्यादिविलक्षणेन रजस्तमोऽनुवेधवैचित्र्यबलाद्द्रुतिविस्तारविकासलक्षणेन सत्त्वोद्रेकप्रकाशानन्दमयनिजसंविद्विश्रान्तिविलक्षणेन परब्रह्मास्वादसविधेन भोगेन परं भुज्यत इति।'. It appears from the Locana that Nāyaka accepted that *Rasa* was the soul of poetry or drama and that it was व्यंग्य. 'रसः। स च काव्यव्यापारैकगोचरो रसध्वनिरिति। स च ध्वनिरेवेति स एव मुख्यतया-

त्मेति ।' (लोचन p. 18) and 'रसस्य शब्दवाच्यत्वं तेनापि नोपगतमिति व्यङ्ग्यत्वमेव' (लोचन p. 23). He differed from the ध्वनि school in two respects, viz. that रस realisation cannot be described and analysed and that रस is the only suggested sense as the soul of poetry and not वस्तु or अलङ्कार as the ध्वन्यालोक admitted (on p. 18). अभिनवगुप्त holds the view that *rasa* is अभिव्यक्त (and not कार्य or ज्ञाप्य).[1] He does not accept the two functions of भट्टनायक (other than अभिधा). He thinks that love and other moods are dormant in the minds of spectators, are roused by the stimulus of विभाव्s etc. and reach the state of *rasa*. Vide काव्यप्रकाश (IV) for a detailed statement of these views and लोचन (pp. 30, 68-70). भरत's view that रस is the soul of poetry was accepted by रुद्रभट्ट in the शृङ्गारतिलक, even by the अग्निपुराण (वाग्वैदग्ध्यप्रधानेपि रस एवात्र जीवितम्, chap. 336. 33), काव्यमी० p. 6 (रस आत्मा), by मम्मट and रुय्यक, by शौद्धोदनि (अलङ्कारस्तु शोभायै रस आत्मा परे मनः ।' अलङ्कारशेखर p. 6) and a host of other writers. अभिनवगुप्त says that *rasa* becomes *abhivyakta* by the power of vyañjanā and one has *rasa* realization (rasapratīti) which can be analysed and described. He gives up the भावकत्व (or साधारणीकरण) of Nāyaka and does not speak of भोग but रसप्रतीति or रसास्वाद or रसचर्वणा. It may be noted that Bharata states (VI p. 71) 'नानाभावाभिनयव्यञ्जितान् वागङ्गसत्त्वोपेतान् स्थायिभावानास्वादयन्ति सुमनसः प्रेक्षकाः तस्मान्नाट्यरसा इति व्याख्याताः ।' and again 'एवमेते काव्यरसाभिव्यक्तिहेतव एकोनपञ्चाशद्भावाः प्रत्यवगन्तव्याः । एभ्यश्च सामान्यगुणयोगेन रसा निष्पद्यन्ते'. भट्टनायक presupposes (नाट्य. vol. I, p. 80 G.O.S.) two व्यापारs viz. भावकत्व (i. e. साधारणीकरण[2]) and भोजकत्व. The principal objections against Nāyaka's view are two viz. there is no evidence to prove that the two व्यापारs are required over and above *abhidhā* and what is called *bhukti* as transcending all knowledge is really nothing but a kind of experience and the latter ultimately ends in the theory of *abhivyakti*.

10 The alaṅkāra school. The word alaṅkāra[3] has had a chequered career. The inscription of Rudradāman cited

1. Vide लोचन p. 69 'अतश्चर्वणात्राभिव्यञ्जनमेव न तु ज्ञापनम्, प्रमाणव्यापारवत् नाप्युत्पादनम् । हेतुव्यापारवत् । ननु यदि नेयं ज्ञप्तिर्न वा निष्पत्तिः, तर्हि किमेतत् ।...अतश्च रसोयमलौकिकः ।

2. साधारणीकरणं चैतदेव यत्सीतादिविशेषाणां कामिनीत्वादिसामान्येनोपस्थितिः । प्रदीप p. 78.

3. The word अलङ्कृति occurs even in the Ṛgveda in the form अरङ्कृति. 'का ते अस्त्यरङ्कृतिः सूक्तैः कदा नूनं ते मघवन् दाशेम' । ऋ. VII. 29. 3.

above shows that in the 2nd centnry A. D. literary गद्य and पद्य were required to be अलङ्कृत. In the नाट्यशास्त्र (chap. 17. 1-5) there is an enumeration of 36 लक्षणs (in two recensions) with which the kāvya to be employed in nāṭya was to be endowed. These *lakṣaṇas* gradually faded out and some of them like हेतु and लेश were accepted as figures of speech by certain old ālaṅkārikas like Daṇḍin. The definition of the very first lakṣaṇa called भूषण or विभूषण is 'अलङ्कारैर्गुणैश्चैव बहुभिः समलङ्कृतम्। भूषणैरिव चित्रार्थैस्तद्भूषणमिति स्मृतम् ॥ (नाट्यशास्त्र 17. 6, G. O. S. vol. II p. 350). This shows that the lakṣaṇa भूषण included both अलंकारs and गुणs. The Nāṭyaśāstra 17. 43 (=K. M. ed. 16. 43 and G.O.S. 16. 40 vol. II.) p. 321 speaks of उपमा, रूपक, दीपक and यमक as four अलङ्कारs of नाटक. Vāmana uses the word alaṅkāra in two senses when he says 'काव्यं ग्राह्यमलङ्कारात्। सौन्दर्यमलङ्कारः।' काव्या. सू. I. 1. 1-2. Here अलङ्कार means 'a thing of beauty.'[1] He also explains that alaṅkāra applies to figures of speech because they beautify kāvya. Similarly, Daṇḍin appears to use the word alaṅkāra in a wide sense also as shown below.

The foremost representatives of this school are भामह and

---

1. Vāmana here asserts that poetry is one of the fine arts which have the expression of beauty as their goal. Controversies have raged round the questions: what are the characteristics of beauty, whether it is objective or subjective, whether the artist (including the poet) as creating beauty must preach morality or whether his province is different from a preacher of morality. I avoid the temptation of going into these questions. The world of Beauty is remote or at least different from the worlds of morality and Truth. Poetry as a department of Fine Arts does not directly aim at inculcating morality nor at ultimate Truth. The poet's duty as a poet is to be true to his own self and to art and to express the visions he sees as best as he can. He may indirectly convey moral ideas by means of his dramas. The ध्व० (III. p. 224) contains the following instructive remarks: 'शृङ्गाररसाङ्गैरुन्मुखीकृताः सन्तो हि विनेयाः सुखं विनयोपदेशं गृह्णन्ति। सदाचारोपदेशरूपा हि नायकादिगोष्ठी विनेयजनहितार्थमेव मुनिभिरवतारिता।'. Vide 'Psychology of Beauty' by Dr. B. L. Atreya in Journal of Benares H. Un. vol. VI pp. 43-55. माघ describes रमणीयता as 'क्षणे क्षणे यन्नवतामुपैति तदेव रूपं रमणीयतायाः।' IV. 17.

उद्भट; दण्डी, रुद्रट and प्रतीहारेन्दुराज may also be held to belong to this school. It is not to be supposed that they were unaware of the theory of *rasa*. Vide p. 341 above. उद्भट defines रसवत् as 'रसवद्दर्शितस्पष्टशृङ्गारादिरसादयम् । स्वशब्दस्थायिसञ्चारिविभावाभिनयास्पदम् ॥' (IV), in which he refers to the technical terms स्थायिभाव, विभाव, सञ्चारि (or व्यभिचारि) भाव and in the next verse names the nine *rasas*. दण्डी also defines रसवत् and ऊर्जस्वि and says 'मधुरं रसवद्वाचि वस्तुन्यपि रसस्थितिः ।' (I. 51). He is quite aware of the eight *rasas* and their स्थायिभावs 'इह त्वष्टरसायत्ता रसवत्ता स्मृता गिराम्' (II. 292); 'प्राक् प्रीतिर्दर्शिता सेयं रतिः शृङ्गारतां गता' (II. 281): vide also काव्या० II. 283, 285, 287. रुद्रट says 'तस्मात्तत्कर्तव्यं यत्नेन महीयसा रसैर्युक्तम्' (XII. 2). These writers were well aware of the existence of *rasa*, but they had not found out how to apply the theory to *kāvya* in general. To them *alaṅkāras* seemed to be the most important part in *kāvyas*, so much so that they made *rasas* subordinate to *alaṅkāras* and defined such figures as रसवत्. भामह and दण्डी hardly made any distinction between अलङ्कारs and *guṇas*. Both भामह and दण्डी regard भाविक as a *guṇa* ('भाविकत्वमिति प्राहुः प्रबन्धविषयं गुणं' III. 52 and काव्यादर्श II. 364); while दण्डी regards the ten गुणs as *alaṅkāras* when the word is used in a wide sense (काव्यशोभाकरान् धर्मानलङ्कारान् प्रचक्षते ।...काश्चिन्मार्गविभागार्थमुक्ताः प्रागप्यलङ्क्रियाः ।' II. 1 and 3). दण्डी in काव्यादर्श II. 367 states that the (64) aṅgas of the *sandhis* in a drama, the (16) aṅgas of *vṛttis* and the (36) lakṣaṇas described in another tradition (viz. dramaturgy in the नाट्यशास्त्र) are all looked upon by him as *alaṅkāras* (यच्च सन्ध्यङ्गवृत्त्यङ्गलक्षणाद्यागमान्तरे । व्यावर्णितमिदं चेष्टमलङ्कारतयैव नः ॥). The अलं. स. (p. 3 and p. 9) says 'इह तावद्भामहोद्भटप्रभृतयश्चिरन्तनालङ्कारकाराः प्रतीयमानमर्थं वाच्योपस्कारकतयालङ्कारपक्षनिक्षिप्तं मन्यन्ते ।...उद्भटादिभिस्तु गुणालङ्काराणां प्रायशः साम्यमेव सूचितम् ।..तदेवमलङ्कारा एव काव्ये प्रधानमिति प्राच्यानां मतम् ।'. The तरल says 'अभाव एव ध्वनेरिति भामहप्रभृतयो मन्यन्ते' (p. 24). This may lead one to think that भामह is ध्वन्यभाववादिन्. But this is not entirely correct. भामह, दण्डी and others were no doubt not aware of the theory that प्रतीयमान sense is the soul of poetry and they do not employ the words ध्वनि and गुणीभूतव्यङ्ग्य in their works. But they do refer to प्रतीयमान sense. In their definitions of अप्रस्तुतप्रशंसा, समासोक्ति, आक्षेप, they included a good deal of प्रतीयमान sense (i. e. गुणीभूतव्यंग्य of ध्वन्यालोक) e. g. यत्रोक्ते गम्यतेन्योर्थस्तत्समानविशेषणः । सा समासोक्तिः' (भामह II. 79). All the rest of ध्वनि they would have included under the figure पर्यायोक्त. जगन्नाथ remarks with great force and truth: 'ध्वनिकारात्प्राचीनैर्भामहोद्भटप्रभृतिभिः स्वग्रन्थेषु कुत्रापि ध्वनि-गुणीभूतव्यङ्ग्यादिशब्दा न प्रयुक्ता इत्येतावतैव तैर्ध्वन्यादयो न स्वीक्रियन्त इत्याधुनिकानां वाचोयुक्तिरयुक्तैव । यतः समासोक्तिव्याजस्तुत्यप्रस्तुतप्रशंसाद्यलङ्कारनिरूपणेन कियन्तोऽपि गुणीभूतव्यङ्ग्यभेदास्तैरपि निरूपिताः । अपरश्च सर्वोऽपि व्यङ्ग्यप्रपञ्चः पर्यायोक्तकुक्षौ निक्षिप्तः । न ह्यनुभवसिद्धोऽर्थो बालेनाप्यपह्नोतुं शक्यते । ध्वन्यादिशब्दैः परं व्यवहारो न कृतः । न ह्येतावतानङ्गीकारो भवति ।' रसगङ्गा० pp. 414-415. Though भामह and दण्डी did not speak of ध्वनि (or व्यङ्ग्य) as the pervading element of poetry, they spoke of वक्रोक्ति or अतिशयोक्ति as all important and as lying at the root of all figures; vide भामह II. 85 (सैषा सर्वैव०) and 'अलङ्कारान्तराणामप्येकमाहुः परायणम् । वागीशमहितामुक्तिमिमामतिशयाह्वयाम् ॥' काव्या. II. 220. For the meaning of वक्रोक्ति, vide section 12 below. रुद्रट defined a figure भाव (vide p. 145 above), in which there is some वस्तु (matter of fact) that is व्यङ्ग्य. He cites an example of implied उत्प्रेक्षा (IX. 13). Therefore he also was not unaware of व्यङ्ग्य sense. The prominence given to *alaṅkāras* by दण्डी and भामह (who says I. 13 न कान्तमपि निर्भूषं विभाति वनितामुखम् ।) persisted, though in a lesser degree, even in later times. Even though मम्मट is a thorough-going follower of the ध्वन्यालोक his treatment of *alaṅkāras* is longer than that of any other topic in his work. The number of *alaṅkāras* separately named by various writers exceeds two hundred. Vide I. A. vol. 41 for 1912 p. 204-208 for further information about *alaṅkāras*, Annals B. O. R. I. vol. I. pp. 87-98 (on 'History and significance of alaṅkāras' by Prof. Sovani); Annals B. O. R. I. vol. II. pp. 69-72 (on classification of *alaṅkāras* by Prof. P. K. Gode), Mookerjee Silver Jubilee vol. III pp. 661 ff), ('Psychological basis of alaṅkāras), History of Sanskrit Poetics' by Dr. De, vol. II pp. 41-94, 'Les Fleurs de Rhetorique dans l' Inde' by Prof. H. R. Divekar (1930), 'Use and abuse of alaṅkāras in Sanskrit Literature' (in 'Indian Culture' vol. III pp. 675-705 by Dr. Raghavan and in his work 'Some concepts &c' pp. 48-91), 'Bhoja's conception of Alaṅkāras' in 'Śṛṅgāraprakāśa' vol. I pp. 361-417.

Several questions arise in connection with *alaṅkāras* viz. the classification of them, difference between *guṇas* and *alaṅkāras*, the number of them and lastly their positioh in the theory of *rasa* and *dhvani*. Only a brief treatment on all these points can be attempted here. It appears that भामह (I. 15 शब्दाभिधेयालङ्कारभेदादिष्टं द्वयं तु नः ।) divided *alaṅkāras* into those of शब्द and those of अर्थ. Vide V. 66 also. दण्डी had the same distinction in view, since he defines arthālaṅkāras at length in the 2nd pariccheda and śabdālaṅkāras like Yamaka in the the third. Udbhaṭa enumerates four śabdālaṅkāras first, then treats of arthālaṅkāras, regards śleṣa (in IV) as an arthālaṅkāra but divides it into śabdaśleṣa and arthaśleṣa, for which he is severely criticized by Mammaṭa. Rudraṭa enumerates śabdālaṅkāras in II. 13 (such as Anuprāsa, Yamaka) and mentions arthālaṅkāras in VII. 9 and introduces four bases of classification in figures of sense (vide p. 143 above). In the सरस्वतीकण्ठाभरण II. 1 Bhoja divides *alaṅkāras* into those of *śabda*, those of *ārtha* and those of both; enumerates, defines and illustrates 24 of each. The most remarkable thing about this classification is that figures like उपमा, रूपक, अपह्नुति, अर्थान्तरन्यास are declared by him to be *alaṅkāras* of both *śabda* and *artha*. A few writers such as the authors of the अग्निपुराण and चमत्कारचन्द्रिका follow him in this respect. Bhoja (in सर. क. V. 8) divides वाङ्मय into वक्रोक्ति, रसोक्ति and स्वभावोक्ति. He elaborates this subject in the शृङ्गारप्रकाश and includes *guṇas* and *rasas* also among *alaṅkāras*. The अलं. स. gives a far more reasonable classification of arthālaṅkāras under seven heads viz. सादृश्य (उपमा, रूपक), विरोध (विरोध, विभावना, विशेषोक्ति), शृङ्खलाबन्ध (कारणमाला, एकावली), तर्कन्याय (काव्यलिङ्ग, अनुमान), काव्यन्याय (यथासंख्य, पर्याय, परिवृत्ति), लोकन्याय (प्रत्यनीक, प्रतीप, मीलित), गूढार्थप्रतीति (सूक्ष्म, व्याजोक्ति). The प्रतापरुद्रयशोभूषण (pp. 337-339) states the basis of classification of *alaṅkāras* and their differences from *guṇas* (सङ्घटनाश्रया गुणाः शब्दार्थाश्रयास्त्वलङ्काराः). For want of space I do not pursue this question further. Bharata mentioned four *alaṅkāras* and ten *guṇas*. Hence he must have made a distinction between them, although he does not express it. Daṇḍin includes *guṇas* under the word *alaṅkara* in the wider sense, as shown above. He defines *alaṅkāras* as काव्यशोभाकरान्धर्मानलङ्कारान् प्रचक्षते । ते चाद्यापि विकल्प्यन्ते कस्तान् कात्स्न्र्येन वक्ष्यति ॥ काव्यादर्श II. 1. भामह's treatment of *guṇas* is meagre. In काव्यालङ्कार II. 1-3 he defines three *guṇas* viz. माधुर्य, प्रसाद and ओजस्. Daṇḍin defines and illustrates ten *guṇas*, the names being the same as in भरत (17. 96=16. 96 of GOS ed. p. 334), काव्यादर्श (I. 41) and वामन (III 1. 4) though the definitions often differ. वामन defines 'काव्यशोभाया कर्तारो धर्मा गुणाः । तदतिशयहेतवस्त्वलङ्काराः ।' काव्या. सू. III. 1. 1-2. He further says that *guṇas* are नित्य and enumerates and defines ten *guṇas* of *śabda* and ten of *artha* (under the same names). The ध्वन्यालोक estblished the relation of गुणs and अलङ्कारs. When by a metaphor it was said that *rasa* or *dhvani* is the soul of poetry, then the *rasa* theorists had to state the place of guṇas and alaṅkāras. The ध्व० (II. 7) states that just as bravery and the like are the guṇas of the soul and bracelets are ornaments put on some limb of the body (wrist &c.), so the guṇas, *mādhurya*, *ojas* and *prasāda* are the guṇas of rasa (तमर्थमवलम्बन्ते येऽङ्गिनं ते गुणाः स्मृताः । अङ्गाश्रितास्त्वलङ्कारा मन्तव्याः कटकादिवत् ॥ ध्व. II 7) and it is further pointed out that mādhurya is pre-eminently appropriate to विप्रलम्भशृङ्गार (love of separated lovers) and करुण (tragic sentiment), the guṇa *ojas* to *raudrarasa* and *prasāda* (perspicuity) is common to all rasas and to all compositions. When the predominant rasa is śṛṅgāra, anuprāsa does not help in its evolution and to employ Yamaka in śṛṅgāra is a great mistake, particularly in विप्रलम्भ (ध्व० II. 15-16). Most of the later writers such as Mammaṭa hold that the *guṇas* are three, that they are the qualities of the soul of poetry like bravery (which is a quality[1] of the spirit), that they are permanently associated with rasa and figures of speech are like ornaments worn on the limbs of the body (ये रसस्याङ्गिनो धर्माः शौर्यादय इवात्मनः । उत्कर्षहेतवस्ते स्युरचलस्थितयो गुणाः ॥ उपकुर्वन्ति तं सन्तं येऽङ्गद्वारेण जातुचित् । हारादिवदलङ्कारास्तेऽनुप्रासोपमादयः ॥ काव्यप्रकाश VIII. 1-2). Most of the *ālaṅkārikas* follow this position.

The number of alaṅkāras has varied from time to time. भरत mentioned only four. There were ancient authors who described only five or eight figures of speech (vide p. 69 n. 2 above). The विष्णुधर्मोत्तरपुराण appears to have known only 18 alaṅkāras (p. 69 above). Bhaṭṭi, Daṇḍin, Bhāmaha, Udbhaṭa and Vāmana speak of between 30 to 40 alaṅkāras. Mammaṭa defines 61, Ruyyaka about 75, the Candrāloka one hundred and the Kuvalayānanda 115. The ध्वन्यभाववादिन् is made to say in the ध्व. p. 9 'सहस्रशो हि महात्मभिरन्यैरलङ्कारप्रकाराः प्रकाशिताः प्रकाश्यन्ते च ।'.

It is noteworthy that the same figure of speech bears different names such as स्वभावोक्ति and जाति, यथासंख्य or क्रम or संख्यान. Sometimes the same name denotes different figures of

---

1. एवमेते ह्यलङ्कारा गुणा दोषाश्च कीर्तिताः । प्रयोगमेषां च पुनर्वक्ष्यामि रससंश्रयम् ॥ नाट्यशास्त्र 17. 108.

speech as in the case of आक्षेप. The व्यक्तिविवेक (p. 88) remarks that although there are many alaṅkāras, yet even a capable poet employs only a few and that Upamā is like the life of alaṅkāras and is extremely enjoyable when it is implied. Vide Dr. Nobel in Z. D. M. G. vol. 66. pp. 283-293 and vol. 67 pp. 1-36 for the study of individual alaṅkāras such as व्याजस्तुति, सहोक्ति, विनोक्ति, प्रतिवस्तूपमा, दृष्टान्त, व्यतिरेक. Vide Prof. S. P. Bhattacharya on 'Neo-Buddhist nucleus in Alaṅkāraśāstra' in JASB. in vol. XXII (Letters 1956) part I pp. 49-66 and 'Influence of Buddhist logic on Alaṅkāraśāstra' by Shri Anantlal Thakur in GOI (Baroda) vol. VII pp. 257-261. The latter paper is full of dogmatic assertions made without any serious effort at research on technical words e.g. it asserts that words स्वसंवेदन, विप्रतिपत्ति, नान्तरीयक, अविनाभाव are exclusively terms of Buddhist logic. नान्तरीयक occurs in महाभाष्य on पा. I. 2. 39 and in श्लोकवार्तिक, वाक्याधिकरण, verse 343. The word विप्रतिपत्ति occurs in the last verse in कौटिल्य's अर्थशास्त्र. One should like to know the Sanskrit Buddhist work composed in 2nd century B. C. in which these two words occur. The word विप्रतिपत्ति occurs several times in the पूर्वमीमांसासूत्र of जैमिनि in the sense of 'conflict or contradiction' in V. I. 18, VIII. I. 32, IX. 3. 15.

11 The Rīti School. Vāmana is the foremost representative of this school. दण्डी also devotes considerable space to what are called *rītis* by others and most later writers on *alaṅkāras* have to say something about them. वामन in his own way made a distinction between *guṇas* and *alaṅkāras* (p. 376 above). Vāmana speaks of ten *guṇas* of word and the same ten *guṇas* of sense, viz. ओजः, प्रसाद, श्लेष, समता, समाधि, माधुर्य, सौकुमार्य, उदारता, अर्थव्यक्ति, कान्ति. दण्डी mentions ten *guṇas* under the same names, but makes no difference between *guṇas* of word and those of sense. The doctrine of *guṇas* was an ancient one. It was shown above that the inscription of रुद्रदामन् (150 A. D.) refers to some *guṇas* such as माधुर्य, कान्ति, उदारता and कौटिल्य also spoke of certain गुणs. It may be noted that कौटिल्य in II. 9. mentions six गुणs of a royal writing (शासन) or order viz. अर्थक्रम, सम्बन्ध, परिपूर्णता, माधुर्य, औदार्य, स्पष्टता, while the नाट्यशास्त्र names ten which include माधुर्य and उदार or उदात्त. This shows that कौटिल्य is much earlier than रुद्रदामन् and the नाट्यशास्त्र in the theory and practice of Poetics. That poets of certain regions cultivated certain poetic features is made clear in his हर्षचरित

by Bāṇa who is earlier than any extant writer on poetics (except भरत). 'श्लेषप्रायमुदीच्येषु प्रतीच्येष्वर्थमात्रकम् । उत्प्रेक्षा दाक्षिणात्येषु गौडेष्वक्षरडम्बरः ॥ (हर्षचरित Intro. verse 7). Here we have two important words, दाक्षिणात्य and गौड. Bāṇa was not a दाक्षिणात्य and hence he cannot be charged with any local patriotism or partiality for दाक्षिणात्यs. दण्डी does not employ the word रीति at all. Instead, he uses the word मार्ग throughout (काव्यादर्श I. 9, 40, 67, 75, 101). He expressly says that there are *several* dictions distinguished from each other by nice distinctions, but that he will describe only two, वैदर्भ and गौडीय, because the points of distinction between the two are very clear. It is interesting to note that he refers to गौडीय मार्ग or पद्धति as पौरस्त्य and employs the word डम्बर found in बाण as regards गौड (इत्यनालोच्य वैषम्यमर्थालङ्कारडम्बरौ । अवेक्षमाणा ववृधे पौरस्त्या काव्यपद्धतिः ॥ I. 50). Vide also काव्यादर्श I. 83 for पौरस्त्य. On the other hand he applies the word दाक्षिणात्य to वैदर्भमार्ग (अतो नैवमनुप्रासं दाक्षिणात्याः प्रयुञ्जते ॥ I. 60). In I. 92 he employs the word वर्त्म and states that the Gauḍas are very fond of अत्युक्ति. Even the काव्यमी. chap. VII. (p. 30) employs the word मार्ग 'किमर्थं पुनरनुपदेश्ययोर्ब्राह्मपारमेश्वरयोर्वाक्यमार्गयोरुपन्यासः—इत्याचार्याः.' The सरस्वतीकण्ठाभरण states that the different ways such as Vaidarbha are known as *mārga* 'वैदर्भादिकृतः पन्थाः काव्ये मार्ग इति स्मृतः । रीङ्गताविति धातोः सा व्युत्पत्त्या रीतिरुच्यते ॥ II. 27th कारिका (Nir. ed. of 1934). The ध्व. (III. 52 p. 290) remarks: 'एतद्ध्वनिवर्णनेन निर्णीतं काव्यतत्त्वमस्फुटस्फुरितं सदशक्नुवद्भिः प्रतिपादयितुं वैदर्भी गौडी पाञ्चाली चेति रीतयः प्रवर्तिताः'. This is probably a reference to वामन. The ध्वन्यालोक makes little of Rītis. Instead it says a good deal on वृत्तिs and सङ्घटना. The नाट्यशास्त्र (17. 96) enumerates the same ten *guṇas*. In the नाट्यशास्त्र *guṇas* and *alaṅkāras* occupy a subordinate position (17. 108). Vide नाट्यशास्त्र K. M. ed. 16. 97-108 and A.B. vol.II (GOS) p.334 chap.16. 96-112 for ten *guṇas*. They are described in the 17th chap. along with 36 other ornaments of poetry, while *rasa* occupies a prominent place in the नाट्यशास्त्र. Daṇḍin gives *guṇas* great prominence (I. 40-101) and the treatment of *guṇas* and *alaṅkāras* takes up almost the whole of his work; his work, however, assigns the most prominent place to *alaṅkāras* of *śabda* and *artha* and practically makes no distinction between *guṇas* and *alaṅkāras* (vide p. 374), while वामन differentiates between them. दण्डी thinks that the ten *guṇas* are the essence of the *vaidarbha* style or way or diction (मार्ग or रीति), while the *gauḍī* style generally presents the opposites or absence of the ten *guṇas* (except अर्थव्यक्ति, उदारता and समाधि which are required by the partisans of both styles) 'इति वैदर्भमार्गस्य प्राणा दश गुणाः स्मृताः । एषां विपर्ययः प्रायो दृश्यते गौडवर्त्मनि ॥ (काव्या. I. 42); *vide* also I. 75, 76, 100. It must be remembered that ओजः was required in prose even in वैदर्भी, but not in पद्य; while the गौडीयमार्ग regards ओजः as highest even in पद्य. He speaks of the *guṇa* समाधि (अन्यधर्मस्ततोन्यत्र लोकसीमानुरोधिना । सम्यगाधीयते यत्र स समाधिः स्मृतो यथा ॥ कुमुदानि निमीलन्ति etc.) as the all-in-all of poetry. But this does not mean that समाधि was the soul of poetry according to him. The words are more or less rhetorical. भामह does not accept that there are two distinct dictions like वैदर्भ and गौडीय (I. 31-33). वामन boldly asserts that *rīti* is the soul of poetry, that *rīti* consists in the special arrangement or combination of words and that the specialty lies in the possession of *guṇas* (रीतिरात्मा काव्यस्य । विशिष्टा पदरचना रीतिः । विशेषो गुणात्मा । काव्या. सू. I. 2. 6-8). He speaks of three *rītis* वैदर्भी, गौडीया and पाञ्चाली and says that the वैदर्भी style is endowed with all the ten *guṇas* while the Gauḍīyā specially affects ओजः and कान्ति, and पाञ्चाली is specially characterised by माधुर्य and सौकुमार्य (I. 2. 11-13). He cites 'गाहन्तां महिषा' (शाकुन्तल II. 6), दोर्दण्डाञ्चित° (महावीरचरित I. 54) and ग्रामेऽस्मिन् पथिकाय (अमरु° 131) as respectively the examples of the three styles. He clearly explains why the styles were so named (विदर्भादिषु दृष्टत्वात्तत्समाख्या' काव्या. सू. I. 2. 10; 'विदर्भगौडपाञ्चालेषु देशेषु तत्रत्यैः कविभिर्यथास्वरूपमुपलब्धत्वाद्देशसमाख्या । न पुनर्देशैः किञ्चिदुपक्रियते काव्यानाम्' वृत्ति). It must be observed that there is considerable difference between the definitions of the various *guṇas* given by the नाट्य°, दण्डी and वामन, though there is agreement in some. For want of space it is not possible to go into details. To take one or two examples: ओजः is defined by the नाट्य° (16. 99) as 'समासवद्भिर्विविधैर्विचित्रैश्च पदैर्युतम् । सा तु स्वरै (सानुस्वारै ?) रुदारैश्च तदोजः परिकीर्त्यते ॥'[1] and by दण्डी as 'ओजः समासभूयस्त्वम्'; while वामन defines as 'गाढबन्धत्वमोजः (III. 1. 5.) and 'अर्थस्य प्रौढिरोजः'. (III. 2. 2). समाधि is defines by she नाट्य° as अभियुक्तैर्विशेषस्तु योर्थस्यैवोपलभ्यते । तेन चार्थेन सम्पन्नः समाधिः परिकीर्त्यते ॥ (16. 97), but वामन defines it as 'आरोहावरोहक्रमः

---

1. This is the definition in the old K. M. ed. of 1894; the Chowkhambha edition defines ओजः as अविगीताविहीनोपि स्यादुदात्तानुभावकः । यत्र शब्दार्थसंपत्तिस्तदोजः परिकीर्तितम् ॥ 17. 103.

समाधिः' (III. 1. 13) and 'अर्थदृष्टिः समाधिः' (III. 2. 7); for दण्डी, vide काव्यादर्श I. 93 and 100. The *alaṅkāra* school looked upon *alaṅkāras*, which are really of secondary importance and without which *kāvya* can very well exist, as very important. The *rīti* school marks a very real advance over the *alaṅkāra* school. Though it did not reach the real essence of poetry, it approached very near it. Instead of looking upon mere *alaṅkāras* as the essence of poetry, it looked upon the *guṇas* as the essence. The *rīti* school was not yet well aware of that to which the *guṇas* belonged, they had only a glimmering or hazy notion about the real essenee of poetry. It is therefore that the ध्वनिकारिका (III. 57) says about the *rīti* school 'अस्फुटस्फुरितं &c'. वामन included in his वक्रोक्ति (defines as सादृश्याल्लक्षणा) all अविवक्षितवाच्यध्वनि and he seems to have found room for *rasas* in the *guṇa* कान्ति (दीप्तरसत्वं कान्तिः' काव्या. सू. III. 2. 14). *Guṇas* really belong to *rāsa* &c. the soul of poetry. The ध्व. pointed out that माधुर्य is a special characteristic of शृङ्गार, that it reaches the highest pitch in विप्रलम्भशृङ्गार and करुण, that ओजः is found specially where रौद्र, वीर and अद्भुत prevail and that प्रसाद is a *guṇa* common to all *rasas* (ध्वनिकारिका II. 8-11). भामह speaks very briefly of *guṇas* and refers to only three of them, माधुर्य, ओजस् and प्रसाद (II. 1-3). Māgha, who as shown above on p. 113, flourished about or before 750 A.D. appears to have only three *guṇās* in view when he says 'नैकमोजः प्रसादो वा रसभावविदः कवेः ॥' शिशुपालवध II. 83. Later writers like मम्मट and हेमचन्द्र reduce the *guṇas* to the above three and show that the rest are either included in the three or are really दोषाभाव. The number of *rītis* varies with different writers. राजशेखर in his काव्यमी. (chap. VII. p. 31) quotes a verse that gives the same names of the three *rītis* as वामन; but in his कर्पूरमञ्जरी he speak of three *rītis* as वच्छोमी (from वत्सगुल्म, modern Basim in Berar), मागही (मागधी) and पञ्चालिआ. रुद्रट and अग्निपुराण (chap. 340) speak of four (लाटीया is added); vide II. 4-6). वाग्भटालङ्कार gives only two like दण्डी. वाग्भट's काव्यानुशासन names three like वामन; while भोज[1] enumerates six, adding आवन्ती, मागधी and लाटी to वामन's three.

We must now say a few words about वृत्ति and प्रवृत्ति and

---

1. The सर. क. II. 27 says: वैदर्भादिकृतः . . . रीतिरुच्यते । quoted on p. 379 above and vide same verse in साहित्यमीमांसा p. 87.

their relation to *rīti*. भरत in नाट्यशास्त्र 22 (=GOS ed. chap. 20) speaks of the mythical origin of the four वृत्तिs called भारती, सात्वती, कैशिकी and आरभटी and their aṅgas (vide p. 34 above). The नाट्यशास्त्र (old K. M. ed. 20. 62) stated that the vṛttis were (like) the mothers of nāṭya[1] (वृत्तयो नाट्यमातरः) and further provides that कैशिकीवृत्ति should be employed in शृङ्गार and हास्य, सात्वती in वीर, रौद्र and अद्भुत, आरभटी in भयानक, बीभत्स and रौद्र, भारती in करुण and अद्भुत. the साहित्यदर्पण (VI. 122-123) also calls them मातृकाः and slightly differs as to the *rasas* for which each is proper. The रसार्णवसुधाकर (pp. 69-71) gives the same rule, offers a mythical origin of the वृत्तिs and fanciful derivations of the names (e. g. भारती from भार burden, कैशिकी from केश). The ध्व. III. 33 remarks that the employment of words and senses that are favourable to a *rasa* and are endowed with appropriateness are known as various vṛttis (रसाद्यनुगुणत्वेन व्यवहारोऽर्थशब्दयोः। औचित्यवान्यस्ता एता वृत्तयो विविधाः स्मृताः ॥); and the वृत्ति on that कारिका runs: व्यवहारो हि वृत्तिरित्युच्यते। तत्र रसानुगुण औचित्यवान्वाच्याश्रयो यो व्यवहारस्ता एता कैशिक्याद्या वृत्तयः। वाचकाश्रयाश्चोपनागरिकाद्याः। वृत्तयो हि रसादितात्पर्येण संनिवेशिताः कामपि नाट्यस्य काव्यस्य च छायामावहन्ति। रसादयो हि द्वयोरपि तयोर्जीवभूताः। इतिवृत्तादि तु शरीरभूतमेव।. This shows that इतिवृत्त (plot) is the body of नाट्य or काव्य, the वृत्तिs called उपनागरिका and others are concerned with the words (वाचक). The ध्वन्यालोक (on III. 19 p. 202) remarks यदि वा वृत्तीनां भरतप्रसिद्धानां कैशिक्यादीनां काव्यालङ्कारान्तरप्रसिद्धानामुपनागरिकाद्यानां वा यदनौचित्यमविषये निबन्धनं तदपि रसभङ्गहेतुः. The नाट्यशास्त्र I. 46 (Ch. ed. 45-46 and GOS ed. vol. I. chap. I. 45-46) states that the कैशिकी can be properly rendered by women (actresses) only. उद्भट (*varga*) I) defines the three वृत्तिs of words as follows: शषाभ्यां रेफसंयोगैष्टवर्गेण च योजिता। परुषा नाम वृत्तिः स्याद् ह्लह्वाद्यैश्च संयुता ॥ सरूपसंयोगयुतां मूर्ध्नि वर्गान्त्ययोगिभिः। स्पर्शैर्युतां च मन्यन्ते उपनागरिकां बुधाः। शेषैर्वर्णैर्यथायोगं कथिता कोमलाख्यया। ग्राम्यां वृत्तिं प्रशंसन्ति काव्येष्वादृतबुद्धयः ॥'. The काव्यप्रकाश (VIII) first shows what combinations of letters are favourable to the *guṇas* called माधुर्य, ओजस् and प्रसाद and then remarks that the उपनागरिकावृत्ति is constituted by letters that

1. In the Ch. ed. (chap. 22. 64=GOS vol. III p. 105 chap. 20-72) the reading is वृत्तयो नाट्यसंश्रयाः. The reading नाट्यमातरः is supported by लोचन p. 226; सागरनन्दिन् (in नाटकलक्षणरत्नकोष) line 1386 reads नाट्यस्य मातरः. अभिनवभारती (vol. I. p. 22 states शृङ्गाररसस्य तु नामग्रहणमपि न तया (कैशिक्या) विना शक्यमिति।'.

are indicative of mādhurya, परुषा by letters indicative of *ojas* and *komalā* (called ग्राम्या by some) by letters other than those indicative of माधुर्य and ओजस्. The काव्यप्रकाश notes that Vāmana and others regard उपनागरिका, परुषा and कोमला as the three rītis respectively called वैदर्भी, गौडी, पाञ्चाली (एतास्तिस्रो वृत्तयो वामनादीनां मते वैदर्भीगौडीपाञ्चालाख्या रीतयो मताः। काव्यप्र. (IX. p. 498)· Rudraṭa (II. 4-6) speaks of four rītis वैदर्भी, पान्चाली, लाटीया and गौडीया based upon the absence of compounds or the presence of a few or many compounded words. Rudraṭa (II. 19) speaks of five वृत्तिs of अनुप्रास viz. मधुरा, प्रौढा, परुषा, ललिता and भद्रा, all of which are based on the employment of certain letters and conjunct consonants, and his मधुरा and परुषा are like उपनागरिका and परुषा of काव्यप्रकाश. But रुद्रट's use of them is restricted to अनुप्रास alone. The नाट्यशास्त्र (14.36) mentions four प्रवृत्तिs, आवन्ती, दाक्षिणात्या, पान्चाली, ओड्रमागधी and states that प्रवृत्ति[1] is concerned with the dress, languages and manners of various countries and that the दाक्षिणात्या प्रवृत्ति is constituted by plenty of dancing, singing and music and with Kaiśikī and *abhinaya* of the limbs which is clever, pleasing and delicate. The सर. क. (II. 3) includes रीति and वृत्ति among the 24 śabdālaṅkāras and then mentions six varieties of रीति (वैदर्भी, पान्चाली, गौडीया, आवन्तिका, लाटीया, मागधी) and six of वृत्ति (viz. कैशिकी and the other three plus मध्यमारभटी and मध्यमकैशिकी). In this welter of conflicting views I should like to quote the काव्यमी. (III. p. 9) 'तत्र वेषविन्यासक्रमः प्रवृत्तिः, विलासविन्यासक्रमो वृत्तिः, वचनविन्यासक्रमो रीतिः'. सागरनन्दिन् (ना. ल .र. को. p. 44) adopts the words विलास...वृत्तिः and provides that भारतीवृत्ति is the aṅga of वैदर्भ, गौडीय and पाञ्चाल rītis (p. 52, lines 1231-33), सात्वती is an aṅga of पाञ्चाली (p. 55 line 1302), कैशिकी is an aṅga of वैदर्भी (p. 57 line 1346) and आरभटी of गौडी (p. 58 line 1325). The विष्णुधर्मोत्तर (III. 20. 53-60) has to say that प्रवृत्तिs are the abode of वृत्तिs.

Vide Dr. Raghavan on vṛttis in J. O. R., Madras, vol. VI pp. 346-370, vol. VII pp. 33-52, pp. 91-112, in 'Some concepts &c.' pp. 182-190, 'Śṛṅgāraprakāśa' pp. 196-215 (for रीति, वृत्ति and प्रवृत्ति). For detailed discussion on *rītis*, vide I. H.

1. प्रवृत्तिरिति कस्मात्। उच्यते पृथिव्यां नानादेशवेषभाषाचारवार्ताः ख्यापयतीति प्रवृत्तिः।...तत्र दाक्षिणात्यास्तावद् बहुनृत्तगीतवाद्या कैशिकीप्रायाः चतुरमधुरललिताङ्गाभिनयाश्च। नाट्यशास्त्र 14. p. 165 (Ch. ed. GOS=vol. II. p. 205, chap. 13 and K. M. ed. chap. 13 p. 216).

Q. vol. III. pp. 375-394 on Gauḍī by Prof. S.P. Bhattacharya; Dr. P. C. Lahiri's 'Concepts of rīti and guṇa' (1937) and his paper in I. H. Q. IX p. 448 ff 'theory of rīti and guṇa in Agnipurāṇa' and pp. 835 ff on 'Vāmana's theory;' Dr. Raghavan in I. H. Q. X pp. 767-779, in Kuppuswami com. vol. pp. 89-118, 'History of Guṇas' in his work on Śṛṅgāra-prakāśa vol. I pp. 258-360 and in 'Some concepts &c.' pp. 131-181 on rīti and pp. 182-193 on 'History of वृत्ति', I. H. Q. vol. 8 pp. 257-266 on 'Kuntaka's conception of guṇas'; Dr. De on 'Gauḍī rīti' in New I. A. vol. I. pp. 74-76. The subject of rīti and guṇa has been worn threadbare by the above writings.

Another word that is employed is पाक. वामन (in काव्या. सू. वृ. I. 3. 15) quotes the following verse: यत्पदानि त्यजन्त्येव परिवृत्तिसहिष्णुताम्। तं शब्दन्यासनिष्णाताः शब्दपाकं प्रचक्षते ॥. This is quoted in the काव्यमी. on p. 20 as the view of वामनीयाः and then the view of अवन्तिसुन्दरी is quoted that this is incapacity (अशक्ति) and not pāka, since great poets are able to express the same matter in many ways. The काव्यमी. (pp. 20-21) mentions several kinds of पाकs such as नारिकेलपाक, क्रमुकपाक, मृद्वीकापाक. The एकावली offers (p. 22) several definitions of पाक which are passed over here. Vide above for reference to अग्निपुराण.

The ध्व. in several places employs the word सङ्घटना (III. 2, 5). This is dealt with below under 'ध्वनि school'.

12 **The Vakrokti theory**. The word वक्रोक्ति has been used in literature from ancient times and bears several meanings. बाण (कादम्बरी para 44 of my edition and Peterson's p. 51) speaks of 'gay men expert in वक्रोक्ति' (वक्रोक्तिनिपुणेन विलासिजनेन). In another place where चन्द्रापीड makes a bantering humorous speech (क्रीडालाप) about the quarrel of the parrot परिहास and the jealous *maina*, the parrot addresses him with the word 'एषापि बुध्यत एवैतावतीर्वक्रोक्तीः, इयमपि जानात्येव परिहासजल्पितानि ।...अभूमिरेषा भुजङ्गभङ्गिभाषितानाम् । Peterson's ed. pp, 195-196. Here वक्रोक्ति is used in the sense of क्रीडालाप or परिहासजल्पित.[1] In the अमरुशतक (23) also the word is used in the same sense 'सा पत्युः प्रथमेपराध-

---

1. It is surprising that in spite of these reference to वक्रोक्ति in the कादम्बरी Dr. De states on p. XI of his Intro. to वक्रोक्तिजीवित (first edition) 'they (i. e. Subandhu and Bāṇa) have not mentioned *vakrokti*.'

समये सख्योपदेशं विना नो जानाति सविभ्रमाङ्गवलनावक्रोक्तिसंसूचनम् ।'. By दण्डी the word is used as opposed to स्वभावोक्ति and he says that श्लेष generally lends charm to वक्रोक्ति (II. 363 श्लेषः सर्वासु पुष्णाति प्रायो वक्रोक्तिषु श्रियम्। भिन्नं द्विधा स्वभावोक्तिर्वक्रोक्तिश्चेति वाङ्मयम् ॥). So वक्रोक्ति is a striking mode of speech, often based on श्लेष, and differing from the plain, matter of fact ordinary mode of speech. भामह used the word in the same sense, saying that वक्रोक्ति sets off to advantage all figures of speech (II. 85). He required वक्रोक्ति to be present in all *alaṅkāras*. Vide the following from भामह 'वक्राभिधेयशब्दोक्तिरिष्टा वाचामलङ्कृतिः ॥' (I. 36); हेतुश्च...नालङ्कारतया मतः। समुदायाभिधानस्य वक्रोक्त्यनभिधानतः ॥' (II. 86); 'वाचां वक्रार्थशब्दोक्तिरलङ्काराय कल्पते ।' (V. 66); वक्रवाचां कवीनां ये प्रयोगं प्रति साधवः ।' (VI. 23). The लोचन (p. 260) quotes भामह (I. 36) and explains 'शब्दस्य हि वक्रता अभिधेयस्य च वक्रता लोकोत्तीर्णेन रूपेणावस्थानम्'. This insistence on वक्रोक्ति emphasises two characteristics of poetry, viz. that, though poetry necessarily takes the words used in common speech, its choice of words is different from that of ordinary speech i.e. its diction is different and that the poet gives expression to striking combinations or relations of things which are beyond the reach of ordinary matter-of-fact men. The वक्रोक्तिजीवितकार used the word वक्रोक्ति mainly in this sense, but he goes too far in making वक्रोक्ति the soul of poetry. In this respect he is similar to the *alaṅkāra* school. Vide above part I. pp. 227-228 for detailed statement of his views. जयरथ says that वक्रोक्ति is due to कविप्रतिभा (p. 9). The अलं. स. p. 9 says वक्रोक्तिजीवितकारः पुनर्वैदग्ध्यभङ्गीभणितिस्वभावां बहुविधां वक्रोक्तिमेव प्राधान्यात् काव्यजीवितमुक्तवान् ।' on which जयरथ after quoting वक्रोक्ति...रूच्यते (p. 227 above) proceeds काव्यजीवितमिति काव्यस्यानुमापकम् । तां विना काव्यमेव न स्यादित्यर्थः । यदाह—विचित्रो यत्र वक्रोक्तिवैचित्र्यं जीवितायते—इति (वक्रोक्तिजीवित १. ४२) । व्यापारस्येति कविप्रतिभोल्लिखितस्य कर्मणः । प्रतिभानिर्वर्तित्वमन्तरेण हि वक्रोक्तिरेव न स्यादिति ।'. कुन्तक's definition of वक्रोक्ति as 'वैदग्ध्यभङ्गीभणितिः' seems to be borrowed from some one like अवन्तिसुन्दरी 'विदग्धभणितिभङ्गिनिवेद्यं वस्तुनो रूपं न नियतस्वभावमिति अवन्तिसुन्दरी' (काव्यमी. p. 46). The word विदग्ध has been used from ancient times as opposed to विद्वत् and means 'versed in *belle lettres*, proficient in poetic or clever speech'. Vide ध्व० 'प्रसिद्धिश्चेयमस्त्येव विदग्धविद्वत्परिषत्सु' etc. (p. 300); ध्व. p. 250 'विदग्धपरिषत्सु'. In the मालतीमाधव (I.) when मकरन्द hears the double-meaning words 'रमणीय एष वः सुमनसां संनिवेशः etc.' he ejaculates 'अहो वैदग्ध्यम्'. For भङ्गि see above quotation p. 384 from कादम्बरी, ध्व. pp. 209, 362 and लोचन p. 224.

The word भणिति occurs in the वासवदत्ता (11th Intro. verse) 'अविदितगुणापि सत्कविभणितिः कर्णेषु वमति मधुधाराम् ।'; vide ध्व. p. 304 'भणितिकृतं वैचित्र्यमात्रं'. वक्रोक्ति is regarded as an अलङ्कार and given a totally different sense by वामन 'सादृश्याल्लक्षणा वक्रोक्तिः' (वक्रोक्ति is indication based upon resemblance) and the instance is 'उन्मिमील कमलं सरसीनां कैरवं च निमिमील मुहूर्तात्' (अत्र धर्मावुन्मीलननिमीलने सादृश्यादिकाससङ्कोचौ लक्षयतः). This would be the समाधिगुण of काव्यादर्श (vide I. 93-94). रुद्रट regards वक्रोक्ति as a *śabdālaṅkāra* and gives two varieties, काकुवक्रोक्ति and श्लेषवक्रोक्ति. He is followed in this by मम्मट, वाग्भटालङ्कार, रुय्यक, काव्यानुशासन of वाग्भट, एकावली and हेमचन्द्र. But रुय्यक regards वक्रोक्ति as an अर्थालङ्कार and remarks 'वक्रोक्तिशब्दश्चालङ्कारसामान्यवचनोपीहालङ्कारविशेषे संज्ञितः' (p. 222). It will be thus seen that the वक्रोक्ति of रुद्रट and रुय्यक is much narrower in scope than the वक्रोक्ति of भामह, दण्डी and of the वक्रोक्तिजीवित.[1] The वक्रोक्ति theory is really an offshoot of the *alaṅkāra* school and need not be separately recognized.

The राघवपाण्डवीय (I. 41) says 'सुबन्धुर्बाणभट्टश्च कविराज इति त्रयः । वक्रोक्तिमार्गनिपुणाश्चतुर्थो विद्यते न वा ॥'. Peterson in his second Report p. 64 quotes from a ms. हरिहारावलि a verse about मेण्ठ attributed to बाण 'वक्रोक्त्या मेण्ठराजस्य वहन्त्या सृणिरूपताम् । आविद्धा इव धुन्वन्ति मूर्धानं कविकुञ्जराः ॥'. The साहित्यमीमांसा p. 115 follows the वक्रोक्तिजीवित in saying that वक्रत्व exists in ध्वनि, वर्ण, पदार्थ, वाक्य, प्रकरण and प्रबन्ध. The सर. क. V. 8 divides all वाङ्मय into वक्रोक्ति, रसोक्ति and स्वभा-

---

1. For four other words that occur very frequently in works on Poetics in a similar sense, are विच्छित्ति and वैचित्र्य, चारुत्व and चमत्कार; vide ध्व. p. 159, लोचन pp. 5 and 9, व्यक्तिविवेकव्याख्या p. 44, अलं. स. p. 58 (for विच्छित्ति) and ध्व. p. 243 and लोचन p. 5 for वैचित्र्य. विच्छित्तिशोभिनैकेन भूषणेनेव कामिनी । पदद्योत्येन सुकवेर्ध्वनिना भाति भारती ॥ ध्व. p. 159 (a परिकरश्लोक)). The word वक्रोक्ति occurs in the verse quoted in ध्व. on p. 10, which the लोचन ascribes to मनोरथ. For चारु vide ध्व. pp. 32, 39, 42, 178 (on III. 10); 'आनन्दो निर्वृत्यात्मा चमत्कारापरपर्यायः' लोचन p. 13; अ.भा. (vol. I p. 281) says 'सर्वथा रसनात्मकवीतविघ्नप्रतीतिग्राह्यो भाव एव रसः ।...तथाहि लोके सकलविघ्नविनिर्मुक्ता संवित्तिः । एवं चमत्कार-निर्वेशरसनास्वादनभोगसमापत्तिलयविश्रान्त्यादिशब्दैरभिधीयते' ।'; काव्यप्र. IV. p. 93 'अलौकिकचमत्कारकारी शृङ्गारादिको रसः' ।; रसग. p. 4 'लोकोत्तरत्वं चाह्लादगतश्चमत्कारापरपर्यायोऽनुभवसाक्षिको जातिविशेषः ।'. Vide Dr. Raghavan in Annals of B. O. R. I. vol. 16 pp. 131 ff, J. O. R. Madras, vol. VI. 218-222 and in 'Some concepts' pp. 268-271.

वोक्ति and states that *rasokti* catches (hearts of सहृदय) most of all. Vide Dr. Raghavan's work on Bhoja's शृङ्गारप्रकाश part I pp. 120-144 'Bhoja and Vakrokti'.

13 The Dhvani School. For an analysis of the ध्वन्यालोक vide pp. 199-201 above. The *dhvani* theory is only an extension of the *rasa* theory. It took over the idea of *rasa* into the field of poetry. The *rasa* theory took account only of a complete dramatic work. The main object of a dramatic work is the evolution of some *rasa*, śṛṅgāra, karuṇa etc. by means of विभाव s, अनुभाव s etc. This naturally presupposes a composition of some length. But if there be a single charming verse, it cannot be said to evolve a *rasa*, although it may suggest some one or more of the constituents that bring about the relishing of a complete *rasa*. Such single pieces would be outside the pale of *kāvya*, if it were said that the soul of *kāvya* is *rasa* alone. It was shown above that *rasa* is always suggested and not directly expressed. Hence, applying the same reasoning, the ध्वन्यालोक said that the best poetry is that which contains a charming व्यङ्ग्य sense. 'अयमेव हि महाकवेर्मुख्यो व्यापारो यद्रसादीनेव मुख्यतया काव्यार्थीकृत्य तद्व्यक्त्यनुगुणत्वेन शब्दानामर्थानां चोपनिबन्धनम्। एतच्च रसादितात्पर्येण काव्यनिबन्धनं भरतादावपि सुप्रसिद्धमेवेति...। रसादयो हि द्वयोरपि तयोः (काव्यनाट्ययोः) जीवभूताः' ध्व. p. 225-226; 'सारभूतो ह्यर्थः स्वशब्दानभिधेयत्वेन प्रकाशितः सुतरामेव शोभामावहति। प्रसिद्धिश्चेयमस्त्येव विदग्धविद्वत्परिषत्सु यदभिमततरं वस्तु व्यङ्ग्यत्वेन प्रकाश्यते न साक्षाच्छब्दवाच्यत्वेनैव।' ध्व. p. 300. Though it is possible to extract some sort of व्यङ्ग्य sense from any sentence or word, still all words or sentences are not necessarily *kāvya*, but only those words, which have particular qualities and are arranged in a particular manner and contain a charming व्यङ्ग्य, constitute *kāvya*. *Vide* लोचन (p. 32) 'तेन सर्वत्रापि न ध्वननसद्भावेपि तथा व्यवहारः। आत्मसद्भावेपि कचिदेव जीवव्यवहार इत्युक्तं प्रागेव।'. The ध्वन्यालोक refutes at great length the theory of some that ध्वनि is गुणवृत्ति or लक्षणा (secondary sense due to the possession of some quality common to two objects); vide ध्व. I. 17 'भक्त्या बिभर्ति नैकत्वं रूपभेदादयं ध्वनिः। अतिव्याप्तेरथाव्याप्तेर्न चासौ लक्ष्यते तया॥'. The ध्व. (p. 18) divided व्यङ्ग्य sense into three varieties, रसादि, अलङ्कार and वस्तु. Under the first are included not only the nine *rasas* but all the *bhāvas* and their *ābhāsas* also. What is meant by वस्तुध्वनि is this that a mere fact is suggested by words that express another sense.[1] What is

1. An example of वस्तुध्वनि is 'पथिक नात्र स्रस्तरमस्ति मनाक्प्रस्तर-

meant by an *alaṅkāra-dhvani* is this that what is suggested is an imaginative thing (not a matter of fact) which if expressed in so many words would assume the form of a figure of speech. The suggestion of *rasa* and others does not require explanation here. The ध्व. seems to hold like Wordsworth that poetry is the spontaneous overflow of powerful feelings (क्रौञ्चद्वन्द्ववियोगोत्थः शोकः श्लोकत्वमागतः ॥ p. 31. When Vālmīki was powerfully affected by the spectacle of the death of the loving क्रौञ्च bird at the hands of the hunter, the sage's imagination was stirred and he burst forth into an impassioned song. But it is not to be supposed that the sage was himself दुःखित nor is it to be supposed that the reader when he reads the impassioned poem is simply दुःखित; for, if that were really so, no one would feel delight in reading the poem. Vide लोचन p. 31 'तेन रस एव वस्तुत आत्मा वस्त्वलङ्कारध्वनी तु सर्वथा रसं प्रति पर्यवस्येते इति वाच्यादुत्कृष्टौ तौ इत्यभिप्रायेण ध्वनिः काव्यस्यात्मेति सामान्येनोक्तम् । प्राथमिकानामभ्यासार्थिनां यदि परं चित्रेण व्यवहारः प्राप्तपरिणतीनां तु ध्वनिरेव प्राधान्येन काव्यमिति स्थितमेतत् ।'. The अलं. स. (pp. 13-14) very clearly and succintly hits off the position of the ध्वन्यालोक as follows : 'वाच्यार्थस्यैव व्यङ्ग्यरूपस्य गुणालङ्कारोपस्कर्तव्यत्वेन प्राधान्याद्विश्रान्तिधामत्वादात्मत्वं सिद्धान्तितवान् । व्यापारस्य विषयमुखेन स्वरूपप्रतिलम्भात्तत्प्राधान्येन प्राधान्यात्स्वरूपेण विदितत्वाभावाद्विषयस्यैव समग्रभरसहिष्णुत्वम् । तस्माद्विषय एव व्यङ्ग्यनामा जीवितत्वेन वक्तव्यः । यस्य गुणालङ्कारकृतचारुत्वपरिग्रहसाम्राज्यम् । रसादयस्तु जीवितभूता नालङ्कारत्वेन वाच्याः । अलङ्काराणामुपस्कारकत्वाद्रसादीनां च प्राधान्येनोपस्कार्यत्वात् । तस्माद् व्यंग्य एव वाक्यार्थीभूतः काव्यजीवितमित्येष एव पक्षो वाक्यार्थविदां सहृदयानामावर्जकः.' The ध्वन्यालोक divided काव्य into three varieties, the best or ध्वनिकाव्य, गुणीभूतव्यङ्ग्य and चित्र. In the last it included all *alaṅkāras* of word and sense. Vide ध्व II. 4 (p. 82 for ध्वनिकाव्य), III 35 (p. 256 for गुणीभूतव्यङ्ग्य), III 42-43 (p. 275-276) for चित्रकाव्य. But the

---

स्थले ग्रामे । उन्नतपयोधरं प्रेक्ष्य यदि वससि तदा वस ॥'. स्रस्तरं कटाद्यास्तरणं पाषाणमयेऽस्मिन् ग्रामे नास्ति किन्तु मेघो वर्षणाय उन्नमतीति दृष्ट्वा यदि वससि तदा वस ।. पयोधर also means स्तन. The expressed sense is 'you will have to lie down on a stone, but a cloud is impending; hence you may not proceed and stay here'; but the suggested sense (वस्तुध्वनि) is यद्युपभोगक्षमोसि तदा आस्स्व.

1. An example of अलङ्कारध्वनि is 'निरुपादानसम्भारमभित्तावेव तन्वते । जगच्चित्रं नमस्तस्मै कलाश्लाघ्याय शूलिने ॥'. शङ्कर has no material and yet he creates this wonderful world. So he is superior to every one. Hence व्यतिरेकालङ्कार is suggested.

ध्वन्यालोक is careful to point out that a true poet should never waste his powers over composing poems that have no relation to *rasa* 'एतच्च चित्रं कवीनां विशृङ्खलगिरां रसादितात्पर्यमनपेक्ष्यैव काव्यप्रवृत्तिदर्शनादस्माभिः परिकल्पितम् । इदानींतनानां तु न्याय्ये काव्यनयव्यवस्थापने...एव न शोभते ।' (p. 277 quoted on p. 166 above). *Vide* his remarks on अनुप्रास and यमक (II. 15-16 pp. 103-104). After having dealt with ध्वनि as the soul of poetry it assigns to *guṇas* and *alaṅkāras* their proper position (ध्व. 75 'तमर्थमवलम्बन्ते &c.); vide p. 378-79 above on which the वृत्ति is 'ये तमर्थं रसादिलक्षणमङ्गिनं सन्तमवलम्बन्ते ते गुणाः शौर्यादिवत् । वाच्यवाचकलक्षणान्यङ्गानि ये पुनराश्रितास्तेऽलङ्कारा मन्तव्याः कटकादिवदिति'. About the *rītis* (III. 47 p. 290) he says that they are explained by the position assigned to the *guṇas* (as the लोचन remarks on p. 290 रीतिर्हि गुणेष्वेव पर्यवसायिता). It speaks of सङ्घटना (ध्व० III. 2, 5, 6) which means nothing more than वर्णरचना or पदरचना[1]. The काव्यप्र. VIII states : अवृत्तिर्मध्यवृत्तिर्वा माधुर्ये घटना तथा and on the following कारिका it says 'विकटा सङ्घटना ओजसि' (p. 486), thus making it threefold (असमासा, मध्यमसमासा, and दीर्घसमासा) and that each of the three is generally suited to some particular *rasa* or *rasas* (though not as an invariable rule) and that *guṇas* are not of the nature of सङ्घटना, nor are they dependent upon सङ्घटना, but that the appropriateness of सङ्घटना is determined by the *rasa* and by the speaker and the subject (vide ध्व. pp. 164-169). The वृत्तिs dependent upon words such as उपनागरिका and those dependent upon sense (such as कैशिकी) are on the same level with *rītis* i. e. like the latter they all depend upon *rasa* as the soul.[1] Compare ध्व. p. 226 'तत्र रसानुगुण औचित्यवान् वाच्याश्रयो यो व्यवहारस्ता एताः कैशिकाद्या वृत्तयः । वाचकाश्रयाश्चोपनागरिकाद्याः । वृत्तयो हि रसादितात्पर्येण संनिवेशिताः कामपि नाट्यस्य काव्यस्य च

1. ध्व. III. 2 says that असंलक्ष्यक्रमध्वनि shines forth in वर्ण, पद, वाक्य, सङ्घटना and प्रबन्ध and the लोचन remarks 'सङ्घटना पदगता वाक्यगता च । सङ्घटितवाक्यसमुदायः प्रबन्धः' (p. 159). ध्व. III. 5 states that सङ्घटना is of three kinds, असमासा, मध्यमसमासा and दीर्घसमासा. On p. 166 ध्व. remarks 'तस्मान्न गुणाः संघटनास्वरूपा न च संघटनाश्रया गुणाः'. The two, सङ्घटना and गुण, are more or less independent (ध्व० p. 169 तस्मादन्ये गुणा अन्या च सङ्घटना). ओजस् is a गुण and is specially suited to रौद्ररस; but as in 'यो यः शस्त्रं बिभर्ति' (वेणीसंहार III.) there is ओजस्, but असमासा सङ्घटना. In 'अनवरतनयनजललवनिपतनपरिमुषितपत्रलेखान्तम् । करतलनिषण्णमवले वदनमिदं कं न तापयति ॥' there is शृङ्गार (in which there should be a few समासs ordinarily) and also दीर्घसमासा सङ्घटना.

च्छायामावहन्ति। रसादयो हि द्वयोरपि तयोर्जीवभूता इतिवृत्तादि तु शरीरभूतमेव ॥'; vide also ध्व. pp. 200 and 291. The three वृत्तिs, उपनागरिका, परुषा and ग्राम्या (called कोमला by some) are spoken of by उद्भट, मम्मट (IX) and other writers; 'शषाभ्यां रेफसंयोगैष्टवर्गेण च योजिता। परुषा नाम वृत्तिः स्याद् ह्लह्वाद्यैश्च संयुता॥ सरूपसंयोगयुतां मूर्ध्नि वर्गान्त्ययोगिभिः। स्पर्शैर्युतां च मन्यन्ते उपनागरिकां बुधाः॥ शेषैर्वर्णैर्यथायोगं कथिता कोमलाख्यया।' उद्भट I. उपनागरिका is appropriate to शृङ्गार, परुषा to वीर and रौद्र, and कोमला to हास्य. रुद्रट (II. 19) enumerates five वृत्तिs (मधुरा, ललिता, प्रौढा, परुषा and भद्रा). The वृत्तिs peculiar to the नाट्यशास्त्र are four, भारती, कैशिकी, सात्वती and आरभटी. All these propositions laid down by the ध्वन्यालोक about the several component parts of a complete theory of Poetics are implicitly followed by all later writers on Poetics. The word ध्वनि has five senses according to the लोचन. According to ध्व. I. 13 (यत्रार्थः...व्यंक्तः काव्यविशेषः स ध्वनिरिति सूरिभिः कथितः॥) ध्वनि means a special kind of काव्य. The लोचन (p. 39) remarks 'कारिकया तु प्राधान्येन समुदाय एव वाच्यरूपमुखतया ध्वनिरिति प्रतिपादितम्।'. The first kārikā asserts that ध्वनि is the soul of poetry ('आत्मशब्दस्य तत्त्वशब्देनार्थं विवृण्वानः' &c. लोचन p. 3). Hence the second meaning of ध्वनि is the essence of काव्य i.e. suggested sense (व्यङ्ग्य). On कारिका I. 17 (p. 60) the लोचन says 'अत्रोक्तप्रकार इति पञ्चस्वर्थेषु योज्यम्। शब्देऽर्थे व्यापारे व्यङ्ग्ये समुदाये च।'. शब्द and वाच्यार्थ are called ध्वनि (ध्वनतीति), व्यंग्य is called ध्वनि (ध्वन्यते इति). ध्वनि also means व्यापार (ध्वनन) as लोचन p. 21 says 'तस्मादभिधातात्पर्यलक्षणाव्यतिरिक्तश्चतुर्थोऽसौ व्यापारो ध्वनन-द्योतन-व्यञ्जनप्रत्यायनावगमनादिसोदरव्यपदेशनिरूपितोऽभ्युपगन्तव्यः'. It is therefore that the रसगङ्गाधर says 'ध्वनिकृतामालङ्कारिकसरणिव्यवस्थापकत्वात्' (p. 425). भामह, दण्डी, उद्भट, वामन and रुद्रट expatiate on शब्द, अर्थ, गुणs, अलङ्कारs and दोषs. The school of ध्वनि regarded these as of secondary importance, they are only the external appearance of poetry and it holds that we must look deeper into the inner or implicit meaning viz. the emotional atmosphere or mood that underlies the best poetry. As in Vedānta, objects of experience are beld to be not the ultimate reality but only manifestations of Reality, so words and the expressed meaning came to be regarded as the mere external appearance of poetry and the emotional mood which a poem communicates to those who read it came to be regarded as the essence of poetry. Poetry came to be regarded as having a double purpose viz. giving the highest delight (सद्यः परनिर्वृति) and also contributing towards a higher mode of conduct and character (उपदेश) in a subtle persuasive way. When ध्वनि or रस is said to be the soul of poetry (काव्यस्यात्मा ध्वनिरिति) it is virtually employing the language of the Upaniṣads about आत्मन् and आनन्द (आनन्दो ब्रह्मेति व्यजानात्). There is a remarkable similarity between the aesthetic experience on reading a poem or on seing a good drama and the spiritual experience derived from the vedānta discipline by one who has realized and contemplates upon the one Reality. It is therefore that Mammaṭa speaks of *rasa* as 'ब्रह्मास्वादमिवानुभावयन्'. But there are differences between the two experiences. Art experience does not last long, vanishes when the stimulus is withdrawn, while the bliss of one who has reached the *brāhmī-sthiti* is permanent. Art experience does not necessarily require moral elevation, while blissful spiritual life is not possible without moral discipline. Before the theory of ध्वनि secured general acceptance, it had to pass through an ordeal of fierce criticism at the hands of प्रतीहारेन्दुराज (pp. 80-86, Nir.), वक्रोक्तिजीवित, भट्टनायक and महिमभट्ट. Vide 'Indian Culture', vol. XI pp. 233-241 on 'a historical and critical survey of Dhvani theory', 'Ānandavardhana's treatment of rasa in relation to Dhvani' J. O. R. Madras vol. 17 pp. 80-91, and 'treatment of ध्वनि, गुण, रीति and वृत्ति' in Journal of Bom. Un. vol. 18 part 2 pp. 57-72, all by Dr. K. Krishnamoorthy.

14 The divisions of Poetry. As in modern works poetry is divided into epic, lyric, dramatic, so in Sanskrit works also it is so divided. Classification of poetry is made from various stand-points. The first divison made by दण्डी is into गद्य, पद्य and मिश्र. While most English critics are agreed that versification is a *sine qua non* for poetry (though Prof. Moulton and a few others maintain the opposite view), all Sanskrit writers on Poetics are unanimous that versification is not a necessary condition of poetry. Not only so but a few like Vāmana say 'गद्यं कवीनां निकषं वदन्ति' (काव्या. सू. on I. 3. 21). दण्डी then speaks under पद्य of सर्गबन्ध (or महाकाव्य an epic) and मुक्तक (a single verse), कुलक (five श्लोकs), कोष and सङ्घात (compilations of unconnected verses). Under गद्य he refers to कथा, आख्यायिका, चम्पू. The मिश्र *kāvya* is constituted by नाटक and other varieties of plays. दण्डी also divides काव्य into संस्कृत, प्राकृत and अपभ्रंश; while रुद्रट (II. 31) divides it into six, संस्कृत, प्राकृत, मागध, पिशाच, शूरसेन and अपभ्रंश. For भामह's divisions of काव्य, vide p. 82 above. वामन divides काव्य into गद्य and पद्य; the former into

three varieties, वृत्तगन्धि (resembling verse), चूर्ण and उत्कलिकाप्राय; पद्य is of various sorts, but he gives two divisions of both गद्य and पद्य into अनिबद्ध (unconnected) and निबद्ध (connected i. e. a प्रबन्ध) and declares that among complete works, the drama is superior (सन्दर्भेषु दशरूपकं श्रेयः' I. 3. 30). हेमचन्द्र (8th अध्याय) divides काव्य into प्रेक्ष्य and श्रव्य, and the former into पाठ्य and गेय and these into numerous varieties; श्रव्य is divided into महाकाव्य, आख्यायिका, कथा, चम्पू and अनिबद्ध. He further speaks of काव्यs composed in संस्कृत, प्राकृत, अपभ्रंश and ग्राम्यापभ्रंश and regards आख्यान, निदर्शन, प्रवह्लिका, मतल्लिका, मणिकुल्या, परिकथा, खण्डकथा, सकलकथा, उपकथा as varieties of कथा. Vide ध्व. pp. 174 ff and the लोचन thereon for several varieties of काव्य.

15 Doṣas. This is an important topic in all works on Poetics. भामह (I. 12) states that, not being a poet does not entail *adharma* or disease or punishment, but to be a bad poet is declared by the wise to be death itself. Similarly, the काव्यादर्श (I. 7) observes that one should not make light of even an insignificent blemish in a poem and that even a handsome body may cause disgust (to the seer) on account of a single leprous spot. भरत speaks of ten *doṣas* (17. 88, GOS 16. 88, vol. II. p. 331). Vide p. 110 above. दण्डी and भामह speaking of ten and eleven *doṣas* rsepectively. But they make no scientific distinction between *doṣas* of पद, of वाक्य, of पदार्थ and वाक्यार्थ. This is done by वामन. This distinction of the *doṣas* of पद, वाक्य and अर्थ is accepted by मम्मट and other later writers. The doctrines of the ध्वन्यालोक that, in a composition in which *rasa* is to be evolved, औचित्य of various kinds has to be looked to (p. 178 ff) and that certain items that conflict (विरोधि) with the main *rasa* should be avoided (p. 199 ff), as they gave rise to the *doṣas* of *rasa*. Vide मम्मट VII for रसदोषs. मम्मट refers (10th उल्लास) to several *doṣas* of *alaṅkāras* and shows that they are included in the several *doṣas* discussed by him in the 7th उल्लास. One cannot avoid doṣas altogether but there are degrees in *doṣas*, the worst being *rasadoṣas*. The साहित्यदर्पण says (I. 2) 'सर्वथा निर्दोषस्यैकान्तमसम्भवात ।'. One has to remember the warning of कुमारिल 'न चाप्यतीव कर्तव्यं दोषदृष्टिपरं मनः। दोषोप्यविद्यमानोपि तच्चित्तानां प्रकाशते ॥' q. by अर्जुनवर्मदेव on अमरुशतक verse 72 and by the व्यक्तिविवेक. On doṣas, vide Dr. Raghavan on 'Śṛṅgāraprakāśa' vol. I. pp. 216-257, Dr. Krishnamoorthy on 'doctrine of doṣas' in I. H. Q. vol. 20 pp. 217-232.

16 The Influence of other Śāstras on Poetics.

The greatest influence has been exercised by grammar. The ध्व. (pp. 47-48) makes it clear that the word ध्वनि was borrowed from the grammarians (vide p. 198 above प्रथमे हि &c.), because they employed the word ध्वनि that manifested the Sphoṭa just as in a poem words manifest the suggested sense (व्यञ्जकत्वसाम्यात्). स्फोट is the all-pervading, eternal and indestructible word principle. ध्वनि (sounds and words) manifest it. The very first verse of the वाक्यपदीय is 'अनादिनिधनं ब्रह्म शब्दतत्त्वं यदक्षरम्। विवर्ततेऽर्थभावेन प्रक्रिया जगतो यतः ॥'. Letters and words are devices used to analyse the operations of our speech. When we utter a word the last letter carrying with it the *saṁskāras* of the letters previously uttered produces an idea in our mind and therefore it is called शब्द.[1] नाद or ध्वनि is अभिव्यञ्जक and स्फोट is अभिव्यंग्य. Vide लोचन p. 47 which quotes several verses from the वाक्यपदीय (e. g. I. 84, 103) and remarks 'व्यक्तशब्दानां तथा श्रूयमाणा ये वर्णा नादशब्दवाच्या अन्त्यबुद्धिनिर्ग्राह्याः स्फोटाभिव्यञ्जकास्ते ध्वनिशब्देनोक्ताः.' The स्फोट theory is very ancient. पाणिनि mentions a predecessor called स्फोटायन 'अवङ् स्फोटायनस्य' (पा. VI. 1. 123). The महाभाष्य tells us that the संग्रह of व्याडि principally dealt with the question whether शब्द was नित्य or कार्य 'संग्रहे प्राधान्येनैतत्परीक्षितम्, नित्यो वा स्यात् कार्यो वेति ।' (vol. I. p. 6, Kielhorn). Vide Śaṅkara's bhāṣya on Vedāntasūtra I. 3. 28. The भागवतपुराण XII. 6. 40 identifies स्फोट with ब्रह्म. The काव्यप्रकाश says: 'सङ्केतितश्चतुर्भेदो जात्यादिर्जातिरेव वा' II. p. 32. This is based upon the महाभाष्य (vol. I. p. 19) 'चतुष्टयी शब्दानां प्रवृत्तिः'. भामह VI. 21 also is based on this. The काव्यप्रकाश (II. p. 33) quotes the वाक्यपदीय 'नहि गौः स्वरूपेण गौः &c.' and also वाक्यपदीय II. 217-218 (काव्यप्रकाश p. 63) 'संयोगो विप्रयोगश्च' as helping in the determination of the meaning of a word that has several significations. The subdivisions of Upamā have been based on grammatical rules by भामह (II. 33 वतिनापि क्रियासाम्यं), उद्भट (कारिका I. 15 ff), the काव्यप्रकाश and साहित्यदर्पण, viz. upon पाणिनि's sūtras about क्यच् &c.

1. पदे न वर्णा विद्यन्ते वर्णेष्ववयवा इव । वाक्यात्पदानामत्यन्तं प्रविवेको न कश्चन ॥ वाक्यपदीय I. 73; नादैराहितबीजायामन्त्येन ध्वनिना सह । आवृत्तपरिपाकायां बुद्धौ शब्दोऽवधार्यते ॥ वाक्यपदीय I. 86. For 'the doctrine of Sphoṭa,' vide Journal, Annamalai University, vol. I pp. 231-240, vol. II pp. 109-119, न्यायमञ्जरी of जयन्तभट्ट (6th आह्निक), वाक्यपदीय I and शब्दकौस्तुभ.

Daṇḍin (II. 227) refers to the words of the महाभाष्य in discussing the verse लिम्पतीव. The definition of विभावना (क्रियायाः प्रतिषेधेपि) given by the काव्यप्रकाश is based on the view of grammarians that 'kriyā' means 'hetu'. Vāmana deals in his 5th adhikaraṇa with the grammatical purity of words and Bhāmaha also (in VI. 30-61) does the same.

Logic (Tarkaśāstra) deals with the power of words (abhidhā). The same subject is discussed in the अभिधावृत्तिमातृका, शब्दव्यापारविचार, त्रिवेणिका, वृत्तिवार्तिक by writers on alaṅkāra. Alaṅkārikas regard anumāna as a figure of speech. The figure काव्यलिङ्ग also is suggested by तर्क phraseology. Mahimabhaṭṭa wrote व्यक्तिविवेक for establishing that ध्वनि comes under anumāna and Śaṅkuka appears to have held that *rasa* is *anumeya* and the vibhāvas are *anumāpaka*. The Sāṅkhya philosophy had not much influence over alaṅkāra, but in dealing with Nāyaka's theory of *rasa* frequent reference is made to सत्त्व, रजस् and तमस् (as on vol. I. p. 279 of अभिनवभारती and p. 283 तत एव कापिलैर्दुःखस्य चाञ्चल्यमेव प्राणत्वेनोक्तं रजोवृत्तिं वदद्भिः). The word भोग or भोगीकृति seems to be suggested by the सांख्य doctrine that पुरुष is भोक्ता and not कर्ता.

The पूर्वमीमांसा system also has lent some doctrines to अलङ्कारशास्त्र. The काव्यप्रकाश view (सङ्केतित...जातिरेव वा) is the पूर्वमीमांसा view (आकृतिस्तु क्रियार्थत्वात्' जै. I.3. 33). The views 'तात्पर्यार्थोपि केषुचित्' (काव्यप्रकाश II.) and 'तात्पर्याख्यां वृत्तिमाहुः पदार्थान्वयबोधने' साहित्यदर्पण II. 20 are derived from the अभिहितान्वयवाद which was supported by Kumārila and Pārthasārathimiśra in his Nyāyaratnamālā.. The अभिहितान्वयवाद and अन्विताभिधानवाद are mentioned in the काव्यप्रकाश II. and V. The काव्यप्रकाश mentions 'लोहितोष्णीषा ऋत्विजः प्रचरन्ति', 'यत्परः शब्दः स शब्दार्थः' (V. pp. 225-227) which are topics discussed in the पूर्वमीमांसा. Vide जै. III. 8. 12 for the first. The words 'फलं संवित्तिः प्रकटता वा' in काव्यप्र. II p. 61 give expression respectively to the theories of प्रभाकर and कुमारिल. अर्थापत्ति is an alaṅkāra acc. to साहित्यदर्पण aud अलं. स.; it is regarded as a प्रमाण by पूर्वमीमांसा. परिसंख्या which is a well-known technical term in पूर्वमीमांसा (as in जै. I. 2. 34, III. 7, 33) is an अलङ्कार according to रुद्रट, काव्यप्रकाश, साहित्यदर्पण and others.

From the Vedānta some works like the चमत्कारचन्द्रिका, the मन्दारमरन्दचम्पू (9th बिन्दु), and रसगङ्गाधर (p. 23) quote the Upaniṣad[1] passage 'रसो वै सः' in order to describe the blissful

1. 'रसो वै सः । रसं ह्येवायं लब्ध्वानन्दी भवति' तै. उप., ब्रह्मानन्दवल्ली 7.

stage of Rasa realization. The काव्यप्रकाश describes रस as ब्रह्मास्वादमिवानुभावयन् (vide p. 360 above). These writers regard रस, आनन्द and आत्मन् as practically identical. The बृहदारण्यकोपनिषद् (IV. 3. 21) has the following very interesting passage 'तद्यथा प्रियया स्त्रिया संपरिष्वक्तो न बाह्यं किंचन वेद नान्तरमेवमेवायं पुरुषः प्राज्ञेनात्मना संपरिष्वक्तो न बाह्यं किंचन वेद नान्तरम् । तद्वा अस्यैतदाप्तकाममात्मकाममकामं रूपं शोकान्तरम् । अत्र पिताऽपिता भवति...तीर्णो हि तदा सर्वान् शोकान् हृदयस्य भवति.' ब्रह्मसूत्र (I. 1. 12-19) deals with the passage of तै उप and others which speak of आनन्दमयात्मा.

———

Index of authors and works on Sanskrit Poetics

In the edition of 1923 works on *abhinaya*, music and *kāmaśāstra* were generally excluded, although in reports on the Mss, works on these subjects are often included under *alaṅkāraśāstra*. Not all works on dramaturgy have been included. The Index is principally based on Aufrecht's Catalogus Catalogorum, on the first volume of the New Catalogus Catalogorum edited by Dr. Raghavan (which mentions authors and works beginning with the letter अ alone) and on the same scholar's numerous papers on Alaṅkāra, on Dr. Harichand's 'Kālidāsa et L' Art Poetique de L' Inde', Dr. De's 'History of Sanskrit Poetics' vol. I. These works themselves except Dr. Raghavan's, are based on other catalogues of Mss. and Reports. Hence I had in many cases to consult the original catalogues such as the I. O. (India Office) catalogue, Mitra's Notices, the catalogue of the Mss. at the B. O. R. I. (Poona vol. XII); Govt. O. Mss. Library, Madras, vol. 22; Mss. cat. vol. VI of the Trivandrum Palace Library; Sarasvatīmahal mss. Library at Tanjore, Cat. vol. 9 and the Reports of Buhler, Bhandarkar, Peterson and others. The entries in catalogues of Mss. are often meagre and misleading. The same work often appears under different names. The word *rasa* appears in names of works on medicine as well as in works on alaṅkāra. The word नाटसूत्र in the विवादरत्नाकर (p. 477) is a mistake for लाटसूत्र (i. e. लाट्यायनश्रौतसूत्र I. 3. 19) as the quotation shows. Dr. Harichand enters नाटसूत्र in his list (on page 35) with a query. Instead of giving two separate lists for authors and works, one consolidated list is presented, the names of authors being put in thick type. I have probably omitted the names of a few commentators, particularly of the Kāvyaprakāśa. I have not given exhaustive references to all printed editions. Obvious abbreviations such as काव्यप्र. for काव्यप्रकाश are not mentioned here, as also those mentioned in the general list of abbreviations. The principal abbreviations employed in this index are :

A. or a.=author; acc.=according to; Ānan.=Ānandāśrama Press edition, Poona; Ano. or ano.=anonymous; Bom. S. S. or Bom. S. Series=Bombay Sanskrit Series; B. O. R. I. cat.—Bhandarkar Oriental Research Institute catalogue of mss.; C. or c. or com.=commentary or commentator according to the context; CC. or cc.=commentary on a commentary; Gode='Studies in Indian Literary History' published by prof. P. K. Gode in 3 vol.; H. R.=Hultzsch, Reports on mss.; I. O. cat.=India Office catalogue of mss.; JGJRI=Journal of Ganganath Jha Research Institute, Allahabad; m.=mentioned; Madras Cat.=Madras Government Sanskrit mss. catalogues; N.=Rajendralal Mitra's Notices of mss.; Nir or Nirn.=Nirṇayasāgar Press edition, Bombay; N. C. C.=New Catalogus Catalogorum ed. by Dr. Raghavan, vol. I; N. I. A.=New Indian Antiquary; p.=page; Pr. or pr.=Printed; R.=Report on mss.; q.=quoted by; q. v.=which see; Tanjore cat.=Tanjore Sarasvatī - mahal Palace Library mss. catalogues; V. or v.=Vide; V. V. R. I.—Viveśvarānanda Vedic Research Institute, Hoshiarpur.

अकबरसाहिशृङ्गारदर्पण of पद्मसुन्दर, a Jain scholar. Pr. in Ganga O. Series No. 1 at Bikaner (1943), edited by Prof. C. K. Raja. Illustrative verses are addressed to the Mogul emperor Akbar. In four उल्लासs. Follows शृङ्गारतिलक of रुद्र; ms. dated 1569 A.D. Accepts nine rasas.

अकवर-साहि-शृङ्गारमञ्जरी a sanskrit version of a Telugu work of the same name composed by a saint Akbar Shah, guru of Sultan Abul Hasan; flourished in latter half of 17th century A.D. Vide Dr. Raghavan's paper in Kunhan Raja presentation volume pp. 325-335 and his edition of the work with an exhaustive Introduction, published by the Arch. Dept. of the old Hyderabad State in 1951.

अच्युत m. by भीमसेन as com. of काव्यप्र.

अच्युतराय a. of साहित्यसार and com. सरसामोद thereon; lived at पञ्चवटी near Nasik; complcted in 1831 A.D.; pr. Nir.

अजितसेन देवयतीश्वर, a. of अलङ्कारचिन्तामणि and शृङ्गारमञ्जरी in 3 chap. for Jain prince Kāmirāya (son of विठ्ठलदेवी), an Ālūpa prince; 10th cen.; vide N. C. C. p. 69 a.

अणुरत्नमण्डन or **रत्नमण्डन**, pupil of रत्नशेखरसूरि, a. of जल्पकल्प-

अलङ्कारकौमुदी (Ano.). At least 7 किरणs.
C व्याख्या (Ano.).

अलङ्कारकौमुदी of वल्लभभट्ट (of recent times). Pr. in ग्रन्थमाला, vol. II, Bombay, 1889.

अलङ्कारकौस्तुभ of कविकर्णपूर alias परमानन्ददाससेन in 10 किरणs. Verses about कृष्ण and राधा illustrate rules; a. born in 1524 A. D. Also wrote drama चैतन्यचन्द्रोदय in 1572 A. D. Ed. by S. P. Bhattacharya (1926). He follows उज्ज्वलं-नीलमणि.
C सारबोधिनी of विश्वनाथचक्रवर्तिन्. Pr. in 1899 at Murshidabad.
C दीधितिप्रकाशिका by वृन्दावनचन्द्र, son of राधाचरण.
C by लोकनाथचक्रवर्तिन्.
C by सार्वभौम, pupil of चक्रवर्तिन्. New Cat. Cat. p. 292.

अलङ्कारकौस्तुभ of वेङ्कटाचार्य, son of अण्णयार्य. Speaks of 6 शब्दालङ्कारs and 108 अर्थालङ्कारs.

अलङ्कारकौस्तुभ of कल्याणसुब्रह्मण्य, patronised by Rāma Varman, king of Travancore (1758-1798 A. D.). Deals with अर्थालङ्कारs only.

अलङ्कारकौस्तुभ of विश्वेश्वर, son of लक्ष्मीधर. Defines and illustrates 61 alaṅkāras; mentions चित्रमीमांसा and रसग०. First half of the 18th century; Pr. in K. M. series.
C विवरण by author.

अलङ्कारकौस्तुभ of श्रीनिवासदीक्षित.

अलङ्कारक्रममाला of दामोदरभट्ट हर्षे
C by a.

अलङ्कारग्रन्थ of काशीलक्ष्मण कवि. End of 17th cen. Examples in praise of Shahaji, king of Tanjore (1684-1711 A. D.).

अलङ्कारचन्द्रिका–V. under कुवलयानन्द.

अलङ्कारचन्द्रिका by गोपीनाथ.
,, by रामचन्द्रन्यायवागीश, son of विद्यानिधि. Same as काव्यचन्द्रिका.
C अलङ्कारमञ्जूषा by रामचन्द्रशर्मन्.

अलङ्कारचन्द्रिका by नारायणदेव

अलङ्कारचन्द्रोदय by वेणीदत्तशर्मन् in 6 उल्लासs.

अलङ्कारचिन्तामणि of अजितसेन, in 5 परिच्छेदs. Pr. in *Kāvyāmbudhi* (N. C. C. I p. 293).
C (Ano.).

अलङ्कारचिन्तामणि by रामचन्द्रराजगुरु, son of गदाधर.

अलङ्कारचूडामणि of राजचूडामणिदीक्षित, son of श्रीनिवासदीक्षित. He wrote many works of which काव्यदर्पण was one.

अलङ्कारचूडामणि-v. काव्यानुशासन of हेमचन्द्र.

अलङ्कारतिलक of भानुदत्त. V. p. 309 above.

अलङ्कारतिलक of अप्पय्यदीक्षित II. V. Pro. of 10th All India O. Conference, pp. 176-180.

अलङ्कारतिलक of वाग्भट, C. on his own काव्यानुशासन q. v.

अलङ्कारतिलक of श्रीकरमिश्र.

C अर्थालङ्कारवर्णन by a.; composed in संवत् 1282 (1225-6 A. D.). Text and C. pr. in G. O. S.

अलङ्कारमीमांसा q. in वासनाभाष्य of योगेश्वर on the भागवत. Vide B. B. R. A. S. mss. cat. pp. 288-89.

अलङ्कारमीमांसा of कृष्णसूरि, son of गोपालाचार्य.

अलङ्कारमुक्तावली of रामसुधी son of नृसिंह.

C रत्नशोभाकर of कृष्णसूरि. For edition, v. N. C. C. vol. I p. 295.

अलङ्कारमुक्तावली of कृष्णयज्वन्; 16th cen. V. 'Brahmavidyā' for May 1943.

अलङ्कारमुक्तावली of श्रीनिवास.

अलङ्कारमुक्तावली of लक्ष्मीधरदीक्षित, son of यज्ञेश्वर.. Vide H. R. vol. III pp. VIII-IX.

अलङ्कारमुक्तावली of विश्वेश्वरभट्ट, son of लक्ष्मीधर. First half of 18th cen. Pr. in Kashi S. Series.

अलङ्कारमौक्तिकमाला of कृष्ण son of रामार्य.

अलङ्काररत्नाकर of शोभाकरमित्र, son of त्रयीश्वरमित्र. In 107 sūtras. Q. in वृत्तिवार्तिक, p.20, रसगङ्गाधर (p. 281 which says that in कुवलयानन्द अप्पय्य follows this work); between 1200 -1550 A. D. It is made use of by यशस्कर in his देवीस्तोत्र, on which रत्नकण्ठ comments; edited by Prof. C. R. Devadhar and pub. by Oriental Book Agency, Poona.

C रत्नोदाहरण by a. Vide B. O. R. I. cat. vol. XII p. 17.

अलङ्काररत्नाकरप्राकृतगाथासंस्कृतीकरण.

अलङ्काररत्नाकर by यज्ञनारायण. Eulogizes रघुनाथनायक of Tanjore. He also wrote साहित्यरत्नाकर; V. Tanjore cat. IX 3974-75.

अलङ्काररहस्य of प्रभाकर, son of महादेव; q. by him in his रसप्रदीप composed in 1583 A.D. (pp. 8-10).

अलङ्कारराघव of चेरुकूरि यज्ञेश्वरदीक्षित, son of कोण्डुभट्ट and brother of तिरुमलयज्वन्. Quotes रसार्णवसुधाकर and साहित्यचिन्तामणि.

अलङ्कारलक्षणानि of शम्भुनाथ. D.C. ms. No. 407 of 1892-95 is dated संवत् 1797 (1740 A.D.)

अलङ्कारवादार्थ Ano; discusses passages of the साहित्यदर्पण.

अलङ्कारवार्तिक-m. by the विमर्शिनी of जयरथ (p. 71) as a work of the a. of अलं. स.

अलङ्कारविचार makes use of प्रतापरुद्रीय. V. Tanjore cat. vol. IX pp. 3978-79.

अलङ्कारवृत्ति or मुग्धमेधाकर of रत्नमण्डनगणि; V. B. O. R. I. cat. XII p. 221 . Middle of 15h cen.

अलङ्कारव्याकरण (in sūtras) by कात्यायन.

C वृत्ति by वररुचि. Spurious. Vide N.C.C. vol. I p. 297.

अलङ्कारशतक. Probably same as चन्द्रालोक.

अलङ्कारशास्त्रसंग्रह of रामसुब्रह्मण्य.

V. p. 138 above. About 925-950 A. D. Pr.

C उद्भटविवेक by राजानकतिलक. About 1100-1125 A. D. V. pp. 138-139 above. Pr. in G. O. S. The काव्यादर्शसङ्केत of सोमेश्वर mentions a कारिका of तिलक on p. 295. Prof. R. C. Parikh in his Introduction to सोमेश्वर's सङ्केत places him between 1135-50 and 1160 A. D.

अलङ्कारसारस्थिति, also called कुवलयानन्दखण्डन, by भीमसेनदीक्षित. Composed at Jodhpur while अजितसिंह (1680-1725 A.D.) was reigning; v. N. vol. X p. 209.

अलङ्कारसारोद्धार by भीमसेनदीक्षित; m. in his काव्यप्रकाशव्याख्यासुधासागर, q. v.

अलङ्कारसुधा- ac. on कुवलयानन्द by नागेशभट्ट.

अलङ्कारसुधाकर-a com. on साहित्यरत्नाकर by कृष्णमिश्र.

अलङ्कारसुधानिधि of गणपति.

.अलङ्कारसुधानिधि attributed to सायण, son of मायण. Illustrative verses praise सायण and are the compositions of भोगनाथ, younger brother of सायण; they form a collection called उदाहरणमाला. Composed about 1358. It is quoted in the रत्नापण (p. 44) and वृत्तिवार्तिक (p. 19). Vide I. A. vol. 45 pp. 22-24, Indian Culture, for 1940 p. 439-44.

अलङ्कारसूत्र of शौद्धोदनि. V. अलङ्कारशेखर p. 315-317 above.

अलङ्कारसूत्र m. in the विमर्शिनी of जयरथ (p. 150).

अलङ्कारसूत्र ascribed to वात्स्यायन; contains 75 सूत्रs (vide H. R. vol. I p. 23).

अलङ्कारसूत्र-Another सूत्र work on which कृष्णावधूत wrote a भाष्य called चमत्कारचामीकर; died in the beginning of this century.

अलङ्कारसूत्र by चन्द्रकान्ततर्कालङ्कार. A recent work. Vide HSP vol. I p 327. Pr. at Calcutta in 1899.

अलङ्कारसूर्योदय by चेरुकूरि यज्ञेश्वर दीक्षित, son of कोण्डुभट्ट. Same as a. of अलङ्कारराघव.

अलङ्कारस्फुरण of रूपनारायण, son of वनाद्रिनाथ. Follows कुवलयानन्द; v. Journal of Ven. R. Institute, Tirupati, vol. 8 Sanskrit part p. 63.

अलङ्कारागम of कवीन्द्राचार्य.

अलङ्कारानुक्रमणिका-Ano.

अलङ्कारानुसारिणी by रुय्यक, a. of अलं. स. V. p. 279 above.

अलङ्काराशय with C. Ano.

अलङ्कारेन्दुशेखर in five प्रकरणs on नायक, काव्यस्वरूप, शृङ्गार, दोषगुण, अलङ्कार; by वेङ्कटनृसिंह, son of दासमाचार्य of श्रीशैल family; Madras Govt. mss. cat. vol. 22 No. 12978.

अलङ्कारेन्दुशेखर by the same a. as above on लक्षणमालिका.

अलङ्कारेश्वर m. by शिवराम in his com. on सुबन्धु's वासवदत्ता p.4.

अलङ्कारोदाहरण by जयरथ, son of शृङ्गार. Refers to his own

उद्भटविवेक of राजानकतिलक. V. pp. 138-139.

उपमन्यु m. in काव्यमी. p. 1 (v. p. 1 above).

उपमासुधानिधि by Śelvappillai Ayyangar.

ऋजुवृत्ति-V. under काव्यप्र.

एकषष्ट्यलङ्कारप्रकाश-- Summary compiled from works of देवनाथ, गोविन्दठक्कुर, जयराम and others. N. vol. 4 No. 1447.

एकावली of विद्याधर. V. pp. 292-293.

C तरल of मल्लिनाथ.

C प्रकाश by प्रभाकर, son of माधवभट्ट and grandson of रामेश्वरभट्ट. Born in 1564 A. D.

एकावली of महामहेश्वरकवि.

औचित्यविचारचर्चा of क्षेमेन्द्र. V. p. 264-266 above.

औद्भटा: m. by काव्यमी. pp. 22,44.

औपकायन m. by काव्यमी. V. p. 1 above.

औमापतम् published in the series of the Govt. Oriental mss. Library, Madras, 1957. In 38 chapters (75 pages in print) mostly in verse; principally on śrutis, svaras, *rāgas*, *veṇu* and vīṇā, *tālas*, Maddala or mṛdaṅga, dance (tāṇḍava and lāsya); four types of dance called Bhāratī, Sāttvatī, Kaiśikī, Ārabhaṭī, poses of body, chest, hams, 43 kinds of hastas; poses of the feet, bhramarī; Mudrās, abhinaya, nartana; nine rasas and their vibhāvas, anubhāvas, distinction between nṛtta' and nṛtya. Work of उमापति m. by कल्लिनाथ in his commentary on सङ्गीतरत्नाकर.

कच्छपेश्वरदीक्षित, son of वासुदेव and grandson of कालहस्तीश्वर; a. of रामचन्द्रयशोभूषण in 3 chapters dealing with *rasas* and *bhāvas*; Madras Govt. mss. cat. vol. 22 No. 12950. Illustrations in praise of बोम्मराज.

कन्दालयार्य a. of अलङ्कारयशोभूषण. He lived at court of वेङ्कट.

कमलाकरभट्ट, a. of numerous works on धर्मशास्त्र and of a com. on काव्यप्र. written for his son. V. p. 275 n. 1 above. He wrote his निर्णयसिन्धु in 1612 A.D.

कर्णपूर or कविकर्णपूर alias परमानन्ददाससेन, son of शिवानन्दसेन. A. of अलङ्कारकौस्तुभ, q. v.

कर्णभूषण of गङ्गानन्द a मैथिल; in five chapters dealing with विभाव, अनुभाव, व्यभिचारिभाव, स्थायिभाव, रस; several verses are addressed to कर्ण himself. In II. 32 he mentions that भानुकवीश्वर regards जृम्भा as the 9th सात्त्विकभाव; written at command of श्रीकर्ण of Bikaner, 1505-1526 A. D.). Pr. Nir.

कर्पूररसमञ्जरी of बालकवि.

कलाधर a. of कारिकावलि of काव्यप्र, V. under काव्यप्र.

कल्पवल्ली m. by भावप्रकाशन on pp. 131, 142 which state that

कविसमयकल्लोल by अनन्तार्य, later than 14th cen.

कवीन्द्रकण्ठाभरण of विश्वेश्वरभट्ट, son of लक्ष्मीधर. Pr. in 8th गुच्छ of K. M. V. under अलङ्कारकौस्तुभ.

C by a.

कात्यायन m. in नाटकलक्षणरत्नकोश as an author on नाट्यशास्त्र.

कान्तिचन्द्र a. of काव्यदीपिका; 19th cen. Pr. at Cal.

कामदेव m. by काव्यमी. p. 1 (v. above p. 1).

कामदेव a. of रतिमञ्जरी.

कामधेनु c. on वामन's काव्यालङ्कारसूत्र. V. p. 147 above.

कामसमूह of अनन्त, a नागरब्राह्मण, son of मण्डनमन्त्रिन्, son of नारायण and pupil of आनन्दपूर्ण. Composed in 1457 A. D. V. Prof. Gode in J. O. R., Madras, vol. 14 pp. 74-81.

कारिकार्थप्रकाशिका of रघुदेव, C. on काव्यप्र.

काव्यकलाप Ano.

काव्यकल्पलता alias कवितारहस्य of अरिसिंह and अमरचन्द्र, in four प्रतान s. Middle of 13th cen. (Bhandarkar's R. for 1883-4. p. 6). Pr. in Kashi S. Series.

C कविशिक्षावृत्ति by अमरचन्द्र. This mentions that some portions of the original were composed by अमरचन्द्र and that the com. was composed in संवत् 1455 (1396 A.D.). V. Bhandarkar's Report 1883-84 pp. 312-313 for extract and I. O. cat. vol. III. pp. 339-341. The dates given in these two viz. संवत् 1455 and 1475 are most porbably the dates of copying the work. Pr. Chowkhamba S. Series.

C परिमल q. in the above.

C मञ्जरी m. by परिमल as the author's work.

C मकरन्द of शुभविजयगणि. 1609 A.D.

काव्यकौतुक of भट्टतौत. About 950 A. D. V. pp. 179, 218-221 above.

C विवरण by अभिनवगुप्त m. in लोचन. V. above p. 179. n. 1 and 2.

काव्यकौस्तुभ of बलदेव विद्याभूषण, known as simply विद्याभषण. In 9 प्रभाs. Also a. of साहित्यकौमुदी on काव्यप्र.

काव्यकौमुदी Ano.

काव्यकौमुदी by देवनाथ; c. on काव्यप्र.

काव्यकौमुदी of रत्नभूषण in 10 परिच्छेदs. First half of 18th cen.

काव्यचन्द्रिका of कविचन्द्र, son of कविकर्णपूर; in 15 chapters. V. previous pages.

काव्यचन्द्रिका of रामचन्द्रन्यायवागीश, son of विद्यानिधि. Pr. at Comilla, 1885.

काव्यडाकिनी of गङ्गानन्दकवीन्द्र, मैथिल. Pr. in सरस्वतीभवन Series. Deals with doṣas in five chapters called दृष्टिs. About first quarter of 16th cen.

काव्यतत्त्वविचार of हलधररथ.

काव्यतत्त्वविवेचककौमुदी of कृष्ण-

C. states he was born in संवत् 1298 (i. e. 1241-42 A. D.).

C दीपिका or जयन्ती of जयन्तभट्ट. Composed in संवत् 1350 (1294 A.D.). His father भरद्वाज was पुरोहित of chief minister of Vāghela king Sāranga-deva of Gujarat (1277-1297 A. D.). Extract in Bhandarkar's Report 1883-84 p. 326.

C by वाचस्पतिमिश्र; m. by चण्डीदास in his दीपिका (p. 131) and by विश्वनाथ in his com. on मम्मट. He is different from वाचस्पति a. of भामती and also from वाचस्पतिमिश्र a. of several धर्मशास्त्र works called चिन्तामणि (such as विवादचिन्तामणि.).

C विवेक of श्रीधर सान्धिविग्रहिक; m. by चण्डीदास in दीपिका (pp. 29, 59, 62, 117) and विश्वनाथ in his काव्यप्र. दर्पण. About 1225 A. D. This has been published in the Sanskrit college Calcutta series, edited by Prof. S. Bhattachacya (1959, only part one containing first four *ullāsas*.

C दीपिका of चण्डीदास. Pr. in सरस्वतीभवन series (Benares). Written at the bidding of his friend लक्ष्मणभट्ट. He also wrote ध्वनिसिद्धान्तसंग्रह. He may be identified with चण्डीदास the younger brother of the grand-father of विश्वनाथ a. of साहित्यदर्पण. He states that his grand-father नारायण defeated धर्मदत्त at the court of नरसिंह king of त्रिकलिङ्ग. His दीपिका (p 118) names खण्डनकृत्. Hence he flourished about or before 1300 A. D.

C दर्पण of विश्वनाथ a. of साहित्यदर्पण. V. pp. 296-304 above. Flourished 1300-1380 A.D.

C संप्रदायप्रकाशिनी of विद्याचक्रवर्तिन्; called बृहट्टीका. He wrote also लघुटीका on काव्यप्र.; 14th cen. Pr. in Tri. S. S.; V. Annals of B. O. R. I. vol. 14 pp. 250 ff.

C साहित्यदीपिका of भास्कर; m. by गोविन्दठक्कुर. Earlier than 15th century.

C विस्तारिका of परमानन्दचक्रवर्तिन्. He mentions दीपिका, विश्वनाथ and प्रतापरुद्रीय. To be distinguished from श्रीविद्याचक्रवर्तिन्, a. of com. on अलं. स. and also on मम्मट. Between 1400-1500 A. D.

C प्रदीप by गोविन्दठक्कुर, a मैथिल, eldest son of केशव and सोनोदेवी, elder brother of a poet श्रीहर्ष

(different from a. of नैषधीय), pupil of his own step-brother in काव्य and साहित्य and friend of रुचिकरकवि. Later than 1400 and earlier than about 1550 A. D.; Pr. Nir. He also wrote उदाहरणदीपिका explaining illustrations.

CC प्रभा by वैद्यनाथ तत्सत् (Pr. K. M. Series).

CC उदाहरणचन्द्रिका by वैद्यनाथ (I. O. cat. III p. 329 No. 1151); 1683-1684 A. D.; Pr. in K. M. Series.

CC उद्द्योत by नागेशभट्ट; pr. in Ānan. Series, Poona.

C तिलक of जयरामन्यायपञ्चानन; q. by श्रीवत्सलाञ्छन and भीमसेन. Between 1500-1700 A. D. V. Peterson's 2nd R. p. 107 for extract.

C सारबोधिनी of श्रीवत्सलाञ्छन or श्रीवत्सवर्मन्. One ms. was copied in संवत् 1665; m. by रत्नकण्ठ and भीमसेन. Later than 1400 and earlier than 1600 A.D.

C by पण्डितराज. m. by रत्नकण्ठ. Different from जगन्नाथपण्डितराज. Vide Stein's cat. p. XXVII and in cat. of Mithila Mss. by K. P. Jayaswal vol. II. p. 24; ms. copied in śaka 1559 (1637 A.D.).

C दर्पण by मनोधर alias रत्नपाणि, son of अच्युत, minister of शिवसिंह, grand-son of भवेश; m. by रवि in his मधुमती. About 1450 A.D.

C मधुमती by रवि, son of मनोधर alias रत्नपाणि and grand-son of अच्युत, minister of शिवसिंह of मिथिला. C. is named after रवि's daughter; m. by कमलाकर. Between 1460-1500 A.D.

C भावार्थचिन्तामणि or आदर्श by महेश्वरन्यायालङ्कार. Earlier than middle of 17th cen. Pr. by Jivananda.

C by कमलाकरभट्ट for his son अनन्त. He wrote his निर्णयसिन्धु in 1612 A. D. Pr. at Benares. V. H. of Dh. vol. I p. 437.

C निदर्शन or शितिकण्ठविबोधन by राजानकानन्द, composed in गतकलि 4766 (i. e. 1665 A. D.). He interprets मम्मट's text as having another mystic meaning referring to शितिकण्ठ (शिव). V. Stein's Cat. pp. XXVI-VII.

C सारसमुच्चय of राजानकरत्नकण्ठ. He states that he drew upon the com. जयन्ती and others. Friend of राजानकानन्द. Between 1648-1681 A. D. V. Peterson's 2nd Report

p. 17 for a list of authors quoted by him.

C नरसिंहमनीषा by नरसिंहठक्कुर, being 5th in descent from गोविन्दठक्कुर. Mentions मधुमतीकार and कमलाकर and is m. by भीमसेन. Between 1620-1700 A. D.

C उदाहरणचन्द्रिका by वैद्यनाथ तत्सत्, son of रामभट्ट, on the illustrations in the काव्यप्रकाश. He wrote also प्रभा on काव्यप्रकाशप्रदीप. Composed in संवत् 1740 (1683-4 A.D.). Pr. in K.M. series.

C सुधासागर by भीमसेनदीक्षित, son of शिवानन्द and grandson of मुरलीधर, a कान्यकुब्जब्राह्मण. C. composed in संवत् 1779 (1722-23 A.D.). Pr. in Ch. S. Series. Names a large number of commentators.

C साहित्यकौमुदी of बलदेव विद्याभूषण or simply विद्याभूषण. Comments only on the कारिकाs calling them भरतसूत्र. He was a follower of चैतन्य school. About 1760 A.D.

CC कृष्णानन्दिनी by a. himself. Pr. in K. M. series.

C उद्द्योत } by नागेशभट्ट or नागोजि. First quarter of 18th cen. V. pp. 324-5 above. Both pr. in Ānan. Series.
C उदाहरणप्रदीप }

C of कृष्णमित्राचार्य, son of रामनाथ and grandson of देवीदत्त.

C of गदाधरचक्रवर्तिन्.

C सारदीपिका of गुणरत्नगणि. See B. O. R. I. mss. cat. vol. XII p. 112. Ms. dated संवत् 1742.

C साहित्यचूडामणि of गोपालभट्ट or लौहित्यभट्टगोपाल; about 1750 A. D. Pr. in Tri. S. Series.

C तिरुवेङ्कट son of चिन्नतिम्म. Mentions गोपाल's com.

C of नारायणदीक्षित, son of रङ्गनाथदीक्षित. Last quarter of 17th cen.

C लीला of भवदेव, son of कृष्णदेव of मिथिला and pupil of भवदेव ठक्कुर; composed in 1649 A. D.

C of भानुचन्द्र.

C of यज्ञेश्वर-यज्वन्. Madras Govt. mss. cat. vol. XXII p. 8623.

C of रत्नेश्वर; m. in his own com. on भोज.

C of राजानन्द.

C of विजयानन्द. Ms. dated 1683 A. D.

C दीपिका of शिवनारायणदास, son of दुर्गादास. Beginning of 17th cen.

C of सुबुद्धिमिश्र, m. by चक्रवर्तिन्.

C अर्थप्रकाशिका of रघुदेव. V. कारिकार्थप्रकाशिका.

C अवचूरि of राघव.

C उदाहरणदर्पण.

in I. H. Q. vol. 15 pp. 512-522 and vol. 24 p. 312.

काव्यशिक्षा of विनयचन्द्र.

काव्यसरणि m. in वृत्तिवार्त्तिक (p. 20) of अप्पय्यदीक्षित as one of the sources. Before 1550 A.D.

काव्यसारसंग्रह of श्रीनिवासदीक्षित in three parts dealing with काव्यलक्षण, वर्णसंग्रह and सुभाषितसंग्रह.. About 1800 A. D.

काव्यसुधा or साहित्यसुधा.

काव्यादर्श of दण्डिन्. V. pp. 84-102. About 660-680 A. D.

C by रत्नश्री, a Buddhist, in 2nd quarter of 11th century; published by the Darbhanga Institute, 1957.

C of तरुणवाचस्पति (ed. by Prof. Rangacharya). First half of 13th cen. (p. 105) above.

C केशवभट्टारक, son of तरुणवाचस्पति; vide JOR (Madras) vol. XIII. part 4 pp. 305-306 (Dr. Raghavan).

C हृदयङ्गमा by an ano. author (ed. by Prof. Rangacharya, on two परिच्छेदs).

C चन्द्रिका of त्रिशरणतटभीम.

C मार्जन of हरिनाथ, son of विश्वधर and younger brother of केशव. V. p. 133. Between 1575 and 1675 A. D.

C दण्ड्यर्थमुक्तावली by नरसिंहसूरि, son of गदाधर.

C रसिकरञ्जिनी of विश्वनाथ.

C काव्यतत्त्वविवेचककौमुदी or विवरण by कृष्णकिङ्करतर्कवागीश. V. p. 133.

C श्रुतानुपालनी of वादिजङ्घल. V. p. 133 above. He refers to दशरूप. Pr. (1936), Srinivasa Pres., Tiruvayyaru.

C वैमल्यविधायिनी of मल्लिनाथ, son of जगन्नाथ. Different from the famous com. मल्लिनाथ.

C by त्रिभुवनचन्द्र alias वादिसिंह, a Jaina. Pr. in Bengali characters.

C by भगीरथ.

C by विजयानन्द. Ms. written in संवत् 1683. V. p. 133 above.

C by यामुन or यामुनेय. V. p. 133 above.

काव्यादर्श of सोमेश्वर. V. under काव्यप्र. above.

काव्यानुशासन of हेमचन्द्र. V. pp. 287-290. Born in 1088 A. D. and died in 1172 A.D. Pr. in K. M. series.

C अलङ्कारचूडामणि by a. } both pr. in K. M.
C विवेक by a. }

काव्यानुशासन of वाग्भट, son of नेमिकुमार. V. pp. 295-296. Probably flourished in 14th cen.

C अलङ्कारतिलक by a.; Pr. in K. M. series.

काव्यामृत of श्रीवत्स. Later than 1400 and earlier than 1600.

काव्यामृततरङ्गिणी-same as काव्यप्रकाशखण्डन q. v.

काव्यार्थगुम्फ of हरिप्रसाद son of माथुर मिश्रगङ्गेश. V. under काव्यालोक.

15th century. Pr. in Bom. S. S.

कुम्भ, a king of Mewad, a. of रसरत्नकोश in 11 chapters. First half of 15th cen.

कुरविराम, a. of a com. on दशरूप and कुवलयानन्द. Vide H. R. I. p. XI.

कुवलयानन्द of अप्पय्यदीक्षित. V. pp. 317-321. Conflict about date. Most probable dates are 1550-1620 A. D.

C अलङ्कारचन्द्रिका of वैद्यनाथ, son of रामचन्द्र. About 1683 A. D. Pr. several times.

C अलङ्कारसुधा of नागेशभट्ट. First quarter of 18th cen.

C कारिकादीपिका of आशाधर, son of रामजीभट्ट. Pr. Nir.

C रसिकरञ्जनी of गङ्गाधर, grandson of a brother of a pupil of अप्पय्यदीक्षित. Hence about 1700 A.D. Pr. at Kumbhakonam.

C विषमपदव्याख्याषट्पदानन्द of नागेशभट्ट काल. This c. is different from the c. अलङ्कारसुधा. Vide Stein's cat. pp. 270-271 for extracts of both.

C काव्यमञ्जरी by न्यायवागीश भट्टाचार्य.

C by मथुरानाथ.

C by रामचरणतर्कवागीश. Composed in 1701 A. D.

C प्रभा by गोपीनाथ.

C लघ्वलङ्कारचन्द्रिका of देवीदत्त.

कुवलयानन्दखण्डन *alias* अलङ्कारसारस्थिति of भीमसेन दीक्षित. About 1723 A. D.; V. under अलङ्कार स्थिति above.

कुवलयामोदिनी.

कूटसन्दोह of रामानुज.

कृशाश्व, a. of a नटसूत्र m. by पाणिनि IV. 3. 111.

कृष्ण, a. of. अलङ्कारमणिहार, q. v.

कृष्ण, a. of अलङ्कारमौक्तिकमाला.

कृष्ण a. of साहित्यतरङ्गिणी.

कृष्णकिङ्कर तर्कवागीश a. of काव्यतत्त्वविवेचककौमुदी, c. on. काव्यप्र.

कृष्णदीक्षित or कृष्णयज्वन् a. of रघुनाथभूपालीय q. v.

कृष्णद्विवेदिन् a. of मधुररसा, C. on काव्यप्र.

कृष्णभट्ट or जयकृष्ण मौनिन् a. of वृत्तिदीपिका.

कृष्णशर्मन् a. of मन्दारमरन्दचम्पू and रसप्रकाश. An inhabitant of गुहपुर and pupil of वासुदेवयोगीश्वर. After 1600 A. D.

कृष्णमिश्राचार्य son of रामनाथ and grandson of देवीदत्त; a. of c. on काव्यप्र.

कृष्णसूरि a. of रत्नशोभाकर, c. on अलङ्कारमुक्तावली.

कृष्णानन्दिनी c. on साहित्यकौमुदी.

कृष्णावधूत a. of चमत्कारचामीकर.

केशवभट्ट, son of हरिवंशभट्ट, pupil of विट्ठलेश्वर, son of वल्लभाचार्य. About latter half of 16th cen.; a. of रसिकसञ्जीवनी, q.v.

केशवदास a. of कविप्रिया, written in 1601 A. D. at the request of Prabin Rai, a गणिका at the court of इन्द्रजित्. V. Dept. of Letters, Cal. Un. vol. 13 pp. 1-34.

गोपीनाथ a of c. सुमनोमनोहरा on काव्यप्र. and on साहित्यदर्पण.

गोपेन्द्रतिप्पभूपाल or त्रिपुरहर० a. of कामधेनु; com. on वामन. Verse 8 of Intro. gives the name as गोपेन्द्रत्रिपुरहर०

गोवर्धन m. in अलङ्कारशेखर (pp. 27, 37).

गोविन्द, a. of काव्यदीपिका.

गोविन्दठक्कुर, a. of काव्यप्रदीप and श्लोकदीपिका. V. above under काव्यप्र.

घण्टक m. by अ. भा.; V. p. 53.

घासीराम, a. of रसचन्द्र, composed in 1696 A. D. and of रसकौमुदी.

चक्रवर्तिन्–vide परमानन्दचक्रवर्तिन् and श्रीविद्याचक्रवर्तिन्.

चण्डीदास, a. of दीपिका, a com. on काव्यप्र., q. v.

चन्द्रकान्ततर्कालङ्कार, a. of अलङ्कारसूत्र q. v.

चन्द्रचूड son of पुरुषोत्तमभट्ट, a. of प्रस्तावचिन्तामणि; Peterson's Ulwar cat. No. 223 (extract).

चन्द्रालोक of जयदेवपीयूषवर्ष son of महादेव. V. pp. 290-292 above. Between 1200-1250 A. D. Pr. frequently,

C शरदागम or प्रकाश of प्रद्योतनभट्टाचार्य, son of बलभद्र. Pr. in Kashi S. series. V. p. 292 above. Patronized by prince वीरभद्र son of रामचन्द्रदेव. V. Adyar Library Bulletin vol. V. miscellaneous Notes pp. 35-36; written in 1583 A.D.

C राकागम or सुधा by गागाभट्ट, Latter half of 17th cen. Pr.

C रमा of वैद्यनाथ पायगुण्ड. About 1750-1800 A. D. Pr.

C शारदशर्वरी by विरूपाक्ष, son of मुद्गलरामचन्द्र. V. Tanjore cat. vol. IX. pp. 4036-4038.

C प्रदीपिका or दीपिका.

C by वाजचन्द्र.

C बुधरञ्जनी by श्रीवेङ्कलसूरि.

चन्द्रिकाकार-a. of c. called चन्द्रिका on ध्वन्यालोक; m. by अभिनवगुप्त. Between 900-950 A. D. V. p. 207 above.

चन्द्रिका-C. on काव्यादर्श q. v.

चमत्कारचन्द्रिका in 8 विलासs by विश्वेश्वर patronized by सिंहभूपाल. It follows भोज except on रस. It gives up शान्त as a रस. It appears to be the earliest work to adduce the Upaniṣad passage रसो वै स: in connection with काव्य. First half of 14th cen. Vide I. O. Cat. vol. VII p. 1507 and Annals, B. O. R. I., vol. 16 p. 131-139 (Dr. Raghavan).

चमत्कारचामीकर, a भाष्य by कृष्णावधूत on अलङ्कारसूत्र.

चारायण m. as an author on नाट्यशास्त्र by नाटकलक्षणरत्नकोश, line 392 and by कामसूत्र I. 1. 12 and 1. 5. 22.

चित्रधर a. of शृंगारसारिणी. Copied in 1743 A. D.

चित्रधर a. of वीरतरङ्गिणी.

चित्रमञ्जूषा by गङ्गाधरकवि in 73

plains the प्राकृत verses in the ध्व. V. p. 208 above.

नखकुट्ट m. in नाट्यशास्त्र (I. 33 G. O. S.) as भरतपुत्र and by सागरनन्दिन् in ना. ल. र. को. lines 2768 and 2904.

नञ्जराजयशोभूषण of नरसिंहकवि alias अभिनवकालिदास son of शिवराम. Illustrations relate to नञ्जराज, son of वीरभूप; नञ्जराज was father-in-law, sarvādhikarī and commander-in-chief of the Mysore ruler Krishnaraja Wadiyar II. V. Poona Orientalist, vol. V. pp. 217-220.

नटसूत्र of शिलालिन् } m. by पाणिनि IV. 3. 110-11. V. p. 335 above.

नन्दिकेश्वर-m. in काव्यमी. p.1 (V. p. 1 above); a. of अभिनयदर्पण in about 330 verses, ed. by Dr. M. M. Ghosh in Cal. S. Series with English translation and Intro.; translated by Messrs. A. K. Coomarswamy andDuggirala Gopalakrishnayya, Cambridge. 1917) सङ्गीतरत्नाकर I. 1. 17 names him as an authority on music. B. O. R. I. transcript of अ. भा. (p. 417 chap. 29) 'इत्येवं नन्दिकेश्वरमतानुसारेणायं चित्रपूर्वरङ्गपूर्वविधिरिति.' His name is affixed to many late wroks on erotics, *abhinaya*, music &c.

नन्दिमत m. in अ. भा. vol. I. p. 171.

नमिसाधु a. of c. on रुद्रट's काव्यालङ्कार. V. p. 155. Composed in 1069 A. D.

नरसिंह or नृसिंहकवि, son of शिवरामसुधी; a. of नञ्जराजयशोभूषण, q. v.

नरसिंह, son of गदाधर and grandson of कृष्ण; a. of c. मुक्तावलि on काव्यादर्श.

नरसिंहठक्कुर a. of नरसिंहमनीषा, c. on काव्यप्र. q. v.

नरसिंह a. of गुणरत्नाकर. q. v.

नरसिंहमनीषा, c. of नरसिंहठक्कुर on काव्यप्र.

नरसिंहसूरि son of तिम्माजि; a. of c. ऋजुवृत्ति on काव्यप्र.

नरसिंहाचार्य or वेङ्कटनृसिंहकवि; a. of अलङ्कारेन्दुशेखर q. v.

नरहरिसूरि a. of रसनिरूपण; m. by रत्नापण (p. 224).

नरहरिसरस्वतीतीर्थ, a. of बालचित्तानुरञ्जनी, c. on काव्यप्र. Born in 1241-42 A.D.

नरहरिभट्ट, a. of श्रवणभूषण, c. on विदग्धमुख०

नवरसतरङ्गिणी-same as रसतरङ्गिणी.

नागरसर्वस्व of पद्मश्री, a Buddhist; divided into 38 परिच्छेदs. Pr. in Calcutta and at Gujarati Press, Bombay. परिच्छेद 13 is on भाव, हाव; most of it is on erotics on the lines of कामसूत्र and is rather filthy in places. It quotes कुट्टनीमत and is quoted often by सागरनन्दिन्, राघवभट्ट on शाकुन्तल and शार्ङ्गधरपद्धति. Earlier than 1100 A. D. and later than 800.

नागराजकेशव, a. of पदवृत्ति, c. on काव्यप्र.

C अञ्जन by a. himself-

नाट्यशास्त्र of भरत V. pp. 10-47. Between 100 B. C. to 300 A. D.

C अभिनवभारती or नाट्यवेदविवृति by अभिनवगुप्त. V. pp. 47 ff. About 1000 A.D.

For commentaries on नाट्यशास्त्र vide pp. 47-55 above.

नाट्यशास्त्र of वसन्तराज; m. by मल्लिनाथ on शिशुपालवध II. 8 as वसन्तराजीय. Metrical. Earlier than 1400 A. D. A. is the same as the king of कुमारगिरि. V. I. O. cat. vol. VII. pp. 1575-76 where काटयवेम says that in his com. on शाकुन्तल he follows नाट्यशास्त्र of वसन्तराज, king of कुमारगिरि.

नाट्यसर्वस्वदीपिका, a. of c. on आदिभरत in 6000 verses, 5 स्कन्धs, 32 chapters. V. p. 27 above. Mentions सर. क., सङ्गीतरत्नाकर and several other works on सङ्गीत.

नाट्यार्णव of नन्दिकेश्वर q. by रसरत्नप्रदीपिका.

नान्यदेव a. of भरतभाष्य or सरस्वतीहृदयालङ्कार. V. pp. 61-63 above.

नायक-V. भट्टनायक.

नायिकादर्पण or नायिकावर्णन of रामकवि in 49 stanzas.

नारद said to be propounder of गान्धर्ववेद. V. pp. 19, 43 above. The भावप्रकाशन says नारद taught भरत the evolution of *rasas* from ब्रह्मा (pp. 47, 58, 69).

नारायणदीक्षित son of रङ्गनाथ; a. of c. on काव्यप्र. About end of 17th cen.

नारायणभट्ट a. of रसतरङ्गिणी, m. in com. of विश्वनाथ on उज्ज्वलनीलमणि (p. 25).

निदर्शन c. on काव्यप्र. by राजानकानन्द.

निर्मलभट्ट-V. त्रिमल्लभट्ट above.

नीलकण्ठ a. of चित्रमीमांसादोषधिक्कार q. v.

नूतनतरि c. on रसतरङ्गिणी q. v.

नृसिंह a. of अलङ्कारसार.

नृसिंहभट्ट a of c. on. दशरूप.

नृसिंहकेशव a. of पाण्डवराजयशोभूषण (पाण्ड्यराज० ?).

नृसिंहठक्कुर a. of नृसिंहमनीषा c. on काव्यप्र.

नेमिसाह a. of साहित्यसुधा, c. on रसतरङ्गिणी.

नौका by गङ्गाराम जडि, a. of c. on रसतरङ्गिणी. Composed in 1742 A.D.

नौका, c. on साहित्यरत्नाकर, by वेङ्कटसूरि, son of लक्ष्मणसूरि. Pr. at Benares in 1884.

पक्षधर, cited by भीमसेन as a. c. on काव्यप्र.

पञ्चसायक of ज्योतिरीश; m. in रसोदधि by मोहनदास.

C लक्ष्यवेधन by साहिबराम.

पण्डितराज alias रघुनन्दन a. of a c. on काव्यप्र; m. by रत्नकण्ठ. Earlier than 1637 A.D.

पदवृत्ति c. by नागराजकेशव on काव्यप्र.

पदार्थदीपिका of गौरनार्य on अलंकारs; Mad. Govt. mss. cat. vol.

pp. 257-263 above. The first was published several times and only a portion of the 2nd has been published so far. Reigned from about 1005 to 1054 A.D.

मकरन्द c. on काव्यकल्पलता by शुभविजयगणि pupil of हीरविजयसूरि who flourished in the reign of the Mogul Emperor Akbar. Composed in संवत् 1665 (1608-9 A.D.).

मङ्खल or मङ्खक said to be a. of वृत्ति in अलं. स. V. pp. 277-78 above. About 1125-1150 A.D.

मङ्गल q. by काव्यमी. of राजशेखर (pp. 11, 14, 16, 20). V. p. 144 above.

मङ्गलमयूखमालिका of वरदाचार्य.

मञ्जीरध्वनिकोमल.

मतङ्ग an ancient authority on नाट्यशास्त्र and music. V. p. 58 above. Before 750 A.D.

मथुरानाथशुक्ल, a. of c. on साहित्यदर्पण and कुवलयानन्द.

मदनोदय m. in कुट्टनीमत verse 122 as an a. on कामशास्त्र along with वात्स्यायन and दत्तक and by राघवभट्ट on शाकुन्तल I.

मधुधारा c. on अलङ्कारमञ्जरी, by सुधीन्द्रयति.

मधुमतिगणेश, a. of c. काव्यदर्पण on काव्यप्र.

मधुमती a c. by रवि son of रत्नपाणि on काव्यप्र. q. v.

मधुररसा a c. by कृष्णद्विवेदिन् on काव्यप्र.

मनोधर alias रत्नपाणि a. of c. काव्यदर्पण on काव्यप्र.

मन्दारमरन्दचम्पू of कृष्णशर्मन् and of चन्द्रदेवशर्मन् in eleven बिन्दुs. An extensive complilation for serving as a handbook for poets. Later than 1600 A. D. Deals with metres, श्लेष, यमक, चित्रबन्धs, नाटक and other रूपकs and their aṅgas, नायक, नायिका, रस, वृत्तिs, अलङ्कारs &c. One verse is 'अथ भोजनृपादीनां मतमत्र प्रकाश्यते । रसो वै स इति श्रुत्या रस एकः प्रकीर्तितः ॥ 9th बिन्दु p. 107. Pr. K. M. series. C माधुर्यरञ्जनी by a. Text and C. pr. by Nir.

मम्मट a. of काव्यप्रकाश and शब्दव्यापारविचार. V. pp. 266-275. Between 1050-1100 A.D. मम्मट appears to have written another work सङ्गीतरत्नावलि; V. Annals, B. O. R. I. vol. 16 at pp. 131-139.

मर्मप्रकाश same as गुरुमर्मप्रकाश q.v.

मल्लराज-see अल्लराज above.

मल्लिनाथ, a. of तरल, c. on एकावली; V. pp. 292-93 above.

मल्लिनाथ, son of जगन्नाथ. A. of वैमल्यविधायिनी, a c. on काव्यादर्श.

महादेव a. of भानुभावप्रकाशिनी, a.c. on रसमञ्जरी and रसोदधि, a.c. on रसतरङ्गिणी.

महिमभट्ट, a. of व्यक्तिविवेक and तत्त्वोक्तिकोश; V. pp. 248-257. The first pr. in Tri. series with c. of रुय्यक. Between 1020-1100 A. D.

महेश्वर a. of आदर्श alias भावार्थचिन्तामणि c. on. काव्यप्र.

रत्नपाणि alias मनोधर son of अच्युत; a. of काव्यदर्पण, a com. on काव्यप्र. q. v.

रत्नभूषण a. of काव्यकौमुदी in 10 परिच्छेदs. A recent writer of middle of 19th cen.

रत्नमण्डनगणि or अणुरत्न० a. of मुग्धमेधाकर and जल्पकल्पलता.

रत्नमाला of लक्ष्मणभट्ट. Deals with अप्रस्तुतप्रशंसा, प्रहेलिकाs &c.

रत्नशाण c. by ano. a. on प्रतापरुद्र-यशोभूषण, q. v.

रत्नशोभाकर of कृष्णसूरि, c. on अलङ्कारमुक्तावलि, q. v.

रत्नाकर-same as अलङ्काररत्नाकर of शोभाकरमित्र.

रत्नापण of कुमारस्वामिन्; c. on प्रतापरुद्रयशोभूषण, q.v.

रत्नेश्वर a. of रत्नदर्पण, com. on सर. क,. who composed it at the request of king रामसिंहदेव.

रमा by वैद्यनाथ पायगुण्ड, com. on चन्द्रालोक q. v.

रवि, a. of मधुमती, com. on काव्यप्र. q. v.

रसकल्पवल्ली of रामगोपालदास (16th cen. A. D.); quotes सङ्गीतदामोदर.

रसकलिका of रुद्रभट्ट. Vide Mad. Govt. mss. Library No. 2241, 3274 and Dr. Raghavan on 'number of Rasas' pp. 53-54.

रसकल्लोल of दीनकृष्णदास written in 1490 A. D., when गजपतिपुरुषोत्तम was reigning. V. I. A. vol. I. p. 215.

रसकौमुदी of घासीरामपण्डित. Describes characteristics of nine rasas.

रसकौमुदी Ano. On alaṅkāras. V. Cal. Oriental Journal vol. III. pp. 35-37 (Prof. Gode .

रसकौमुदी of श्रीकण्ठ. Combines साहित्य and सङ्गीत in 10 chapters divided into पूर्वखण्ड and उत्तरखण्ड. Ms. dated 1596. A. D. and work composed between 1569-1596 A. D. V. B. O. R. I. mss. cat. vol. XII. pp. 463-466. A. was patronized by शत्रुशल्य) 1569-1608 A. D.) Jām (Sattarsal) of Navānagar. V. Annals, B. O. R. I. vol. 14 p. 129.

रसकौस्तुभ of वेणीदत्त Cat. of Mithila mss., vol. II p. 44 No. 34

रसगङ्गाधर of जगन्नाथपण्डितराज. V. pp. 321-324; flourised 1620-1665 A. D.

C मर्मप्रकाश of नागेशभट्ट who was supported by prince राम of शृङ्गवेर. Pr. in K. M. Series.

रसगन्ध

रसचन्द्र of घासीरामपण्डित. Composed in 1696 A. D. in four chapters dealing with नायक, नायिका, अनुभावादिगण and रस.

रसचन्द्रिका of विश्वेश्वरभट्ट, son of लक्ष्मीधर; quotes अप्पय्य and जगन्नाथ; beginning of 18th cen.; pr. in Kashi S. Series.

रसतरङ्गिणी of गोपालभट्ट son of हरिवंशभट्ट. This is a com. on the शृङ्गारतिलक of रुद्रभट्ट.

रसतरङ्गिणी a. of c. on रुद्रट's काव्या-

Pr. in Benares S. Series. First quarter of 18th cen.

C भानुभावप्रकाशिनी by महादेव.

C रसिकरञ्जन of व्रजराजदीक्षित son of कामराज and father of जीवराम. First half of 18th cen.

C रसिकरञ्जनी of गोपालभट्ट son of हरिवंशभट्ट, द्राविड ब्राह्मण.

C विकास or विलास by गोपाल alias वोपदेव, son of नृसिंह; 1572 A.D.; quotes प्रदीपकार, वत्सलाञ्छन, साहित्यदर्पण.

C व्यङ्ग्यार्थकौमुदी of अनन्त son of त्र्यम्बक; Pr. in Benares S. Series. Composed in काशी in संवत् 1692 i.e. 1635-36 A.D.

C व्यङ्ग्यार्थकौमुदी or समञ्जसा by विश्वेश्वर son of लक्ष्मीधर. Vide N. IX. p. 122.

C व्यङ्ग्यार्थदीपिका by आनन्दशर्मन्, son of त्र्यम्बक.

C स्थूलतात्पर्यार्थ

C by रमानाथवैद्य

रसमञ्जरी of लक्ष्मीधर, son of यज्ञेश्वरदीक्षित, grandson of तिम्मय and pupil of कोण्डुभट्ट. Patronized by तिरुमलराज. Later he became a यति called रामानन्दाश्रम.

रसमहार्णव of गोकुलनाथ, son of पीताम्बर. Lived and wrote at Benares. Last quarer of 17th and first of 18th cen.

रसमीमांसा of काशीश्वर, *guru* of विश्वेश्वर author of चमत्कारचन्द्रिका. V. Annals, B. O. R. I. vol. 16 at pp. 139-140. About 1300 A. D.

रसमीमांसा of गङ्गारामजडि in 114 verses. Pr. at Benares in 1885. Second quarter of 18th cen.

C छाया by himself.

रसरत्नकोश of राजाधिराजकुम्भ or कुम्भकर्ण, in 11 chapters on rasas, नायक, नायिका, अभिनय. This is part of his सङ्गीतराज. Vide Annals, B. O. R. I. vol. 14 pp. 258-262 (Dr. Raghavan). About 1428-1459 A. D. Mentions कीर्तिधराचार्य and अभिनवभरताचार्य. V. Regnauds' 'La Rhetorique' p. 379.

रसरत्नप्रदीपिका or रसरत्नप्रदीप of अल्लराज or मल्लराज, son of king हम्मीर. In 6 परिच्छेदs, prose and verse. Between 1250-1350 A. D. Pr. in the भारतीयविद्याभवन series, Bombay, ed. by Dr. R. N. Dandekar. Quotes stanzas from कविकङ्कण, चण्डकौशिक, and भावप्रकाशन and is quoted by कुम्भ in रसिकप्रिया c. on गीतगोविन्द.

रसरत्नहार of शिवराम त्रिपाठिन्, son of कृष्णराम and grandson of त्रिलोकचन्द्र. In verses on रस, भाव &c.

C लक्ष्मीविहार by a. himself. Later than 1st quarter of 18th cen.; quotes रसमञ्जरी and its टीका व्यंग्यार्थकौमुदी. Pr. in K. M. series, 6th गुच्छ p. 124.

रसरत्नावली of वीरेश्वरपण्डित son of लक्ष्मण. Deals chiefly with शृङ्गाररस and नायिकाs

रसविलास of शुकलभूदेव, son of सुकदेव. In four स्तबकs;

रसिकसर्वस्व cited in रसिकप्रिया, c. by king कुम्भ on गीतगोविन्द; v. pp. 51, 55. 56 of Nir. ed. of 1949.

रसोदधि by गणेश on रसतरङ्गिणी; ms. dated 1698 A. D.

रसोदधि by महादेव on रसतरङ्गिणी.

रसोदधि of मोहनदास. V. Auf. cat. of Bodleian mss. part I p. 143 a.

रहस्य-cited by मल्लिनाथ on किराता-र्जुनीय III. 60 and XIV. 41 and by अलङ्कारशेखर pp. 40 and 83.

रहस्यदीपिका of जयराम, also called तिलक. C on. काव्यप्रकाश.

रहस्यप्रकाश by जगदीश on काव्यप्र.

राकागम by विश्वेश्वरभट्ट, c. on चन्द्रालोक q. v.

राघव, a. of an अवचूरिटिप्पण on काव्यप्र.

राघवचैतन्य a. of. कविकल्पलता.

राजचूडामणिदीक्षित son of श्री-निवासदीक्षित and कामाक्षी; a. of अलङ्कारशिरोमणि (or-चूडामणि), काव्यदर्पण, चित्रमञ्जरी and many other works.

राजशेखर, a. of काव्यमीमांसा. V. pp. 208-218; 900-925 A. D.

राजशेखर, a. of अलङ्कारमकरन्द. About 1760-1772 A.D.

राजहंसोपाध्याय a. of a c. on वाग्भटा-लङ्कार. Ms. dated 1430 A.D.

राजानन्द a. of a c. on काव्यप्र.

रामकर्ण a. of यशोवन्तयशोभूषण q. v.

रामकवि or रामशर्मन् a. of नायिका-दर्पण or-वर्णन.

रामकृष्ण a. of c. भावार्थ or कवि-नन्दिनी on काव्यप्र. q. v.

रामचन्द्र a. of नाटकदर्पण or नाट्य-दर्पण q. v.

रामचन्द्र a. of काव्यप्रकाशसार, c. on काव्यप्र. and अलङ्कारमञ्जूषा, a c. on अलङ्कारचन्द्रिका.

रामचन्द्रदीक्षित a. of शब्दभेदनिरूपण.

रामचन्द्रन्यायवागीश a. of काव्य-चन्द्रिका.

रामचन्द्रयशोभूषण of कच्छपेश्वर-दीक्षित. Illustrations in honour of बोमराज.

रामचरण, a. of c. on साहित्यदर्पण. 1700 A.D.

रामनाथविद्यावाचस्पति a. of c. रहस्यप्रकाश on काव्यप्र. First quarter of 17th cen.

रामदेवचिरञ्जीवभट्टाचार्य a. of काव्य-विलास and शृङ्गारतटिनी.

रामपण्डित a. of रसकौमुदी.

रामसुधीश्वर a. of अलङ्कारमुक्तावली, q. v.

रामसुब्रह्मण्य a. of अलङ्कारशास्त्रसंग्रह.

रामानन्द a. of रसतरङ्गिणी.

रामानन्दाश्रम i. e. लक्ष्मीधरदीक्षित, a. of. अलङ्कारमुक्तावलि and रस-मञ्जरी.

रामानुज a. of कूटसन्दोह.

राहुल a. on dramaturgy cited by अभिनव, and by ना. ल. र. को.; V. p. 54 above.

रीतिवृत्तिलक्षण by विट्ठलेश्वर or विट्ठलदीक्षित.

रुचक-Vide. रुय्यक

रुचिनाथमिश्र m. by प्रभाकर in रसप्रदीप (pp. 6, 7, 9,).

रुचिमिश्र m. as a. of c. on काव्यप्र. by भीमसेन.

रुद्रट, a of काव्यालङ्कार V. pp. 151-160 above.

रुद्रभट्ट a. of शृङ्गारतिलक V. pp. 156-160 above.

वररुचि m. as an ancient writer on Poetics along with काश्यप by the c. हृदयंगमा on काव्यादर्श.

वल्लभदेव, son of राजानक आनन्ददेव, and called परमार्थचिह्न, a. of c. on रुद्रट's काव्यालङ्कार. V. p. 155 above. Between 900-930 A. D.

वल्लभभट्ट a. of अलङ्कारकौमुदी.

वसन्तराज, king of कुमारगिरि, a. of a नाट्यशास्त्र called वसन्तराजीय.

वसन्तराजीय, a नाट्यशास्त्र of वसन्तराज. Not later than 1400 A.D.

वाग्भट, son of सोम, a. of वाग्भटालङ्कार. V. pp. 286-7 above. Flourished in first half of 12th cen.

वाग्भटालङ्कार-Vide the preceding.

C by आदिनाथ or जिनवर्धन who was a priest of खरतरगच्छ in 1405-1419 A. D. Pr. in ग्रन्थमाला, Bombay; ms. copied in संवत् 1610 (1553-4 A.D.). B. O. R. I. mss. cat. 12 p. 323.

C by सिंहदेवगणि. Pr. in K. M. sreries.

C समासान्वयटिप्पण by क्षेमहंसगणि.

C विवरण by गणेश, son of अनन्तभट्ट ; ms. copied in 1713 A.D.

C by राजहंसोपाध्याय, pupil of जिनतिलकसूरि; ms. copied in 1430 A. D. (V. Bhandarkar's R. for 1883-4 pp. 156, 279.). Between 1350-1400 A. D.

C by समयसुन्दर, pupil of सकलचन्द्र; composed at Ahmedabad in 1636 A.D.

C अवचूरि by unknown a.

C by कृष्णशर्म.

C ज्ञानप्रमोदिका by वाचनाचार्य ज्ञानप्रमोदगणि, composed in संवत् 1681 (1624-25 A.D.).

वाग्भट, son of नेमिकुमार, a. of काव्यानुशासन. V. pp. 295-6 above; 14th cen.

वाचस्पति a. of a c. on काव्यप्र.

वात्स्यायन, a. of अलङ्कारसूत्र q.v.

वाजचन्द्र, a of c. on चन्द्रालोक.

वादिजङ्घल a. of c. on काव्यादर्श.

वामन, a. of काव्यालङ्कारसूत्र with वृत्ति by himself. V. pp. 139-147.

वासुकि m. as a writer on dramaturgy by भावप्रकाशन (pp. 37, 47, 69) and रत्नापण (p. 122). The verse (नानाद्रव्यौ० .. नयैः सह) cited as वासुकि's by the भावप्रकाशन p. 37 is नाट्यशास्त्र VI. 39 (G.O.S. vol. I p. 294).

विजयवर्णी a. of शृङ्गारार्णवचन्द्रिका. V. N. C. C. p. 69a.

विजयानन्द a. of c. on काव्यादर्श.

विठ्ठलेश्वर or विट्ठलदीक्षित, also called अग्निकुमार, a. of रीतिवृत्तिलक्षण and शृङ्गाररसमण्डन. A. was son of the famous वल्लभाचार्य and was born in 1515 A. D. Author of numerous works. V. Aufrecht's cat. I. p. 572 a and b.

विदग्धमुखमण्डन of धर्मदाससूरि (a Bauddha) in four परिच्छेदs

with गाम्भीर्यादिगुणs. रीतिs and दोषs ; cat. of Mithila mss. vol. II p. 65 no. 46.

वीरनारायण a. of साहित्यचिन्तामणि.

वीरेश्वर a. of. रसरत्नावलि.

वृत्तिदीपिका of कृष्ण or जयकृष्णमौनिन्.

वृत्तिवार्तिक of अप्पय्य दीक्षित; vide p. 317; 1550-1620 A. D. Pr. in K. M. series.

वृन्दावनचन्द्र तर्कालङ्कार, a. of दीधितिप्रकाशिका c. on अलङ्कारकौस्तुभ.

वेङ्कटनृसिंहकवि, a of अलङ्कारेन्दुशेखर c. on लक्षणमालिका.

वेङ्कटसूरि a.of नौका, c. on साहित्यरत्नाकर.

वेङ्कटाचार्य, son of अण्णायाचार्य of श्रीशैल family. a. of अलङ्कारकौस्तुभ.

वेङ्कटाचलसूरि a. of c. on काव्यप्र.

वेङ्कपय्यप्रधान a. of अलङ्कारमणिदर्पण.

वेङ्कलसूरि a. o बुधरञ्जनी on चन्द्रालोक.

वेचाराम a. of c. on कविकल्पलता.

वेणीदत्तशर्मन् a. of अलङ्कारचन्द्रोदय and c. रसिकरञ्जनी on रसतरङ्गिणी. About 1583 A. D.

वैद्यनाथतत्सत् son of रामचन्द्र and grandson of विट्ठल; a. of c. प्रभा on the काव्यप्रकाशप्रदीप of गोविन्दठक्कुर and of the उदाहरणचन्द्रिका explaining the illustrations in the काव्यप्रकाश. The K. M. ed. of प्रभा clearly ascribes it to वैद्यनाथतत्सत्. For the उदाहरणचन्द्रिका, vide Peterson's R. II. p. 108, Cal. Sanskrit College mss. Cat. VII. 54, Ulwar Cat. No. 1044 and I. O. Cat., vol. III, No. 1151; these give the above pedigree the उदाहरणचन्द्रिका was composed in संवत् 1740 i. e. in 1683-84 A. D. (I. O. Cat. vol. III. No. 1151 p. 322 gives this date).

वैद्यनाथ पायगुण्ड, a. of c. रमा on चन्द्रालोक and of a c. called अलङ्कारचन्द्रिका on कुवलयानन्द. In the Gujarati Press edition (1939) of रमा, his parentage is not mentioned; while in Jīvananda's edition of the अलङ्कारचन्द्रिका, वैद्यनाथ is described as the son of रामभट्ट. I, believe that the two Vaidyanāthas are different, though some mss. make a confusion between the two. Aufrecht (II p. 146a) makes the confusion worse by remarking 'वैद्यनाथ पायगुण्ड of the तत्सत् family'. पायगुण्ड is a well-known surname in महाराष्ट्र. Peterson's R. II p. 108 and Cal. S. College mss. cat. vol. VII p. 54 have the colophon 'धर्मशास्त्र-·पारावारीणतत्सद्विट्ठलात्मज' &c.

वैमल्यविधायिनी by मल्लिनाथ son of जगन्नाथ; a c. on काव्यादर्श.

वोपदेव another name of गोपाल, son of नृसिंह, a of c. विकास (or विलास) on रसमञ्जरी; composed in 1572 A.D.

व्यक्तिविवेक of महिमभट्ट. V. pp. 248-256 above. Between 1020-1100 A. D. Pr. Tri. S. S.

nning of 18th cen. From extract 236 in Ulwar cat. it appears that he composed over 30 works.

शितिकण्ठविबोधन alias निदर्शन, of राजानकानन्द; a. c. on काव्यप्र; composed in 1665 A.D.

शिवनारायणदास a. of c. on काव्यप्र. Beginning of 17th cen.

शिशुप्रबोधालङ्कार of विष्णुदास, son of माधव. Vide Auf. II p. 156b which says that the Florentine ms. contains only chap. 6 and 7.

शिशुप्रबोधालङ्कार of पुञ्जराज, son of जीवनेन्द्र..

शुभविजयगणि a. of परिमल, c. on काव्यकल्पलता.

शृङ्गारकौस्तुभ.

शृङ्गारचन्द्रोदय q. in प्रस्तावचिन्तामणि.

शृङ्गारतटिनी of चिरञ्जीवभट्टाचार्य. First half of 18th cen.

शृङ्गारतरङ्गिणी of श्रीनिवासाचार्य.

शृङ्गारतिलक of रुद्रभट्ट. Vide pp. 156-160 above. Flourished sometime between 950 and 1110 A. D.

C रसतरङ्गिणी by गोपालभट्ट, son of हरिवंशभट्ट.

शृङ्गारदर्पण of पद्मसुन्दर. Vide-अकबरसाहिशृङ्गारदर्पण above.

शृङ्गारदीपिका of भानुदत्त. Whether the same as the a. of रसमञ्जरी is a question.

शृङ्गारदीपिका of वेम, son of पेद्दकोमटि. Vide E. I. vol. XI at p. 315.

शृङ्गारपवन.

शृङ्गारप्रकाश of भोज. Vide pp. 259-60 above. Ruled 1005-1054 A. D.

शृङ्गारभेदप्रदीप of हरिहर on the ten *avasthās* of विप्रलम्भ, q. by रसचन्द्रिका p. 55.

शृङ्गारमञ्जरी of विश्वेश्वर; q. by his own रसचन्द्रिका (p. 90).

शृङ्गारमञ्जरी of अजितसेन in three chapters and 128 stanzas dealing with दोषs, गुणs and अर्थालङ्कारs. Latter half of 10th cen.

शृङ्गारमञ्जरी of अकबरसाहि; vide above अकबरसाहिशृ०

शृङ्गारमण्डन of मण्डन, prime minister of a king of Malva; composed between 1400-1448 A. D.

शृङ्गारमाला by सुखलाल, son of बाबूराय; in 3 विरचनs; written in संवत् 1801. Ulwar cat. No. 1083, extract 230.

शृङ्गाररत्नाकर.

शृङ्गाररसमण्डन or शृङ्गारमण्डन of विठ्ठलेश्वर, son of वल्लभाचार्य, the famous religious teacher; in 10 उल्लासs. Author was born in 1515 A. D. B. O. R. I. mss. cat. XII. pp. 350-351.

शृङ्गाररसविलास of देवदत्त

शृङ्गारलता of सुखदेवमिश्र.

शृङ्गारविधि.

शृङ्गारसरसी of भावमिश्र, son of भटकमिश्र.

शृङ्गारसार of वेङ्कटनारायण दीक्षित of गोडवर्तिकुल, son of कामेश्वर. In six उल्लासs; mentions his own fuller work. He is said

षट्पदानन्द (विषमपदव्याख्यान) by नागेशभट्ट, a c. on कुवलयानन्द q. v.

षट्सहस्रीकृत् i. e. भरत's नाट्यशास्त्र. Vide धनिक on दशरूप IV. 2.

सङ्केत c. of माणिक्यचन्द्र on काव्यप्र. q. v. V. p. 274.

सङ्केत–c. of रुय्यक on काव्यप्र. q.v. V. p. 279.

सङ्गीतदामोदर of शुभङ्कर, son of श्रीवर कविचक्रवर्तिन्; 15th cen. A. D. Edited by Principal Gaurinath Sastri and Dr. Govindagopal Mukhopadhyaya and published in the Cal. Sanskrit College Research Series, 1960; in five स्तबकs; Introduction pp. 13-40, text pp. 1-124 and pp. 125-136 sourses and references. Deals with भाव, हाव, अनुभाव, नायिका, नायक and dramaturgy, रस, besides सङ्गीत.

सङ्गीतरत्नाकर of निःशङ्क शार्ङ्गदेव who was patronized by यादव सिङ्घण (1210-1247 A. D.). Pr. by Ānan.

C कलानिधि by चतुरकल्लिनाथ a resident of विजयनगर. Pr. in Ānan. Earlier than 1608 A. D.

C सुधाकर of सिंहभूपाल. Pr. (in part) by Adyar Library. About 1330 A. D.

ञ्जीवनी or सर्वस्वञ्सजीवनी C. by विद्याचक्रवर्तिन् on अलं. स. Before the end of 14th cen.

सदलङ्कारचन्द्रिका.

सदाशिवदीक्षित a. of. बालरामवर्मयशोभूषण,, q. v.

समयसुन्दर a, of c. on वाग्भटालङ्कार q. v.

समयसुन्दरगणि a. of अष्टलक्षार्थी alias अर्थरत्नावली. No. 1353 in Kathavate's Report (1891-95). Composed in संवत् 1646 (1589-90 A.D.) at लाभपुर (Lahore).

समुद्रबन्ध a. of c. on अलं. स. Pr. in Tri. S. S. About 1300 A. D.

संप्रदायप्रकाशिनी (बृहती टीका) c. on काव्यप्र. by विद्याचक्रवर्तिन् q. v.

समञ्जसा or व्यंग्यार्थकौमुदी by विश्वेश्वर a. of c. on रसमञ्जरी of भानुदत्त.

समासान्वयटिप्पण, c. on वाग्भटालङ्कार by क्षेमहंसगणि.

सरसामोद by अच्युतरायमोडक, c. on साहित्यसार, q.v.

सरस्वतीकण्ठाभरण of भोज. Vide pp. 257-264 above.

C by. आजड

C रत्नदर्पण by रत्नेश्वर. 14th cen. Vide p. 263 above. (3 परिच्छेदs in K. M. edition).

C of जगद्धर (on 4th परिच्छेद in K. M. edition).

C by भट्टनृसिंह. Vide Dr. Ragahvan on Bhoja's Śṛṅgāra-prakāśa vo. I pp. 418 ff. particularly pp. 432-434.

C मार्जन by हरिनाथ.

C दुष्करचित्रप्रकाशिका by लक्ष्मीनाथभट्ट. Before the middle of 17th cen.

हरिकृष्णव्यास a. of a c. on सरस्वतीकण्ठाभरण.

हरिश्चन्द्र m. in शृङ्गाररत्नाकर of ताराचरण.

हरिदास, son of पुरुषोत्तम; a. of प्रस्तावरत्नाकर composed in 1557 A. D. V. Aufrecht's Cat. Cat. I p. 360 a.

हरिनाथ a. of c. मार्जन on काव्यादर्श and c. मार्जन on. सर. क.

हरिप्रसाद, son of माथुर मिश्रगङ्गेश; a. of काव्यार्थगुम्फ, काव्यालोक. About 1718-1728 A. D.

हरिलोचनचन्द्रिका-V. रमा above.

हरिहर a. of शृङ्गारभेदप्रदीप q. v. एकावली p. 242 quotes a verse on दीपक from हरिहर.

हर्ष-same as श्रीहर्ष,, a. of a वार्तिक on नाट्यशास्त्र. V. pp. 59-60 above. सागरनन्दिन् mentions हर्षविक्रमनराधिप and भावप्रकाशन. p. 238 mentions हर्ष as a writer on नाट्य०.

हलधररथ a. of काव्यतत्त्वविचार.

हृदयंगमा c. on काव्यादर्श. Pr. by Prof. Rangacharya at Madras.

हृदयदर्पण of भट्टनायक. V. pp. 221-225. Between 900-1000 A. D.

हेमचन्द्र a. of काव्यानुशासन with वृत्ति अलङ्कारचूडामणि and c. विवेक. V. pp. 287-290. Flourished 1088-1172 A. D.